MONTAGNAIS

C R E E

MICMAC

MALECITE

O J I B W A

O J

ALGONQUIAN

ABNAKI

PENNACOOK

MENOMINEE

OTTAWA

HURON

IROQUOIS

MAHICAN

MASSACHUSET

MOHEGAN

ITEE

KICKAPOO

51

POTAWATOMI

NEUTRAL

METOAC

IOWA

MIAMI

ERIE

CONESTOGA

DELAWARE

ILLINOIS

MOSOPELEA

NANTICOKE

MISSOURI

MONACAN

POWHATAN

OSAGE

SHAWNEE

CHEROKEE

PAMLICO

TUSCARORA

QUAPAW

CHICKASAW

CATAWBA

YUCHI

CADDO

49

CREEK

CUSABO

TUNICA

CHOCTAW

50

HITCHITI

YAMASEE

NATCHEZ

MOBILE

BILOXI

APALACHEE

TIMUCUA

ACOLAPISSA

ATAKAPA

CHITMACHA

Location of North American Indian Groups

CALUSA

. . . so long as the waters shall flow
and the sun shall shine . . .

THIS LAND WAS THEIRS

A Study of Native Americans

SIXTH EDITION

Wendell H. Oswalt
University of California, Los Angeles

Sharlotte Neely
Northern Kentucky University

Mayfield Publishing Company
Mountain View, California
London • Toronto

Library of Congress Cataloging-in-Publication Data

Oswalt, Wendell H.
 This land was theirs : a study of Native Americans / Wendell H. Oswalt,
 Sharlotte Neely. — 6th ed.
  p. cm.
 Includes bibliographical references and indexes.
 ISBN 0-7674-0504-8
  1. Indians of North America. I. Neely, Sharlotte.
 II. Title.
 E77.O8   1998
 970'.00497—dc21   98-25731
                                                                CIP

Manufactured in the United States of America

10 9 8 7 6 5 4 3 2

Mayfield Publishing Company
1280 Villa Street
Mountain View, California 94041

Sponsoring editor, Janet M. Beatty; production editor, Linda Ward; manuscript editor, Elaine Kehoe; design and art manager, Susan Breitbard; cover designer, Cynthia Bassett; manufacturing manager, Randy Hurst. The text was set in 10/12 ITC Garamond Light by G&S Typesetters, Inc. and printed on 45# Highland Plus by Malloy Lithographing, Inc.

Cover: Photo of Crow woman on horseback (upper right) courtesy of the Field Museum, Chicago, neg. no. 2784. Photo of Yupik children (middle right) © Elizabeth Wolf/Alaska Stock. Photo of Navajo family (bottom) courtesy of Museum of Northern Arizona Photo Archives, Earl Forrest Collection, neg. no. MS-143-11-1-2953. All other photos courtesy of Wendell H. Oswalt.

In memory of
Edward H. Spicer
and
John J. Honigmann

Preface

When the first edition of *This Land Was Theirs* appeared in 1966, it introduced a different approach to the study of Native Americans. The emphasis was, and continues to be, on both traditional and modern Indian lifeways. The tribes chosen for chapter-length presentation represent varied geographical areas, ecological adaptations, and degrees of cultural complexity. The selection of tribes depended to a great extent on the scope of the available information. The reader will find that no particular theoretical orientation dominates in this book; ecological, ethnohistorical, functional, and other perspectives are incorporated as appropriate.

The two opening chapters address the most commonly asked questions about Native Americans, including such matters as Indian identity, linguistic ties, treaties, and current issues, including Indian casinos. This background information introduces twelve chapters devoted to specific tribes. Each of these chapters begins with an ethnohistorical sketch followed by old and new reports about tribal life. The final chapter, new to this edition, provides an overview of the Native American past, present, and future.

The sequence of chapters reflects evolutionary differences in socioeconomic life (band, tribe, and chiefdom). In order of presentation, the tribes selected are as follows. The Chipewyan, who live in northwestern Canada, represent subarctic hunters and fishers. The Kuskowagamiut of southwestern Alaska are Eskimos whose lives centered on salmon harvests. The Cahuilla inhabit an arid area of southern California and were primarily gatherers of plant products; a segment of the modern tribe is noteworthy because some of its members are exceedingly wealthy. The Crow of the northern Plains represent foragers who adopted the horse in historic times and emerged as outstanding bison hunters and warriors. The Yurok of northern California and the Tlingit of southeastern Alaska provide a comparative dimension for salmon fishers on the Northwest Coast. The Hopi of the Southwest were arid-area farmers who in many ways typify Pueblo Indian life. The chapter about the Navajo in the Southwest acknowledges their present-day numerical importance and stresses their comparatively recent emergence as a tribe. The Mesquakie (Fox) were farmers and hunters, selected here because they are one of the few tribes to survive into modern times in the eastern sector of the Midwest; unlike most Indians, they purchased the land that they occupy. The Iroquois of the Northeast were farmers who not only reflect an inordinate political complexity but are also important in the development of ethnographic studies, as well as in colonial American history. The Cherokee of North Carolina were farmers who are included because some of them continue to live in their southeastern homeland and have retained a clear sense of Indian identity. Finally, the Natchez of Mississippi were farmers with one of the most complex ways of life reported among Native Americans north of Mexico; they were among the many tribes destroyed by Western colonialists.

| A Note about *Indian* and Other Usages

The use of certain words in this book requires comment, especially the word *Indian*. The term originated with Christopher Columbus, who though he had reached the East Indies, islands off Asia. He termed the people *los Indios,* and, even after the error was realized, the Spanish continued to use the word *Indios* for all New World peoples; the word became *Indian* in English. Alternatively, the words *savage, heathen,* and *barbarian* were popular for identifying Indians and emphasizing their "noncivilized" and "non-Christian" status. By the late eighteenth century, the "noble savage" designation became an increasingly popular way to glorify and romanticize Indian life, especially in art and literature. By the 1970s the word *Indian* was becoming politically incorrect in the United States. In this book, *Indian, Native American,* and *American Indian* are all terms used to refer to indigenous peoples in the New World. Significantly, Indians usually call themselves Indian.

When generalizing, the distinctions just cited include Aleuts and Eskimos, as is an accepted convention. The Canadian government distinguishes between Eskimos and Indians in some contexts but applies the term *First Nations* to both. Less significantly, the word *maize* is used far more often than *corn,* and *bison* rather than *buffalo,* to provide a modicum of exactness.

| New to This Edition

The differences between this and previous editions are considerable and deserve comment. Most important, the discussion of Indian life from the 1950s through the 1970s has been abridged so that we could put more emphasis on what has happened between the 1980s and 1997. A major challenge in preparing the sixth edition was obtaining updated information about the extant peoples described in Chapters 3 through 13; for most tribes, published studies dealing with the recent past do not exist. Thus in 1996 and 1997 Oswalt obtained current information during brief visits to the Cahuilla, Chipewyan, Crow, Hopi, Iroquois, Mesquakie, Tlingit, Navajo, and Yurok. (The Yurok chapter has been restored at the fervent request of some users.) Finally, readers of recent editions have complained about the absence of a concluding discussion about American Indians. The last chapter now attempts to examine the current scene in broad context.

This edition also incorporates some new reader aids. In addition to the maps on the inside covers, a glossary of potentially unfamiliar words has been added, along with a pronunciation guide to a list of words that may be troublesome. An *Instructor's Manual* includes not only possible test questions but also video and film listings (with annotations) and information about where these visual aids may be obtained.

In closing, it is gratifying to note that among non-Indians there is a resurgent interest in Native Americans. Hopefully, this revised edition will further a sympathetic understanding of Indian life both *past* and *present*.

| Acknowledgments

Whereas the previous edition was revised almost entirely by Sharlotte Neely, Wendell Oswalt made virtually all of the changes in the present edition. In both editions, reviewers provided invaluable help. We'd especially like to thank the following colleagues for their help with this edition: Richard W. Jefferies, University of Kentucky; Alan Lamb, North Idaho College; Stephen C. Lensink, University of Iowa; and Beverly A. Smith, University of Michigan, Flint.

Individuals who were especially helpful in providing specifics about particular tribes for this edition are as follows:

Chipewyan: Margaret Ann Beaudette, René Fumoleau, K. B. Morrison, Adeline Jonasson, and Bill Simpson

Kuskowagamiut: Michael W. Coffing, Ted Horner, A. Oscar Kawagley, and Ann Fienup-Riordan

Cahuilla: Lowell John Bean, Don Magee, Ginger Ridgeway, and Bud Robbins

Crow: Denis L. Adams, Magdalene Medicine Horse-Moccasin, Timothy P. McCleary, and Janine Pease-Pretty on Top

Yurok: Thomas M. Gates

Tlingit: Roger Drapeaux, Steve Henderson, Andy Hope III, Marie Olson, Wallace M. Olson, Thomas F. Thornton, and Liana Wallace

Hopi: Hubert Taylor

Navajo: David Tsinnie

Mesquakie: Gladys Benson and Johnathan Buffalo

Iroquois: Joanna Bedard, Richard Hill, Amos Keye, Angie Monture, and Jake Thomas

Eastern Cherokee: Lou Ellen Jackson and Ned Long, Sr.

Natchez: Jim Barnett and Jean Simonton

Current Realities: James W. VanStone

Janet M. Beatty, Senior Editor, Mayfield Publishing Company, deserves special thanks. Members of the staff at Mayfield Publishing Company who have been especially supportive include Linda Ward, production editor; Susan Breitbard, design and art manager; and Elaine Kehoe, copy editor.

Unattributed photographs in the text were taken by Wendell H. Oswalt.

Contents

Chapter 7   The Yurok: Salmon Fishers of California 214

Chapter 8   The Tlingit: Alaskan Salmon Fishers 249

Chapter 9   The Hopi: Farmers of the Desert 292

Chapter 10   The Navajo: Transformations among a Desert People 329

Chapter 11   The Mesquakie: Warriors and Farmers of the Woodland Fringe 367

Chapter 12   The Iroquois: Warriors and Farmers of the Eastern Woodlands 404

Chapter 13   The Eastern Cherokee: Farmers of the Southeast 447

Chapter 14   The Natchez: Sophisticated Farmers of the Deep South 477

Chapter 15   Current Realities, Fears, and Hopes 501

1 Questions about Native Americans

*We ask only an even chance
to live as other men live.
We asked to be recognized as men.*

Chief Joseph, Nez Perce Tribe, 1877

THIS ANTHROPOLOGICAL STUDY begins by focusing on general questions about American Indians living north of Mexico. How have we been influenced by Indians? Who is a Native American? How long have their ancestors been in the New World, and where did they originate? The answers to these questions, and others, are the subject of this chapter. They provide essential background information for the account, in the next chapter, of what happened as Indians became deeply involved with non-Indians.

| How Are We Influenced by Native American Cultures?

Our thoughts about Indian influences on our lives commonly focus on artifacts borrowed from them, such as birch-bark canoes, moccasins, parkas, snowshoes, and toboggans. The shortness of this list reflects the vast technological differences between the life-styles of aboriginal Americans 500 years ago and those of contemporary Americans. Our industrial technology is so foreign to Indian culture that they could not be expected to have contributed a great deal to it. Furthermore, most of us have lost an intimate association with the land, a quality that typified Native American life. Nevertheless, we should neither minimize nor deny the place of Indians in our cultural heritage.

We tend to forget that we are most indebted to American Indians for our country itself, because this land was theirs. Yet, it is doubtful that the thoughts of most non-Indian Americans linger on Indians for very long. We take them for granted, which is a clear indication that they are an intimate part of our lives. We may learn about their ways in grade school and something about their history in high school. At Thanksgiving we feast on foods exploited by Native Americans: beans, cranberries, maize (corn), pumpkin, and turkey. We may visit Indian reservations and read novels about Indians. These are the ways in which Indians often intrude on our thinking. Another dimension of their presence is worthy of attention. Native Americans are a challenge because our responses to them represent a homegrown experiment in tolerance, understanding, and compassion.

In historical perspective, one enormously important borrowing by non-Indian Americans occurred along the eastern seaboard during colonial times. Precariously established early European settlers acquired the knowledge and technology associated with maize from local Indians. They were taught by Indians how to cultivate and store corn and how to prepare it as food. This Indian contribution may not seem significant today, but at the time it was immensely important to non-Indian survival. In addition, maize has emerged as one of the most important food crops in the modern world.

The list of Indian discoveries and inventions in all of the Americas becomes longer with the inclusion of American Indian cultures in Central and South America, which were the most elaborate cultures. To the inventory are added most species of beans, chili peppers, chocolate, peanuts, potatoes, sweet potatoes, tobacco, and tomatoes, as well as a few material items, such as hammocks, pipes, and the rubber syringe. Important medicines include cocaine, curare, ipecac, and quinine. The list is still not long, but some of the plants and rubber products are of immense economic importance in the modern world.

It may be asked why, from a global perspective, North American Indian culture was comparatively less elaborate than those further south. It was not from any lack of intelligence among Indians but rather because of the nature of their environmental setting and its possibilities for development. The New World was largely devoid of animals with great potential for domestication, such as cows and pigs; nor did there exist such grains as barley and wheat. More important, in the New World the animals and plants that did have potential as domesticates were *not* concentrated in one restricted geographical area. A contrary situation existed in the Old World, where the basis for most of Old World civilization emerged in the Near East about 8000 B.C. New World developments, however, are not to be cast aside as failures. One must recognize that in aboriginal Mexico and Peru, complex societies emerged with large populations and elaborate life-styles; in these regions the environmental potential for indigenous cultural developments was far greater than in settings to the north.

American English words and phrases based on a background of Indian contacts persist. Examples such as *Indian summer, happy hunting ground, medicine man, speaking with forked tongue,* and *burying the hatchet* are known widely. When place-names are added, the list becomes staggering; included are the names of not only lakes and rivers but also states and cities. Indian trails were important not only for their names but also as routes for future highways.

Indians played an important role in shaping the belief system of one of the few large and important religions originating in the United States, the Church of Jesus Christ of Latter-day Saints, or Mormons. *The Book of Mormon* relates that Indians originated from a Jewish population that entered the New World before Christian times. According to Mormon beliefs, Indians descended from the Lamanites; although these were thought to be a degenerate people, the Mormons have been inordinately kind in their dealings with Indians. As noted by A. Irving Hallowell (1958, 461), the inclusion of population theory in a religious dogma "could hardly have occurred anywhere but in early nineteenth-century America."

In early American literature no subject had greater appeal than the Indians, but their literary image has been far from uniform. The Indian entered into American literature through speeches recorded during treaty deliberations. The oratorical skills of Indians were appreciated, and the texts were printed for general circulation in the eighteenth century. Because Indians were close at hand in the eastern states and were an obstruction when whites coveted more land, they soon were viewed as foes. As the frontier expanded westward in the first half of the nineteenth century, the image of the Indian reverted to that of a nonantagonist, in fact to a romantic figure. Drawing on accounts about Indians, James Fenimore Cooper wrote his great novels and conceived the character of Leatherstocking, a white Indian without literary equal. *The Song of Hiawatha,* by Henry Wadsworth Longfellow, appeared in 1855 and was a literary marker of this era. One of the most popular nineteenth-century American plays was *Metamora,* and playwrights have continued to build plots around Indians. Included in the first American opera, *Tammany,* performed in 1794, was a Cherokee melody, and the Indian exists in such American folk songs as Charles Cadman's "From the Land of Sky Blue Waters" and "Red Wing" by Thurland Chattaway and Kerry Mills. Other Indian contributions to the arts are now a part of American history; these include Wild West shows, the Indian medicine show, the cigar-store Indian, and the romantic Indian as a subject for painters.

Along the western frontier, Indians came to be regarded as they had been in the East by non-Indian Americans who sought land. According to these settlers, the Indian impeded progress and was a form of vermin to be exterminated. After Indians had been defeated in skirmishes and wars and remnant Indian populations were confined to reservations, these people again could be viewed romantically; even before the West was colonized, the Indian was a figure in nearly half of the 320 dime novels originating in the 1850s. The Indian theme never died but was recast with the introduction of motion pictures and radio. Needless to say, American television owes a great debt to the Indian; nor is the Indian forgotten in contemporary novels.

The contemporary popularity of Indians quite possibly began to spread broadly after the Boy Scouts of America incorporated in 1910. Scouting placed considerable emphasis on Indian crafts, dances, lore, and other customs. In this manner, Indians entered the mainstream of childhood socialization for countless non-Indian males. For females, the programs of the Girl Scouts and Camp Fire Girls likewise stressed Indian culture. These influences appear to have helped give rise to "the hobby," words used to identify non-Indians interested largely in American Indian arts, crafts, dances, and songs. As noted by William K. Powers (1988, 557), the hobbyist movement emerged after World War II. Every major city has or has had such an organization, especially in the Midwest; they sponsor powwows in which Indian costumes and dances represent a focal activity. This development in turn contributed to the expanding popularity of events organized by Indians and others for Indians and non-Indians alike. No one knows for certain how many powwows are held in the United States and Canada each year, but in 1997 the estimate was 2000 such events. A prominent feature usually is Indian dance performances; parades, rodeos, and the sale of craft items are widely included. Among the largest powwows is the one held by the Mashantucket Pequot, the owners of the extremely profitable Foxwoods casino in Connecticut. This four-day gathering is inspired by a traditional corn festival. In 1997 it attracted over 2000 dancers for prize money in excess of $850,000. For outsiders, powwows provide entertainment above all else; but for the Indians themselves, the purpose may be educational and a means to revitalize select aspects of Indian life. These events, furthermore, are an important element of Pan-Indianism (see also Chapter 2).

| Who Is a Native American?

In the sixteenth century, as ever-increasing numbers of European maritime explorers ventured to the Americas, there was no difficulty in establishing who was a Native American. The racial, linguistic, and cultural differences separating Africans, Europeans, and indigenous peoples were apparent to all observers. Native Americans belonged to the Mongoloid racial stock, in contrast to the Caucasian racial background of most intruders. Indians spoke languages that differed widely from one tribe to another, but none could be understood by the explorers. Indians dressed in an unfamiliar manner, and their bodily adornments were unusual, if not bizarre, to a traveler from England, France, or Spain. Then, too, the main crops that Indians raised, maize and beans, were not cultivated in Europe. Thus, the people of the New World stood in striking contrast to Europeans and their ways.

The problem of classifying a person as an American Indian became more complex with the arrival of African slaves and European adventurers, fishermen, missionaries, settlers, traders, and trappers. Three conditions resulting from these contacts were important. First, outsiders mated with Indian women to produce persons of mixed genetic heritage; second, Indians sometimes captured blacks and whites and made them "Indians"; and third, some Indians lost their identity by assimilation into the intrusive society. To identify an Indian with clarity after the period of early historic contact, we must deal primarily with racial and sociocultural factors. Socially, we can imagine that foreigners who were assimilated into an Indian tribe were considered Indians, in spite of their race. Likewise, Indians who disassociated themselves from other Indians came to be judged as non-Indian. For individuals of mixed Indian and white or black ancestry, the distinctions were clear as long as they consistently followed one life-style or the other. Such persons could, however, behave as Indian in one context and non-Indian in another, as Indian or non-Indian exclusively throughout their lives, or as Indian at one time in life and non-Indian at another. The identification of a Native American has become a matter of definition and is most reasonably considered in a legal sense.

Before we consider Indian identity further, one point requires clarification. Non-Indians classify Aleuts and Eskimos* as separate from Indians

---

*Canadian Eskimos and numerous white Canadians are adamant that Eskimos be called Inuit, their name for themselves, and not Eskimo. In this book, *Eskimo* is used as the generic designation of these northern peoples because all Eskimos are *not* Inuit; many who live in Alaska and small numbers in Siberia are Yuit, a designation comparable to Inuit yet distinct from it. Therefore, to use the word *Inuit* for Eskimos in general is incorrect.

because of their dissimilar physical appearance and cultures. In racial terms, Aleuts and Eskimos are the most Mongoloid of indigenous New World peoples, having been the last to arrive from Asia, and their economic adjustments stand apart from those of other aboriginal Americans. However, the cultural differences separating some Indian tribes from each other are greater than those that separate Aleuts and Eskimos from many Indians. Thus, Aleuts, Eskimos, and Indians all may reasonably be called Native Americans. In Canada the preferred term is First Nations.

It merits note that in North America by the early seventeenth century, Native Americans commonly were called "blacks" or "negroes." Subsequently, Indians also might be termed "free people of color," in the manner of some blacks, or "mulattoes." Likewise, individuals of Native American and African ancestry could be called "negroes." In the 1980 U.S. census, a person who checked the "black" and "Indian" categories on the census form was counted as "black." Until recently the official classification of Native Americans and blacks clearly was a product of Euro-American racism.

In the history of United States Indian law there was no uniform definition of an Indian. In general, however, if a person is considered an Indian by other individuals in the community, he or she is legally an Indian. The degree of an individual's Indian genetic heritage may be important, but under most circumstances this is secondary to sociocultural standing in the community in which he or she lives. Regardless of heredity, a person who "acts white" may not be considered a "real Indian" by the rest of the community. Examples will illustrate why there is so much confusion. If an individual is on the roll of a federally recognized Indian group, then he or she is an Indian; the degree of Indian genetic heritage is of no real consequence, although usually the person's heritage is at least partly Indian. *Federal Indian Law* (U.S. Department of the Interior 1958) states that a person may, on some reservations, be considered an Indian even if records show that fifteen of sixteen immediate ancestors were not Indian. Add to this the fact that individual states often have different criteria for Indian status than the federal government does, and it becomes apparent how difficult it can be to define who is a Native American (Barth 1969). However, the real need for defining an Indian is with reference to a specific piece of legislation at a particular time. A person who is on the roll of a tribe and lives on a reservation clearly is an Indian; if that person moves from a reservation but remains on the roll, he or she continues to be an Indian. If he or she receives a clear title to allotted reservation land, he or she may or may not subsequently remain an Indian, depending on the circumstances. Indian status also is lost by voluntary disassociation from other Indians and by identifying with some other social segment of society.

In the United States, all Native Americans did not become citizens until 1924, when the Citizenship Act was passed by Congress. Previously, about 250,000 Indians had become citizens by other means; the act made citizens of about 125,000 more persons. As early as 1817 individuals were granted citizenship under treaty arrangements if they met certain provisions, such as the acceptance of title to individual lands in contrast to living on tribal lands. For many years the prevailing opinion of the federal government was that Indians who followed tribal customs and were not under the control of the state or territory in which they lived could not be citizens. Becoming a citizen was given a different basis with the passage of the Dawes Act in 1887. This act was designed to divide reservation lands into individual and family holdings. After a man received a clear title to land, he became a citizen, or, if he adopted Euro-American ways and lived apart from any tribe, he also became a citizen. Because he was an Indian he might still retain a special status and receive treaty or other benefits. Thus, he was a citizen with special privileges not granted to other citizens. In 1888 a law was passed making Indian women citizens if they married citizens, the assumption being that these women were following the path of "civilization." As noncitizens, Indians were not inducted into the armed services during World War I. However, those who volunteered were made citizens by congressional action. By 1938 seven states still refused to allow Native Americans to vote, and only in 1948 were voting rights granted to Indians in Arizona and New Mexico. Opposition to Indian suffrage was based on their special relationship to the federal government.

One provision in the Canadian Indian Act of 1876 was that any Indian who had a university education or its equivalent thereby became a citizen. In other instances an individual, or the band by majority vote, initiated enfranchisement proceedings; this method required a probationary period before becoming effective. When a man with a wife and minor unmarried children became enfranchised, his family was granted the same legal status. These provisions were not generally applied to the Indians of British Columbia, Manitoba, or the Northwest Territories. For the next fifty years Canadian Indian policy fluctuated between voluntary and forced enfranchisement. Finally, as a result of the Indian Act of 1951, Canadian Indians became subject to the same general laws that applied to other Canadians. They could vote in national elections and could consume intoxicants legally for the first time. In 1985 a dramatic change was made in Canadian Indian law. One result was that Indians who had become non-Indian could once again regain their Indian identity (see Chapter 2 for the details).

| Population Figures

At the time of early European contact, around A.D. 1500, estimates of the Indian population north of Mexico range from about two to more than four million people; the latter figure may be more accurate. The Native American population in the United States reached its lowest point around 1900 with about 240,000 people. The U.S. government now recognizes about 300 tribes in the contiguous states and about 225 Native Alaskan villages (sometimes called tribes). Based on a 1994 estimate, some 2,275,000 people in the United States identified themselves as Native Americans; nearly half of that number were not members of a federally recognized group. The Navajo, with about

250,000 people, are the most populous federally recognized tribe. Some groups have achieved federal acknowledgment only in recent years; in 1984, for example, the 2000-member Poarch Creek of Alabama was recognized. Others, such as the 600-member Shawnee Nation United Remnant Band of Ohio, achieved state identity in 1980 but did not seek federal recognition. Many people consider themselves American Indians but have no formal affiliation with any Indian community, organization, or tribe, and some cannot document their claim to be Indian. Most Native Americans in the United States live in urban areas. About 25 percent live on or near reservations or traditional lands. The states with the highest percentages of Native Americans in 1990 were Alaska (15.6), New Mexico (8.9), and Oklahoma (8.0).

In Canada the First Nations (Native American) population reached its lowest point around 1900 with about 100,000 people. The First Nations population in 1996 was about 805,000; of these, 554,000 were North American Indians, 210,000 were Metis (persons of mixed heritage), and 41,000 were Inuit (Eskimos). About 70 percent of the First Nations people lived on or near reserves (reservations). The provinces with the largest populations were Alberta, Manitoba, and Saskatchewan.

Today, about 50,000 Inuit (Eskimos) live in Greenland, a province of Denmark, having recovered from a population low of about 10,000 in 1900.

| Where Did Native Americans Originate?

Speculations about the origins of Native Americans have had lasting romantic appeal. Humanists, the general public, and scientists alike have long puzzled over the original Indian homeland. Surprisingly, each of the theories that have been advanced to explain their derivation involves something that is lost to modern times; thus, the supportive evidence can only be indirect.

Conjecture about a lost continent of Atlantis (or Antillia, the word on which Antilles is based) predates the discovery of the Americas. After Europeans learned of the existence of Native Americans, the idea that Atlantis had been a stepping-stone for early migrants from the Old to the New World seemed logical. Atlantis was thought to be a vast island beyond Gibraltar, where a complex civilization developed before it was destroyed by a cataclysm. The idea lingered among the Romans and was accepted by some persons in medieval Europe. Christopher Columbus may have sailed toward its presumed position, and some people thought that the land he discovered was Atlantis. The thesis that Native Americans were from Atlantis was clearly expounded in the writings of Francisco Lopez de Gomara, published in 1552. He proposed, for example, that the word *atl,* which was the word for water among Indians in one sector of Mexico, was a lingering remembrance of their homeland. By the 1880s the island's disappearance was still being attributed to a major cataclysm that had occurred after the people destined to become American Indians had left its shores. Each author who supported the theory was struck by the cultural similarities between American Indians, usually those in Mexico, and some early Old World civilization, usually Egyptian.

Another theory proposed that Indians were descendants of the Lost Tribes of Israel. The evidence for this idea was summarized long ago by Samuel F. Haven (1856). According to this theory, ten tribes of Israelites, defeated by the Assyrians, became lost by wandering into Asia. They ventured to a point nearest the Americas, where they crossed the waters into the New World. Evidence to support the Hebrew ancestry of Indians was found in certain customs, words, and idioms. The theory has been popular and continues to find support among members of the Church of Jesus Christ of Latter-day Saints.

A host of conjectures has been advanced to explain the origins of American Indians. James Churchward (1931) proposed that there once was a great Pacific island called Lemuria, or Mu. However, his evidence was fanciful and gained little acceptance. Other speculators have identified seafaring peoples such as the Carthaginians or Phoenicians as responsible for the original occupation. Cotton Mather, in colonial America, advanced a unique explanation for Indian origins. He wrote that "probably the *Devil* decoyed those miserable salvages* hither, in hopes that the gospel of the Lord Jesus Christ would never come here to destroy or disturb his absolute empire over them" (Drake 1837, 9).

In 1570 the Jesuit missionary Father Joseph de Acosta went to Peru, and about 1580 he began to write his *Historia natural y moral de las Indias*. The book appeared in its first Spanish edition in 1590, three years after he returned to Spain. Acosta reasoned that since Adam was the original ancestor of humanity and since Indians were people, then they must have come from the Old World, which Adam's descendants had peopled. He reasoned that the New World and the Old World had been connected, or separated, by a narrow strait, because certain land mammals were the same in the respective hemispheres. He felt that people and animals alike had traveled along the same route. The human entry was visualized as having taken place slowly, caused by overpopulation, famines, or the loss of former living areas. Thus, Acosta was the first to advance a land-bridge theory to explain why and how people entered the New World. He also theorized that the original occupants were hunters who later developed a more complex way of life. Therefore, any comparisons between New and Old World civilizations could not be very meaningful.

Modern anthropologists support the general thesis of Indian origins first advanced by Acosta. People did not evolve in the New World but migrated there. The bones of *all* the distant human ancestors that have been found are reported in the Old World. Bones that are clear markers along humankind's

---

*Middle English spelling of "savages."

evolutionary trail have been found repeatedly in Africa. In the same context, the earliest human remains in the New World date from about 9000 B.C. and belong to individuals who were essentially modern in physical appearance. From the fossil record, we must conclude that people entered the Western Hemisphere in relatively recent times. Furthermore, geological evidence indicates that continents did *not* formerly exist in either the Atlantic or Pacific oceans. Thus, there could not have been either a continent of Atlantis or of Mu to serve as stepping-stones to the New World.

The vast majority of professional archaeologists contend that the first people to arrive in the New World entered over a land bridge in the Bering Strait area. These migrants lingered in Alaska for a considerable length of time and eventually followed western mountains southward into Canada, ventured on into the western United States and Mexico, and finally continued into South America. The economic lives of the earliest migrants were based on hunting, and the Bering Strait entryway served as a cultural filter through which only hunters could pass.

| What Later Influences Came across the Seas?

Although the ancestors of most historic Indians arrived in the New World via the Bering Strait area, in the popular literature about Indians speculations about all-water migration routes have persisted. The idea of pre-Columbian voyages to the New World has almost boundless popular appeal. To think of people setting sail in small boats, headed they knew not where, is spine-tingling. The romance of the idea has led commentators to visualize voyages originating from diverse sectors of the Old World. Even after setting imagination aside, the realities of what may have been are in themselves inviting.

The only pre-Columbian voyages beyond reasonable dispute are the ones made by Viking, or more properly Norse, explorers. Iceland was settled in the ninth century by Scandinavians, and within a hundred years Greenland had been discovered. After becoming involved in a series of homicides, Eric the Red was exiled from Iceland for three years. He spent the time, A.D. 982–985, exploring southwestern Greenland, and on his return he organized a colonizing expedition. It left for southwestern Greenland in 986, and additional settlers arrived later. The Greenland colony was occupied by the Norse until about 1540 and had a maximum population of about five thousand persons. Given the turbulent weather in the north Atlantic, many ships heading toward Greenland were lost or blown off course. One vessel strayed to the coast of North America but did not land. About the year 1000, the son of Eric the Red, Leif Erikson, purposely sailed for continental North America. In the centuries to follow, a number of planned trips were made to northeastern North America from Greenland, especially to obtain building timber. The Norse appear to have settled briefly in northern Newfoundland at L'Anse aux Meadows, which was discovered and partially excavated by Helge Ingstad. Radiocarbon dates indicate that the site was occupied about A.D. 1000. The presence of a few

Norse artifacts and wrought iron at the site leaves little doubt that these were Norse remains. However, no clear evidence exists to suggest that these Europeans had any influence on the cultures of aboriginal Americans.

If voyagers from the Old World, apart from the Norse, did arrive in the New World during pre-Columbian times, we might expect to find artifacts that they brought with them. Conversely, if travelers ventured in the opposite direction, we would expect to recover objects in the Eastern Hemisphere that were made in the Americas. Despite the thousands of excavations in which millions of artifacts have been recovered, not one such artifact has been found in a clearly valid context. Admittedly, these objects may exist in unexplored sites, and if any are found, our thinking will need to be revised or even reversed.

If there were substantial Old and New World contacts, we would expect to find evidence in linguistic ties. Relationships between languages cannot be postulated based on a small number of words with the same form and meaning, because such parallels may be accounted for by chance alone. To demonstrate historical connections between languages, clear phonemic and grammatical similarities as well as numerous parallels among words must exist. Is there any evidence of this nature to link pre-Columbian peoples of the two hemispheres? The answer is a cautious "yes," in the Bering Strait region. The Eskimo–Aleut language family that spans the American Arctic and the Chukchi–Kamchatkan family in northeastern Siberia appear to be related. Thus, the New and Old Worlds may be joined in linguistic terms but not in a way that speculators might assume.

Expecting to find Old World artifacts in prehistoric New World sites may be unreasonable, if only because few objects probably survived long ocean voyages. Similarly, the speakers of Old World languages could have arrived, but their languages might have passed out of existence when the original migrants died. This raises the question of whether there were *influences* from the Old World reaching the Americas. As we consider the question, we must first make one critical observation. Innumerable examples exist of people in one part of the world inventing artifacts similar to those independently conceived and produced by a distant people. Thus we must be cautious in deducing that a form had a single place of origin and spread from there. Furthermore, evidence that coherent *groups* of Old and New World artifacts are similar is of greater potential significance than are similarities between isolated artifact types or design motifs.

Perhaps the best evidence for prehistoric Old and New World contacts is the presence of certain Asian-like artifact types in sites along the coast of Ecuador, dating about 200 B.C. As Emilio Estrada and Betty J. Meggers (1961) noted, this cluster is largely restricted to Ecuador. Included are pottery models of houses with saddle-shaped roofs and columns, figures with one leg folded above the other, and the "coolie" yoke. These finds suggest that ocean voyagers from Asia landed in Ecuador and successfully introduced these and other novel ideas.

Another approach to the problem centers on evidence of a different nature: domestic plants and animals transported by pre-Columbian peoples to the New World. In a symposium that he organized, Carroll L. Riley and his associates considered cultigens. A quotation from their summary remarks follows (Riley et al. 1971, 452–453): "The consensus of botanical evidence given in this symposium seems to be that *there is no hard and fast evidence for any pre-Columbian human introduction of any single plant or animal* across the ocean from the Old World to the New World, or vice-versa. This is emphatically *not* to say that it could not have occurred." Thus, the case rests on a largely negative note.

| Precontact History North of Mexico, An Overview

The earliest human migrants to the New World came from Siberia, and they were hunters. These statements seem beyond reasonable doubt. Likewise, ancestral Native Americans filtered southward to occupy inhabitable areas of the Americas. By early historic times, Indians had made innumerable adaptations, depending on localized resources, contact with other Indians, and other factors. This section provides a brief synopsis of pre-Columbian cultural developments, with the emphasis on the regions north of Mexico.

PALEO-INDIANS   Controversy surrounds the question of when the earliest migrants first entered the Americas. It is widely accepted that in the vicinity of the Bering Strait a land bridge existed from about 75,000 to 45,000 years ago. Yet there is no current evidence to suggest that this bridge was used by people entering the New World. In the same region, a land bridge was known to have been exposed from about 25,000 to 11,000 years ago, and it was during this time span that the earliest humans probably entered northern North America. During this and earlier cold periods, glacial ice covered large areas of the Northern Hemisphere, and worldwide sea levels were lowered by as much as 300 feet. In eastern Siberia and western Alaska, there were no major glaciers because conditions were unfavorable for their formation: the amount of annual precipitation was low, and the land was relatively flat. When the land bridge, called Beringia, loosely connected the continents, it served as a pathway and a cultural filter. Hunters who lived by killing large herbivores, such as bison, caribou, mammoth, and horses, were quite possibly the earliest migrants.

A critical year in the discovery of evidence about prehistoric humans in the Americas was 1926. It was then that J. D. Figgins, a paleontologist excavating a site in northern New Mexico, uncovered the bones of an extinct bison that was much larger than modern bison. The site had been located in 1908 by George McJunkin, an African American cowboy who was the foreman at the ranch on which the discovery was made; unfortunately, McJunkin died before the site was investigated. Ultimately, Figgins found four flint points near bison bones, and a fifth point was embedded *in* bone. This evidence has never been seriously challenged. The projectile points were named Folsom, after the discovery site, and date around 10,500 years ago.

Excavations at the Folsom site demonstrated that Native Americans had considerable antiquity in the New World. The next question was and remains: When did people begin to occupy the New World? Unfortunately, we do not know. Archaeologists are rather confident that the sporadic claims that some sites were occupied 30,000 years ago or in the even more distant past are incorrect. Pre-Folsom artifacts made from flaked stone occasionally have been found in the far north and relatively near Beringia. Widely accepted examples are artifacts from Bluefish Caves in the northern Yukon Territory, Canada, that date around 13,500 years ago; those at Dry Creek in the Nenana River valley of central Alaska date around 11,200 years ago. Much farther south, especially in Arizona, distinctive projectile points, termed Clovis, repeatedly have been excavated in association with mammoth bones and date around 11,000 years ago. Finally, there is the Monte Verde site in southern Chile. The occupants hunted small game and collected plant products; they lived there at least 12,500 years ago.

Considering the location and approximate date for the Monte Verde site, if the ancestors of these Native Americans traveled by land from Siberia and Alaska, they probably arrived in the Americas much earlier than 12,500 years ago in order to reach southern South America by this time. One reasonable explanation would be that there are older and yet-to-be-discovered inland sites. Another far more speculative possibility is that at least some early migrants traveled by water, not by land. In this context, it is widely accepted that the initial human occupation of Australia was by watercraft at least 50,000 years ago. Could it be that watercraft existed long, long ago along the eastern fringe of Siberia? The possibility exists. If so, early migrants may have boated along the Siberian coast, island-hopped along the north Pacific area of Alaska, and continued southward in the Americas.

THE ARCHAIC TRADITION   As the West and the Southwest became drier, hunting diminished in importance. By about 6000 B.C. a way of life adapted to the western deserts had developed, one that has been termed the Desert culture. The primary foods were wild plant products and small game. As small groups of people moved about to exploit varied resources, they occupied open sites or camped in caves and rock shelters on an opportunistic basis. Grinding stones became key technological forms in processing seeds, nuts, and other plant or animal products to render them edible. Small animals were stunned with missile sticks or captured in fencelike nets, and spears harvested large game, such as antelope or bison. Basketry became important for winnowing wild seeds, cooking foods, and for storage. This eminently successful lifeway, the Archaic tradition, persisted in many parts of the West until after the arrival of Europeans. The Cahuilla Indians (Chapter 5) represent one form of this life-style as it continued into historic times. In the northwestern Plains, Archaic tradition bison hunters persisted into historic times, but their lives changed dramatically beginning about A.D. 1730, when domestic horses, of colonial Spanish origin, were introduced from the south. The Crow (Chapter 6) represent one such people.

Along the northwest coast from the Gulf of Alaska to northern California, prehistoric maritime cultures emerged, probably from an Archaic base. By 1000 B.C. sea mammals were hunted and salmon fished with expanding intensity. Woodworking tools were well established by about 200 B.C., suggesting the manufacture of plank houses and large dugout canoes. These developments provided the general background for the emergence of historic Northwest Coast Indian cultures such as the Yurok (Chapter 7) and the Tlingit (Chapter 8).

In the eastern United States and Canada, along rivers and coastal areas, Indians lived as hunters and gatherers from about 8000 to 3000 B.C. These Archaic economies varied widely because of differences in local resources. In some areas, shellfish, fish, or large game were the dominant foods, whereas in many others, wild plants predominated. The oldest sites had relatively brief spans of occupation, but by about 3000 B.C. some settlements, especially those along major rivers with abundant food resources, were being occupied for generations. These people are noted especially for their ground and polished stone woodworking tools, such as adzes, axes, and gouges. The technology of these people was far more developed than that reported among Paleo-Indians.

THE NORTHERN HUNTERS The distant descendants of some pioneer hunters in the north remained hunters or became hunters and fishers. Early evidence about them is associated with inland areas and dates from as long ago as 13,500 years. Some reasonably early finds recall Archaic tradition artifact types. Other tools are similar to finds in Siberia and thus support an archaeological link with northeastern Asia. It is thought that the Na-Dene Indians, the northern hunters who were the ancestors of modern Athapaskan Indians, were living in interior Alaska and northwestern Canada by at least 5000 B.C. These distinctly inland people hunted caribou or moose, depending on the locality, and fished; for most of them, their fishing activities increased during times of food stress. The Chipewyan Indians (Chapter 3) are a historic example of Athapaskans who were caribou hunters and fishers. The Navajo (Chapter 10) appear to have been northern hunters before they entered the Southwest, where they became part-time farmers during prehistoric times and herders during the historic era.

The oldest finds associated with coastal hunters in the Bering Strait region are identified with the Arctic Small Tool tradition. The sites date from as early as about 2000 B.C. They are associated with the emergence of Eskimo culture, whose bearers spread to southwestern Alaska and eastward into Greenland. These people primarily were sea mammal hunters, but they harvested caribou on an opportunistic basis or fished for salmon whenever possible. The large, open skin boat (umiak) and small, one-person skin boat (kayak) became important aids to hunting, as did the weapon called the toggle-headed harpoon. Eventually many Eskimos burned the oil from sea mammals in lamps, thereby freeing themselves from a dependence on wood for fuel. Winter mobility increased with the introduction of dog-team travel in comparatively recent prehistoric times. The impermanent tents of early Eskimos were replaced by semisubterranean houses built of turf and stone or driftwood, depending on the area. Eskimos are famous for their varied adaptations to differing arctic and subarctic conditions. The Kuskowagamiut (Chapter 4) are an example of a people who made a major ecological adaptation.

THE FARMERS   Among Indians in many areas, the most radical prehistoric economic change occurred when hunting and gathering were replaced by a primary dependence on domestic plant products. Maize was domesticated in Mesoamerica about 4000 B.C.; the common bean may have been domesticated at about the same time in Peru, where squash could have been a cultigen somewhat earlier. By about 1000 B.C., the cultivation of maize had spread from the south into the American Southwest; later, beans and squash were planted there. These were the primary crops raised north of Mexico. Some western Indians developed more productive hybrid strains of maize that enabled them to become increasingly sedentary. In the Southwest this led to the Hohokam cultural tradition in the deserts of Arizona and the Mogollon tradition best associated with highland areas of Arizona and New Mexico. The Anasazi tradition, which represents the ancestors of modern Pueblo Indians such as the Hopi (Chapter 9), arose primarily from various groups of gatherers identified with the Basketmaker culture. The Pueblo Indian cultures that emerged between A.D. 700 and 1400 are most often associated with pueblo-type dwellings, separate ceremonial chambers or *kivas,* and elaborate pottery.

In the eastern United States, some Archaic peoples became gardeners, and by 2000 B.C. they were raising sunflowers for food, as well as a variety of squash, maygrass, and sumpweed. By A.D. 100, maize was cultivated, but beans did not become evident until about A.D. 1000. The Woodland tradition began to coalesce about 1000 B.C., with its burial mounds and distinctive pottery. The Adena people, concentrated in the Ohio River drainage area, became prominent mound builders who flourished until about A.D. 100. They traded widely for raw materials and probably were well organized, possibly with chiefs as leaders of political and religious life.

In the same general area, the successors to the Adena people represented the Hopewell tradition that flourished from about 200 B.C. to A.D. 500. They were probably farmers living in relatively permanent communities, and they are famous for their elaborate earthworks. They were organized into distinctive social classes and accorded prominent attention to certain of the dead. We do not know why the Adena and Hopewell traditions declined rather abruptly at their centers, although disease may have been a contributing factor. Some Hopewell Indians survived, however. Their descendants may have included the Fox or Mesquakie Indians (Chapter 11). Other Hopewell branches persisted in the Northeast, and one group probably provided the background for Iroquois Indian culture (Chapter 12).

Prehistoric Indian culture in the United States climaxed in the Mississippian tradition, found in parts of the Midwest and Southeast from about A.D. 900 to 1500; their economy was based on the cultivation of maize, beans, and squash. The Mississippians probably were organized into complex social and political units, each with a clear sense of national identity. Social ranks existed, with priests and other elites topping the hierarchy. Their ceremonial centers must have required years to plan and construct, with the labor of many people required to build their elaborate terraced temple mounds, as well as the house mounds of the elite. The Natchez Indians, examined in Chapter 14, represent a remnant population within the Mississippian tradition. It had spread widely in the Southeast, and a more peripheral manifestation led to the emergence of the Cherokee (Chapter 13).

SUMMARY This brief review of the prehistory of Native Americans north of Mexico should demonstrate that the original American Indian culture developed from that of Asian migrants who were hunters. Farming emerged much later and was based primarily on crops domesticated in Mexico and Peru. The diversity of American Indian life observed by Columbus and his successors represented adjustments to different ecological and social settings as these groups occupied the continent. Eventually, hundreds of distinct Indian cultures appeared. Thus no fanciful lost continents, lost tribes, or large-scale shipborne migrations in prehistoric times are required to explain the presence and diversity of Indians in the New World.

| How Have Native American Cultures Been Studied?

No matter where Europeans settled in North America, it soon became apparent that Indians were well entrenched and quite different culturally. Some Native Americans were primarily fishers, whereas others farmed and still others hunted or gathered. They spoke many different languages and organized themselves in diverse ways, ranging from small, mobile, autonomous communities to large, stable nations or confederations. To better understand this variability and how it has been described, it is helpful to introduce a number of concepts.

Any reasonably systematic account of the lives of a people is called an *ethnography*. Their artifacts, language, social and political organization, art, knowledge, and myths are each an ethnographic dimension. An ethnography is overwhelmingly descriptive and pertains to a brief period of time. In more exact terms, an ethnography is a descriptive framework for behavioral information about a population at a particular point in time. The peoples considered by ethnographers ideally are aboriginal, and the time span examined is a typical calendar year. Ethnographic data are collected as systematically as possible and are checked for internal consistency; for these reasons, most accounts by explorers, travelers, or journalists do not qualify. There are two general categories of ethnographies: baseline studies made about life at the time of historic contact and others made for later points in time. A *baseline ethnography* describes a people before they had any significant contact with representatives of literate societies. Thus, the data represent conditions *before* the people studied were influenced or disrupted by Europeans, Euro-Americans, or the members of other clearly foreign groups. In a strict sense, a baseline ethnography should be compiled before European trade goods or diseases of European origins prevail. Yet capable observers seldom were present to record a broad range of information about a Native American population in a systematic manner before their customs were altered by agents of Western culture. The first comprehensive ethnography of an Indian tribe, or of any aboriginal people for that matter, that made a significant impact on anthropology was written in 1851. The author was Lewis H. Morgan, and his study was of the Iroquois Indians in New York state. Thus, ethnography as a distinct intellectual pursuit is comparatively recent in origin.

Trained investigators did not begin making thorough studies of American Indians until around 1900. Usually they attempted to collect verbal information about Native American life at the time of historic contact, or at least for a period as far back in time as an informant could recall. An ethnographer talked with Indians about the past, observed current customs, and consulted written sources. By using these data he or she assembled a *reconstructed baseline ethnography*. The primary difficulty in such an enterprise was obtaining reliable information about the early historic period. Most ethnographies written by anthropologists about American Indians are reconstructions made long after the first historic contacts of the groups studied. A major difficulty was to validate informants' statements, especially when documentary sources had not been studied thoroughly, a typical failing of early ethnographers. The time factor often could not be held constant for the early historic period, and as a result many descriptions were actually composites of customs at various times. Traditional ethnographies began changing character by the early 1930s, but it was not until much later that most anthropologists realized what had happened. The long-term ideal of reconstructing aboriginal baseline accounts rarely could be realized after about 1940.

Quite obviously, ethnographic information has been recorded by many observers with varied backgrounds and at different times, which leads to a note of caution about their findings. If the biases of an observer are readily apparent, they can be taken into account when evaluating his or her descriptions. In some instances, however, the biases may be so subtle that they escape the attention of someone using the material. In still other cases an ethnographer may be mistaken in what she or he reports. Because a misrepresentation of Indian life may result from these conditions, it is most desirable to check one source against another, if this is possible. Alternatively, the general reliability of the observer must serve as the primary guide to the validity of data. Cultural anthropologists understandably are cautious in their interpretation of field data and seek the most valid data base.

As the lives of Native Americans changed following prolonged firsthand contact with exotic complex societies, the Indians were said to be undergoing the process of acculturation; the end product was either stabilized pluralism or assimilation into the dominant society. Thus, we may consider *acculturative ethnographies* as a type of ethnography. They present a description of life relating to a brief span of historic time and may be assembled from documents or by observations and interviews.

The first person to focus a field study on contemporary Indian lifeways was Margaret Mead. In 1930 she worked among the Omaha Indians and subsequently published *The Changing Culture of an Indian Tribe* (New York, 1932). This was a watershed in North American Indian studies and anticipated hundreds of broadly similar works about Indian acculturation. By 1940 even the most remote Indians had had substantial contacts with Euro-Americans for at least forty years, and indirect contacts had introduced Anglo-American trade goods and exotic diseases long before. Historic changes loomed large in many ethnographic accounts that attempted to reconstruct aboriginal conditions; thus, they were inaccurate as aboriginal baseline studies. Yet, the training of ethnographers continued to stress interviews with informed persons, observant participation, genealogical techniques, reasonable efforts to learn the language of the people studied, and the usually superficial analysis of pertinent historical writings. Because original fieldwork was nearly essential to gain professional status, it remained a dominant training device but with a shift to acculturative field studies of tribes or communities as the aboriginal ideal was replaced by acculturative realities. As ethnographers became methodologically more sophisticated, the emphasis shifted further. Problem-focused studies began to dominate, with one or more aspects of Indian life singled out for detailed attention.

Clearly, the data base of old has disappeared, and the study of urban Indians or certain aspects of modern reservation life, such as health or land tenure, has been one response. Another approach, called *ethnohistory* and favored by persons more interested in traditional Indian life, has been the study of pertinent historical documents, often with accompanying field studies for additional information, to plot changes in a people's lifeway. The study of historical records long has been the purview of historians, and some of them, such as William T. Hagan, Roy H. Pearce, Lewis O. Saum, and Wilcomb E. Washburn, have a keen understanding of the Indian in American history. For American anthropologists concentrating on Indians north of Mexico, an appreciation of historical developments has been comparatively recent. One of the earliest studies was that carried out in 1928–30 by Felix M. Keesing (1939) concerning the Menominee of Wisconsin. The next major work was by Oscar Lewis (1942) and dealt with Blackfoot culture change. Thus, ethnohistory as an anthropological focus is a comparatively new development; *Ethnohistory,* a journal devoted to the subject, originated in 1954.

Ethnohistory has only recently emerged as a significant focus among anthropologists. In addition to archival and library research, field studies often are recognized as valuable; some Native Americans clearly remember many customs and historical events that had never found their way into written records. The study of historical records has led to major revisions in our understanding about some tribes early in their history. It probably is true that every tribal ethnography for aboriginal or early historic times could be made far more accurate after a careful study of existing archival and published records. Thus, superior accounts for many tribes are yet to be written.

Two other terms need defining to round out our consideration of how Indian cultures have been studied. *Ethnoarchaeology* is the use of archaeological techniques to acquire ethnographic data about a particular population. The time range represented by the artifacts recovered is of no consequence in a study of this type; the major consideration is that the artifacts must be identified with a particular people. If broad or narrow generalizations are drawn from ethnographies, the study is termed *ethnology,* which is the comparative study of ethnographic data.

Thus far the units for study have not been defined precisely, but their clear identification is desirable. Different groups of Indians usually are termed tribes, yet no one set of criteria for a tribe accommodates all North American Indians. The difficulties in deriving a concept that encompasses the diversity of social norms and cultural forms may be illustrated by a rather typical definition. Alfred L. Kroeber (1925, 474) stated that a true tribe "has a name, a dialect, and a territory." Yet, among the nearly fifty major Indian groups in California, only the Yokuts of the San Joaquin Valley had all three characteristics. Most California Indians did not have a distinct tribal name; they identified themselves only as members of a particular community. Efforts to define a tribe on the basis of political cohesiveness are equally unrewarding. As John R. Swanton (1953, 1–2) pointed out, the reported variability seems to defy the use of a single label. The Creek confederation comprised dominant and subordinate tribes; the name Powhatan embraced about thirty tribes or subtribes united by conquest; the name Ojibwa (Chippewa) included small groups of people who had little if any sense of political unity; each Pueblo village governed its own affairs and was in a sense a small tribe.

Kroeber (1955, 303) attempted to bring some order to the terminological maze. He wrote, "What are generally denominated tribes really are small nationalities, possessing essentially uniform speech and customs and therefore an accompanying sense of likeness and likemindedness, which in turn tended to prevent serious dissensions or internal conflicts." Within such nationalities were smaller sovereign states, usually termed bands or villages, that were in fact economically self-sufficient and had a recognized territory and political independence. Kroeber reasoned that a tribe was rather like a German state before the consolidation in 1871: each state functioned independently although they shared a common language, culture, and ideology. In the United States these Indian units were more properly regarded as nations in the seventeenth and eighteenth centuries. Actually, the concept of a tribe or nation most often was a product of white contact; government officials grouped tribes, bands, or villages so they could more conveniently negotiate treaties, arrange resettlements, and so on. Aboriginal decision making most often was at the band or village level, although some peoples were consolidated into larger political aggregates. In the subsequent chapters, the difficulties in defining a tribe are not overwhelmingly important, but the reader should be aware that the label *tribe* does not always mean the same thing when applied to different peoples. Those interested in pursuing the topic further are referred to a volume on the subject edited by June Helm (1968).

Another aspect of studying Native Americans that has led to confusion because of its overall inconsistency is any attempt to view the time of historic contact collectively. Historic contact with Indians differed widely in time from one region to another. Many tribes in the eastern United States had been destroyed by disease and homicide or displaced from their lands before others to the north and west ever heard of white people or knew of the diseases that they carried. Historic contact began about A.D. 1000 in northern Newfoundland, while in the Southwest it was 1540, and it was 1885 in one sector of central Alaska. Thus, no single decade or century represents the contact period. This means that there is a *sliding historical baseline* for the beginnings of Indian history on a regional basis. Swanton (1953, 3–6) has suggested that if A.D. 1650 is taken as a base date, it is possible to establish the indigenous Indian boundaries for the southern and eastern United States as well as for eastern Canada. In the northwestern sector of the continent, no major relocations of peoples appear to have occurred between 1650 and the time of their actual historic contact, making it possible to tentatively include them under this date as well. For the balance of the continent north of Mexico, the date of 1650 is less satisfactory. An adjustment backward in time to around A.D. 1540 might be more accurate to accommodate the peoples of the Southwest. The Plains area would require several dates over a considerable time span. The most important conclusion is that the boundaries and positioning of many tribes on standard ethnographic maps, including those in this volume, are not entirely accurate for any single time period. Instead, they attempt to represent the area of any particular tribe at the moment in history when it was surveyed and located on a map.

What Do We Know of Native American Languages?

By conservative estimates 2 million Native Americans lived north of Mexico when first contacted, and they spoke about three hundred different languages. In some sectors, such as among Eskimos along the Arctic rim, the same language was spoken over a wide area. In other regions, as in northwestern Canada, people spoke different but closely related languages. Elsewhere, highly distinct languages might exist in a limited area. In California, for example, far greater linguistic diversity existed than is found in all of modern Europe.

European settlers could ignore Indian customs if they wished since they lived in separate communities, but they could not ignore Indian languages if they hoped to communicate with them. Since typical colonists felt superior to Native Americans, they seldom attempted to learn an Indian language; most often Indians or persons of mixed heritage became bilingual. Yet, for Christian missionaries intent on converting Indians, it was essential to learn the languages of peoples among whom they worked. The first landmark in American Indian linguistics was the publication in 1663 of a Bible translated into Massachuset, an Algonquian language, by the missionary John Eliot; in 1666 he published an Algonquian grammar.

The first prominent student of Indian linguistics was Thomas Jefferson. He was concerned that Native American languages were disappearing rapidly, and before he became president in 1801 he had collected considerable linguistic information. Jefferson (1801, 149) reasoned that preserving linguistic data from Indians in the Americas would make it possible to trace the relationships among these peoples. The first comparative linguist of stature in the United States was Peter S. Du Ponceau. French by birth, he served in the Revolutionary War and later practiced law in Philadelphia. Among the notable conclusions drawn by Du Ponceau in his study of languages was that a relationship existed between the Chukchi of Siberia and Eskimos in arctic America. However, no Asian language was identified as spoken in North America, and he suggested tentatively that no South Pacific area languages were spoken along coastal America.

The next linguist of note was Albert Gallatin, the first person to analyze and classify varied Indian languages of North America. This Swiss-born language teacher became a businessman, later the Secretary of the Treasury, and finally a minister to France and then to England. In 1836 Gallatin published a classification of languages in North America north of Mexico and east of the Rocky Mountains. He also supported Du Ponceau's conclusion about the essential homogeneity of American Indian languages compared with those found elsewhere in the world. When John Wesley Powell published his definitive study of American Indian linguistic families in 1891, he credited Gallatin as the person who previously had contributed the most to the subject. The essence of Powell's classification has withstood the test of time, but he deserves credit primarily for assembling sources rather than for making a highly original contribution. Powell prepared a map on which fifty-eight language families were identified; it has been revised and reproduced on innumerable occasions. The general classification that prevails at present is by C. F. Voegelin and F. M. Voegelin (1966); it appears in simplified form as Figure 1-1. Subsequent studies have led to modifications of this map, and they are summarized by Lyle Campbell and M. Mithun (1979); their revisions are cited in the presentations about particular tribes. (Campbell and Mithun did not compile a revised map based on their findings.)

About half of the three hundred native languages survive into the present, and yet for most of them few speakers remain. The most widely spoken examples are Eskimo subgroups (Yupik and Inuit-Inupiaq), Navajo, and Chippewa. Although some tribes have indigenous-language programs in the classroom, they have neither lasted very long nor been very successful. However, radio broadcasts in tribal languages are increasingly common and appear to provide a better context for learning. News items about Native Americans have been broadcast since the early days of commercial radio in the 1920s, but regularly scheduled programs for Indians did not begin until the 1960s. Native-owned radio stations and noncommercial public and tribal stations began to appear in 1971. By 1998 in the United States there were thirty tribal radio stations, including eight in Alaska. Canada has about two hundred stations dominated by First Nations peoples. In both Canada and the United States, many Indian-dominated stations air native-language programs. They also increasingly broadcast programs that emphasize cultural revitalization. These developments hold promise for greater Indian-language vitality.

| How Can We Group Tribes?

Linguists first established relationships among tribes on a sound basis by identifying families of related languages, thereby reducing the immense diversity of languages to an almost manageable whole. By 1896 Otis T. Mason had formulated a means for grouping ethnographic information based on environment and culture. The idea of describing Indians in terms of geographical clusters was relatively well accepted at this time, but Mason was the first to detail the characteristics of each area. A culture area is a geographical sector of the world whose occupants exhibit more similarities with each other than with peoples in other such areas. Culture areas were in theory determined on the basis of baseline ethnographies and by taking the sliding historical baseline into consideration. The concept was applied to American Indians most systematically by Clark Wissler (1938, 1942), and it has served as the organizational basis for most continentwide discussions of Indians. The system has the advantage of fitting all tribes into a relatively small number of groups. Its major disadvantages are that it refers to a single point in time and tends to stress material culture. We find, too, that one area may include peoples with

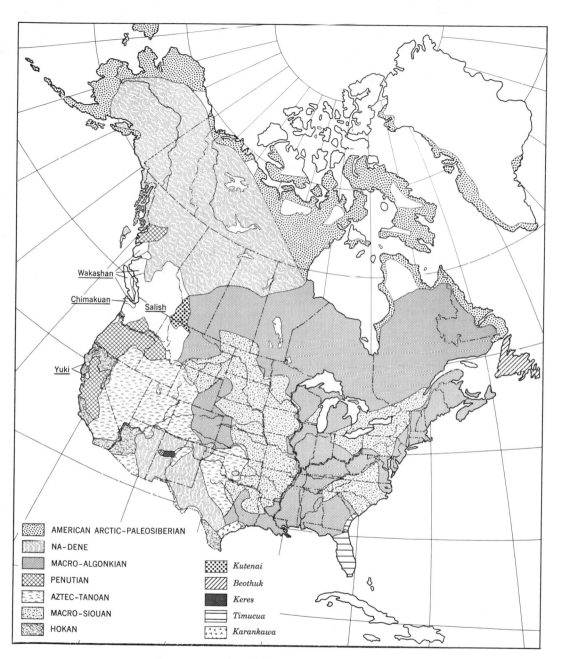

Figure 1-1 | Major linguistic groups for aboriginal North America north of Mexico. The widespread phyla are designated in capital letters; the phyla for which there is a single representative language are in italics, and the families for which there are no established phyla are underlined. (After Voegelin and Voegelin 1966; reproduced by permission of the American Ethnological Society. Not for further reproduction.)

different ways of life and that tribes along boundaries may share the characteristics of two areas. Finally, those doing the classifying seldom agree on the precise boundaries for areas, a situation that partially reflects the impressionistic basis of the evaluations. A culture-area classification is presented in Figure 1-2, and the major characteristics of each area are reported in Table 1-1.

| Ethnographic Studies, An Overview

Early professional ethnographers (ca. A.D. 1900–1930) collected information from Indians with inordinate zeal because they thought that Native American lifeways would soon disappear. At least some Indians who helped them shared this dire perspective. Likewise, as products of their times, ethnographers were biased in how and what they recorded. For example, women's viewpoints and perspectives on sexual activities seldom were presented in a systematic manner. Subsequently, attention shifted to how Native American lifeways were changing in response to intensive contact with Euro-Americans and other outsiders. The 1930 study of the Omaha Indians by Margaret Mead is the best marker of this new approach. By the 1950s ethnographic studies of Indians typically had become narrower in scope, far more historical and problem-oriented, increasingly dependent on statistical approaches, and sometimes concerned with resolving Indian "problems."

By the 1990s a shift in emphasis and approach was emerging. By then it was abundantly clear that American Indians were *not* a vanishing race, and many tribes had retained their cultures with far greater vitality than had been predicted. As a result, ethnographers are returning to Indian studies with a new respect for the "survival" of old traditions and customs. Indians sympathetic to a more accurate recording of their tribal ways can be quite knowledgeable, and they are numerous. As never before, Indians and ethnographers have become full collaborators in data collection. Likewise, Indians are in a unique position when they hire anthropologists to work for them. This exciting development has one serious potential flaw: How accurate is a "remembered culture"? One study (Driver 1939) suggests that Native American memories about the distant past can be quite reliable.

| Additional Sources

The best published bibliographic sources by tribe are the fourth edition of the *Ethnographic Bibliography of North America* (New Haven, 1975), by George P. Murdock and Timothy J. O'Leary, and its supplement, by M. Marlene Martin and Timothy J. O'Leary (New Haven, 1990). The best widely available anthropological and historical source about Native Americans is the multivolume *Handbook of North American Indians* (Washington, DC), under the general editorship of William C. Sturtevant. The first of the proposed twenty volumes appeared in 1978. Although it is not clear whether all the volumes will be published, nonetheless, this source should be consulted first. *Ancient North America* (New York, 1995) by Brian M. Fagan is an excellent source about prehistory. *Indian Givers* (New York, 1988) by Jack Weatherford chronicles

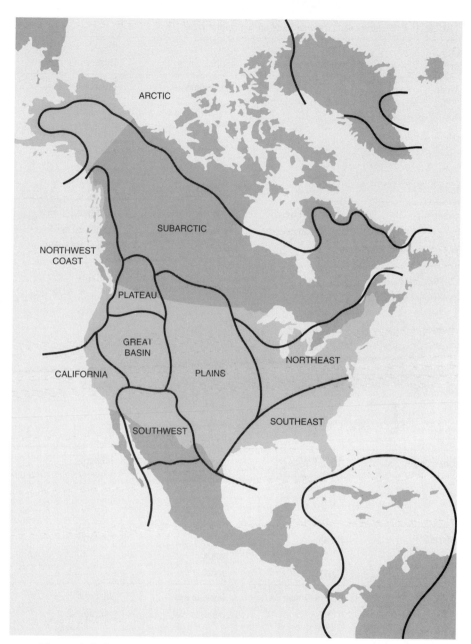

Figure 1-2 | The Indian culture areas for North America north of Mexico.

TABLE 1-1. Summary of characteristics of the ten culture areas.

Culture Area	Languages	Subsistence	Descent
Arctic	Eskimo-Aleut	sea mammals caribou fish	bilateral
Subarctic	Na-Dene in west Algonquian in east	caribou moose fish	matrilineal in west patrilineal in east bilateral in both
California	highly varied	acorns mesquite beans game marine resources	bilateral
Great Basin	Aztec-Tanoan	pine nuts rabbits antelope	bilateral
Plateau	Salish	salmon game roots	bilateral
Plains	Macro-Siouan	bison in west maize in east	bilateral patrilineal
Northwest Coast	Na-Dene in north Salishan in middle Wakashan in south	salmon land mammals sea mammals	matrilineal in north patrilineal in south

Political Organization	Religion	Housing	Manufactures & Other
charismatic leaders bands	shamans good & evil spirits ceremonies in west	wood, stone, sod in east & west snowhouse in central area	tailored clothing elaborate harpoons umiaks, kayaks, dog-sleds sinew-backed bows feuds over women infanticide
charismatic leaders bands	shamans Nakani in west shaking tent divination in east	double lean-to & rectangular log-frame in west conical tent in east	semitailored clothing toboggans, snowshoes bark canoes deadfalls & snares birch-bark baskets cannibalism during famines spruce-root baskets in west hunting dogs in east
bands	shamans diverse supernaturals elaborate female puberty ceremonies	impermanent brush, bark, grass	developed basketry seed-grinding stones sinew-backed bows
bands	shamans elaborate female puberty ceremonies	impermanent brush, bark, grass	basketry seed-grinding stones sinew-backed bows nets for land mammals
villages	shamans diverse spirits	semisubterranean winter reed- or mat-covered summer	basketry important bark fiber clothing
bands band alliances military societies raiding important	vision quest guardian spirits emerging ceremonialism	skin tepee	developed bone & skin working dog-drawn travois game surrounds hide shields
villages	potlatch elaborate ceremonial round complex masks	rectangular, plank multifamily	elaborate woodworking dugout canoes social classes, slaves

TABLE 1-1. (continued)

Culture Area	Languages	Subsistence	Descent
Northeast	Macro-Algonquian Macro-Siouan	maize, beans, squash game fish	matrilineal patrilineal
Southwest	Hokan Aztec-Tanoan	maize, beans, squash game	matrilineal bilateral
Southeast	Macro-Algonquian Macro-Siouan	maize, beans game fish	matrilineal

Indian contributions to the world. *The Columbian Exchange* (Westport, CT, 1972) by Alfred W. Crosby, Jr. is a valuable book for the impact of Old World diseases, animals, and plants on American Indian life. *Black Africans and Native Americans* (Oxford, England, 1988) by Jack D. Forbes is the key source about this complex topic. *The Native Population of the Americas in 1492* (Madison, WI, 1992), edited by William M. Denevan, examines this difficult problem.

| Selected Bibliography

Barth, Fredrik, ed. 1969. *Ethnic groups and boundaries: The social organization of culture difference.* Boston.

Campbell, Lyle, and M. Mithun. 1979. *The languages of Native America.* Austin.

Churchward, James. 1931. *The lost continent of Mu.* New York.

Drake, Samuel G. 1837. *Biography and history of the Indians of North America.* Boston.

Driver, Harold E. 1939. Culture element distributions: VIII, The reliability of culture element data. *Anthropological Records* 1:205–19.

Driver, Harold E., and William C. Massey. 1957. *Comparative studies of North American Indians.* Transactions of the American Philosophical Society, n.s. 47, pt. 2. Philadelphia.

Estrada, Emilio, and Betty J. Meggers. 1961. A complex of traits of probable transpacific origin on the coast of Ecuador. *American Anthropologist,* n.s. 63:913–39.

Political Organization	Religion	Housing	Manufactures & Other
tribes confederations	developed ceremonial round harvest stress secret societies dogs eaten ceremonially	dome-shaped wigwam multifamily palisades	hide clothing bark canoes
villages	elaborate ceremonial round kiva masked dancers	pueblo-type	developed pottery & basketry cotton garments domestic turkeys irrigated farmland
tribes confederations warfare important	complex ceremonies sun worship priests	rectangular multifamily fortified	feathers over netting for clothing houselike storage facilities "black drink" cmetic

Fritz, Gayle J. 1994. Are the first American farmers getting younger? *Current Anthropology* 35:305–09.

Gallatin, Albert. 1836. A synopsis of the Indians within the United States east of the Rocky Mountains and in the British and Russian possessions in North America. *American Antiquarian Society Transactions and Collections* 2:1–422.

Hagan, William T. 1961. *American Indians*. Chicago.

Hallowell, A. Irving. 1957. The impact of the American Indian on American culture. *American Anthropologist*, n.s. 59:201–17.

———. 1958. The backwash of the frontier: The impact of the Indian on American culture. *Annual Report of the Smithsonian Institution, 1957–58*, 447–72.

———. 1963. American Indians, white and black: The phenomenon of transculturalization. *Current Anthropology* 4:519–31.

Haven, Samuel F. 1856. Archaeology of the United States. *Smithsonian Contributions to Knowledge* 8:1–159.

Helm, June, ed. 1968. *Essays on the problem of tribe*. Seattle.

Holmes, William H. 1893. The World's Fair Congress of Anthropology. *American Anthropologist* 6:423–34.

Jefferson, Thomas. 1801. *Notes on the state of Virginia*. New York.

Keesing, Felix M. 1939. *The Menomini Indians of Wisconsin*. Memoirs of the American Philosophical Society, vol. 10. Philadelphia.

Kinkade, M. Dale. 1991. The decline of native languages in Canada. In *Endangered languages,* R. H. Robins and E. M. Uhlenbeck, eds., 157–76. New York.

Kroeber, Alfred L. 1925. *Handbook of the Indians of California.* Bureau of American Ethnology Bulletin no. 78. Washington, DC.

———. 1955. Nature of the land-holding group. *Ethnohistory* 2:303–14.

Lewis, Oscar. 1942. *Effects of white contact upon Blackfoot culture.* Locust Valley, NY.

Mead, Margaret. 1932. *The changing culture of an Indian tribe.* New York.

Pearce, Roy H. 1965. *The savages of America.* Baltimore.

Powell, John W. 1891. Indian linguistic families of America north of Mexico. *Bureau of American Ethnology, 7th Annual Report,* 1–142.

Powers, William K. 1988. The Indian hobbyist movement in North America. In *Handbook of North American Indians,* William C. Sturtevant, gen. ed., 4:557–61. Washington, DC.

Riley, Carroll L., J. Charles Kelley, Campbell W. Pennington, and Robert L. Rands, eds. 1971. *Men across the sea.* Austin.

Saum, Lewis O. 1965. *The fur trader and the Indian.* Seattle.

Swanton, John R. 1953. *The Indian tribes of North America.* Bureau of American Ethnology Bulletin no. 145. Washington, DC.

U.S. Department of the Interior. 1958. *Federal Indian Law.* Washington, DC.

Voegelin, C. F. and F. M. 1966. *Map of North American Indian languages.* American Ethnological Society.

Washburn, Wilcomb E. 1984. A fifty-year perspective on the Indian Reorganization Act. *American Anthropologist,* n.s. 86:279–89.

Wauchope, Robert. 1962. *Lost tribes and sunken continents.* Chicago.

Wissler, Clark. 1938. *The American Indian.* New York.

———. 1942. The American Indian and the American Philosophical Society. *Proceedings of the American Philosophical Society* 86:189–204.

Yarnell, Richard A. 1978. Domestication of sunflower and sumpweed in eastern North America. In *Early food production in North America,* R. I. Ford, ed., 285–99. Ann Arbor, MI.

Zepeda, Ofelia, and Jane H. Hill. 1991. The condition of Native American languages in the United States. In *Endangered languages,* R. H. Robins and E. M. Uhlenbeck, eds., 135–55. New York.

2 Indian–Non-Indian Relations

Don't you ever
you up in the sky
don't you ever get tired
of having the clouds
between you and us?

Frances Densmore (1939, 278)

SOON AFTER DISCOVERY of the New World, a great debate raged in Spain about the humanness of Indians. Regardless of the manner in which the conquistadores were received, they argued that Indians were irrational, heretical, and tainted with mortal sin. This attitude served to justify inhumane treatment of Indians and seizure of their land or property. Francisco Vitoria, a professor at Salamanca and a founder of international law, argued against this thesis. He noted that in Europe heretics were privileged to own property and could not be punished for sins without a trial. Implicit in Vitoria's argument was the acceptance of Indians as human beings. When the exploiters of Indians maintained that the pope of the Roman Catholic church had granted title to all newly discovered lands to the kings of Spain and Portugal, Vitoria countered that the pope had no power over the aborigines and their land and that title by discovery could apply only to unoccupied lands. In a papal bull of 1537 Pope Paul III proclaimed "that the Indians are truly men and that they are not only capable of understanding the Catholic faith, but according to our information, they desire exceedingly to receive it" (Cohen 1960, 290). Considering Indians as human beings gave the church new millions of immortal souls to be saved. This acknowledgment of Indian humanness, combined with an acceptance of Native American land ownership, served as a guide for colonial governments in of the Americas. In the years to come, the course of Indian–non-Indian relations was to take many twists and turns, as this chapter demonstrates.

| Early Contact

European maritime explorers found the Indians fascinating because they felt that Indians embodied what people could be like when stripped of Christian and "civilized" behavior (see Figure 2-1). Indians were considered savages; although human in form, they were barely human in their customs, according to these biased observers. The land they owned was attractive, and many intruders felt that Indians were a blight on it. A brief review of early contact in different areas provides an overview of Indian–white relations that fosters greater understanding of the subsequent course of history.

The Virginia Charter of 1606 provided for bringing God to Indians because adopting Christian ways was equated with being civilized. Land was purchased from the Indians, and settlers were certain that they could live in harmony with Indians who would soon be Christianized. Before long, about fifty missionaries were sent to work primarily with children because it was felt that children would learn more readily than adults. The colonists were convinced that their efforts were succeeding, since there were no serious hostilities. Actually, the most powerful Indian leader, Powhatan, was waiting and hoping that the colony would fail, but the English grew more firmly entrenched with each year. In 1622 Powhatan's successor decided he had waited long enough, and attacked the colonists. Nearly 350 whites were killed, and the only reason the colony was not destroyed was that a Christian Indian

Figure 2-1 | This 1493 woodcut accompanied the Italian printing of the first letter by Christopher Columbus about his New World discoveries. In the background is one of the earliest representations of aboriginal Americans. (From Winsor 1889.)

warned the English at the last moment. To the colonists the massacre was clear evidence of inborn Indian treachery, and the settlers now felt justified in destroying these savages whom they no longer sought to understand. The Indians in Virginia were viewed as an impediment to the march of civilization, and within the next fifty years they were systematically destroyed or displaced. This pattern was repeated time and again.

"The Indian experience" of each colony was different because of the settlers' backgrounds and the Indians encountered. It might be anticipated that the Quakers, granted the land comprising Pennsylvania in 1681, would be more successful in making Indians into Christians, given their commitment to nonviolence and humanistic tolerance of others. The Quakers stressed the common denominators that unite all people and did not seek to identify differences between themselves and Indians. They offered the Indians love and peace; nevertheless, they were unable to win very many converts. Moreover, the Quakers remained neutral when non-Quakers fought the Indians in their midst and at their frontiers.

The Puritans of New England believed that God would guide their affairs with Indians, who were viewed as fallen people in the grip of Satan. When many Indians died in a "wonderful plague" of smallpox, the Puritans saw it as God's way of furthering the goals of the settlers. The Puritans believed that Indian lands were intended for Christian English use. Nevertheless, to keep peace they purchased land from the Indians rather than taking it. On the other hand, they did not hesitate to initiate raids and wars against the Indians or to foster dissension for their own purposes. They also insisted that Indians should be "civilized." Missionaries like John Eliot began working among Indians in 1632, but the number of converts was small and success transient. Puritan efforts to integrate the Indians into transported Western European culture failed for obvious reasons.

The Spanish who first entered the Southwest in 1540 expected to find barbarians or savages and felt a strong obligation to civilize them. Church and civil authorities accepted this as their primary goal after realizing that the area was not going to yield great riches. The gross pattern of Spanish life was to be introduced, and the advance agents usually were Roman Catholic missionaries. They built churches and quarters near established pueblos, instructed certain individuals in Catholic doctrine, and soon recruited Indians as catechists and helpers. The missionaries especially were responsible for introducing new crops and novel crafts; their goal was to create self-sufficient Roman Catholic communities. The missionaries in New Mexico usually were accompanied by soldiers who reinforced Spanish authority; in general, the priests treated Indian transgressions harshly. Soon the Eastern Pueblos were paying tribute to the king of Spain, a good indication of the program's effectiveness.

Apart from the mission environment, Spanish frontiersmen impinged on the Indians of New Mexico through the policy of giving land grants to soldiers for services rendered. The great *encomienda* grants, made to Spanish colonists in New Mexico as a reward for services rendered, did not include any of the large pueblos; but the people who lived in the small communities in the midst of such grants were forced to work these lands for the Spanish, usually with little or no compensation. Before long, Spanish employees of encomenderos were marrying Indians and acquiring their lands. Abuses of the encomienda system engendered a great deal of hostility in some pueblos and eventually led to its abandonment. Spanish towns, with Santa Fe as the prime example, formed another setting for cultural contact, but because the Indians were drawn to them only for services, their impact was relatively minor.

When the Mexican War for Independence ended in 1821, Indians in the Southwest were granted the full rights of Mexican citizens. All persons born in Mexico became citizens, irrespective of their culture or race, and efforts were made to incorporate Indians into national life. This goal was not achieved in New Mexico, however. Anglo-Americans began to penetrate New Mexico in the 1840s, and their attitudes contrasted rather strikingly with those that previously had prevailed. The mission settlement had no place in their plans. They regarded the pueblo-dwellers as moderately "civilized" but considered most of the less sedentary Indians "wild." The Anglo-American policy was to push Indians aside, either peacefully or by force, to facilitate westward expansion.

Effective Spanish intrusion into California in 1769 was guided by the same policies that the Spanish had introduced to the Southwest. A primary purpose of the Spanish colony in California was to Christianize Indians and to settle them at self-sufficient missions; thus Indians were very much a part of the economic order. Yet most of the people who were drawn to the missions, either voluntarily or by force, were unlikely to adapt to a sedentary life in crowded conditions with a rigid work routine. The experiment had clearly failed by the time the missions were secularized, beginning in 1834. Souls had been saved, but the cost in human life had been great.

In the northern portions of the continent, the English, French, and Russian ventures were of a different order. Here the fur trader, not the settler or missionary, usually was the most important advance agent of Western culture. Irrespective of their national origins and time of contact, fur traders viewed Indians very differently from most other white intruders. Indians and traders were *joined* by economic ties that profited them both. The areas where the fur trade dominated longest were those unsuitable for large settlements of whites, and thus the Indians' way of life was not disrupted by large groups of intruders. Furthermore, the fur trader and the Indian could maintain their relationship only as long as the Indians remained trappers and retained the essence of an aboriginal way of life. Regardless of nationality, fur traders could be intolerant or tolerant, cruel or kind, depending on their personalities and their experiences with Indians.

Unlike the white settler on a farm or the land-hungry pioneer pushing westward, whether into Ohio, Manitoba, or California, the trader lived among Indians and became a part of their way of life. A trader was reasonably tolerant of his clientele, if only to further his enterprise; at times his very survival depended on aid from Indians. These were practical men of action, not philosophers; they had the hearts and heads of merchants. In their judgment some Indians and tribes were good while others were bad—it was that simple. They were parsimonious with their praise and often characterized Indians as "scoundrels" and "rascals," on occasion even as "monsters" or "inhuman." Yet, an active and productive Indian was an essential ingredient to a successful trading enterprise, and the Indians as well as the traders appreciated this fact. These generalizations about traders apply only to those of English and French origin, who were important over most of the continent. The Russian fur trade requires a brief discussion.

When the men who accompanied Vitus Bering on the Russian expedition of 1741 returned to Kamchatka the following year, they brought with them the pelts of sea otter. To obtain more of these valued pelts, a host of small-scale expeditions soon reached the Aleutian Islands, and the Alaskan mainland along the northern Pacific Ocean was discovered. The men who launched these ventures were *promishleniki,* the Russian counterpart of the

Figure 2-2 | The earliest known illustration of Eskimos, printed in Germany probably in 1567. (From Sixel 1967.)

French *coureurs des bois;* the Russians, however, were bold and cruel. The atrocities that the promishleniki committed against the Aleuts and Pacific Eskimos were numerous. Not until the founding of the Russian—American Company in 1799 were the most gross transgressions against aboriginal Americans curbed with a certain degree of effectiveness. During the latter part of the Russian era the administrators were naval officers, but it apparently was common for ordinary employees to be criminals from Russia who chose to work for the company in Alaska rather than go to jail in Russia. A number of men who held high posts in the company were "creoles," or persons of mixed Russian and aboriginal Siberian or American ancestry; these men appear to have been much more evenhanded in dealing with the fur trade clientele than were their Russian counterparts. Eventually the Russians assumed a stern but essentially paternalistic attitude toward the native people. They were anxious to expand the fur trade but not at the expense of drastically altering the economic foundations of the Eskimos and Indians with whom they dealt (see Figure 2-2).

| Subsequent Destruction and Displacement of Peoples

It seems likely that after initial historic contact far more Indians were killed by diseases introduced by whites than by bullets. It also appears that more Indians were killed by other Indians than by outsiders, although many such murders unquestionably were abetted by whites. Every tribe probably was subjected to at least one severe epidemic, and there were very few Indians whose way of life was not altered dramatically, or even destroyed outright, soon after contact.

Throughout this volume, the impact of disease on specific peoples is documented, and its disruptive force should not be underestimated. Certain diseases long prevalent among Europeans eventually became less virulent among them but deadly to a virgin population; measles and whooping cough are examples. Other diseases, such as malaria, raged through Indian and white populations alike. Tuberculosis was a dreadful killer of Indians but was less lethal among whites.

Records of tribes destroyed by diseases are not difficult to locate; one depressing example will illustrate the speed of impact. The Massachuset, with an estimated population of three thousand in 1600, were reduced to five hundred by 1631 as a result of a terrible epidemic, possibly smallpox; soon thereafter another wave of smallpox reduced their number even more. By 1663, when John Eliot published the Bible in their language, they were nearly extinct.

Even though an epidemic might not destroy a tribe, it could kill so many people that they could not defend themselves against outsiders or continue their cultural traditions. For example, a malaria epidemic struck in the Central Valley of California and along the Columbia River in the early 1830s. A mortality rate of about 75 percent made it impossible for the survivors effectively to resist subsequent white intrusions or to maintain their ways of old.

The extinction of a population unquestionably is tragic, but another consequence of white dominance was nearly as sad. Because of the intimate associations of Indians with their traditional homelands, their displacement to other areas was often heartrending. One example will suffice. In aboriginal times the Delaware lived in New Jersey and adjacent areas, but in the early 1700s the Iroquois dominated them politically and sanctioned their displacement by white settlers. Before long many Delaware settled in eastern Ohio, but only after wandering largely homeless for some time. By 1820 some lived in Arkansas, and others had ventured on to Texas. Some fifteen years later many of them had settled on a reservation in Kansas, from which they were moved to Oklahoma in 1867. Most of them remain there today, but there are Delaware Indians scattered from eastern Canada to Montana, far from each other and from their eastern homeland.

The personal and cultural trauma wrought by purposely displacing a tribe from its home is tragic in itself. But the federal policy of moving all the Indian tribes from one vast area into another violates the very principles on which the United States was founded. Yet this happened, and the drama began to unfold with clarity about 1800. One overwhelming argument was advanced to justify assuming control of Indian lands, and it *never* has changed: Indians obstructed the progress of whites who could use land much more effectively, and thus it was the God-given right of the settlers or real estate promoters to obtain such ground. Displacement became a blanket policy with the Indian Removal Act of 1830. New England whites could deplore this policy elsewhere because they had long ago resolved their "Indian problem" by killing many local Native Americans, displacing them, or tolerating small remnant Indian populations. It was the residents of the southeastern states and settlers in the Midwest who became the wanton destroyers of Indian rights. Most surviving tribes with large landholdings east of the Mississippi River were bribed and intimidated into moving west. By 1831, the states of Alabama, Georgia, and Mississippi had forced the removal of the Choctaw, Chickasaw, and Creek. Mesquakie and Sauk reluctance to forsake their lands led to the Black Hawk War (see Chapter 11), and Cherokee resistance to removal was strong but largely unsuccessful (see Chapter 13).

| U.S. Treaties

Although virtually all inhabitable country in North America was occupied by Indians when Europeans arrived, Indians now possess only a very small portion. Most land was obtained by whites through treaties, with land in one area being substituted for that in another, often with monetary compensation as added inducement. An overview of the changing status of Indian land is presented in historical perspective.

In northeastern North America in the 1700s, the Dutch and English administrators held that Indian tribes were sovereign nations and the legitimate claimants to the lands they occupied. Land acquired from Indians was obtained on a national, not an individual, basis. The pre–Revolutionary War treaties of the British dealt primarily with the questions of boundaries and the acquisition of Indian lands. As early as 1670, during the reign of Charles II, England was concerned that those tribes desiring her protection should receive it; her treaties and agreements with New England tribes date from 1664. By 1755 a bureau had been founded to deal with Indian matters, and formal recognition of Indian title to land was to guide policy in Canada and the United States.

Between 1778 and 1871 the United States government negotiated formal treaties with Indians in the same manner as with foreign powers (see Table 2-1). Tribes were classified as dependent nations, and treaties were considered in the same light as other statutes of the U.S. Congress. In some instances early treaties prohibited United States citizens from trespassing on Indian lands without passports, but more often the subordinate position of Indian nations to the United States was made clear by the provisions. It may come as a surprise that, despite the conflicts between the federal government and various tribes, the United States never formally declared war on hostile Indians.

Many treaty obligations still are being met by the federal government in the United States, although no new treaties have been made with Indians since 1871. Furthermore, treaty arrangements became a primary basis for federal Indian law. In treaties the federal government reserved the right to regulate Indian affairs, and seldom was this right relinquished to a state. Once a treaty was negotiated and ratified, it could not be nullified by the Indians, even if duress, fraud, or improper Indian representation took place during the

TABLE 2-1. Major events in Native American relations with the federal government of the United States

1778	The first U.S. treaty with Indians, the Delaware tribe
1824	The Bureau of Indian Affairs was created to "civilize" Indians
1830	The Indian Removal Act was designed to relocate southeastern Indians to land west of the Mississippi River; the purpose was to open the land to white settlers
1849	A Navajo treaty permitted the federal government, for the first time, to influence the internal affairs of a tribe
1871	The last treaties with Indians
1879	The Carlisle Indian School was founded and became the most famous Indian boarding school; its purpose was to acculturate children rapidly
1887	The Dawes Severalty Act was designed to allot reservation lands to individual Indians and thus break up reservations; "surplus" land was opened to Euro-American settlers
1934	The Indian Reorganization Act attempted to reverse the impact of the Dawes Act by restoring land to reservations and to encourage tribes to form federally recognized tribal governments
1946	The Indian Claims Commission Act was created to settle outstanding Indian claims as a step toward ending federal responsibilities to Indians
1953	House Concurrent Resolution 108 included a timetable for ending federal obligations to Indians
	Public Law 280 transferred civil and criminal jurisdiction to select states as a major step in terminating federal responsibilities
1975	The goals of the Indian Self-Determination and Education Assistance Act were to foster tribal self-government and to transfer many of the functions of the Bureau of Indian Affairs to individual tribes
1983	President Ronald Reagan declared that the termination of federal responsibilities to Indians was no longer a goal and proposed greater funding for tribal self-government and resource development
1990	The Native American Graves Protection and Repatriation Act provided for the return of skeletal remains and artifacts by universities and museums to the tribes requesting them
1997	A proposal by Senator Slade Gorton (R-Wash.) would indirectly "tax" economically successful tribes and force a tribe to waive its sovereign immunity to receive Bureau of Indian Affairs funding; the proposal was rejected

negotiations. Treaties might be renegotiated by mutual government and Indian consent. Treaties or treaty rights also have been repealed by Congress, with or without the consent, involvement, or agreement of Indians; this is called abrogation. Indian treaties, like all other treaties, have the same status as any other federal statute and can be repealed or modified by a later statute. Yet it has been a general policy of the government to interpret ambiguities in treaties in favor of Indians and to consider the circumstances under which a treaty was negotiated. The courts could not interpret a treaty in a manner not intended in the original wording, however.

Treaties with Indians were negotiated by the president of the United States and were binding when approved by the Indians and two-thirds of the U.S. Senate. It is important to note that a treaty could not provide funds for Indians; monetary commitments required separate congressional action. Nearly 400 treaties were negotiated. The greatest number, nearly 260, were arranged during the great westward expansion of white settlers following the War of 1812. The majority of these treaties, 230, involved Indian lands. A block of

76 treaties called for Indian removal from their lands and resettlement on other lands. As early as 1818 a treaty reserved land for a specific tribe, but most reservations were established much later. Nearly 100 treaties dealt primarily with boundaries between Indian and white lands and affirmed the friendly relations between a tribe and the United States. Two tribes, the Potawatomi and Chippewa, negotiated 42 treaties each, a record number.

The first treaty in which the federal government sought to control the internal affairs of a tribe was with the Navajo in 1849. It stipulated that the federal government could "pass and execute in their territory such laws as may be deemed conducive to the prosperity and happiness of said Indians" (U.S. Department of the Interior 1958, 163). By the mid-1800s, it was becoming apparent that treaties with tribes were unrealistic because of the increasing dependence of Indians on the federal government. The last treaty was negotiated and ratified in 1871. Treaty making came to an end when the U.S. Senate and the House of Representatives could not agree on the appropriations specified by a treaty.

An interesting sidelight in federal dealings with Indians was the attempt to create Indian representation at the national level. The first treaty of the United States with Indians was with the Delaware in 1778. It provided that at a future date this tribe might consolidate with others and form a state, with the Delaware as the leaders; the state would have congressional representation. However, nothing ever developed from the possibility. Treaties of 1785 and 1830 proposed that Indians send a representative to Congress, but again this possibility was never realized.

In the United States, Indians have land rights based on aboriginal possession, treaty, congressional act, executive order, purchase, or the action of some colony, state, or foreign nation. Reservations were created by treaty arrangements before 1871, by acts of Congress after that time, and by executive orders of the president. In almost every instance the federal government retained the title to reservation lands. Statutory reservations usually consisted of public domain or land purchased by the federal government for use by designated Indians. The legality of reservations established by executive orders was uncertain, but their validity was established in the General Allotment Act (also known as the Dawes Severalty Act or Dawes Act) of 1887. Reservations were created by executive order between 1855 and 1919. This practice met resistance from Congress, however, and was brought to an end except for the addition of some Alaskan reservations. From time to time Indians have purchased lands with their own funds for the group as a whole, and these properties have been supervised by the federal government (see Chapters 11 and 13). Since nearly all of the land that is now the United States was held earlier by European-based powers, the rights of Indians under British, Dutch, French, Mexican, Russian, and Spanish rule have been taken into consideration when a transfer of sovereignty has occurred. In each instance at least some recognition has been given to aboriginal rights of occupancy by the Indians.

As a closing observation about treaties with Indians, it must be noted that they seldom were negotiated in any meaningful sense. Representatives of a particular tribe or tribes were assembled, and a treaty was offered for their approval. The signers seldom had any realistic opportunity to modify the terms. Then, too, treaties often were made through "chiefs" who were sympathetic to the whites, and in certain areas of the United States it was not uncommon for intoxicants to be distributed freely at treaty-making sessions. In addition, the interpreters often could not or did not set forth the fine points of an agreement in true detail or spell out the implications of what the Indians were losing and what they were gaining. A most important final observation along these lines is that most Indians had *no concept* of the permanent alienation of land. Since they had never bought and sold land, their concept was that they were granting whites the rights to its use. Thus many such agreements were not treaties in a strict sense of the word.

| Administration of U.S. Indian Affairs

In 1775 the Continental Congress created three agencies, on a geographical basis, to deal with Indians. Among the commissioners were Benjamin Franklin and Patrick Henry, an indication of the importance attached to Indian matters. The commissioners were to make treaties, to establish friendly relations with Indians, and to prevent them from aiding the British. In 1786 Indian administration was placed under the secretary of war. With adoption of the Constitution, the War Department maintained jurisdiction over Indians. The first Congress in 1789 appropriated funds for negotiating treaties and placed the governors of territories in charge of local Indian affairs. The next year Congress, in an important step toward federal control, began licensing traders among Indians. The Bureau of Indian Affairs (BIA) was created in 1824 within the War Department, and its administration passed into civilian control at the newly created Home Department of the Interior in 1849. Flagrant corruption and mismanagement within the bureau led to the creation of the Board of Indian Commissioners that functioned from 1869 to 1933. They oversaw the expenditure of funds and made policy decisions.

The BIA remains the federal agency most responsible for Indian affairs. However, bureau mismanagement again was endemic by the 1980s. A federal study in 1984 demonstrated that *two-thirds of the BIA budget was consumed by the bureau itself*. As a result of this finding and the excessive regulatory power of the bureau, administrative changes were launched. The major thrust, continuing into the 1990s, has been to turn over most BIA responsibilities to the tribes. This trend, coupled with widespread national concern about the federal budget deficit, has meant that the funds for the BIA have declined, as have direct payments to tribes.

| Canada, The First Nations

In recent years, the "First Nations" has become the standard designation for the indigenous peoples of Canada. As Allan G. Harper (1947) noted, the Canadian government was not especially generous in its treaties with Indians;

however, it did generally honor its promises. Typically, treaties were arranged with Indians before the arrival of Euro-Canadian settlers, and as a result there were no great conflicts between Indians and outsiders. The first treaty between the Canadian government and Indians was negotiated in 1781; the final treaty in this series was made in 1921.

The earliest significant grant of land to Indians was made in 1680 by Louis XIV of France to a band of Iroquois, who still live on that land. The first large British grant was in 1784 to the Six Nations, who were primarily Iroquois. They received nearly 700,000 acres as a reward for their loyalty to the British during the American Revolution (see Chapter 12).

A cornerstone of British policy toward Indians is embodied in the Proclamation of 1763. It includes specific guiding principles for Indian–white relations: Indians possessed the rights to all lands *not* formally surrendered; land could be surrendered only to the Crown; Indians could not grant land to individual whites unless it had been surrendered. Under the terms of the proclamation, settlers in what is now the United States could not readily occupy Indian lands; this provision eventually became one of the causes of the American Revolution. Noteworthy too is that large sectors of Canada *never* have been legally ceded by Indians to the Crown; examples include the western portion of the Northwest Territories and British Columbia.

Under the Canadian Act of 1870, reserved land could be held by a particular Indian in an allotment system, with an allottee having the exclusive right to use and occupancy. An allotment could only be passed on to heirs or sold to another Indian within a group. Indians with more land than necessary might surrender acreage and use the money from the sale to benefit the group. Under certain conditions, an individual Indian obtained clear title to land. For example, an Indian could request full Canadian citizenship (enfranchisement); if it was granted, the individual could obtain title to the land.

With the confederation of Canada in 1867, Indian administration passed to the Dominion of Canada. Soon thereafter the dominion Parliament alone became responsible for rights and services under the Indian Act of 1876. The administration controlled the management of Indian lands. This act also recognized that the dominion government was responsible for relief, education, health services, Indian-based agriculture, and industry. Finally, the Parliament was made responsible for the enfranchisement of Indians. A Department of Indian Affairs was founded in 1880 with a minister who was the superintendent general of Indian matters. Following numerous administrative changes over the years, the Department of Indian Affairs and Northern Development was established by an act of Parliament in 1967.

Canadians with both European and Indian ancestry merit special attention because they were treated differently from full-blooded Indians in some contexts. In general, people of mixed heritage, or *Metis,* were given the rights of Indians, and those Metis who lived as Indians had the right to be treated as Indians. Efforts by the Metis to protect their land rights were largely responsible for the Red River Rebellion of Manitoba in 1869. As a result of this uprising, the rights of the Metis were more fully recognized in Manitoba. Their success led Metis living elsewhere to press their claims in terms of money or land settlements. Those who received money or land had their aboriginal rights extinguished.

The next major change in Indian policy, the Indian Act of 1951 with revisions, was the legal basis for more recent policy. The act sets forth the authority and power of the governor in council, the minister, and the minister's field representatives, the superintendents. Robert W. Dunning (1962), in discussing the effects of the act on Indians, stressed the power of the superintendent on a reserve in formulating and implementing local policy. A reserve superintendent determined who could become members of a band (i.e., federally recognized Indian group), screened enfranchisement applications, and administered welfare, relief, and education on a reserve. A superintendent furthermore accepted or vetoed the nomination of an Indian to a band council.

In 1985, Bill C-31 became law and embodied fundamental policy changes regarding the First Nations. Discrimination was largely removed by the bill, and each band controlled its own membership. Thus the process of enfranchisement was abandoned. For instance, the band membership of a woman who had lost her band status by marrying a non-Indian was restored by the federal government although not necessarily by her particular tribe. The children of such a woman usually obtained band status. Subsequent legislation in the 1990s led to far greater self-government by select bands, and this policy probably will be extended to all bands. Another fundamental administrative change is to take place in the eastern portion of the Northwest Territories. In 1999 it will become a separate territory, Nunavut, whose population will be about 85 percent Eskimo (Inuit). They are to receive $1.15 billion for social and economic development. Most important, these Eskimos are to control the surface title to land and the subsurface title to a portion of it; the latter is exceedingly important with respect to the development of mineral resources.

It must be stressed that the central Canadian government has far less control over the provinces than the federal government of the United States has over the states. One result has been that treaty negotiations began between British Columbia Indians and the provincial government only in 1996. They surely will become drawn-out, complicated, and divisive. Throughout much of Canada, the estimated 800,000 Indians have become increasingly vocal and politically active in seeking nation-to-nation negotiations.

| Greenland, A Brief Summary

Norse people from Scandinavia settled Greenland beginning in A.D. 986, but Eskimos had occupied portions of the island since at least 2000 B.C. The original Norse colony was neglected over the years and had disappeared by about 1540. Greenland began to be resettled in 1721 by Norwegian Lutheran missionaries; at that time Norway was under the political control of Denmark. Danish sovereignty over much of Greenland, however, was not established until 1921, and it was a closed country until after World War II. The Danes dominated most aspects of Eskimo life from the beginning and were concerned primarily with saving souls and with commercial profits. The deplorable health and living conditions of the Eskimos did not begin to be acknowledged in a realistic manner until 1953, when the colonial status of Greenland was abolished. In that year, Greenlanders became full citizens of Denmark, and their living conditions began to improve dramatically. Finally, home rule was extended to Greenland in 1979. Contemporary Greenland is occupied by about 50,000 Greenlanders, persons of Eskimo or combined Eskimo and European descent.

| Landmark U.S. Indian Policies

Indian tribes were relatively free and independent nations until the War of 1812 ended. Soon thereafter they became "domestic, dependent nations" and lost realistic control over their destiny. The Indian Removal Act of 1830 was a clear indication of the change in relations between Indians and the federal government. The end of treaty making in 1871 was another plateau, but the General Allotment Act (Dawes Severalty Act or Dawes Act) of 1887 had the greatest impact on changing Indian life.

THE DAWES ACT   Under the terms of this act, the president was authorized to allot most reservation land to individual Indians. Indians were to select their acreage, and the federal government was to hold a trust title for at least twenty-five years, during which time the land could not be encumbered. Surplus reservation lands then were sold, and the funds derived were held in trust for the tribe, subject to use for educating and "civilizing" the tribe when Congress approved these uses. The Dawes Act was modified over the next ten years to allow allotted land to be leased. Indian education began to be stressed. Schools were provided, and the attendance of children virtually was forced; but federal support for church schools was withdrawn. An important supplement was made to the act in 1906 that permitted the president to extend the trust period for allotted lands. The aim of the Dawes Act was to bypass tribal organizations and make land allotments to individual Indians. The act was designed to *destroy* the tribes by doing away with the land base held collectively and, at the same time, to integrate Indians into the dominant society. Many whites who truly were concerned with Indian welfare felt that the sterile and depressing quality of reservation life should be destroyed and that the best means to accomplish this goal was to make individual Indians property holders and farmers.

THE INDIAN REORGANIZATION ACT (IRA)   The goals of this act were the direct opposite of those of the Dawes Act. The IRA of 1934 was intended to *end* the alienation of Indian lands through the allotment process. In fifty years of allotments, Indians had lost nearly 90 million of their 138 million acres of land, and about half of the remaining land was desert. The most effective means to permit retention of the land base was to extend the period of trust holding, which the act did. Furthermore, the act acquired additional land for Indians, declared it exempt from taxation, and placed it under federal control.

The commissioner of Indian affairs from 1934 to 1944 was John Collier, who was deeply committed to the reformulation of American society in a less competitive mold with greater social justice. He hoped in fact that restoring vitality to Indian societies could make them a model for community living for other Americans. Two guiding principles of the IRA were self-government with democratic ideals and parliamentary procedures and communal enterprises as the best avenue to bettered economic conditions. Tribes were encouraged to form chartered corporations and to operate essentially as local governments; revolving credit funds helped those choosing to incorporate. One key condition of the original law was that it would apply only to those tribes that by majority vote decided to come under its provisions. Initially, 181 tribes accepted and 77 rejected the IRA. Fourteen groups came under it because they did not vote, and the act was extended in 1936 to include Alaskan and Oklahoman peoples without their vote of approval. Since Indians in general had come to distrust the federal government, the Indian response to this enlightened legislation was not as positive as had been hoped for by its creators. Some tribes favored allotments and were able to obtain clear title to their land in spite of the IRA. Other tribes, such as those that stressed individual wealth, did not even agree with the principles behind the IRA.

World War II disrupted the implementation of IRA goals, and in the period between the end of this war and the late 1960s the federal government generally pursued policies designed to assimilate Indians into the greater American "melting pot." However, the IRA has remained the legislation with the most critical effect on reservation Indian life. As Wilcomb E. Washburn (1984) observed, acceptance of the IRA by reservation Indians in general over the years has led to the revival of tribal life or its creation among them. The act has contributed significantly to the vitality of tribal political structure. As will become evident in numerous chapters to follow, many tribes probably would have been destroyed by now had it not been for the IRA.

FEDERAL INTRUSION AND INDIAN IDENTITY   Since the 1930s the concept of acculturation has been prominent in anthropology. It came to mean the steps by which native peoples are gradually absorbed into the dominant sociocultural pattern. With assimilation, acculturation is complete. Yet few anthropologists are satisfied with the concept because it fails to define the stages leading to assimilation or to explain the persistence of tribal identity in the face of hundreds of years of pressures to negate it. Quite clearly, the idea of acculturation does not allow for the lasting quality of Indian identity. By far the most bold and innovative approach to the general problem has been conceived and articulated by Joseph G. Jorgensen (1971).

The central idea of Jorgensen's thesis is that tribes were in fact assimilated into national economic and political life as soon as they came to be controlled by the United States. Conversely, it would seem that Indians have maintained their strongest sense of identity in those areas where federal intrusion has been least successful. Jorgensen attributes the deplorable conditions under which most Indians live to the economic order imposed on them. Efforts to gauge relative degrees of acculturation fail to recognize that Indians are enmeshed in a political system that essentially is colonial. He identifies the metropolis as the center where economic and political power are concentrated; the manipulators of this power are able to promote legislation to sustain their goals and ensure their growth. Thus the politically weak rural areas are exploited by the metropolis for its growth, and this applies as well to the rural areas in which Indians live. Indians are subject to the same laws that apply to everyone else, in addition to those imposed by federal control through the BIA.

The BIA attempted to promote industrial development on and near reservations, but Jorgensen noted in 1971 that the program was mostly talk; this has remained essentially true. With economic conditions often so bad on reservations, it is understandable that Indians have moved to cities in large numbers. Because these migrants have few skills, little confidence, and a foreign cultural tradition, they are not likely to succeed. Often they make a little money and then return to their reservations. If they remain in urban centers, they usually have the poorest paying jobs and very little job security. In essence, as a result of white political and economic intrusion, Indians are enveloped in a culture of poverty, and the move from a reservation to a city has substituted an urban ghetto for a rural one.

Beginning in the 1950s, the BIA launched a program to relocate Indians to urban areas, and the program came to include vocational and on-the-job training. By the early 1970s, about ten thousand Indians participated each year. The obvious goal was to force their assimilation. The BIA maintained that the relocation program was voluntary, which simply is untrue; people were encouraged to leave the reservations, and quotas were established for relocated Indians. By the mid-1970s, the program was being terminated. Despite all the pressures for assimilation, especially with the relocation program, many Indians in cities and on reservations retained their distinct identity. Their adaptation is one of biculturation, that is, living in two cultures, rather than acculturation; although it contributes to maintaining Indian identity, biculturation may also contribute negative aspects to their life-style.

Compatible with the goals of the relocation program, the federal government made a move to "get out of the Indian business" by settling old claims with the Indian Claims Commission Act of 1946. Then in 1953 a federal policy was launched that had a far more immediate impact—House Concurrent Resolution 108. It was designed with a timetable for ending federal responsibilities to Indians. As Randall H. McGuire (1992, 825) noted, "If Indian people would not vanish, then the Congress would terminate them." Termination of the Klamath and Menominee reservations was one result; these reservations included major stands of timber that were being sought by lumber companies. In addition, other reservations were terminated, such as those in western Oregon and in Nevada. For some Indians, Public Law 280 in 1953 transferred civil and criminal jurisdiction to select states, including California, Minnesota, Nebraska, and Oregon. Largely through efforts by the Menominee, the termination policy was itself terminated in 1974, and reservation status was restored to such tribes as the Menominee and Klamath.

| Forces Fostering Native American Identity

Compared with European intruders, early historic cultural diversity among Native Americans north of Mexico was great. Indians not only spoke many unrelated languages and had varied social conventions but also reflected different social and political norms. By contrast, the cultural background of Europeans was homogeneous; their linguistic differences were minor, while social and political ideals were broadly similar. Thus, compared with Europeans, the Indians were fractured and fragmented along many dimensions. The agents of Western civilization often exploited these differences to divide Indians still further. In the face of European threats to their cultural integrity, Indians came to recognize what different tribes had in common and to develop a new sense of identity as Indians that transcended tribal lines.

PAN-INDIANISM   This concept refers to a general sense of Indian cultural identity that unites the members of different tribes. Since the word *Indian* long has been a generic designation for Native Americans based on cultural similarities, the prefix *pan* is actually redundant. Nonetheless, *Pan-Indianism* is a term that gained prominence in the 1950s and was applied to a condition that had originated much earlier. A more accurate designation might be pantribalism because participation brings together Indians with different tribal backgrounds. Pan-Indianism began in the mid-1700s and eventually emerged as a movement that has become a primary source of Indian identity for many of its members. This has been true especially for those Indians with a weak sense of tribal identity, such as those raised off reservations, and for other persons who consider themselves Indian although they lack the customary biological or cultural heritage.

Over the years varied factors have contributed to the rise of Pan-Indianism. Among the early influences were religious prophets who emerged repeatedly and advocated what Indians must do to free themselves of external control. One such person was Neolin, better known as the Delaware Prophet. By the 1760s, when he came into prominence, the Delaware and other Algonquians had been displaced from the East by whites and were living in Ohio. They expected a surge of whites into their adopted homeland and were uncertain how to respond. Neolin, like other contemporary Delaware prophets, urged his people to abandon European customs and return to their aboriginal ways. God had revealed to him that if Indians once again lived a simple life, recited certain prayers, and dispelled whites, then game would return and the purity of Indian ways would prevail. His message was appealing to many Indians in the Ohio Valley, especially the Ottawa chief Pontiac, because the message served as partial justification for political action. In 1763, Pontiac planned a general uprising. The Indians took a number of forts and massacred their garrisons, but their attempt to take the outpost of Detroit by siege failed. Indian dominance was of brief duration, since the confederation was organized so loosely that the British soon divided the Indians and were able to reconsolidate their position. This is but one example of individual Indians who represented different tribes but attempted to cooperate in furthering a common goal.

As western Indians came into increasing conflict with non-Indians, other prophets came forth, especially those associated with the Ghost Dance. The first Ghost Dance was originated in 1869 by Wodziwob, a Paviotso (Northern Paiute) who was said to have died, along with a disciple, and then returned to the land of the living. They reported that if a particular dance was performed, whites would disappear, fish and game return in abundance, and the dead come back to earth. Although the doctrine spread to California and Oregon, it did not have wide impact (see Chapter 7). The Ghost Dance of 1890 that originated with a Paiute from Nevada named Wovoka (Jack Wilson) became far more important. Wovoka reportedly died during an eclipse of the sun in January 1889 and went to heaven, where he saw dead Indians living in an idyllic state. God reportedly said that if Wovoka returned to earth and taught the people to perform the Ghost Dance, the dead and living would be reunited. He cautioned people not to fight with each other or with non-Indians; neither should they lie or steal. If these instructions were obeyed, there would be no more illness, old age, or death. Performing the Ghost Dance was to hasten the dawning of this new world. Although some tribes embraced the dance with fervor, it inevitably failed.

Much of the background for Pan-Indianism may be traced to Indian prophets, but there were essential non-Indian elements as well. The most important of these was the formal education process imposed on Indians. In government and mission schools instruction was in English, which became the language for communication between the members of different tribes. Boarding schools likewise had a profound influence. None was more famous than the Carlisle Indian School in Pennsylvania. It was founded in 1879 by Richard H. Pratt, an army officer, whose philosophy was encapsulated in his slogan, "Kill the Indian and save the man!" The school was organized along military lines and attended by the members of far-flung tribes. It was intended to be a way station between the reservation and assimilation. Carlisle often is thought of as a college because its football team played university teams, but it was largely a secondary school that stressed vocational training and the fundamentals of English. Indians who attended Carlisle and other boarding schools often had a difficult time readjusting to reservation life. Although some went "back to the blanket," meaning that they reverted to Indian ways, others were assimilated into the white world, and many worked for the federal government in Indian administration.

The boarding schools in the United States and residential schools in Canada were exceedingly powerful institutions for the systematic destruction of traditional Native American cultures. The military model, with its repressive environment, is as sad as it was dreadful. The most powerful person at a school might be the disciplinarian, not the teachers. Children, young and old, frequently wore uniforms, were punished, sometimes severely, for speaking their native languages, and might be confined to a school for years on end. Furthermore, and of singular importance, many children were unable to learn the subsistence activities, social norms, or religious conventions of their parents. It appears that much of the social disorganization on contemporary reservations and reserves may be traced directly to these schools.

Christianity was an especially important influence on Indians in the late 1800s in a number of different ways. Indians from different tribes came to be identified with each other because they were members of the same church denomination. Likewise, mission advocates helped foster Indian identity by working for their well-being. Missions maintained many schools, and diverse white organizations with Christian backing were concerned with Indian life. These included the Women's National Indian Association (founded in 1879), the Indian Rights Association (1882), and the Lake Monhonk conferences (1883), all of which lobbied for Indian justice. At the same time, members of these organizations sought to *assimilate* Indians, and most members had little tolerance for Indian customs. These white activists in Indian affairs supported the principles of the Dawes Act but deplored the injustices of its administration. As Hazel W. Hertzberg (1971, 22) has noted in the best study of this era, "All unwittingly the reformers—the Indians' chief friends in court in the white world—thus helped to break down Indian self-respect and Indian attempts at self-help." Many Indian leaders were Christian, but at the same time they often were unwilling to abandon their Indian heritage. They sought accommodation with Euro-American customs, and their general approach has endured among many Indians seeking to retain their identity. For many others assimilation into white society was desired and realized.

Indians of many tribes with different historical backgrounds were drawn into Pan-Indianism through the peyote cult. The peyote plant, which grows in central Mexico, is a spineless cactus with "buttons" containing alkaloids that are stimulants or sedatives in varying proportions. When consumed, buttons produce a wide range of reactions. A common response to taking peyote is exhilaration and an inability to sleep for about twelve hours; depression and hallucinations, sometimes including color visions, follow. This non-habit-forming drug was consumed in Mexico in aboriginal times but was not widely used in the United States until more recently. It became popular among Indians of the southern Plains between 1850 and 1900 and spread to other western tribes. Early use in the Plains appears to have been associated with warfare, and it was taken only by men. Indians began using peyote more widely when they were suffering in the dismal aftermath of military defeat, physical displacement, and confinement to reservations. The Bureau of Indian Affairs, Christian missionaries, and white reformers all were actively opposed to the peyote cult, and its adherents were harassed. In spite of the oppression by whites and some Indians, there were about twelve thousand members in 1918. Efforts were made in 1916 and again in 1917 to pass a federal law against the use of peyote, but these bills failed. In 1918, as a response to white opposition, a group of participants incorporated as a formal religious institution, the Native American church. Although a number of states soon passed laws against the use of peyote (for example, Kansas, 1920; Arizona, 1923), seven states had chartered Native American churches by 1925. As members of a formal religious organization, Indians were afforded far greater protection from persecution than previously.

A typical peyote service among Plains tribes was held in a tepee and lasted all night. Participants sat around a central fire, and peyote buttons were passed for each person to take as many as he chose. A special gourd rattle and a drum were used to produce distinctive music. One person after another chanted his sacred song either in English or in his tribal language. Bibles and crosses might be part of the ceremonial equipment. The goals of the ceremony were to achieve physical and spiritual well-being and to promote harmonious relations with others. Brotherly love, self-reliance, and a disapproval of alcohol all were important values held by participants. The psychedelic experience gained through the use of peyote was never an end in itself.

According to Hertzberg, the peyote religion had appeal because old tribal religions had lost their meaning and Christian teachings seemed remote from reality. Furthermore, this was an Indian religion that united members of different tribes in a common sense of brotherhood. Peyote often was considered a powerful medicine for the diseased, and the rituals also provided an opportunity for social gatherings. Some Indians, such as the Pueblo peoples, Five Civilized Tribes in Oklahoma, and Iroquois, were relatively untouched by the peyote religion, but it had become *the* religion for many Indians by 1934 (see Chapter 10).

The anthropologist James H. Howard (1955) was one of the first to identify the Pan-Indian movement and to define the material traits associated with it. He identified the movement's roots as being in Oklahoma, especially among the small tribes originally from the East. Howard felt that racial discrimination against Indians was an important factor fostering solidarity among them. Coupled with poverty, apartheid tended to bind Indians of diverse backgrounds together. Other contributing elements were the peyote religion, intermarriage between members of different tribes, the use of English as the common language, and schools. Pan-Indianism was identified best with particular traits associated with powwows. The war dance, which possibly began among the Pawnee, originally had religious associations with a men's war society but became a social dance. Men danced as a group, yet each man performed in his own style to the accompaniment of singers and a drum. Thus no rehearsals were necessary, which made the dance ideal for persons from diverse tribes performing together. A modified Plains Indian scalp dance, the buffalo dance, and stomp dance were likely to be performed; the latter was once a religious dance among tribes in the East. The feather roach headdress, feather shoulder bustle and back bustle of feathers, choker neckband, and hard-soled Plains-type moccasins were common among the performers. Indians and non-Indians alike found that the Plains Indian dances were the most exciting and the costuming from this area the most visually appealing.

In addition to the artifacts and dance styles, other characteristics are associated with the Pan-Indian movement. The making of Indian bread is an example. It is a flour-based dough that is fried in fat and is popular at Indian gatherings, but it was not an aboriginal food. Behavior patterns typical of Pan-Indian movement members include tolerance of idiosyncratic behavior, consensus-seeking in group decisions, and joking patterns. Many of the qualities associated with pantribalism were strengthened by the civil rights movement. On college campuses, for example, Indians from varied tribes often began at this time to identify closely with one another and to form organizations to further their general goals, a pattern that has endured into the present.

THE INDIAN IMAGE   The Plains Indian has come to symbolize Indians to most Americans, and we might take a moment to consider how it has happened that Indians in one sector of the country have become representative of all Indians.

Indians of the Great Plains were seen first by Spanish and then by French and English explorers, yet they were nearly unknown until after the Louisiana Purchase of 1803. In 1821 members of Plains tribes visited Washington, DC, and none was more popular than Petalesharo, the Pawnee who rescued a Comanche girl from being sacrificed to the Morning Star. In three paintings of him by different artists, he wore a flowing feather headdress (see Figure 2-3), and according to John C. Ewers (1965) this probably was the first pictorial record of the feather "war bonnet." Many other Indians in the same party had their portraits painted, and their exhibit long was a popular attraction in Washington. The earliest picture of a Plains tepee appeared in 1823 (see Figure 2-4), and the first illustration of a Plains Indian on horseback was printed in 1829 (see Figure 2-5). This beginning possibly never would have led to the emergence of the Plains tribes in popular fancy were it not for the efforts of Karl Bodmer and George Catlin, who painted Plains Indians in the 1830s. Catlin especially was important, for he not only painted many pictures of Indians but also exhibited his Indian gallery widely in the United States and then in London and Paris. His book *Manners, Customs and Condition of the North American Indians,* first published in 1841, had a wide distribution, and this two-volume work with over three hundred engravings was reprinted

Figure 2-3 | Painting of Petalesharo, a Pawnee, by John Neagle, 1821. (Courtesy of the Historical Society of Pennsylvania.)

again and again. To Catlin the noblest Indians clearly were those of the Plains. His paintings and those of Bodmer were copied or modified and also inspired other artists to venture west to paint Indians.

The Plains Indian symbol crystallized in Buffalo Bill's Wild West Show, which opened in 1883. It was seen by millions of people in Canada, the United States, and Europe during its run of more than thirty years. William F. Cody, or "Buffalo Bill," was a colorful frontier figure who became the hero of innumerable dime novels. The show, a reenactment of episodes in Plains life, was highlighted by an Indian attack on a stagecoach and its dramatic rescue by cowboys led by Buffalo Bill. Other Wild West shows that imitated the original and Indian medicine shows intensified and spread the Plains Indian image (see Figure 2-6). By the turn of the twentieth century Indians all over the country were beginning to dress as Plains Indians for special occasions.

Figure 2-4 | The first illustration of a Plains Indian tepee to be published, appearing in 1823. (From Ewers 1965.)

Figure 2-5 | Probably the first published illustration of a Plains Indian warrior on horseback, appearing in 1829. (From Ewers 1965.)

Figure 2-6 | In 1896 these Rosebud Sioux were put on display at the Cincinnati Zoo, demonstrating village life by day and performing in Wild West shows at night. (Photo by Enno Meyer. Courtesy of the Cincinnati Museum Center.)

Contemporary images of Indians are based not only on historical paintings and drawings and on the Plains Indian stereotype but also on many additional sources. One of these is the "Noble Savage" concept of Indians that gained prominence in the United States in the 1700s, especially as it was applied to Native Americans living north of Mexico. Although the concept has a long history in artistic and literary contexts, it has been given new emphasis in recent years by Euro-American environmentalists. That "Indians were the first American environmentalists" is stressed in television commercials, magazine articles, press releases, and public television programs. Native Americans understandably embrace this sympathetic position.

Examples of conservation practices are not difficult to locate in ethnographic reports. Some aboriginal Indians who were salmon fishers purposefully left openings in fishweirs so that many salmon could reach their breeding areas. Beaver trappers might take only a few animals from a lodge so that the survivors could reproduce. When a nest of duck eggs was discovered, some eggs could be left to hatch. These clearly were conservation practices. At the same time, aboriginal Native Americans usually did not have the technological capacity to disrupt the balance of nature in a serious manner. For example, a great deal of time was required to make and to maintain fish nets. Indian nets typically were relatively short and fragile and usually made from rawhide or plant fiber. As a result, these nets could not trap vast numbers of fish in the manner of modern long nets that are made from synthetic materials.

Today environmentalists forcefully and avidly condemn the burning of tropical rain forests throughout the world as a means of converting forests into productive farmland. In eastern North America, however, aboriginal Americans typically and systematically burned vast areas to produce arable land. Burning forests was, and remains, a highly effective means to clear land. The same was true for Euro-American pioneers, whether they were settling in Ohio or Oregon. Among both Indians and whites, the practice was not confined to farmers. It was commonplace among Indians to burn grasslands in order to drive out animals that could then be killed for food. Likewise, expanses of coniferous forests in Alaska and Canada often were burned to entice big game to the new plant growth that resulted from a burn. An area also might be burned on occasion to keep down the mosquito population. Thus, Native Americans were thorough vegetation burners, just as are many other peoples throughout the world.

Most Euro-Americans probably think that Native Americans harvested only enough fish, game, and birds to provide necessary food and raw materials. For some tribes this was true beyond doubt. But not for others. Justifiably, we condemn white hunters in the 1870s who killed countless bison for "pleasure." But did some Indians also kill animals needlessly? The answer is a clear "yes." However, we must step back and place such killings in their context. Although not everyone would agree, a good argument can be made that killing per se is learned behavior. Assuming this is so, the sooner a child in a society of hunters learned to kill nonhuman species, the greater the person's survival potential. Thus, when a small child found a nest of ducklings and systematically pulled the live birds apart, the process became a learning experience. The child was praised, not reproved, by adults. In sum, among hunters killing became a way *to* life and a way *of* life.

It is not difficult to document the destruction of game by Native Americans in early historic times. A Chipewyan example will suffice. Samuel Hearne (1958), on his travels from Churchill along western Hudson Bay to the Coppermine River and the Arctic Ocean, reported Chipewyan wastefulness soon after their first contact with the British. He reported that caribou were so abundant that Indians "frequently [killed] great numbers merely for the fat, marrow, and tongues" (p. 75); "[i]ndeed, they were so accustomed to kill every thing that came within their reach, that few of them could pass a small bird's nest, without slaying the young ones, or destroying the eggs" (p. 76); and caribou "were very plentiful on the whole way [south]; the Indians killed great numbers of them daily, merely for the sake of their skins" (p. 127). Despite these quotes, it must be added that the Chipewyan believed, based on their creation myth, that game would always be abundant (see also Chapter 3).

Not only was the reckless destruction of fish, game birds, and big game commonplace in aboriginal times among some Native Americans, but the practice continues into the present in certain areas. Why is this practice, as selective as it may be, not generally recognized? One answer is that ethnographers usually do not publish information about overkills, of which they are fully aware. Their rationale is to protect Native Americans and thus not betray them to law enforcement agents and others.

| Other Recent Developments

The feelings of non-Indians toward Native Americans seem to swing between sympathy and resentment. During the height of the civil rights movement in the 1960s and early 1970s, many Americans regarded Indians with sympathy, if not with compassion. Motion-picture stars, such as Marlon Brando, rallied to tribal causes; the depressed economy of Indians was the subject of television documentaries; and the Indian folksinger Buffy Sainte-Marie, who recounted old and new injustices, became popular. Members of the U.S. Congress less often urged Indian assimilation into the American "melting pot." Indians flexed their political muscles in an unprecedented manner: Native Alaskans formed an "ice block" in the statehouse, the Iroquois wanted their wampum back from museums, and Canadian Eskimos sought to establish their own political unit in the Arctic. Indian demands received more thoughtful attention from politicians and administrators than they had previously.

As the 1970s drew to a close, the civil rights movement had lost its thrust, and social justice diminished as a major American concern. With this new climate and a downturn in the economy, Native Americans and other minorities began to elicit more resentment than sympathy. One particular development in 1977 seems to have decreased American support for Indians. In that year a special White House study group issued a report about the land claims of the Passamaquoddy and Penobscot Indians of Maine. A settlement was proposed that would have given four thousand Indians millions of dollars and vast tracts of land. State officials in Maine labeled the proposal as "really outrageous" and "crazy." The suggested settlement received widespread and intense media attention, and many non-Indians shared the attitudes expressed by Maine officials. In the 1980 settlement, the Indians received $81.5 million from the federal government, a decision which elicited ill feelings toward Indians in general, especially among people not familiar with the merits of the case.

Anti-Indian feelings crystallized during this time, especially after other tribes realized that the Maine settlement represented legal precedent and pressed their own claims against illegal land seizures. Non-Indian constituents urged members of Congress to do something, and there was a serious proposal that the United States abrogate *all* Indian treaties. This approach failed, and in the 1980s a concerted federal effort was made to vitalize reservation life. The programs offered were complicated, expensive, and often misguided, and ultimately they have been relatively ineffective. By the mid-1990s, the widespread political discontent in the United States with the size, intrusive-

ness, and cost of federal programs was clear. Few federal agencies were regarded as sacred by politicians. For Indians, one result has been "termination
by budget massacre." Barring a dramatic shift in federal goals, Indians must increasingly devise their own solutions for many problems facing reservation
residents. One appealing option for numerous tribes has been to operate gambling facilities on their reservations. Another trend, especially in the Southwest, has been for tribes to develop more effective means to profit from the
millions of tourists who visit reservations each year. Indians have launched
their own museums, more tourist-oriented businesses, fairs, and powwows to
profit the tribes.

POLITICAL ACTIVISM   The Pan-Indian movement of the 1930s appears
to have been a major source for the Red Power movement of the late 1960s.
A major contributing factor was the impact of World War II and the Korean
War on Indians who were members of the armed services and who afterward
refused to fit back into the Indian stereotype. Some began to search for their
cultural roots. College-educated Indians resented the way the BIA treated
them. The most radical group to emerge was the American Indian Movement
(AIM) in 1968; its goal was to seek equality for Indians in the civil rights arena.
The most dramatic confrontation, and one that has stuck in the minds of non-
Indians, began in 1973. AIM seized the small town of Wounded Knee on the
Pine Ridge Reservation in South Dakota. (At Wounded Knee Creek, about
300 Siouan men, women, and children were massacred by U.S. Army troops in
1890; this episode and the site have long symbolized white injustice.) In a
71-day standoff, between 250 and 400 Indians held out against 125 Federal
Bureau of Investigation agents, 40 BIA police, and 150 U.S. marshals. The
siege resulted in hundreds of arrests, and the two major leaders, Dennis Banks
(see Figure 2-7) and Russell Means, spent fifteen years in court trying to vindi-
cate themselves in politically motivated trials by the federal government. By
the end of the 1970s, AIM had few members and diminished political impact.
(In 1979 the Federal Bureau of Investigation files in Washington, DC, contained 17,725 pages of information bearing on the activities of AIM, which was
said to be a revolutionary organization.) Dennis Banks went on to found another organization, Sacred Run, devoted to environmental issues and spiritual
renewal.

In 1978 Congress passed the American Indian Religious Freedom Act
(AIRFA), which was designed to review and update federal policies so that Native Americans would have the legal right to practice their traditional religions,
possess sacred objects, and gain access to sacred sites. Policies were reviewed,
and several recommendations were made. However, in 1988 and again in
1990, the U.S. Supreme Court ruled that AIRFA is a policy statement and not
law, and as such it does not afford rights to the protection of sacred sites or
the religious use of peyote in the Native American Church. The Native American Graves Protection and Repatriation Act (NAGPRA), passed in 1990, was a
notable exception.

Figure 2-7 | Dennis Banks, founder of Sacred Run, speaks in Santa Fe, New Mexico, at the culmination of a run from Alaska to the Southwest to commemorate the 500th anniversary of Columbus' landing in the New World. (Photo by Thomas C. Donnelly, 1992.)

NAGPRA requires that all federal agencies and all organizations receiving federal funds (most museums and universities, for example) conduct an inventory to determine what Native American skeletal remains and sacred objects are in their collections and the modern tribes with which the remains and objects are affiliated. The tribes involved must then be consulted about what is to be done with the remains and objects. While some groups have elected to leave items with museums and universities, others have requested their return for tribal museums or reburial.

TRIBAL SELF-DETERMINATION The current emphasis on greater tribal control over Indian lives may have been an indirect response to the civil rights movement, with its stress on ethnic diversity. In 1968 President Lyndon Johnson spoke of Indians as "The Forgotten Americans" and proposed changes in policies, including self-determination. Yet it is an old concept for Indians to manage their own affairs. Government-to-government negotiations took place in colonial times and in early U.S. history, when Indians had full jurisdiction over their internal affairs. As noted earlier in this chapter, tribal autonomy began to be eroded with a Navajo treaty in 1849. The current policy is set forth in the Indian Self-Determination and Education Assistance Act of 1975. It was designed to foster greater self-government and to free Indians from pervasive BIA control. A major barrier to self-determination had been the Alaskan Eskimo and Indian land claims that were resolved in 1971 (see Chapters 4 and 8). In 1983 President Ronald Reagan stressed that termination of federal responsibilities to Indians was no longer a goal, and he proposed that a greater percentage of the federal budget be earmarked for tribal self-government and resource development. However, the money for Indian programs actually was decreased.

The label "self-determination" is deceptive, because it does not mean that Native Americans are gaining unlimited control over their destiny. It does mean that the federal government has taken a somewhat more humane political attitude toward Indians. Again, the concept of "tribal sovereignty" is misleading. It is inconceivable that Indian reservations will become sovereign in a strict sense, despite a 1940 U.S. Supreme Court ruling that sovereign immunity is necessary for self-governance. Sovereignty really has come to mean that in some contexts Indians are regaining a degree of local autonomy at the state and federal level. These changes, however, are set against a complex historical backdrop: there are nearly 400 ratified Indian treaties; some 5000 federal statutes deal with Indians; and some 2000 court decisions have been rendered. The constitutions of tribes and lesser Indian political entities must be considered as well.

Courtrooms increasingly have become a prominent Indian battleground, and sovereignty issues have been salient. In general, federal courts have been sympathetic to Indian rights, whereas state courts have been, and remain, largely anti-Indian. For example, in 1980 the White Mountain Apache in Arizona, together with a timber company, sued the state, maintaining that state motor carrier and fuel taxes did not apply on the reservation. The U.S. Supreme Court agreed on the basis that the federal government controlled such taxes on reservations. In 1996, the U.S. Supreme Court ruled that in Oklahoma tribal-owned service stations were exempt from paying the state gasoline tax. Thus, federal court rulings have, on occasion, made non-Indians subject to Indian laws and regulations on reservations. Further examples are presented in later chapters.

A long-established aspect of sovereignty is represented by tribal courts that arose during the treaty-making era; initially they emerged from traditional Indian customs and laws for particular tribes. By the latter part of the nineteenth century, Indians on reservations were typically resolving their own internal legal disputes. In 1883 the BIA formally launched the Courts of Indian

Offenses with Indian judges appointed by the federal government. These courts sometimes, possibly often, were used to suppress traditional Indian laws and were under the control of local Indian agents. The contemporary court system emerged in 1934 with the Indian Reorganization Act. This system was far more responsive to Indian customs and legal norms and was controlled by each tribe. These courts seek to resolve civil disputes and have limited jurisdiction over criminal law on reservations. Most cases seem to be alcohol-related or concerned with child custody and divorce. One recurrent problem is the difference between Indian customary law and the demands of the Euro-American legal system.

An unexpected and positive aspect of self-determination has been the emergence of tribal colleges. The Navajo Community College was founded in 1968 because tribal leaders realized that formal education was one key to the future. Leaders were frustrated because many young people lacked the knowledge and skills to cope with Euro-Americans (see also Chapter 10). Before long the federal government acknowledged the potential of Indian colleges, especially in the Tribally Controlled Community College Assistance Act of 1978. As a result, twenty-four tribal colleges were founded, most of which are in Montana and the Dakotas. Typically, the libraries have relatively few books, most faculty are non-Indian, and the physical plants are inadequate. But because most reservations are located in rural areas with no ready access to four-year colleges, tribal community colleges provide an exceedingly valuable post–high school learning environment (see also Chapter 6).

INDIANS AND ALCOHOL   Treaties and laws referring to Indians in Canada and the United States often made reference to the consumption of intoxicants. In Canada, Indians who were not enfranchised could not buy liquor legally for ordinary consumption until 1951. The Indian Act of 1951 permitted the provinces or territories, with the approval of the governor in council, to allow Indians to consume intoxicants in public places. This condition existed over most of Canada until 1958. Between 1958 and 1963 the restriction was lessened in most provinces and territories to permit Indians to buy alcoholic beverages in the same manner as Canadian citizens in general—that is, either in a public place or from a package store. A band has the option of prohibiting intoxicants on its reserve lands.

In the United States the first federal regulation of intoxicants among Indians occurred in 1802. The law was modified periodically to ease enforcement and to cover loopholes. The federal government did not repeal this law until 1953. Prohibition still was possible on any reservation under local option. Before Indians could consume intoxicants in some states, state laws against the sale of liquor to Indians had to be changed.

To Native Americans the right to drink has been important symbolically as well as literally. For hundreds of years whites have expressed the opinion that Indians have a tolerance of alcohol lower than their own. Some whites have gone so far as to use the stereotype of the drunken Indian to rationalize not attempting to resolve depressed social and economic conditions among Indians. The question of Indian tolerance of alcohol has been the subject of many studies, but the one by Lynn J. Bennion and Ting-Kai Li (1976) deserves particular attention. They compared the rate of alcohol metabolism in thirty whites and thirty full-blooded Indians who had had some prior exposure to alcohol. They wrote, "Since our study showed no significant difference between American Indians and whites in rates of alcohol metabolism, the conclusion cannot be drawn that racial variations in proclivity to alcohol abuse can be accounted for by racial variations in alcohol metabolic rates" (1976, 12). Subsequent comparable studies validate these findings.

Thus the effects of excessive alcoholic beverage consumption by Indians are best attributed to nonbiological factors, but, as Philip A. May (1994) has stressed, alcohol abuse by Indians is a complex issue. The most recent comprehensive studies date from the late 1980s, when about 18 percent of Indian deaths were attributed to alcohol use compared with 5 percent for the general U.S. population. As these percentages are compared, it is essential to be fully aware of the major contributing factors. First, the Indian population is quite young, with a median age in the early twenties compared with a median age in the early thirties for the United States in general. As in the general population, young Indians are the most likely age group to be risk takers and careless drinkers. Second, many Indians live in rural areas of western states, and when they are involved in accidents, aid often is delayed. Third, many Indians live in poverty, which makes them prime candidates for alcohol abuse that leads to accidents, suicides, and homicides. In addition, although broadly based statistics about Indian drinking suggest that the vast majority of Indians are heavy drinkers, this does *not* seem to be the case. The reason is that heavy drinkers inflate the apparent total number of drinkers in arrest and treatment records. That *non-Indians are probably heavier drinkers than are Indians* is suggested in one study: for the Navajo adults in 1984, 52 percent drank, whereas for the United States in general at the same time 67 percent of adults drank.

The federal government has recognized the problem of Indian drinking, and by 1986 it had established more than two hundred programs in thirty-four states to combat it. Increasing numbers of these programs have been turned over to Indian management and adjusted to local conditions. Alcoholics Anonymous (AA) is a widely popular alcoholic therapy program for Indians and other U.S. citizens. However, by the late 1990s, there never had been a scientific study of the AA success rate; it appears that AA is no more successful in general than are other approaches to alcoholism.

RESERVATION GAMBLING OPERATIONS   Although bingo is hardly an ancient American Indian game, it attracted intense Indian interest beginning in 1979 when the Florida Seminoles initiated high-stakes bingo. A 1982 U.S.

Supreme Court decision held that reservation Indians could sponsor bingo if the game was permitted elsewhere in a state. There was no direct state or federal control over Indian gambling, nor were Indians subject to any taxes on gambling except those that Indians approved. As a result, the Indian gambling industry was born.

In 1988 Congress passed the Indian Gaming Regulatory Act, which made Indian gambling the most rigidly controlled form of legal gambling in the United States. This act permits Indians to operate gambling businesses in any state that permits legal gambling. Specific games in such states could be negotiated with state authorities. As Indian gambling expanded, opposition by non-Indians has mounted. Church and other groups that run charity bingo games objected because their gains were diminished. States objected to their inability to tax the operations. Furthermore, gambling operators in Nevada, New Jersey, and elsewhere objected to the competition from Indians. Yet most non-Indians do not realize that Indian gambling in the United States represents *less than 10 percent* of the legal gambling in this country.

By 1997 the tribes with gambling operations numbered 184. Eight casinos accounted for 40 percent of the total income, and it was estimated that the Foxwoods casino of the Mashantucket Pequot in Connecticut earned more than $1 billion a year. These gambling businesses employed about 140,000 people, 85 percent of whom were *non*-Indian. When it sanctioned Indian gambling, Congress stipulated that the revenues are to be used primarily for tribal programs or operations, general welfare, and economic development. One survey revealed that many non-Indians have been quite sympathetic to Indian gambling because of the benefits to Indians. At the same time some tribes, such as the Hopi and Navajo, have rejected gambling on their reservations based on moral grounds.

In states with Indian gambling, state officials object for one simple reason: they cannot tax these operations. But states have devised ways to circumvent this problem. For example, the Grand Ronde tribe in Oregon operates the Spirit Mountain Casino. Since there is a state lottery and video poker in Oregon, the state negotiated with the Grand Ronde to permit them to provide craps, roulette, and forms of poker not permitted elsewhere in Oregon. The state in turn receives 6 percent of the gambling profits, about $1.5 million in 1997. Thus the state has a "sweetheart" arrangement with the Grand Ronde. This "revenue-sharing" clearly is a veiled tax. What is just as alarming, however, is that the Grand Ronde have surrendered a portion of their sovereignty to the state, as also is the case for Indian casinos in other states.

OUTSTANDING INDIANS At present and in the comparatively recent past, innumerable Indians have achieved prominence in many fields. It is feasible to include only a small cross-section of individuals here. (Indians who have been successful anthropologists are discussed in the next section of this chapter.)

Sherman Alexie (1966–), of Spokane and Cour d'Alene ancestry, is a prominent young author. His books of poetry have been widely praised, and his collection of short stories, *The Lone Ranger and Tonto Fistfight in Heaven* (New York, 1993), and his novel *Reservation Blues* (New York, 1995) are both humorous and heartrending. Robert L. Bennett (1912–), an Oneida, was the BIA commissioner of Indian affairs from 1966 to 1969. Subsequently he became the director of the American Indian Law Center at the University of New Mexico. Ada Deer (1935–), a Menominee, played a critical role in the restoration of the Menominee Reservation after it and other reservations had been terminated by the federal government. Her efforts led to the reinstatement of additional terminated reservations. She currently is an assistant secretary of Indian Affairs in the Department of the Interior.

Vine Deloria, Jr. (1933–), a Standing Rock Sioux, is possibly the most celebrated Indian writer. He is an attorney and professor best known for his book *Custer Died for Your Sins* (New York, 1969; reprinted Norman, OK, 1988), which includes a vigorous attack on anthropologists. Deloria is an author of ten additional books, and the ones that address the legal issues involving Indians are especially notable. Walter Echo-Hawk (1948–), a Pawnee, is a lawyer with the Native American Rights Fund, the most important advocacy group managed by Indians for Indians. Joy Harjo (1951–), a Creek, is most recognized for her award-winning poetry. She also is a screenwriter and plays saxophone with her band, "Poetic Justice."

Ira Hamilton Hayes (1923–55), a Pima, was a U.S. Marine hero during World War II. He participated in the assault on the island of Iwo Jima and was one of the marines (in a famous photograph) who raised the U.S. flag at the summit of a volcano under heavy Japanese fire. William L. Hensley (1941–), an Eskimo (Inuit), was born in northern Alaska and played a significant role in resolving native claims in Alaska during the 1960s. He later served in the Alaska House of Representatives and remains an outstanding spokesman for native Alaskan issues. Russell Means (1940–), an Oglala–Yankton Sioux, is best known as one of the American Indian Movement leaders who confronted federal agents at Wounded Knee, South Dakota, in 1973. He also played a dominant role in subsequent confrontations while supporting Indian causes.

N. Scott Momaday (1934–) is a Kiowa raised in the Southwest who attended the University of New Mexico and became an outstanding novelist. His best-known book is *House Made of Dawn*. Momaday also is a widely respected poet. William Lewis Paul, Sr. (1885–1977), a Tlingit, became a lawyer and did more than any other individual to further Tlingit rights and those of other native peoples in Alaska. He was a pioneer in the 1920s in addressing civil rights issues.

William Penn Adair Rogers (1879–1935) was an Oklahoma Cherokee; known as Will Rogers, he was one of the most famous American humorists. He also was a prominent writer and actor. Buffy Sainte-Marie (1942–), a Cree, is an award-winning folksinger and a songwriter of note. She is an articulate advocate of Indian rights as well. Will Sampson (1934–87), an Oklahoma Creek, was a notable motion picture actor best known for his role in the 1975 film *One Flew over the Cuckoo's Nest*.

James Francis Thorpe (1888–1953), a Sauk and Mesquakie (Fox) from Oklahoma, was regarded as the greatest athlete in the world after winning gold medals in the 1912 Olympics. Although he was later stripped of his medals on a technicality, they were restored posthumously. From 1907 to 1912, Thorpe played football for the Carlisle Indian School in Pennsylvania; at that time there were only about 250 students in the school old enough to play football. Carlisle football teams played against major universities and seldom lost a game. The teams of 1911 and 1912 were among the best in the history of football.

| Native Americans and Anthropologists

American anthropologists have had a deep and abiding interest in American Indians for obvious professional and less obvious personal reasons. Since Indians in the United States and Canada have been quite accessible and usually considerate hosts, they have served as the subjects for thousands of ethnographic studies. A well-established tradition in cultural and social anthropology is the study of people in at least one other society as a part of professional training. In this manner the observer not only gains meaningful cross-cultural experience but also assembles a body of information that contributes to a broader understanding of humanity. The personal dimension is important because ethnographers typically develop a great affinity for the people among whom they work; they empathize with Native Americans in a way that most others do not. The field study of an ethnographer has two primary goals: to record the activities of people and to employ this information for the solution of theoretical or practical problems. Some Indians are resentful of anthropologists, and we need to ask: What do anthropologists do that may displease Indians?

Describing Native American life, the main purpose of ethnographers, would seem to be a relatively neutral activity. It is important if only because customs are reported that otherwise might go unrecorded and be lost to history. To preserve disappearing information has been a real concern of many investigators, especially those convinced that they were witnessing the rapid disappearance of aboriginal ways of life. Some ethnographers, especially those in the early 1900s, became secular crusaders who devoted their lives to recording cultural ways before they were gone forever. Surely this is a worthwhile, if not noble, goal.

With aboriginal customs as their focal point, many ethnographers recorded behavior that lived only in the memories of Indians. Counting coup (showing bravery by striking or touching a live enemy), scalping an enemy, bison hunts, and feather headdresses were given emphasis in descriptive accounts, conveying the impression that these forms and norms typified Native American life in the recent past. Modern Indians may justly object, because in their lifetimes or during the lives of their grandparents these customs no longer existed. Such ethnographers misrepresented Indians because they froze them in time; this was true of most pre-1930 studies. In retrospect, we can say that anthropologists did not lack compassion, but, unfortunately, they did produce a distorted picture of past practices lasting into the present.

Directly contributing to this misunderstanding is the fact that aboriginal or more recent Indian life often was described in terms of the "ethnographic present." This means that even though an ethnographer was describing extinct customs, the information was reported in the present tense as a literary technique to impart vitality to an account. Criticisms of this technique clearly are valid, especially because so much has happened to Indians historically and in the recent past. It distorts contemporary realities and contributes further to unrealistic views of Native Americans.

D'Arcy McNickle (1970) suggested that the use of the ethnographic present, and the failure by ethnographers to present the *adaptive* changes in Indian lifeways, has led to another unfortunate result, that of abetting the advocates of Indian assimilation. Acculturation studies have been important to ethnographic fieldwork since the early 1930s, and most of them have stressed the negative aspects of reservation life. This hardly has been a criticism of the Indians involved, however, nor was it intended as a prop for assimilation programs. Instead it often was an expression of dismay about federal programs as they were administered at the time.

Older Indians often are quite sympathetic when an eager ethnographer arrives to collect information about the past, but younger ones often have neutral or hostile attitudes toward these efforts. The older people see what they regard as the essence of Indian life disappearing, and they are well aware that their children or grandchildren often have little or no interest in their cultural heritage as Indians. Thus, an old man or woman finds it very satisfying to talk about the past to an ethnographer and have the conversations recorded with care. The attitude of many younger Indians about such information can be one of disinterest or of shame about old customs. If or when these younger people decide to learn about their past as Indians, it is probable that they will have to rely on the writings of the very ethnographers that they now resent.

In a discussion of anthropologists and Native Americans, it should be noted that a number of Indians have emerged as outstanding anthropologists with ethnography as a specialization. Anthropologists long have encouraged—and continue to encourage—Indians to join their ranks. Ethnographers are keenly aware that in many contexts a perceptive insider may be a better reporter and interpreter of Indian life than an outsider. The names of a number of Indian anthropologists come to mind. Francis La Flesche (1857–1932), an Omaha, first collected information about Indians with Alice Fletcher and then worked for eighteen years at the Bureau of American Ethnology. William Jones (1871–1909), of Mesquakie and white ancestry, earned a PhD at Columbia in 1904 and is noted for his research among Algonquian Indians. He was killed by the Ilongots on a field trip in the Philippine Islands. J. N. B. Hewitt (1859–1937), of Tuscarora and white ancestry, was an authority on the Iroquois. Edward P. Dozier (1916–1971), born at Santa Clara Pueblo, was noted for his writings about Pueblo Indians. Alfonso Ortiz (1940–1997) was a part-Hispanic member of the San Juan Pueblo and a specialist in Indians in the Southwest.

Prominent Indians today who are professional anthropologists are numerous. They include Edward D. Castillo (1947–), a Cahuilla and Luiseno, who holds a PhD in anthropology and is best known for his studies of California Indians. Nora Dauenhauer (1927–), a Tlingit, is recognized for her voluminous and insightful studies of the Tlingit. Jack D. Forbes (1934–), Powhatan and Lenape, earned a PhD degree in anthropology and is the chair of Native American Studies at the University of California, Davis. He is best known for his insightful historical studies of Indians. Shirley Hill Witt (1940–), a Mohawk, earned her PhD in anthropology and became a member of the U.S. Commission on Civil Rights. She has been especially active in supporting the rights of women. These are but a few examples.

An important question remains: If anthropologists know so much about Indians, why have they not played a more prominent role as "experts" on culture change among Indians? The basic reason is straightforward. For many years the guiding principle behind federal Indian policy in the United States was assimilation, the sooner the better—a position that anthropologists found distasteful. When the Indian Reorganization Act of 1934 became law, a number of outstanding anthropologists did work for the BIA to further the provisions of the act, because it was designed to restore vitality to reservation life. However, World War II diverted national attention from this program, and the early 1950s ushered in the termination policy, which found little support among anthropologists. In theory and in fact, the BIA was long committed to Indian assimilation, but like most bureaucratic organizations, it has in truth devoted a great deal of energy and funds to its own expansion. Furthermore, bureau personnel often regarded anthropologists as "Indian lovers" and neither sought nor welcomed their advice. Anthropologists in turn have had little sympathy with the bureau policies in general and have preferred not to become involved in most of their programs.

Anthropologists clearly have served Indians in useful and positive ways. They spoke out against the termination policy, although in retrospect not as strongly as they might have. They have worked to increase the effectiveness of health programs, given evidence to support Indian land claims and identity, testified in vigorous support of the Native American church, and often served as advisors to Indians in economic development programs. In recent years anthropologists have aided Native Americans in their efforts to obtain aboriginal resource utilization rights opposed by the federal and state governments. Furthermore, anthropologists have played an important role in interpreting Native American life to non-Indians, both in and out of the classroom.

| Comparing Cultures

In each of Chapters 3–14, a particular tribe is discussed in detail. You will be reading about Indian conventions that seem quite ordinary, reasonable, and even self-evident. In these cases, your reaction no doubt will be one of appreciation and understanding, because you are familiar with these Indian ways; they will seem "normal." On the other hand, you will also be reading about Indian behavior that seems strange, bizarre, and possibly barbaric. In these cases, your response probably will range from negative to abhorrent. An additional cautionary note is fitting. Not infrequently we think that some types of human behavior, especially those associated with our biology, "occur everywhere." Yet this may not be true. An example is instructive. Youthful Navajo males stand to urinate while older men kneel on one or both knees. Young Navajo women squat but older women urinate while standing. Thus, something as basic and ordinary as urinating may, and sometimes does, vary from one culture to the next.

To better understand American Indians—or any other unfamiliar people—it is desirable to be as objective as possible. Three concepts are introduced for your consideration. The first is ethnocentrism, meaning that one's own lifeway is the basis for judging all other lifeways. This is a commonplace human reaction when exposed to persons in other cultures, especially those quite different from the one in which you were born and raised. Ethnocentrism is "good" in some ways; it gives you a strong sense of personal identity with a particular culture (or subculture). But ethnocentrism is "bad" in other ways; it fosters irrational prejudice, contempt, or hostility toward other peoples. The phrases "a good Indian is a dead Indian," "America right or wrong," and "ethnic cleansing" serve as examples. The "bad" of ethnocentrism overwhelms the "good."

The second concept is cultural relativism, which holds that human behavior always occurs within the context of a particular culture and should be considered within such a framework. Thus every culture has its own standards, attitudes, and particular logic. Stated differently, a culture is considered from an insider viewpoint. Examples illustrate the concept. We might say that the people in some cultures "smell bad," and we in turn may be accused of "smelling bad." There is no universally accepted standard for how people smell. Euro-Americans cut wood with a handsaw on the push stroke while the Japanese would cut with a handsaw on the pull stroke; the contrast represents different motor habits to achieve the same goal. The people in one culture may believe that "little people" inhabit a hinterland, whereas another people may label such an idea as "nonsense." Is one right and another wrong? No, because the ideas are culture-bound. Ethnographers embraced cultural relativism because it helped them avoid biases built into their own culture. However, as Paul R. Turner (1982) points out, the concept of cultural relativism is in essence ethnocentric.

Turner suggests a third approach. Universalism holds that certain categories of values are universal; they are found in all cultures. A value is a shared concept of what is desirable or undesirable by a people; when combined, all of their values provide a worldview. The universal value categories are the following:

1. power (participation in decision making)
2. enlightenment (access to information)

3. wealth (income, including goods and services)
4. well-being (health and safety)
5. skill (proficiency in any practice)
6. affection (love, friendship, and loyalty)
7. respect (recognition by others)
8. rectitude (ethical behavior)

With this list of value categories in mind, it becomes possible to view the behavior of people, any people, without reference to culture-specific standards. It encourages nonbiased comparisons. In sum, we would encourage you not to be ethnocentric as you read about Indian life. You may take a cultural relativist view, or, better yet, consider universalism as an approach to understanding human lifeways.

| Additional Sources

The best widely available general source about Indians in historical perspective is volume 4 of the *Handbook of North American Indians* (Washington, DC, 1988), under the general editorship of William C. Sturtevant. One brief but effective history is *American Indians* (Chicago, 1961) by William T. Hagan. For Canada, *The Canadian Indian* (Don Mills, Ontario, 1972) by E. Palmer Patterson II is worth consideration. For the colonial era, the best ethnohistory is *The European and the Indian* (New York, 1981) by James Axtell. The emergence of the Pan-Indian movement is detailed best in *The Search for American Indian Identity* (Syracuse, 1971) by Hazel W. Hertzberg. A relatively recent and valuable source is *The Politics of American Indian Policy* (Cambridge, MA, 1982) by Robert L. Bee. A classic study of Indian law by Felix S. Cohen, published originally in 1942, has been updated and republished as *Felix S. Cohen's Handbook of Federal Indian Law* (Charlottesville, VA, 1982), edited by Charles Wilkinson. Another outstanding source about Indian law is *American Indians, American Justice* (Austin, 1983) by Vine Deloria, Jr., and Clifford M. Lytle. The sovereignty issue in particular is addressed in *The Indian and American Society* (Berkeley, 1985) by Francis Paul Prucha. Settlement of Passamaquoddy and Penobscot Indian claims against the federal government is presented vividly by Paul Brodeur in *Restitution* (Boston, 1985). Donald L. Fixico's *Urban Indians* (New York, 1991) focuses on contemporary issues.

| Selected Bibliography

Bee, Robert L. 1982. *The politics of American Indian policy.* Cambridge, MA.

Bennion, Lynn, and Ting-Kai Li. 1976. Alcohol metabolism in American Indians and whites. *The New England Journal of Medicine* 294:9–13.

Brookings Institution. 1928. *The problem of Indian administration.* Baltimore.

Cohen, Felix S. 1960. *The legal conscience.* Lucy K. Cohen, ed. New Haven. Reprinted as *Felix S. Cohen's handbook of federal Indian law,* Charles Wilkinson, ed. Charlottesville, VA, 1982.

Cook, S. F. 1955. *The epidemic of 1830–1833 in California and Oregon.* University of California Publications in American Archaeology and Ethnology, vol. 43, no. 3.

Cumming, Peter A., and Neil H. Mickenberg, eds. 1972. *Native rights in Canada.* Toronto.

Deloria, Vine, Jr., and Clifford M. Lytle. 1983. *American Indians, American justice.* Austin.

Densmore, Frances. 1939. Nootka and Quileute music. *Bureau of American Ethnology Bulletin* 124.

Donaldson, Thomas. 1886. The George Catlin Indian Gallery in the U.S. National Museum. *Annual Report of the Board of Regents of the Smithsonian Institution, 1885,* pt. 2 appendix.

Dunning, Robert W. 1962. Some aspects of governmental Indian policy and administration. *Anthropologica,* n.s. 4:209–31.

Ewers, John C. 1965. The emergence of the Plains Indian as the symbol of the North American Indian. *Smithsonian Report for 1964,* 531–44.

Foreman, Grant. 1932. *Indian removal.* Norman, OK.

Harper, Allan G. 1947. Canada's Indian administration: The treaty system. *American Indigena* 7:129–48.

Hearne, Samuel. 1958. *A journey from Prince of Wales's Fort in Hudson's Bay to the Northern Ocean.* Richard Glover, ed. Toronto.

Hertzberg, Hazel W. 1971. *The search for American Indian identity.* Syracuse.

Howard, James H. 1955. Pan-Indian culture of Oklahoma. *Scientific Monthly* 81:215–20.

Jorgensen, Joseph G. 1971. Indians and the metropolis. In *The American Indian in urban society,* Jack O. Waddell and O. Michael Watson, eds., 66–113. Boston.

Kroeber, Alfred L., and Edward W. Gifford. 1949. World renewal. *Anthropological Records,* vol. 13, no. 1.

La Barre, Weston. 1960. Twenty years of peyote studies. *Current Anthropology* 1:45–60.

May, Philip A. 1994. The epidemiology of alcohol abuse among American Indians. *American Indian Culture and Research Journal* 18:2, 121–43.

McAuliffe, Dennis, Jr. 1996. For many Indian tribes, the buffalo are back. *Washington Post National Weekly Edition,* Mar. 18–24, 8–9.

McGuire, Randall H. 1992. Archeology and the first Americans. *American Anthropologist,* n.s. 94:816–36.

McNickle, D'Arcy. 1970. American Indians who never were. *The Indian Historian* 3(3): 4–7.

Mooney, James. 1896. The Ghost Dance religion and the Sioux outbreak of 1890. *Bureau of American Ethnology, 14th Annual report,* pt. 2, 641–1110.

Pearce, Roy H. 1965. *The savages of America.* Baltimore.

Saum, Lewis O. 1965. *The fur trader and the Indian.* Seattle.

Sixel, Friedrich Wilhelm. 1967. Die deutsche Vorstellung vom Indianer in der ersten Hälfte des 16, Jahrhunderts. *Annali del Pontificio Museo Missionario Etnologico già Lateranensi* 30:9–230.

Sorkin, Alan L. 1971. *American Indians and federal aid.* Washington, DC.

Spicer, Edward H. 1962. *Cycles of conquest*. Tucson.

Taylor, Theodore W. 1972. *The states and their Indian citizens*. Washington, DC.

Turner, Paul R. 1982. Anthropological value positions. *Human Organization* 41:76–80.

U.S. Department of the Interior. 1958. *Federal Indian law*. Washington, DC.

Washburn, Wilcomb E. 1984. A fifty-year perspective on the Indian Reorganization Act. *American Anthropologist,* n.s. 86:279–89.

Winsor, Justin. 1889. *Narrative and critical history of America,* vol. 2. Boston.

3 The Chipewyan: Subarctic Hunters

*Before the flood, caribou were easy to
hunt with the bow and arrow, but after
it the arrows could not pierce them: it
was just as if they were nothing but
bone. The hunters had to aim at their
heads and hit a vein to make them
bleed to death. Then the raven said,
"We cannot kill the caribou because
they are only bone," and while all
others were asleep it stayed up and
made magic all through the night. It
was the raven that gave the caribou
their present form with flesh on their
bones, through which the arrows could
go. After that they were easy to hunt.
This is what we know about the raven.*

A myth about caribou and the raven.
(Birket-Smith 1930, 88)

THE CHIPEWYAN HAVE been chosen to represent the subarctic culture area for cultural, ecological, historical, and social reasons. They are one of the numerous Athapaskan tribes that inhabit interior Alaska and northwestern Canada. Most subarctic peoples depended on caribou and fish for food, and the Chipewyan were reasonably typical in this respect, although caribou were far more important in their diet. We know more about them than about most other Northern Athapaskans largely because of historical chance. They were reasonably well described by Europeans soon after historic contact, and in 1960 a thorough study was made of a modern community. Furthermore, anthropologists have made comparatively recent ethnohistorical studies and additional field researches among these people. We do not have information of comparable scope for any other Northern Athapaskan tribe. The sociocultural reasons for describing the Chipewyan are equally significant because their lifeway was considered one of the simplest reported for North American Indians. Typically described as a band-level society, they formed temporary groups of extended families and exhibited marked local variability in social organization. Furthermore, the Chipewyan provide an opportunity to analyze the impact of the fur trade, which changed them from caribou hunters to beaver and marten trappers.

| People, Population, and Language

Chipewyan is a Cree word meaning "pointed skins," a reference to the dangling point at the front and back of the poncholike garment men wore. These people called themselves Dene, meaning "humans," and were unified on the basis of language and life-style. Most, but not all, individuals were related by blood or marriage to other persons who called themselves Chipewyan, and this formed a primary basis for their identity. The major subgroups were territorial and were based on the exploitation of regional caribou herds. By the time of contact with Europeans, the Chipewyan numbered about forty-five hundred and had one of the lowest population densities among North American Indians. Today the Chipewyan population approaches eight thousand.

The Chipewyan language belongs to the Na-Dene linguistic phylum and the Athapaskan family. The Na-Dene lived from near the Bering Strait to the western shore of Hudson Bay and were scattered southward to the Mexican border. They were primarily inland peoples and were relatively recent migrants to the New World. Some Athapaskan peoples spread south to form the Pacific group, and another cluster went on to the Southwest. The extremely close cultural and linguistic bonds between the Chipewyan and Yellowknife lead some modern ethnologists to consider them as a single people.

| Chipewyan Country

The early historic range of the Chipewyan is shown in Figure 3-1. Chipewyan country is a vast expanse of tundra extending as much as seven hun-

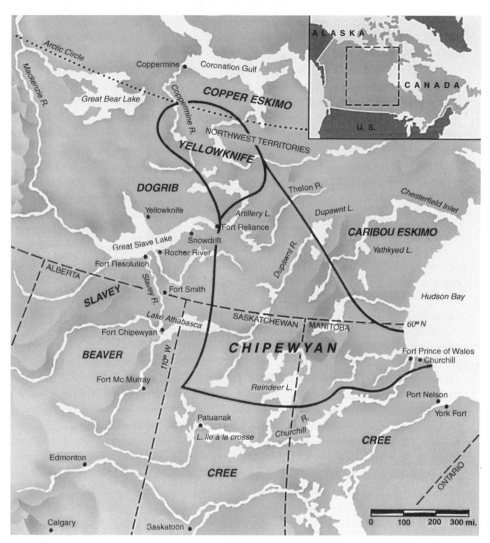

Figure 3-1 | Early historic range of the Chipewyan Indians.

dred miles from east to west and nearly six hundred miles from north to south. The climate is continental, with long, cold winters and short, hot summers. The extremes range from the high 80s (°F) in summer to −60°F in winter. Everywhere networks of waterways—foaming as well as hesitant streams and rivers, great lakes, and countless smaller lakes—interlace. Barren rocks show obvious signs of glacial wear on their smoothed or striated surfaces. Results of glacial action are especially evident in the north, where rolling masses of bedrock give way to boulder-strewn valleys with adjacent lines of eskers. Lichens alone grow on highlands, but valleys are covered with dwarf birch, mosses, lichens, and willows. This region is known to the Chipewyan as the

Barren Grounds, a fitting term incorporated in geographical writings. Along river bottoms on the southern Barrens, stands of spruce appear as outriders of their species; this is the taiga, where the tundra and northern forest meet. Still farther south the spruce are dense, and aspen, birch, and juniper stands are fringed by marshy bogs and upland tundras. The forested area was foreign to the aboriginal Chipewyan, but it became important to them in historic times. Above all, Chipewyan country was dominated by great caribou herds that meant survival for these Indians. Interestingly, and contrary to the title of this book, the Chipewyan maintained that they did not own the land but that the land owned them.

| First Contact with Fur Traders and Missionaries

According to nearly all standard sources, the Chipewyan lived in the northern forests at the beginning of their history and were driven into the Barren Grounds by the Cree after the latter received firearms. However, ethnohistorical studies by Beryl C. Gillespie (1970, 1976) have shown this was not the case. Instead, the Chipewyan lived in the taiga and tundra during early historic times and began to exploit interior forests only under fur traders' influence. The Chipewyan were first encountered by Europeans in connection with the Hudson's Bay Company efforts to expand the fur trade. Company administrators at York Fort, founded in 1684 along southern Hudson Bay, were anxious to have the Chipewyan trade at the post, but these Indians were afraid to travel through territory occupied by their enemies, the Cree. In 1715 William Stewart visited Chipewyan camps with a Chipewyan woman, who induced her people to settle their differences with the Cree and to trade at York Fort. Thus the country south of Great Slave Lake soon was open for trade. The next move of the Hudson's Bay Company was to establish a trading center on one margin of Chipewyan country. They selected the former whaling station of Churchill along the western shore of Hudson Bay, and built a post in 1717. The great stone fort named Fort Prince of Wales was erected nearby between 1732 and 1771.

Still, the heart of the Chipewyan area had not been brought under realistic European control. As a few "Far Indians" began trading at Churchill, they told about the great area to the northwest and about a major copper deposit. The Chipewyan, however, were making tremendous profits as middlemen in the trade with more distant tribes and were reluctant to guide company explorers. In 1768 the English felt that it might be profitable to locate the copper deposits. When approval for a land expedition was given, the name of Samuel Hearne became intimately associated with the Chipewyan, with copper, and with the exploration of northwestern Canada.

Samuel Hearne was born in London in 1745, and after naval service in the Seven Years' War he joined the Hudson's Bay Company. In 1766 he became a seaman on a small vessel engaged in trading and whaling along the western shore of Hudson Bay. In 1769 and 1770 he made abortive attempts to penetrate Chipewyan country, then launched a third, more rewarding, try. The ultimate success of this venture hinged on the Chipewyan guide Matonabbee, who had his own opinions about how to travel. The key to his plan was to take women along to relieve the men of the many burdensome chores. Matonabbee had six wives at that time. The trip to the Coppermine River and Coronation Gulf was completed successfully in mid-1772 and is one of the most noteworthy feats of individual exploration anywhere at any time. Hearne's maps were not accurate, and for this he has received periodic criticism, but, far more important, his book (1795) is a classic in exploration literature and the first comprehensive account of the Chipewyan. Hearne died a month after his manuscript was accepted by a publisher in October 1792.

The map Hearne prepared and his knowledge of the country facilitated further expansion to the northwest. The first trader to settle in the midst of Chipewyan territory was Peter Pond, who established himself near Athabasca Lake in 1778. The organization of the North West Company in 1783 introduced an era of fierce competition with the Hudson's Bay Company, and not until their amalgamation in 1821 did trading conditions become stabilized. The history of Chipewyan country centered about a failed quest for mineral wealth, the expanding fur trade, and disappointing searches for a water passage to the Pacific Ocean. Later, missionaries began the search for souls to save. In 1846 Roman Catholic missionaries founded a permanent mission at Lake Ile a la Crosse, and the Anglicans located at Churchill in 1912. Thus fur and souls attracted most outsiders to Chipewyan country.

| Aboriginal Life

When the Chipewyan were encountered by Europeans, their economy, based on caribou and fish, was well established and probably had been much the same for thousands of years. The baseline ethnographic account to follow examines each major aspect of their sociocultural lives. Although much of the information is based on observations by Hearne, his findings are supplemented by those of later observers as they relate to aboriginal conditions. Introducing the Chipewyan with ethnographic baseline data establishes a point of departure for examining more recent historical developments among these people.

ORIGIN MYTH   Most people have at least a passing concern about their beginnings and seek some rationale for their existence. In the absence of a strictly historical perspective, they usually explain their presence in legendary or supernatural terms. Most often a creation myth accounts for their genesis.

The Chipewyan regarded the primordial world as centering about a woman who lived in a cave and subsisted on berries. As the myth goes, in time a doglike creature followed her into the cave and lived with her. She thought that she dreamed this animal turned into a handsome young man who had sexual intercourse with her, but it was no dream, and the woman became pregnant. At this juncture a giant man approached; he was so tall that his head reached nearly to the clouds. With a stick he outlined the bodies of water and caused them to fill. The giant tore the doglike being to shreds and threw its internal organs into the water, creating various fish. He tossed the flesh on the land in bits and it became land animals, and he tore the skin and threw it into the sky to become birds. The giant told the woman that her offspring would be able to kill as many of these creatures as they required and she need not worry about the animals' abundance, since it was his command for them to multiply. The giant returned from whence he had come and was never seen again. In this way, order in the world emerged, and the abundance of game was assured. This tale justified the Chipewyans' indiscriminate killing of game and led to a supernatural association with dogs, since the woman's human offspring were descended from a creature related to the dog. The creation myth was not only taught to children but also used to guide thoughts about the adult world.

CLOTHING   Chipewyan garments were made from the skins of caribou killed in the early fall when the hides were strong and the hair dense but not long. Eight to ten skins were required to outfit an individual for winter. The upper garment of a man consisted of a loose-fitting, sleeved poncho with the hair side out and the skins cut to a point in front and back. He sometimes wore a fur boa when the temperature was low, and his ears might be protected by a fur band or cap. His ankle-length leggings were of dehaired skins, and moccasins were sewn on at the bottom. In severe weather he draped a caribou skin cape over his shoulders. The garb of a woman included a sleeved dress that reached her knees or ankles; to hold a long dress up from the ground she wore a belt around her waist. Her leggings reached from below the knee to the ankle and may not have had attached moccasins. She also wore a cape, and both sexes used mittens of double thickness. They could slip their hands out of the mittens without the chance of losing them because each was attached to a leather harness that hung about the neck. Gloves were unknown among American Indians until their introduction by Europeans.

SETTLEMENTS AND MANUFACTURES   Habitations ranged from isolated family dwellings to clusters of as many as seventy units, but large aggregates usually were of brief duration. The size of a community was above all else a function of the time of year and the local availability of food. People lived in a subarctic variety of the tepee best known from the American Plains. A Chipewyan tent was framed with poles set in a circle and bound near the top. The cone was covered with as many as seventy caribou skins sewn together, and it measured over twenty feet across at the base. An opening at the apex of the cone permitted smoke from the central fireplace to filter upward. If spruce boughs were available, they were placed around the fire and covered with caribou skins; on these people relaxed, worked, and slept.

Most manufactures could be found in and around the tents. A well-supplied camp included tripods of poles from which hung caribou-skin bags filled with meat. Among the possessions of women were cooking and storage containers of birch bark or skin. The women commonly used a basket of folded and sewn bark for cooking by filling it with water, preheated stones, and raw meat. They probably had skin bags in which they kept sewing awls and thread of caribou sinew. The men's tool kits included antler wedges for splitting planks from logs; a crooked knife with a copper blade and antler handle, the most important form of knife; a curved, wooden-handled knife with a beaver incisor for a blade, another highly useful tool for cutting small sections of wood; and a hand drill with a copper bit and an antler handle, the only drill form known. Awls were of copper, and a copper ax head was hafted on a wooden or antler handle. These uses of native copper, and its use in icepick points, arrow points, spearheads, and spoons, reflect a reliance on this metal. The copper tools were made by pounding a raw lump of the metal into shape. These people never heated or smelted copper but processed it as they did stone.

CONVEYANCES   The little that is known about aboriginal Chipewyan boats suggests that they had only small skin-covered canoes with wooden frames. These vessels probably served primarily to ferry people across rivers and for hunting caribou as they crossed lakes. The toboggan for winter transport was up to fourteen feet long and about fourteen inches wide. It was made from thin juniper planks that were steamed and bent upward at the front. The planks were joined to crosspieces, probably with thongs. Chipewyan men, or women if the occasion arose, pulled the toboggans; they presumably did not use dogs as traction animals because of their supernatural associations. If wood was unavailable, the people could make toboggans by using sewn caribou leg skins as a substitute. The cariole, which is a more complex toboggan with sides and a back, was a European invention.

Snowshoes were essential for travel over deep snow. The Chipewyan made them by lacing babiche (thin, dehaired caribou-skin strips) through holes in birch-wood frames. These snowshoes had slightly turned-up tips and were asymmetrical in outline; the outer edge flared, but the inner edge was relatively straight. Men prepared the frames, and women laced the babiche into place with eyed snowshoe needles. When traveling on snowshoes, the men jogged along at a pace that was faster than a walk, and they traveled in this manner for hours at a time.

HOUSEHOLD LIFE   In camp, women prepared meals and cared for children, as did their counterparts throughout most of the world. To these obligations was added one of their most important activities, the task of processing skins, particularly those of caribou. After a caribou had been killed by a man, his wife recovered it, skinned it, and removed bits of flesh and fat with a bone scraper. If the hair was to be removed, the woman propped a wooden beam obliquely in the ground, draped the skin over it with the hair-side up, and removed the hair with a scraper. A dehaired skin often was smoke-cured by hanging it over a pole framework under which decayed wood smoldered. A skin to be used with the hair intact was scraped, softened in water, wrung out and dried, and a paste of partly decayed caribou brains was rubbed on the inner surface. Later the skin was dried once again and finally scraped with a copper-bladed end scraper. The skin probably was rubbed by hand to make it pliable and relatively soft. This process of skin preparation was a key technological complex for the Chipewyan, who relied on caribou skins not only for clothing but also for bedding, dwelling covers, containers, and ropes. American Indians did not tan skins in the technical sense.

Favorite foods largely were caribou products: the head and fat from the back, a fetus, and grubs from beneath the skin. The Chipewyan did not consider steaks and chops luxuries. They ate caribou meat or fish both raw and cooked. In addition to boiling it in a birch-bark container, they roasted flesh over an open fire. The Chipewyan diet rarely included plant products, although a moss soup is reported and moss could season meat soup.

Although women prepared meals at camp, men ate first. This was customary because if men were not reasonably well nourished, especially in times of food stress, they could not hunt or fish as effectively. The women received what the men had not consumed, which might at times be nothing. However, because women typically prepared meals, we might assume that they ate at least some food in the process.

Pemmican was an important food in the subarctic, although it usually is associated with Plains Indians. Pemmican, from a Cree word meaning "manufactured grease," was made from lean meat that had been cut into strips and dried by the sun or near a fire. The dry meat was pounded into a powder, mixed with fat, and stuffed into caribou intestines; this highly concentrated food was a favorite of travelers. Dried meat had the advantage of being light and portable. Many Chipewyan considered it more desirable than fresh meat.

SUBSISTENCE ACTIVITIES   When the Chipewyan could not find caribou, they located their summer camps near lakes or rivers, and fish became the staple. The principal fishing device was a gill net, which was made from strips of babiche and strung with wood floats and stone sinkers. The men set these nets across narrow streams, at eddies in rivers, or at spots in lakes favored by lake trout, northern pike (jackfish), and whitefish. Gill nets had the general appearance of modern tennis nets. The dimensions of the openings, or mesh, depended on the size of the species of fish for which a net was set. When these fish attempted to swim through the netting, their heads were held fast by vertical netting strands that caught in their gills.

The Chipewyan felt that each net had its own personality; they did not join one net to another because they believed that jealousy between the nets would prevent fish from being caught. Additional precautions included attaching charms to the corners of a net; without them, the Chipewyan believed, no fish would be taken. Charms often were attached to antler, bone, or wooden fishhooks, and the first fish caught with a new net or hook was boiled, the articulated bones removed intact and burned. Other fishing implements included dip nets used for fish confined by weirs, which were brush fences across shallow stretches of water. The Chipewyan shot barbed fish arrows from bows and used leisters (fish spears) from canoes.

Fish were an important food in times of stress, but the Barren Ground caribou were the staff of life. The word for meat was derived from that for caribou, and some Chipewyan said that they preyed on caribou herds in the manner of wolves. In the early spring, bands of hunters prepared to range over the Barrens to intercept caribou. At a birch grove on the northern forest edge, a party would cut tent poles and make canoes for crossing deep or swift water. As many as two hundred persons might assemble, including women taken along primarily as bearers. A strong woman carried about 140 pounds of camping equipment, an impressive burden considering the nature of the terrain. While traveling, the men hunted on both sides of the trail taken by the women and young girls as they pulled the heavily loaded toboggans along the most direct route. Dogs, laden with parcels of tent skins, containers, and poles, accompanied the women. The female–male division of labor on a winter trail may seem to have been more stressful for women; however, this does not appear to have been the case. Women and girls pulled toboggans along the most direct route, and the noise they made scattered game along the way. Men on snowshoes traveled much farther, pursuing game adjacent to the trail. Thus, there may have been a reasonable balance between the energy expended on the trail by each gender.

In the fall, six hundred persons might gather at well-known caribou crossings and camp in a single locality. Families seeing each other for the first time in months or years followed an established etiquette at their reunion. At first they sat apart from each other and said nothing. Then an older person of one party recounted all of their personal traumas since the last meeting, and women of the other group wailed on hearing of the misfortunes. The fate of the second party next was recounted and responded to. Men then greeted one another, and women exchanged presents as well as good news. When caribou appeared, their number might be truly fantastic. Sometimes so many were killed that only the skins, long bones, fat, and tongues were taken, and the carcasses were left to rot. As the caribou moved, the Indians followed, drying as much meat as they could conveniently carry.

When caribou rutted in October, a hunter sometimes attached lengths of caribou antler to his belt so that they rattled as he walked. A bull caribou in the vicinity would think he heard two other bulls fighting over females and would boldly approach, expecting to lead off the females. A bull could be killed more readily this way than by the usual method of stalking against the wind. At these times hunters used the self bow, a one-piece wooden shaft strung with babiche. Caribou-killing arrows had unbarbed bone or stone points and were vaned with feathers. An alternative and preferable fall hunting method was to drive large herds of caribou into water and kill them from canoes with spears.

In the eastern sector, winter and early spring camps were established on promontories along the forest edge, in localities frequented by caribou and near lakes containing fish. People moved only once or twice during the winter from an ideally situated camp, one accessible to lakes or wide rivers along which caribou normally passed. Here funnel-shaped caribou surrounds were built. Converging lines of brushy poles were erected, with poles at about twenty-yard intervals. When caribou approached the wider end of a funnel, they were unaware of the poles, which sometimes spanned three miles. As animals entered the surround, the women, boys, and some men appeared from behind to herd them. The caribou were driven into a trap, which was a large enclosure of branches at the end of the funnel, with snares set at narrow exits. After the entrance was blocked with trees, snared caribou were speared, and arrows were shot at loose animals.

When the snow was soft and deep, men, on snowshoes, sometimes tracked caribou. This meant following a single animal until it was exhausted from floundering in the snow. In the winter, the men might set gill nets beneath the ice of lakes or jig for fish through holes in the ice with hooks. In the western area of Chipewyan country, fishing was more important than among the eastern bands. Secondary means for taking game included the use of deadfalls for bear, marten, squirrels, and wolverine. The Chipewyan used nets for taking beaver in summer, but in winter, after they had broken open the beaver lodges, they took the animals from retreats beneath the ice along stream or lake edges. They set babiche snares to entangle hares or ptarmigan. Even though these Indians reached Hudson Bay at Churchill, they did not hunt the sea mammals abundant there at certain seasons.

It is important to note the advantage, in food-getting activities, of using devices that do not require the presence of a person. Set nets, snares, traps, and deadfalls are examples of "untended facilities" that operate when no one is present, and no danger, waiting, or pursuit are required in their use. By contrast, spears and bows and arrows must be operated by hand and may be dangerous for the user—for example, against a bear. Thus, under most circumstances, it is preferable to use untended facilities when possible. Note that the Chipewyan used snares and deadfalls.

Additional details of Chipewyan hunting and fishing activities could be presented, but it already is obvious that caribou, and fish to a lesser extent, were the primary staples. Although recent research indicates that the subarctic environment may have been more productive than outsiders realized, relying as they did on very few species, the Chipewyan sometimes found food to be scarce, and people starved. Famine probably was more common among Northern Athapaskans than among any other group of American Indians. At these times the people ate berries, mosses, or other plant products and later consumed items of clothing; under extreme conditions they turned to cannibalism.

SOCIAL DIMENSIONS The Chipewyan were described in less than glowing terms by Europeans, who characterized Chipewyan men as patient and persevering but also as morose and covetous. The Chipewyan firmly believed that they were more intelligent than the intrusive outsiders. The Chipewyan were peaceful within their own community, at least in terms of not shedding blood. When angry with one another, the men wrestled, pulled their opponent's hair or ears, or twisted his neck. As far as honesty went, among the eastern tribes of the Northern Athapaskans, the Chipewyan were ranked as superior to all others; they abhorred a thief. However, they considered whites to be not quite human and did not really consider taking their property to be theft.

No description of these people would be complete without commenting on the status of women as recorded by Hearne in the eighteenth century. According to him, women were subordinated in every way, were treated cruelly, and were held in gross contempt by men. Female infants were occasionally permitted to die, a practice viewed by adult women as kindly. In fact, they are said to have wished their mothers had done it for them. Women were beaten frequently, and although it was considered an odious crime to kill a Chipewyan man, it was regarded as no crime for a man to beat his wife to death. We probably will never know whether this was typical behavior toward women, but we may suspect that Hearne exaggerated or that his description was based on the actions of Matonabbee and men associated with him. Matonabbee unquestionably was a very powerful and self-centered person. The treatment of women as recorded by Hearne seems inordinately severe and out of character for Indians north of Mexico. Furthermore, a similar pattern did not exist among the Chipewyan in more recent historic times. Contemporary researchers have suggested that while women may have been devalued symbolically, in everyday life they had considerable influence and power (Sharp 1988).

As was typical for many foragers (collectors, fishermen, and hunters) around the world, the constraints on individual behavior were defined largely on the basis of age and gender. Each household was self-sufficient and could exist in isolation until a member sought a spouse. Group responsibilities or community cohesion hardly existed, and individuals had a great deal of flexibility in their behavior. A man, however, was responsible for his family and typically dominated his wife. Environmental resources were open to exploitation by everyone on an equal basis; family hunting or trapping territories did not exist.

POLITICAL ORGANIZATION Aggregates of people structured in a formal manner and functioning as cohesive units did not exist among the aboriginal Chipewyan. Instead, as studies by James G. E. Smith (1970; 1976a; 1976b) and others have indicated, local groups were amorphous and highly flexible. In ecological terms, it is important to note that regional bands were defined largely on the basis of the separate herds of caribou exploited, and a regional group was divided further into localized bands of one hundred or more people who hunted together. Seasonally, when great numbers of caribou were available, several localized bands might assemble for a hunt. However, when caribou did not follow their expected migration routes, people divided into smaller hunting groups. Conditions influencing the movements of caribou included fires, weather variations such as sudden thaws or blizzards, and, in all likelihood, cyclical variations in their number. The most important observation about the nature of a band was its flexibility in number as a function of local food resources.

Families might unite under the aegis of a charismatic leader. Such a man was above all else an outstanding provider with an inordinate ability to take game and fish. Hearne's guide, Matonabbee, is an example. He supported himself, six wives, seven biological children, and two adopted children. Once a man's reputation as a leader was established, fathers of marriageable daughters sought him as a son-in-law. This was to the personal advantage of the father-in-law because the pattern of marriage residence was for a husband to join his wife's natal household (matrilocal residence). Subsequent wives could be sisters of the first, but other women could also be chosen. Such a man had to be physically strong because he was obligated to validate his claim to a wife, especially a younger wife, by wrestling if challenged by another man. Less successful hunters, relatives, and nonrelatives cast their lot with him for greater security. An important characteristic of this form of leadership was that it was transient. A man could keep his wives and other followers only as long as his powers of persuasion, hunting skills, and physical strength endured. As he began to fail physically, he sometimes could retain his position of authority by craft and intrigue, but this was only a temporary respite before he slipped into obscurity.

The Chipewyan were a tribe, but only in a general sense, and comparatively little political integration existed among the member bands. Conflicts with non-Chipewyan took the form of raids and generally were carried out by the members of a single band. An account by Hearne illustrates this type of hostility. He was accompanying a group of Chipewyan to the Coppermine River mouth when they raided an Eskimo camp. Matonabbee was the undisputed leader, and the raiders were unusually cooperative as they lent equipment to one another. Beforehand each man painted his shield in black and red, adding one or more figures representing supernatural aids. They painted their faces red, black, or with a combination of the two colors, and took off most of their clothing or lightened it so that they could run fast. They launched the attack in the middle of the night and caught the Eskimos asleep. Once alarmed, the twenty or so Eskimos ran naked from their tents only to be speared to death by the attackers. Afterward the Indians plundered the camp and departed. As was typical among northern Indians, the Chipewyan attacked these Eskimos for individual prestige, plunder, potential glory, and tribal security; territorial gain was not a goal.

DESCENT, KINSHIP, AND MARRIAGE   The Chipewyan calculated their ancestry through both female and male relatives (bilateral descent); the descent group (kindred) was like that which prevails in the United States today. When a man married, he attached himself to the household of his parents-in-law (matrilocal residence), and his ideal mate was his father's sister's daughter (patrilateral cross-cousin). In *recent* times at least some Chipewyan called a father's sister's daughters and mother's brother's daughters (cross-cousins) by the term for sweetheart, a convention that gives strength to the assumption of cross-cousin marriage. As the anthropologist Fred Eggan (1937) has pointed out, a man relied on his son-in-law for support, and the son-in-law in turn was aided by his wife's brother's son. While there was regional variation, it appears that, in general, in the aboriginal system of kinship terminology, the cousin terms were of the Iroquois type. Father's brother's children and mother's sister's children were termed the same as siblings, but different terms were employed for a father's sister's children and mother's brother's children. This terminology would be compatible with cross-cousin marriage. For the generation above an individual, the kinship terms for father and father's brother are alike (bifurcate merging), and mother's brother is distinct. Mother, mother's sister, and father's sister are all termed differently (bifurcate collateral). This terminology indicates that probably siblings and parallel cousins of the same sex (who were terminological siblings), particularly if they were males, extended mutual aid to one another and regarded their cross-cousins as possible mates. With the further presence of wife exchange, we find an integrated network of blood relatives on an individual's generational level. On the parents' generation the same social distance separated aunts and uncles from one another as from parents. The inference is that these individuals were not as important socially or economically as near relatives of one's own generation.

The Chipewyan system of kinship terminology is diagrammed in Figure 3-2. The symbols in this and all subsequent kinship diagrams follow the same pattern. Each diagram represents the kinship terminology that prevailed

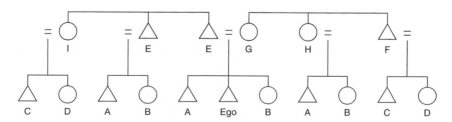

Figure 3-2 | The early historic Chipewyan system of kinship terminology.

in early historic times. A circle symbolizes a female, a triangle, a male. Short parallel lines represent marriage. The long horizontal lines and short vertical ones represent descent. The point of departure for examining a diagram is a male "Ego." Each letter represents a kinship term. For example, a male sibling of a Chipewyan Ego is designated as *A* and a female sibling as *B*. These terms are broadly comparable to "brother" and "sister" in English, but note that they are extended to include father's brother's and mother's sister's children; thus, the terms *A* and *B* are applied to some individuals that English speakers would identify as first cousins.

SUPERNATURALISM   External threats to the Chipewyan came from the neighboring Cree and Eskimos. The hostility stemmed in part from the belief that the shamans of these people sent evil by supernatural means to cause illness. The Chipewyan believed that death or disease occurred from natural causes only among the aged. Thus in theory each physical disorder of a younger person resulted from the hostile activities of a foreign shaman. Chipewyan shamans attempted to negate the effects of such evil by acting through personal spirits that they controlled. When someone fell sick, a shaman sang and danced to summon his supernatural aids or "shadows," who were animal, bird, or imaginative familiars. He then sucked and tried to blow the intrusive disease substance from the patient. For serious cases a shaman treated an ill person in a special small square tent built with no opening at the top.

Death and disease led the Chipewyan to frequent hostilities with non-Athapaskan neighbors, and they made sporadic forays into the lands of their tormentors. In the raid on Eskimos reported earlier, the attackers carried wooden shields on which they had painted designs representing their individual guardian spirits. After the encounter the raiders observed numerous taboos to placate the spirits of those they had killed. A raid of this nature united the participants against a common enemy but did not require elaborate organization.

In the Chipewyan view of the supernatural world, animistic spirits hovered about constantly, and some were more potent than others. Because the spirits of wolves and wolverine were considered dangerous, these animals usually were not hunted or killed. The bear, too, was considered dangerous; when one was killed, its skin might be burned and the large bones scattered in the four directions. A woman could not touch or step over a bearskin; thus, one placed before a door was a means of keeping women from entering a tent. The spirits of a shaman were powerful, and the spirit of an ordinary person was sometimes feared. Only a vague notion existed of a future life, a life like that on earth but free from cares, according to one observer. Not all accounts agree, however. One states that the Chipewyan believed that the soul of the deceased crosses a river, and if the individual has been good on earth he reaches an island on which life is free from worry. If he has been evil, he struggles in the river forever.

ENTERTAINMENT   Games and other forms of amusement were few, and the only dancing was a step borrowed from the Dogrib Indians. A widely popular pastime was the hand game, a guessing game in which two opponents sat opposite each other with ten to twenty counters beside them. One man had an object in one hand and, behind a skin, shifted it. His opponent then guessed the hand that contained the gaming piece. A correct guess gave the winner one counter, and the game was won when one man had all of the counters.

LIFE CYCLE   Tracing the pattern of typical lives from birth to death provides invaluable insight into the forms and norms that produced and sustained the sociocultural system identified as Chipewyan. No ethnography is reasonably complete unless such a sketch is included. While information about aboriginal Chipewyan life histories is not balanced or complete, it does lend itself to presentation in brief.

The Chipewyan, like all other North American Indians, realized that conception resulted from sexual intercourse. As the time of delivery approached, a small tent or brush-covered structure was erected away from the main camp for a pregnant woman. Here she bore her offspring and remained apart from normal camp routine for about a month. Her isolation was enforced whether the group was traveling or at a relatively permanent camp. The mother was cared for by other women, but she had no contact with men. The father did not see his infant until the period of isolation had ended. Similar isolation was the norm for menstruating women and for girls at menarche. The blood associated with women at these times was considered antipathetic to fish and game, and men avoided contacts with females in these conditions. Apparently the women were successful in keeping the true nature of the menstrual cycle a secret from men. When a woman sought to avoid her husband, which might be several times in one month, she simply crawled out of the tent beneath a side, to indicate that she was beginning to menstruate, and went to the menstrual hut.

During the first year of life an infant was carried on its mother's back next to her skin; the baby was held in place by a belt that passed from the middle of the mother's back over her breasts. In this secondary "womb," a baby wore only a moss-padded diaper. A female infant was typically named after a form or characteristic of a marten, such as Marten's Heart, Summer Marten, or White Marten. The names for males were taken from the seasons, places, or animals. Unfortunately, little is known about the social environment of children. Males clearly occupied a favored position compared with their sisters, but children in general were treated as adults. Conversations in the presence of children were free and frank.

Childhood betrothals were customary, and parents were careful to prevent a girl from participating in sexual intercourse before she married. Matches were made by parents or other relatives; a girl had no choice. The usual marriage was between a pubescent girl and a man who was at least twice her age. Since there was no marriage ceremony, the man simply attached himself to his wife's household. A marriage assumed stability only after an infant was born. Offspring seldom were born during the early years of marriage, and from this it may be presumed that the young bride's adolescent sterility tended to delay conception. A nuclear family (a husband, wife, and children) was neither a stable nor a long-lasting unit. The possibility of death by accident, disease, or starvation always existed, and life expectancy was probably less than thirty years on an average. (High infant mortality rates often account for a statistic such as this one.) Dislike of a spouse could rupture a household, and wrestling to retain one's wife whenever challenged did not lead to familial stability. Skill in wrestling was developed during youth, and the rule was that the man first thrown to the ground was the loser. An opponent could be downed most readily by grabbing his hair—thus it was cut short—or by seizing his ears—so they were greased. The woman being fought over had no voice in these matters but was expected to follow the winner dutifully.

A wrestling match for a wife did not always end well. In one case the husband killed a potential rival. He and his wife then were forced to live in isolation, and whenever other Chipewyan happened on the couple, they would take everything they owned except their clothing. Women deserted their husbands, but because of the physical isolation of most camps this was a dangerous undertaking. The woman might be caught and beaten by her husband or seized by another man before she found safety with a man she desired. Men guarded their wives jealously, not allowing them out of their sight if the opportunity for adultery existed. Wives generally were faithful to their husbands, but a particular wife sometimes shared her husband with as many as seven co-wives. The exchange of wives for a night perhaps helped temper any urge to seize a woman for sexual purposes alone. Wife exchanges were made by men and had implications that were more economic than sexual. The bonds between men resulted in continuing friendship and mutual aid. If one of the men died, his partner assumed the responsibility, at least temporarily, of caring for the widow and her children.

As individuals aged and became less capable of caring for themselves, they were regarded as a burden. Old people had the poorest of tattered clothing and were given the most undesirable food. When a camp was moved, they might be left behind in a small shelter where they would starve alone. The corpse of a person who had died in isolation was not buried when it was found, and the corpse of one who died in camp was simply placed on the ground. In both cases, the bodies were eaten by animals. Property of the deceased was destroyed, and immediate relatives also destroyed their personal property. A widow cut her hair short as a sign of bereavement, and the shorn hair might be placed beside the deceased. She wailed about camp, stripped of her clothing and other possessions, to be aided and soothed by relatives and friends but not to remarry for a year.

In drawing the Chipewyan life-cycle discussion to a close, it is appropriate to comment on the manner in which these people behaved toward one another, especially on men's treatment of women and the general treatment of the aged. We should realize fully that the area in which these people lived offered either feast or famine. It was one of the most difficult sectors of North America in which to live in aboriginal times because of food uncertainties. The men, as the hunters and primary providers, presumably were often anxiety-ridden about their capacity to feed their families. This at least provides a partial explanation for their harsh treatment of women and the aged. We also must recognize that early writers about the Chipewyan were European men whose own attitudes toward these segments of the population possibly colored their accounts.

| Early Historic Changes

Until recently Chipewyan history was unknown except in terms of obvious sources such as the work by Samuel Hearne. Recent ethnohistorical studies, however, make it necessary to correct and revise accounts about the Chipewyan, in terms of both baseline and acculturative ethnographies. The thoughtful analyses of historical sources by Beryl C. Gillespie, Henry S. Sharp, David M. Smith, and James G. E. Smith provide a dramatic illustration of what may be learned from existing but previously ignored or underused sources. These works reveal configurations of patterned change that are considered here.

THE PULL OF CONFLICTING ATTRACTIONS   James G. E. Smith (1976b, 14) aptly characterized the course of Chipewyan life from contact to the recent past in his statement that "one may view the history of the Chipewyan from the early 18th century to the present as one of conflicting attractions to the caribou of the taiga-tundra ecotone on the one hand and to the fur trade and the fur bearers of the full boreal forest on the other." In early historic times the Chipewyan occupied a major portion of the Barren Grounds and the adjacent taiga; their precise distribution remains disputed. Some bands began moving south and west into the northern spruce forests in the late 1700s, but the change was made slowly and reluctantly by many groups. The Chipewyan wanted European trade goods, however, and by 1721 Hudson's Bay Company agents were encouraging them to trap beaver and marten in the northern forests. The Chipewyan could trap marten without serious disruption of their caribou-based economy, but trapping beaver meant a commitment to life in the forests, where these animals were abundant, which led to an accompanying decline in hunting caribou.

A major technological change aided these people as they sought to participate effectively in the fur trade. It was a shift from walking to the use of a small, one-person canoe and subsequently to the use of large canoes capable of carrying at least two persons, pelts, and supplies. When the Chipewyan first

Figure 3-3 | A man carrying a small birch-bark canoe in early historic times. (From Hearne 1796.)

traded at Churchill, they arrived on foot. By the 1700s they were building small birch-bark canoes (see Figure 3-3), and by the 1790s they were using much larger canoes to travel in the summer.

EPIDEMICS AND FAMINES   Early in their history, the Chipewyan abruptly lost much of their vitality as a result of exposure to new diseases. A severe smallpox epidemic struck in 1781, and an estimated 90 percent of the people died. While this estimate may have been exaggerated by whites who only observed Chipewyan living near the trading posts, there is no doubt of the horrendous effect of the 1781 epidemic. In 1819, another smallpox epidemic "carried away whole bands" (Simpson 1938, 81). Thus they had become a remnant people early in their history. Weakened by disease, they were less able to support themselves and more subject to famines. Another momentous change took place as a direct result of the fur trade. When they began to trap intensively, they spent less time hunting caribou and lived within a more tenuous economic system. They desired trade goods and trapped to obtain them, but thereby they deprived themselves of the opportunity to acquire their basic foods. Thus, if they did not take large numbers of fish and caribou at certain seasons, they faced starvation. Famines made devastating inroads into the vitality of the society; although famines were not new, they now occurred more often. At Fort Resolution in 1833 some "forty of the choicest hunters" died in a famine (Back 1836, 209), and between 1879 and 1881 "many died in hunger and misery."

CHANGES IN LEADERSHIP   In aboriginal times the charismatic leader was respected because of his unique abilities, and a number of such individuals, among whom Matonabbee was an outstanding example, are reported. With the advent of the fur trade, a different form of leadership developed. Traders preferred dealing with a group representative, not with individuals,

Figure 3-4 | A 1913 photograph of Chief Squirrel, a Chipewyan trading chief. (Courtesy of the Canadian Museum of Civilization, neg. no. 26070.)

and this led to the emergence of trading chiefs (see Figure 3-4). Traders strengthened a trading chief's standing by deferring to him and presenting him with clothing, medals, and a formal reception on his arrival at a post. By the late 1880s, the "chiefs" were distributing the meat of caribou and moose to whomever they chose, irrespective of the wishes of the men who killed the game, although the hunters personally kept the skins of animals. If this was the norm, we must conclude that a chief possessed authority and some form of power. By 1908 chiefs represented groups in dealings with officials of the federal Indian Affairs Branch, but, as we would expect, they were not very effective.

CHANGING STATUS OF DOGS   It is revealing to consider the changing status of dogs among the Chipewyan. Recall that a doglike creature was thought to have fathered these people, and the dog, along with bears, wolves, and wolverine, had strong supernatural associations (Sharp 1988). In the 1820s the people were convinced by a powerful man that they should not use such closely related animals to do their work, and consequently they destroyed all of their dogs. For this reason, during the early period of contact the people had very few dogs or none at all. Apparently, dogs were not widely used as beasts of burden, nor did they pull toboggans, until sometime in the mid-1800s. Yet, Hearne mentioned that in his time dogs hauled birch poles as hunters moved into the Barrens. Certain taboos still surrounded dogs in the early 1930s. For example, dogs were not shot, and to feed a dog a moose head or bear intestines was thought to bring ill fortune.

CHANGES IN SUPERNATURAL BELIEFS   The unformalized supernatural system of the aboriginal Chipewyan population absorbed Cree concepts, and by the early 1800s they had borrowed the concept of manitou, a supernatural force that pervades the natural world. An evil manitou was blamed for sickness, disease, or bad luck. By 1908, some Chipewyan had learned many of the Cree folktales, including tales that involved a trickster-hero. In these accounts, one animal tricks another, or a supernatural force creates something, and thus becomes a mythological hero. Christianity was introduced by Roman Catholic missionaries, and most Chipewyan became converts by the 1920s, at least in name. Yet many traditional supernatural beliefs continued to prevail; Catholicism was integrated with the old religion, a typical pattern among Indians.

In early historic references to caribou hunting, taboos were rarely reported. Later in history, caribou remained the key food, but numerous taboos surrounding them appeared. For example, in one area if a woman's skirt were to pass over a hunting knife, there was fear that the caribou would not migrate in that direction during that year. A woman was supposed to pierce the caribou's eyeball before she butchered the carcass to prevent the spirit of the deceased animal from reporting its fate to others. The implication might be that these taboos emerged as caribou hunting became less dependable.

| Becoming Modern at Snowdrift (Lutselk'e)

The character and texture of Chipewyan life began to assume its contemporary form as the people abandoned seasonal camps to settle in villages. The first detailed study of emerging contemporary Chipewyan life was made from 1960 to 1962 by James W. VanStone at the community of Snowdrift. His findings represent an acculturative baseline and therefore are reported at some length. His study demonstrates the increasing integration of one community of Chipewyan into the fabric of modern Canadian life.

SNOWDRIFT HISTORY   The settlement of Snowdrift, beyond the margins of aboriginal Chipewyan country, is in a forested area along the eastern portion of Great Slave Lake. The people had traded at Fort Resolution, founded in 1786; but after the Hudson's Bay Company built a post at Snowdrift in 1925, families began trading there. Yet it was not until 1954 that most people began to settle at Snowdrift. They did so in response to pressure from the federal Indian Affairs Branch agent at Yellowknife, who stressed the advantages of more sedentary living. In 1960 the village consisted of twenty-six predominantly log houses, Hudson's Bay Company buildings, a Roman Catholic church, and log cabins used seasonally by Euro-Canadian sport fishermen and mining entrepreneurs.

The commitment to settled village life was a dramatic shift from being mobile caribou hunters. The move to Snowdrift radically altered the social, religious, and economic life of old. Many people now were clustered to exploit limited local resources. One result was that it became increasingly difficult to maintain their previous standard of living. Furthermore, they came under far more direct control of federal authorities.

THE SETTLEMENT   At Snowdrift, family dwellings had an air of permanence unknown in the recent past. About 1912 the first ridged commercial canvas tent was bought locally, and soon this style replaced the conical tent of old. After 1950 most families began to construct more substantial dwellings with federal support for the construction or renovation of the cabins. The Indians were at first reluctant to participate in the program because they were hesitant to commit themselves permanently to the village. Most of the dwellings were one-room log cabins with board floors. They were furnished with homemade beds, chairs, tables, and shelves. Light was supplied by kerosene lamps, and heat was furnished by wood-burning sheet-iron stoves. Trunks or bags for extra clothing and bedding, a battery-powered radio, a hand-operated sewing machine, and utensils were common household items. In nearby log storage sheds were frozen or dried fish, dog harnesses, outboard motor parts, traps, snowshoes, fishnets, and rifles. Quite clearly, with all of the new material goods, a family became far less mobile.

CLOTHING   Most garments were quite unlike aboriginal forms, although a few men wore hooded and sleeved caribou skin ponchos rather than manufactured parkas. From the Hudson's Bay Company store, men bought long underwear, shirts, trousers, and sweaters. Women purchased briefs, cotton stockings, dresses, petticoats, shoes, skirts, and sweaters. The most important locally made items of aboriginal derivation were moccasins for men and skin slippers worn by women during the summer. Young girls wore clothing like that of the women, with the addition of slacks and colorful lightweight jackets. Young girls often curled their hair, and young women as well as girls wore lipstick. Young women used commercial perfumes and set off their appearance with brooches, earrings, and finger rings. Young men were particularly fond of wide leather belts with large buckles and short, ornamented, black leather jackets. The implication of the modern clothing styles is at once obvious. The people obtained most items from the store and needed to have something that the outside world valued for their purchase.

CONVEYANCES   In 1960 each Snowdrift family owned a large commercially made canoe, an outboard motor, and a small canvas-covered canoe. Although a form of toboggan existed, it was purchased from the store and was more correctly a cariole, for it had a rear panel and canvas sides. Dogs, not women, pulled the carioles. Each family owned about five dogs, which were chained near the homes. The use of dog teams and outboard motors as sources of power unquestionably had greatly increased the families' mobility. In addition, canvas-covered canoes were being replaced by aluminum boats, which required substantial cash to purchase.

SUBSISTENCE ACTIVITIES   Traditional Chipewyan economic life had centered about caribou and fish, and with the addition of trapping furbearers, these foci persisted. Trapping was a major source of cash, and although it was important, hunting remained a significant part of family welfare. Most men would abandon their traplines if caribou appeared in the vicinity.

Trapping was a difficult occupation. A trapper was obligated to depend largely on game birds for food while on a trapline, and he fed his dogs by fishing through the ice with a gill net. One to three days of dog-team travel were required to reach a trapline, where commercial steel traps or wire snares were set for lynx, marten, mink, white fox, and wolverine. Cross, red, or silver fox were not sought, since their market value was low. Trapping was surrounded by many uncertainties. Wolverine sometimes ate the animals caught in traps or sprung a line of sets and ate the bait. Gray jays or other creatures might also spring a trap. Furthermore, the living conditions on a trapline were difficult. A canvas trapping tent was small and impossible to heat adequately, and men found it difficult to work alone for weeks on end. Previously a man had been accompanied by his entire family on a trapline, but often this was no longer possible because school age children were obligated to attend classes. Because of all these problems, men tended to trap only for short periods in November and December, when the pelts of most furbearers were prime.

Trapping was linked to the Hudson's Bay Company store, the only local trading center. Hearne's account of the Indian–trader relationship was in many ways similar to the observations made by VanStone. Indians attempted to outwit the trader and resorted to subterfuges to obtain credit. In Indian eyes, the only good traders were generous ones. Despite opposing goals, the Indian and the trader were economically dependent on each other. The price of pelts was not very high; for the trapping season that ran from the fall of 1959 to the spring of 1960, the average take per trapper was worth about $320. The most important furbearer trapped in the spring was beaver, upon which there was a harvest limit. In theory no man could take more than five animals, and each pelt was tagged before being exchanged at the store. Energetic trappers, however, bought unused tags issued to others and increased their take in this manner. The income from trapping was not sufficient to meet subsistence needs and made no major contribution to the welfare of the community. Thus the one contribution of these people to the world economy had declined and had not been replaced.

In the early 1960s dependence on caribou remained great, and the late summer hunt was of prime importance. A household head felt that he required about one hundred caribou per year, yet harvests of this magnitude were no longer realized. The people traveled by large canoes to the Fort Reliance area for caribou, and if there were no animals available, they portaged east to the vicinity of Artillery Lake. Burdened by their families, large amounts of equipment, and big canoes, they were unable to reach the best hunting grounds. As a result they were not likely to kill many animals. The meat obtained was smoked and brought back to the village to be stored in the Indian Affairs Branch cold-storage unit. In 1960 nearly half of the households were unrepresented in the fall caribou hunt, although some families shared in the take of others because they had provided a hunting party with equipment.

In the late fall, men set nylon or cotton gill nets in the lake (see Figure 3-5) or along nearby rivers and filled them with stone sinkers, wooden floats, and large anchor stones at each end as in aboriginal times. They caught lake trout and whitefish most frequently, hung them out for partial drying, and then stored them as winter food for dogs and people.

Most men began to prefer wage-labor jobs to hunting, fishing, and trapping. Few such positions existed, however, and most were temporary. Construction jobs were few after the community physical plant was completed; work on commercial fishing vessels was unpredictable and physically demanding. Fire fighting was sporadic and important but seasonal. Serving as guides for tourist fishermen had limited potential. Thus, making a living by wage labor was even more uncertain than following subsistence pursuits of old.

Aboriginal foods were increasingly replaced by purchased edibles. People preferred fish and meat with each meal, but since these often were unavailable, bannock became an important staple. Bannock ("Indian bread"), the standard fare of poor Eskimos and Indians throughout Alaska and Canada, is made of white flour and baking powder mixed with water into a paste and spread in a greased skillet to be fried. Often this was the only food at a meal; bannock and tea are the bread and water of depressed subarctic living. The dominant method of cooking was by boiling. When families were able, they purchased prepared foods from the store. The imported items most desired were flour, sugar, tea, coffee, crackers, peanut butter, canned meats and fruits, evaporated milk, and seasonings.

DESCENT, KINSHIP, AND MARRIAGE   The people of Snowdrift traced their descent along both the female and male lines (bilateral descent), as they had in early historic times. Cousin terminology, however, was of the Eskimo

Figure 3-5 | A Snowdrift man, Louison Abel, checking a gill net set beneath lake ice in 1960. (Photograph by James W. VanStone, © The Field Museum, Neg. no. A95940.)

type (similar to the current classification of cousins in the United States). Preferential cousin marriage no longer existed; in fact, people did not recall it as an aboriginal practice. The one hundred years of contact with Roman Catholic missionaries who spoke against cousin marriage probably had produced the change, yet premarital fornication between cousins prevailed.

When a person married, he or she was most likely to select a mate within the community (village endogamy), and immediately after marriage the couple lived with the in-laws who were best able to receive them (temporary bilocal residence). As soon as possible the couple built a separate dwelling and lived alone (neolocal residence). In 1961 most households were nuclear or nuclear core families, the latter comprising a nuclear family to which were added a near relative or two of the husband or wife. Plural marriages no longer existed, and capable providers did not attract followers who lived with them. The overall impression is that the nuclear family was still the most important social unit, although it was not as autonomous as before.

SOCIAL DIMENSIONS   With subsistence activities and material culture changing so much from aboriginal times, we would expect to and do find equally significant differences in other aspects of living. The old attitudes toward women and their harsh treatment as described by Hearne are not reported. Although VanStone was not explicit on the subject, he conveyed the impression that domestic harmony existed. Certain activities, such as food preparation and child raising, remained female obligations, but men performed these tasks as the need arose. Women could profit monetarily from their own labors. A woman who processed a moose or caribou hide or sewed skin garments for someone outside her family was paid directly and retained the profits. The favorable position of women at Snowdrift may have resulted from the fact that they were a distinct minority; for unknown reasons there were fewer young women than men. Because it was difficult to obtain a wife, she was treated with care (see Figure 3-6).

Social bonds beyond those based on kinship were new and of expanding importance. Village life produced feelings of unity, and people thought of themselves as economically, morally, and physically superior to persons in adjacent settlements. Other evidence of village cohesion was the widespread sharing of locally available foods. By the time a successful moose hunter beached his boat he had given away most of the meat, and the same applied to a catch of fish. Food had been shared in aboriginal times, but apparently not in as pervasive or egalitarian a manner. Furthermore, an intensive pattern of reciprocal borrowing had developed, and this included major as well as minor items of material culture. These attitudes and their behavioral manifestations clearly were integrating the community on a social and economic basis.

POLITICAL LIFE   The Snowdrift Chipewyan were included in Treaty Number 11, which was signed by the Indians in 1921 and provided them with direct monetary and other benefits. The Indians gave up their aboriginal rights to the land but at the same time were protected in their exploitation of local resources. In exchange, they received tangible benefits such as formal education, health services, and material goods. Each year a band member received a cash payment of five dollars, the band chief received twenty-five dollars, and counselors, fifteen dollars each. The Indian Affairs Branch began to provide fishnets, ammunition, and items such as roofing and doors for house

Figure 3-6 | A Snowdrift woman, Mary Louise Rabesca, sitting in front of a smokehouse in 1976.

construction. Furthermore, families in need, as defined by the Indian agent, received a "ration" from the Indian Affairs Branch through the store. A national program of old-age assistance provided for the welfare of persons sixty-five years of age or older. Even more important was the "baby bonus," or Family Allowance, which was a national program. Every month, each family received six dollars for each child under ten and eight dollars for those ten through sixteen. The program was designed to improve child care, and it probably served this end at Snowdrift.

One result of living in a stable community was intensified contact with the Indian agent. Stationed at Yellowknife, he visited Snowdrift and called meetings on matters of villagewide concern. Attendance usually was poor, and it was difficult to conduct a general meeting because each Indian was inclined to raise issues of personal interest, usually specific requests for aid. Thus, the process of democratic group action failed. Unity, when it was manifested, consisted of a stand against a proposal rather than any positive approach. The Chipewyan preferred to deal with the agent on a private, almost secret, basis concerning specific requests. They felt that an agent was in a position to grant favors, and for him not to do so was regarded as pure stubbornness.

Visits to the village by the Royal Canadian Mounted Police (RCMP) in the 1960s were more a show of power than the result of actual need. Crimes as defined in the Canadian legal system were rare, and the most common cause for arrest was the manufacture of home brew. Since everyone was secretive when making home brew and avoided being seen intoxicated when the police were present, few arrests were made. The Chipewyan felt that it was wrong to appeal to Canadian legal authorities for the settlement of personal disputes, and they rarely did so, although they might threaten such action.

In 1960 the bands were reorganized to allow for the movement of people from one band to another. Under the reorganization, Snowdrift Indians had their own chief and two counselors or advisors. The Indians had a clear formulation of what they considered to be ideal behavior for a chief: he did not interfere in the affairs of villagers, but he adopted a stern attitude toward Euro-Canadians in general and toward the Indian agent in particular. Whites, by contrast, expected a chief to be cooperative; if he was not, they bypassed him and acted through the trader or teacher. This pattern by whites of accomplishing their purposes undermined Indian authority and contradicted the purpose of having a chief, counselors, and recognized Indian authorities.

For years the Canadian government encouraged the development of local political power at the band level. However, in 1969 federal administrative obligations shifted largely to the government of the Northwest Territories, and this government fostered the democratic process through local settlement councils that were in direct competition with the band. Furthermore, a regional native rights organization became increasingly militant in fostering Indian interests. These competing institutions above all else intensified local factionalism and divided the community in terms of effective political action.

RELIGION AND SUPERNATURALISM   Everyone at Snowdrift was a participating, but nominal, Roman Catholic. A priest visited the community frequently throughout the year and sometimes stayed for two months; he always was present during the Christmas and Easter seasons. Church dogma and belief were understood poorly by the people, but participation in formal ceremonies was high. In general, the Church was regarded as something beyond the context of daily living. The Chipewyan felt that the Church was wealthy and that people should be paid for any labor performed on its behalf. Thus, the feeling of belonging to a church and strengthening its purposes was not understood by the members. Interestingly enough, it was in the supernatural sphere that the Chipewyan admitted openly that they were different from whites. The concept of a "bush man" prevailed here as it did among other Northern Athapaskans. In their conceptualization, this creature was a man who wore manufactured shoes and appeared at a distance during the summer. He kidnapped children, but apparently he did not harm adults as long as they remained beyond his reach. The Indians believed that certain supernatural beings could harm them but did not affect whites. They also held beliefs about trapping practices, but these were unknown by whites.

The curing of physical illness had passed out of the hands of shamans, who no longer existed, into the domain of the Indian and Northern Health Services and a lay dispenser, usually the Hudson's Bay Company manager. If a case was considered serious, the nurse at Yellowknife was contacted by radio, and she decided what course of action was to be followed. This nurse, sometimes accompanied by a medical doctor, visited the village at intervals. These Indians were concerned about their health but did not use patent medicines or turn freely to Euro-Canadians for aid. They seemed to enjoy talking about their aches and pains, but they sought treatment only when they were quite ill.

ENTERTAINMENT   Square dancing was a popular pastime, and the steps probably had been learned from commercial fishermen, who often stopped for a few days of relaxation during the summer. Men played guitars or violins and learned dance music by listening to village phonographs or broadcasts from the Yellowknife radio station. The square dances were called expertly by village men, and participation at dances was good. Less formal entertainment included nightly card games, which were extremely popular, particularly blackjack and gin rummy. Men and women often played together, and the stakes ranged from small change and ammunition to three-dollar hands in gin rummy games if men were affluent. While adults were playing cards, children sometimes gambled by pitching coins to a line. The hand game of old was known but seldom played; card games were considered more exciting (see Figure 3-7).

The consumption of alcohol was as much a ritual as a form of entertainment, and prescribed drinking patterns were rarely ignored. The only alcoholic beverage regularly consumed was home brew, produced from yeast, raisins, sugar, and water. It was made secretly by two or three men and allowed to age for about twenty-four hours. It was thought better if it aged longer, but anticipation negated the possibility. The men drank the brew in the home of one of the makers or in the brush during the summer; the object was to become intoxicated. A man would dip a cup into the three-gallon pail, drink the beverage, and pass the cup to the next participant. Normally, some brew was stored in bottles, to be consumed after the brew pail had been drained. When participants became reasonably intoxicated, they visited one house after another, regardless of the time, and drank as they chatted with their reluctant hosts. Sometimes they offered to share their brew, but this was

Figure 3-7 | A summer card game at Snowdrift circa 1960. (Photograph by James W. VanStone, courtesy of the Field Museum, Chicago, neg. no. A107881.)

not consistent. The conversations of intoxicated men were about village life, and they became more outgoing during drinking sprees than at any other time of their adult lives.

| Contemporary Lutselk'e

The village of Snowdrift (Lutselk'e) had begun in 1925 as a trading post of the Hudson's Bay Company and by 1954 had become the home of numerous local Chipewyan. Settled village life was above all else an artifact of federal Canadian Indian policy. Initially, houses and other incentives were provided to induce families to take up residence. Since the early 1980s especially, the government has been creating a novel physical setting, and the quality of homes has improved a great deal. Householders eventually were provided with water and fuel delivery, sewage disposal, electricity, and roads (see Figure 3-8). By 1996 there were 286 residents, including 10 Euro-Canadians. With federal and territorial support, buildings had been constructed for band administration. There was a school that educated students through the ninth grade, along with a permanently staffed nursing station, a local RCMP office, and an airport with mail service six days a week (see Figure 3-9). Accompanying these developments, old-age assistance benefits were provided, in addi-

Figure 3-8 | The community of Lutselk'e (Snowdrift) in 1996.

Figure 3-9 | By 1996 Lutselk'e had mail service six days a week.

tion to varied forms of relief for the needy. The Child Tax Credit (previously Family Allowance) was a nationwide program to foster the welfare of children; the amount received depended on family income. Quite obviously, government policies and practices had dramatically altered what it meant to be a Chipewyan. In sum, the federal goal had been to recast the people into a generalized Euro-Canadian mold.

In the government effort to transform villagers into "standard" Canadians, the system of formal education became a major catalyst. In 1935 families began to be encouraged by the Indian agent to send their young children to a residential (boarding) school managed by Roman Catholic missionaries. About 10 percent of village children lived at the school ten months of the year. Instruction was in English, and children were discouraged from speaking Chipewyan. Thus during their formative years these children spent only about two months at home each year. Residential schooling intensified after school attendance became compulsory in 1960. The fund of traditional cultural knowledge conveyed to a child depended to a great extent on his or her family background and ranged from being comprehensive to comparatively superficial. A federal village school was opened in 1960 to end residential schooling for most young children. However, by 1996 a free high school education could be obtained only at the government residential school in Fort Smith; during that year, thirty-four high school students studied there. The school system in general, with its stress on Euro-Canadian values, did little to foster or sustain traditional Chipewyan life. A partial indicator is that most younger people do not speak Chipewyan.

To transform mobile hunters into sedentary villagers in less than two generations was achieved with high social and cultural cost. For many adults, possibly most, life had lost much of its purpose; they could no longer pursue their old ways, nor could they truly become Euro-Canadians. A widespread reaction was one of futility and hopelessness and a pervasive dependence on a government that always would provide in times of physical need. A direct by-product of this situation was rather clearly a growing dependence on the consumption of alcoholic beverages imported from Yellowknife. (The home brew produced and consumed locally in the 1960s was far more a social activity than a drinking "problem.") It is widely agreed that the situation had become critical in the 1970s, and an effort was made to prohibit the importation of alcoholic beverages and the making of home brew. The problem remained acute despite a 1980 band-council prohibition law. Then, in the 1980s, multiple deaths were directly attributed to excessive drinking, and the violence level associated with intoxicants became alarming. However, by the mid-1990s intoxicant consumption had *decreased* significantly, although it remained a disturbing factor. By then about 25 percent of adults had been abstinent for about five years. During the first eight months of 1996, most of the police action cases involved alcohol, and about twenty individuals were the most frequent offenders. It may well be that the numerous antialcohol programs administered by the band have made an important difference. There appears to be at least a short-term trend toward less social turmoil associated with intoxicants.

In addition to the programs to reduce alcoholism, numerous other positive factors seem to have contributed to its decline and to an accompanying rise in community integration. Most prominent have been major changes in federal Indian policies, with far greater administrative authority being shifted to the local level; but there is no local control. A number of examples are il-lustrative. In 1991 a symbolic but meaningful change was made. The official village name was changed from Snowdrift to Lutselk'e, Chipewyan words meaning "the place of small fish," a nearby locality. In that same year we also find that an effort was being made by the First Nations (Indians and Eskimos) in the Northwest Territories to renegotiate their treaty rights, including a trans-fer of land ownership to the indigenous peoples. The federal government has been reasonably sympathetic with these efforts, and a shift toward more ad-ministrative power is taking place. A major change in the local economy has already occurred. The Hudson's Bay Company store closed in 1973, and, after a brief period of private ownership and with financial assistance from the gov-ernment, it became a member of a network of arctic cooperative stores. Thus the people became the store owners. Management of the local school is super-vised by a community educational authority that administers the budget and hiring. With respect to local government, a band manager was trained, and the band council has emerged as a municipal government with territorial funding and expanding administrative control over local affairs. The band council in-cludes representatives from the major family groups, as well as women, and the council has been working together far more harmoniously than ever before. Likewise, a Chipewyan holds the office of justice of the peace, and a local Dene is being trained as a law enforcement officer. In sum, changes in federal policies have led to far more local responsibilities than would have been conceivable thirty years ago.

Socially, it is not insignificant that five white women had married Chipe-wyan men by 1996, and four Dene women once were married to white men. Furthermore, while we do not associate respect for most older persons with the early historic Chipewyan, the villagers of today appear to be changing their attitudes toward their elders (see Figure 3-10). Finally, the position of women is strong. This may be a product of a higher sex ratio for men, as in the early 1960s. More women than men have had post–high school training; one local Chipewyan woman has earned a college degree.

By the mid-1990s local food resources remained of critical importance for many families. In the early 1960s game was scarce in the vicinity, and the area continues to be a "land of feast or famine." Since about 1980 the fall cari-bou migration has shifted to nearby localities and has included many animals; in addition, some caribou winter locally. Moose likewise have become more readily available as a source of meat. Coupled with an abundance of lake trout, this is a land of plenty, at least for the time being. Accompanying these increases has been a decrease in pressure on food resources from hunting and fishing in the settlement area from a generation ago. This is because a smaller number of families depend on these activities for their primary food supply. Others depend far more on federal and territorial monies, both earned and un-earned. Historically, the harvest of furbearers was the major source of cash for the local people, but by 1996 trapping was a primary activity for only ten men. Nearly one hundred others set at least a few traps.

Figure 3-10 | Lutselk'e men in 1996: Alfred Boucher (left) and his father Joe Boucher.

Although employment opportunities were limited in the mid-1990s, the number of year-round jobs had become far greater than it was previously. The band employed some twenty persons, including an elected chief, social worker, and an alcohol-abuse counselor. The cooperative store grossed about one million dollars a year and employed seven persons on a full-time basis. The school employed four teachers. To maintain the infrastructure, workers provided water and heating oil delivery and power plant and airport mainte-nance. In addition, summer construction projects were a source of employ-ment, and ten men were available to fight forest fires. There previously had been commercial fishing at the eastern end of Great Slave Lake, but it was dis-continued to help preserve the lake trout. Yet there were a number of local fishing lodges for sport fishermen, and some men in the community worked as guides for these fishermen.

Some cultural anthropologists have a reputation for emphasizing the changes in Indian life that were introduced by Westerners at the expense of traditional Indian culture. One reason is that the changes are often so over-whelmingly evident and important. One result of this focus has been to down-play or ignore the continuing vitality of traditional Indian ways that may be far less obvious. One example of Lutselk'e will illustrate the point. As a long-term observer of Athapaskan (Dene) Indians in the Northwest Territories, Fa-ther René Fumoleau, noted, "the most important thing in life is mobility." The capacity to move about remains a fundamental value in the 1990s, just as it was in much earlier historic times. To go to Yellowknife by airplane, boat, or snowmobile on the spur of the moment, to suddenly decide to hunt, fish, or visit someone, or to allow a child not to attend school on a particular day are part of this deep-seated pattern that remains Chipewyan, despite the span and intensity of Western influences.

Clearly the dramatic shift in federal Canadian policies regarding the First Nations, especially in the last twenty years, has led to far greater local autonomy. The Chipewyan of Lutselk'e have embraced many of these changes to their distinct advantage, have a greater sense of purpose as a result, and have become more Canadianized in the process. Likewise, with greater present-day local food resources and the availability of numerous jobs, they are more economically secure. However, new uncertainties have arisen. About 120 miles north of the community, diamonds have been discovered, and, although the deposits are untapped, they appear to be major. To develop the mines, it is anticipated that small lakes will be drained, up to five open pits excavated, and at least two underground mines developed. The federal and territorial governments understandably are concerned about the impact of mines on the Indians and the environment. Public hearings have been held, but they were a window-dressing exercise; Indian claims are a relatively minor problem given the power of mining companies in Canada. About one thousand jobs are to be involved in the construction phase. By 1998 at least one diamond mine was to be operational, and two-thirds of the eight hundred employees were to be from the north. What all of this will come to mean at Lutselk'e is critical but unpredictable.

| Additional Sources

The key source about the aboriginal Chipewyan is *A Journey from Prince of Wales's Fort in Hudson's Bay to the Northern Ocean* by Samuel Hearne (London, 1795; Dublin, 1796; Toronto, 1911; and Toronto, 1958). For a historical overview of Northern Athapaskans, the best widely available source is the *Subarctic* volume (6) of the *Handbook of North American Indians* (Washington, DC, 1988), William C. Sturtevant, general editor. The book *Athapaskan Adaptations* (Chicago, 1974) by James W. VanStone is a superior source for comparisons among these Indians. *The Changing Culture of the Snowdrift Chipewyan,* National Museum of Canada Bulletin no. 209, 1965, by VanStone is a comprehensive account of life in the early 1960s. For more recent studies, the reader is referred to the Selected Bibliography in this chapter, especially those written by Robert Jarvenpa, Henry S. Sharp, David M. Smith, and James G. E. Smith.

For additional ethnographic sources dealing with the Chipewyan and all the other peoples considered in this book, the interested reader should consult the fourth edition of the *Ethnographic Bibliography of North America* (New Haven, 1975) and its 1973–1987 supplement (New Haven, 1990).

| Selected Bibliography

Back, George. 1836. *Narrative of the Arctic Land Expedition*. London.

Birket-Smith, Kaj. 1930. *Contributions to Chipewyan ethnology.* Report of the Fifth Thule Expedition, vol. 6, no. 3.

Eggan, Fred, ed. 1937. *Social anthropology of North American tribes.* Chicago.

Franklin, John. 1823. *Narrative of a journey to the shores of the Polar Sea.* London.

Fried, Jacob. 1963. Settlement types and community organization in northern Canada. *Arctic* 16:93–100.

Gillespie, Beryl C. 1970. Yellowknives: Quo Iverunt? *Proceedings of the 1970 Annual Spring Meeting of the American Ethnological Society,* Robert F. Spencer, ed., 61–71.

———. 1976. Changes in territory and technology of the Chipewyan. *Arctic Anthropology* 13:6–11.

Hearne, Samuel. 1795. *A journey from Prince of Wales's Fort in Hudson's Bay to the Northern Ocean.* London. (Other editions: Dublin 1796; Toronto 1911; Toronto 1958.)

Jarvenpa, Robert. 1976. Spatial and ecological factors in the annual economic cycle of the English River band of Chipewyan. *Arctic Anthropology* 13:43–69.

———. 1977. Subarctic trappers and band society. *Human Ecology* 5:223–59.

———. 1982. Intergroup behavior and imagery. *Ethnology* 21:283–99.

Jenness, Diamond, ed. 1956. The Chipewyan Indians: An account by an early explorer. *Anthropologica* 3:15–33.

King, Richard. 1836. *Narrative of a journey to the shores of the Arctic Ocean.* 2 vols. London.

Lowie, Robert H. 1909. The Chipewyans of Canada. *Southern Workman* 38:278–83.

———. 1909. An ethnological trip to Lake Athabasca. *American Museum Journal* 9:10–15.

Mason, John A. 1946. *Notes on the Indians of the Great Slave Lake area.* Yale University Publications in Anthropology, no. 34. New Haven.

Rich, Edwin E. 1960. *Hudson's Bay Company, 1670–1870.* 3 vols. Toronto.

Richardson, Richard. 1854. *Arctic searching expedition.* New York.

Sharp, Henry S. 1975. Introducing the sororate to a northern Saskatchewan Chipewyan village. *Ethnology* 14:71–82.

———. 1977. The Chipewyan hunting unit. *American Ethnologist* 4:2:377–93.

———. 1979. *Chipewyan marriage.* Mercury Series, Canadian Ethnology Service Paper, no. 58. Ottawa.

———. 1986. Shared experience and magical death: Chipewyan explanations of a prophet's decline. *Ethnology* 25:4:257–70.

———. 1988. *The transformation of Bigfoot: Maleness, power, and belief among the Chipewyan.* Washington, DC.

———. 1991. Memory, meaning, and imaginary time: The construction of knowledge in white and Chipewyan cultures. *Ethnohistory* 38:2:149–76.

———. 1995. Men and women among the Chipewyan. In *Women and power in native North America,* L. Klein and N. Ackerman, eds., 46–74. Norman, OK.

Simpson, George. 1938. *Journal of occurrences in the Athabasca department, 1820 and 1821*. Publications of the Champlain Society, Hudson's Bay Company Series, no. 1.

Smith, David M. 1973. *INKONZE: Magico-religious beliefs of contact-tradition Chipewyan trading at Fort Resolution, NWT, Canada*. Mercury Series, Ethnology Division Paper, no. 6. National Museum of Man, Ottawa.

———. 1976. Cultural and ecological change: The Chipewyan of Fort Resolution. *Arctic Anthropology* 13:35–42.

———. 1982. *Moose-Deer Island house people: A history of the native people of Fort Resolution*. Ottawa.

Smith, James G. E. 1970. The Chipewyan hunting group in a village context. *Western Canadian Journal of Anthropology* 1:60–66.

———. 1976a. Introduction: The historical and cultural position of the Chipewyan. *Arctic Anthropology* 13:1–5.

———. 1976b. Local band organization of the caribou eater Chipewyan. *Arctic Anthropology* 13:12–24.

———. 1981. Chipewyan. *Subarctic (v. 6), Handbook of North American Indians*. William C. Sturtevant, gen. ed. Washington, DC.

Smith, James G. E., and Ernest S. Burch, Jr. 1979. Chipewyan and Inuit in the central Canadian Subarctic, 1613–1977. *Arctic Anthropology* 16:2:76–101.

Tyrrell, Joseph B., ed. 1916. *David Thompson's narrative*. Publications of the Champlain Society, vol. 12.

VanStone, James W. 1961. *The economy of a frontier community*. Northern Coordination and Research Centre, Department of Northern Affairs and National Resources.

———. 1963. Changing patterns of Indian trapping in the Canadian subarctic. *Arctic* 16:159–74.

———. 1965. *The changing culture of the Snowdrift Chipewyan*. National Museum of Canada Bulletin no. 209.

———. 1974. *Athapaskan adaptations*. Chicago.

4 The Kuskowagamiut: Riverine Eskimos

*When someone has something that is
particularly good to eat they take a pinch of it
and toss it away, saying "to the dead people
who we love the most."*

Offerings to the dead according to an old man.
(Oswalt field notes)

ESKIMOS* MOST OFTEN are regarded as a happy people who wear skin clothing, hunt seals, live in snowhouses, munch on raw meat, and count wife-sharing among their customs. This characterization of Eskimos has a clear historical basis in the United States, thanks primarily to the American explorer Robert E. Peary. Between 1886 and 1909, he made seven voyages to northwestern Greenland in an effort to discover the North Pole. For someone from the United States to be the first person to reach this pole became a national obsession that received intense press coverage for many years. The aid Peary received from the local Polar Eskimos led Americans to view these Eskimos, *not* those in Alaska, as the stereotype. This was an unfortunate development because the aboriginal Polar Eskimos and those with a similar lifeway were atypical of most Eskimos. Of the nearly 52,000 Eskimos at the time of historic contact, only about 4,500 lived much like the Polar Eskimos. By contrast, nearly half of all Eskimos, some 21,000, occupied southwestern Alaska, where salmon was their staple and wooden houses were their homes. Thus there are good, even compelling, reasons to present such a group as more typical of the Arctic culture area and the Eskimo lifeway, especially since a single chapter here is devoted to Eskimos.

The Eskimos described in this chapter, the Kuskowagamiut, were primarily salmon fishers. Not only were salmon runs predictable, but great numbers of them literally swam next to Eskimo settlements. Thus we have a clear contrast in subsistence base between this group and the one depicted in the accepted stereotype. Further differences between these Eskimos and others will become apparent as we examine the Kuskowagamiut culture.

| People, Population, and Language

In the manner of Alaskan Eskimos in general, those living along the Kuskokwim River in the southwestern sector had recognized boundaries (see Figure 4-1) and a group name, the Kuskowagamiut, but their dialect was shared by other Eskimos in the region. No one is certain of their aboriginal population total, but an early Russian explorer estimated their number at seven thousand, which seems reasonable. These people possibly numbered about three thousand in 1880, but the population had declined to about six hundred by 1910, largely as a result of epidemics. Their number has increased steadily since 1920 and now approaches ten thousand.

The Kuskowagamiut and all other Alaskan Eskimos southward from the vicinity of Nome spoke two distinct languages called Yupik. General Central

---

*Canadian Eskimos and numerous Euro-Canadians are adamant that Eskimos be called Inuit, their name for themselves, and not Eskimo. In this book, *Eskimo* is used as the generic designation of these northern peoples because all Eskimos are *not* Inuit; many who live in Alaska and small numbers in Siberia are Yuit, a designation comparable to Inuit yet distinct from it. Therefore, to use the word *Inuit* for Eskimos in general is incorrect. The Kuskowagamiut call themselves Yuit.

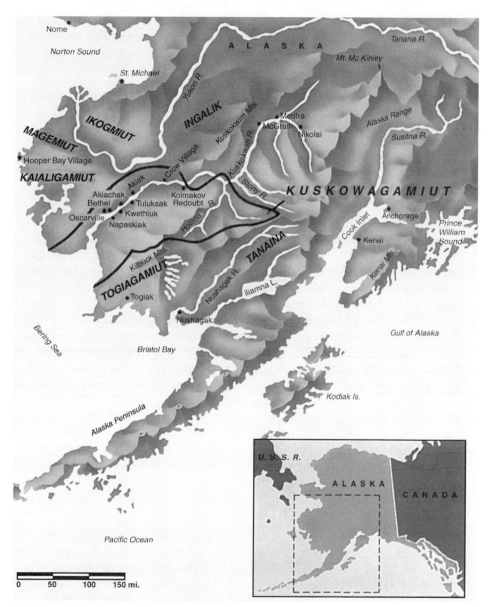

Figure 4-1 | Range of the Kuskowagamiut Eskimos.

Yupik included the Kuskowagamiut. Pacific Yupik was spoken south of the Alaska Peninsula. The early historic Yupik population total may have been about twenty-nine thousand, including two thousand in Siberia. In Alaska north of Nome and extending across Canada to Greenland, the Eskimos were Inupik speakers with relatively minor dialectic differences, and they may have numbered about thirty thousand. In linguistic terms, Inupik and Yupik belong to the Eskimo-Aleut language family and the American Arctic–Paleosiberian linguistic phylum.

| Differences among Eskimos

As suggested in Chapter 1, the culture-area concept often masks or ignores significant local and regional differences among the occupants of a single culture area. This failing of the classification is well illustrated by the differences among Eskimos in the Arctic culture area. They subsisted on fish and game, had few if any designated political leaders, and depended largely on shamans to intercede with supernatural forces. Yet beyond shared characteristics such as these, many significant contrasts were evident. For example, diverse kinds of settlements existed in early historic times, and food-getting activities varied widely. In one sector of east Greenland the Eskimos occupied communal houses built of wood, stone, and turf, and there could be a single house per settlement. Here the people subsisted primarily by hunting seals from kayaks. Eskimos in central Canada lived on the sea ice in snowhouses most of the year and hunted seals at their breathing holes in the ice. They moved about frequently as small family groups and had no permanent settlements. Eskimos along the northern coast of Alaska maintained permanent villages and built houses of wood and turf; a number of small families lived in each house. They hunted great whales, seals, and walrus; whale hunting in particular required cooperation and coordination of effort. Additional differences in food-getting patterns existed among Eskimos, and contrasts in dependability, abundance, and distribution of food resources led to divergences in social life, leadership, and religious behavior from the basic patterns that they shared. Thus what was typical of some Eskimos was unheard of among others.

| Russian Contact

The first direct contact between Kuskokwim Eskimos and outsiders was made with explorers and fur traders. In 1819 Russians founded Alexander Redoubt (or fort; modern Nushagak), their first settlement north of the Alaska Peninsula. From here the Russian-American Company expanded the beaver trade northward, and soon distant Eskimos were trading at the Nushagak station. In the summer of 1830, Ivan F. Vasilev led a small party to explore the Kuskokwim region. He reported favorably on the fur resources of the area, and the company began building Kolmakov Redoubt along the central Kuskokwim River in 1841. The redoubt was operated by the Russians until 1866, when they withdrew in anticipation of the purchase of Alaska by the United States.

| Aboriginal Kuskokwim Eskimos

After early historic accounts were consulted, it became possible to re-construct a portrait of aboriginal Kuskowagamiut life; the emphasis is on the people who lived along the lower Kuskokwim River.

ORIGIN MYTH   No known traditions account for Eskimo movements to the Kuskokwim River system, but one myth does explain the origins of the people, the land, and its configurations. The tale reports that in primeval times the only creature in existence was Raven. He flew about in darkness until he grew so weary that he created land in order to rest. He became discontented because his creation could not be seen, and so he went off to find the sun. As he returned to earth with it, some light was detached and formed the Milky Way; the holes burned in the sky by the sun became stars. Once Raven saw the bleakness of his creation, he made mountains and valleys, caused plants to grow, and made all the rivers flow into the sea. In order to share the world with others, he created animals, birds, and fish. Raven's effort to make people of stone failed, and so he created them from mud. He created spirits to govern all living things, and if people were to prosper, they could not offend these spirits.

APPEARANCE AND CLOTHING   These Eskimos are relatively short in stat-ure, with long torsos. The men are lean and muscular, but some women may be plump. Eskimos, as the most Mongoloid of New World aboriginal popu-lations, often have high cheekbones, epicanthic folds, and shovel-shaped in-cisor teeth, all reflections of a genetic affinity with Asian populations. They are dark-skinned only on their faces and hands, where they color deeply from weathering. Many men have rather heavy beards, and in aboriginal times whiskers were removed with clamshell tweezers. They wore their hair long over the shoulders or tonsured with bangs over the face. Women did not cut their hair and might gather it at the back; they often wore glass beads sus-pended from a hole in the nasal septum. In this period before direct contact was made with the Russians, these beads were obtained in trade from Siberia. Women usually had pierced ears from which earrings or strings of beads were hung. Their faces were tattooed with lines from the lower lip to the chin, and they wore one or more labrets, or lip plugs, beneath the lower lip (see Fig-ure 4-2). A man might wear a medial labret or lateral ones beneath the lower lip, but he was not tattooed. Note that bodily adornments were confined to the head, which is understandable considering their garments.

The winter garment most typical for both sexes was a loose-fitting sleeved parka reaching the calves or ankles, made from ground squirrel skins with the claws and tails often attached (see Figure 4-3). The parkas of women were hooded, frequently trimmed with caribou hair and fur strips, and split up

Figure 4-2 | An 1884 photograph of a woman with beads suspended from a hole in her nasal septum and a labret beneath her lower lip. (Courtesy of the Moravian Archives, Bethlehem, PA.)

the sides; men's parkas were hoodless and had no slits in the sides. A man protected his neck from the cold with a bearskin collar sewn onto the neck opening of his parka, and he wore a head cover of skin or fur. Men apparently wore short caribou-skin undertrousers, in addition to their skin trousers that reached just below the knees. They wore socks of caribou skin or woven grass inside knee-length caribou-skin boots with sealskin soles. Women preferred sealskin boots that reached the hips. Both men and women wore caribou-skin mittens. Garments intended for summer use included hooded rain parkas made from sewn strips of intestine or from fish-skins. During rainy weather, people also wore socks and boots of fishskin, a popular material because it was strong, lightweight, and waterproof when sewn with blind stitches. The word *parka,* incidentally, is an anglicized Russian word meaning a loose fitting upper garment of skin.

Figure 4-3 | An 1880 illustration of men in long squirrel-skin parkas. The parka of the man on the left is adorned with pieces of cloth and squirrel tails. The other man has his parka bottom held up with a belt around his waist, which was the custom when walking. (From Petroff 1884.)

LAND, VILLAGES, AND ARTIFACTS The Kuskowagamiut live along the central and lower Kuskokwim, a broad and gently flowing river in these sectors. The lower river and estuary land is low and laced with diverging waterways, lakes, and ponds. In unprotected areas, a tundra vegetation flourishes, but sheltered spots support willow thickets, rare stands of birch, and dwarf spruce. Animal species of economic importance include caribou, muskrat, mink, hare, and river otter. Migratory waterfowl pass through the country in the spring and again in the fall, while spruce hens and ptarmigan live in the region throughout the year. Salmon contributed the most to economic welfare, and the most important species were king (chinook), dog (chum), red (sockeye), and silver (coho). In the main river, lakes, and sloughs, blackfish, burbot, northern pike, and whitefish abound at certain seasons. The only other fish of importance are smelt, which ascend the lower river to spawn in the early spring and were taken in dip nets.

Settlements were built on high ground whenever possible and at spots with ready access to food, especially salmon. Typically the houses were occupied by adult women, their daughters, and young sons. These dwellings

Figure 4-4 | A settlement photographed in 1884, with houses and caches in the background. In the foreground is a sled for portaging kayaks, with kayaks resting on supports behind it. (Courtesy of the Moravian Archives, Bethlehem, PA.)

looked like mounds of dirt because they were built partially underground (see Figure 4-4). The main room, of post and beam construction, was built in a rectangular excavation, and the log framework was covered with grass and then with sod. A skylight in the center of the roof had a removable wooden frame covered with sewn fishskins or animal intestines. Beneath the skylight was a fireplace where meals were cooked, and smoke from the wood fire drifted out this opening. Extending around the walls, just above the dirt floor, were low benches covered with grass, grass matting, and animal skins; it was here that residents lounged, worked, and slept. A house generally included a wood-framed anteroom and a passage to the main room that prevented cold air from penetrating the living area.

To an outsider, the odors in a house would have been the most striking feature. The smells of stale urine, skin clothing, and dried salmon offered a pungent combination. The interior was dark from soot on the walls and ceiling. Some light penetrated the skylight cover, which was set aside during warm sunny days for light and heat. Artificial light came from the fireplace fire or from bowl-shaped clay lamps. The lamps were placed on stands, and oil, preferably seal oil, burned on a wick of moss. On the floor were cups, food trays, wooden water containers, and pottery cooking vessels. Common household items included a woman's sewing equipment, her semilunar slate-bladed knife or ulu, wooden cutting boards, chipped and ground stone scrapers for processing skins, and awls for sewing.

The men's house or kashgee was the home of most adult males and older boys. The largest building in a village, it also served as a bathhouse, ceremonial chamber, and workshop. A large kashgee might measure as much as thirty feet on a side. The walls were made of planks and split logs set vertically, and the roof was cribbed. Access was through a tunnel either at ground level or beneath it, and some men's houses had both varieties of entrance. The floor of a kashgee was covered with planks except for an area some four feet square at the center. Here was a fire pit that could be planked when not in use, and above the fire pit was a skylight. Kashgee furnishings included two or three tiers of benches around the walls and at least two large bowl-shaped oil-burning lamps to provide artificial light.

In a kashgee were the tools and equipment used by the men. Conspicuously absent were cooking vessels and eating containers, for these were brought in by females at mealtime and removed after the men and boys had eaten. The most important woodworking tools included the ubiquitous crooked knife, wedges, mauls for driving wedges, slate-bladed adzes, whetstones, and engraving tools. Near each man's assigned position on a bench were his sinew-backed bow and arrows, spears, and other weapons. Hanging from the ceiling on exhibit until a later ceremony were the bladders of animals and the stuffed skins of birds and small animals.

At scattered places about a settlement, pits were dug to preserve silver salmon caught so late in the season that they could not be dried. Salmon taken earlier were sun-dried and placed in caches erected on four posts. A wooden platform built on the posts supported a rectangular wooden structure with a gabled plank roof (see Figure 4-5). Inside a cache were stored dried or frozen fish, herbs, and equipment such as snowshoes and nets. Sleds often were stored on the cache platform beyond the reach of hungry dogs who would eat the lashings.

From late spring until late fall, these people traveled almost exclusively by water, using rivers, sloughs, and lakes. Each man owned a kayak made by covering a driftwood frame with dehaired sealskins. An extended family unit owned a large, open skin boat or umiak. The only other vessel was an improvised umiak made by hunters after big game had been killed. Fresh skins stretched over a rude wooden frame served to carry meat and men from a distant hunting camp to a village.

The usual winter conveyance was a wooden sled with a built-up bed on stanchions that were mortised and bound to the bed and to the runners with babiche (thin, dehaired caribou-skin strips). Sleds with low flat beds were used to carry boats over the snow. Families went to their fall camps by umiak before freeze-up or else waited until later and traveled by dogsled. Three or four dogs were harnessed to a sled by attaching individual towlines to stanchions at the *sides*, an inefficient hitching method. This practice seems to be an example of "cultural blindness," a behavior that appears illogical in its cultural context. In all likelihood, a man pushed at the rear of a sled as women and older children pulled at the front. Not until about twenty years after the arrival of Russians were dogs harnessed in tandem at the front of a sled, as in

Figure 4-5 | Women photographed in front of a cache in 1907. Smelt are drying on the pole. (Courtesy of the University of Pennsylvania Museum, Philadelphia.)

eastern Siberia. Finally, birch-framed snowshoes webbed with babiche were essential for traveling in timbered areas when the snow was deep and fluffy.

HOUSEHOLDS In a strict sense, household life focused narrowly on females, since the only males present were young boys. A man lived with his wife and their unmarried children only at camps away from a village. Ideally, daughters remained with their mothers after they had married and raised the next generation of children in the same house. Only when the number of females crowded a dwelling or when a house became uninhabitable did they move. A line of females lived in lifelong intimacy. The normal obligations of women in these close-knit domestic units included the preparation and processing of food, caring for children, manufacturing and repairing clothing, picking berries and a few other plant products, and collecting firewood. Men were expected to provide their wives with fish, fowl, and land mammals, but their duty did not extend beyond bringing such items to the settlement. Once a harvest was at hand, a man's wife had total responsibility for and control over its preparation and distribution.

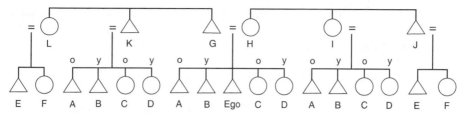

Figure 4-6 | The historic Kuskokwim Eskimo system of kinship terminology.

DESCENT, KINSHIP, AND MARRIAGE Aboriginal Kuskowagamiut marriage and residence patterns have been reconstructed from comparatively recent sources, and the accounts may not be entirely correct. These people appear to have attempted to arrange marriages within a community (village endogamy). Since households comprised the female lines, a man became associated with his wife's natal unit (matrilocal residence), whether he had been raised in her settlement or elsewhere. Some men, especially shamans, had more than one wife (polygyny); where this occurred, the other wives were often sisters of the first (sororal polygyny). Relatives were traced along both the father's and mother's line (bilateral or nonunilineal descent) to a given degree of collaterality; this meant that each person, except for brothers and sisters, was a member of a different bilateral kin group (personal kindred).

As the kinship terminology is examined, we find that cross-cousins (mother's brother's and father's sister's children) are distinguished by sex. Parallel cousins (mother's sister's and father's brother's children) are equated with siblings, and, in addition, age distinctions are made. Thus, a mother's sister's older daughter is termed the same as Ego's older sister. Although parallel cousins were termed the same as siblings, the people were fully aware that parallel cousins were not biological siblings. Yet essentially the same social bonds bound parallel cousins and siblings. Kuskokwim Eskimo cousin terminology is classified as Iroquois, not "Eskimo." Mother, father, aunt, and uncle terms were each different. This is a bifurcate collateral terminology for the parental generation. Since parallel cousins were equated with siblings, one might assume that their parents would be called either "mother" or "father," but obviously this was not the case, and one would assume that the terms were in a state of flux (see Figure 4-6).

SUBSISTENCE ACTIVITIES In the spring, after the ice breakup on the main river and after the high water had dropped, the people returned from their tundra camps to riverbank villages or to fish camps along the river in anticipation of the first runs of fish. Gill nets with netting made from the inner bark of willows or rawhide had wooden floats and caribou-antler sinkers. A net, probably about thirty feet long and six feet deep, was set in a river eddy and tended daily from a kayak. If possible, a net was set in the same eddy used the previous year; otherwise, a man lost his claim to the spot. Because the river channel shifted frequently, no eddy had any real permanence. The first species caught was most likely the sheefish, and those taken were boiled for immediate consumption.

A fisherman was most anxious to take king salmon in his net. After he had caught a number of these fish, he tied all his king salmon netting together. He then placed the longer net in his kayak and paddled to a straight stretch of river with no obstructions. He paid out the net and drifted at right angles to the current. When he saw a float bob violently, he knew a fish had struck the net, and he detached the net rope from his vessel, tied a large wooden float to the end, and threw it overboard. Paddling to the spot where the fish had thrashed, he gently lifted the net from the water and either clubbed the salmon to death or stuck a bone bodkin into the base of its head. He tried to kill the fish as efficiently as possible, for if it thrashed violently it was likely to destroy a section of the net. The fisherman took the dead fish aboard and straightened the net to drift evenly with the current. After a drift of about two miles, he hauled the net in and repeated the process if the take had been small. This fishing technique, called drift netting, was possibly the most important means for taking salmon. King salmon were caught in this manner; dog, red, and silver salmon were harvested with smaller-meshed gill nets. Reports indicate that men fished for salmon only until they felt that they had a winter's supply. If a man took a large number of king salmon, his fishing for later, smaller species was desultory. A king salmon might weigh fifty pounds, with the edible portion probably averaging about seventeen pounds. For smaller species, the average edible portion was about six pounds; thus it was less worthwhile to expend time and work to take smaller fish. Salmon always ascended the river to spawn, but high water made it difficult to net them in certain years. However, failure of salmon runs apparently did not lead to starvation.

Returning to his base with the catch, a man put the fish in a wooden bin and covered them with a grass matting as protection from flies. His wife or daughter processed the fish to boil for immediate consumption or dried them for later use. The roe was mashed and mixed with oil, and then dried as food for travelers. The heads might be dried for dog food or buried to make "head-cheese." After the heads decayed, they became "stink fish," as whites would term them. When asked how they could tolerate the smell as they ate these fish, the Eskimos' standard reply was, "We don't eat the smell."

During early winter, the men sledded to tundra camps, where they set funnel-shaped fish traps in small streams leading from lakes to take blackfish. These small fish were caught in great quantities and stored frozen in woven grass bags. Later in the winter they served as food for both people and dogs. Another fall activity of the men was to snare hares, marmot, and squirrels; mink and river otter were caught in fish traps or in smaller traps of the same design. Ptarmigan snares were set in clusters around willow thickets, and if beaver were nearby, they were captured in nets set beneath the ice. Whenever possible, men hunted caribou with bows and arrows in the late fall when the animals were fat, their skins prime, and their meat at its best, but caribou were not abundant. By midwinter, people were gathering at their riverbank settlements where caches usually were well stocked with food, and as the weather grew colder they depended almost entirely on stored edibles. This was the ceremonial season, and when supplies were plentiful, few cares disturbed the tranquillity of winter.

With the approach of spring, villagers grew restless and were anxious to return to their tundra camps. They went by dog team before the trails became free of snow and before the sloughs and rivers were covered with melt water. Here, as the last snow disappeared, they harvested ptarmigan and migratory waterfowl with arrows or snares. Women collected berries, especially the high-bush cranberries clinging to the dried bushes from the year before, and men refurbished blackfish traps that they set in small streams leading to lakes. They set gill nets in larger sloughs for northern pike and whitefish; the surplus fish were dried for later use. Men traveled by kayak once there was open water, hunting and snaring fur animals. When they judged that their take was sufficient or when they simply wearied of the tundra camps, they returned to their riverbank communities. They did so, however, only when reasonably certain that the river ice had broken up and the flood waters had subsided.

MALE SOCIAL LIFE   In a village men lived in the kashgee, or men's house, and thus apart from women. In the building each man or boy occupied an assigned spot that changed over the years. Early each morning, before anyone else was up, someone placed a wand across the exit, indicating that no one was to leave, and old men began to talk to an audience that appeared to be sleeping. In monologues or dialogues they discussed life from childhood to maturity. They spoke of traditional customs and of new rules in response to changing conditions. Discussions might be of behavior in public or on trips and of actions necessary in case of accidents or other emergencies. Afterward those men who planned to travel a considerable distance that day dressed and left the kashgee as others split wood for a sweat bath. Preparations for a bath included removing the planks that covered the fire pit, setting aside the skylight cover, and building a great fire. After the wood had burned to a bed of coals, the gut window was fitted back in place, and men stripped to bathe. In the intense heat their ears might blister before they began to perspire. As the room became hotter, men wailed loudly for the dead, who were missing a fine bath. When the heat subsided, they washed in urine and in the winter might sit in the snow to cool off.

After hunting or fishing during the day, men returned to the settlement and went directly to the men's house. A wife or close female relative unloaded the catch and put away the equipment of each man, and after the men had bathed women brought in the evening meal and dried the men's clothing. In the early evening men told of what had happened to them during the day, and the old men commented on what was said. As everyone settled down to sleep, an old man began telling a traditional story. The audience at first responded with "e-yee" to encourage the storyteller, but before he had finished, most men and boys were asleep.

POLITICAL LIFE   With villagers living together for at least half of each year, one might expect a certain degree of political integration, but group decisions that affected an entire community do not appear to have been commonplace. A partial explanation may be that subsistence activities were individual, not community, endeavors, and most families were related. A man most likely guided the activities of his sons, and an older brother, in the absence of a father, guided a younger brother. It is probable, too, that older men informally resolved routine problems, such as a dispute over fishing rights. Possibly a wider range of opinion was sought concerning differences with persons in other settlements or the formalities of arranging ceremonies. If one individual had a prominent voice in the decision making, it may have been a male shaman because of his supernatural affiliations. The nonconformity of any individual would lead first to gossip and then to mild ridicule, which was usually sufficient to bring deviant behavior into line with community expectations. If a father was annoyed at the behavior of a son, he would express his dissatisfaction to a close friend during a sweat bath, and this person would make known the father's feelings to the son. Ridicule songs appear to have been sung as a more forceful and face-to-face means of pointing up individual failings.

The most likely secular leader was a highly successful hunter and fisherman who could feed orphans and widows, provide oil for the kashgee lamps, and furnish food for feasts. Such an individual took an active role in all village activities and thereby earned the worthy title of "a man indeed!"

The most serious rupture of social harmony occurred when a person was murdered by an outsider, but such an occurrence appears to have been rare. If it happened, an influential relative of the deceased assembled the men from his and adjacent communities, entertained them, presented each with a gift, and requested their aid in exacting blood revenge. Balance was restored after someone in the family of the murderer was killed, and there were no additional murders. Sometimes revenge flared out of hand, and a family feud erupted. This would cease only with the flight or murder of one faction. Formal warfare did not exist.

SUPERNATURALISM   When defined as dogma, rules, a ceremonial round, and ritual leadership, religion played a critical role in Kuskokwim Eskimo life. As so often is the case, some aspects of these Eskimos' religious life were integrated with economics and entertainment. Ceremonies and feasts followed a well-developed calendrical cycle, whereas shamanistic activities, the other ritual events, took place primarily at critical and unscheduled times.

Shamans   Shamans were reported to be far more powerful among the Kuskokwim Eskimos than among most others, and male shamans often were members of particular families. Very little is known about female shamans, although some old women clearly did become powerful specialists in supernaturalism. A young boy with a predilection to shamanism was apprenticed to a successful practitioner and did not perform independently until he reached adulthood. During his training he acquired supernatural aids, learned to drum and sing, and practiced performing tricks. Shamanistic sessions were held to diagnose, predict, and cure by supernatural means, as well as to demonstrate a shaman's power. It also was a shaman's duty to make certain that people observed the necessary behavioral norms, and he became a secular practitioner in performing certain cures that did not require supernatural aids. Other persons, especially elders, also might function as secular curers. When a settlement included more than one shaman, people turned to the one regarded as most capable in times of greatest crisis.

When someone's illness had no obvious cause, a shaman's help was sought. If the patient did not improve or died, the shaman might be accused of witchcraft, in which case he or she could be murdered. A curing session involved apprentices who drummed and sang the shaman's songs while he or she summoned a spiritual helper. When this force had entered the shaman's body, he or she behaved strangely, reflecting the motions and sounds of the helping spirit, which was often an animal. The disease substance was driven from the sick person's body by sucking or brushing it away. It sometimes happened, too, that a shaman, when possessed by a spirit, learned that a villager had caused the illness by breaking a taboo; after the offender confessed, harmony was restored to the universe. Shamans also interpreted unusual events. An eclipse of the moon was thought to anticipate illness and death, an earthquake was an ominous sign, and comets foretold hunger.

Shamans, as interpreters of extraordinary events, played a highly positive role in village life. They sought to understand and explain what seemed to be abnormal behavior in people and unusual happenings in the natural world. Their performances included trickery, such as vanishing acts or sleight of hand, but these possibly are best regarded as mood-setting techniques rather than proof of supernatural powers. Men who were shamans provided for their families in the manner of other men in addition to being well rewarded for the services they performed. Unlike all other married men, male shamans lived in the houses of their wives, which clearly set them apart from other men.

Witchcraft was the ultimate form of antisocial behavior, and shamans who reportedly used their powers against other persons were considered dangerous. The malevolence of a witch in a distant village could be countered by a powerful local shaman, but if he or she were unsuccessful, the victim might die. If a witch exerted power locally, the situation was even more traumatic. Although this form of witchcraft seems to have been rare, if villagers were convinced that one among them was a witch, he or she might be clubbed to death, after which the joints of the body were severed, and the body burned.

Figure 4-7 | Mask representing a spirit that the Kuskowagamiut believed lives in the ground and leaves no hole when it emerges. According to their belief, this spirit sometimes dislikes men and will jump through them without leaving a mark but killing them in the process. (Courtesy of the National Museum of the American Indian, Smithsonian Institution, neg. no. 29931.)

Ceremonies The Kuskowagamiut ceremonial round is known incompletely but in enough detail to realize that it was well developed. Ceremonies commonly spanned four days, and people from one or more adjacent villages were guests. The villagers prepared for the celebration by storing large quantities of food, composing songs, and manufacturing dance masks (see Figure 4-7), along with practicing their roles until they were perfected. The general supervision was in the hands of a dance leader who as host made certain that the activities were carried out in a traditional manner. This office tended to pass from father to son. The most important ceremonial event was the Great Ceremony for the Dead, performed every four to ten years, depending on the number of deaths and the time required to assemble the assets for holding the event. In alternate years reciprocating villages held a Sending-a-Messenger Ceremony as the climax to yearly ceremonials.

The Great Ceremony for the Dead was designed to free the souls of the dead so that they could rest forever in a world in the sky. The Sending-a-Messenger Ceremony was in honor of the recently deceased and included the institutionalized giving of gifts. The person or persons hosting the celebration were relatives of the deceased and had accumulated food and property in large quantities. Messengers were sent to the guest community with a mnemonic stick on which symbols were carved or appended. An announcement was made formally, and the signs on the stick were to convey the details of the invitation. When the guests arrived, they were greeted ceremonially, and during the evenings of festivities they watched dances and songs commemorating the dead and denoting his or her merits. If the deceased was not a noble person about whom any good could be recounted, the praises of his or her ancestors were sung. The climax of the ceremony came a few days later when gifts were distributed to the guests in honor of the deceased; there was no obligation to make a return gift.

The Bladder Ceremony that was so important at adjacent coastal Eskimo communities also was held by these riverine people. The bladders of all important animals killed were saved because it was thought that an animal's soul was in its bladder. The first birds and small animals killed by boys also were preserved after the meat and intestines were removed. The skins and bladders were hung in the kashgee during the time of the festivities. Included were sporting events, songs, storytelling, gift exchanges, and feasting. On the tenth and final day everyone assembled in the men's house for a feast, and bits of food were thrown on one wall for the dead. The purpose of the ceremony was to renew the game killed, and at the end the bladders probably were submerged in a hole in the river ice. The focus of the event on bladders was not entirely appropriate for Kuskokwim Eskimos since they depended so heavily on salmon, which were not specifically honored. This seems to be an example of a ceremony maintained even though key aspects of its original purpose were no longer fully relevant.

LIFE CYCLE A woman gave birth at home, aided by her mother or another female relative. She delivered in a squatting position, and downward pressure was applied to her abdomen if the process was delayed. If there were already daughters in a family, or if it was a lean time of the year, female infanticide might be practiced. Infanticide was not restricted to the newborn but could occur during the first two or three years of life. The attitude was that since part of the soul of a deceased individual returned to the body of the next one born, this was no real destruction of life. A baby was named after the person who had died most recently in the local area, and the relatives of the deceased behaved toward the namesake as they had toward the deceased. Parents were known by the name of their firstborn, a custom termed teknonymy. Thus, if the firstborn was named Kamoucha, the mother was called Kamoucha's mother. Names obviously were not gender-linked, and they were changed if their bearers were plagued with misfortune. Growing up in a household dominated by older females, infants and small children were pampered and catered to; this treatment was based as much on supernatural beliefs as on affection. Since an infant was believed to have the soul of a recently deceased individual, he or she mirrored the feelings of the deceased and was appeased in order not to offend the watching spirits. This association decreased in importance as the individual matured and acquired a distinctive personality of her or his own.

A maturing girl soon was integrated into the household routine of the older females. Her toys usually were facsimiles of the artifacts used by her mother, and by the time she was nine years old she was a reasonably capable housekeeper. Indications are that the bonds between a maternal grandmother and granddaughter were extremely close. The granddaughter's activities and worldview appear to have been molded largely by this older woman, who occupied the rear platform in a large household. Recognition of the grand-mother's importance stems from a study of stories told by contemporary Eskimo girls. These stories, or storyknife tales as they are known, were illus-trated with stylized representations of people, boats, houses, and other forms. The drawings were made on a mud or snow surface with an oblong-bladed implement known as a storyknife. Storyknife tales were a vital part of the women's world, and their content suggests that grandmothers originated them and taught them to their granddaughters. No evidence exists of males either telling or listening to storyknife tales. The stories told by a grandmother enter-tained and also instructed. The main characters most often were a grand-mother and her granddaughter; repeated messages in stories were that one should offer food to visitors, that nonrational behavior is expectable from males, and that a granddaughter who disobeys her grandmother brings harm to the grandmother.

By the time boys were ten years old, they had left their natal homes and moved into the kashgee. Here they came under the supervision of the older men in the family and the indirect control of all the older kashgee residents. The boys were no longer regarded as children. After a male had killed one of each animal species, he was considered marriageable. Ceremonial recognition was given a girl when she picked the first of each species of berry, but a more important event was the ceremonial acknowledgment of her menarche. At this time she probably was restricted to one corner of the dwelling, wore old clothing, and observed food as well as behavioral taboos. Possibly at about this time a girl had sexual intercourse with a male shaman; this was essential for a maiden before she could be admitted to kashgee ceremonies.

A female was nubile at about the age of fourteen, but a male was likely to be at least four years older and sometimes as much as twenty years older than his bride. The marriage itself was without ceremony and was arranged by the families of the couple or by an older man directly with the girl's family. Thereafter the man slept with the girl in her mother's house; she was respon-sible for preparing his meals, caring for his clothing, and processing the sub-sistence items he obtained. In the event that either member of the couple became dissatisfied with the other, they ceased cooperating and cohabiting. A marriage might also be terminated with a wrestling match. Any man was free to challenge another to wrestle, and the man thrown to the ground was obli-gated to give up his wife. Women do not appear to have had any voice in these matches. Usually men wrestled only for young women without children. No stigma was attached to divorce, and most individuals had at least two partners during their lifetimes. A marriage tended to stabilize after the woman bore a child, particularly if it was a son.

Figure 4-8 | Grave goods above burials, photographed in 1907. (Courtesy of the University of Pennsylvania Museum, Philadelphia.)

The activities of adult marriage partners were complementary, and even though marriages may have been brittle, an adult did not willfully remain unmarried for long. In the early years of marriage the partners might be cool toward one another, but as time passed they were more likely to become congenial partners. The personality of an adult Eskimo manifested a phlegmatic realism, and an even-tempered, jovial person was the ideal. Verbal aggression or physical dominance was abhorred, and to be withdrawn or caustic was considered symptomatic of illness. Aged people were not killed but often came to be respected for their knowledge. Some old men were great storytellers and passed the traditions of their fathers on to the men and boys of the next generation. Old women held forth from the rear platforms of their dwellings with advice and criticism, both of which were offered freely.

A dead person's body was flexed, with the knees bound up to the chest. The women wailed, and the men killed the dogs of the deceased. Clothing and other property, except those items that were kept as mementos, were destroyed or deposited on the grave. The body was removed through a hole made in the wall of the kashgee or dwelling; according to Kuskowagamiut belief, after the opening was closed, the spirit of the deceased could not find its way back into the structure. The small plank coffin was placed above the ground on four short poles in the cemetery, usually located on a hill or rise near the settlement. At the head of the coffin a board might be placed between two poles; on it were pegged wooden carvings of human faces (see Figure 4-8).

| The Early Impact of Colonialism

Major changes in Kuskokwim Eskimo traditional life first resulted from direct Russian contact and intensified with the arrival of Euro-Americans. These outsiders introduced desirable trade items and novel institutions, but the impact of new diseases nearly overwhelmed the people. Their recovery was slow and often traumatic.

THE RUSSIANS As Russian-American Company agents ranged northward beyond the Alaska Peninsula, their singular goal was commercial—to expand the fur trade. To achieve this goal, they began building Kolmakov Redoubt along the central Kuskokwim River in 1841. The redoubt, or fort, included a blockhouse fortified with two small cannons, a store, living quarters, bathhouse, and outbuildings. Far from being a northern bastion, the redoubt was the most remote company fort in Alaska, and it was typically staffed with about a dozen employees of Russian, Eskimo, or mixed racial background; soldiers were never stationed there. The most important trader was Semen Lukin, who may have been of Eskimo or Eskimo and Russian ancestry. His major obligation was to obtain beaver pelts, which is a probable reason why the post was built so far inland. Kolmakov Redoubt never thrived because the worldwide demand for beaver was declining when the fort was founded. In Europe the gentry were turning from beaver to silk hats at this time. In addition, the Russian–American Company never was able to supply this trading center with a substantial inventory of trade goods. Imports consisted largely of small, highly portable, and not readily destructible items; beads, tea, knives, needles, and copper ornaments are examples. To help sustain the operation, traders dealt in local products, such as dried fish. The general impression is that the Russians did not radically alter local Eskimo material culture.

In local history the long-range impact of the Russian Orthodox church was of far greater importance than was the fur trade. The first resident trader, Lukin, was a deeply religious man authorized by the Orthodox church to baptize converts. Before a chapel was built, he led weekly church services in the store. He was well regarded by the local Eskimos, and although there were intermittent rumors of pending attacks on the settlement, none materialized. An Orthodox priest and later a hieromonk, a monk who also was a priest, visited the area and won many converts. By the end of the Russian era most Kuskokwim Eskimos along the river considered themselves to be Christians. They had been baptized and given Russian names but probably did not understand Christian dogma very well.

Many reasons probably account for the conversion of Eskimos to Orthodox Christianity. In all likelihood, one reason was that the Eskimos had a deep respect for Lukin as a person and as a trader. Another reason is that most of the leaders of aboriginal religious ceremonies probably perished during the 1838–39 smallpox epidemic. During these years, at least half of the riverine

Eskimos died of smallpox. This provided Orthodox workers a greater opportunity to win converts among the survivors, if only because shamans who survived lost prestige because they had failed to stop the epidemic. On the other hand, Kuskokwim Eskimos initially held the Russians responsible for the epidemic and were bitter against most of them, which no doubt delayed conversions or made the process superficial.

A particular custom introduced by the Russians deserves mention—the steam bath. A bathhouse was constructed by Lukin at Kolmakov Redoubt. The Eskimos trading in this post were familiar already with bathing in intense heat, but the Russian bath was somewhat different from the sweat bath in the kashgee. It was taken in a small structure, and stones were heated above a stove or in an open fire. When water was poured over the rocks, bathers sat back and enjoyed the hot air moistened by the steam. Initial Eskimo reaction probably was unfavorable, but as time passed the Russian bath was to assume more importance.

THE EARLY EURO-AMERICAN ERA   For nearly twenty years following the 1867 purchase of Alaska by the United States, the only American interest in the Kuskokwim was commercial. The Russian–American Company, which had held a monopoly on the Alaskan trade since 1799, soon became the Alaska Commercial Company. Kolmakov Redoubt continued as a trading center, but the main post was located nearer the river mouth at a village that came to be called Bethel. These stores were not a great source of profit, and consequently their inventories were modest. The change from the Russian to the American period brought no abrupt break in trading patterns; in fact, two of the three traders during the early American period were Russian or of Russian–Eskimo extraction.

The Russian Orthodox church became a foreign mission for the Russians after the United States gained control of Alaska, and Eskimo converts were badly neglected by the church for some twenty years. This enabled missionaries representing denominations in the United States to establish Alaskan missions. Along the Kuskokwim, Moravian missionaries dominated. The Moravian church was an early Protestant denomination founded in Europe in the early 1400s; eventually they established missions among Eskimos in Greenland and Labrador. Moravians who had settled at Bethlehem, Pennsylvania, decided to launch a mission among Alaskan Eskimos. In 1885 two Moravian missionaries, William H. Weinland and John H. Kilbuck, and their brides founded a mission at Bethel. After a deep-water channel from the sea to Bethel was discovered in 1908, the settlement became a major regional center for education, health, and other services. The Moravians soon realized, however, that most local Eskimos already were members of the Russian Orthodox church. Over the years the Moravians converted many Kuskokwim Eskimos to their religion, and yet some villagers, such as those at Napaskiak (see the next section), remained Orthodox.

The feverish search for Alaskan gold around 1900 brought profound changes in varied regions, but major deposits were not found along the Kuskokwim. Yet prospectors were numerous in the 1910s, and they introduced an important new fishing device—the fish wheel. It had long been known in Europe and the eastern United States before being introduced to the Pacific Northwest and Alaska. In essence, a fish wheel consists of wood-splint baskets set on a raft and propelled by river current. As a wheel rotates, fish are lifted from the water into a basket and deposited in a bin at one side of the wheel. A fish wheel can best be used where the water is opaque and gently flowing along a riverbank. In those sectors of the Kuskokwim above tidewater, the time required to harvest salmon declined abruptly with this new device. Yet the work of women intensified because they had so many fish to process at one time. Great numbers of salmon could be caught with a fish wheel, and their sale to miners and other outsiders made an important contribution to the local Eskimo economy.

A second major change brought to the region by Euro-Americans was the introduction of reindeer herding. Reindeer were domesticated in northern Eurasia, and they are of the same species as caribou. Reindeer imported from Siberia were first introduced by missionaries among northern Alaskan Eskimos in 1892. In 1901 Moravian missionaries at Bethel received nearly two hundred reindeer as part of a program to provide local Eskimos with a more dependable economic base than fishing for salmon and trapping furbearers gave them. By the 1930s some forty thousand reindeer reportedly grazed along the Kuskokwim River system. The number of animals, however, declined precipitously in the early 1940s, possibly because they had depleted the major source of food, lichens. By the end of the decade, reindeer had disappeared. In retrospect, the enterprise probably was doomed from the beginning. Local Eskimos could not adapt to the nomadic way of life required of herders.

In addition to the dreadful 1838–39 smallpox epidemic, disease struck again in the early twentieth century. Between 1900 and 1901, white miners introduced influenza, whooping cough, and measles epidemics that devastated the riverine population. At that time, a medical doctor reported the deaths of *all* babies and half of the adults; some villages were abandoned as a result. The accompanying sociocultural loss must have been great and ruptured riverine Eskimo continuity with the past.

These epidemics seem to have contributed to Eskimo expansion inland. The Indians farther up the river apparently were harder hit by the diseases because their population was much smaller; this enabled Kuskokwim Eskimos to migrate up the river. Their inland movement was facilitated because neighboring Indians were not regarded as enemies. By 1970 Kuskokwim Eskimos had settled at the trading center of McGrath and in the Indian villages of Nikolai and Medfra. Eskimo genealogies suggest a pattern of Indians marrying Eskimos and adopting Eskimo ways. Thus we see the continuing adaptability of Eskimos with their penetration deep into interior Alaska.

| Life at Napaskiak

The emphasis now shifts to the village of Napaskiak to plot continuity with the past and further changes. In 1955–56 Oswalt lived there to collect information about contemporary conditions. At the time Yupik was the first language of all children, and only six adults among the permanent residents were able to speak and read English. At the BIA school, launched in 1939, only English was taught; by the mid-1950s it was a "school language" for most children.

The oldest villagers reported that the settlement had been occupied for many generations and that their ancestors previously had lived at nearby abandoned villages. The residents had no tradition of moving into the area. Moravian missionaries often visited there but were unable to make a significant number of lasting converts, and by the 1950s nearly all villagers were members of the Russian Orthodox faith. Directly across the river from Napaskiak was the settlement of Oscarville, important to Napaskiak because of its trading post. An Orthodox church had been built at Napaskiak in 1931, and a Bureau of Indian Affairs school had opened there in 1939.

THE SETTLEMENT AND MANUFACTURES Napaskiak stretches along the southeastern bank of the Kuskokwim River, and in 1956 the twenty-seven frame and seven log houses were occupied by 141 persons. The most imposing structures were the Russian Orthodox church and the Bureau of Indian Affairs school with its adjoining residence. Scattered around the houses were caches, fish-drying racks, privies, smokehouses, and bathhouses (see Figure 4-9).

Closely related nuclear families tended to live in adjacent houses, and the dwellings of larger families usually included two or three rooms, with the second or third rooms serving primarily for sleeping and storage. Each house had an attached anteroom or storage shed that contained a jumble of objects. A gasoline-powered washing machine often was the largest item in the shed; stored there as well were foods soon to be eaten, winter parkas, a chamber pot, and assorted woodworking tools. The rectangular houses usually had at least one curtained window on each side, plank floors, and walls and ceiling usually covered with painted wallboard. Furnishings included a table and chairs, cast-iron woodburning stove with a clothes-drying rack above, a homemade wooden cupboard, and a washstand with an enameled basin. Overhead hung a gasoline lantern that supplied the only light in most households; two families owned gasoline-powered generators to furnish their houses and those of near relatives with electricity. Each house contained trunks or suitcases piled somewhere and filled with clothing not then in use. On one wall was always an Orthodox church calendar, around which hung prints of icons and a container of holy water.

Figure 4-9 | A Napaskiak scene in 1956. In the foreground are racks for drying gill nets and salmon, with a cache and houses behind.

Eskimos justifiably are famous for the sophistication of their traditional material culture, and yet at Napaskiak by the 1950s it had nearly disappeared. The artifact types of old that they continued to make and use were few and technologically uncomplicated, such as wooden dippers, ladles, mauls, paddles, and spatulas. Kayaks were still made, but the wooden frames were lashed with cords and covered with painted canvas. The large plank boat made of spruce and powered with an outboard motor had long since replaced the umiak. Raised caches retained their form of old, as did gill nets, although the netting was made from cotton, linen, or nylon. Hunting weapons were rifles and shotguns. A few boys used bows and arrows, but they preferred slingshots or air rifles. Most of the equipment necessary for living off the land was purchased ready-made from nearby stores, and even items of local manufacture such as plank boats, sleds, or fish traps were constructed from imported materials.

CLOTHING   Most men and younger women wore ready-made garments and footwear bought from local stores or mail-order houses. Sealskin boots most likely were worn by older persons, and conservative women, young or old, wore handmade cotton bloomers and petticoats. Many women, especially those middle-aged and older, had squirrel-skin parkas adorned elaborately with calfskin trimmings, but skin parkas were being replaced by ready-made jackets. In summer, particularly when cleaning fish, a woman wore a hooded cloth parka over her dress. A male child had the same type of clothing as his father but was more likely to wear skin boots, and a girl's garments were similar to those of conservative women.

SUBSISTENCE ACTIVITIES   Village men fished for salmon, trapped, and hunted to support their families. The cash earned from trapping and wage labor was used to buy imports from the local stores and mail-order houses. Male economic flexibility was a key to family success, and to obtain at least a few hundred dollars in cash was essential. When trapping was poor, a man virtually was forced to seek wage-labor jobs. In this context, and with regard to subsistence activities in general, it was exceedingly difficult to fall back on the gains from a previous year.

The male subsistence round illustrates the varied skills required. Beginning in the late fall, before the waterways froze, some men boated to tundra camps, where they had small houses built of wood and sod; a particular camp might be shared by a number of men. They shot waterfowl, and more important, set fish traps for blackfish as winter dog food. When it was safe to travel by dog team, they returned to the village with a portion of their catch. Men who remained in the village set blackfish traps in nearby sloughs but harvested far fewer fish than those camping on the tundra. In earlier years, entire families went to fall camps, but this was no longer the pattern because children were obligated to attend school and women usually did not like the hardships of fall camp life.

With the approach of winter, men and boys sledded to nearby stands of alder, where they spent many hours chopping firewood that was hauled back to the village to heat houses. Men also chiseled holes in the river ice to set baited hooks for burbot, a highly desirable fresh fish at this time of the year. In November many men traveled by dog team to trap mink at tundra camps. In general, the farther a man ventured, the greater his harvest. A mink sold for about twenty dollars at local stores; the average catch yielded about three hundred dollars. The men usually returned to the village in time for the Christmas holidays. From late December until spring, few subsistence activities were profitable. Only the least successful providers were forced to hunt and fish in the dead of winter.

Spring brought welcome opportunities to obtain fresh food once again; by then people were weary of a diet dominated by dried salmon. Ptarmigan were shot, hares were snared, and an occasional owl was killed as food. Beneath the ice, blackfish traps were set once again, and burbot were hooked while women jigged for northern pike. As the days lengthened and the snow began to melt, families prepared to occupy tundra camps, usually the ones men had visited in the fall. Arriving at camps by sleds on which boats were hauled, people lived in cloth tents and small houses. Most everyone was busy. Women and girls collected the past year's berries that were still on bushes, while men hunted waterfowl, set gill nets for pike and whitefish, and hunted muskrats. After the ice had cleared from waterways, the people returned by boat to the village and arrived shortly after the breakup of the Kuskokwim River ice.

They now made preparations for the salmon-fishing season. The fishing was largely based in the village rather than at fish camps because of the

Figure 4-10 | A Napaskiak woman filleting salmon in 1956. The fillets were held open with small sticks to assure uniform drying.

mobility provided by wooden boats with outboard motors. Gill nets were set and later drifted for king salmon; with an abundant harvest, fishermen were far less intent on taking the later and smaller salmon species. The last salmon of the season, silvers, were buried in old oil drums and served as winter dog food. Local Orthodox beliefs kept men from fishing on Saturday afternoon or night so that women were not obligated to process fish on Sunday (see Figure 4-10); nor did most men fish on Sundays.

The need for cash led to a partial decline in the importance of salmon fishing by 1956. About twenty men earned around one hundred dollars each unloading supply ships anchored at Bethel. Nearly the same number were flown to Bristol Bay salmon canneries, where a man earned from three to six hundred dollars for the season. (There was no commercial salmon fishing season along the Kuskokwim River at this time.) Money received from territorial and federal agencies provided additional income that was unassociated with the immediate environment. Thirteen persons over the age of sixty-five received Old Age Assistance funds from the territorial government, and eight families received Aid to Families with Dependent Children. In addition, two men and three heirs of qualified men received social security payments, and two others obtained aid for the blind. The total was about eighteen thousand dollars a year; thus the government was a significant source of cash for some villagers.

Salmon remained the basic staple in virtually all households, but people considered salmon alone to be plain fare. They ate unleavened bread for breakfast and drank coffee or tea, preferably coffee, when finances allowed. Every family considered sugar, flour, salt, canned milk, tea, coffee, tobacco, and cooking oils to be necessities. They also bought canned foods, crackers, and candy, depending on their resources.

SOCIAL DIMENSIONS   As of old, descent was traced equally through the male and female lines (bilateral). The kinship terminology included separate terms for father and mother, as well as uncle and aunt terms for the brothers and sisters of one's parents (lineal type). Cross-cousins were called cousins, whereas parallel cousins were grouped with siblings (Iroquois cousin terms). The most important set of relationships seems to have been between males who were classificatory or biological siblings, as previously mentioned. By the time a girl was thirteen she usually was courted by older boys, but since marriages still were arranged by older women and parents, courtship did not lead directly to marital ties. If at all possible, parents found mates for their children in the village (community endogamy); alternatively, the girl moved to another village, or, very rarely, to Bethel. A bride was expected to move into the house of her husband's family (temporary patrilocal residence) until the couple could build a house of their own (eventual neolocal residence).

Only the persistence and good fortune of a male family head enabled a household to prosper. The relationship between a father and his son, therefore, was critical. A son learned subsistence skills largely through informal instruction from his father. In his father's company a young man was unassuming and rarely, perhaps never, overtly expressed his dissatisfaction in a face-to-face situation. The pelts that a son trapped and the wages that he earned were at the disposal of his father; likewise, a father had first call on equipment use. Ideally, an aged father was cared for by his son, but in all likelihood the old man received Old Age Assistance. With this cash income, a father might continue to dominate household management. The relationship between a father and daughter was cooler and more distant. A girl married and moved to her husband's household, offering a father few comforts in his old age.

The mother-daughter ties were close and warm. After bearing a son, every mother hoped for a daughter, and affection bound the pair. A mother sought a spouse for her daughter within the village and vigorously defended the daughter against real or imagined abuse from her in-laws. Mothers also were the most outspoken defenders of their sons but did not express the same warmth toward a son as toward a daughter. The relationship between siblings, which extended to parallel cousins, was one of friendship and mutual aid. Married male siblings might share a house, food, and equipment. Siblings of the opposite sex were not socially close as adults, but they could depend on each other in times of crisis. The ties between cross-cousins were looser, and the degree of closeness was largely dependent on the personalities of the individuals involved. These persons joked with one another and, if called on, rendered mutual assistance.

After the village kashgee burned around 1950 it was not rebuilt, a good indicator that by then men and boys were increasingly integrated into the households of their mothers and wives; male solidarity diminished. A partial substitute for the kashgee were the Russian-style bathhouses. The nine bathhouses each accommodated about a dozen men at a time, and most men bathed four or more times a week. Here they talked at length and enjoyed the company of each other. Women sometimes bathed with one another, sometimes with their husbands; rarely would a woman bathe with a man who was not her husband. For everyone, bathing was an enjoyable pastime in a relaxed atmosphere away from the bustle in a household.

Villagers and government officials alike considered tuberculosis the most pressing health problem. The combined Napaskiak and Oscarville population in 1956 was 180; of these, 45 persons were diagnosed as having active cases of TB. Villagers did not understand the germ theory of disease and tried various means to cure this and other serious diseases. They usually turned first to patent medicines and their traditional pharmacopoeia; then they might take steam baths, consult a shaman, drink holy water, or pray. Finally, they might turn to the teacher for medicine or go to the Bethel hospital. Tuberculosis control with chemotherapy, instituted by the U.S. Public Health Service, was new in the village.

The nearby town of Bethel, with its stores, hospital, theaters, and pool halls, was an attractive place that represented the white world. Here people met friends from other villages and obtained intoxicants flown in from Anchorage. Visits to other riverine settlements were largely of a social or religious nature. Men also boated upriver to hunt moose or downriver to hunt seals, and a few flew to distant towns to work. The yearly U.S. National Guard encampment at Anchorage was important for members of the local unit. The only other direct and distant contacts were made when someone was hospitalized or attended National Guard training sessions in the contiguous states.

In this general context, it may be noted that among persons of European background, swearwords are a long-established part of one's potential vocabulary. One might assume that swearing is a universal form of linguistic expression. Yet aboriginal Eskimos along the Kuskokwim apparently did not have swearwords in their vocabulary. To refer to someone as a "bastard" was either true or untrue but not profane. The nearest approach to swearing was when one child said to another, "your ass stinks," but adults did not use this phrase. As Eskimos in the region became exposed to profanity in English, some people began to use it. Handling a dog team could be extremely frustrating; the same was true of outboard motors that failed to start. Some forty years ago and in these contexts, Eskimo men who spoke no English often used English swearwords in remarkably innovative combinations.

Not all exotic contacts necessitated leaving the community. One could listen to a battery radio, found in most houses, and learn what was happening beyond the local area. "Tundra Topics," broadcast from Fairbanks, was especially popular, for it presented news about isolated settlements. Then, too, people came to the village from urban areas in connection with governmental work. The only outsider to reside in the community was the BIA teacher, but the bureau also sent supervisors and maintenance workers to the settlement on occasion. U.S. Public Health Service field nurses and those working with the special program for the control of tuberculosis made regular visits. Scientists were frequent callers; their work usually had to do with some aspect of public health. An occasional U.S. National Guard officer or enlisted man from the Bethel headquarters came on official business, and the same applied to the U.S. deputy marshal from Bethel. Sometimes a stray tourist was seen in the village.

POLITICAL LIFE When most males lived in the kashgee, a small number of older and influential men, especially those with large extended families, constituted an informal council whose judgment was not likely to be challenged. Apparently, when differences between families were irreconcilable, members of the weaker faction moved elsewhere. In 1906 an Orthodox priest appointed the first "chief," who seems to have been the head of a large extended family. His primary duty was to oversee church matters, a purpose his successors continued to fulfill. With BIA encouragement, in 1945 the villagers elected a council, but it did not request formal recognition under the Indian Reorganization Act and would become known as a "traditional council." Some people thought the council leader was the village head, while others considered the Orthodox church leaders as responsible for most local matters. The church officials probably were more important because they had the reputation of helping people. They met often, whereas the council met intermittently to address problems such as intoxicants when pushed to do so by one family or another. Villagers much preferred to settle each contentious issue in an informal manner.

Warfare became an intimate part of village life early in World War II. The Alaska Territorial Guard was organized locally as a scouting unit for the U.S. Army when a Japanese invasion of the Alaskan mainland seemed possible. In the village unit, older men were appointed as officers, and the younger ones became enlisted men. Little military discipline was practiced, but large quantities of military equipment were issued. Men were permitted to use the military clothing and guns daily, which was a real economic advantage to members. After the war this organization was replaced by the U.S. National Guard, and the policies changed drastically. The older men were discouraged from reenlisting, especially if they spoke no English. Promising younger men were sent

Figure 4-11 | Napaskiakers and the Russian Orthodox bishop of Alaska in 1956.

to special training schools, and regular drills became a routine part of membership. The village unit came to reflect military norms and emerged as a disruptive institution in village life, particularly since it encouraged the overt authority of young aggressive men, an unprecedented village behavior pattern. Younger men regarded the National Guard as romantic and the yearly two-week encampment near Anchorage as a great adventure. The older men who remained in the unit did so because of the monetary rewards.

RELIGION Christianity was introduced to the Kuskokwim Eskimos in its Russian Orthodox form, and in the 1950s all of the people at Napaskiak, including a practicing shaman, considered themselves Christians (see Figure 4-11). Since there had never been a resident missionary, Orthodox dogma was not well understood. Most villagers agreed that helping other people when in need was one of the most important Christian ideals. The people also believed that after an individual died, the soul automatically went to hell if he or she had not been baptized or if death was from suicide; otherwise, God evaluated a person's deeds, and on this basis admitted the spirit to heaven or hell. At times the ghost of a dead person was thought to have returned to the community; to decrease the likelihood of a visitation the windows of the deceased's former abode were opened after death and closed after burial. An icon was hung on the door to prevent the spirit from returning through the doorway.

The ceremonial cycle duplicated the Orthodox church calendar elsewhere in the world. Along with regular church services, special observances were held at Russian Christmas and New Year's, the Epiphany, the Easter season, and during the annual church conference. Russian Christmas was of far greater importance than any other ceremonial event, and preparations were elaborate. During three days of processions, the choir announced the birth of Christ in each household by singing Christmas songs while carrying a guiding star made of metal. Since the singers and their followers were fed at each house, most of the three nights were taken up with eating vast quantities of food. The Russian New Year was celebrated by putting lighted kerosene lanterns on the graves of the dead, as was done also at Russian Christmas. At about midnight, fireworks and guns were shot off, while the Christmas trees that had decorated the houses for the season were burned in front of the village. The climax of the event was a short service in church about the ideals of behavior for the coming year.

One reason for the ineffectiveness of the village council was that the Orthodox Church Brotherhood had long cared for the crisis needs of the community and held monthly meetings to deal with ongoing problems. The general purpose of this organization was to coordinate church activities and to provide welfare aid for members. Because all of the families participated in at least some Orthodox church functions, with only one man claiming membership in another church, the welfare provision embraced everyone. The brotherhood had elected officers with established duties. The specific obligations of its members were to prepare coffins and bury the dead, to arrange for the annual trip of the bishop to the area, to aid the aged, to maintain the church structure, and to perform certain ceremonial obligations. From the time of its organization in 1931, the brotherhood provided food and funds to families without means of support until this function was assumed by the Alaska Department of Welfare and the BIA shortly after World War II.

Alaska Native Land Claims

Among Eskimos and indigenous peoples the world over, land represents the fundamental basis for identity. Thus, a brief review of Alaskan Eskimo claims is desirable. When Alaska was purchased from Russia by the United States in 1867, the treaty provided that "the uncivilized tribes will be subject to such laws and regulations as the United States may, from time to time, adopt in regard to aboriginal tribes in that country." No effort was made by the federal government to consider aboriginal claims until 1906, when Eskimos and Indians were allowed to claim 160-acre plots; but few selections were made because the grants were inadequate in terms of Eskimo needs.

The first effort by Native Alaskans to organize for their rights was in 1912, when the Alaska Native Brotherhood was founded; but this effort, discussed in Chapter 8, was limited largely to the Tlingit of southeastern Alaska. The Indian Reorganization Act encouraged the establishment of reservations, but few Alaskan Eskimos or Indians claimed land under its provisions. The greatest threat to their landholdings came when Alaska was admitted as a state in 1959. The new state was granted the right to select 103 million acres of land from the public domain, and no meaningful allowance was made for the claims of Indians and Eskimos. In 1962 Howard Rock, a Point Hope Eskimo, founded the newspaper *Tundra Times,* and in 1966 the Alaska Federation of Natives was organized. These efforts were directed primarily at achieving a settlement of native claims throughout the state. The first key victory was the federal "land freeze" on state selections. Finally, after years of proposals and counterproposals, the Alaska Native Claims Settlement Act was passed by Congress and became law in 1971. The major provisions were that Alaskan natives were to receive fee simple title to 40 million acres of land and that $962.5 million was to be paid to the Alaska Native Fund over a period of years as compensation for extinguished claims. The money was to come from congressional appropriations and 2 percent of the mineral revenues from certain federal and state lands in Alaska. U.S. citizens in or from Alaska of one-fourth or more Aleut, Eskimo, or Indian heritage were enrolled and became stockholders in regional corporations and usually village corporations as well. In general, the regional corporations held mineral rights to village lands. Payments were from the Alaska Native Fund to regional corporations on a per capita basis; the regional corporations retained part of the money and turned the balance over to village corporations and to individuals. Above all else, as far as non-natives were concerned, the settlement was essential before construction of the Alaskan oil pipeline could begin.

By 1985, Calista, the local regional corporation established under the settlement act, had lost nearly $43 million from total assets of about $70 million because of incompetent management. The typical Kuskokwim Eskimo has not benefited monetarily from the settlement act. One of its provisions was that stock shares, which represented land as well as money, could be sold to the public after 1991. However, the original act was amended in 1987 to prevent stock sales to outsiders without the approval of the majority of stockholders in a corporation. In the 1980s many if not most Kuskokwim Eskimos regarded the act as seriously flawed. It abruptly forced villagers into the business world, with disappointing results. A key *grassroot Eskimo response* was to form the Yupiit Nation in 1983 at the villages of Akiakchak, Akiak, and Tuluksak. Their major goals were to gain greater control over the land, to achieve far more political autonomy, and to foster the continuity of Eskimo culture. The nation's goals were widely appealing and soon expanded to include nineteen villages, but the effort had lost its momentum by the late 1990s. The state and federal governments have been reasonably cooperative in some respects, such as granting the control of schools to villagers. A major problem for Native Alaskans in dealing with the state is that they represent only about 15 percent of the total Alaskan population, and legislators have not been sympathetic to their goals.

| Additional Recent Changes

Beginning in the mid-1960s at Napaskiak and other riverine Eskimo villages, changes became more rapid and dramatic than ever before in historic times. We focus briefly on major developments apart from the settlement act.

The Great Society program launched by President Johnson in 1965 had a profound impact on life in these small communities. Federal government studies indicated that living conditions in western Alaskan villages were the *poorest in the nation,* a finding that led to a proliferation of programs for directed culture change. First and foremost, many substandard houses were replaced by new dwellings (see Figure 4-12), wells were drilled for safe water, and generators were installed to provide electricity. It became apparent, however, that not all of these projects would lead to lasting benefits. Many of the new houses were poorly built, costly to heat, and difficult to maintain. The wells and electrical plants often were unreliable, and the same was true of the sewage systems that had been installed. Neither the federal government nor the local people had the capacity to maintain the infrastructure, and the result by the 1980s was not as positive as the federal planners had expected.

New construction of clinics, churches, community halls, post offices, and schools continued. Although some old-style bathhouses and caches remained, most other evidence of traditional material culture had disappeared. Within the houses, changes were especially notable in the quality of imported furnishings, including the addition of oil-burning heaters and television sets. Household inventories were much larger than ever before, reflecting a considerable investment. Families also spent more money on aluminum boats and

Figure 4-12 | By 1970, new houses at Napaskiak were heated with oil stored in drums. Caches were at ground level, and outhouses were built behind dwellings. A house had few windows and multiple doors with substantial locks as protection from roving drunks.

larger outboard motors and on the snowmobiles that had largely replaced dog-team travel.

By the mid-1980s the riverine Eskimo population had increased dramatically, due in part to a decline in the infant mortality rate and to better health maintenance. The younger adults, who came from large families, began to raise large families of their own. Tuberculosis, long a primary killer and crippler, was virtually eradicated. Through U.S. Public Health Service efforts, the death rate from tuberculosis, which among native Alaskans in 1950 was 653 per 100,000 (compared to 22.5 for all races in the United States at that time), was reduced to 3.7 in 1969 and became relatively rare thereafter.

The dramatic population increase that began in the 1960s was accompanied by a growth in affluence. Family incomes typically increased, despite a decline in the amount of trapping brought about by comparatively low fur prices and disaffection with the rigorous physical activity required. In large measure, family incomes grew because of the many village construction projects for which local people were hired. In addition, commercial salmon fishing in the Kuskokwim River began in 1959; this was a new major source of income, especially along the lower river, where the harvest quota was greatest. By 1982 the commercial salmon harvest was worth about $4.2 million to fishermen of the region, with the average income ranging between $3000 and $5000. Commercial fishing was the most important source of locally earned income. However, by 1998 there was a significant decline in this source of cash. There were many reasons for the situation: operating expenses at Bethel were the highest in Alaska; the worldwide demand for wild salmon had diminished with the increased efficiency of fish farms in raising salmon; and the state had shortened the permitted fishing hours to protect the escapement of sufficient salmon to spawn. The future of commercial salmon fishing in the region does not appear to be bright.

The consumption of alcoholic beverages appears to have been relatively low until soon after World War II. Then residents began to order intoxicants by airfreight from Anchorage or Fairbanks, and public drunkenness became commonplace. In 1964 thirteen drownings were attributed directly to drinking. A municipal liquor store opened at Bethel in 1963; although it soon closed, it was reopened a number of times. By 1996 Bethelites could possess and consume alcoholic drinks, but the sale of intoxicants was banned. From the 1950s to the present, villagers have often gone to Bethel to drink. This especially has been true since 1981, when the state passed a local option law. As a result, most Kuskokwim Eskimo villages have banned the possession and/or the sale and importation of alcoholic beverages. Most riverine villages are "dry," but alcohol-related incidents remain commonplace.

A decision by the Ninth U.S. Circuit Court in 1996 was a dramatic recent development. The court ruled that the native government of Venetie in Alaska had the right to levy taxes. This ruling meant that the 226 federally recognized "tribes" (read "villages") in Alaska were "Indian country," comparable to reservations. Thus these villagers would gain a significant degree of autonomy; for

Figure 4-13 | In this 1997 photograph, Jerry N. Jerry of Bethel is fishing for burbot in the Kuskokwim River. (Courtesy of Ted Horner.)

example, they would have powers of taxation, land use regulation, and law enforcement. State officials were convulsed over the ruling because it would deprive them of control over much of rural Alaska. In 1997 the state appealed the ruling. Early in 1998 the U.S. Supreme Court upheld the appeal, declining to recognize tribal lands in Alaska as Indian country.

Historically, a notable aspect of Eskimo culture had been their capacity to live off local food resources (see Figure 4-13). Their diet changed a great deal as imported foods became available at trading posts and stores. A pertinent question is: How important are local food resources in their present-day economy? A partial answer is provided in a 1985–86 study by Michael W. Coffing (1991) for the Kuskokwim Eskimo village of Kwethluk. He reported that the vast majority of the 540 residents were Eskimo and that the median wage employment income per household was about seventeen thousand dollars, with most earnings coming from government-funded jobs. At the same time, the cost of living was more than twice the U.S. average. Members of each of the 112 households harvested wildlife, especially salmon and other fish, as food. The wildlife harvest was 800 pounds edible weight per capita, which was high even for rural areas in Alaska. Thus, it is clear that living off the land continues to be a key factor in their economic lives. (See also Chapter 8, Subsistence Issues, pages 286–287.)

Dramatic changes launched in 1965 with the Great Society programs, including food stamps, better housing, and improved health services, loomed especially large. By the 1990s the physical transformation of villages had become even more apparent. A. Oscar Kawagley (1995), a Kuskokwim Eskimo who received his PhD from the University of British Columbia, described the community of Akiak located a short distance upriver from Napaskiak. He reported the dominance of frame houses heated by oil furnaces. Some homes had septic systems. Many houses included refrigerators, microwave ovens, freezers, televisions, and VCRs. Akiak had a high school with a gymnasium, a community laundry, and local government offices. Additionally, the village had an airport, clinic, library, Moravian church, post office, stores, and a water well. In gross physical terms Akiak resembled many other small communities in the United States.

In communities such as Akiak the dominance of Euro-American culture marches onward. A prime example is the village school complex, which is the primary employer; schools are "the big business" along the river. The teachers, cooks, maintenance personnel, secretaries, bilingual-language program aides, and others associated directly with schools are prominent in each community. Most important, the teacher turnover is high, and teachers are primarily non-Eskimo with little appreciation or sympathy for Eskimo culture. Kawagley (1995, 54) wrote of the "guilt and shame" exhibited by younger persons that stems from a loss of their Eskimo identity. The formal system of education is a compelling force in the lives of youth as they attempt to fit into both the "white" and Eskimo worlds.

Despite the dramatic physical changes at Akiak and in other riverine settlements and the pervasive impact of the traditional American educational system, being Eskimo remains a prominent aspect of village life. Numerous programs, both in and out of school, have been designed to impart an ongoing sense of being Eskimo. Traditional subsistence and survival techniques are taught to youth, the dances and songs of old are increasingly emphasized, and Eskimo-language programs are expanding. Yet current state and federal government efforts strive to make the Kuskokwim people into standard Americans. As Ann Fienup-Riordan (1990, 192–200) vividly conveyed in an essay about the Yupiit Nation, a great deal of cultural vitality continues to prevail and to blend the old with the new in a novel Eskimo cultural configuration (see Figures 4-14 and 4-15).

| Additional Sources

Alaskan Eskimos in the Bering Sea region are well known for the complexity of their technology; the best account of their material culture is by Edward W. Nelson (1899). The earliest comprehensive report about Eskimos in the Kuskokwim area during the Russian era is by Lavrentiy A. Zagoskin (Toronto, 1967). The *Arctic* volume (5) of the *Handbook of North American Indians,* William C. Sturtevant, general editor (Washington, DC, 1984), is the best single source for descriptions and comparisons of the Eskimos in southwestern Alaska and elsewhere. An ethnoarchaeological study by Oswalt and VanStone (Washington, DC, 1967) provides some insight into material culture changes introduced by the Russians and Anglo-Americans. *Alaskan Eskimos* (San Francisco, 1967) by Oswalt examines aboriginal conditions among this segment of the population. Oswalt's *Napaskiak* (Tucson, 1963a) reports about life in one village during 1955–56, and *Mission of Change in Alaska* (San Marino, 1963b) is a historical reconstruction of Kuskokwim Eskimo culture from 1884 to 1925. Anglo-American educational programs among these Eskimos are presented by John Collier (New York, 1973)

Figure 4-14 | The Kuskokwim area Eskimo skin-working tradition survives to a great extent in handcrafted dolls. Lucy Beaver, a Bethel resident, is shown with one of her dolls in 1997. (Courtesy of Ted Horner.)

Figure 4-15 | Dog teams as a winter transportation mainstay have been largely replaced by snowmobiles. Dog-team races remain popular, as shown in this 1997 photograph of a race along the lower Kuskokwim River. (Courtesy of Ted Horner.)

and more recently by A. Oscar Kawagley (Prospect Heights, IL, 1995). Ann Fienup-Riordan (Norman, 1991) offers an insightful study of early Moravian missionaries in the area. Her *Eskimo Essays* (New Brunswick, 1990) probably is the most knowledgeable analysis of Eskimos in southwestern Alaska. Oswalt's *Bashful No Longer* (Norman, 1990) concerns Kuskowagamiut ethnohistory from 1778 to 1988.

| Selected Bibliography

Anderson, Eva G. 1940. *Dog-team doctor.* Caldwell.

Arnold, Robert D., et al. 1976. *Alaska native land claims.* Anchorage.

Coffing, Michael W. 1991. *Kwethluk subsistence.* Alaska Department of Fish and Game. Juneau.

Collier, John. 1973. *Alaskan Eskimo education.* New York.

Fienup-Riordan, Ann. 1983. *The Nelson Island Eskimo.* Anchorage.

———, 1990. *Eskimo essays.* New Brunswick.

———. 1991. *The real people and the children of thunder.* Norman, OK.

Kawagley, A. Oscar. 1995. *A Yupiaq worldview.* Prospect Heights, IL.

Nelson, Edward W. 1899. *The Eskimo about Bering Strait.* Bureau of American Ethnology, 18th Annual Report, pt. 1.

Oswalt, Wendell H. 1963a. *Napaskiak: An Alaskan Eskimo community.* Tucson.

———. 1963b. *Mission of change in Alaska.* San Marino, CA.

———. 1964. Traditional storyknife tales of Yuk girls. *Proceedings of the American Philosophical Society* 108:310–36.

———. 1967. *Alaskan Eskimos.* San Francisco.

———. 1990. *Bashful no longer: An Alaskan Eskimo ethnohistory, 1778–1988.* Norman, OK.

Oswalt, Wendell H., and James W. VanStone. 1967. *The ethnoarcheology of Crow Village, Alaska.* Bureau of American Ethnology Bulletin no. 199. Washington, DC.

Petroff, Ivan. 1884. *Report on the population, industries, and resources of Alaska.* United States Department of the Interior, Census Office.

Wrangell, Ferdinand von. 1839 (German edition). *Statistical and ethnographic data concerning the Russian possessions on the Northwest Coast of America.* St. Petersburg.

Zagoskin, Lavrentiy A. 1967. *Lieutenant Zagoskin's travels in Russian America, 1842–1844,* Henry N. Michael, ed. Anthropology of the North: Translations from Russian Sources, no. 7. Arctic Institute of North America, Toronto.

5 The Cahuilla: Gatherers in the Desert

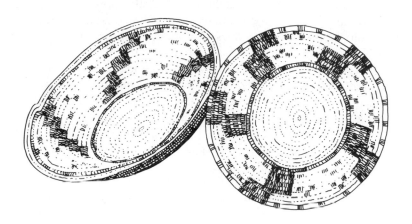

His food gave out, his water gave out,
Leave him now, go away from him:
Isilwelnet. [enemy name]
[repeated as many times as desired]

Bury him now, plant him now:
And then they buried him, and then they planted him:
Pehuetematewilwish.

There stands the whirlwind, there stands the whirlwind
Where they burned him, where they burned him:
Puchueulchalmalmia.

> Three "enemy songs" among the Desert Cahuilla
> collected by Lucile Hooper. (1920, 345)

A MAJOR REASON for selecting the Cahuilla to represent the California culture area is the quality of the information available about them. Yet we must stress that tremendous variability existed in California Indian lifeways; no individual tribe was "typical." Not only is the ethnographic and historical data about the Cahuilla superior, but over the years they have attracted inordinate Anglo-American attention. In historical context, the Cahuilla gained literary recognition in the novel *Ramona*. Once exceedingly popular, it depicts the life of a Cahuilla woman. Its author, Helen Hunt Jackson (1884), brought southern California Indians to national attention. The Palm Springs group (Agua Caliente Band) have been the focus of attention of bankers, land speculators, lawyers, municipal officials, and judges, especially in the resort city of Palm Springs; this interest has been, above all else, monetary.

Considering the course of Native American history, it might be expected that the Palm Springs Band of Cahuilla are relatively disadvantaged, but nothing could be further from reality. The land allotted to individual band members is valued at *billions of dollars*. In addition, the band owns a casino, spa hotel, and other tribal operations. The combined assets of the nearly three hundred band members are astronomical. "Lo the poor Indian" clearly is not a phrase that applies to these Indians.

Historically, three Cahuilla subgroups have been recognized: the Desert, Mountain, and Pass populations. In this chapter, the emphasis is on the Desert Cahuilla, who lived in the vicinity of Palm Springs. However, it was not always possible to determine from a source whether a specific trait was expressed in both the general desert area and at Palm Springs. As is true of most ethnographic reconstructions, this chapter does not apply in detail to a single community, but it does represent a composite for the desert dwellers.

| Population and Language

Six thousand, or possibly fewer, Cahuilla lived in the interior of southern California (see Figure 5-1). By 1888 their number had declined to its lowest point, about one thousand. By 1997 there were twenty-five hundred persons enrolled as Cahuilla.

The Aztec-Tanoan linguistic phylum, which is represented widely in the western United States and Mexico, includes the Cahuilla. They belong to the Uto-Aztecan language stock and the Takic family.

| Early Historic Contact with Non-Indians

The Cahuilla often are classed as Mission Indians, but this is not an entirely accurate label. They were not subject to the mission environment in the manner of coastal Indians in southern California, and most Cahuilla had only indirect contact with Roman Catholic missionaries. The first Europeans to travel into the Cahuilla region were Pedro Fages in 1772 and Juan Bautista de Anza in 1774, but neither made any known impact on these Indians. De Anza attempted without success to establish an overland route from Mexico to Alta

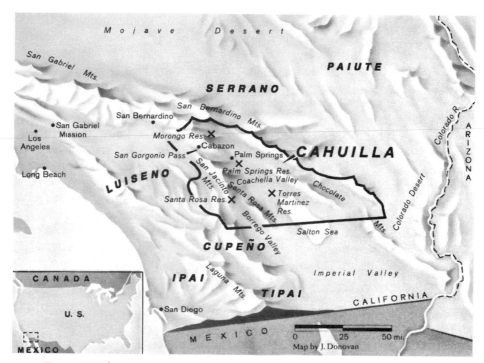

Figure 5-1 | The Cahuilla area with major reservations indicated.

California. Following the War for Independence in Mexico and the establishment of a republic in 1823, attention again turned to the interior of southern California. At the request of Indians in the San Bernardino area for a mission, an outpost or rancho was established among them in 1819. Jose Romero was charged with opening an overland route, and a small party set out from Tucson in 1823. An expedition member's diary makes apparent that the Desert Cahuilla, at least those as far south and west as Palm Springs, were in close contact with the San Bernardino mission rancho. Some of the people in the Coachella Valley were raising maize and pumpkins, crops that they probably acquired from Colorado River area Indians, and the Cahuilla of the desert were growing watermelon, an Old World domestic plant introduced by Europeans to the New World.

Before 1834 the California missions were under the control of Franciscans, who introduced most European ideas and technology to the region. After this date some missions, including the one founded at San Gabriel in 1771, became secularized, and the missionaries lost control. In 1834, the San Bernardino rancho was sacked and burned by Indians. With secularization the rancho passed into private ownership, and marauding Indians raided the herds of livestock. A Mountain Cahuilla leader, "Captain" Juan Antonio, and his small band were recruited to end the raids, which they did with great success. In 1846 the United States acquired California, and a few years later, in

1852, the San Bernardino rancho was purchased by Mormon settlers. During the late Mexican and early American periods, raids by Mohave, Paiute, and Yuma for livestock, especially horses, contributed to the hostile attitude of whites toward most Indians in southern California. The Cahuilla were not combative and apparently played an insignificant part in these raids. Since they did not intrude on the activities of whites, the Cahuilla were left very much to themselves.

In 1850 the U.S. Congress sent a special commission to California to negotiate treaties with Native Americans and assign lands to them. A treaty arranged in 1852 set aside an area about forty miles long and thirty miles wide for the Cahuilla. The U.S. Senate, however, refused to ratify any of the eighteen treaties with California Indians. Congressional resistance stemmed from a number of factors: the commissioners had committed the government to spend a great deal of money; white Californians vigorously opposed the treaties; and it was thought that some of these lands might contain gold.

In 1852 Edward F. Beale was appointed superintendent of Indian affairs in California, and he selected Benjamin D. Wilson as the subagent for the southern part of the state. Wilson, a former mayor of Los Angeles, was a landowner and merchant married to a Spanish American. In a report that may have been written by Wilson's friend Benjamin Hays, we have contemporary comments about the Cahuilla and a good account of conditions among southern California Indians. The Wilson Report noted that the last ties with missionaries had been severed in 1834 and that old ethnic groups had been disrupted by 1852. Living among the Desert Cahuilla were Ipai and Luiseno Indians; one of the Cahuilla leaders was a Yuma. The elders and many others spoke Spanish by this time. The Indians worked as underpaid laborers and domestics on the ranchos of whites and were frequently intoxicated. The report pointed out that under Spanish law the Indians had rights to their settlements and pasture lands, and in theory the State of California recognized Indian land rights. The report characterized state laws as "*All* punishment. *No* reform!" But the positive recommendations of the Wilson Report made no recognized impact on early American policy, probably in part because of the recent rejection of California Indian treaties by the U.S. Senate.

In late 1852 Beale recommended that lands be set aside for Indian occupation; this was *the beginning of the modern reservation system* in the United States. The lands would be military reservations as well as places where Indians could be instructed in farming and other skills. Soldiers were to be stationed there to maintain order, and the military would be supported from surplus Indian harvests. The first reserve opened at Tejon in 1853, and after initial success Beale's political enemies charged that he was making a personal profit from the reservation. Although he finally was vindicated fully, the reservation system had lost its impetus and did not become important in California.

In the mid-1850s, Cahuilla men reportedly numbered about thirty-five hundred. These figures unquestionably included many non-Cahuilla, but in any event Indians far outnumbered the local white settlers. The Indians were discontented after the federal government failed to set land aside for their exclusive use; they complained that they had not received farm equipment as promised and that whites were trespassing and squatting on traditional Indian lands, as well as taking water and wood. In 1862 a smallpox epidemic spread from Los Angeles, and although the number of people who perished was not recorded, the epidemic probably was a significant factor in eroding the people and their way of life. Throughout the latter part of the nineteenth century, some Cahuilla worked on the ranches of whites, the men as laborers and the women as domestics. The men also tended orchards and vineyards, cut mesquite wood, and labored at salt works. When the Southern Pacific railroad was being built through the area in the 1870s, they were employed as laborers. They continued to collect products of the desert and farmed some of the better-watered localities.

| Aboriginal Life

Cahuilla tradition states that these people originally lived in the desert but were forced to flee to adjacent mountains by a great flood, a probable reference to the emergence of the inland sea that once covered much of the present lowland and subsided about five hundred years ago. The San Jacinto and Santa Rosa mountains where they sought refuge consist of steep granite ridges and barren tablelands at medium elevations, but higher up are streams, open meadows, and forests of oak and pine. After the flood subsided, the Desert Cahuilla moved into the Coachella Valley, a desert environment in which cacti, mesquite, and screw beans were economically important plants. The region has very little precipitation, and summer temperatures may reach 120°F. Precipitation, when it does come, is often torrential and causes widespread erosion. Furthermore, severe dust storms may whip across the valley. Some sectors, particularly in the eastern part of the Desert Cahuilla range, are devoid of vegetation. The Pass Cahuilla occupied the country surrounding San Gorgonio Pass; here were open grassland and some oak groves as well as desert areas.

ORIGIN MYTH   In the Cahuilla culture, ties with the mythological past were very important. Their well-developed origin myth goes as follows. In the beginning, there was no earth or sky or anything or anybody; only a dense darkness in space. This darkness seemed alive. Something like lightning bolts seemed to pass through it and meet each other once in a while. Two substances that looked like the white of an egg came from the lightning bolts. They lay side by side in the stomach of the darkness, which resembled a spider web. These substances disappeared. They were produced again, and again they disappeared. This was called the miscarriage of the darkness. The third time they appeared, they remained, hanging there in this web in the darkness. The substances began to grow and soon were two very large eggs. When they hatched two men emerged, Mukat and Tamaioit. They were grown men from the first and could talk. As they lay there, both at the same time heard a noise like a bee buzzing; this was the song of their mother, Darkness (Hooper 1920, 317).

With this great event the natural world began to emerge as an orderly system; at least this was said to be so by the Iviatim, the descendants of Mukat and Tamaioit, who have come to be known in the ethnographic literature as the Cahuilla (Coahuillas, Kawia), a word that may have meant "masters."

Once the twin creators existed, Mukat reached into his mouth and then into his heart to remove a cricket, another insect, a lizard, and a person. These creatures were charged with driving away the darkness, but they failed. From their hearts the creators removed tobacco, pipes, and a coal to light one pipe. Mukat and Tamaioit argued over which one was born first and which was the more intelligent. Mukat became associated with making things black, and Tamaioit made forms that were white. Together they created the earth, ocean, sun, moon, people, and some plants and animals. Finally Mukat and Tamaioit disagreed so violently that Tamaioit disappeared beneath the ground, taking with him many of his creations. It was then that mountains emerged, the earth quaked, and water from the ocean overflowed, forming streams and rivers. After this Mukat lived in a big house with people and animals who had human qualities. The moon was there as a lovely female who instructed women about marriage, child rearing, and both menstrual and pregnancy taboos. Mukat, who had created her, desired to make the moon his wife. She knew this but said nothing. Since she could not marry him because he was her father, she traveled to her present home in the sky. When she was asked to return, she said nothing; she only smiled. One day, while in a humorous mood, Mukat caused the people to speak different languages. As the sun grew hot, some of these people sought shelter and were transformed into different plants and animals. Those who stayed with Mukat remained human. He told the people how to make bows and arrows and how to shoot at each other, which led to the first deaths. It was about this time, too, that the sun turned people different colors. Those people who were nearest the sun's rays became black people, those who were far away stayed white, and the Indians turned brown because they were in between.

The people became angry with Mukat after he had caused a rattlesnake to bite a friendly little man, the moon woman to leave, and people to kill one another. They decided to kill Mukat but did not know how to do it. Mukat lived in the middle of the big house and only went outside to defecate when everyone was asleep; this a white lizard discovered. One night a frog caught the feces of Mukat in his mouth, and Mukat grew ill. The shamans pretended to try to cure him, but Mukat became sicker. As he was dying, he sang songs and told the people how to conduct a mourning ceremony in memory of the dead each year. After his death, Mukat was cremated, the big house was burned, and the essence of the world was established.

SETTLEMENTS AND MANUFACTURES Cahuilla villages usually were located near canyon mouths or in a valley where flooding was unlikely. Where

Figure 5-2 | Palm Springs Cahuilla homestead, ca. 1900. (Courtesy of the Southwest Museum, Los Angeles, CA, neg. no. 33934.)

water was scarce, settlements clustered near water holes or hand-dug wells. Their dwellings were substantial rectangular structures with fork-top corner posts to receive roof beams. Along the sides and on the beam tops were arranged lengths of brush held in place with horizontal poles (see Figure 5-2). On some houses the brush was smeared with mud, and a layer of dirt was added to the roof. At the front of a house was a ramada or porch constructed like a house but walled only on the windward side. A settlement included a post-and-pole bathhouse built in a shallow pit and probably covered with brush and a layer of earth. A fire was built in the fireplace, and smoke drifted from the doorway until the people were ready to bathe. Cahuilla caches were highly distinctive. They usually were raised above the ground on a pole platform and were made by intertwining small branches; they looked very much like birds' nests some two to four feet high and were used to store plant products (see Figure 5-3). The only other structures were a brush enclosure used for certain ceremonies and a large enclosure walled on three sides and attached to the house of a male leader. Among the Palm Springs Cahuilla in 1925, the social and ceremonial leader occupied the dance house, which was about forty feet in diameter with walls of fitted boards and a palm-thatched roof. At the back was a room where the sacred (medicine) bundle was kept; in front of the structure was a fenced enclosure.

An aboriginal house remained relatively cool even in the hottest weather. The inside was dark from soot on the walls, and natural light filtered in only through the doorway. On one side of the entrance were a woman's food-grinding stones. People the world over who collect seeds as food often

Figure 5-3 | A 1907 Desert Cahuilla granary. (Courtesy of the Phoebe A. Hearst Museum of Anthropology, University of California at Berkeley.)

used a set of stones to crush the shells. The Cahuilla spread seeds on a flat or slightly concave stone called a milling stone (metate, quern) and pulverized them using a smaller stone called a hand stone (mano, rubbing stone). On the other side of the doorway was a pottery vessel for water. Toward the center of the room, fire-blackened cooking pots encircled the fireplace; at the back of the house, blankets and animal skins served as mattresses. Attached to the roof beams or in the thatch were bundles of plants or dried meat for future use. Near every house a section of log set vertically into the ground served as a mortar: the top was flat except that the center was hollowed out a foot or more in depth. A smooth pole some two feet long served as the pestle. The combination was designed to pulverize mesquite beans, which were an important item in the diet.

Most artifacts around a settlement were made from plant fibers. Baskets, usually fashioned by coiling and often having black geometric designs woven on the sides, were the most varied cluster of forms. Among the more common styles were globular baskets used as utensils or containers for small objects and round forms for food or seed storage (see Figure 5-4). Mescal fiber nets used as carrying baskets looked like small hammocks and had loops at each end for cinching cords. A woman carrying a basket passed the cord over her forehead and rested it against the front of a flat-topped cap made of basketry that she wore.

The only domestic animal, the dog, served as a pet and watchdog rather than an aid in hunting. The dog was not an ordinary pet because it was believed to possess certain supernatural powers. According to Cahuilla belief, dogs could understand human conversation but could not speak, and like people, they had souls. In the origin myth, at the time of Mukat's death, the

Figure 5-4 | A Cahuilla woman, Louisa Costa Rice, making baskets for the tourist trade in 1938 at the Soboba reservation. (Photograph by Maxine and Gerald A. Smith, courtesy of the San Bernardino County Museum and A. K. Smiley Public Library, Redlands, CA.)

people had only one dog, and among the modern Desert Cahuilla, some dogs still were named after the first dog. Other dog names referred to their appearance or to some behavioral characteristic.

CLOTHING In aboriginal times, clothing seems to have been nonexistent, although it is possible that women wore short skirts of plant fiber and men wore breechclouts. A more certain item of apparel was footwear, which consisted of sandals made from mescal fiber pads. Women sometimes wore the basketry hats mentioned earlier. They were tattooed on the chin, and certain men, most likely leaders, had their nasal septums pierced and a deer bone inserted in the opening. Both males and females wore strings of beads in their pierced earlobes. The beads were thin curved and circular pieces of shell received in trade from the coastal regions of southern California.

SUBSISTENCE ACTIVITIES The Cahuilla identified three primary seasons: the budding of trees, hot days, and cold days. Some persons divided the year into eight more specific seasons, each associated with the development of mesquite beans. The beginning of a season arrived when a particular star appeared; this was a moment for rejoicing and a time to make preparations for an appropriate collecting activity. Star watching was especially important in the spring when food supplies might be low and edible plants were ripening. It is estimated that 80 percent of all edibles were harvested within five miles of a village.

The most important Desert Cahuilla food plant was the mesquite tree, which grew in groves from the desert floor to elevations of thirty-five hundred feet in better-watered areas. Stands were particularly numerous near springs or streams and in washes. In the early summer, the people roasted mesquite blossoms in a pit of heated stones, formed them into balls, and stored them in pottery containers as food. After mesquite beans ripened, entire families harvested them. Children helped by climbing trees to dislodge the pods from higher branches. They did not gather pods indiscriminately; the beans of some trees were regarded as more palatable than those from other trees. The pods might be stored from one year to the next because the trees of a particular grove were not equally productive every year. The pods might be ripened artificially, picked ripe, or gathered after they had fallen from trees. They pulverized ripened pods in an upright wooden mortar with a pestle and processed the juice as a beverage. Most pods were stored in raised caches and later processed in a mortar or on a milling stone. When the meal had dried, it was formed into a cake and stored in the rafters of a house. People broke off sections of the cakes to eat as snacks or for food when traveling. The meal could also be made into a gruel or soaked in water to make the mesquite juice beverage. Loose ground meal was stored in pottery or basketry containers to be made into gruel later.

The Desert people also ate screw beans that grew under the same general conditions as the mesquite and were processed in the same manner. Ethnographic studies of California Indians often specify acorns as the most important staple. This clearly was the case over much of the state, but among the Cahuilla acorns were less important. The groves were controlled by patriclans (groups of families related through the male lines), and each family owned particular trees. In the fall, men climbed the trees to dislodge the acorns. Women cracked the acorns between two stones, spread the kernels out to dry for several weeks, and then pulverized them with pestles in stone mortars. To remove the bitter tannic acid, they spread the meal on a loosely woven basket or in a depression made in sand. In either case, grass or leaves were placed in the leaching basin to prevent the meal from washing away. Then they poured water repeatedly over the meal and stirred the mixture. The capabilities of a woman were gauged by her skill in leaching and grinding acorn meal. Finely ground meal was made into cakes and baked in hot coals, while coarse meal was made into a gruel. Acorns that were not ground at gathering time were stored in platform caches.

Mesquite and screw beans were the most important foods, but over sixty different plants played a part in the diet. Growing in well-watered localities was a species of *Chenopodium* locally called careless weed. The seeds were collected, ground, and baked in cakes. One of the most important seed-producing grasses was chia, a member of the sage family. A seed beater dislodged the seeds from the whorls onto a flat basket. They were parched and ground to be baked into cakes or mixed with water to make a nourishing drink. When the century plants or agave of the canyons produced stalks, the stalks and "cabbages" were roasted in sand pits heated with stones. To this list of foods could be added many others, but the examples cited suggest the broad range of plants collected and the varied means of food preparation.

Contrary to expectations, the overwhelming emphasis on plant foods did not mean that hunting was neglected nor that the inventory of weapons and traps was impoverished. Adult males trapped animals and also stalked, chased, and intercepted them. The principal weapon was a shaft (self) bow with a plant fiber bowstring. The arrowshafts were vaned with split feathers, and shafts simply sharpened at the point probably were meant for birds and small game. Arrows with cane shafts and wooden arrow points probably were used against large game and enemies; some arrows apparently were tipped with poisons made from rattlesnake venom and other toxic substances. Another weapon was the nonreturning boomerang, commonly called a throwing stick when reported in western North America. It was a flat, curved piece of wood thrown at birds and small game. Hunters also used calls and decoys to lure game near enough to kill with arrows. Additional facilities for taking game included nets set along trails, deadfalls, and snares. Hunting was surrounded by numerous restrictions. For example, the Desert Cahuilla regarded mountain lions and grizzly bears as shamans and avoided killing them. When a mule deer was killed, people gathered to sing all night and eat the deer the following morning. In general, a man or boy did not consume any of the animals that he killed. Rabbits, squirrels, and other small game taken by a young boy in a communal hunt usually were given to his mother's family. The kills of an adult male were given alternately to his own family and to his wife's family.

DESCENT, KINSHIP, AND MARRIAGE All the peoples described previously traced their descent through their father's *and* mother's hereditary lines; this is the bilateral (nonunilineal) descent system familiar to us, since it currently prevails in the United States. (Our descent system should not be confused with our pattern of typically taking our father's surname. This practice may give some added stress to the father's line, but a mother's line may be equally or more important in the lives of some individuals.) Many people around the world give special stress to the male *or* female lines. The Cahuilla emphasized one line and thus had a unilineal descent system. Since they considered the male line far more important, their descent system was patrilineal, and a married couple resided with or near the husband's family (patrilocal residence). A typical Cahuilla settlement was formed around a group of males

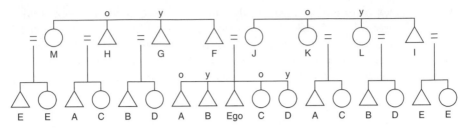

Figure 5-5 | The early historic Cahuilla system of kinship terminology.

who traced their descent to a *known* common ancestor (patrilineage). Closely related patrilineages with a *presumed* common ancestor composed a larger unit (patriclan), which was the most important social and ceremonial group.

In the kinship terminology, a male individual distinguished among his older and younger male and female siblings and made similar distinctions between his father's brothers and mother's sisters. He employed still other terms for his father's sisters and mother's brothers; these did not take relative age into consideration. A male individual referred to his father's older brother's and his mother's older sister's son and daughter by the same term as for his older brothers and sisters. Similarly, he referred to the son and daughter of his father's younger brother and mother's younger sister by the same terms as for his younger brothers and sisters. In essence, parallel cousins (children of father's brother and mother's sister) were termed the same as siblings, with the same age distinction as for siblings. For cross-cousins (father's sister's and mother's brother's children), the male–female kin terms were the same but different from those for siblings or parallel cousins. This cousin terminology is of the Iroquois type, while the terms on the first ascending generation are bifurcate collateral. The Iroquois cousin terms make particular sense since moiety exogamy (marriage outside each of the two basic tribal subdivisions) existed. Thus certain near relatives, such as father's brother's children and mother's sister's children, were of one's own moiety and reasonably called brother and sister. Cross-cousins, on the other hand, were of a different moiety and termed differently, but in spite of the terminological difference one could not marry a cross-cousin (see Figure 5-5).

SOCIAL DIMENSIONS   In the Cahuilla origin myth, Mukat and Tamaioit were associated with the wildcat and coyote, respectively, and all Cahuilla identified with one or the other of these groups (moieties). Among the Desert Cahuilla, the Wildcat moiety included eight clans, and the Coyote moiety consisted of ten clans. In aboriginal times the members of each clan theoretically occupied a single settlement, but in actual fact, persons from a number of clans might live in one settlement. We may presume that at one time all the members of a patriclan lived in a single village. As their number increased and they could not support themselves at the village site, the surplus, most likely members of a junior patrilineage, formed a new village or joined another clan at its settlement. A clan section or patrilineage founding a new village might eventually become so expanded that it qualified as a clan, with its own name and leader, or clan "chief," called a *net*. The office of net usually passed from father to eldest son (primogeniture), and it included extremely important obligations. Nets lived in dwellings with dance houses attached and were the trustees of sacred clan bundles. A net directed subsistence activities, settled conflicts between members, represented the clan before other clans, and was responsible for the correct performance of ceremonies.

In sum, the core population of a village consisted of small family groups related through male lines descending from a known common ancestor (patri-lineage). In the same settlement might be the members of other patrilineages assumed to have had a common male ancestor (patriclan). Moiety exogamy prevailed, which meant that a Wildcat was obligated to marry a Coyote and vice versa. Persons in opposite moieties maintained a joking relationship and friendly rivalry.

POLITICAL LIFE Hereditary leaders did not exist above the clan level, and in instances where the activities of one clan impinged on those of an-other, the differences were resolved by the nets in council. Decisions of a clan as a collectivity were made by the net, who ideally was a man of exceptional abilities. A net was required to know the boundaries of all clan lands, all clan traditions, and a broad range of esoteric facts important to the clan's viability; he also was expected to be a good orator and fair-minded. He did not possess more material property than anyone else, but families presented him with the initial harvest (first fruit) of any plant, which was partial compensation for the time he devoted to clan activities. At the rear of the net's house was a small room where sacred objects, termed the "heart" of the clan, were kept. Eagle feathers were a vital part of each sacred bundle. Clearly, the net, as conveyer of clan knowledge and guardian of the most sacred clan objects, was the para-mount leader.

A second important political and religious functionary was the *paha*. His role existed only in certain localities, and his exact duties have not been re-ported in detail. Apparently, where the office existed the paha was primarily responsible for ceremonial preparations and the maintenance of order on such occasions. In addition, he was a leader of hunting parties and a spokesman and messenger for a net. Upon his death he was replaced by a son or another close male relative.

Formalized warfare or even feuds with neighboring ethnic groups were rare. To the east the desert area had no permanent occupants as far as the Col-orado River; here the aggressive Yuma lived. The Cahuilla feared the Yuma, but the intervening desert was an effective barrier to intensive contacts. The Chemehuevi, who lived to the east along the Colorado River and into the deserts of California, were friendly with the Desert Cahuilla. The southern neighbors of the Desert Cahuilla were the Tipai, but contacts with these people have not been described in any detail and are assumed to have been infrequent.

RELIGIOUS ACTIVITIES Shamans were responsible for dealing with intermittent disaster and personal trauma, while the net and paha guided ceremonies focusing on the life cycle and belief system. The Eagle-Killing Ceremony belongs to the latter category and was a highlight in religious life.

The Eagle-Killing Ceremony symbolized the continuity of a lineage. According to Cahuilla belief, the eagle was one of the species originally created by Mukat. It was said that the eagle lived forever, and by permitting itself to be "killed" by people it assured them of life after death. Thus, although lineage members died, the lineage would continue as had the eagle as a species. Furthermore, the flight of the eagle symbolized the magical course of shamans when they led human souls to the land of the dead. The ceremony also provided a means of obtaining eagle feathers, essential for replacing ceremonial artifacts that had worn out, been destroyed, or exchanged in previous rituals.

In the higher country controlled by some clans, eagles' nests were closely watched by a clan member. This person notified the others of the clan when the eggs had been laid. A feast was then held, and after the nestlings were well feathered, one was removed and raised in a cage by the net's family. After the bird had grown, festivities were held with the members of a neighboring clan, or clans, as guests. At the appointed time, special songs were sung about the death of eagles, and dances were performed. The climax came after the eagle was rolled into a ceremonial mat held by the close family members of the net. They danced with the encased eagle and at dawn the bird screeched and died; it probably was gradually squeezed. The bird was skinned, and the net kept the feathered skin in the sacred clan bundle. Some feathers might be made into a ceremonial skirt, and others were kept to adorn images during the Mourning Ceremony.

Among the Desert group the status of a shaman was not hereditary, and a number of practitioners might belong to a single clan. A shaman often was a man who had been ill frequently as a child, and the healer who treated him had become aware of the child's potential as a curer, magician, and seer. As a young man the novice dreamed of a song that became a tangible manifestation of his inordinate powers. Mukat was responsible, in Cahuilla belief, for implanting the dreams and guardian spirits identified with shamans. A novice danced before the people of his clan for three nights and afterward was qualified to pursue his calling. In his dreams he eventually learned other songs, dances, feats of magic, and bewitching methods. In his dreams, too, a shaman learned of herbal cures for particular ailments or at other times of harmful or curative spells. Certain creatures, such as the coyote, fox, hummingbird, and owl, were considered to be messengers who brought shamans warnings of impending illness. When not drawing on his pharmacopoeia, the shaman attempted to cure by sucking on the afflicted part of a patient's body. Reputedly, he removed the disease object without breaking the skin. Only a few plants were used in curing, despite the Cahuilla's extensive botanical knowledge and their many uses of plants as food. As a youth a shaman did not receive compensation for his services; but as he grew older and became established, he would charge a fee.

If a shaman became malevolent, he posed a threat to a community. In the latter part of the nineteenth century, one old man was considered the world's most powerful shaman. When shamans exhibited their skills, he always performed last and challenged the others to kill him. None was able to do so because he was protected by spirits on all sides. Finally, the old shaman was told by a man of a different clan to stop killing people. The man who gave the warning was soon struck by a "pain" that no shaman could remove, and he died. Everyone knew that the old shaman was responsible. A man from the shaman's clan and men from other clans met and decided that he must be killed. The executioner was to be the net of another clan because he was strong and brave. This man and another visited the sorcerer and were invited to spend the night. After everyone else was asleep, the net crushed the old man's skull with a stone pestle. At the head of the victim's bed were found a variety of small feathers and the skin of a gopher snake, objects used by the old man to make pains. As they were trampled into the ground, a thunderlike sound was heard. In the morning people came to view the body, and later the same morning the body and the house were burned. This is one of the rare recorded instances in which collective action was taken for the good of all the people.

ENTERTAINMENT   Of all the forms of recreation for the Cahuilla, the most important was peon, a hand game that was played at secular gatherings and during ceremonies. A team from one village played against one from another settlement. A peon was a small bone attached to a string with a piece of wood tied to the opposite end. The goal was for a member of the opposite team to guess which clenched fist held a peon. Bets were made, and shamans aided their respective sides while women sang at certain times during the game. A mediator kept a fire burning by which the game was played, held the stakes, and settled disputes. A particular game ended when one side had lost all the peons of the four players or had won a series of tally sticks. Then a new game was started, and new stakes were put up. Peon was frequently played throughout the night, and as one player tired, he was replaced by another.

Other games included races between two groups of men. Each group kicked a wooden ball for several miles and then back again to the starting point. The men on each team took turns kicking the ball, and the team that finished first was the winner. Another race took place on the night of a new moon. The first boy to see the moon would call the others, and they would race to a spot where they could swim. After swimming they raced home, and by so doing they supposedly brought good luck in the coming month. Cat's cradles were made by persons of both sexes. This skill had supernatural implications, since the people believed that before a person's spirit could pass into the world of other spirits, it was required to make string figures.

LIFE CYCLE   At critical times during an individual's life, he or she followed numerous rules, and one of these periods was pregnancy. A future mother refrained from eating any more than necessary; she drank only warm water, ate very little meat, and consumed no salt. In Cahuilla belief, if a pregnant woman ate fruit pecked by a bird, her infant would have sores; if she ate meat from the legs of game, a breech presentation would result; but if she was industrious when pregnant, her offspring would be energetic. These were but three of the rules to insure a safe delivery and a normal offspring. As soon as a woman gave birth and expelled the placenta, she lay in a specially prepared trough dug in the floor of a house. The depression was lined with hot sand, and after the woman stretched out, more hot sand was piled over her body. Here she remained for about ten days, leaving the trough only to urinate and defecate, to have the sand reheated, and to be bathed with hot water each morning. During the month following parturition, the mother remained subject to food taboos, and the father could eat no foods containing salt. A nursing mother did not have sexual intercourse with her husband, for to do so was thought to spoil her milk. She was the object of teasing if she weaned her infant early.

The naming of a child was enmeshed in ritual. After a number of children had been born into a clan, the parents began accumulating food and wealth for a formal naming ceremony. This meant that a child was between four and twelve years of age before he or she was named. A child who had not been named by the age of thirteen would always be known by a nickname. The ceremony was in the father's clan dance house with the couple's clans represented. Female names most often referred to plants or artifacts, whereas males tended to be named after animals, birds, or insects. Amidst singing and dancing, the net held up a child and shouted his or her name three times; the name was repeated by the audience. To prevent an "enemy" clan from learning a child's true name, a disgraceful revelation, and incorporating it in their songs, a net might not say the child's real name. In these instances, a false name would be shouted and the true name revealed in secret. After the namings, food and gifts were distributed to the guests to conclude the ceremony.

When a Desert girl approached adolescence, she was tattooed by her mother's sister as guests from the operator's clan watched. The tattoos were made with cactus thorns pricked in straight or angled lines from the lower lip to the chin, and black paint was rubbed into the wounds. At this time the earlobes of a girl were pierced. When a girl menstruated for the first time, the net summoned the clan of the girl's mother to a ceremony that began in the evening. A fire was built before the net's house to heat the ground, and afterward a trough was dug. The girl was placed in the depression, and her body was covered with hot sand. Throughout the night the members of the girl's clan danced and sang around the pit. In the morning the girl was removed, bathed in warm water, and her head covered with a white paint. For the next three weeks she was subject to food taboos very much like those surrounding pregnancy. The girl stayed in or near the house, and she scratched her head with a special implement rather than her fingernails to prevent her hair from dropping out. Subsequent menstrual periods were surrounded by the same taboos, and in addition, a married woman was forbidden to touch her husband when she was menstruating. The good health of a couple supposedly depended on how well the woman obeyed these rules.

Some Desert Cahuilla do not appear to have initiated adolescent males, but an appropriate ceremony occurred at Palm Springs. Boys between the ages of ten and eighteen were selected by elders for initiation and taken to a brush enclosure outside the dance house. The boys were secluded there for five days and saw only those persons who brought them special foods. Throughout three nights the old people danced until morning. The climax came on the fourth night when the initiates were brought out and given a drink of cooked jimsonweed, or *toloache* as it is known in Spanish. After taking it, the boys danced briefly, but they became dizzy and were placed in a corner while the older people continued to dance. The following evening the effects of the jimsonweed had worn off, and for the next five nights the boys were taught how to dance, sing particular songs, and behave correctly as adults. This ceremony seems to have symbolized the initiates' death as children and their rebirth as knowledgeable adults. The only forms of body mutilation among males were piercing the ears and the nasal septum. The latter operation was not common and was performed only on young boys with promise as leaders. In the opening at the base of the nose pieces of deer bone were inserted.

When members of different clans assembled, especially for the tattooing of a girl or the piercing of a boy's nasal septum, songs known as enemy songs might be sung. Between clans, especially those geographically removed from one another, a rivalry of unknown origins existed. Members of competing clans composed derisive songs in which they incorporated the personal names of individuals in rival clans. These names had been bestowed by a net in secret, and the fact that they were known to the members of other clans was shameful. First one clan performed and then the other, with victory going to the side mentioning the most names of rivals and heaping the greatest abuse or to the clan whose members were physically able to sing longer. Enemy songs were an obvious means for giving vent to aggressive behavior in a socially approved manner. (These were not comparable to the dueling songs sung by two hostile Eskimos in some sectors of the Arctic.) The joking relationship between moiety members served the same purpose in a friendlier atmosphere.

The Desert Cahuilla marriage pattern included not only moiety exogamy but a prohibition against seeking a spouse from known relatives on either side of the family. Since genealogies were not remembered over many generations, one could marry a distant cousin in the opposite moiety. A thirteen-year-old girl was most likely to wed a man of eighteen from a nearby community. The match was arranged by parents, and after the formalities had been settled, the bride was led into the groom's house (patrilocal residence). She sat facing a corner with her back to the assembled relatives of the groom. The groom then sat next to the girl, and the couple was given food as the boy's relatives ate. When the feasting was over, the couple was considered married, and that night the newlyweds were given a single blanket with the theory that if affection did not bring them together the cold desert night would. A girl who was unhappy in the home of her in-laws might return to her mother's home, but if she did this repeatedly, the presents that had been given were returned and the marriage considered dissolved. The groom and his parents had the right to expect the bride to bear an infant within two or three years. Failure to do so might annul the marriage and again mean a return of the wedding presents. A man could, if the woman's parents agreed, receive a younger sister of his wife if the latter died (sororate). It was less common for a woman to marry her deceased husband's brother (levirate). Among these people monogamy was the prevailing form of marriage, and familial relationships appear to have been quite stable.

In the routine of adult life, a woman was the outsider in the extended family household of her husband. The husband and wife were expected to be reserved in the presence of others, and the wife generally was retiring when with her in-laws or around men. Ideally, younger persons were thoughtful and unselfish in their dealings with older persons; these values were instilled in children when they were small. Young boys who hunted or collected the first plant products of the season were expected to take them to the aged (see Figure 5-6). The most respected adults were those men who hunted best and those women who could work most efficiently.

In early times, death brought immediate destruction of a Cahuilla household: on the morning following the death of a person, the body of the deceased and the house in which the death had occurred were burned. In later aboriginal times, however, this pattern was modified. When an individual died, the members of his or her and other clans assembled, bringing presents. The body was washed, dressed, and taken to the clan dance house of the deceased. Here the assembled mourners sang over the body throughout the night. If a man had died, the creation narrative was sung; for a woman, a song about the moon was sung, since it was the moon who had originally instructed women. The body was burned the morning following death, and within a week the person's house and possessions were burned.

Each fall or winter a seven-day Mourning Ceremony was held for clan

Figure 5-6 | Pasqual, a Cahuilla man said to be ninety years old, circa 1890. (Courtesy of the San Bernardino County Museum and A. K. Smiley Public Library, Redlands, CA.)

members who had died during the previous year. This was the most complex Cahuilla ceremony, and an essential feature was a narration of the origin myth, in which Mukat had described the proper death rituals, which had been performed for the first time at his death. The clan net, paha, and others began preparations months in advance for the yearly ceremony. Guests were persons from other clans who were related to the deceased by marriage and those individuals who had brought gifts following the death. Members of each clan arrived on a specific night so that the assembled group was not overwhelming. The first three nights, shamans of the host clan or other clans performed tricks, danced, and attempted to communicate with the spirits of the dead. At one Mourning Ceremony a shaman tied a band about his head and inserted clusters of owl feathers in it. He attached another cluster of owl feathers to a stick about eight inches long that he held in his hand. As he sang and shuffled around the fire, he began trembling violently and then pushed the stick down his throat three times. The third time he brought up a small black object said to have been a lizard. After the "lizard" was removed from his heart, he stopped shaking. A more common performance upon such an occasion was for the shaman to place live coals in his mouth and swallow them (see Figure 5-7).

Throughout the following three nights, different clans sang all night long. Those individuals singing the last night aided the relatives of the deceased in making images of each person who had died and for whom the ceremony

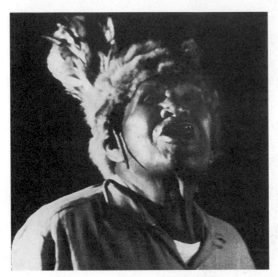

Figure 5-7 | A Cahuilla shaman, Salvador Lopez, with a live coal from a wood fire in his mouth, photographed in 1963, possibly during a Mourning Ceremony. (Courtesy of the Phoebe A. Hearst Museum of Anthropology, University of California at Berkeley.)

was being held. The images, made from reed mats, were nearly life-size and clothed with deerskins. A male image included an eagle-feather headdress and a bow and arrows, while a female image included baskets decorated with eagle feathers. On the final day at sunrise, guests were fed and given presents. Then a procession was formed in which each image was carried by a surviving relative to a spot near the clan dance house. Subsequently, songs were sung and dances performed as mourners wailed. Afterward the images were taken elsewhere and burned; the ceremony ended as each guest received a string of shell beads from the hosts. The souls of the honored dead now were released, their names no longer mentioned, and mourning for them ceased.

In a person's life, evidence for the existence of a soul was thought to be manifest in dreams or when someone fainted; the soul was thought to be wandering. A soul might stray at other times as well, producing an illness that required the intervention of a shaman to return the soul to the person's body. Likewise, the Cahuilla believed that the soul left the body during the months before death. A soul beyond recall was considered to be seeking a place created by Mukat where two mountains joined and separated from one another. Here a deathless guardian questioned and tested a soul seeking entry. Subsequently, a soul passed between the clapping mountains; and those persons who had lived by Mukat's rules survived unharmed, while others were crushed to become bats, butterflies, trees, or rocks.

| Early Historic Changes

Following Spanish entry into the region and the 1862 smallpox epidemic discussed previously, the establishment of reservations in the 1870s was the next major episode in Cahuilla ethnohistory. By then Anglo-Americans had usurped much of the local land for their own purposes, particularly raising cattle. The Cahuilla economy of old underwent profound changes as numerous men worked for white cattle ranchers or became agricultural workers and some women became domestic servants for whites. Social life likewise moved in novel directions. The rule of moiety exogamy declined, and money was substituted for the gifts formerly presented to a bride's family. A girl's family received thirty dollars around 1900, but a generation later a female infant scornfully was termed "a paper," meaning a marriage license that no longer brought a gift. Leadership roles had long been impinged on by outsiders, but tribal leaders did not emerge, although whites appointed chiefs or captains with whom they dealt. As late as the 1920s these leaders were not effective spokesmen for their groups. By 1925 clan ownership of farmland was still the rule, but the amount of arable land was small because water was scarce. Changes in dwelling forms were notable by then, since frame houses had replaced the aboriginal type; a frame house was not burned until three members of a household had died. In the desert, a clan dance house continued to be occupied by a net and his family, but it looked different from the houses of old because the roof now was pitched like that of a shed.

Ceremonial life reflected disintegration and reintegration during the same period. A major shift occurred as unrelated ceremonies were combined with the Mourning Ceremony into a fiesta week. For example, among the Pass Cahuilla in the late 1880s, the Eagle-Killing Ceremony was joined with the Mourning Ceremony; the eagle feathers were used to decorate the images, which were burned two days later. In aboriginal times the people had cremated their dead; under Spanish, Mexican, and Anglo-American influence, they began to bury the dead. Interment sometimes included placing food, clothing, and bedding with the body in the hope that these things would be useful to the spirit if it did not soon find a permanent resting place. Changes in the Mourning Ceremony included dressing the images in manufactured clothing, such as hats and veils. Indian-owned lunch counters sold food and coffee to participants and observers. By 1931 the Mourning Ceremony at Palm Springs had become biennial and was held by alternating clans for the dead of the two previous years. Among the Desert Cahuilla, one of the last nets died in 1958. He had directed local ceremonial life, but when he died, the ceremonial structure, his house, and all of the ceremonial equipment were burned, an end not only to his life but also to the net ceremonials. Today most Cahuilla are Roman Catholic. Funerals continue to be an important rite of passage, however, and at death the personal possessions of an individual are burned as traditional Cahuilla songs are sung.

As the 1990s unfold, land holdings best symbolize the identity of the Cahuilla as a people, as well as their Indianness in general. In a broader cultural context, some Cahuilla, possibly most youth, are largely uninterested in their Indian background. Those elders who have such an interest find it difficult to convey to the younger generation. Most Cahuilla no longer speak their language, their distinctive craft skills have died out, and they have not had a ceremonial house since 1958. The last shaman died in 1984, but one woman had learned the ceremonial songs, and she carries on this part of the old religious tradition to this day.

Palm Springs Cahuilla Land

In the course of Desert Cahuilla history, especially for the Palm Springs group, a dominant theme since the late 1860s has been Indian rights to land. In 1869 the superintendent of Indian affairs for California hoped to set aside lands for Indians before further white encroachment took place. He succeeded in establishing small reservations in San Diego County the following year. Then in 1875 President Ulysses S. Grant authorized the founding of the Agua Caliente (Palm Springs) and Cahuilla reservations. A Mission Indian agency began to function out of San Bernardino in 1879. For the first time slight but realistic efforts were being made to recognize the needs of Indians in southern California. In 1881 Helen Hunt Jackson published a book entitled *A Century of Dishonor*, a scathing indictment of the treatment of American Indians. Because of her crusading interest in Indians, she was retained to report to the commissioner of Indian affairs about the Indians of southern California. She conducted her study with Abbott Kinney, and their report, partly a chronicle of wrongs against Indians and partly a series of recommendations, was submitted in 1883. This study did not make the impact on Indian policy that Jackson felt was essential, and so she decided to write a novel about the plight of these people. As a novel, *Ramona* was highly successful, but it failed to bring about the reforms Jackson advocated (see Figure 5-8).

EARLY LAND DISPUTES   The problem of Palm Springs Indian land rights is complex, and the most critical legal developments must at least be summarized. The modern reservation, created in 1896 under the Mission Indian Relief Act of 1891, set aside thirty-two thousand acres in essentially a checkerboard pattern in and around the town of Palm Springs. The act was based on the Dawes Act of 1887, and the keystone of this act was the allotment of reservation lands to family heads. After twenty-five years an allottee could in theory receive a fee patent to the land and become the legal owner. Allotments were first issued in 1923, and the land per family was limited to 160 acres. Allotments were made irrespective of whether or not the band members agreed with the idea of dividing land into individual parcels. Furthermore, the allotments were *not* of comparable value. In 1927 allotments were made only to Indians who requested them; nearly half of the members made requests.

Figure 5-8 | The Cahuilla woman Ramona Lubo at her home, probably photographed around 1900. Her life was fictionalized in the novel *Ramona* by Helen Hunt Jackson. (Courtesy of the Southwest Museum, Los Angeles, CA, neg. no. 24329.)

These allotments consisted not of 160-acre parcels but of packages of a 5-acre parcel of irrigable land, a 40-acre parcel of dry land, and a 2-acre lot in the town of Palm Springs. The 1927 allotments were not approved by the federal government. Meanwhile, the Indian Reorganization Act of 1934 opposed allotments, and the Indians took legal action in the 1930s to force allotment approval. The Indian legal battle reached the U.S. Supreme Court, and in a subsequent decision in 1946 allotments were declared valid. Some allotments were approved in 1949. The ones that were unapproved involved conflicting claims; finally, however, selections were approved for the entire band.

One of the suits involving allotments resulted in a 1950 court decision that allotted lands should be of *approximately equal value,* since this was the original intent of the law. The allotment values, based on 1949 estimates, ranged from about $17,000 to $165,000, with a total value of lands allotted and pending allotment being about $7.4 million. To equalize the allotments, the BIA proposed that a tribal corporation be created and all tribal assets conveyed to it. A bill in 1957 before Congress in essence would have established a liquidation corporation and ended the tribal identity of the Cahuilla involved. It was rejected by Congress.

In 1959 two new bills were introduced in Congress, and these became law. The major provisions of one of them, the equalization bill, were that (1) allotments would be made to all band members who had not received them, but no future-born members would receive allotments; (2) equalizations would be made on the basis of 1957–58 appraised land values, and the cemeteries, Roman Catholic church, hot springs, and certain canyons were to remain tribal reserves not subject to allotment, but all other lands were to be allotted regardless of prior acreage limitations and in proportion to the highest monetary value of the prior allotments. The second bill provided that reservation lands could be leased for a period not exceeding ninety-nine years except for grazing land, which could be leased for not more than ten years. The 1957–58 allotment appraisals ranged from approximately $75,000 to $630,000, in contrast with the 1949 appraisal range of $17,000 to $165,000. Obviously, the land was rapidly becoming fantastically valuable. Even with the passage of the first bill, it was impossible to equalize the allotments fully. Some 80 percent of the band obtained allotments valued at not less than $335,000; the remaining 20 percent of the allotments had values in excess of $335,000. Most of the land was still in trust status by 1962 and thus was not producing income. However, changes in leasing laws made it likely that over the next ten years individuals would derive considerable profit from it. The first large leasing enterprise was the Palm Springs Spa complex at the hot springs. The spa was completed in 1960 at a cost of $1.8 million, and an adjacent hotel, also on Indian land, was completed in 1963. In 1961 the City of Palm Springs purchased lands allotted to eight Cahuilla adults and twenty-two Cahuilla children for $2,979,000, which was shared by the allottees.

WOMEN'S LEADERSHIP ROLE   The most notable aspect of all the Palm Springs land disputes is the leadership role assumed successfully by women. When the issues were coming to a climax in 1957, the band included only thirty-two adults and sixty-four minors. At that time there were ten adult men and twenty-two women; of the men, two were in the U.S. Navy, two were over seventy years of age, and two were incapable of handling their own affairs. At this point only two courses of action were possible: either the band could trust the BIA and its lawyer to handle its business affairs completely or the women could assume the role of leaders. The Cahuilla decided to pursue the latter alternative. Aboriginal sociopolitical life had set no precedent for female leadership, except that a woman did occasionally hold an office in trust for a son and old women sometimes were very active in clan ceremonies. The net was always a man, and in the early historic period whites appointed Indian men to act as intermediaries and later as reservation leaders. These persons seem to have been clan leaders. In the Cahuilla acculturation process a differential rate of adaptation for women and men appears to have developed. The men continued to follow a "collecting" pattern in their economic activities; they worked only sporadically as grape pickers, ranch hands, wood-cutters, or railroad laborers. In their jobs they interacted most often with other Indians, not whites. Women, by contrast, often worked as domestics in the homes of whites and therefore became much more familiar with the new ways. This was possibly an important reason why women could become the stable core around which the society was reorganized. In 1935 a woman became secretary to the band business committee, and by 1954 an all-woman tribal council had been elected, with Vyola Olinger as chairperson. Mrs. Olinger, who was an active member of the band, was an apt choice, for she was not only intelligent and articulate but also willing to work constructively with the BIA officials. The men had by this time come to distrust virtually all proposals by the bureau. Under the tribal council of women the major land disputes were resolved. In 1961 a young man was elected to the council, and this brought an end to the era of all-female political dominance, but it was the women who had handled the vital issue (see Figure 5-9).

ISSUES IN THE 1960S   By the early 1960s a small group of determined Indians had gained a settlement, and seemingly the avarice of whites had become just another episode in our blemished past; justice had prevailed. Alas, it was not to endure. In 1967, George Ringwald, a reporter for the *Daily Enterprise* of Riverside, California, wrote a series of articles about the administration of Palm Springs Cahuilla lands and funds. He demonstrated beyond any doubt that greedy whites still were taking grossly unfair advantage of Indians. Among the individuals involved in the immoral and often illegal handling of Palm Springs Cahuilla affairs were BIA personnel, a Superior Court judge, a municipal judge, a former mayor of Palm Springs, a Palm Springs real estate broker, and a host of attorneys-at-law. As a result of Ringwald's journalism the BIA was forced to conduct an investigation into the system of court-appointed guardians and conservators. It was demonstrated, for example, that a municipal judge and one attorney had, over a seven-year period, collected $485,000 in fees. From 1956 to 1967, approximately 40 percent of the $10.8 million received by eighty-four estates had gone to conservators, guardians, or their attorneys under the supervision of the Riverside County Superior Court. Congressional action in 1968 put an end to the conservator and guardian management of these valuable lands.

A fair-minded person would hope that Palm Springs Indian problems with the BIA, some local developers, and city officials would have ended by the 1960s, but such was not the case. When Palm Springs incorporated as a city in 1938, its governing body included Indian land as part of the city without consulting the Indian owners. The city passed zoning ordinances and a master plan that included control over Indian land in the city. The Palm Springs Indians in turn formed a zoning commission and prepared their own zoning ordinances that did not agree with those of the city. In 1966 the Indians won a

Figure 5-9 | The all-woman Palm Springs Tribal Council in 1955. From left to right are Eileen Miguel, La Verne Saubel, Gloria Gillette, Elizabeth Monk, and Vyola Olinger. (Courtesy of the Agua Caliente Cultural Museum.)

judgment against the city with reference to zoning procedures, but by 1972 the city had not made the required modifications. The Indians initiated further zoning litigation, in which they accused the city of preventing the development of Indian land and thereby decreasing its value. The issue finally was settled in 1977 when the U.S. Supreme Court decided, in another case, that neither the state nor its political subdivisions could regulate Indian trust lands.

THE MODERN SCENE By the late 1990s major developments built by the band in and near Palm Springs included the Spa Hotel & Casino (see Figure 5-10), the Marquis Hotel, and the Canyon Country Club. The casino payroll in 1997 was $10 million. This enterprise will be relocated to a nearby site in 1998 at an estimated cost of $20 million. In recent years, the Palm Springs Cahuilla and the city have worked together reasonably well on land developments of mutual interest.

To enhance the value of the land owned collectively by band members, the Agua Caliente Development Authority was formed in 1989, a major administrative innovation. BIA managers in Palm Springs play a major role in leasing land belonging to the band. Their office is the only one in the country

Figure 5-10 | The Spa Hotel of the Agua Caliente Band as it appeared in 1997.

funded entirely by the Indians involved. It supervises residential and commercial leases, as well as the development of Indian land, which comprises about ten square miles in scattered plots within Palm Springs—more land than is held by any other single landowner in the city. Yet the Indians remain confronted with a major problem: allotments and their equity. After allotments were made to 131 band members, the available land for allotments was exhausted. As a result, those band members born after 1959 have no land allotments except by inheritance. Their greatest hope for financial gain is to share in the profits from the development of land held by the band collectively. By the 1980s most original allotments had been sold or subdivided among heirs, so that individual plots tended to be small and scattered. Since developers prefer large land units, numerous owners of small adjacent allotments must agree to the joint lease or sale of their holdings. One major project on land belonging to sixteen allottees is the "Eye of the Desert" development on 480 acres east of the city. The project was launched in 1996 and will cost a minimum of $250 million. The complex is to include a hotel, amusement park, restaurants, theaters, Indian nation displays and stores, and numerous other attractions.

The Palm Springs Cahuilla are proud of their cultural heritage, but it understandably has diminished significance in their lives. Only one band member speaks Cahuilla fluently, and the essence of their culture virtually has disappeared. They are at the same time highly protective of the scenic beauty of the palm-lined canyons that they own; in many ways these canyons best symbolize band identity. They also have developed the Agua Caliente Cultural Museum Center as a means to preserve their Cahuilla heritage.

By the late 1990s, there were about 320 enrolled Agua Caliente Band members, most of whom owned allotted lands whose total value was in the billions of dollars. The band understandably is unwilling to release figures about total band assets. At the same time, it must be noted that numerous band members do not have allotments, and therefore the money they receive from the band depends on the collective investments that they share. Thus, not all Palm Springs Cahuilla are wealthy. Some rich band members, however, share their riches with those who are less affluent. They may buy them new cars each year, provide them with money for vacations, and pay their medical expenses. Yet the band collectively has not been helpful in alleviating the depressed living standards of other Cahuilla, some of whom are depressingly poor. In sum, the contemporary Agua Caliente people apparently do not subscribe to a traditional emphasis on generosity within the tribe.

It would be unfair to end on such a negative note. It is more fitting to paraphrase positive statements by an articulate Mountain Cahuilla woman about the Palm Springs Band. She said that she did not resent the wealth of the Agua Caliente people because they struggled for many years to obtain their wealth, and they are fortunate to have so much money. She was glad for them.

| A Note about Clan

The word *clan* was defined in this chapter as a unilineal descent group with a presumed common ancestor, and it will be used in this manner throughout the book. A clan may be traced along either the male line (patriclan) or female line (matriclan); in this book a prefix is used when the rule of descent of a particular people is first identified and thereafter if required for clarity. Originally the word clan was restricted to people who traced descent through females, and the word *gens* was used when these ties were traced through males. The word gens is no longer employed, and clan is now applied to both cases.

George P. Murdock, in *Social Structure* (1949), proposed that clan be more rigidly defined. In his terms a genuine clan has a unilineal rule of descent uniting a core of members; residential unity, meaning that residence and descent are consistent (for example, matrilineal descent and matrilocal residence), and social integration, especially in the acceptance of in-marrying spouses. Murdock proposed that *sib* be used to refer to a unilineal descent group through males (patrisib) or females (matrisib) if the other qualifications for a clan were not met, and there is good precedent for this usage. Following Murdock's definition, the Cahuilla did not have clans, since in-marrying spouses were not integrated into membership; instead they had patrisibs. The differentiation by Murdock has not been widely accepted, however, and in terms of the more standard pre-1949 definition of a clan the Cahuilla had clans.

| Additional Sources

Lowell J. Bean is the most prominent student of Cahuilla life. The best place to begin searching for information about these people is the book by Bean and Lisa J. Bourgeault (1989). The *California* volume (8) of the *Handbook of North American Indians,* William C. Sturtevant, general editor (Washington, DC, 1978) includes a Cahuilla summary by Bean, and the volume provides a wealth of information about other California Indians. Bean's 1972 study is an insightful ethnographic reconstruction with considerable emphasis on worldview and values. Bean and William M. Mason (1962) examine Spanish influences in their presentation of the Romero expedition accounts. For traditional Cahuilla material culture, the monographs by Lucile Hooper (1920) and Alfred L. Kroeber (1908) are the best sources. A pioneering ethnobotany was written by David P. Barrows (1900), and it is supplemented by an article published by Bean and Katherine S. Saubel (1961).

| Selected Bibliography

Barrows, David P. 1900. *The ethno-botany of the Coahuilla Indians of southern California.* Chicago. Reprinted by Malki Museum Press, Banning, CA, 1967.

Bean, Lowell J. 1963. Cahuilla ethnobotanical notes: The aboriginal uses of the mesquite and screwbean. *Archaeological Survey, Annual Report 1962–1963,* Department of Anthropology and Sociology, University of California, Los Angeles, 55–76.

———. 1972. *Mukat's people.* Berkeley.

———. 1991. *Cahuilla landscape.* Menlo Park, CA.

Bean, Lowell J., and Lisa J. Bourgeault. 1989. *The Cahuilla.* New York.

Bean, Lowell J., and William M. Mason. 1962. *Diaries and accounts of the Romero expeditions in Arizona and California.* Los Angeles.

Bean, Lowell J., and Katherine S. Saubel. 1961. Cahuilla ethnobotanical notes: The aboriginal uses of the oak. *Archaeological Survey, Annual Report 1960–1961,* Department of Anthropology and Sociology, University of California, Los Angeles, 237–49.

———. 1972. *Temalpakh: Cahuilla Indian knowledge and usage of plants.* Malki Museum Press, Riverside.

Beattie, George W., and Helen P. Beattie. 1951. *Heritage of the valley.* Oakland.

Ellison, William H. 1922–23. The federal Indian policy in California, 1846–1860. *Mississippi Valley Historical Review* 9:37–67.

Gifford, Edward W. 1922. *California kinship terminologies.* University of California Publications in American Archaeology and Ethnology, vol. 18.

Hooper, Lucile. 1920. *The Cahuilla Indians.* University of California Publications in American Archaeology and Ethnology, vol. 16, no. 6.

Jackson, Helen H. 1881. *A century of dishonor.* New York. (An 1890 edition contains the *Report on the conditions and needs of the Mission Indians of California.*)

———. 1884. *Ramona.* Boston.

James, Harry C. 1960. *The Cahuilla Indians.* Los Angeles.

Kroeber, Alfred L. 1908. *Ethnography of the Cahuilla Indians*. University of California Publications in American Archaeology and Ethnology, vol. 8, no. 2.

Murdock, George P. 1949. *Social structure*. New York.

Ringwald, George. 1967. *Riverside Press-Enterprise* and *Riverside Daily Press* articles.

Rush, Emmy M. 1932. The Indians of the Coachella Valley celebrate. *El Palacio* 32: 1–19.

Shinn, George H. 1941. *Shoshonean days*. Glendale.

Strong, William D. 1929. *Aboriginal society in southern California*. University of California Publications in American Archaeology and Ethnology, vol. 26.

Transmitting report by Subcommittee on Indian Affairs. State of California, Senate Committee on Rules, Resolution No. 8. Sacramento.

Wilson, Benjamin D. 1952. *The Indians of southern California in 1852*. John W. Caughey, ed. San Marino.

6 The Crow: Plains Raiders and Bison Hunters

I wonder how my grandchildren will turn out. . . . They have only me, an old woman, to guide them, and plenty of others to lead them into bad ways. The young do not listen to the old ones now, as they used to when I was young. I worry about this, sometimes.

Observations by Pretty-shield, an elderly woman in the early 1930s. (Linderman 1932, 23)

PLAINS INDIAN LIFE has long captivated Euro-Americans and Europeans, sometimes to the point of indifference to all other Native Americans. The image of warriors astride horses recklessly chasing herds of bison or enemies across the plains conveys a sense of daring and freedom. The Crow typify this lifestyle shared by other Siouans* and Algonquians such as the Blackfoot, Cheyenne, and Gros Ventre. The Crow are presented because any book about American Indians would be incomplete without including a people of the northern Plains. Their lifeway, based on hunting herd animals from horseback, and their emphasis on warfare represent a major regional configuration in North American Indian culture, that of the Plains culture area. The Crow also illustrate the flexibility of some Indians in making ecological adaptations. About seventy-five years before their first contact with whites, the Crow began receiving domestic horses, and they molded their economy around this animal in a remarkably brief period.

| Origin Myth, Population, and Language

The Crow call themselves Apsaalooke (Absaroka), which commonly is translated as "children of the large-beaked bird." The term probably refers to the "raven," however, rather than the "crow." A misinterpretation of this term by early trappers led to the Apsaalooke being called the "Crow." According to the Crow, their origins began with Old Man Coyote. While most of his adventures reflect his trickster character, Old Man Coyote also was the creator of the world. In the Crow origin account, there was first Old Man Coyote, who was traveling alone in a cold, wet world with no place to rest. He asked three species of duck to dive beneath the waters and bring up earth, but each failed. At last he asked a grebe to bring up some earth. The grebe dove deep, was down a long time, and surfaced with a small piece of mud. With this earth, Old Man Coyote was able to travel from east to west to make the land, its mountains and rivers, its animals and plants, and to give them life. The world was still a lonely place. So Old Man Coyote molded from the earth an image he liked and blew a small breath into it. The first man moved. Old Man Coyote still was not satisfied. He tried again and made an image he liked even more. The first woman moved. Now Old Man Coyote was no longer alone. He taught the people how to live and pray. He gave them their language and clans. Finally, with the help of mice, Old Man Coyote showed the people how to do the Sun Dance.

Before Euro-Americans made lasting contact with the Crow, the tribe suffered a series of terrible smallpox epidemics. The early French trader Fran-

---

*The Crow are Siouan in the sense that they are linguistically related to the Sioux, the popular name for the Dakota Indians. The Siouan linguistic family includes the Crow and Dakota plus the Assiniboine, Hidatsa, Mandan, and Omaha.

çois A. Larocque (1910) estimated that they occupied three hundred tepees in 1805, but he reported that two thousand tepees had existed just before the first smallpox epidemic. In 1833 the Crow had eight hundred tepees with an estimated population of sixty-four hundred. By the early 1930s their number had declined to about sixteen hundred, but in 1998 there were about ten thousand Crow. Their language belongs to the Macro–Siouan linguistic phylum and to the Siouan family. Their closest linguistic relatives are the Hidatsa, and in the comparatively recent past the Crow and Hidatsa probably were one people.

| Life before Historic Contact

Varied opinions exist about Crow origins and prehistoric movements. Traditional Crow history, referring to the not-so-distant past, states that they came from a place with many lakes, which is thought by some to have been the Lake Winnipeg area in Manitoba, Canada. They settled briefly in earth lodge communities along the Missouri River as farmers and hunters who came to be called the Hidatsa. Differences between two chiefs led one of them to separate with about five hundred followers; this new group emerged as the Crow. Perhaps the split occurred in the 1700s, since some Crow remained closely identified with the Hidatsa as late as the 1830s. We can assert with reasonable confidence that the Crow began moving south and west about 1700 and began living in their historic homeland about 1750 (see Figure 6-1).

As domestic horses introduced into the New World by Europeans reached the Crow soon after 1730, Crow life began to assume its historic orientation. In aboriginal times they were a hunting people, with dogs to bear packs and pull travois. The Crow were accustomed to a mobile way of life, and the horse vastly increased their movements. A host of Plains tribes raided for horses or exchanged horses for firearms and other imported manufactures. The availability of horses at the eve of direct white contact heralded a virtual cultural revolution. As mobile hunters the Crow had a distinct advantage over sedentary Indians who farmed at earth lodge communities and were stationary targets—for example, the Pawnee, who were semipermanent farmers. With horses, Crow economic and combative activities expanded. They could strike a distant enemy suddenly or travel far to hunt. By the same token, they were subject to raids by other equally wide-ranging equestrian hunters, and these widespread contacts facilitated the rapid spread of deadly new diseases. With horses as pack animals the Crow could transport large quantities of dried meat, accumulate more property than before, and build larger tepees. The aged were no longer a burden; they could be transported easily by horses. With old people living longer, the basis for cultural learning broadened. The horse, as a unit of wealth and an object of prestige, resulted in social distinctions between those who had many horses and others with few animals.

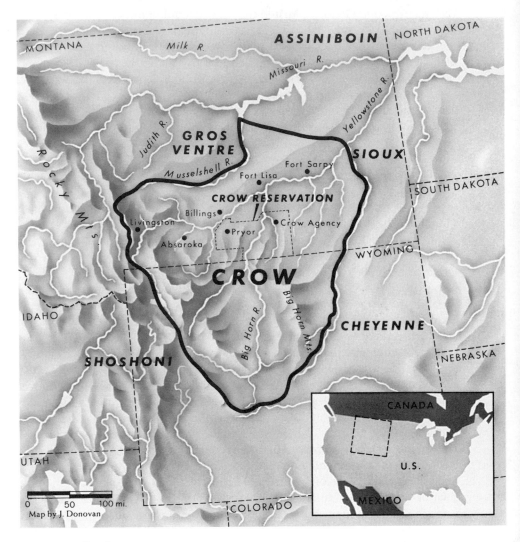

Figure 6-1 | Historic homeland of the Crow Indians.

| Early Contact with Non-Indians

Initial contact with non-Indians apparently took place in the 1740s, and the Crow soon earned a reputation as a clever and deceptive people and shrewd traders. Early in their history they also had the distinction of disdaining alcohol, which they called "white man's fool water." By the early 1800s the heart of Crow country reportedly was in the Big Horn Mountains, and they lived there as a loosely integrated tribe. About 1825, two rival chiefs, Arapooish and Long Hair, had a disagreement, and the people split into two groups. The Mountain Crow, followers of Long Hair, ranged south of the Yellowstone River in southern Montana. The followers of Arapooish, the River Crow, lived farther north, along tributaries of the Missouri River.

In the early decades of the nineteenth century, non-Indian fur traders and trappers (collectively "mountain men") were attracted to Crow country in their quest for beaver pelts. The impact of the fur trade was not great, however, because access to the region was difficult, some Indians were hostile, and the market for beaver pelts was declining. The first fort in Crow country was built in 1807, but it and numerous others of the period failed. The original Fort Sarpy, for example, was abandoned in 1855. It had proved to be very difficult to move goods along the dangerous rivers; in addition, persons stationed there often were the virtual prisoners of surrounding Indians.

One observer reported a terrible smallpox epidemic in the early 1830s, and smallpox struck again in 1837 and in 1848. In 1849 an influenza epidemic was said by one observer to have killed 150 persons; another reporter said 600. In addition, the Crow were greatly outnumbered by their enemies, the Blackfoot and the Sioux.

The United States began to assert control over the region in 1825, sending a government agent up the Missouri River. Long Hair signed a treaty of friendship, but Arapooish refused to sign. Among the treaty conditions was recognition by the Crow that the United States controlled Crow country and had the right to regulate trade and intercourse. The Crow further agreed not to harm white Americans locally or to trade with aliens. Late-nineteenth-century Crow prophecies about white Americans further encouraged the Crow to accommodate Euro-Americans rather than fight them. By and large the Crow were faithful subjects, and the eventual protection provided by the U.S. Army probably saved them from extinction at the hands of the Sioux.

Father Pierre-Jean DeSmet (1905) was the first Christian missionary to seek out the Crow. He visited them in 1840 and in 1842, being well received on both occasions. They were friendly and admired him, but he had no impact on their life-style. After hearing the tenets of Catholicism, one man responded that there were only two Crow men who would not go to hell for killing, stealing, and other non-Christian behavior.

In 1851 the first Treaty of Laramie was negotiated; in it, land in northern Wyoming, southern Montana, and western South Dakota was set aside for the Crow. By agreeing to the conditions of this treaty, the Crow and other tribes involved were granted annuities, while the federal government obtained the right to build forts and roads in the region. The treaty was amended in 1852, limiting the annuities to ten years, but the Crow refused to sign the revision. They gradually abandoned the Big Horn Mountains because of pressure from the Sioux, because game animals were disappearing, and because non-Indians were moving into the area on their way to a gold strike in western Montana. The second Treaty of Laramie in 1868 confined the Crow to a reservation south of the Yellowstone River in southern Montana; they have continued to live on a small portion of this area to the present day.

Early Historic Life

By the time Euro-Americans became familiar with the northern Plains in the early 1800s, the lifeways of local Indians already had begun to change as a result of indirect contact with outsiders. Pressures brought about by other Indians who were forced westward by whites were beginning to build, and the fur trade was making an impact in the region. Most of all, however, domestic horses received earlier from the south had altered Crow cultural ways dramatically. The ethnographic account presented in this section attempts to describe Crow life before the direct impact of white influences became intense.

APPEARANCE AND CLOTHING   To the Crow, a handsome man was tall and had a straight nose and a face free from blemishes or scars. The noble appearance and bearing of Crow men attracted favorable comment from most early travelers. Men greased their long hair and sometimes made it even longer by gluing on additional human or horse hair. One great chief, Long Hair, was inordinately concerned about the length of his hair because his inordinate abilities were attributed to his long hair. Thus he grew it to about ten feet in length. Men plucked their whiskers, and both sexes apparently removed axillary hair. Strings of ornaments hung from the hair on each side of a man's head, and his ears were adorned with abalone-shell earrings cut into angular designs. Men painted their faces red and highlighted their eyelids with yellow paint. Bear-claw and bone-disk necklaces, as well as bone pendants, were popular. Men in general, and young men in particular, were fastidious about their appearance. Men wore hair-trimmed leggings held up by tucking the top ends into a belt. Other items of male clothing included a shirt, moccasins, and a bison robe.

Crow women were not pleasingly portrayed and were often reported as wearing dirty, greasy clothing. When they mourned the loss of a relative, which was often, their hair was cut short, and their faces were spotted with clay and dried blood from self-inflicted wounds. Dresses of deerskins or mountain sheep skins reached from the neck to mid-calf. The most distinctive characteristic of their dresses was that the fronts and backs were decorated with rows of elk teeth; openings on each side of a woman's dress were for nursing an infant. Women wore moccasins and leggings from their thighs to their knees. Young boys went naked until they were about nine and then wore the clothing of men; girls dressed in the manner of women.

SETTLEMENTS   The Crow had no permanent villages but moved from one campsite to the next in search of game. After so many people died from smallpox, most of the tribe camped together for protection against enemies. Camps were dominated by tepees that were framed with about twenty poles, each some twenty-five feet long, set in the form of a cone and covered with bison skins. An opening was left at the top as a smoke hole, and two external poles were attached to flaps at the top of the cover to open or close the smoke

Figure 6-2 | A Crow tepee, after a painting by Catlin. (From Donaldson 1886.)

hole (see Figure 6-2). Before the Crow had horses to haul tepee poles and covers, it appears that their dwellings were much smaller. There was a fireplace at the center of a tepee, and along the sides toward the back were hide mattresses beneath sleeping robes; the seat of honor was at the back and center. Other structures of importance were circular arbors with conical roofs made from boughs and used as sun shades and small dome-shaped sweat lodges where men bathed in a ritual context by pouring water over heated stones.

When a band moved, the caravan might extend for miles. Scouts kept a lookout for enemies, and hunters scattered in search of game. Men wore their best buckskin garments and carried their weapons in case of a sudden attack. Women rode astride horses, as did men, and from the saddle of a wife's horse hung her husband's shield and sword, if he owned one. Small children were tied to saddles, but five-year-olds rode alone. Meat, tools, utensils, and other property were packed in skin containers tied to horses. One horse carried a tepee cover and another dragged the poles. Some horses pulled pairs of tent poles with a frame attached to carry wounded or ill persons; this conveyance, a travois, was in earlier times pulled by dogs. The most important purpose of dogs appears to have been to warn of the approach of enemies or strangers.

USE OF HORSES   Wild horses lived on the North American Plains during the Pleistocene era, but they disappeared about 8000 B.C. or perhaps in more

Figure 6-3 | A Crow woman on horseback. (Courtesy of the Field Museum, Chicago, neg. no. 2784.)

recent times, possibly hunted to extinction by Indians. The domestic horses used by Indians in North and South America all were descendants of those introduced by Europeans in historic times. The Spanish took domestic horses to Mexico in A.D. 1519, and by the end of the century large herds of domestic and feral animals ranged over northern Mexico. Thus, North American Indians did not begin to use domestic horses until the early 1500s. Horses began to filter into the historic Crow area by 1730, and therefore these people had only had access to horses for about seventy-five years before they began to be described in reasonable detail by whites.

Crow men, women, and children always were described as excellent riders who depended on horses so much that their ability to endure long periods of walking had diminished (see Figure 6-3). Their saddles were high in the front and back but were not used for hunts or during war. Most horses could be guided without a bridle. A rider leaned in the direction in which she or he wanted to turn, and the horse turned in that direction until the rider sat upright.

Around 1850 a horse was worth from sixty to one hundred dollars and was the major form of wealth, as well as the standard medium of exchange. In a proper marriage, a groom presented horses to the brothers of the bride. In later times, ten good arrows equaled a horse in value, and a woman skilled at preparing hides for a tepee cover might receive a horse for her labor. Personal conflicts in a camp, which usually involved women, might be settled with horses. If a man eloped with the wife of another, the offended husband took all his rival's horses; in doing so he had not only the support of his clan members but also the backing of most persons in the camp. The offender kept the woman, and his clansmen gave the new husband horses to compensate for his loss, although eventual repayment was expected. The same pattern prevailed if all a man's horses were stolen.

By the mid-1800s the Crow had more horses than any other tribe east of the Rocky Mountains. A poor person owned at least twenty animals, and a middle-aged man had up to sixty. The Crow received horses in trade from the Flathead and Nez Perce, but they more often obtained them during raids. Raids for Crow horses by the Blackfoot and other tribes, especially the Sioux, meant that younger men spent a great deal of time guarding the horses. When an enemy raid was expected, the best horses were tethered at the entrance of their owners' tepees so that riders could pursue horse thieves quickly at any time. Once it was realized that horses had been stolen, Crow warriors gave pursuit, each riding his fastest horse and leading another. They rode day and night, and when the first horse was exhausted they rode the other; when it gave out they might continue on foot. If they caught up with the thieves, they first attempted to recover their horses and then killed and scalped an enemy if it was possible to do so without the threat of losing one of their number.

SUBSISTENCE ACTIVITIES   Part of the Crow habitat in the 1840s was described by Denig (1961, 139) as "perhaps the best game country in the world." He reported immense herds of bison from the Rocky Mountains to the mouth of the Yellowstone River and herds of hundreds of elk along the river, as well as many black-tailed and white-tailed deer. Antelope covered the prairies and badlands near the mountains, while in the mountains were many bighorn sheep and grizzly bears. The truly majestic Rocky Mountains, high valleys, fast-flowing streams and rivers, meadows, hot springs, and great forests characterized this idyllic land.

The Crow economy was based on hunting large game, especially bison, deer, elk, and antelope; in fact, they did not eat fish or berries. Except for the maize that they obtained by trading with the Hidatsa, the most important use of plant products was as seasoning for meat dishes. Cooperative hunts were the norm, and the purpose was to kill or maim herd animals by driving them over cliffs or riverbanks. Alternatively, animals were driven into a valley with a single narrow exit, and a fence was erected after the animals were confined. The planning and coordination required for large-scale hunts was supervised by the members of military sodalities, and hunting rituals were performed to further ensure success.

The bow and arrow was the primary weapon for the hunt or for war. The wood-shafted arrows were tipped with points of bone or stone. Bows were fashioned from bison or mountain sheep horn or elk antler; pieces were cut, smoothed, spliced, glued, bound together, and then backed with sinew (composite, sinew-backed bow). Arrows were carried in skin quivers that were ornamented with porcupine quills.

A woman's life was physically demanding. She supplied the household with firewood and water, cooked the food, cared for children, collected plant products, and made and repaired all the clothing, skin containers, and tepee covers. Women were also responsible for erecting and taking down tepees. A woman groomed her husband, saddled his horse, and took off his leggings and moccasins in the evening. Women usually followed men on bison hunts and skinned the animals killed. One of women's most highly developed skills was working skins. Depending on the skin involved and the purpose served, hides or skins were dehaired, prepared on one or both sides, smoked or not smoked. To break down its texture and make it supple, a skin was spread with a preparation made from bison brains and liver. In addition to processing bison hides for tepee covers and skins for clothing, women made small skin pouches for pipes and sacred objects. The best-known rawhide container, termed a parfleche, was folded, often painted with designs, and used primarily for storing and transporting dried meat or pemmican. Although other American Indians were skilled in basketry, pottery, weaving, and elaborate wood carving, the Crow did not practice these crafts.

For men, camp life was as leisurely as it was busy for women. They made tools and equipment, but these were not time-demanding activities. Some men were part-time specialists in making bows or arrows. The major pursuits of men, hunting and fighting, usually took place at a distance from a campsite.

DESCENT, KINSHIP, AND MARRIAGE   Descent was traced through women (matrilineal system), since each person was identified with the mother's clan (matriclan). Thus an individual was a member of the same clan as his or her mother, mother's sisters and brothers, mother's mother, mother's mother's brothers and sisters, and so on. The thirteen named Crow clans reported for both the Mountain and River Crow included Thick Lodge, Sore-Lip Lodge, Tied-in-a-Knot, and Bad War Honors. Clan members usually were dispersed over a broad area; in other words, Crow clans were not localized.

It appears that by the seventeenth century the Crow lived farther north, and their primary economic focus was on crops raised by women. Presumably the cultivated plots were relatively stable. Daughters learned horticultural skills from their mothers. In this reconstruction, women produced the food staples; when a man married he went to live with his wife. The resulting focus on the female line led to or sustained a matrilineal descent system with matrilocal marriages. However, as the Crow became bison hunters on horseback in the mid-eighteenth century, the emphasis dramatically shifted to men, and the Crow began to be patrilocal. Because whites were fast becoming a dominant force in Crow life, subsequent changes in their descent system and kinship terminology were forced rather than occurring naturally and logically.

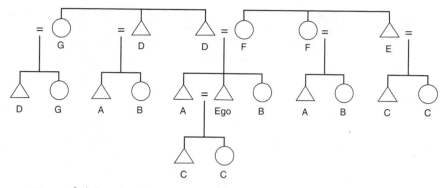

Figure 6-4 | The early historic Crow system of kinship terminology.

Clans were grouped into two, or in one case, three units (phratries) that were not named; one of the two-clan clusters may have been a single clan. It was most common for a spouse to be from another clan (clan exogamy). Yet, the bonds between some paired clans seem to have been so close that members could not marry each other (phratry exogamy).

The kinship terminology employed by the Crow has come to be called the Crow type, and it is shared by other people around the world. The Crow termed father and father's brother alike and used a different word for mother's brother. Likewise, father's sister was termed differently from mother and mother's sister, who were termed alike (bifurcate merging). Furthermore, father's sisters' daughters and their daughters' daughters were termed as father's sister; the term really designated women of the father's clan from his generation downward. The same logic applied when father's sister's husband was termed father, as was his son. The ignoring of generational distinctions in these contexts made clan members equivalents. In a like manner, the term mother was extended to her clan sisters (see Figure 6-4). The most rigid behavioral taboo prohibited a man from talking with or having any contact with his wife's mother or her grandmothers. Likewise, a woman did not interact with her daughter's husband or her daughter's daughter's husband.

SOCIAL DIMENSIONS   The worst possible insult was for one Crow to say to another, "You are without relatives," meaning that the accused had no merit. Supportive relatives protected one from slander, came to one's defense in times of conflict with others, and provided material aid in times of stress. A matriclan was the largest integrated social unit, and one's obligations to it were great. Although members of the same clan do not appear to have camped adjacent to one another, they often ate together.

The bonds within a clan were most severely tested when a person from one clan killed someone from another clan. In these rare instances, the members of the murdered person's clan were obligated to kill either the offender or one of his clansmen. Despite their matrilineal focus, a father had close ties with his sons. When someone asked a special favor, a common phrase was, "By the love you bear your children, I beg you" (Lowie 1935, 18).

"Sodalities" are special-purpose groups in which membership might be either voluntary or required. Among the Crow most men were either Lumpwoods or Foxes. These were military sodalities into which young males were recruited by established members. Each sodality had distinctive adornments, dances, and behavioral characteristics.

In the fall after the first snow, Lumpwood men met and ate in the tepees of one member and then another. The membership was distinguished partially on the basis of age grades, and officers served for one year. The four pairs of officers were called elders, straight-staff bearers, hooked-staff bearers, and rear men. Being offered a pipe and smoking it were symbolic of selection and acceptance of an office. Men often were reluctant to become staff bearers because after a straight shaft was planted in the ground by its bearer during a battle he could not retreat from the spot unless another Lumpwood rode between him and the enemy. After a hooked staff had been placed in the ground, it could not be moved, and the bearer defended it until he was killed. Because of the danger involved, the bearers of these staffs counted a double coup if they struck an enemy.

Sodality members extended mutual aid to fellow members in stressful times; they sometimes fought together, and they honored by excessive mourning a member killed in battle. One Lumpwood behavioral peculiarity was that when a member mourned the loss of certain relatives, the other Lumpwoods had the right to make jokes about the loss to his face. This behavior would have been insulting to anyone else, irrespective of the circumstances.

The Foxes were organized much the same as the Lumpwoods, and competition between the two sodalities was keen. This was most dramatically expressed in the abduction of wives. In the spring either group could initiate the proceedings, and any man was free to abduct the wife of a member in the other fraternity if he had been her lover. Sometimes a woman was kidnapped without cause, and women sometimes hid to avoid abduction. A wife might also successfully plead with a potential abductor and not be taken away. Men who suspected that their wives would be abducted often made a point of being away because they had no desire to see their wives seized. Yet, if a man was present, custom dictated that he should make no effective effort to prevent his wife's capture. These women were paraded about and were received as brides by their abductors' families. A stolen wife could not return to her husband; a man caught sleeping with such a woman was tied up and smeared with feces. This period of license lasted about two weeks, and then the Lumpwoods and Foxes went on the warpath, each attempting to count coup (touch a live enemy) first so that they could ridicule their opposites. After the first snows fell the rivalry abated, only to surge again the next spring.

WARFARE The Plains Indian stereotype is that of a bloodthirsty killer for whom war was by choice a dominant cultural focus. Yet economic factors best account for the intensity of warfare on the plains and prairies. We find that the Crow rarely killed whites, even though they often had ample opportunity and just cause, especially for killing mountain men in their midst. This situation contrasted with the animosity between whites and the members of surrounding tribes. Furthermore, when the Crow were at peace with another people they appear never to have initiated a new conflict. Their primary reason for launching a raid was to avenge the death of a Crow killed by the members of another tribe. Unlike most Plains Indians, the Crow killed men but usually captured women and children; the children were adopted and captive women worked beside Crow wives. An adopted boy who was raised as a Crow did not hesitate to kill men from the tribe of his birth. In rational terms, by not initiating a war and by assimilating captives, the Crow compensated for their relatively small number and their losses in war. They went to war most often for a combination of three purposes: revenge, glory, and horses.

The word translated as "chief" really meant "good, valiant," and to achieve this title a man had to perform four feats: lead a successful raid, capture tethered horses from an enemy camp, be the first to count coup, and take a bow or gun from a live enemy. Warriors who performed each of these deeds at least once were chiefs; but this did not mean that they were political leaders. The greatest living chief in 1910 was Bell-rock; he had led at least eleven war parties, taken at least two tethered horses, counted coup six times, and seized five guns. Such a man boasted of his achievements at public gatherings, depicted his brave deeds on a robe that he wore, and had distinctive adornments on his clothing. To take a scalp was important to the tribe but was not ranked as a major personal achievement, and when a man listed his war honors he did not mention scalps. It should be noted that scalping an enemy was especially widespread in the Northeast culture area (see Chapter 12).

The foremost weapon of war was the bow and arrow, but it soon was replaced by the gun. Spears sometimes were used, but they apparently were not very important (see Figure 6-5). For close combat it was customary to use a war club with a stone head bound at one end of a wooden shaft. The shields men carried had a purpose more supernatural than practical, except in defensive circumstances. These circular pieces of bison hide might have bird skins, feathers, or animal tails hanging from them. Either a shield or its leather case was painted with symbols or scenes revealed to its owner in a vision (see Figure 6-6). Men also went into battle with ornamental sticks used to count coup. These were tied together at intervals with skin strings ornamented with quills.

Ideally, each youthful male longed to achieve personal honor in battle and believed that the greatest glory was achieved by dying young in warfare. Yet every effort was made to prevent the death of a Crow in combat, and a war party was never considered successful if it lost a single member. Those who were fearless in battle were persons convinced of their invincibility on supernatural grounds or who were reckless by nature. Still, the positive value placed on an early death was a recurrent theme in Crow child rearing. Typically, a young man eagerly sought his first opportunity to join a party of

Figure 6-5 | George Catlin (1926, vol. 1, 216) wrote of this painting of a Crow warrior, "I have painted him as he sat for me, balanced on his leaping wild horse with his shield and quiver slung on his back, and his long lance decorated with the eagle's quills, trailed in his right hand." (From Ewers 1965.)

raiders. As a novice he performed menial tasks, such as carrying the meat supply and hauling water. He likewise was the butt of jokes as a part of his informal initiation into the life of warriors.

An attack was organized by a raid planner, who usually achieved his position after having a dream or vision that detailed the tribe to attack and the booty to be gained. An ambitious warrior not blessed with a personal vision could turn to a shaman and succeed by following the shaman's instructions.

Some warriors might doubt an announced leader's abilities and decline to follow him, but recruiting a war party does not appear to have been difficult, especially for previously successful war leaders. Raiders typically set off on foot with a supply of moccasins often carried by dogs. As they approached enemy territory, the scouts were especially watchful. Once an enemy camp was sighted, the war leader performed sacred bundle rituals. For example, the leader of a raiding party might place his sacred bundle on a rock, whistle or sing toward an enemy camp, and then relate how many enemy horses he hoped to obtain. To further ensure success, each participant attached sacred

Figure 6-6 | This is one of the finest Crow shields, and it was famous for its power. It belonged to the chief Arapooish and is said to represent the moon. Attached to the left side of the cover are the head and body of a crane. At the top right is an eagle feather, and below it is a deer's tail. (Courtesy of the National Museum of the American Indian, Smithsonian Institution, neg. no. 29656.)

objects to his body and painted himself in an appropriate manner. One or two warriors were chosen to enter the enemy camp, usually late at night, and to drive off as many horses as possible without being discovered. The party made its escape by riding the remainder of the night, all the next day, and the following night before relaxing. As the warriors approached their home camp, they shot guns into the air and paraded the captured horses. The booty belonged to the raid leader, but he freely gave horses to the participants. These raids often were dangerous ventures. If a horse was not captured for each raider, some warriors were forced to return on foot and risked being overtaken by the pursuing enemy. Raiders sometimes went for days without food and rode so long and hard when attempting to escape that their "buttocks were worn out" (Lowie 1935, 222).

As warriors the Crow were daring and merciless enemies. In open battles, especially if a number of Crow were killed, they slaughtered every man and then tortured the wounded to death. Hands and feet were cut off, eyes gouged out, and intestines exposed to be pierced with sharp sticks. The brains and hearts of the dead were hurled in the faces of the living while the victors scorned their victims. It should be added that in defeat Crow warriors suffered a similar fate.

A newly taken scalp was the focus of a three-day celebration. Warriors carrying their weapons and wearing their finest clothing, their faces painted black, danced in a partial circle to the accompaniment of drums and rattles. The scalp was carried on a pole, and the warrior who had made the kill mounted a horse and was led by a chief in the midst of the dancers. That night young men walked around the camp, and at each chief's tepee they sang songs about his particular accomplishments. During the next day the scalp was tied to the bridle of a horse on which a young man rode while beating a drum and singing. When many scalps were taken in a battle, the celebration was far more elaborate and sometimes included a reenactment of the conflict.

Denig (1961) reported that a Gros Ventre girl was captured by the Crow at about the age of ten and became a great chief. As a child she preferred the activities of boys, and her adopted father encouraged this behavior. She soon was playing with bows and arrows and riding fearlessly. As a youth she was trusted to guard horses. As an adult she always wore women's clothing, and when her adopted father was killed she became the head of his household. Later in a raid against the Blackfoot she killed and scalped one enemy and counted coup over another. She came to be known as Woman Chief after she consistently distinguished herself in other raids. Before long she sat as an equal in the council of chiefs. Woman Chief deplored the idea of doing woman's work and obtained first one woman as a "wife" and then three more. Thus she lived as an honored person for twenty years, until she tested a peace with the Gros Ventre and was killed by them after they discovered her origins.

When a man was killed by an enemy, everyone in the camp mourned as the body rested in state outdoors. The face of the corpse was painted; he was clothed in his best garments and was especially honored by members of his military society. They cried and sang over the body as drums were beat. They pierced their limbs and bodies with arrows or cut themselves with knives. These men also distributed the dead man's property. Relatives took the body to a tree or scaffold for interment and wept. Their period of mourning did not end until a member of the enemy tribe that had killed him was murdered. Thus, it was near relatives who most encouraged warriors to avenge deaths.

POLITICAL LIFE   Control of the day-to-day Crow social unit or band was in the hands of a man who had performed each of the four honored deeds in war and had demonstrated the qualities of a leader. His authority expanded further if he was generous with booty, a shaman of note, and an able narrator of tales. Thus individual achievement, open to nearly all, was the avenue to honor and prestige in a political context. Tacit agreement determined who was to be band chief, and no formal installation ceremony existed. A band chief decided when a campsite was to be abandoned, where to move, and the placement of tepees. Yet he apparently had little control over people, since he neither judged nor punished in a manner often associated with chiefly powers. It appears that as long as the people who camped together enjoyed good fortune, their chief retained his office. When he failed, he was replaced quietly and informally. One of his most important duties was to appoint the members of a particular military society to take charge of the spring bison hunt. At larger camps the chief appointed an outstanding man as a crier; his duty was to ride among the tepees repeatedly making announcements about matters of public interest and making the chief's opinions known about matters of current concern.

Within a camp or band of the Mountain or River Crow, members of the thirteen clans formed the largest political entities. They dealt with each other as equals, and they recognized no superior authority to which they all were responsible. Feuds between clans were the greatest threat, but intermediaries attempted to settle conflicts as quickly as possible before they became emotionally charged and out of hand. Language, culture, and common social norms unified clans. Crow survival was partially contingent on cooperation among clans for the common good. If a segment of a clan separated from the main body, it could muster comparatively few warriors and would be destroyed by enemies. The tranquillity of camp life in tribal tradition was upset the most when an aggressive person with a small number of related followers dominated. This was especially true of a person who was regarded as having powerful supernatural guardians. Such individuals might seize the horses or wives of others, but, as Lowie (1935) pointed out, such a man was a de facto but never a de jure leader.

The members of the military sodality policing a bison hunt could and did severely punish nonconformity. The worst offense was for men to hunt bison alone or in small groups, because this scattered the herds and made it difficult for others to kill bison on the legitimate communal hunts. Likewise, on a group hunt, if a man broke and charged a herd prematurely, he might scatter the animals and ruin the opportunities of others. These nonconformists might be whipped, their weapons destroyed, and the kill seized. The warrior sodality in charge also had the right to prevent raiding parties from setting forth at inopportune times, and they attempted to settle differences between the people in camp peacefully, especially when a feud threatened to erupt between clans. Disagreements between members of different clans may have been reasonably common, but for one Crow to kill another was almost unknown. Any crime, except murder, could be compensated for with an exchange of property.

When the Crow split into two major bands, the River and the Mountain, it was Arapooish (Arapoosh, Sore-belly, Rotten-belly) who led the River Crow. A brief sketch of his life illustrates the qualities of leadership that he possessed. Arapooish was a retiring and even surly person who said little but spoke in an authoritarian manner. As a relatively retiring shaman, he controlled powerful supernatural forces, and he apparently had many wealthy clansmen. He was fearless in battle. Time and again he successfully raided horses from enemies without any loss of Crow life. He saw to it that the Crow always were on the alert for enemies and that raiders who approached were killed. Arapooish was a confident aggressor and able tactician in the large battles that he planned. In a battle against the Cheyenne, more than 1,000 horses were captured, 200 Cheyenne men killed, and 270 women and children captured; the Crow lost 5 men. But Arapooish was a man possessed; when he charged a Blackfoot fortification in 1834 shouting "One last stroke for the Crow Nation" (Denig 1961, 183), he was killed. Arapooish came to be known as *the* Chief.

RELIGION   The basis for Crow supernaturalism centered on personal rapport with a guardian spirit. An unsought spirit aid might reveal itself, but far more often it was gained in a vision quest. All personal glory, power, and wealth ultimately were attributed to valid visions. Thus, religion among the Crow was not a tightly integrated system of beliefs with accompanying dogma. In Crow linguistic expression, a vision or a dream of supernatural portent were the same. A youthful male sought a personal spirit aid as he began to emerge into the world of adults. If he was fully successful, he might never seek another vision in his life. Were he to do so, it might be to cure a sick child or in an extraordinary quest for vengeance.

The Vision Quest   A vision seeker sometimes, perhaps most often, first purified himself by taking a sweat bath. Ideally he then went to a mountaintop, where he abstained from food and water and wailed. Lightly clad and covered only with a robe at night, he slept until the sun began to rise. The seeker next chopped off the final joint of his left forefinger, placed it on a buffalo chip, and held it up as an offering to the rising sun with an accompanying prayer for glory and success in life. As the blood flowed, he fainted and was unconscious until evening. He could not sleep because of the cold of night. Three nights passed; on the fourth one, with sleep coming late because of the cold, a vision came to him.

Alternative ways of obtaining a vision existed. One man might have another cut slits in his chest or back through which one end of a thong was passed, the opposite end being tied to a pole. The aspirant ran around the pole until he tired; he rested, only to run again and again. He might or might not tear the thong free in his quest. Another means to the same end was to pierce the back with two holes and tie a thong from them to a bison skull that was dragged about in the first stage of the search for power.

A supernatural visitant might assume the form of an animal such as a bear or bison, a bird, an insect, or the earth, moon, or stars. A person could be blessed by association with more than one such power, and literally anything might be revered by an individual. The sun was the supernatural to whom a direct appeal was made, but it rarely was the source of power received; thus it was not a god worshipped in the usual sense. The supplicant might be taught a sacred song, learn of a symbol that could be represented graphically, or be instructed to follow certain taboos. A feather, a stone with a strange shape, a braided rope, or a weasel skin, among other forms, symbolized the receiver's power and formed the core of a sacred (medicine) bundle. A bundle and its power could be transferred to a near relative after proper instruction or purchased by a nonrelative; thus the control of supernatural forces could pass from one generation to the next. The degree to which any particular bundle was revered depended directly on the fortunes of its possessors.

Tobacco Ceremonialism   Among the Crow their sacred tobacco, one of the two species known to them and identified by the Crow as "Short Tobacco" (Lowie 1935, 274), had inordinate supernatural power. The Tobacco Society, of which some thirty chapters existed in the 1870s, sought to focus that power. Each had its distinctive rituals, but the general pattern was much the same. The yearly plantings of sacred seeds was thought to be vital to prosperity because society members collectively had the power to influence the natural world, such as to ward off disease and renew the supply of game. Therefore, the survival of the Crow as a people was intimately associated with the plantings.

The role of tobacco planter was hereditary, but a person could purchase the right to be adopted into the society. Before initiation, a novice was instructed in the rites and rituals of the group and then formally presented to it. Typically a married couple was inducted together, and membership normally was for life.

A chapter of the Tobacco Society began its yearly rituals by sowing seeds in the spring. Then they built a huge tepee that could accommodate as many as three hundred people and decorated the interior lavishly. Here the participants ate and danced for three days to the music of bells, drums, rattles, and whistles in a deafening combination. The people then began to move away,

Figure 6-7 | A Crow man in ceremonial costume smoking a pipe. (Courtesy of the Field Museum, Chicago, neg. no. A2790.)

going a short distance each day, indicating their reluctance to leave the sacred plants. To encourage the seeds to germinate, a society member was placed in charge of rainmaking and was given valuable property to sacrifice to the rain clouds. If he was successful, all the gifts became his property, and he gained great fame. If he failed, he blamed the other participants for improper behavior during the rituals. In late August the society members returned to the tobacco plot, harvested the crop, and collected the seeds.

Tobacco was smoked only by men (see Figure 6-7). The most important times for smoking were when making peace with other tribes, during rituals, or by shamans in curing severe illness. Even when tobacco was smoked on less ceremonious occasions, the first puffs were dedicated to the earth, heavens, spirits, and the sun. Each man present took only four puffs and then passed the pipe on to the person on his left because this was the direction in which the sun moved. Furthermore, each man had personal smoking habits. One man would not smoke if a pipe had touched grass, another would not smoke if women were present, and another would insist on emptying his pipe on bison dung. These details were dictated by individual relationships with guardian spirits.

The Sun Dance   The sun as a powerful if remote supernatural was the focal point of the most sacred Crow ceremony. A man pledged that he would hold a Sun Dance in return for obtaining a special vision that revealed how to avenge the killing of a relative. The commitment was so great that an elderly person might have witnessed only about six performances. The person making the pledge was called a whistler, and he sought out a shaman who owned at least one sacred doll. These small wooden or skin-covered figures had painted features, Morning Star designs, and feathers attached to them; they also were used to bring war parties success. A doll served as the vehicle through which the whistler obtained his vision. The shaman and whistler were the central actors in a great ceremony that attracted all the tribe. As the preparations began, the whistler fasted and became haggard in appearance. Bison tongues were collected as special food for each noonday meal during the ceremony. A special kilt was made for the whistler, and after many preliminaries involving incense and smoking, a special lodge was built a few miles away. The whistler, painted with cross-shaped designs symbolizing the Morning Star, blew a whistle and danced slowly toward the lodge while holding a wooden hoop with the doll figure representing the sun attached at the center. He tied the doll to a lodge pole at eye level. At the same time, other men who sought visions had their bodies daubed with white clay and slits cut in their chest or back to receive skewers tied to lines attached to lodge poles. Each man pulled against his skewer until it ripped free. The whistler neither ate nor drank water after entering the lodge; here he gazed at the doll and danced before it as one chief and then another described his deeds of valor and acted out his moments of glory. The whistler, who was not skewered, slept at the lodge, and a sham battle was fought the next day as the whistler danced on. His performances might extend over days until he finally received a vision that he usually did not reveal. At this point the ceremony ended, and the whistler sought out the enemy.

Shamans   Physical disabilities and death usually were attributed to supernatural causes such as ghosts or breaking taboos. One category of health care practitioners depended primarily on secular knowledge. They used plant products, lanced a swollen part of the body, or applied a poultice as ordinary treatments. A particular root that was considered a cure-all was rubbed on sores, placed on an aching tooth, or chewed and swallowed to cure a cold. The botanical pharmacopoeia was extensive and most often appears to have been applied in a secular context. Other curers, more properly shamans, had the ability to treat specific traumas because of revelations they received in visions. They might be able to cure snake or spider bites, wounds, or disease caused by a foreign object in a patient's body. Shamans were adept at sleight of hand; they appeared to transform bark into meat or mud balls into beads in either public or private performances. Competitive exhibits of their skills often were dramatic contests. These were men who had the most powerful guardian spirits, and it was primarily in this respect that shamans stood apart from persons who had less potent spirit aids.

Sorcery sometimes was practiced by ordinary persons to settle grudges against other Crow by supernatural means, but it appears to have been relatively uncommon. One technique was to draw the figure of an antagonist along a riverbank near the water's edge, burn incense, and blow smoke toward the figure. As the water washed the drawing away, the victim was expected to die. Other magical practices supposedly could cause lifelong disabilities in the target person. The only sure safeguard against sorcery was considered to be for the victim to have more powerful supernaturals working in her or his behalf.

LIFE CYCLE   As the time for a birth approached, the husband, other men, and boys were excluded from a tepee, and the woman was aided by a male or female specialist who was well paid. The woman knelt over padding and grasped two sticks. To hasten delivery she might be given potions or her back might be rubbed with a special preparation. The particular aid used depended on the techniques that the birth specialist had learned in a vision or had obtained by purchase from someone else. A woman present at the delivery cut the umbilical cord, and part of it was encased in a container that hung from the cradleboard of a baby girl and later from the back of her dress. The new mother observed food and behavioral taboos for a brief period, but the father's activities were not restricted. Within a few days and without ceremony, a neonate's ears were pierced with a hot awl; the holes were held open with small greased sticks until earrings could be inserted. Offspring were placed in cradleboards and rocked to sleep with lullabies. Water was poured into the nose of a small child who cried often, and such a child soon learned to stop crying when someone said, "Bring the water!"

A few days after a birth an infant was named, but names were neither sex- nor clan-specific. The father asked a noted warrior to select a name based on one of the warrior's personal achievements and gave the warrior a horse in return. Names often were descriptive phrases; for example, a newborn girl might be named Captures-the-Medicine-Pipe or a boy His-Coups-Are-Dangerous. As a name was given, the infant was tossed into the air four times (four was a sacred number among the Crow), each time higher than the last. Women changed their names when someone with a like name died, and men assumed new names to commemorate brave deeds or to improve their fortunes. Nicknames, often based on unusual behavior, might be more commonly used than formal names. For example, a man who took an old dog with him to carry his moccasins on the warpath came to be called Old Dog as a result.

Adults placed few constraints on the behavior of children. Children might interrupt adult conversations at any time and typically were both forward and self-confident. The freedom of boys was especially boundless. Denig (1961, 154) wrote, "The greatest nuisance in creation is Crow children, boys from the ages of 9 to 14 years. These are left to do just as they please. They torment their parents and everyone else, do all kinds of mischief without either correction or reprimand." Boys swam and played water games, hurled sticks at each other with the ends covered with mud or mud and live coals. Individually or in teams they shot at targets with arrows, and the arrows were stakes for the winner. In the winter boys coasted down hills on toboggans made by covering bison rib frames with rawhide. Every youthful male ate part of a raw grizzly bear heart to bring him strength and a clear head in times of trouble. Thus, he could say "I have the heart of a grizzly" in the face of adversity. When meat was plentiful in a camp, boys might cover themselves with mud so that they could not be identified and run into camp where meat was hanging to steal as much as possible before they were chased by old women. The thieves cooked the meat away from camp, and the boy who had stolen the best piece ate the choice parts first. Boys hunted small game, and after a bison hunt they might ride out to kill the calves, bringing home the meat and giving the skins to girls for tepee covers. A pair of boys sometimes became close friends, and the bond could extend into adult life when they fought together and shared the same woman, either as a wife or mistress; these men referred to each other as "Little Father" and were closer than with any other persons.

At about the age of ten, boys and girls began imitating the camp life of adults, an activity called "calfskin tepee." Girls from affluent families had small tepees that they set up at a distance from the camps of their parents. Boys pretended to be their husbands and took food from their families for their "wives." The boys organized themselves in the manner of men, even to the point of kidnapping girls belonging to another group. When the boys killed a coyote or wolf, they returned in triumph with a piece of the pelt as a "scalp," and the girls danced with it in imitation of women dancing with scalps obtained by warriors.

Puberty went unacknowledged for males and females alike, although when a girl or woman menstruated she was prohibited from approaching sacred objects and avoided a wounded man or men preparing for a war party; most persons denied that women were isolated physically during menstruation. Girls appear often to have married before they reached puberty, and while marriage to a person in one's own clan was forbidden (clan exogamy), it also was considered in bad taste, at least in the eyes of some persons, to seek a spouse from the clan of one's father. To marry someone from a father's clan with whom no blood ties could be traced was acceptable although not desirable.

Marital arrangements varied, although the parents of a girl often seem to have had some influence, if only because a daughter was so young when she married. A man might meet a girl while she was alone and propose that they elope, offering her a horse for going off with him. A couple could summarily announce that they were going to live together, or a man might seek the aid of a go-between to make the arrangements. Young men seldom hunted before they married. They slept late and spent most of the day grooming themselves to show off on their horses. They courted girls with flute music and sometimes did not return home until daylight.

The most proper marriage proposal, especially for a woman of virtue, was for a man to offer horses to the girl's brother and meat to her mother; these arrangements produced the most lasting marriages. A man who had offered wealth for his bride had the right to claim her younger sister in marriage (sororal polygyny), and the girls' parents were likely to agree when the first daughter was well cared for. In the early 1800s perhaps half of the men had more than one wife, and apparently a few men had as many as twelve. They did not all live together, and some might simply have been betrothed to him. A woman could marry her deceased husband's brother (levirate), but she would not be forced into the union.

Crow sex life was free and open, especially for men, but women were far from pawns. Men and women alike might have many love affairs and made little or no effort to conceal their feelings and sexual activities; their philandering ways were often noted. When a married woman took offense at the affairs of her husband, she might hold him up to ridicule in songs about his behavior. Men and women alike hurled "a fine variety of beautiful epithets" at each other, according to Denig (1961, 151) and other observers. A woman could leave her husband and take her children as well as her property, including horses, skins, and the tepee, with her; boys not fully dependent on their mother joined their father. Yet, after a couple had separated, irrespective of the reason, they could not live together again without bringing disgrace on them both. As noted previously, during a particular time each year, a Fox or Lumpwood could abduct and marry another man's wife if she previously had slept with him. If he did seize her, the woman could not return to her husband. Divorce was common, except among virtuous women, and could be initiated by either partner. Just as a marriage was without ceremony, so was a divorce. Men were expected to be unfaithful to their wives; in fact, for a man to keep the same wife for many years was considered unmanly and a source of ridicule. Yet some men were jealous of their wives to the point of always taking a favorite wife along on a hunt and strongly resenting it when she committed adultery.

Male transvestites, or berdaches, were reasonably common among the Crow and were not regarded as abnormal but as a third sex. According to Denig (1961), some boys preferred the company of girls in their preadolescence and eventually were dressed as girls by their parents. They then embarked on a lifetime of female activities and might "marry" a man. It also should be noted that there were sacred aspects of being a berdache. For example, in the Sun Dance certain rituals could be performed only by a berdache.

The hand game was a very popular form of entertainment, with garments and beadwork commonly bet on the outcome. To the accompaniment of beating drums and songs, a pair of male or female players participated. One person held an elk tooth or bone gaming piece in one hand and gestured wildly while switching the piece from hand to hand. If the guesser failed to identify the hand that held the piece, he or she lost a tally stick; the person who obtained all the tally sticks, three or ten in number, was the winner. One dice game played by women involved placing six dice that were marked on one side and plain on the opposite face in a wooden bowl and shaking them. The game was scored with tally sticks according to the combination of plain or marked dice facing up. A popular game called shinny (stickball) was played by women in the spring. The object was for the members of two teams to drive a ball to opposite goals by using curve-ended sticks. Another widespread game played by men was hoop-throwing, and they bet on the outcome. The object was to throw a dart through a rolling hoop that might have webbing in the middle. The man whose dart entered the hoop or passed nearest to it won a tally stick.

When someone died, the body was painted, clothed in fine garments, and shrouded in part of a tepee cover. The spirit was told not to turn back, and the body was removed under a side of the tepee to prevent further deaths in the household. Interment was either in the crotch of a tree or a scaffold above four support poles. After the body had decayed, the bones were sometimes removed and placed in a rock crevice. Mourners from the immediate family pulled out their hair or cut it short, slashed themselves with knives, and often cut off finger joints. The practice of removing a finger was so common that scarcely a person had complete hands. However, men usually did not mutilate their thumbs or the fingers used to draw a bow or shoot a gun. The soul of a person was believed to first linger near the corpse, perhaps giving an owl-like cry, but to later go to the camp of the dead. The Crow had little interest in the fate of souls; although they believed that ghosts might return to harm the living, they also considered ghosts to be a source of helpful visions.

The expectation in this matrilineal society was for material property to be passed down along the female line, going to brothers, sisters, and their heirs rather than to a man's sons. But a dying man's request to pass his property to nonclan members was honored. A man could bequeath horses to his wife or sacred objects to an eldest son. Even when bequests were not made along the maternal line, they usually were made to an immediate family member.

| Later Historic Changes

Effective federal control over the Crow began with the second Treaty of Laramie in 1868. This treaty established a clearly defined reservation. The town now called Crow Agency became the administrative center of this community in 1884. From the beginning of the reservation period, the federal goal was to destroy the traditional basis for Crow life. Christian church services were to replace heathen ceremonies, the people were to wear "civilized" clothing and live in log cabins, the men were to become farmers, and the children were forced to attend school (see Figure 6-8).

Figure 6-8 | Crow schoolchildren. From left to right: unknown, unknown, Russell White Bear, Henry Shin Bone, Annie Wesley, Addie Bear-in-the-Middle, Fanny Butterfly, Kitty Deer Nose. (Courtesy of the Montana Historical Society.)

A number of factors contributed to the decline of Crow culture during this time. The most crushing blow was a precipitous drop in the number of bison in the region due to overhunting by whites for pleasure, hides, tongues, and, to a lesser extent, meat. Furthermore, many whites favored the destruction of bison to make way for cattle. By 1883 bison were nearly gone. An immediate result was privation among the Crow. The people became dependent on Indian agents, who controlled food and goods that were assured by treaty and essential for survival. These agents were powerful and often corrupt, and they withheld aid to those Crow who were uncooperative with federal policies. The presence of whiskey traders nearby also contributed to declining living conditions. Within ten years of passage of the Homestead Act of 1862, whites were surging into Montana Territory seeking land. The new settlers resented the magnitude of Crow holdings. Under pressure from the homesteaders, Congress repeatedly reduced the amount of land designated for the Crow. Between 1882 and 1904, the size of the reservation was reduced three times. Congress liberalized lease laws and granted land for railroads and a dam. By 1968 two million acres remained of the eight million that the Crow had once occupied.

After the disappearance of bison in the early 1880s, the Crow faced additional threats and challenges to their way of life. Perhaps the greatest trauma was psychological. With the destruction of bison, a sense that life had lost its meaning dominated the community. Farming was proposed as a new economic base, but the first politically appointed agents usually knew little about either Indians or farming. The monetary rewards offered people to farm went begging, and during the early reservation years only agency employees planted crops. The most appealing work for men was to serve as scouts for the U.S. Army. In time, however, some Indians turned to agriculture, and one of the first to do so was the great chief Plenty Coups. His example encouraged others because he faced the white world in a painfully realistic manner. Indian agents made great efforts to persuade the Crow to abandon their tepees and live in log cabins. Even when houses were built for them, many people preferred to camp in nearby tepees (see Figure 6-9). The cultural geographer John W. Stafford (1972, 132) summarized the prevailing white attitudes in terms of "good" and "bad" Indians. "The idea of a good Indian was nurtured. To the 'good' Indian who cooperated by cutting his hair, sent his children to school, and took up farming were given special monetary rewards, wagons, and cattle. Other 'good' Indians were given jobs in the agency. Leaders who cooperated were flattered with trips to Washington. On the other hand 'bad' Indians were threatened with loss of rations."

The Dawes Act of 1887 attempted to make the Crow and other Indians farmers and to destroy tribal life by treating each family individually. The head of a Crow household was forced to accept a 160-acre land allotment, but most people still did not recognize farming as a legitimate occupation. As soon as they could, many persons leased or sold their allotments to whites. A revised Crow Allotment Act of 1920 increased the size of the Crow holdings to about 1,000 acres per person, of which 320 acres could not be alienated for twenty-five years. Crow who were declared competent could sell their remaining 680

Figure 6-9 | A Crow camp in 1901–02. (Courtesy of the Field Museum, Chicago, neg. no. 2770.)

acres, and many did so as soon as it was legally possible. As a result, white and Indian lands form a checkerboard on the reservation. Over the years, even those Crow who have attempted to keep their land have been faced with one problem above all others: as land has been inherited, the plots have been divided time and again.

| The Background to Modern Life

The hallmark of Crow life in the twentieth century has been their resistance to assimilation. Despite pervasive changes, the essence of Crow culture has remained intact. Their tenacity may be attributed, at least in part, to a pragmatic approach to Euro-Americans that began to emerge in the nineteenth century, as well as to their continuing sense of a separate identity. A prime illustration of this approach dates from 1857, when Plenty Coups, then nine years of age, had a vision that anticipated dramatic changes and provided guidance: learn from the mistakes of others and establish peaceful relations with whites. He foretold that the greatest defense of Crow culture would be achieved through education. By adhering to the Crow lifeway as much as possible while adjusting to Euro-American policies and practices, the Crow pursued and realized the vision of Plenty Coups.

TRADITIONAL CULTURE   Continuity with the past quite possibly is best reflected in the conventions surrounding personal relationships, especially those involving clan and kinship bonds. A unifying principle is conveyed in the Crow term for clan, *ashammaleaxia;* it literally means "as driftwood lodges." In the Yellowstone and Bighorn rivers, an individual piece of driftwood has difficulty surviving a battering by boulders in the current; but a log finds security when it becomes tightly lodged with other pieces of driftwood along a river. So too an individual Crow may have difficulty surviving the river of life with its potential adversaries—once the Blackfoot and Siouans, now discrimination, substance abuse, and unemployment. Yet an individual is nurtured in an extensive web of kinship ties maintained through gift exchanges. It is a system comprising social and spiritual kin and expressed throughout the fiber of Crow culture.

The clan values are conveyed clearly in the oral literature of the Crow. The "buffalo-days" stories, many of which were first recorded by Robert Lowie, are still told with animation and anticipation. The story of Burnt Face is especially illustrative. A badly burned young boy is scarred and ostracized by his playmates. Alone, Burnt Face fasts from food and water for several days in the Big Horn Mountains. While there, he assembles what is known now as the Big Horn Medicine Wheel. Having given of himself, Burnt Face is adopted by the Little People, who remove his scars. Subsequently he returns to his people and becomes a great shaman.

In the social world of the Crow, joking relationships, respect, and mutual aid are critical in the matrilineal clan system. The prereservation clan network first described by Lowie (1912; 1917) remains vital. Of all the kinship relations, that of clan aunt and uncle is predominant. All male and female members of one's father's clan are considered clan aunts and uncles. They are to be respected, like "medicine," and acknowledged through gifts of blankets and food at giveaways held throughout the year. In turn, clan aunts and uncles bestow on each niece and nephew an Indian name that will protect the individual; sing praise songs for their accomplishments; and offer prayers for them before a meal, with a lit cigarette at sunset, or during a sweat bath. The strength of this critical relationship is particularly evident in the giveaways held and praise songs sung during the Crow Fair, which will be discussed shortly.

Clans likewise play a significant role in religious life. To assist a closely related clan member, a person may offer prayers in Christian churches or in the Native American church (peyote religion). A fast may be offered as a sacrifice so that a loved one may be helped. The sweat bath especially is an important setting to offer prayers for spiritual and physical cleansing. Medicine bundles are opened regularly and prayed over for individual and family well-being. Young women and men continue to seek visions in a semitraditional manner.

As recently as the 1970s the Crow language, Apsaalooke, was spoken by about 90 percent of the people. The language continues to be used on a daily basis by many adults at various meetings, family gatherings, and church services. However, a 1989 survey found that only a third of Indian students under the age of ten who lived on or near the reservation spoke Crow. In recent years, efforts to introduce the Crow language in grade schools have been reasonably successful on a limited basis. Mathematical concepts, for example, have been taught in both Crow and English. Although far fewer children than in the recent past are learning to speak Crow at home, nevertheless the language maintains a vitality that comparatively few other tribal languages can match.

The horse remains a focus of cultural identity. Photographs of family members on horseback are often seen on the walls of homes (see Figure 6-10). During the Crow Fair, horses are adorned with the finest beadwork and ridden with pride during the parades. Certainly the horse is no longer economically pivotal, nor is it a clear marker for male prestige. (The last bison hunt was in 1883, and the last coups were counted in 1886 during a Piegan and Siouan raid.) Nonetheless, by 1900 the Crow had approximately forty thousand horses. In 1919 the federal government instituted a livestock reduction policy, and horses were either shot or railed to canneries. By 1921 an estimated one thousand horses remained to the Crow, yet in recent years the number of horses has rebounded considerably.

In 1904 an Indian agent began the Crow Agricultural Fair as a means of encouraging farming. Over the years, the Crow Fair, as it is now called,

Figure 6-10 | Kevin (Crow Boy) Old Horn in 1985.

became primarily a showcase for expressing cultural pride rather than an exhibition of agricultural produce. "Powwow culture" was introduced in the context of these fairs. For six days each August, a host of Crow families and many Indians from Canada and elsewhere in the United States attend the fair in what is known as the "Tipi Capital of the World." Furthermore, the event attracts thousands of Euro-American visitors. The fair includes Indian dances, an all-Indian rodeo, dance-parades, family reunions, and giveaways. The Crow make little effort to sell traditional crafts such as beadwork, yet at the fair lavishly beaded dance costumes are worn by young and old during the dances and parades. As a further indication of the tribal commitment to the fair, the council allocates significant funds for dance and rodeo prizes.

For better or worse, the influence of Euro-Americans and other Indians has changed what it means to be a Crow. As mentioned previously, the Crow language is spoken far less widely now than it was in the recent past. We also understandably find that the technological skills of old have nearly disappeared. The traditional foods that were prevalent not so long ago are now served primarily on special occasions. Likewise, Tobacco Society activities that once were so sacred are on the verge of extinction. Concurrently, however, arranged marriages still occur, and some small children are fluent speakers of Crow. Without a doubt a detailed study of customary Crow life, especially in isolated sectors of the reservation, would reveal that many of their past ways retain considerable vitality.

Figure 6-11 | A Crow Sun Dance Lodge in the summer of 1994. (Photo by Rodney Frey.)

SUN DANCES   The last traditional Sun Dance was held in 1875. By the 1940s, however, it had regained prominence (see Figure 6-11). Fred Voget (1984) has documented the introduction of the Wind River Shoshoni Sun Dance to the Crow. Key to the revitalization were the efforts and dedication of several persons, especially William Big Day (1891–1967). Disillusioned with the Roman Catholic church, Big Day traveled to Wyoming in 1938 and witnessed the Wind River Shoshoni Sun Dance. Subsequently at one of these dances Big Day reportedly was cured of chest pains by John Trehero (1883–1985), a medicine man of Shoshoni and Mexican ancestry who sponsored the event. Big Day pledged to hold a Sun Dance if his adopted son, Heywood, survived a desperate illness. The boy recovered, and with the help of Trehero, Big Day organized a Sun Dance on the Crow Reservation during the summer of 1941. In 1943 another Crow held the dance to help ensure the safe return of his sons fighting overseas during World War II; others held similar dances. In 1991 Heywood Big Day held a Fiftieth Anniversary Sun Dance in honor of his father.

Trehero further aided the Crow with the Sun Dance by giving them his medicine bundles, songs, and the right to hold the dance. Thomas Yellowtail (1903–1993) played a major role in reestablishing the dance, as did his brother Robert Yellowtail (1887–1988). The latter, as tribal chairman and BIA superintendent for the reservation, gave official sanction to the new Sun Dance (Yellowtail 1991). Notably, in 1993 descendants of Trehero sought and received

Crow help in revitalizing the dance among the Wind River Shoshoni. What the Shoshoni had helped bring to the Crow, the Crow were able to return to the Shoshoni.

The Shoshoni–Crow Sun Dance has become fully integrated into Crow religious life and is now identified simply as the Crow Sun Dance. It has emerged as a cornerstone for Crow spiritual expression, as from 40 to 120 men and women dancers participate in three or four Sun Dances each summer. Dances typically last three days, and participants offer collective morning prayers for the welfare of all peoples and other prayers especially for family members. In addition, the ill are treated by medicine men, and individual dancers may receive visions.

POPULATION AND ECONOMY The Crow population reached an all-time low of 1625 in the early 1930s, but improved health care has helped to reverse this trend. In 1969 the reservation population had increased to some 3500, and by the late 1990s their number on and near the reservation was about 10,000. Over 80 percent of the Crow live on the reservation. Contrasting with population trends, for many years the reservation land base was in continual decline. By 1961 a large portion of the two-million-acre reservation was owned by Euro-Americans, and much of the remaining land had little water for farming or for grazing. The federal government then began to prohibit the sale of reservation land to outsiders; between 1961 and 1968 the tribe bought back about fifty-five thousand acres that previously had been purchased by whites.

The leasing of reservation land to whites for farming or grazing became both a significant source of income and a horrendous problem. The first land lease was to the U.S. Army in 1882 for grazing cattle. To expand food production during World War I, thousands of acres were leased to whites for raising wheat. The Crow Allotment Act of 1920 permitted "competent" Indians to lease or sell their land. Those who leased land often were persuaded by whites to sign leases at low rates. Because the Crow usually did not have the resources to raise stock or to farm on a large scale, lease arrangements appealed to them. About 90 percent of land allotments had been leased to whites for farming or grazing cattle by 1962.

The Crow were fully aware that leases profited whites at their expense but could do little about the situation. To give an example, a white might own land along a stream, whereas a Crow might own the adjacent land without water. The Indian's holdings are of little value without access to water, but for a white who has water, leasing the Indian land at a low rate would be highly profitable. The same applied to small, scattered parcels of Indian-owned land. Such parcels could not be used effectively by the Indians and were again leased by whites at low rates. Leases as a major source of income became the established pattern.

The allotment process was a gross intrusion on the integrity of the Crow tribe—as it was meant to be—but the problems created for later generations were overwhelming. A basic problem was the failure of the federal government to make reasonable allowances for birth, death, and population growth rates. No land was set aside for future generations as was the pattern in some Canadian treaties. An extreme case will illustrate the problem. One 160-acre allotment made in 1887 had passed to 245 heirs before 1967, at which time it was consolidated into 86 claims. Of these claims, the largest was for about 11 acres, and the smallest was for 0.0014 acre! The land was not divided physically, but all the heirs held an interest and shared any income derived from it. Most land with multiple owners was leased by the BIA, and the annual payments were made to the heirs. At a rent rate of fifty cents per acre, the yearly profit for the person owning the 0.0014 acre previously mentioned would be less than one cent. The same conditions held for leasing both dry farmland and small parcels of irrigated land.

The leasing arrangements finally became an administrative and financial burden for the BIA and an absurdity for the Crow. Federal legislation beginning in 1983 eventually led to the consolidation of fractionated leases. The end result was that when more than five Crow owned a lease, it was consolidated; if the owners could not agree on the terms, the land reverted to the tribe. These arrangements seem reasonable and should resolve a long-standing problem.

The reservation now includes somewhat more than two million acres, and most of the land is held in trust by the federal government. The acreage leased to whites for farming or grazing has declined to about 35 percent of the total. It is particularly important that the tribe has the first right of purchase when land that once had been a part of the reservation comes up for sale. In 1996, for example, some 62,000 acres were added to the reservation in this manner; but at the same time about 1000 acres of fee patent land owned by individual Crow were sold to outsiders.

By the late 1990s local job opportunities were few, and the unemployment rate on the reservation ranged from about 70 to 80 percent. The major employer was the tribe, with about 600 permanent and temporary employees. The Indian Health Service hospital employed about 250 people, and the BIA had some 120 employees. Furthermore, the Crow casino employed about 65 people, the Little Big Horn College employed 30, and local businesses had hired a comparatively small number of additional persons. In each instance, most of the workers were Crow. It might appear that there were many jobs on the reservation, but such was not the case; nearly half of the Crow had a living standard beneath the national poverty level.

GOVERNMENT   Electing *not* to adopt most of the specific provisions of the Indian Reorganization Act of 1934, the Crow wrote their own constitution in 1948 and amended it in 1961. It established a somewhat distinctive general-council government in which every adult member of the tribe is a council member and entitled to vote at the council meetings. In turn, the council elects four officers: a chair, vice-chair, secretary, and vice-secretary, who each serve two-year terms. The council also established various governing committees that are responsible for specific activities such as education, housing, industrial development, land purchases, and tribal enrollment. Council meetings are usually held quarterly and deal with issues of tribal concern. Along with the tribal court, the council governs the internal affairs of the tribe not under the jurisdiction of the BIA.

During the twentieth century, the Crow have had great leadership, as exemplified by Plenty Coups, Pretty Eagle, Joseph Medicine Crow, Robert Yellowtail, Angela Russell (a State Senator), and Bill Yellowtail (a nephew of Robert Yellowtail, a former State Senator, and later a Regional Director of the Environmental Protection Agency). Each in his or her own way has sought to preserve the tribe's cultural and natural resources in order to secure economic self-sufficiency.

With respect to tribal politics, the sale of reservation land to the federal government for Yellowtail Dam construction in the 1950s produced a deep division within the tribe between those who opposed and those who favored the dam. Their differences were based largely on family ties and Christian-church membership. This conflict introduced political factionalism that continues into the present. However, the administration of the tribal chairwoman, Clara Nomee, who began her fourth two-year term in 1996, has produced greater internal stability than has existed for many years. At the same time, differences within the tribe remain divisive.

RECENT DEVELOPMENTS   The nationwide debate about the size, spending, and intrusive nature of the federal government is having a major impact on reservation life (see also Chapter 2). For the Crow it has led to a reduction in BIA programs and funding. Because the BIA has long been considered a bloated and ineffective bureaucracy, it has been a prime target for reorganization and retrenchment. The ultimate fate of the bureau is uncertain, but it appears that far greater autonomy at the tribal level will result. It seems likely that most, perhaps all, of the bureau's functions will be assumed by the tribes. Concurrently in the late 1990s the Crow and some other tribes have been *supplementing* the BIA appropriation with tribal money.

For about forty years the Crow have fought vigorously for their legal rights. A major land claim settlement was made in 1961, when $9.2 million was awarded to the tribe. They also received $2 million for land sold to the federal government for the construction of the Yellowtail Dam and Reservoir, completed in 1965.

Furthermore, the Crow have launched innovative means of funding reservation enterprises. A prime example resulted from the energy shortage of the 1970s. The Crow Reservation lands contained millions of tons of low-sulfur coal. In 1977 the State of Montana enacted a severance tax on coal-mining operations. A complex legal issue arose with the mining company, Westmoreland Resources, over whether the state or the Crow had the legal right to the coal severance tax. After years of litigation, approximately $30 million in protested tax money that had been held in an escrow account for coal severance taxes since 1982 was finally awarded to the Crow. Litigation is pending over the Crow's claim to earlier coal severance funds and the accumulated interest on this money. If the Crow prevail, they may receive as much as $400 million. Since 1988 Westmoreland has been paying a portion of the severance tax to the Crow. By the late 1990s the tribe was receiving about $2.5 million a year from this source.

Further Crow efforts have also expanded community income appreciably. In 1993 the tribe began to tax railroad and utility property on the reservation at 3 percent of the market value; this tax has generated about $1 million each year. Then in 1995 the tribe imposed a 4 percent tax on gross sales of some 60 tourist-related businesses on the reservation, such as campgrounds, guest ranches, fishing lodges, and motels. This resort tax should produce about $500,000 a year. Numerous businesses have challenged the validity of the tax and refused payment; yet the tax appears to be valid, and overdue receipts will be collected. The ability of the tribe to collect taxes is a *critical factor* in the recognition of Indian sovereignty over reservation land.

Another major development has been the resolution of the "107th meridian" problem. This problem stemmed from an inaccurate survey of the eastern boundary of the reservation, which deprived the Crow of about 45,000 acres of land. The problem was resolved in 1996 when the federal government established an $85 million trust fund for the land the Crow had not received. The tribe will initially receive over 5000 acres of land in a complex land exchange involving the federal and state governments. The Crow also are in the process of developing a coal mine in the southeastern corner of the reservation. As a result of the 107th-meridian settlement, the Crow plan to issue bonds based on interest from the trust to fund numerous projects, including a commercial bank, community center, nursing home, and family housing.

The relative isolation of the reservation made it difficult for most young people to obtain a post–high school education. To help remedy this situation, the tribe chartered Little Big Horn College as a community college in 1980; major funding was provided by a congressional act of 1978 intended to support Indian institutions. By 1996 there were about 250 full-time students, virtually all of whom were Crow (see Figure 6-12). About 30 individuals earn Associate of Arts degrees each year. Requirements for graduation included courses on the Crow language and Crow studies. The college president was a Crow, Janine Pease-Pretty on Top, who was the recipient of a MacArthur Foundation grant in 1994.

For tourists, a major attraction in the area is the Little Bighorn Battlefield National Monument (known as the Custer Battlefield until 1991), which is adjacent to Crow Agency. The battlefield typically attracts about 400,000 visitors a year and provides significant income locally from tourist dollars. To attract visitors to the reservation, the Crow opened the Little Big Horn Casino in 1994. It has poker and keno machines, but, since these forms of gambling are widespread in Montana, the profits for the Crow have not been great.

Figure 6-12 | India Hill was a Crow student in general studies at Little Big Horn College in 1996. American Indian history was her major interest.

In recent years, the Crow finally have gained political power in Big Horn County, Montana. This development is partially a result of a county redistricting of voting areas that had previously favored Euro-American voters. As a result of the change, two of the three county commissioners were Crow. In many ways the Indian majority is more symbolic than anything else, but it does have practical aspects. For instance, county roads to Indian households are now more likely to be comparable to the roads that lead to the farms and ranches of whites.

Crow initiative and enterprise unquestionably have bettered economic conditions on the reservation, and more substantial positive changes appear to be in the offing. But, as previously mentioned, it must be remembered that about half of the Crow live below the national poverty level. There also continues to be widespread substance abuse, high unemployment, and ongoing tribal factionalism. Furthermore, the general anti-Indian attitude of state officials and discrimination and prejudice by most local whites against Indians are constant factors in Crow life. One may reasonably ask: Why do so many Crow continue to live in the area? An anthropologist familiar with the modern Crow, Tim McCleary, responded to this question by saying, "The Crows like each other and they consider poverty [as] not having relatives nearby." Thus the concept of driftwood lodging in a river of adversity persists, and cultural revitalization may arise as the Crow enter the twenty-first century. The Crow are anything but a vanishing people. As Tom Yellowtail foretold in 1993, "great stories will come."

| Additional Sources

The ethnography by Robert H. Lowie (1935, 1956) is the standard Crow source, and the ethnohistorical study by Frederick Hoxie (1989) is outstanding. The *Plains* volume (13) of the *Handbook of North American Indians,* William C. Sturtevant, general editor (Washington, DC, forthcoming) provides an overview of Crow life and includes a wealth of information about the Plains Indians. Reliable early historic accounts by fur traders are by Edwin T. Denig (1961) and Zenas Leonard (1959). Outstanding historical discussions of the Crow include a book by Charles Bradley (1991) and a monograph by C. Adrian Heidenreich (1971). Joseph Medicine Crow was the first Crow to graduate from college, and he is the tribal historian. In a 1992 study, he combines oral traditions and written records to present an insider view of Crow life. The Shoshoni–Crow Sun Dance presentation by Fred Voget (1984) includes excellent biographical sketches of the key individuals involved. Thomas Yellowtail (1991) writes about his life, with particular emphasis on the Sun Dance. A primary contemporary researcher among the Crow is Rodney Frey (1987); in this important work he emphasizes worldview in modern life. Dale D. Old Horn and Timothy P. McCleary (1995) present a brief and notable account of social life, past and present.

The massacre of Lieutenant-Colonel George Custer and his command at Little Big Horn in 1876 is of some interest in Crow history because Custer's scouts were Crow. A great deal has been written about the Battle of Little Big Horn; the events leading up to the massacre are well described in the journal of Lieutenant James H. Bradley, edited by Edgar I. Stewart as *The March of the Montana Column* (Norman, OK, 1961).

| Selected Bibliography

Bonner, Thomas D. 1972. *The life and adventures of James P. Beckwourth*. Lincoln, NE.

Bradley, Charles. 1991. *The handsome people: A history of the Crow Indians and the whites*. Billings, MT.

Catlin, George. 1841. *North American Indians*. 2 vols. London. (Later editions in 1880, 1903, 1913, and 1926.)

Crummett, Michael. 1993. *Sun Dance: The 50th anniversary Crow Indian Sun Dance*. Helena, MT.

Denig, Edwin T. 1961. *Five Indian tribes of the upper Missouri*. John C. Ewers, ed. Norman, OK.

DeSmet, Pierre-Jean. 1905. *Life, letters and travels of Father Pierre-Jean DeSmet, S. J., 1801–1873*, vol. 1. Hiram M. Chittenden and Alfred T. Richardson, eds. New York.

Donaldson, Thomas. 1886. The George Catlin Indian Gallery in the U.S. National Museum. *Annual Report of the Board of Regents of the Smithsonian Institution, 1885*, pt. 2 appendix.

Ewers, John C. 1965. The emergence of the Plains Indian as the symbol of the North American Indian. *Smithsonian Report for 1964,* 531–44.

Frey, Rodney. 1987. *The world of the Crow Indians: As driftwood lodges.* Norman, OK.

——. 1995. *Stories that make the world: Oral literature of the Indian peoples of the inland northwest as told by Lawrence Aripa, Tom Yellowtail, and other Elders.* Norman, OK.

Heidenreich, C. Adrian. 1971. *Ethno-documentary of the Crow Indians of Montana, 1824–1862.* PhD dissertation, University of Oregon.

Hoxie, Frederick. 1989. *The Crow.* New York.

Larocque, François A. 1910. *Journal of Larocque.* Publications of the Canadian Archives, no. 3, L. J. Burpee, ed.

Leonard, Zenas. 1959. *Adventures of Zenas Leonard, fur trader.* John C. Ewers, ed. Norman, OK.

Linderman, Frank B. 1930. *Plenty-Coups.* London.

——. 1932a. *Pretty-Shield: Medicine woman of the Crows.* Lincoln, NE.

——. 1932b. *Red Mother.* New York.

Lowie, Robert H. 1912. *Social life of the Crow Indians.* Anthropological Papers of the American Museum of Natural History (APAMNH), vol. 9, pt. 2. New York.

——. 1917. *Notes on the social organization and customs of the Mandan, Hidatsa, and Crow Indians.* APAMNH, vol. 21, pt. 1. New York.

——. 1918. *Myths and traditions of the Crow Indians.* APAMNH, vol. 25, pt. 1. New York.

——. 1919. *The Tobacco Society of the Crow Indians.* APAMNH, vol. 21, pt. 2. New York.

——. 1922a. *The religion of the Crow Indians.* APAMNH, vol. 25, pt. 2. New York.

——. 1922b. *The material culture of the Crow Indians.* APAMNH, vol. 21, pt. 3. New York.

——. 1922c. *Crow Indian art.* APAMNH, vol. 21, pt. 4. New York.

——. 1924. *Minor ceremonies of the Crow Indians.* APAMNH, vol. 21, pt. 5. New York.

——. 1935. *The Crow Indians.* New York. (Revised, 1956.)

Maximilian, Alexander P. 1906. *Travels in the interior of North America.* In *Early western travels, 1748–1846.* Reuben G. Thwaites, ed., vols. 22–24. Cleveland.

Medicine Crow, Joseph. 1992. *From the heart of the Crow country: The Crow Indians' own stories.* New York.

Nabokov, Peter. 1967. *Two-Leggings: The making of a Crow warrior.* New York.

Old Horn, Dale D., and Timothy P. McCleary. 1995. *Apsaalooke social and family structure.* Crow Agency, Montana.

Russell, Osborne. 1955. *Journal of a trapper.* Aubrey L. Haines, ed. Portland.

Stafford, John W. 1972. *Crow culture change.* PhD dissertation, Michigan State University.

Stewart, Omar. 1987. *The peyote religion: A history.* Norman, OK.

Thwaites, Reuben G., ed. 1905. *Original journals of the Lewis and Clark Expedition, 1804–1806,* vol. 5. New York.

Voget, Fred. 1984. *The Shoshoni–Crow Sun Dance.* Norman, OK.

Wildschut, William. 1960. *Crow Indian medicine bundles.* Contributions from the Museum of the American Indian, Heye Foundation, vol. 17.

Yellowtail, Thomas. 1991. *Yellowtail: Crow medicine man and Sun Dance chief: An autobiography as told to Michael Oren Fitzgerald.* Norman, OK.

7 The Yurok: Salmon Fishers of California

*To make deer-hunting medicine, first you learn
to see the bush that's in front of you, then the
bush behind that bush, then the deer behind the
bush behind the bush that's in front of you, then
the spirit of that deer. Now you can call the deer,
his spirit, and he'll walk up to you. The people
with the strongest medicine learn to fly out,
their spirits, and find the deer that way. A well-
educated person learns to see two sides to everything while at the same time seeing the whole.*

(Buckley 1979, 37)

THE CULTURE OF Northwest Coast Indians is best known for massive totem poles and giveaway feasts, or potlatches; yet behind the commonalities lies a great deal of local variability. Indians along the Northwest Coast had far more abundant and dependable sources of food than did other hunting, fishing, and collecting peoples north of Mexico. Salmon were the key to plenitude, but other species of fish and land and sea mammals were important elements in their diet. The Eskimos described in Chapter 4 lived near the northern limit of Pacific salmon and depended largely on salmon for food. Because of numerous constraints, they did not develop a highly complex life-style. The Yurok, who approached the southern limit of salmon in northwestern California, represent an amalgamation of Northwest Coast Indian emphasis on wealth and prestige and a simpler material culture more typical of northern California Indians and those of the adjacent Plateau culture area. The comparatively unelaborate nature of Yurok technology and their complex social conventions make them worthy of particular attention.

The Yurok's emphasis on aristocratic social standing and wealth is a fascinating aspect of their culture. As Arnold R. Pilling (1978, 141) pointed out, there were notable parallels between aboriginal Yurok aristocrats and those of Europe in the recent past. The elite of both cultures owned heirlooms as treasures, and they lived in named houses located on high ground. Both had special manners when eating, a richness of vocabulary in their speech, and pride in an ability to speak another language. Aristocrats were ceremonial hosts, and religious specialists were selected from among their number. These and other similarities provide an example of parallel social developments between cultures that were otherwise quite different. In this general context, it should be noted that ethnographers usually worked among Yurok aristocrats who lived along the Klamath River. Thus a bias exists in accounts about them that tends to exclude ordinary people.

| People, Population, and Language

The name Yurok means "downstream" in the language of the Karok, their neighbors to the interior. The aboriginal Yurok may have numbered about three thousand persons who lived on some seven hundred square miles of land dominated by Douglas fir and redwood forests. By 1910 approximately seven hundred Yurok remained, and their land base had been reduced drastically. By 1996 their numbers had risen to somewhat more than three thousand; they now are said to be the most populous indigenous Indian group in modern California. Most contemporary Yurok do not live on their traditional lands, and may have been marrying outsiders for generations.

In early historic times most Yurok lived along the Klamath River, although some coastal villages were relatively populous (see Figure 7-1). Their language is most closely related to that of the Wiyot to the south. The Yurok and Wiyot are members of the Macro-Algonquian linguistic phylum, but they are far removed from their linguistic relatives in the eastern United States, such as the Mesquakie.

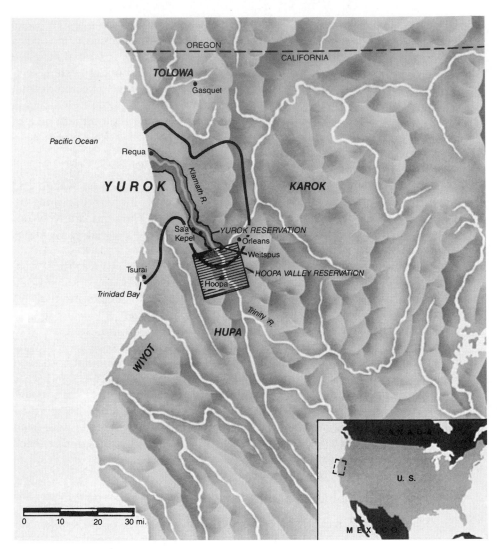

Figure 7-1 | Aboriginal range of the Yurok Indians.

| First Contact with Outsiders

The Portuguese explorer Sebastian Cermeno probably discovered Trinidad Bay in 1595. The area was revisited by Spanish explorers in 1775 and by the English navigator George Vancouver in 1793. From 1800 to 1817 the Yurok were involved in the fur trade. Between 1818 and 1848, they apparently had little contact with Euro-Americans, but in 1849 the mining of placer gold on the Trinity River made Trinidad Bay the most important transshipment point for goods and equipment destined for the mines. The Yurok as a whole had little contact with outsiders prior to 1849, but from that time forward exotic influences expanded greatly, both in scope and intensity.

| Aboriginal Life

For the aboriginal Yurok, the center of the world was near the Klamath and Trinity river junction, and from there the earth was thought to extend in a seventy-five mile radius. Surrounding this mountain and forest country was supposedly an ocean of water and then a sea of pitch. Westward beyond the water lived a culture hero, the Widower across the Ocean, and north of his home lived the salmon, then dentalium shells, and finally another supernatural to the northwest. At the edge of the land to the south was the country of geese; on their migration north the geese were believed to fly through a hole in the sky and disappear. Thus was the world conceived by these stay-at-home Indians.

ORIGIN MYTH According to the Yurok origin myth, the Widower across the Ocean made soil that he kept in a deerskin container, and by spilling it he created the firm earth of the world. Since he could not see his creation, he caused the sun to give light in the daytime and made the moon to give light at night. The earth was without life, and to replace the desolation he created the varied landscape, with streams flowing to rivers, and these emptying into the ocean. He made the forest and the animals. The first animal he created was a white deer, and then a red eagle to command the skies. After creating other animals and plants the Widower formed the first real man of soil and then created a woman to keep him company. This couple wandered from their home in the north and finally came to settle in the Klamath River valley.

GEOGRAPHIC CONCEPTS The Yurok view of the world was exact: the land was a flat, circular expanse that rested on water and was surrounded by it. As breakers rolled in from the sea, people observed the gentle rise and fall of the land. Instead of designating regions, the Yurok concentrated on naming particular localities or spots on the landscape. Thus they did not name the Klamath River but conceived of it in terms of particular locations along it or on adjacent streams. According to the Yurok, to traverse their country in a canoe along the Klamath River, a distance of approximately 150 miles, required twelve days. As would be expected, the Yurok were not great travelers; they had contact with their neighbors but apparently did not journey deep into the territory of other peoples. Not only did they refuse to go abroad, but they regarded strangers as a threat, thinking that normal people stayed close to home with relatives and friends.

Directions were not conceived as cardinal points on a compass but in terms of water flow: there was an upstream and there was a downstream, and it did not matter to the Yurok if a river meandered in different directions.

Calculating direction in terms of water flow was applied to the coast also, north being regarded as downstream. People usually traveled by boat, but they also maintained a well-developed system of trails. As Thomas M. Gates (1995, 393–423) has noted in his detailed analysis, trails served many customary functions. Trails provided access to settlements and a means to carry out subsistence activities or to trade and were used as paths to ceremonial events. Furthermore, trails were "like people" and had designated rest stops; to pause at a spot that was not a traditional resting place invited ill fortune.

APPEARANCE AND CLOTHING Yurok women wore basketry hats over their hair, which they braided and adorned with flowers. They pierced their ears for ornaments and had necklaces of bone, shell, or small pieces of fruit. A young girl was tattooed with three parallel bands from the lower lip to the chin to indicate she was marriageable. After a woman had children, and as she aged, additional lines were tattooed on her chin to produce a dark band. Women wore a short apron of skin with shells, nuts, and pieces of obsidian attached to the fringe. A longer skin apron was placed over the first and partly obscured the inner garment. On ceremonial occasions women wore elaborate shell-covered aprons and many strings of shell beads (see Figure 7-2). Little girls wore aprons after they were about two years of age, but boys went without clothing, except for furs worn during the winter, until they reached puberty.

Men wore their hair long and loose over the shoulders or else tied it in a knot on top of the head; in his hair a man might wear a garland of flowers or feathers. Facial hair was plucked with hinged mussel-shell tweezers. A man's earlobes were pierced to hold ornamental pins of bone or shell. Men painted their faces red to indicate joy and black for war. Several lines were tattooed on a man's arm to serve as gauges for measuring lengths of dentalium shells that were used as money. Most young men folded skins around their hips, but older males, as well as some younger ones, wore no clothing. When traveling overland a man wore skin moccasins, and when hunting in deep snow he wore knee-length leggings and used snowshoes. During cold weather both men and women wore skin capes.

SETTLEMENTS Yurok villages were built along the Klamath River, bordering coastal lagoons or where streams and rivers flowed into the sea. Most settlements had three to seven houses, sweat houses, and menstrual huts (see Figure 7-3). Each home was identified with a specific male line (patrilineage). Villages appear to have been abandoned often as a result of floods or disease; in addition, families might be forced to relocate because of quarrels with other families.

The rectangular, gabled, and post-framed houses were built in deep excavations and covered with planks. People entered a house through a round hole cut into a front wall plank at a gabled end. The outer entrance was paved

Figure 7-2 | A Yurok woman, Alice Frank Spott, dressed in her finest garments. (Photograph by Pliny Goddard at Requa, Del Norte County, 1901. Phoebe A. Hearst Museum of Anthropology, University of California at Berkeley. [15-3344].)

with flat stones. An opening in the center of the roof allowed sunlight to enter and smoke from the fireplace to escape. The inside of a large house had partitioned rooms for firewood and equipment storage. These rooms provided entry into the living area, which was dominated by a fireplace some five feet deep and ten feet square that had a notched log ladder descending into it. Over the stone-lined fire pit a pole frame was suspended from the ceiling for drying fish. Family members ate around the fireplace, while women and children usually slept there. Scattered about were wooden serving trays for meat,

Figure 7-3 | Wahsekw, a Yurok village. (Photograph by Alfred L. Kroeber, 1907. Phoebe A. Hearst Museum of Anthropology, University of California at Berkeley. [15-1421].)

twined cooking baskets for preparing acorn meal, and similar but smaller baskets in which food was served. Spoons were made from antler, a mussel shell, or the top of a deer skull. Wooden bowls nearby were used for washing one's fingers after eating, and small redwood stools served as seats. At the side of a house sometimes was a lean-to of planks that served as a menstrual hut; in other cases, the menstrual hut was a separate structure built a short distance from a dwelling.

A sweat house served from one to three dwellings, and it was here that adult males lounged and men and boys slept (see Figure 7-4). No prohibition prevented women from being in sweat houses, and they sometimes slept there on cold nights.

Figure 7-4 | A reconstructed Yurok sweat house in the foreground and a dwelling in the background; Patrick's Point State Park, California.

A sweat house was rectangular with a gabled roof and was built largely underground of posts, beams, and planks. An old canoe was placed facing downward along the gable to prevent water leakage along the ridge. The floor of a sweat house was paved with stones or planked and was reached by stone steps or a rampway. Near the center of the building was a stone-lined fire pit. A small round exit hole was cut in one of the end wall planks. The only furnishings were pillows made from stone or blocks of redwood. Men collected the wood for a bath and sang songs of good fortune as they returned to the sweat house. The men built a fire, and after the wood was reduced to a bed of coals, they undressed and entered. They placed covers over the entrance and exit and sat in the intense heat for about half an hour. After crawling from the exit, they lounged on the stone paving and repeated the songs they had sung while gathering firewood. After cooling off, they swam in a stream and returned home to an evening meal.

CONVEYANCES   The most time-consuming craft item to produce was a dugout canoe made from a redwood log. The log was split with antler wedges and stone mauls, and then a fire was built along the center of one section of the split log. The charred wood was removed with a shell- or stone-bladed adz until the vessel was hollowed out. A typical canoe was eighteen feet long and three feet wide, with a rounded bottom and sides some fifteen inches high. At the front of a canoe on the inside, a small knob of wood was left, with a shallow hole in its center. This was the "heart" of the canoe, and without it a vessel was thought to be "dead." Pitch from conifers was used to caulk cracks in the wood, while crosspieces fore and aft prevented the sides from warping. These vessels were propelled by men standing in the front using poles or long-bladed paddles; a man seated in the stern used a shorter paddle as a rudder. These canoes were designed for river travel and drew as much as six inches of water when fully loaded. Given the rounded bottoms of these boats, a man sitting in the stern could quickly change course to avoid obstructions in the rushing water. When they traveled in the ocean, men sang songs and recited formulas to prevent their larger boats from capsizing and to keep the water smooth. Considering how ill-adapted such a vessel was to ocean travel, these precautions seem quite reasonable.

The only other manufactured form for travel was the snowshoe. Used by men hunting in deep snow, snowshoes were small with grapevine outer frames and wooden crosspieces.

SUBSISTENCE ACTIVITIES   The most important food was salmon, termed "that which is eaten" (Waterman 1920, 185), followed by elk, deer, and acorns and then by the far less important game and plant products. Success in getting food depended to a large extent on access to sites with exploitative potential. These usually were owned by an individual, family, or community and included fishing spots along the river, oak groves, seed collecting areas, places for snares along game trails, and stretches of riverbank extending about a mile inland. The most important riverine localities were sites where salmon could be dip-netted easily. Pools with an eddy where salmon rested while ascending the river to spawn were particularly important spots to own. A platform was erected over the pool, and it was fished with a long-handled dip net lowered into the water (see Figure 7-5). As soon as a fish was caught, the fisherman jerked the net from the water and clubbed the salmon over the head. In a single night a fisherman might take as many as a hundred salmon this way. The right to use an eddy was owned by an individual or a group of individuals and could be sold for money, inherited, or bartered away. Its worth was determined by the number of fish that could be taken. As many as ten men might jointly own an excellent dip-net site, but these pools were not everlasting, for a shift in the river channel could change the productivity of an eddy. Gill nets were also used, and these, as well as the netting for dip nets, were made from iris leaf fibers. The nets were weighted with stones, and floats most likely were made from short sections of wood. Men also used seines and toggle-headed harpoons to take salmon. The harpoon shafts were as much as twenty feet long, and at the forward end were two slightly diverging foreshafts. To each foreshaft was attached a toggle harpoon head with a line leading from the head to the shaft. When a salmon was struck, the harpoon head detached, and it was drawn in with the hand line. Salmon were

Figure 7-5 | Umits, Yurok man of Sa'a, raising a dip net. (Photograph by Alfred L. Kroeber, 1906. Phoebe A. Hearst Museum of Anthropology, University of California at Berkeley. [15-2730].)

split with a flint-bladed knife, dried, smoked on a rack over the fireplace in a house, and then packed in baskets.

Kroeber (1925, 87) wrote with economy and precision, "Acorns were gathered, dried, stored, cracked, pulverized, sifted, leached, and usually boiled with hot stones in a basket." Unshelled acorns were stored in large baskets inside the house and were later processed by removing the nuts from their shells and pounding the meal on a stone slab with a pestle. They leached the bitter acid by packing the ground meal in a sand basin and pouring hot water over it. Acorn meal was cooked with hot stones in a basket containing the meal and water. The mixture was stirred with a spatula to prevent the stones from burning the woven container.

The Yurok hunted land animals with a bow and arrows, but the practice does not appear to have been important. The hunting bow was strung with a

Figure 7-6 | A young Yurok man with bow and arrows for hunting land animals. The swordlike object in his right hand probably is an obsidian blade. (Drawn by Seth Eastman form a sketch by George Gibbs in 1851. Courtesy of the Smithsonian Institution, National Anthropological Archives, neg. no. 2854-F-27.)

sinew cord and backed with strips of sinew (sinew-backed bow); a feather-vaned arrow had a separate wooden foreshaft with a stone arrow point attached. They carried arrows in a quiver made by turning the skin of a small animal, such as a fox, inside out (see Figure 7-6). They used dogs to chase deer and elk but probably more often took those animals with snares. Dogs were never eaten since their meat, like that of reptiles, was considered poisonous.

A fish or mammal killed for food was not, in Yurok thinking, really destroyed. The spirit continued to exist, leaving only its physical form behind for the hunter or fisher. A number of restrictions on the taking of salmon will be cited later, but here it is appropriate to mention some of the observances surrounding deer. This animal was thought to have many likes and dislikes that had to be accommodated to kill it successfully. Deer supposedly did not like a house that seemed unoccupied; they were attracted to hunters from dwellings where there was smoke. The reason for washing one's hands in flowing water after eating deer meat was to avoid drowning the deer. Deer meat was eaten from wooden platters, and care was taken during a meal so that none of the meat dropped to the floor. It was thought that only by observing these and other taboos could deer be taken successfully.

The Yurok were not farmers, but they planted tobacco. The plants were cultivated and the crop harvested for use by the grower or for sale to others. The mature leaves were dried in the sun or by a fire, pulverized, and placed in baskets. The cultivated species apparently was the same as the local feral tobacco, but they did not smoke the latter for fear that it might have grown on a grave. People smoked tobacco in tubular pipes that most often were made from wood, and they inhaled the smoke. Most men smoked just before bedtime, but some old men were addicted to tobacco and smoked more often. Old female shamans appear to have been the heaviest smokers; other women did not smoke.

MONEY AND WEALTH   In the broadest sense, money is a divisible and portable class of objects having a standardized value and acceptable in exchange for goods or services. In terms of this definition, money clearly was important among the Yurok, and dentalium shells were the most widely circulated form. These small mollusks had tusk-shaped shells that ranged up to about three inches in length. They were most abundant in the coastal waters off British Columbia and were collected there with a rakelike device that was thrust into the sandy ocean bottom to impale as many dentalia as possible. In western North America the shells were traded throughout the area from the subarctic to southern California. Among the Yurok, as with most Indians, the shells were named and graded according to size, with the largest shells having the greatest value. An eleven-shell string, with each shell 2½ inches long, was valued at about $50 during the early American period; a string of the same length with fifteen 1⅞-inch shells was worth only about $2.50. Other monetary units included redheaded woodpecker scalps that ranged in value from 10¢ to $1.50 each. Ordinary deerskins, after being prepared for ceremonial use, were worth from $50 to $100; skins of albino deer were valued at from $250 to $500, although they were never sold. Blades flaked from black obsidian were worth $1 for every inch in length until they reached a foot; blades longer than this were worth a great deal more.

Many, if not most, items of material culture were scaled in value against dentalium shells. Around 1900, a small dugout canoe was worth a thirteen-shell string or three large redheaded woodpecker scalps; a house was valued at from three to five strings of shells; an oak grove from one to five strings; a fishing spot from one to three strings; a shaman's fee from one to two strings; a slave one string; and a woman's basketry cap filled with tobacco one small shell. A few items were so valuable that they normally could not be exchanged but were passed along a patrilineage. These were most important as exhibits during ceremonial occasions. Fine albino deerskins with transparent hoofs and huge obsidian blades nearly a yard in length were among these treasures.

The preceding account of money is a traditional one that is not incorrect, but it fails, as John and Donna Bushnell (1977) have noted, to take into account the overwhelming symbolic importance of wealth among the Yurok. The ownership of wealth not only indicated social worth but symbolized the presence of those spiritual qualities needed to acquire it. Furthermore, the land of dentalium shells, called Dentalium Home and supposedly located across the ocean, was a supernatural figure sometimes regarded as a creator. Therefore, the shells and other highly valued objects, according to the Bushnells (1977, 128), "are intimately linked to the world of immortals and characteristically emit supernatural power that redounds to the good fortune and wealth of those who possess them."

LEGAL SYSTEM   Yurok customary law was based on the idea that wrongs were committed against individuals. Disputes ranged in intensity from minor to major in highly varied contexts. Efforts to resolve lesser differences before they expanded typically involved rock-throwing episodes between disputants. Rock throwing was institutionalized and surrounded by numerous conventions, including songs, procedures for selecting rocks, and magical means to make them strike their target. Yurok stories often included accounts of rock throwing. More serious offenses were settled with the exchange of specific forms of property.

Any major deviation from a behavioral norm necessitated a compensatory settlement, and extenuating circumstances were rarely considered. The age, sex, and previous behavior of an offender were unimportant, but his or her wealth was relevant. Finally, once a dispute had been settled, no further recourse was possible. The major grounds for claims were murder, seduction, adultery, saying the name of a deceased person, trespassing, or a shaman's refusal to treat a person who was ill. Failure to ferry someone, even an enemy, across a river led to a claim. If someone injured himself while on the land of another, the owner was responsible for compensation. This was true even of a trespasser, but in such cases the landowner would likely press a counterclaim for trespassing. If a shaman refused to accept the responsibility for treating a patient and the person died, the shaman was liable. To pass before a village by boat when a family in the village was mourning a death from natural causes was grounds for a claim. If a person became hopelessly in debt because of some drastically antisocial act, he could, in lieu of payment, become the slave of the one he had offended. For example, if a poor person struck the son of a rich man, he could settle his debt through "debt-slavery" of himself or one of his female relatives. "Slaves" were never killed or abused but performed the more difficult subsistence tasks. A slave owner was free to integrate the individual into his household or to maintain his or her status as a slave. Foreigners of prisoners from raids were never made slaves. The former

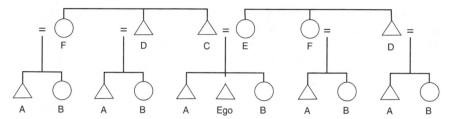

Figure 7-7 | The early historic Yurok system of kinship terminology.

always were killed if they arrived unannounced, and prisoners were held for ransom.

DESCENT, KINSHIP, AND MARRIAGE In the Yurok social system the most important ties were those along a line of males. It is tempting to regard the descent system as strictly patrilineal, and unquestionably a man was most concerned with his relatives along a male line. Still, there was ample recognition of a wife and her relatives in calculating social ties. Perhaps it would be best to characterize these people as patrilineal with a distinct and recognized tendency to consider relatives on both sides of a family as important (bilateral descent).

In the kinship terminology, a man referred to his father by one term; for his father's brother and his mother's brother, he used another term. For the mother's side of the family, the terminology was comparable to that on the father's side (lineal terms). Thus, the Yurok employed terms for the parental generation that are of the same type as those used in the United States today. In an individual's generation, the term for sister extended to all female first cousins, and the word for brother extended to all male first cousins (Hawaiian cousin terms). It would seem that if cousins were called brother or sister, the parents of these individuals would be referred to as mother and father, but such was not the case (see Figure 7-7).

The only bar to marriage was the prohibition against taking a spouse from among near relatives. An individual in a small settlement was obligated to seek a mate from elsewhere, since all the occupants were near relatives; but a partner could be found easily in another village or another tribe. At the same time the tendency in large settlements was to find a mate in one's home community (village endogamy). It has been reported also that men tended to seek their wives from downstream settlements. Ideally, the couple lived in the settlement and house of the groom (patrilocal residence), but alternative arrangements were not unusual. Were a man's wife to die before she bore three or four offspring, the woman's family was obliged to offer one of her sisters or female relatives to replace her (sororate). Conversely, when a married man died, his brother was expected to marry the widow (levirate).

SOCIAL DIMENSIONS Personal ambition and extreme individualism dominated Yurok social life. The core members of each community were persons who traced their descent along the male line to a known common ancestor (patrilineage); within this unit were lines of familial authority, with a wealthy old man most likely to have jurisdiction over other members of the unit. A hamlet contained one or more patrilineages, each structured as the other, but no organized system of villagewide authority existed. An individual also was bound in a network of kinship ties with persons in other settlements through bonds of blood and marriage.

The Yurok also were grouped into five political units that became known as "districts." Each was headed by an especially well-educated aristocratic leader, sometimes referred to in English as a "real man." As will be discussed in a subsequent section, a well-educated person was considered to be one who knew a great deal about the law. Although the available information is not the most reliable, it suggests that real men mediated major disputes before important ceremonies were held each year; this procedure became a means of resolving differences before they exploded. Furthermore, a village or village cluster cooperated in rivalries with other villages or village clusters. In sum, while individualism dominated, it was constrained by allegiances based on kinship and residence.

Within a patrilineage and beyond it, worth was based on ownership of material property, and families were rich, well-to-do, or poor. It was difficult to move up in social standing, since everyone coveted wealth and was reluctant to part with it; but the possibility of a poor boy acquiring riches through persistence and supernatural aid did exist. The Yurok believed that constant thoughts about money led to its acquisition. Meditating about wealth when preparing for, taking, or resting after a bath was thought to be most propitious. An ambitious young man was urged to fast and work hard for ten days while concentrating on dentalium shells. When he gathered wood for the sweat house, he collected it from the upper branches of trees where he visualized the dentalia to be hanging. As he bathed, he thought of shells, and when peering intently into the river, he imagined that he saw huge dentalium shells. Such a person would say to himself, "I want to be rich," and he would make a tearful invocation for wealth, but not to any particular spirit or supernatural. Most importantly, however, according to Gates (1995, 464–65), visions of this nature "were not of the items of wealth, but are feelings of what lies behind the items; what the wealth items indicate. That is, consciousness focuses on the richness of the land and good feelings that come from participating with paradise in a centered way." Women were viewed as a complication in a male's quest for this richness. A young man seeking wealth was warned not to have anything to do with women, and an adult man was not to copulate with his wife in the house where his wealth was kept.

The nature and texture of life varied widely from one Yurok family to another. An almost insurmountable social barrier separated very rich, aristocratic families from the poor, and poverty was thought to have a genetic basis.

A person supposedly was poor, lazy, and ill—except for instances of sorcery—because these conditions prevailed in his or her family line. The economic distinction was apparent in various dimensions of life. The speech of aristocrats was different from that of commoners, and the rich were wary and guarded in what they said. Rich people were "high class" and lived "clean" lives. An aristocrat knew the law and adhered carefully to its letter, while poor persons were far less familiar with it and also were careless, unclean, and lacked social graces. To prevent an ambitious commoner from reaching a position of power, wealthy men practiced sorcery to dissipate the commoner's wealth or cause deaths in his family. Thus, social distinctions ran deep throughout a Yurok's life, and to improve one's condition was quite difficult.

As would be expected, formal warfare did not exist in this society where political ties were muted. Conflicts between families might develop into small or great feuds, depending on the size of the families involved, their wealth, and how quickly a settlement could be arranged by men identified as "judges." Fighting was with bows and arrows except for hand-to-hand combat, when short stone clubs were used. Protective armor was made either from elk hide or vertical wooden rods bound together, and it seems to have been worn only during prearranged battles. Murders, committed either in the heat of anger or by witchcraft, could set off serious feuds and prompt the near relatives of the dead person to seek revenge. They might approach their enemy's village secretly and attack before the defenders could rally, or they might ambush the offending family on the trail. Following a successful raid or ambush, the contending parties might negotiate a meeting to settle their differences. The two sides armed themselves, pained their faces, and formed lines separated by the distance an arrow could be shot. They sang songs and performed a dance of settlement; at this point fighting might resume if the arrangements broke down. Otherwise, negotiations continued uninterrupted. The contesting parties carried with them the full amount of property necessary for a settlement. The side that had killed the most people and destroyed or seized the greatest amount of property was the "winner" but was at the same time required to relinquish the most property. This pattern represents a southern extension of the Northwest Coast Indian potlatch system (see Chapter 8). The items to be distributed were placed in baskets and held over a fire as songs were sung and a dance performed. This ritual was to cast away any feelings of hostility and to make any lasting feelings of vengeance the responsibility of the other party. If all went well, the settlement was made, and neither side could make further claims or hold a grudge.

RELIGION AND SUPERNATURALISM The only time that diverse Yurok families cooperated fully was in fulfilling ceremonial obligations. Collective rituals were held to renew and perpetuate the natural world with its resources as an orderly system. The principal ceremonies were performed to prevent disease, famine, and cataclysms such as earthquakes and floods. The ceremonial procedures supposedly were based on precedents set by immortals before the present race of people occupied the country, and the formulas recited concerned these immortals. Ceremonies were fixed calendrically and usually were held at the spots where they reportedly had been enacted for the first time. During certain ceremonies men displayed their wealth and greatest treasures, and Deerskin and Jumping Dances might be held. Curing and sorcery were also a part of Yurok belief.

Ceremonies The most elaborate Yurok ceremonial cycle was associated with a fishweir at Kepel along the Klamath River. Here the river was wide and shallow and had a gravel bottom, an ideal place for weir construction. Beforehand, a ceremony was performed at the mouth of the Klamath River to remove a prohibition against eating salmon caught that year. The designated weir chief dominated both the ceremonial and technical aspects of weir building and its use. He achieved his position by learning the formal recitations required; this knowledge was passed on to one of his sons. The weir chief wore a special deerskin robe throughout the ceremonies and, with the aid of a man and woman as assistants, became deeply involved in the ritual obligations. The chief and his assistants visited sacred places, burned incense, fasted, recited formulas, and bathed in a special manner. After determining where the weir support poles were to be cut, they announced to adjacent villages when construction would begin. On the appointed day, participants were assigned to build particular and named weir sections, and for the next five mornings they worked at cutting and barking weir support poles. They also collected hazel shoots and made them into mats that were placed along the weir to hinder salmon escapement. On the fifth day, the weir chief cut poles for the weir ends and the center pole; workers prepared the other poles. After this work was completed, they joked with one another for the remainder of the day. No offense could be taken at jokes at one's own expense, irrespective of how abusive they may have been.

On the sixth day, construction began. The weir chief prayed for salmon and drove the first stake in place with a special maul. Workers drove the remaining weir stakes into the gravel. Afterward the weir chief and his male assistant tied the first stringer in place along the pole tops, and workers bound stringers to all the remaining poles. Ten wooden fish traps were then built on the downstream side of the weir. Each trap was about twelve feet long and fourteen feet wide with a moveable opening at each end. The hazel shoot mats were fitted in place along the weir to complete construction. An opening was left near one riverbank so that boats could pass by and some salmon could escape upstream.

On the tenth day, boys, girls, and the female assistant participated in a set of competitive rituals. This was followed by the male assistant removing the first salmon caught. The salmon was taken by the female assistant as her evening meal, but it was not until the following day that others could begin eating freshly caught salmon.

The catch from three traps was reserved for the principal participants and their relatives. Salmon were removed from the traps each morning with dip nets, and fish not taken in this manner from a trap were allowed to escape. Great numbers of salmon were harvested at Kepel and processed for future consumption.

The next event was a Deerskin Dance held nearby; a similar dance was held farther downstream. A Deerskin Dance was a colorful event, with each male dancer wearing the skin of a civet cat or deer around his waist. The dancers were not clothed above the waist, but around each man's neck hung massive strings of dentalium shells. Each man's head was adorned with a fur browband and a stick on which eagle or condor feathers were arranged to appear as one long feather. Each dancer carried a pole with a stuffed deer head at the top and a deerskin hanging loose that swayed back and forth as the pole was moved. A singer and assistants provided music as a line of dancers performed. Two other men paraded before the dancers, blowing crane bone whistles and holding obsidian blades. During a Deerskin Dance, as at ceremonies in general, members of the host community danced and were followed by performers from each represented village. Morning and evening dances were given by each group for a twelve-day period. On the final day, men danced with their finest white deerskins, and others displayed their most beautiful obsidian blades.

Formal ceremonies at the Kepel fishweir ended with the performance of a two-day Jumping Dance held near Kepel. Dancing men wore a double layer of civet cat skins about their hips and many necklaces of dentalium shells. Each man wore a deerskin headband covered with woodpecker scalps and trimmed with a white band of deerskin; a white plume extended above his head on a stick. From the sides of his headpiece hung long skin flaps that swung rapidly as he performed. In one hand a dancer carried a cylindrical basket with an opening along one side (see Figure 7-8). Two steps were performed in the Jumping Dance; both involved hopping or jumping as the baskets were lowered.

After this final ceremony, most of the participants in the fishweir returned to their homes. Only the weir chief and his male assistant remained until the weir was destroyed by rushing water, about two or three months later.

While the Kepel fishweir ceremonies were the most elaborate, portions of the Yurok population participated in other ceremonies as well. At the junction of the Trinity and Klamath rivers in a community called Weitspus a ceremony was held to renew the world each September. It was designed specifically to avert natural disasters and disease. At two coastal villages, a village at the Klamath River mouth and another a little less than halfway between the Trinity junction and the sea, four other world-renewal ceremonies were held. Yurok participation in these and other ceremonies produced a form of integration along sacred, not secular, lines.

Another popular celebration, called the Brush Dance by Anglo-Americans, was held to treat an ill child, but it also served as entertainment for most participants. The event was held in a dwelling from which the roof and part of the sidewalls had been removed. On the first night a formula was recited for the ill child, and men danced about the fire holding boughs. Nothing

Figure 7-8 | Jumping Dance performers, circa 1900. (Courtesy of the A. W. Ericson Collection, Humboldt State University Library.)

took place the second night, but on the third and fourth nights the Brush Dance continued until dawn. On each night a series of three dances was performed by competing sets of dancers. The sick child was integrated into the performances with the recitation of formulas and the waving of torches above him or her.

Formulas were very important in the Brush Dance, as well as in calendrical ceremonies, and they also served individual needs under other circumstances. Some formulas involved the recitation of a list of sacred spots that someone long ago had visited to accomplish a particular purpose. Others were recitations or prayers, including the spirit responses. Offerings of tobacco and the use of plant products were associated with the formulas.

Curing Among the Yurok, women were the primary shamans. Such a woman usually acquired her power in a dream, either unanticipated or sought after, about a dead shaman. From this deceased curing specialist the potential shaman obtained a "pain," considered a tangible object that entered her body and became the nexus of her power. Once she had acquired power, the next step was to bring it under control by fasting and dancing in a sweat house for ten days under the supervision of other shamans. The goal was for the novice to be able to vomit forth her pain and to swallow it again. As a further step the aspirant and a male relative visited a supernatural spot on a mountain for one night during the summer. On the mountain the woman recited a formula, smoked, and danced near a fire. Another ten days in the sweat house, performing as before, was followed by a dance around a large hot fire to bring the pain fully under the woman's control. This dance was the final step in becoming a shaman.

When a woman was asked to heal a patient, she negotiated the amount of payment with the relatives of the sick person before she attempted a cure. A female curer's equipment consisted of a pipe, two strings of feathers in her hair, and an ankle-length skirt. She effected a cure by changing over the patient, smoking, and dancing for as much as six hours. A long session sometimes was necessary to see into the body of the patient and to locate the pains that caused the disease. The pain, or pains, were then removed by sucking. If the shaman was unable to remove the pains, she referred the patient to another curer. If a patient died, the shaman returned her fee.

In a secondary category of curers were men who probably did not acquire their power from supernatural sources but intensified it by supernatural means. They visited mountaintops, recited formulas, bathed ritually, and smoked in order to reinforce their power. These men relied on a pharmacopoeia consisting of plant and mineral products. This knowledge and the position were passed from father to son or to another close male relative. Like a female shaman, the male was paid before he attempted a cure and returned the payment if he was unsuccessful. Among the illnesses treated were wounds, snakebites, and chronic diseases, as well as other forms of unidentified sickness. One source states that male curers served as a check on the ambitions of female shamans. Apparently, the duties of female and male shamans were distinct, females handling cases of psychological ailments with supernatural cures and males treating physical disabilities due to natural causes.

Sorcery Some female shamans had the reputation of using their powers for antisocial purposes, the motivation being material profit. These shamans allegedly made a person ill and then collected a fee to cure her or him. Another technique was to leave one of multiple pains in the body of a person who was treated in order to be called back when this pain became troublesome. Other persons were more truly "devils"; they reportedly acquired a malignant object by purchase or special knowledge and used it to kill individuals. If the possessor of such a power went out at night, the power was thought to appear as sparks or as a bluish light. It could be placed on the end of a miniature arrow and shot from a small bow at the home of the victim. It was thought that the victim would die if not treated by a shaman. A person also could be harmed by a poison made of crushed meat from a dog, frog, rattlesnake, or salamander. After the poison was added to a victim's food, the individual would supposedly remain healthy for a year but then become ill and die if not cared for by a very powerful shaman.

When a person's rights were violated and just compensation could not be obtained by legal means, the only alternative was to turn to a sorcerer. These usually were men, and they customarily charged as much as a bride price, which meant that their services could be commanded only by aristocrats. A sorcerer was either of high social standing or was attempting to achieve higher status. He owned two to twelve "poisons" that ranged in effectiveness from very mild to lethal; each strength was represented by a different miniature arrow. The mildest form was said to produce a headache or cold and the middle level to cause chest pains that led to the victim's confinement. From the eighth level upward, all were lethal and were associated with behavior while sleeping. Once the fee and the degree of illness to be induced were agreed upon, the sorcerer went outside the victim's house disguised as a dog. He shot the mildest arrow from a miniature bow and returned at specified intervals to shoot arrows until he reached the level of illness desired. When the victim showed symptoms of illness, a shaman was hired to extract the "pains," but very few shamans had the power to remove lethal arrows. If a shaman could suck the pain from a victim, she spit it out of her mouth, and the arrow supposedly rose into the air and flew back to its maker, with only the shaman seeing the return. It was essential for a sorcerer to handle the objects of his power with great care. When not in use, they were buried in a cache of stones, but it was necessary for the owner to use the force of the poison at least once a month. If he did not, it was thought that the power would harm his children, or himself if he was childless. This form of sorcery possibly developed during the early historic period when the economic position of aristocratic families was threatened by white intruders who began to control key economic resources.

LIFE CYCLE   The first time a woman conceived, her offspring was born after ten months, according to tradition, but later births followed nine-month pregnancies. Most births were in the spring, but not because a mating season existed, as was once suggested. The reason is that a man stored his material wealth in his house, and riches were believed to be diametrically opposed to sexual activity. To have sexual intercourse in the house was to invite poverty, and thus couples were most likely to copulate in the summer when sleeping outdoors. A pregnant woman worked hard, ate little, and was concerned about how her physical actions might affect the fetus. For example, she worried that she might bear a large neonate if she ate too much and slept excessively.

In giving birth, a woman rested on her back with her feet braced against a midwife and her arms bound with leather straps suspended from the ceiling. During labor the midwife told her when to lift herself with the thongs. The newborn was steamed over wild ginger, and a preparation made from ground land snail was applied to the navel. The severed cord was put inside a pine tree branch that had been split to receive it. Because these people thought that the colostrum from the mother's breast was harmful to ingest, an infant was fed hazelnut soup for the first ten days and then was nursed. After twenty days

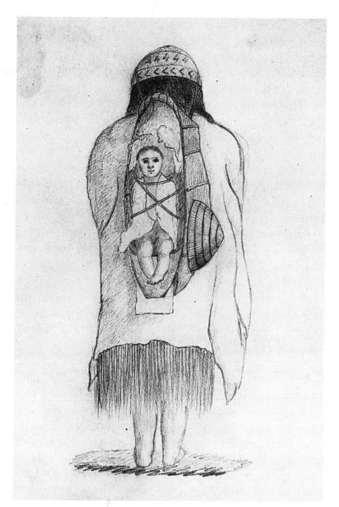

Figure 7-9 | A woman with her child in a baby basket (cradleboard). (Drawn by George Gibbs in 1851. Courtesy of the Smithsonian Institution, National Anthropological Archives, neg. no. 2854-F-21.)

a grandmother, probably most often the paternal grandmother, began to massage the infant's leg muscles to encourage it to crawl. Between the time of birth and the healing of the navel, parents observed food taboos, and they were prohibited from having sexual intercourse until the baby crawled. Cradleboards ("baby basket" is the term used by the Yurok) were made in such a manner that the infant sat with its legs hanging free (see Figure 7-9). The baby could move its legs at any time, which was in keeping with the desire to have it crawl at a tender age. Many, if not most, aspects of rearing an offspring were designed to encourage self-reliance. This attitude clearly was reflected by the practice of weaning at one year, which was earlier than among most American Indians.

A child was named when he or she had clearly demonstrated a systematic recall capacity, probably at about eight years of age. The names for males were selected by fathers, and for females by mothers; each family seems to have had its own set of personal names. Nicknames of girls often contained some reference to their marriage, such as Married a Rabbit. Personal names were used in referring to or addressing individuals, but they were dropped when someone married.

The Yurok believed that each child had a unique personal spirit derived from the energy of the Universe, which acted against itself and sent its waves through everything. According to Thomas Buckley (1979), an ethnographer of the Yurok, this infusion of energy was thought to occur ten weeks after conception. At an early age a child was not considered capable of learning systematically. His or her readiness to learn was based on a capacity to remember, not on chronological age; the process of learning began as she or he matured. At this time each child was taught on an individual basis, since each one was viewed as diffcrent from the others. The information taught primarily involved ways to think and behave in particular situations. It was uncles and aunts who taught children; parents were considered too close to them, while grandparents were too emotionally involved with grandchildren to be routine teachers.

A child was taught comparatively little in a formal way; the Yurok felt quite strongly that an individual could learn only by experience. For example, aristocratic families placed an inordinate emphasis on table manners, and a child was expected to learn the proper etiquette by observing others. If a maturing offspring seized food greedily, ate greedily, ate rapidly, and did not chew thoroughly, his or her meal basket was turned upside down as an indication of parental disapproval. It was up to the child to determine what she or he had done wrong and to correct this behavior. Some instruction was formal, however. A child might be shown rocks shaped like figures and told they formerly were persons who did not follow social norms. One rock in particular was pointed out as once having been an errant child. Animals and birds, too, were the subjects of stories about proper behavior. One particularly vivid tale concerned the greedy buzzard who put his entire head in his soup while it was still hot. He scalded the top of his head and henceforth could eat only old, rotten food. Another dominant concern of parents was to ensure that a child learned not to offend the dead. Any direct statement about the dead or reference to items associated with death was considered a form of swearing. A rude gesture used as a means of swearing was to hold out one's hands with the fingers outstretched and the thumbs together, since this was thought to be how the dead swore. The probable reason for disapproving of such behavior was that it led to claims by the relatives of a deceased person. To discourage words or gestures of this nature, a mentor placed nettles against a child's lips or hands, a very effective punishment.

A child sooner or later came to understand what the people conceived of as the law; everything was subject to this law. The essence of the law, which was above all else an expression of the Universe, was *truth*, because it was correct and proper at all times. As Buckley (1979, 30) has noted, "All education and training must move in respect of each unique person's individuality while, at the same time, insuring the success of the results as far as this is possible. That is, the interface between individual and society is specified by culturally defined truth expressed in a legal idiom." An individual who learned a great deal of the law was called a "well-educated one," which was an exalted achieved status. The key to education was to learn to perceive "facts" in perspective. In this context, objects as well as behaviors, thoughts, and feelings were objectified as *things* to be seen and understood. A child first learned to comprehend the nature of material things as an essential step toward understanding things that were nonmaterial. To draw distinctions between the two, such as between a tree in a physical sense and a spiritual one, a child was encouraged to be reflective and was given clues, not answers, by instructors. Youths were encouraged to be contemplative, to do their own thinking, and especially to be true to themselves. This was how they not only became upright adults but acquired the spiritual power that brought them both wealth and inner contentment.

The most important skill to be acquired by a young girl was basket weaving, since a great deal of prestige accrued from making excellent baskets. After watching older women make baskets for years, a girl attempted to weave her first one when she was about six years old. She tried a simple form, and often after the first few rows were completed, her mother ripped out the poor weave and gave the basket back to the girl to do again. The learner received little credit for "trying" because a basket either served its purpose or it did not. If a girl's interest and abilities were sustained, a skilled basket weaver instructed her informally. Only one set of weaving techniques existed, and therefore all baskets were similar, differing only in quality and to a lesser degree in design elements. Not all girls became good basket weavers.

When a girl first menstruated, she spent most of ten days sitting silently in a corner of the house, facing away from the fire. Whenever she needed to scratch, she used a special stick, and she wore a skirt of inner bark like that of a female shaman. The girl moved about as little as possible but brought in a load of firewood each day. For at least the first four days she ate no food, under the assumption that the longer she fasted the more wealth she would accumulate later in life. When she did eat, it was at the bank of a roaring river where she would hear no sound but the water. Each night she bathed the number of times equal to the days of her confinement, except that on the ninth night she bathed ten times. At dusk of the tenth day each small child living nearby washed her back. Finally, her mother or another woman told her she would have ten boys and ten girls.

The preceding account is based on traditionally accepted writings about the initial menstruation of Yurok females, which imply that during their first and subsequent menses women were isolated because of their capacity to contaminate anything with which they had contact. For a menstruating woman to seduce an unknowing man was considered odious; thus, the impact of menstruation on women and men alike was interpreted largely negatively. However, a field study among the Yurok by Buckley in 1978 (Buckley 1982), coupled with his examination of unpublished field notes collected by A. L. Kroeber in 1902, leads to a reevaluation of published accounts about menstruation and sheds new light on Yurok social and religious life. Buckley emphasizes that the data are not the best and his reconstruction of the menstrual complex is tentative, but his nonetheless is an important interpretation to consider.

On her "moontime," as the Yurok called menstruation, a woman was isolated from males for ten days and ate separate meals prepared in particular containers. Furthermore, men were expected to refrain from hunting or participating in ceremonial activities when their wives or daughters were menstruating. One rationale for isolating women at this time was negative: menstruating women were considered highly polluting. Yet a positive reason existed as well: a menstruating woman was thought to be at the height of her power because the flow of blood purified her. This was why she refrained from ordinary tasks and concentrated instead on the purpose and meaning of her life. The Yurok drew a clear analogy between the purification men sought in their sweat houses and that sought by women in menstrual isolation. Men seeking wealth secluded themselves in a sweat house, avoided contact with fertile women, and ate special foods for ten days. In a similar fashion, Yurok women during their menses attained purification and supposedly had the greatest capacity to attract wealth.

From these data it becomes obvious that if the women of a household menstruated at different times, the normal household routine frequently would be disrupted. Buckley suggests that this may not have been the case because of a menstrual synchrony among the fertile women in a household group. (Menstrual synchrony is widely recognized as occurring among women who interact frequently, such as in college dormitories. A female pheromone can diffuse through a large room with sufficient strength to synchronize the menstrual cycles of women who customarily occupy the room.) Presumably, the women in a Yurok household, or in clusters of closely related households, interacted often. Furthermore, it may be, as Buckley cautiously suggests, that Yurok women synchronized their menses by being exposed to the full moon. (It has been demonstrated that the exposure of a woman to light while she is asleep may affect the onset of menstruation.) The lunar cycle was known to be highly significant among the Yurok in calculating time, and this awareness of lunar change may have led them to use photic stimulation to influence the onset of menstruation as required for synchrony. In any case, the menstrual synchrony that apparently existed meant the absence of all fertile adult females from the household at one time, which may have been more advantageous than constant disruptions of routine.

A maturing girl of good breeding was watched carefully by her parents to make certain that she did not fornicate. The prohibition was not so much a matter of morality as to prevent the girl from becoming pregnant and thereby decreasing the amount of bridewealth she would bring. A girl who conceived before marriage attempted to abort by placing headed stones on her abdomen; if successful, she threw the fetus in the river.

Property exchanges at marriage were critical because a person's social standing depended on the amount of bridewealth offered at the time of his mother's marriage. At the bottom of the scale was a nonlegitimate offspring who had no formal standing. Next was a poor person, whose father had offered little for his wife; he in turn could provide his son with very little bridewealth. A third level of prestige was achieved by persons whose fathers had offered substantial wealth. Finally, some persons' rich fathers provided far more wealth than was necessary to consummate a marriage. Marital arrangements were not a simple offering of a given amount of wealth to the bride's family; instead there often were manipulations and compromises. According to the ideal, a man with wealth suggested a suitable amount of material goods to the girl's relatives, had it accepted, and took the girl to reside in his settlement (patrilocal residence). Such was a "full marriage." Any particular groom was unlikely to possess enough wealth of his own to satisfy the girl's relatives, but his father or father's brothers ideally gave the young man the necessary balance. The bride of a wealthy man brought with her a considerable amount of property, which partially offset the outlay of the groom and his relatives. A girl of high social standing might bring ten baskets of dentalia, otter skins, a canoe, deerskins, and other small assorted valuables. It was possible also for a man with a small daughter to be deeply in debt to a man with a young son and to offer the girl in marriage when she was quite young. In this case, the girl would grow up in the household of her prospective in-laws and would marry the boy after puberty. Sometimes a father was so covetous of his wealth that he refused to give his son a sufficient amount for a full marriage. If the son worked hard, sweated often in the sweat house, cried for wealth, and fasted, after about four years the girls' relatives might feel sorry for him and permit a full marriage.

Another form of marriage was "half marriage," which meant usually that the groom could not accumulate the necessary wealth to make a full-marriage payment and was forced to be content with lower social standing. He offered his potential father-in-law all the wealth he possessed and went to live in the girl's village, either in the same house or in a nearby house (matrilocal residence). In a typical marriage of this sort, the children of the couple were affiliated with the wife's family, and the bridewealth given at the marriage of their daughter went to the wife's kinsmen. Furthermore, the woman in a half marriage could correct her husband openly and supervise his subsistence activities, while the children were under her direct control even concerning their marital arrangements. A half marriage sometimes was negotiated quickly if a girl was pregnant, to prevent the social stigma of bearing a bastard. Finally, a greedy father of a girl who was a successful shaman might force a half marriage upon her to continue his claim on her earnings. In a record of 356 marriages, 25 percent were half marriages, indicating that either the number of persons with little wealth was small or that extenuating circumstances often were involved in a marriage. At the same time, full marriages were not all equal, for very rich men would offer far more than the minimum amount of wealth necessary in order to acquire increased prestige for themselves and their children.

Possibly the most common grounds for divorce was failure of the wife to conceive, and if she could not be replaced by a kinswoman, the bridewealth was refunded. If a man abused his wife in a full marriage so much that she returned home, the husband was obligated to pay the woman's family an additional amount before he could receive her back. If he did not do so, the girl's family probably would return part of the bridewealth, and the couple was considered divorced.

Following a death, the corpse was washed, but it was touched as little as possible. The deceased was painted, clothed, wrapped in a skin, and placed on a plank for twenty-four hours. Mourners wailed before the body, and then it was removed from the house through an opening made in the wall and buried near the house. During burial the mourners wept, sang appropriate songs, and said good-bye to the deceased.

The spirit of a good person was believed to travel a narrow, winding trail north until it climbed a ladder into the sky to a peaceful afterlife. The soul of an unworthy individual supposedly traveled a broad trail to a river where an old woman and a dog lived. Sometimes the dog drove the soul back into the dead person's body, and he or she came to life again. This was rare, and if it did happen, the person was not happy and would meet a sudden death. When the old woman had control of the soul, she sent it across the river in a waiting canoe of the Yurok type but without a "heart" near the bow. A young man propelled the canoe and landed the soul in a damp, depressing land where food, although plentiful, was unpalatable. As described, these beliefs about the fate of souls sound as if they might be of Christian derivation.

Early Historic Influences

Early historic influences on Yurok life were brought to bear by contact with whites, Chinese, and other Indians. Some of these contacts resulted in friction, some in a sharing of religious ideas, and some in conflicts over land rights.

FRICTION WITH FOREIGNERS   When gold miners moved into the Trinity River country in 1849, the most dramatic effect on the Yurok was the realization that foreigners, equated with enemies, were permanently in their midst. Their primary contacts were with traders, who offered not only useful material goods but intoxicants as well. These Indians not infrequently fought whites when either or both were intoxicated. Another serious problem was that of compensation in Indian terms. In one instance a trader hired Indians to transport supplies for his store from the coast, and when the canoemen drowned, the trader was held responsible. When he would not compensate the relatives of the deceased, they laid siege to his store. He summoned U.S. Army soldiers as protection, and finally the Indians retaliated by killing a white who had nothing to do with the affair. Problems such as these during the early period of intensive contact appear to have been relatively common.

THE 1870 GHOST DANCE   Within a generation of the first intensive contact with Euro-Americans, the Yurok were exposed to the Ghost Dance that Wodziwob, a Paviotso Indian (Northern Paiute) originated in 1869. He and a disciple were said to have returned from the place of the dead to report that the dead would come back to earth if a dance was performed to hasten their return. As the doctrine spread in California, it changed from its original form. Yurok reaction to the basic tenets is revealing. The dogma spoke of an end to the present world when nonbelievers, including whites, would turn to stone; believers would survive and be joined by the dead. Some Yurok, however, thought that all people would die, and others that everyone would survive the world's end. All Yurok thought that if individual wealth were not exposed during the Ghost Dance performances, it would be worthless in the new world. To facilitate the return of the dead, the Yurok removed fences from graves in some localities. The message appears to have won support for a short time, with the strongest adherents being the young and the poor, but the Ghost Dance of 1870 made no lasting imprint on Yurok life, possibly because the doctrine had no precedent in their mythology and was without the traditional formulas that formed the core of Yurok supernaturalism (see also Chapter 2).

RESERVED LANDS   By executive order, in 1855 the Klamath Reserve was established, extending from the mouth of the Klamath River to twenty miles upstream and one mile on each side of the river. Farther inland, the Hoopa Valley Reservation was created by Congress in 1864 in an area occupied by the Hupa (Hoopa) and Yurok. Then in 1876 the Hoopa Valley Extension was created by executive order for local Indians between the Klamath Reserve and the Hoopa Valley Reservation; administratively, the Klamath Reserve became a part of the Hoopa Valley Extension.

| Later Historic Life

Published anthropological information about the Yurok that was collected between the 1940s and the 1970s is scarce. Fortunately, however, two anthropology students at the University of California, Los Angeles, Cynthia Burski and Dorothy Hosler, visited the Yurok in 1965 and graciously made their field notes available. Most of the information that follows is from their work.

RELIGION AND SUPERNATURALISM In 1927 the Indian Shaker church gained converts among the Yurok, and by the 1930s it had enough adherents to become influential in local life. One results was that sorcery by professionals almost disappeared, although knowledge about it remained widespread. It apparently was not uncommon for a person to whistle near an "enemy's" house at night as a means of frightening the occupants, but this "deviling" was more often mischievous than harmful. Among the Yurok in the late 1960s persons still were suspected of practicing sorcery if they had threatened somebody who became ill months or even years later. Individuals also were suspect if they behaved in a suspicious manner—for example, if they wandered alone late at night. Suspected sorcerers, who most often were old, poor, and lived alone, were avoided.

Attendance at Christian church services seemed to be the most important form of organized religious activity. The world-renewal ceremonies had died out long ago, but the Deerskin Dance still was held sporadically. One was given in 1955, and the next was held during seven days of August 1964. Reportedly, in 1955 most of the Yurok's boats were lost in a flood, and their destruction made traveling to a dance difficult. The same year, much of the ceremonial equipment was destroyed by fire; this caused the long delay between Deerskin Dances.

During December of 1964 a severe flood occurred along the Klamath River. The amount of Yurok property swept away or damaged by the flood was great, and the region was designated as a national disaster area. Some thirty-five Yurok houses along the Klamath were completely destroyed. The people were appalled by their material losses but were able to receive temporary supplies and clothing through the disaster relief program. Some Yurok had predicted that disaster would follow the cutting of a road through a sacred mountain by the Division of Highways two years before. Other Yurok offered a host of other possible causes for the disaster. They noted, for example, that a Deerskin Dance held at Hoopa had not lasted the traditional number of days. Furthermore, in the fires built during a recent Deerskin Dance, driftwood, not the traditional timber from the mountainsides, had been burned. Another mistake connected with this dance was that water had been sprinkled on the dance area by a truck before the event. Then, too, one man had refused to display his wealth at the dance, which again had invited disaster. The people were distressed also because cemeteries were washed away by the flood and the bones of the dead were exposed. The tradition-oriented Yurok explained the continuing rains of January 1965 as being caused by the exposure of bones of the dead; they thought the rains would continue until the bones once again were covered.

ATTITUDES: YUROK AND WHITE The views of many local whites about these Indians were stereotypic and fell into an expectable pattern. The Indians were considered drunkards with little or no respect for the law; dirty, irresponsible employees; and generally unreliable. Unquestionably, the opinions of the whites had a certain amount of truth to them, for the consumption of intoxicants did seem to be important to many Yurok, and the attitudes of many of them toward wage labor were not shared by whites. The Yurok considered whites to be greedy and felt that they looked down upon Indians. More important to the Yurok were their specific complaints against the Hupa, who they felt were unjustly favored by the BIA, and against BIA officials for both real and imagined injustices.

SOCIAL LIFE AND SUBSISTENCE Yurok social life still was built on the nuclear family residence unit, but Yurok of both sexes showed a striking tendency to marry whites. Yurok clothing did not differ from the garments of whites in the area, since both men and women wore store-bought clothing exclusively. Yurok homes were large, rectangular frame dwellings with four or more rooms. One characteristic of households was their cluttered appearance, the result of a great accumulation of material goods. Household furnishings included both expected items such as refrigerators, stoves, tables, and chairs and many seemingly useless items. The clutter apparently was compatible with older housekeeping norms. Houses contained collections of baskets, an overt sign of their Indian heritage. Production of baskets was limited, since few women retained the skill to make them, and they were sold primarily to Yurok. The sweat houses, which once were so extremely important, had largely ceased to function. Stools, which were one of the few items of aboriginal furniture, were occasionally seen in the dwellings, but they were regarded more as heirlooms than as furnishings. The traditional forms of Yurok wealth, such as elaborate ceremonial costumes, dentalium shells, and white deerskins, existed as treasures.

Subsistence fishing for salmon had become less important, although certain family fishing spots were owned, and trespassers were prosecuted. The timber industry was the primary source of employment, followed by road construction. During the summer months, numerous men served as hunting and fishing guides for tourists. In the mid-1960s, loggers earned $3.50 an hour, and in a nine-month season an individual might accumulate as much as $7,000. This was the most lucrative type of employment, especially when wages were supplemented by unemployment insurance payments for the balance of the year.

| Modern Developments

In recent years, concerted Yurok attention has focused largely on two long-standing conflicts with the federal government: the Gasquet-Orleans

(G-O) Road and land claims. These issues were finally resolved, and they merit primary attention.

THE G-O ROAD The Yurok and their Indian neighbors united against the U.S. Forest Service in opposition to the completion of a fifty-five-mile road between Gasquet and Orleans in the Six Rivers National Forest. The primary purpose of the road was to provide access to timber for logging; secondarily, it would serve as a scenic drive for tourists. By 1974 the road had been completed everywhere except in the Chimney Rock area. The Indians objected to the road's completion because the last six-mile segment would cross land that was sacred to the local tribes. It was to the Chimney Rock area that Indians traveled when they were "called." Apprentice female shamans went there to acquire power, and men visited its sacred places to experience the "power, beauty, and essence" that represented a core of their traditional religious life.

In a federal court suit to halt completion of the road, Indians and environmental groups joined forces. Years of complex litigation culminated in 1988, when the U.S. Supreme Court ruled on the basis of the First Amendment to the Constitution, the free exercise clause. The court determined that despite the religious importance of the area to Indians, the government *could* permit road construction and timber harvests in the area. However, the decision became moot with passage of the California Wilderness Act of 1984, which precluded building and use of roads in the area. Subsequent legislation protected the area from exploitation; entrances to the road are blocked by locked gates to prevent its use. Thus the Indians "won," but in essence were denied federal protection of religious sites on federal lands.

THE YUROK RESERVATION The Hoopa Valley Extension and the Klamath Reserve became the Yurok Reservation in 1988 following passage of the Hoopa-Yurok Settlement Act by the federal government. The reserve and the extension originally were designated for local Indians, not specific tribes. By the 1940s Hoopa Valley Reservation timber had become valuable, and, as trees were harvested, the BIA limited profits from the sales to Hupa enrolled on their reservation. The Yurok contended that they deserved to profit from the timber sales. This led to a suit, filed by Jesse Quinn McCoy Short, for a share in timber sale profits; she was one-quarter Yurok and one-quarter Hupa. This case was one of the most drawn-out litigations in American legal history, lasting for thirty-two years. A complication was that the Yurok had never organized as a tribe, and therefore they found it difficult to act against the Hupa. For the Yurok not to have organized was in keeping with their strong sense of individualism and the factionalism among powerful family lines.

In 1973 the U.S. Supreme Court ruled that the Yurok had a legal claim to the profits from the Hupa timber sales. A 1987 court decision stated that the legitimate Yurok claimants were owed timber-harvest payments and the interest from these monies dating back to 1958. In 1991 about thirty-five hundred

Yurok were judged eligible for individual payments of between four and fourteen thousand dollars in a complex distribution arrangement. The final settlement was completed in 1995, and the payments were made in 1996.

The Hoopa-Yurok Settlement Act also authorized the Yurok to organize as a tribe under the amended Indian Reorganization Act. A Yurok committee drafted a constitution that was adopted by the tribal members in 1994, and a tribal council became their governing body. In some ways the Yurok were advantaged by their relatively recent organization as a tribe. One compelling reason is that as a result of federal legislation in 1975 the BIA had been turning their administrative functions over to local Indians. By 1996 the Yurok had become deeply involved in self-government, enabling them to help guide their destiny to a far greater extent than ever before. They have been able to achieve expanded control over Indian law enforcement, the development of tribal courts, a greater share in forest management, and a more dominant voice in fishing regulations—the latter having been a long-standing conflict with the federal and state governments. These developments represent positive strides toward Yurok autonomy, even partial sovereignty. Yet their future, like their past, is linked to federal Indian policies, to their funding, and to the general political climate, none of which can accurately be anticipated.

As is the case with many reservations, the size of their modern land-holding is a major problem for the Yurok. Most Yurok sold their land allotments, typically to whites; most of the land eventually came to be owned by large timber companies. The original land base on the extension and old reserve consisted of about 57,000 acres. By 1994 nearly 49,000 acres had been alienated. Tribal lands accounted for 4400 acres and allotted lands comprised 3300 acres. Thus the tribe and individual Yurok together held about 13.5 percent of the extension and reserve land but only 2.5 percent of the original 300,000 acres that they occupied early in their history.

Many Yurok stoutly maintain that allotment holders have been repeatedly swindled out of their land, in part because they were nonliterate. The most recent cases were in the early 1950s, when BIA personnel and timber company agents visited allottees with timber holdings. The whites claimed that the timber was needed for the Korean War effort and that it would be unpatriotic for the Indians to hold on to their timber. This convinced numerous persons to sell what they *thought* were timber rights; in fact, they also were selling their land. The courthouse in which the records of these transactions were kept subsequently was destroyed by fire.

As the land base has declined dramatically over the years, there has been a corresponding significant decrease in the resident reservation population. By 1996 residents numbered about 750. However, their unemployment rate has been estimated at about 85 percent because so few job opportunities exist. This may help explain why an additional 1900 Yurok live in the general area where logging service jobs offer greater employment opportunities. At the same time, the definition of a Yurok has changed over the years, so that a person with one-eighth Yurok genetic heritage may now be on the tribal roll. The loss of genetic identity suggests that numerous tribal members have abandoned their sense of Indianness except in select contexts.

The diminished scope of traditional Yurok culture is readily apparent. Fewer than twenty individuals speak their aboriginal language. Traditional dances are still performed at public events, but the last Deerskin Dance to be held in its appropriate context was in 1906. They continue to make old-style baskets and other craft items, but these efforts do not seem to be an important part of life. Female shamans, who once played a central role in curing, have nearly disappeared. One woman remains a practicing shaman; she has a few apprentices who seek to become practitioners.

Despite these examples of eroding continuity with the past, for numerous, perhaps many, Yurok the sense of tribal identity remains strong and appears to be becoming stronger. Influential factors unquestionably have been settlement of the Jessie Short case in their favor and their recent organization as a tribe. The latter is especially critical because the Yurok are now able to control their own destiny in critical issues more than ever before; such issues include fishing regulations, forest management, and tribal courts. The fact that traditional Yurok ways have tenuous continuity may not matter all that much when they confront the modern world as reservation Indians (see Figure 7-10).

Since organizing as a tribe, the Yurok have devoted appreciable attention to the revitalization of traditional culture. To focus this effort, they formed

Figure 7-10 | Desmon (Merk) Oliver, in a 1996 photograph, was a Yurok living at Requa.

a tribal cultural committee and hired a cultural anthropologist, Thomas M. Gates, PhD, who administers the Tribal Heritage Preservation Office. This office assumed the responsibilities previously held by the state. A major effort has been made to pinpoint and document pertinent archaeological and ethnographic information about sites in traditional Yurok country. The cultural committee likewise has been developing other programs, such as one to revive Yurok as a spoken language. The devotion of the cultural committee to encouraging the furtherance of their traditions is clear.

| Additional Sources

The Yurok article by Arnold R. Pilling in the *California* volume (8) of the *Handbook of North American Indians,* William C. Sturtevant, general editor (Washington, DC, 1978) provides an excellent overview of these Indians and neighboring tribes. The best general ethnography is by Robert Spott and Alfred L. Kroeber (1942). The book by Lucy Thompson (1916), a Yurok woman, is an exceptional narrative by an Indian about her people. Superior presentations about particular aspects of Yurok culture are: material culture, Kroeber (1925); personality, Erik H. Erikson (1943); basketry, Lila M. O'Neale (1932); and placenames on the land, Thomas M. Gates (1995) and Thomas T. Waterman (1920).

| Selected Bibliography

Buckley, Thomas. 1979. Doing your thinking. *Parabola* 4(4):29–37.

———. 1982. Menstruation and the power of Yurok women. *American Ethnologist* 9:47–60.

Burski, Cynthia, and Dorothy Hosler. 1965, January. Field notes.

Bushnell, John, and Donna Bushnell. 1977. Wealth, work, and world view in native northwest California. In *Flowers of the wind,* Thomas C. Blackburn, ed., 120–82. Socorro, NM.

DuBois, Cora. 1939. *The 1870 Ghost Dance.* Anthropological Records, vol. 3, no. 1.

Erikson, Erik H. 1943. *Observations on the Yurok: Childhood and world image.* University of California Publications in American Archaeology and Ethnology, vol. 35, no. 10.

Gates, Thomas M. 1995. *Along the ridgelines.* Ann Arbor, MI.

Gifford, Edward W. 1922. *California kinship terminologies.* University of California Publications in American Archaeology and Ethnology, vol. 18.

Goldschmidt, Walter. 1951. Ethics and the structure of society: An ethnological contribution to the sociology of knowledge. *American Anthropologist* 53:506–24.

Heizer, Robert F., and John E. Mills. 1952. *The four ages of Tsurai.* Berkeley.

Kroeber, Alfred L. 1925. *Handbook of the Indians of California.* Bureau of American Ethnology Bulletin no. 78. Washington, DC. (Reprinted 1953, Berkeley.)

———. 1976. *Yurok myths.* Berkeley.

Kroeber, Alfred L., and Edward W. Gifford. 1949. *World renewal, a cult system of native northwest California*. Anthropological Records, vol. 13, no. 1.

O'Neale, Lila M. 1932. *Yurok-Karok basket weavers*. University of California Publications in American Archaeology and Ethnology, vol. 32, no. 1.

Pilling, Arnold R. 1978. Yurok. In *Handbook of North American Indians: California*, vol. 8, 137–54. Washington, DC.

Spott, Robert, and Alfred L. Kroeber. 1942. *Yurok narratives*. University of California Publications in American Archaeology and Ethnology, vol. 35, no. 9.

Thompson, Lucy. 1916. *To the American Indian*. Eureka, CA. (Reprinted 1991, Berkeley.)

Titiev, Mischa. 1963. *The science of man*. New York.

Valory, Dale K. 1970. *Yurok doctors and devils*. PhD dissertation, University of California, Berkeley.

Waterman, Thomas T. 1920. *Yurok geography*. University of California Publications in American Archaeology and Ethnology, vol. 16, no. 5.

———. 1938. *The Kepel fish dam*. University of California Publications in American Archaeology and Ethnology, vol. 35, no. 6.

Waterman, Thomas T., and Alfred L. Kroeber. 1934. *Yurok marriages*. University of California Publications in American Archaeology and Ethnology, vol. 35, no. 1.

8 The Tlingit: Alaskan Salmon Fishers

Tlingit rattle (from Lisianskii 1814)

The world is rolling around for all the young people; therefore let us not love our life too much, hold ourselves back from dying.

A song about the earth composed by Dry Bay George. (de Laguna 1972, 792)

WE PROBABLY HAVE more information about the Tlingit from early historic to modern times than we have for any other Northwest Coast salmon fishers. The Tlingit are an excellent example of a people in a land of plenty who stressed wealth as well as social achievements within family lines. Yet they were not politically organized at the tribal level; instead, narrowly defined bonds of kinship focused their economic, political, and social lives. Totem poles and potlatches, characteristic of Northwest Coast Indians in general, predominated among the Tlingit. While Tlingit totem poles usually are assumed to have been an aboriginal characteristic of Northwest Coast Indians, this chapter shows that they were a relatively recent development, quite possibly stimulated by the fur trade. The Tlingit's complex social network and ceremonial life invite comparison with the other salmon fishers represented in this book—the Kuskowagamiut and the Yurok. In addition, the Tlingit capacity to cope with members of Euro-American society contrasts with the less successful adaptation of most peoples described previously.

| People, Population, and Language

Tlingit means "the people." Their language appears to be distantly related to the Na-Dene phylum. They possibly numbered ten thousand early in their history, and by the late 1990s about fifteen thousand people identified themselves as Tlingit (see Figure 8-1).

| Early Contact with Explorers and Fur Traders

As early as 1582 a Spanish explorer sailed along the Tlingit coast, but he apparently made no contact with the people. An expedition led by Vitus Bering sailed from Kamchatka in 1741 to determine whether the Asian and North American landmasses were continuous. The ship that Bering commanded anchored off Kayak Island, at the northern fringe of Tlingit country; and although the sailors saw no people, they found a camp with a burning fire. The commander of the other vessel, Alexei Chirikov, anchored off the southern shores of Tlingit country. He sent two boats to investigate the coast, but neither boat returned. Indians later paddled two canoes toward Chirikov's ship but withdrew before making contact. On the return voyage Bering and his crew were forced to winter on what came to be known as Bering Island off the coast of Kamchatka. Here Bering died, but his men returned to Kamchatka the next year with valuable pelts of sea mammals. Russian adventurers hastily formed trading and hunting expeditions and sailed to the Aleutian Islands in a quest for furs, especially for sea otter pelts, which were extremely valuable in China. Before many years passed, Russian fur hunters and traders had reached the Alaskan mainland. In the late 1700s competition from European and American trading vessels seeking sea otters increased.

The following account by the northern Tlingit recalls the visit to Lituya

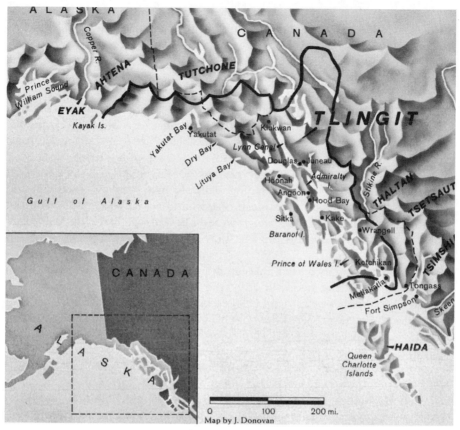

Figure 8-1 | Range of the Tlingit Indians.

Bay by Captain Jean de La Perouse of the *Astrolabe* and Paul-Antoine de Langle on the *Boussole,* the first Europeans to visit the locality. One day during the summer of 1786 a Tlingit hunter looked seaward from Lituya Bay on the Gulf of Alaska and was startled by what he thought he saw. Imitating the call of a wolf to signal important news, he ran to a nearby village. As people gathered, he called, "Raven is coming." He told them that Raven was white and could be seen on the western horizon. Everyone knew that Raven had been white before he turned black, and thus his reappearance as white was not surprising. This was a great moment because Raven, their creator and culture hero, had said he would return to reward people who obeyed his teaching and to turn the others into stone. Some persons looking seaward peered at the white object through hollow stalks of kelp so that they would not be blinded by Raven's brightness. As Raven came into the bay, he folded his wings. Those individuals who expected to be turned into stone stood erect and cut their chests with stone knives; others who felt no guilt began painting their faces to receive this great and honored visitor. One wise old man decided to go out to Raven and ask to be turned into stone so that others might be spared. He paddled a canoe to Raven and was lifted, canoe and all, from the water onto Raven's body. Here the old Tlingit saw men with white faces, brown hair, and blue eyes; their clothing was strange to him. The old man began to wonder whether he truly was in Raven's midst. A man far better clothed than the others appeared, and the old man assumed him to be Raven. The old man asked for mercy, but the man in fine clothing sent for food. One of the foods seemed to be a section of a human skull, and something else looked like maggots. Finally he was offered a red liquid that looked like blood; he declined to partake of anything. The well-dressed man then crossed his hands in the air twice, and the old Indian knew that this was not Raven after all since the sign he made was the one used for trading. The old man exchanged his hat and garments of sea otter skin for a piece of iron and a small bell. Then, without clothing, he got into his canoe, was lowered into the water, and paddled back to the village. He carried his prizes ashore and told the people of his great experience.

As competition increased, Russian merchants moved to gain firm control over the north Pacific trade. In 1799 the Russian-American Company was granted a monopoly by Czar Paul I. The company was dominated by one man above all others, Alexander Baranov, who had established the first permanent base on Kodiak Island in 1791. The major fort and trading post were built at Sitka in 1799. As long as Baranov was there, the Indians, who respected his bravery, were afraid to attack. When he left temporarily in 1801, the Indians destroyed the fort and killed the members of the small garrison.

When Baranov returned in 1804, with nearly nine hundred men, the Tlingit withdrew to a nearby fort. The Russians founded their hilltop settlement, New Archangel (Sitka). Anchored before Sitka was the *Neva,* under the command of Urey Lisianskii, the first vessel to sail to Russian America from European Russia. The Indians sought to drive the Russians away, but they could not withstand the bombardment from the *Neva* and withdrew from their fort.

After Baranov's retirement in 1818 a succession of administrators controlled the fortunes of the Russian-American Company, and relations with the Tlingit fluctuated with the abilities of the chief administrator. Throughout the latter part of the Russian period, Sitka was the primary trading center for the Tlingit, but American trading vessels and traders of the Hudson's Bay Company competed successfully for Tlingit pelts. The destructive Indian and Russian hunting techniques led to a rapid decline in the fur trade. When the Russian flag at Sitka was lowered on October 18, 1867, and the flag of the United States was raised, one era came to an end as another began.

| Aboriginal Life

Among all the aboriginal peoples of the world who lived as hunters, fishers, and collectors, those of the Northwest Coast of North America achieved the highest level of cultural complexity. Their lifeways were in many respects more complex than those reported among numerous aboriginal farming groups. The Tlingit are reasonably typical of these Indians; as was true of other Northwest Coast populations, the richness of their culture was based on the abundance of salmon and the reliability of this major food source.

ORIGIN MYTH   According to the Tlingit, the first people simply existed, and no explanation was sought for their origin. Among these people, according to one account, was a woman whose sons were killed by her brother. She decided to commit suicide, but an old man told her to swallow a heated beach pebble. The woman followed his instructions and became pregnant. She bore an offspring, who was Raven in human form. When Raven was older, he visited his uncle despite his mother's warnings that this man had killed his ten older brothers. The uncle attempted to kill Raven, but because of his supernatural powers Raven saved himself. Finally, Raven caused a flood, and all the people perished except for Raven and his mother, who donned bird skins and flew into the air. Raven stuck his beak in the sky and hung there for ten days. After the water subsided, he fell to earth and landed on a heap of seaweed. Raven went to the house of Petrel, a man who had always existed. In a small locked box on which he sat, Petrel kept water, and when Raven was thirsty, Petrel gave him only a little. Raven tricked Petrel into thinking that he, Petrel, had excreted in his bed. While Petrel was outside cleaning his blanket, Raven drank more than his fill of water and then flew to a tree with pitch in it. Petrel built a fire beneath the tree, and the smoke turned Raven from white to black. Later the trickery of Raven released the stars, the moon, and finally the sun into the sky. Raven was a creator or releaser of forces in the world, a culture hero, and an inordinate trickster.

APPEARANCE AND CLOTHING   The Tlingit were lean, medium to tall in stature, and had skins no darker than those of many persons in southern Europe. Women wore their hair loose and had striking adornments. From a woman's pierced earlobes hung ornaments of shell, stone, or teeth, and her nasal septum was pierced to receive a bone pin. Each woman also wore a large medial labret (lip plug) inserted through a hole beneath the lower lip (see Figure 8-2). The initial opening was made about the time of puberty and was fitted with increasingly larger labrets until the hole was as much as four inches across; as one observer noted, these women could not kiss. Men wore their hair loose and rubbed it with grease; while their whiskers were not numerous, they were nonetheless plucked. When a male was young, his nasal septum was pierced, and through the opening a small ring was suspended. Men wore ear ornaments like those of the women, and a man of great achievements might have bits of wool or small feathers stuck in several small holes around the outer edge of each ear. Facial paints were worn by men and women on special occasions and as protection from temperature extremes and insects.

Figure 8-2 | A girl in the Yakutat area with earrings, a nose pin, and labret. Sketched by Don Tomás de Suría in 1791. (Courtesy of the Beinecke Rare Book and Manuscript Library, Collection of Western Americana, Yale University.)

Adults of both sexes dressed in long-sleeved shirts of dehaired skin, over which they wore sea otter skin capes with the fur facing outward. The processed skin undergarments of women reached from the neck to the ankles. During severe weather they wore moccasins made by interior Indians or styled after their footwear. Tlingit hats, worn for hunting and ceremonies, were woven from roots or bark and were shaped like a truncated cone with a flat top. Their clothing hardly seems adequate to an outsider, but these people conditioned themselves to accept temperature extremes. They not only bathed in cold or icy waters but lived in scorching houses.

LAND AND SETTLEMENTS   Tlingit country is a mass of mountains that reach a sea marked by islands, deep bays, and glaciers. This verdant land with its tranquil and turbulent waters had rich exploitative potential. Along the northern third, impressive mountains abruptly meet the sea, and sheltering bays are rare. In the balance of Tlingit country innumerable large and small islands front a fractured coastline. The mild temperatures and heavy precipitation produce a lush and varied vegetation, including stands of red cedar and Sitka spruce. Considering the geographical configuration, it is understandable that travel by boat was far more important than walking, although trails to the interior existed along certain rivers and over low divides and were negotiated for trading or raiding ventures.

Winter villages were built along bays, inlets, or the lower courses of rivers, near good fishing grounds and where canoes could be landed safely. The square plank-covered houses had gabled roofs. At small villages, houses were built in a line facing the water, but the houses in larger settlements were arranged in rows. The plank-covered floor of the small dwellings was at ground level, but the central area of the larger houses was dug down about three feet. Along the sides at ground level were board- or mat-enclosed compartments for sleeping, bathing, or storage. Around the fire pit were stones to be heated in the fire and placed in containers for cooking food. Hunting and fishing devices were stored overhead along the beams, and fish might be hung from the roof beams to dry. Among the northern Tlingit, in particular, the house of a leading lineage was likely to have decorated wall partitions or panels called heraldic screens. It appears that behind a screen was the apartment of the house chief. Around the entry to a house, or even around an entire village, were palisades to protect the occupants. A bough-covered structure might be leaned against the outer wall of a house or built nearby for women during menstrual periods or childbirth. Scattered about a settlement were pole racks for drying fish, and a short distance away, either toward the forest or sea, were clusters of graves. At summer camps, where they caught their winter supply of fish, families lived in flimsy plank structures, some of which were walled only on the windward side.

Among the Tlingit the most important geographical unit was the *kwaan* (kwáan, kon), the people of a place or area, irrespective of their clan or moiety affinities. A kwaan was in many respects comparable to a "tribe," in which case the Tlingit collectively would be a "nation." From north to south the first kwaan was Yakutat, with its most important settlement along Yakutat Bay. The most powerful kwaan was that of the Chilkat, with four major villages along the shores of the upper Lynn Canal. One of these, Klukwan, had sixty-five houses and about six hundred residents. The only interior group, the Inland Tlingit, lived around a series of lakes and occupied the largest area. The other kwaans, each of which had at least one large village, were the Auke, Taku, Huna, Killisnoo, Sitka, Kake, Kuiu, Stikine, Henya, Tongass, and Sanya.

Within a village the land was owned by groups of persons who traced their descent to a presumed common female ancestor (matriclan), and land was subdivided among house groups. Plots of ground near houses were owned by the adjacent households, but village paths were common property. Community members as a group cleared the trails, and everyone was free to use the beach. Each kwaan had its geographical boundaries, and each village controlled the sector it exploited. Within the domain of a village, each represented clan had particular localities defined as its own. Unclaimed sectors could be exploited by anyone. A clan, or portion thereof, owned fishing streams; land of a stream's drainage used for hunting; sealing islands; mountains inhabited by mountain goats; ocean banks; berry patches; and house sites. They conceived of ownership in terms of specific spots used rather than as geographical areas exploited.

MANUFACTURES AND HOUSEHOLD LIFE   Tlingit artistic skills rank high among tribal peoples anywhere in the world. Their manufactures in bone, stone, and wood are justly famous. A wide variety of wooden containers filled a typical aboriginal household. One style was made from a thin plank of cedar that was steamed and bent into a rectangular form, then overlapped and sewn with root. A wooden bottom was fitted into place and a top sometimes added. Some of these boxes had bulging sides that were painted or carved. The largest and most elaborately decorated boxes were used for the storage of valuables, and others were used for cooking or food storage. Another common wooden form was made from a single piece of wood and ranged from round to oval to rectangular in outline. To these basic forms were adapted various animal shapes, such as a beaver lying on its back, with its head at one end, legs on the sides, and tail opposite the head. Other household items included dishes, spoons, and ladles of mountain sheep or goat horn. Oval lamps of pecked and polished stone furnished light as fish or seal oil burned on a moss wick.

Family members gathered around the fire pit to rest, eat, or work during the day. At the fireplace, they prepared meals at irregular times of the day for as many as thirty house occupants. Boiled foods were cooked in wooden or woven containers. They poured water into the containers and dropped hot stones in to simmer the meat or fish before putting on the lid. Fish were boiled, roasted, or dried, and served as the principal food, supplemented by flesh from land and sea mammals. They also ate shellfish, vegetable products, and fruit, particularly a wide variety of berries. These foods were relatively unimportant; however, shellfish became important in times of food stress. Boiled foods were dipped from their cooking containers in large spoons, which served as plates, and people consumed large quantities of water at every meal.

ART   Northwest Coast Indian art has long attracted the attention of Westerners because of the monumental aspects of the totem poles produced by men and the fine workmanship evident in the robes and woven baskets manufactured by women. The dominant materials worked by women were flexibles such as wool and cedar bark or the root fibers of spruce. Their most famous woven products were Chilkat robes, which were made from mountain goat wool with symbolic patterns produced by using wool dyed black and yellow. A single robe required six months or longer to make (see Figure 8-3). Women also wove baskets, making named patterns of geometric design. Men usually worked hard materials such as red cedar, copper that was pounded and incised, horn, and ivory. They often included symbolic patterns, especially

Figure 8-3 | Chilkat woman weaving a dance robe. (From Krause 1885, vol. 1.)

clan crests, as decorative elements on their totem and house poles, canoe parts, and ladles.

The crest of a clan was carved on any object by a member of the opposite moiety who held a rank equal to that of the individual requesting the carving. By preference this would be a wife's brother; if such an individual was not a capable carver, he could hire someone else of either moiety to make the object. The man who was first asked to do the work paid the craftsman and in turn was paid by his brother-in-law. Carvings produced in this manner fulfilled ritual obligations, and the labor involved was ceremonial.

Among the common elements in symbolic art were symmetrical, stylized figures. Animals most often were the subject matter, but human figures also appeared. Sometimes these seem to have been portraits of individuals. Tlingit art was not as complex as that produced by Indians to the south; neither was it so monumental, possibly because of the scarcity or absence of great cedar trees in most of the Tlingit area. The Tlingit did excel in producing a wide variety of imaginative masks used by performing shamans. The human faces might be supplemented with animal figures, which were the familiars of shamans. The carvings on utilitarian objects served to enhance their beauty and bring prestige to their owners. Distortion was an important consideration in Tlingit creations, since traditional forms were adapted to diverse surfaces. Carving a bear on a totem pole was very different from fitting the bear motif on a rectangular vessel, the handle of a horn spoon, or a flat screen painting. Another characteristic of artistic symbolism was that it emphasized features of an animal as a key to its identification. The beaver was characterized by its incisor teeth and tail, while the killer whale was keyed to its prominent dorsal fin. So it was with other totemic representations. Prominent and recurring characteristics included the skeletal motif, the use of joint markers, and the prominence of stylized eyes. Tlingit craftsmen employing these motifs produced outstanding works of art.

CONVEYANCES   The most important Tlingit manufacture for subsistence activities was the canoe, normally built in the winter when unhurried production allowed them to make attractive and sound vessels. The best wood came from a straight-grained red cedar blown over by the wind or felled by building a fire at the base. A builder would hew and scrape the log with a stone-bladed adz. To spread the sides of the hollowed log he filled the cavity with water and dropped hot stones into it. As the log expanded, pieces of wood were wedged across the gunwales to give the sides the desired degree of flare. The outer sides might be painted with designs and the bow carved. A small canoe carried two or three persons, whereas larger ones held sixty persons and were forty-five feet long. Canoes were propelled with paddles, and an extra-long paddle was used for steering. When not in use, a canoe was covered with mats or blankets to protect it from the sun, and water was sprinkled over the sides. A small canoe made from a cottonwood log was used for fishing and river travel.

Snowshoes were essential for overland mobility during the winter, especially among the Chilkat, who went inland to trade at this time of year. The maple or birch snowshoe frames were heated over a fire and shaped; the netting was made from rawhide thongs. The shoes were about four feet long and ten inches wide at their broadest point, with rounded toes that turned up at the front and pointed heels.

SUBSISTENCE ACTIVITIES   Terrestrial fauna included black and grizzly bears, fox, wolves, wolverine, lynx, and deer on some islands. Scattered caribou herds occupied mainland plateaus, and mountain goats as well as mountain sheep frequented the coastal ranges. Smaller species included hare, squirrel, ermine, porcupine, muskrat, and a few beaver. Among the marine mammals were whales, hair and fur seals, sea lions, and sea otter. Of all the fish the most important were the salmon and candlefish (eulachon); halibut, haddock, trout, and herring also were caught. Along the edges of the sea were edible algae, crabs, sea urchins, mussels, and cockles. Avifauna included the bald eagle, raven, owl, and migratory waterfowl that summered in the area.

The subsistence cycle ebbed during the winter, and even March did not offer reliable weather for fishing. Nonetheless, it was during March that the subsistence year began anew. Canoes were repaired, fishing gear was readied, and men waited anxiously. In calm weather they fished for halibut along the coast fronting the Pacific Ocean. Two men fished from a canoe, maintaining about fifteen lines with baited V-shaped hooks and a wooden floater for each. When a fish was hooked, they paddled to the bobbing float, raised the line, and clubbed the fish to death as it was boated. Trout fishing with baited hooks also was important at this time. Following the ice breakup in March women fished for trout with gill nets of rawhide with inflated bladder floats and stone sinkers. One woman usually paddled a canoe as a second handled the drifting net. They collected clams and mussels in large quantities and either dried and smoked them for future use or steamed them in a pit by pouring water over hot stones and applying a leaf covering. The pelts of fur animals were prime in March; fox, mink, wolf, and river (land) and sea otter all were sought. Some of these animals were trapped in deadfalls, but sea otter were hunted with harpoon darts.

Candlefish were a rich source of the oil that was drunk during feasts but more commonly served as a dip for dried salmon. These small fish were taken in traps or dip nets in the spring as they ascended rivers. Their processing began by placing the fish and water in a canoe half-buried in the sand. Heated stones repeatedly were dropped into the mass, and as the oil from the cooked fish came to the surface it was ladled into wooden containers. In mid-April herring spawned in shallow bays and were so numerous that they could be impaled on sharp tines set in the side of a pole. The tine-studded pole was drawn back and forth in the water, and the pierced herring were shaken off into the canoe. They either were eaten soon after being caught or were strung on ropes and dried.

Auke, Chilkat, and Stikine men traveled inland trading fish oil to Athapaskan Indians in exchange for caribou skins, moccasins, sinew, and lichens to be used for a particular form of dye. During the summer they paddled great canoes south to Haida and Tsimshian country, and in early historic times they ventured as far as Puget Sound in trading canoes. They carried copper from the Copper River and other local products to exchange for dentalia, haliotis, shark teeth, and slaves.

Sea mammals usually were hunted with harpoon darts that had a line running from the detachable dart head to the shaft. When an animal was struck, the barbed dart head held beneath its skin, and the shaft was dragged through the water as the animal sounded. When it surfaced, the captive was harpooned again or killed with a spear or club. The most important species hunted were dolphin, seals, sea lions, and especially sea otter in early historic times. From the ethnographic accounts it seems that sea mammal hunting was not very important or that inland hunting was important at most settlements. If bears or mountain goats were pursued, they were cornered with the aid of dogs and killed with bone-pointed spears.

In the late summer people collected berries and stored them with candlefish oil in airtight boxes. Salmon eggs, oil, and berries were similarly mixed and preserved. If large land mammals were killed, their flesh usually was cut into strips and sun-dried or else boiled and stored in oil. Some foods were stored for winter at this time of the year, but it was not until September that the winter food supply became a major concern. They took diverse species of salmon during the summer but made no great effort to catch and dry quantities of them until September. The species available included dog (chum), humpback (pink), king (chinook), silver (coho), and sockeye (red), and these were taken from July through December. The principal salmon-fishing device was a funnel-shaped trap set with the mouth opening downstream. The stream was blocked with a weir, which opened only at the trap. Fish caught in September were cleaned and hung on racks to dry or were smoke-cured in the house. After being dried or smoked, they were bundled and stored. As soon as a house group had obtained enough salmon for the winter, the members left their fishing camp and settled down in their village until April. Very little food apart from shellfish was gathered during the winter months, for this was the season for rituals, feasting, storytelling, and recreation.

In subsistence activities men dominated as the procurers of edibles, and women played the key role in households. The principal wife of the Keeper of the House was responsible for allocating domestic female tasks. The capacity of these women to process food, especially salmon, was a critical factor in the prosperity of a household. As Frederica de Laguna (1983, 81) has noted, "The whole Tlingit economy of subsistence and luxury wealth rests ultimately on the stores of dried salmon prepared by the women."

DESCENT, KINSHIP, AND MARRIAGE   The people of each kwaan were divided into two groups (moieties) that were represented in each of the geographical areas. The moieties were named Raven and Wolf, with the Wolf moiety called Eagle in the north; these were in turn divided into named descent groups traced through females (matriclans). The Tlingit associated specific personality characteristics with the moieties. Raven people were expected to be wise and cautious, and the Wolves quick-tempered and warlike. According to Aurel Krause (1885), the clans of the Raven moiety included the Frog, Goose, Owl, Raven, Salmon, and Sea Lion. Clans of the Wolf moiety included the Auk, Bear, Eagle, Shark, Whale, and Wolf. These lists, although far from complete, identify the important clans in early historic times. An outsider, who was not a member of any clan, was addressed as uncle or son-in-law, reflecting his in-marrying status. At Klukwan the most important clans were the Wolf and Eagle; these were divided into named subgroups that probably were lineages. Within each clan the lineage with the greatest wealth was most influential. Ideally, the leadership of a lineage was passed from a man to his sister's son, but apparently this practice could be bypassed by appointing a new chief while the old one was still alive. Each settlement with a number of clans represented had more than one chief, but one dominated because of his wealth and personality. A person in one moiety was obligated to seek as a mate someone in the opposite moiety (moiety exogamy); further ramifications of marital arrangements are presented in the section about the life cycle.

Each clan recognized a particular settlement as the place of its origin. Although a clan was identified initially with a specific site, by the time of historic contact a number of different clans usually were represented in most villages. If a clan was large in a particular settlement, it was divided into lineages represented by house groups. In theory, the clans of each moiety possessed distinctive titles and associated design motifs that only members could use. These might be lent temporarily or even usurped by a more powerful clan. Again in theory, only members of the Raven moiety had the right to the raven design, and only those of the Wolf moiety, the wolf design. House names usually were derived from a clan myth, from the clan's name, or by assuming the name of another clan's house for legendary or historical reasons. Moieties were each divided into a number of matriclans that in turn were divided into house groups composed of nuclear families, again related through females.

Nuclear family unity did not exist among the Tlingit because the parents were of different clans and moieties. Since various clans were represented in most areas, geographical groupings acted as a unit only in those rare instances when a feud affected all sections of the clan. A clan had no common leader or unified territory, and even crests often were identified with localized lineages rather than with the clan as a whole. Finally, each clan included persons ranked as nobles, "commoners," and slaves, depending on the social standing of particular lineages.

In the kinship system we find that a single term embraced all the people of the grandparent generation. To these persons the individual was attentive and respectful. The ties between a mother and her son were close even though the son might leave home to live with his mother's elder brother, who was for him the most powerful individual in Tlingit society and his authority figure. Fathers were considered too lenient to discipline their sons effectively, and of course a father did not belong to his son's clan or moiety. Parents were especially concerned about the welfare of a daughter, who would command a large bride price only if she were well-mannered and a maiden; thus, she always was watched by someone. A mother's sister was called by a term for diminutive mother and was treated as one's mother. The "little mother" term was extended to all the other women of her moiety in her generation. A mother was aided and advised in raising children by her sister. A father's sister

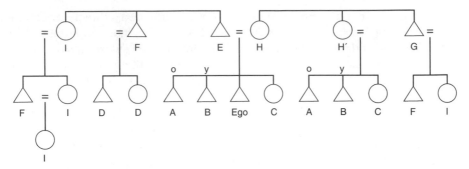

Figure 8-4 | The early historic Tlingit system of kinship terminology.

was termed differently from mother and mother's sister, with the father's sister word extended to all women of her moiety in both her generation and descending generations. The father term was unique while the term for father's brother was extended to the other men of his moiety of his generation as well as the next lower one. A man treated his father's brother with respect, and a girl on rare occasion married her father's brother.

A man ideally married his father's sister, and because she was a potential mate, their relationship was always warm. At one's generational level a man distinguished between older and younger brothers, and these terms were extended to the other men of one's generation and moiety. Older and younger male sibling distinctions were highly important because an older brother had the first rights of inheritance, greater authority, and more ceremonial responsibilities. A woman made the same distinction among sisters. There also was a particular term for a man's sister and one for a woman's brother; these were extended to all the members of that sex of the individual's generation and moiety. Brothers were socially and physically close since they were of the same clan and lived in the same house; with a sister a man was supposed to be distant and withdrawn, although he was concerned for her welfare. A mother's sister's children were termed brother and sister, and the boys were raised in the same household as the mother's children. The terminology for the first ascending generation was essentially bifurcate merging, and the cousin terminology was of the Crow type (see Figure 8-4). One overriding principle governed the kinship terminology of the Tlingit: to separate blood relatives in one's own moiety from those in the opposite moiety. The average adult avoided using relationship terms in direct address in everyday conversation for fear of offending someone, since a great deal of emphasis was placed on an exact ranking of individuals. Thus, nicknames and given names were in common use. Relationship terms were employed primarily on ceremonial occasions.

SOCIAL DIMENSIONS   The most important social and economic unit was the household, and it had a significant place in the ceremonial life of the clan and moiety. A house group ideally was composed of a male and his brothers, as well as his mother's sister's sons who were classificatory brothers, and the sons of the sisters of these individuals, plus the sons of the daughters of these sisters. All were members of one matrilineage, and there were additionally the in-marrying spouses. A household of this nature functioned as an economic unit, with members working for their common welfare. In particular it was brothers, led by the eldest, the Keeper of the House, who aided one another in feuds, potlatches, and other matters of house group concern. The importance of the Keeper of the House in directing house group life cannot be over-estimated. He directed the economic activities of household members and was deferred to by the other men in his residence unit. The house group leader allotted items obtained in trade, was given choice foods, and was freed from any humble form of household labor. It was this man, the eldest brother, who represented the household in ceremonial activities as well as in clan councils. Furthermore, when he died the rights to his position fell to the next oldest person called brother. In addition to the position of Keeper of the House, the wealthiest of the local household heads in any clan, and thus the ranking Keeper of the House, was designated Rich Man. These men more than any others were responsible for the fortunes of their clan units.

Within a household the Keeper of the House and his principal wife outranked all other members. Older brothers and sisters outranked younger ones, while bastards and slaves ranked lowest. The same system prevailed between the members of a leading lineage and of the secondary ones within a clan. The highest-ranking persons were aristocrats, chiefs, and the wealthy. Their status was based on birth, personal character, accomplishments, age, and either inherited or acquired wealth. "Commoners" as such did not exist; instead, most persons within lineages were junior members who could be ranked against other persons in broadly similar positions. Furthermore, just as households and lineages were ranked against one another within a clan, so it was among the clans of a moiety. The members of lowly clans were poor, whereas those of lofty clans were rich, hosted elaborate potlatches, and had splendid artifacts as clan heirlooms. The leading members of some aristocratic clans reportedly could not sleep at night because they thought so intently about their greatness.

Men clearly were the overt Tlingit leaders, but the importance of women behind the scenes was exceedingly strong, so much so that they may be considered the dominant gender. Judgments by women were critical in trading relations; they were the keepers of household wealth, and they made critical decisions in social life. The prominence of women was in keeping with Tlingit matrilineality. Thus, moiety, clan, and lineage matters were in their firm grasp. Unfortunately, however, their position is not well reported in the early ethnographic record.

In this social setting, based as it was on rank, classes did not exist. Instead, wealthy and prestigious households competed with one another within a clan and beyond it for high status that changed with the fortunes of these

units. In the absence of social classes, the rank of a household, a clan segment, or a whole clan relative to another such unit constantly was being re-
assessed. The comparative wealth and prestige of these units was tested in
numerous ways, such as in potlatches and, to a lesser extent, in the erection of
totem poles.

TOTEM POLES   Among the Tlingit, the most valued possessions were
clan or lineage crests. Crests were represented on canoes, dishes, ceremonial
garments, and totem poles, as well as on other artifacts. The most important
crests for the Raven moiety were the raven, owl, and whale. Wolf moiety
crests included the eagle, wolf, and bear. Crests represented Tlingit totems that
were honored in ritual contexts, but totems were not worshiped.

No aspect of Northwest Coast Indian life has fascinated Westerners more
than totem poles. The size of the totem poles, their boldly sculptured figures,
and their design motifs have made them memorable cultural monuments. Edward L. Keithan (1963), in a comprehensive account of Tlingit poles, identified
six primary types.

1. The four main vertical support posts for a house usually were plain,
but they might be faced with carved pillars (or panels) bearing clan crests
that could include abalone shell inlays. *Carved house pillars* were one of the
two prehistoric types.

2. The second prehistoric type was the *mortuary pole*. The pole body
was plain. A box was set at the top of the pole in which were placed the
cremated remains of the person honored. A crest figure might be carved on
the upper portion of the pole. The earliest example was reported in 1791
(see Figure 8-5).

Figure 8-5 | The earliest illustration of a Tlingit mortuary pole and graves,
1791, for the Yakutat area. (From Malaspina and de Bustamante y Guerra 1885.)

3. A *memorial pole* honored a deceased house group leader and was raised under the sponsorship of a younger brother or maternal nephew of the dead person. Such a pole usually was not erected at the interment site. Its purpose was to honor the deceased and, equally important, to validate the succession of the house group leader.

4. A *heraldic pole* was raised at the front and center of a house. A myth or tale associated with the house group was represented by the carved and painted pole.

5. The *ridicule pole* usually was raised to force another house group to settle a debt. One particular example was said to have been erected to shame a white trader for not repaying a potlatch held in his honor.

6. The *potlatch pole* was the most recent type to appear. They were raised to enhance the prestige of a family group that had accumulated and distributed wealth from the fur trade or by working directly for whites (see Figure 8-6).

Totem poles in general did not become commonplace among the Tlingit until the late 1800s. In 1881–82 one pole was reported among the Chilkat, none among the Sitka or Killisnoo groups; however, they were numerous at one Stikine village. Some observers have suggested that great totem poles may not have been carved until iron-bladed tools became widely available as a result of the fur trade. Yet a well-developed woodworking technology predates the Northwest Coast Indian fur trade.

For the Tlingit, erecting a totem pole was an end in itself. A pole that was carved and raised for a particular purpose was thereafter unimportant as a physical object. As a pole tilted with age or threatened to fall, it was not supported in any manner. Restoration necessitated ceremonial involvements and an outlay of wealth equal to that expended when the original pole was raised, and therefore it was more sensible to erect another pole and bring even greater honor to the house group. Since poles deteriorated rapidly in this damp area and comparatively few new poles were raised after the turn of the present century, most have rotted away.

The totemic symbols exhibited on poles were associated with one or the other of the moieties, with clans, or with house groups. All of the Raven moiety members employed the Raven design as their primary symbol. The Wolf moiety had the Wolf as its chief totem in the south and the Eagle in the north. Not only the actual crests but also the names of animals associated with a clan were important, and their uses were validated through the potlatch system. These honorific names, often drawn from the clan or moiety totems, tended to pass from great-grandfather to great-grandson. The animals associated with a moiety could be killed and eaten by moiety members, however, and the uniform eating habits of all the tribe indicate no taboo on eating one's totemic species.

ENTERTAINMENT Gambling was an important pastime among adult Tlingit males, and some men were so addicted that they sometimes lost prized

Figure 8-6 | Chief's house with painted front and totem poles in 1899. (Courtesy of the Smithsonian Institution, National Anthropological Archives, neg. no. 43,548-H.)

possessions, even including wives. The most important form of gambling was a hand game in which one man guessed which hand of an opponent held a uniquely marked stick. The game was played by teams, but only one man of each team handled the sticks at any one time. Other adult diversions included dice games and a ball game in which the purpose was to drive a ball along the tidal flats to the opponent's goal. Boys played a game that involved throwing a stick at a rolling wad of grass. They also wrestled, hunted, and swam for entertainment. A favorite diversion among little girls was to arrange beach pebbles in the form of figures.

POLITICAL LIFE Conflicts between Tlingit moieties were common, and modern Tlingit liken these disputes to relations between European nations. For real or imagined injuries, either material goods were exchanged or a life was taken. The nature of a settlement depended on the ability of the guilty to pay and the power of the offended to collect. Minor conflicts eventually were settled at feasts that included property settlements. When a person was grievously offended, the only acceptable retribution was the offender's murder, but this was bound to lead to a retaliatory killing. If those murdered were of unequal rank, there was the further problem of establishing a value for each death. Sometimes when an individual felt badly wronged and had no means to retaliate, he committed suicide, and his relatives then pressed for compensation. On occasion, clan disputes were settled by a duel between warriors who represented each group. Murders were from ambush, as were raids against other clans or tribes. The only crimes occurring within a clan were incest and witchcraft, each punishable by death. It should be stressed that overall political unity did not exist within a moiety, and some of the bloodiest feuds were between clans of the same moiety.

Raids were conducted to avenge deaths and to obtain slaves. Preparations for impending conflict involved fasting and abstaining from all contact with women. In addition, a warrior conditioned himself for combat by bathing in the sea, even at the coldest time of the year, and by being whipped by an older man. As a raiding party traveled, it seized property from camps along the way irrespective of whether the residents were friendly or not. A shaman always accompanied the party and predicted events of the near future. Plans for an attack on an enemy community were kept secret, and the foray was launched at dawn. Rod or skin armor protected a man's body; his face was covered with a mask, and his head with a wooden helmet. All the enemy men who did not escape were killed with daggers; women and children were taken as prisoners. A reprisal attack would be expected to avenge the murders.

Copper-bladed daggers, spears, and war clubs appear to have been the most important weapons. Scalps were taken at times, and the scalped person's head sometimes was impaled on a stick and exhibited. The men in a war party sang of victory as they returned to their village, and the paddle of each warrior killed was propped up at the spot he had occupied in the boat. To bind peace, hostages might be exchanged and kept for a year or longer. Peacemaking followed a pattern of ceremonialism, which climaxed with the exchange of hostages, termed "deer" since they were to behave as timidly as these animals.

Most slaves were captured in raids or purchased from peoples to the north or south. Others were the children of indebted men who could find no way out of their dilemma except to offer themselves and as many of their children as necessary to cancel the debt. These slaves, unlike the captives, might be redeemed. Slaves usually were well cared for by their masters since they were a valuable form of property. Yet, some reports picture the lot of slaves as extremely difficult since they performed all odious tasks and might at any time be killed at their owner's fancy. Sometimes slaves were killed to emphasize the importance of their owner—for instance, when he built a new house. To gain prestige one man might kill a number of slaves; his rival would be obligated to kill a greater number, and so it went until one contestant had no more slaves. The ownership of slaves apparently provided prestige more than economic gain. The proportion of slaves to free persons is not known, but ten slaves in a house was a large number.

RELIGION AND SUPERNATURALISM   The Tlingit crystallized their knowledge about the natural world and integrated it into a loosely ordered system. They thought of the world as a flat expanse with the sky as a dome above the earth. They believed that everything that existed in all this space was alive: spirits lived on the sun and moon; stars were the lights of distant towns or houses. They sometimes named clusters of stars, and they identified Venus. A rainbow was thought to be the path of dead souls to the upper world, and the northern lights, human spirits playing. For the Tlingit, everything on earth was possessed by a spirit quality, which had subordinates or helpers; each trait, every fire, and everything that one did had its main spirit and helpers.

Tlingit shamans reputedly were the most powerful on the north Pacific coast, and their effectiveness came from the spirits they controlled. The usual manner in which a clan acquired a new shaman was for the spirit of the clan's shaman to leave his body at death and enter the body of an upstanding clan youth. Nephews who aspired to the position went into trances around the dead man's body, and the one who remained in a trance the longest was most likely to be named the successor. After this supernatural visitation the novice and certain near relatives went into the forest, ate little, and searched for a sign. The most propitious was to see a bird or an animal drop dead; the spirit of this creature henceforth aided the novice. After the young man demonstrated that he had his uncle's power, he inherited the ceremonial equipment.

Shamans controlled the spirits represented on their masks (see Figure 8-7), and while most spirits served specific clans, some could be controlled by any shaman. The latter category included a spirit associated with the souls of persons who were lost at sea or died alone in the forest. The primary protecting spirit was represented as the main figure on a mask, and helping spirits also might appear. A secondary spirit might be posed around the eyes of a mask, thereby increasing the vision of the primary spirit. A shaman neither cut nor combed his hair, and about his neck he wore a bone necklace and a small whetstone, the latter used for scratching his head. A shaman owned rattles that

Figure 8-7 | Shaman's mask of painted wood. (Courtesy of the Field Museum, Chicago, neg. no. A98082.)

had spirit associations and were used in his performances. The split tongues of animals, especially the river otter, and the claws of eagles were sources of power; both appear to have been placed in bundles of cedar bark, grass, and devil's club. After a shaman bathed, he rubbed himself with the bundle, and he used it in all his rituals. Among the spirit helpers were those of the sun, the sea, and the crest animals of the shaman's clan. After summoning his spirit helpers, a shaman cured an afflicted individual by blowing, sucking, or passing an object over the locus of the disease, which drew out the cause. Other services of a shaman included locating food sources and predicting the future. A shaman and his family usually lived in a separate residence, and in the forest near the house was his shrine. From time to time shamans retreated for extended periods to intensify their spirit relationships.

A number of charms appear to have been employed by ordinary persons. Made from parts of plants, they were used in such diverse activities as foreseeing the future, attracting a woman, making one wealthy, or improving hunting abilities. A few additional items seem to have served as secular cures, but these were rare and apparently unimportant. In general, it would appear that curing and supernaturalism were shamanistic matters. It is interesting that salmon, which were the all-important subsistence item, were not dealt with in a sacred manner. They simply were accepted as present and were caught and eaten. Even in Tlingit mythology, salmon play a relatively unimportant role; they seem to have been regarded as a constant part of the environment.

Witchcraft was most often performed by obtaining an item intimately associated with the victim and using it in a representation of the victim in the form desired. If a person became ill, the cause was attributed to sorcery, and the offender was named by the curing shaman. Persons accused of being witches usually were women, children, or slaves. They were tortured to extract a confession or killed if a confession was not forthcoming. An accused witch was bound by clan members and given no food or water for eight days or longer. If the person was a witch and did not confess, death was expected at this point; if the accused confessed, the bewitching substance was scattered in the sea, and the individual presumably resumed an ordinary status.

LIFE CYCLE   Childbearing was prohibited within the mother's home because it supposedly would bring ill fortune to the men of the house. Thus, a birth took place in a shelter never visited by men. During the birth, slaves and a midwife, always a member of the opposite moiety and preferably the woman's husband's sister, aided the woman. Inside the structure a pit was dug and lined with moss, and a stake was driven into the center of the hole. While giving birth, the woman squatted in the pit, holding the stake. After the birth the umbilical cord was cut and placed in a bag hung around the neonate's neck for eight days; the umbilical cord of a boy later was placed under a tree where an eagle had nested to make the boy a brave adult. To prevent a baby from crying repeatedly, the first cry was caught in a container and buried where many people walked so that it would be smothered as the baby grew. The baby was wrapped in skins, with moss for a diaper, and was tied to a board. The mother carried the cradleboard with her or hung it from a roof beam when she was in the house. She placed woodworm burrowings on her nipples so that as the baby nursed she or he would swallow the burrowings and would be neat in later life. A child was nursed for three or four years and was given its first solids after about a year. An infant born to a woman without a husband normally was suffocated. A baby was named after a maternal ancestor; the name itself was taken from an animal associated with the clan. With the birth of a son the parents referred to themselves by the son's name, as the father or the mother of the son (teknonymy).

Children were encouraged to behave in a manner appropriate to adults of the same sex. They were taught to restrain signs of emotion, to be dignified and aloof. They were expected to take cold baths daily from the time they learned to walk and were physically punished if they refused to bathe in the winter. When boys moved to the household of their mother's brother, they were whipped with a switch by this man after bathing and were forced to run up and down the beach. After this exercise, they were instructed by older men in the customs and history of the clan, and they learned certain skills by watching men perform routine tasks. As a boy grew, he came increasingly under the influence of his maternal uncle and performed tasks for this older man rather than for his father. A boy tended to gravitate toward a particular uncle whom he wished to emulate in his exceptional skills relating to carving, hunting, or the supernatural. The uncle gave honorific names to his young charges and taught them clan lore, but no secret initiations took place. The most important nephew was the oldest, for he would inherit from his maternal uncle not only material property and wives but titles as well. Even while young, boys were free to use a maternal uncle's tools with permission. If a mother died, the father was obliged to place the offspring in the custody of the mother's siblings.

When a girl first menstruated, she was confined to a brush-covered shelter or to a compartment in the house behind the heraldic screen. Her face was covered with charcoal, and she was attended by female relatives and a slave if her parents were wealthy. A high-born girl was isolated for a year, and one of lower birth was confined for at least three months. She drank water through a bird-bone tube and went outside only at night, even then wearing a broad-brimmed hat so that she would not taint the stars with her gaze. During isolation her mother instructed her about proper female behavior and taught her clan myths and songs. At the beginning of her confinement, her lip, nasal septum, and possibly her earlobes were pierced by a woman of the opposite moiety. When she came out of seclusion, she wore new clothing, and her slave attendant, if she had one, was freed. The girl would marry soon, and to ensure that she remained chaste she slept on a shelf above her parents' bed. The rank of a person was reckoned through both sides of the family and depended largely on the amount of bride price paid by one's father for one's mother; thus, parents attempted to provide a daughter with all the advantages of careful rearing and wealth.

Moiety exogamy was strictly observed, and a match was initiated by the suitor, who used a go-between to approach the girl and her family. If favorably received, he sent presents to his future father-in-law. The most desirable marriage partners, in decreasing order, were a father's sister, brother's daughter, father's sister's daughter, and finally, mother's brother's daughter. In the ideal form of marriage with father's sister, the groom assumed the role of his mother's brother. However, the most common marriage was with a father's sister's daughter, and this was preferred by a young man. Marriage to near relatives served two important functions: to keep wealth concentrated and to provide spouses of nearly equal rank.

A wedding ceremony was held in the bride's house. Here relatives of the groom assembled as he sat in the middle of the floor wearing his most elaborate ceremonial garb. The bride was concealed in a corner of the house and was lured to sit beside the groom by the singing and dancing of the assembled group. The guests were feasted, but this was not a formal potlatch event. A month after the ceremony the couple was considered married. Marriage residence was with the family of either spouse (bilocal), depending on the wealth and standing of the principals. If the couple moved into the man's household, the bride's relatives presented him with property equal to or exceeding the value of that presented by his relatives. A man of wealth might have multiple wives (polygyny), with the first wife holding a rank superior to that of any subsequent spouses; five wives appear to have been the maximum. A woman sometimes had more than one husband (polyandry) but only if the second husband was a brother (fraternal polyandry) or near relative of the first. A widow customarily married her late husband's brother (levirate), and if the deceased husband did not have a brother, his sister's son married the widow. If neither category of individual was available, a widow could marry any man of her former husband's clan. If his mother's brother died, a man was obligated to marry the widow even though he might already have a wife, and he inherited his uncle's wealth. In spite of the ideal that a man should live in the house of his mother's brother, inherit his wealth, and marry his daughter or another person in this line, his father's clan attempted to lure him into its domain. This especially seems to have been true for a boy who had married into the community. When a married woman was seduced, blood revenge might be exacted by her husband, or the seducer might make a property settlement. If the seduction was by a near relative of the husband, the offender was expected to become the woman's second husband.

To outsiders, the Tlingit (Kolosches) were not likable. Physicians for the Russian-American Company at Sitka in 1843–44 described the people as follows (Romanowsky and Frankenhauser 1849, 35): "The Kolosches are proud, egoistic, revengeful, spiteful, false, intriguing, avaricious, love above all independence and do not submit to force, except the ruling of their elders." Still, adults were patient and persistent; they never seem to have hurried; and they became angry only with provocation. During the fishing season they worked long hours, but winter was a time for leisure. During the winter women made their famous robes and baskets; in general, women appear to have had less free time than men. The social position and respect that a woman commanded depended on her personality and standing within her clan; a woman with abilities was listened to by men. Women had well-defined rights, and relatives were willing to come to their defense in case of any injustice from the husband's side of the family. An individual, whether male or female, was expected to behave in accord with his or her rank. Persons were of higher rank if their clan was large, wealthy, and powerful. Still, not all such persons were noble in their behavior, in which case they were treated as though they belonged to a lesser clan. Were a person from a high-ranking clan to behave coarsely as judged by fellow clan members, he or she might be killed by them.

Death, as a major aspect of the life cycle, was given elaborate focus in funeral ceremonies, memorial feasts, and especially memorial potlatches. Collectively, these involvements provide insight into the substance and symbolism of Tlingit culture. The conventions surrounding Tlingit dead in the nineteenth century have been reconstructed by Sergei Kan (1983; 1986), who emphasizes the meaning behind the rituals and ceremonies.

Figure 8-8 | A man lying in state amidst his wealth, circa 1890. (From Porter 1893.)

A corpse embodied specific qualities and was considered dangerous to lineage members. The flesh was regarded as soft and wet compared with the bones, which were solid and dry. Bones were intermediate between the flesh and spirit; with cremation, bones, which were pure, found release from the polluted flesh. A ghost dwelled with the bones and, by cremation, became warm in the afterlife. The fireplace in a house served as the medium through which to communicate with the deceased of a lineage; burning food and gifts became a means for the living to provide for the dead.

Shortly after a death a body was prepared by members of the immediate lineage. The ghost of the deceased was thought to remain in the dwelling for four to eight days, while the body rested in state at the back of the house surrounded by personal wealth and by lineage and clan possessions (see Figure 8-8). The principal mourners were closely related lineage members who painted their faces black, fasted, and observed other customs as they wailed and sang "crying songs." One important ritual was to burn food and tobacco in the fireplace as offerings to matrilineal ancestors. At this critical time, parental and affinal relatives (members of the opposite moiety) performed routine household activities to free mourners from ordinary and thus polluting concerns. Members of the opposite moiety also visited the mourners each evening to comfort them and received token gifts for their efforts.

Following a wake, the body was removed through a temporary opening made in the back of the house or through the smokehole above the fireplace. Males of the opposite moiety cremated the corpse, and some of the person's possessions were burned. Females of the opposite moiety collected the ashes and bones, which were put in a box and temporarily placed in a grave house.

Afterward, the primary mourners bathed, dressed normally, and hosted the first of a series of small feasts for those who had helped them. At these events, food and tobacco again were offered to the matrilineal ancestors of the deceased. This series of small celebrations ended when the spirit of the deceased was believed to have entered the "village of the bones' people," the Tlingit term for a cemetery. The dead usually were buried behind the house of their clan, although the ashes and bones of aristocrats might be placed in mortuary poles. In their afterlife, the dead were believed to follow the life-style of their immediate descendants. Obligations to the recently deceased did not end until a new box, a repaired grave house, or a mortuary pole was provided for the remains. This was taken care of by the same group from the opposite moiety that had aided the bereaved relatives throughout the wake.

The memorial potlatch, for which extended preparations were made, was given to compensate moiety opposites for their help at the time of a death. A second purpose was to end the period of mourning, and a third one was to transfer the names and certain items of property of the deceased to a successor.

The word "potlatch" is of European and anthropological origins. The Tlingit word is *kueex,* meaning to call or invite to a ceremony that focused on marriage, death, or the investiture of an heir. The hosts sent delegates near and far to extend formal invitations to named guests. When guests arrived, songs and dances of greeting were exchanged and a mock battle enacted. Although a potlatch spanned only four days, the hosts entertained and fed their guests for about a month. The formalities began as the hosts cried and sang sad or "heavy" songs to indicate that their period of mourning was nearly over. Guests offered condolence speeches, followed by speeches of gratitude from the hosts. The hosts also placed food in the fire for the deceased, who were considered to be present. The tenor of the rituals then shifted, as the guests coaxed the mourners back to a normal state with jokes and "lighter" songs. The climax of the potlatch came when hosts transferred the titles and ceremonial objects of the deceased to his or her successor and to others in the maternal group. The hosts also ceremonially presented gifts to specific guests according to their rank; the number and quality of gifts a person received became a marker of his or her status. Some gifts were burned in honor of lineage ancestors, who were believed to receive the essence of the goods. When the potlatch ended, guests received any excess food and expressed thanks to their hosts (see Figure 8-9).

By the end of a potlatch, the bones and ghost of the honored dead were thought to be at home in the village cemetery, and the person's spirit had reached the "village of the dead." Another noncorporeal entity was believed to return to the living to be reincarnated in matrilineal descendants of the deceased, while names, ceremonial titles, and lineage or clan artifacts went to his or her immediate successor. Kan (1986, 198) writes, "The rebirth of the deceased and the death's failure to interrupt the continuity of the matrilineal group were dramatically expressed by addressing the new owner of the title or the regalia as if he were the deceased himself."

Figure 8-9 | Two Tlingit men in ceremonial garments before 1895. The man on the left wears a painted hide tunic and wooden hat. The one on the right with a nose ring and facial paintings wears a woven dance shirt and holds a rattle. Both men are wearing leggings decorated with porcupine quills. Photograph by Lloyd V. Winter and Edwin P. Pond. (Courtesy of the Alaska State Library; PCA 87-296.)

The potlatch was foremost a memorial ceremony that allowed a group of hosts to honor all of their recently deceased relatives and individuals, but it also was to honor their particular ancestors. Thus, it provided continuity between the living and the dead of a matrilineal group and gave mourners the opportunity for a profound expression of sorrow. It was during a potlatch, too, that the successor validated his or her claim to a particular rank and status by assuming specific titles or the management of ceremonial equipment.

In analyzing Northwest Coast Indian potlatches, ethnographers often have placed the greatest emphasis on competitive aspects, both within the host group and between the hosts and their guests, as individuals or groups vied for rank, status, and prestige. Competition seems to have been most keen among host lineages of nearly equal rank in their efforts to "grab" a high-ranking name, rather than between hosts and guests. Although this element clearly was important, Kan emphasizes that among hosts and guests there also was a major stress on group or individual "love and respect" for ancestors. Finally, reciprocity in different forms was a pervasive aspect of potlatch traditions. Reciprocity between the living and the dead of a lineage or clan and reciprocity between hosts and guests were especially prominent. In sum, a potlatch fostered both competition, to separate, and cooperation, to unite, the participants.

| Early Historic Changes

Aboriginal Tlingit life inevitably changed as a result of early Spanish and then Russian and Euro-American influences. The material culture changed with trade, religion changed with the arrival of Christian missionaries, and patterns of settlement, social life, and subsistence changed as the Tlingit adapted to colonialism.

TRADE AND GOVERNMENT From the time the Russians reestablished themselves at Sitka in 1804 until 1867, Sitka was virtually the only Russian center in southeastern Alaska. During the early era of contact, iron was the most desired trade item among the Tlingit. Russians and shipborne European or Euro-American traders were most eager to obtain sea otter pelts from the Indians, and they found the Tlingit to be cunning and dangerous hagglers. Furthermore, women were usually at the forefront in making commercial transactions. As trade contacts intensified, the people were increasingly selective. They wanted woolen blankets because they were trading away their animal pelt clothing; they also desired firearms and were able to obtain them from non-Russian sources. Standard early trade items included axes, metal containers, tobacco, glassware, and clothing. The Russians never gained political control over the Tlingit, who governed themselves. The Russians could only try to minimize the violence around the Sitka area.

In 1867 ownership of Alaska was formally transferred from Russia to the United States. The ceremony took place at Sitka. The Tlingit were not permitted in Sitka for the ceremonies, but they watched from canoes in the harbor. Russian inhabitants of Alaska had the option of either returning to Russia within three years or becoming U.S. citizens; nearly all of them left soon after the transfer. For ten years civil government did not exist, and the U.S. military garrisons at Sitka, Tongass, and Wrangell were more often a source of trouble than a means to establish order. The Tlingit clashed repeatedly with the military over Indian deaths that went uncompensated, which led to murders and the destruction or threatened destruction of Tlingit settlements. After the troops departed, the U.S. Revenue-Cutter Service vessels and the collector of customs usually represented legal authority. In 1878 the customs officer at Wrangell stated that within the space of a month he had a thousand complaints from Indians but had no way to deal with them. The difficulty became acute with the influx of miners who wintered that year at Wrangell. In 1880 gold was discovered near the present city of Juneau, which brought more miners and confusion; still, it was not until 1884 that a civil government began to function in the more populous areas of Alaska.

CHRISTIAN INFLUENCE   Russian-era efforts to Christianize the Tlingit never were very successful because of the strong aboriginal religious system, the limited scope of Russian influence, and the scarcity of clergy. A Russian priest made an unsuccessful attempt to vaccinate the people of Sitka against smallpox in 1834. In 1835 a smallpox epidemic struck. No Russians died, but nearly half of the Tlingit may have perished. When the Indians realized their shamans could not cure the disease, they turned to the Russians for vaccinations.

The Presbyterian Sheldon Jackson established a mission at Sitka in 1878, and a school was founded in 1880. Missionaries found that Tlingit women were more receptive to Christianity than were men. Because women were influential in this matrilineal society, working through them became an important avenue of culture change. Girls attended school more often than boys and became interpreters more often than men, which gave them increased standing and influence. Certain biblical messages were readily understood. For example, the sacrifice of Jesus Christ for the sins of humankind was fully comprehensible in terms of compensation. A Tlingit also considered it much better to give than to receive, which again was a Christian ideal, although with a different meaning. They began to expect rewards for becoming Christian. When asked to attend church, an old Tlingit was likely to respond, "How much you pay me?" Parents also expected compensation for permitting their children to attend school. Presbyterian mission schools became widespread and a key institution for the introduction of systematic changes. Instruction was in English, and students were punished for speaking Tlingit. It was through these schools that missionaries were most successful in winning converts.

One of the problems faced by missionaries was the condition of Tlingit slaves. Except in rare instances, slaves were not freed when Alaska was purchased by the United States because there was no effective governmental agent to force emancipation. The missionaries also took a firm stand against cremation, shamans, the potlatch system, polygyny, and intoxicants.

SOCIAL LIFE, SETTLEMENTS, AND SUBSISTENCE   By the early 1880s, the most obvious changes in Tlingit life were the changes in material culture. Women had stopped wearing the labrets that had begun to go out of fashion fifty years earlier. Bracelets and finger rings made from silver coins became popular. Skin garments rapidly were replaced by cloth clothing, and imported woolen blankets served as capes. The people raised vegetables, especially potatoes, which had been introduced by the Russians. Women were the gardeners. Intoxicants, unknown in aboriginal times, had become an important item of trade. A discharged American soldier taught the people to distill alcohol, and this drink, called hooch in English, became extremely popular.

Settlements apparently had begun to consolidate in late prehistoric times, and this pattern intensified. Early in the twentieth century the forces that led to population concentrations included a decline in Tlingit number due to warfare and disease; the availability of better boats for greater mobility; the efforts by outsiders to encourage larger settlements for more efficient trade and administration; and the economic advantages of settling near Euro-American towns. During the same time frame, nuclear-family dwellings were built from lumber (see Figure 8-10), but at some villages, such as Hoonah, people remained in clan houses until relatively recently. In 1944 most of Hoonah was destroyed by fire, and subsequently nuclear-family houses were built.

As mentioned earlier, the house group was the most functionally integrated social unit in traditional Tlingit life. It was also the basic economic and ceremonial unit within a clan. In aboriginal times, however, each man in a house group supplied pelts for his own nuclear family. As trapping became a primary means of livelihood, individual trappers built cabins on clan lands and claimed local areas for their exclusive exploitation. Thus the economic focus shifted from the house group to the individual, and house group cohesion declined—a factor that contributed to the construction of nuclear-family dwellings.

The economy continued to center on fishing and the sea, but people were beginning to learn new fishing skills. They had begun to use plank boats, and the halibut hooks of old were replaced by modern metal hooks. Women and men began working in salmon canneries, and some men were attracted to jobs in the local gold mines. A few men hunted sea otter until 1911, when laws were introduced to protect these animals that were clearly headed for extinction. The skills of the men as wood-carvers and metalworkers led some of them to produce craft items for the tourist trade, while women wove robes and baskets for the same market. Knowing the independent nature of the Tlingit, it is understandable that they were not reliable employees. To be ordered about was to be insulted, and as domestic servants or laborers they usually did not satisfy their white employers.

Figure 8-10 | A funeral picture at Yakutat before the Thunderbird House screen of the Wolf clan. The house was built in about 1919. Photograph by Fhoki Kayomori. (Courtesy of the Alaska Historical Library.)

The potlatch system continued with much of the pageantry and drama of aboriginal times. The predilection for borrowing and imitating the songs, dances, and costumes of foreigners continued. For example, some ship-wrecked Japanese arrived at Dry Bay in 1908. The next year Tlingit women displayed a memorable imitation of Japanese clothing and hairstyles. Changes

Figure 8-11 | The totem pole erected at the town of Kake in 1971 is 136 feet high and is the tallest pole ever raised. (Courtesy of the Alaska Division of Tourism.)

were also evident in the form that potlatch gifts took. Blankets from traders came to be more important than Chilkat robes; silver dollars were a favorite gift item, followed closely by store-bought food. However, totem poles were still erected occasionally (see Figure 8-11).

| Becoming Modern

Perhaps the best means of tracing Tlingit entry into the modern world is to begin with a discussion of church-centered voluntary associations. As noted earlier, the Russian Orthodox and Presbyterian churches introduced Christianity to the Indians. Missionaries from these churches emphasized eliminating traditional aspects of Tlingit life; they were met with resistance. Still, the pressures to convert were great, and most Tlingit did so sooner or later. The Orthodox church was the first to establish brotherhoods among the converts to help them live a Christian life; the Presbyterian church soon followed suit. Yet in the long run, the Alaska Native Brotherhood was the most successful in fostering Indian assimilation into the white way of life.

BROTHERHOODS   Early Russian efforts to Christianize the Tlingit people made no realistic headway until after the terrible smallpox epidemic between 1835 and 1837. By the end of the Russian era in 1867, over five hundred Tlingit, most of whom lived in or near Sitka, had become members of the Russian Orthodox church. Orthodox success was relatively modest, however, because members of most kwaans had retained their political independence and had limited contact with priests. Following the purchase of Alaska by the United States, Tlingit participation in Orthodoxy temporarily declined, especially after most Russians departed.

By the late 1800s Orthodox membership began to grow again, partially as a reaction to the muscular Christianity of the Presbyterians. In the 1890s especially the Presbyterians became closely identified with the civil government centered at Sitka, and both groups were far less sympathetic to traditional Tlingit life than were the Orthodox. One result was an abrupt increase in Orthodox church membership. Because the pressures to convert to Christianity were great to begin with, many Tlingit decided it was in their best interest to convert to Orthodoxy. By the early 1900s most of those who lived in Sitka were members of this church.

One of the most active Orthodox priests was Anatolii Kamenskii, who felt that the traditional Tlingit culture and the excessive consumption of alcoholic beverages by many of them were major barriers to their living a Christian life. His approach was to establish church brotherhoods devoted to temperance and mutual aid. The idea was not new locally; persons of Russian descent had previously had such organizations. The first seventeen members of the initial Orthodox brotherhood at Sitka were sworn in in 1896; among them were three leaders, one from each of the most prominent local clans. The Tlingit majority apparently refused to join because of Kamenskii's emphasis on eliminating traditional aspects of Tlingit life. Internal competition led to a second brotherhood at Sitka in 1904, and the competition led to increased membership in both brotherhoods. Despite growth of the brotherhoods, the priests remained unsuccessful in their attempts to stifle traditional Tlingit ceremonial life (see Figure 8-12).

Somewhat later, high-ranking Tlingit joined the first brotherhood because they realized the potential for influencing village life in new ways through this organization. Although the Russian church workers were pleased to receive them, their membership meant that compromises were required with respect to brotherhood goals; for example, these aristocrats could not be expected to abandon potlatches. Quite obviously, brotherhood membership was viewed differently by the Tlingit members and by Orthodox organizers. High-ranking Tlingit membership conferred legitimacy on brotherhoods in the

Figure 8-12 | In a Russian Orthodox church, traditional Tlingit artifacts were placed with the corpse of a high-ranking Sitka Tlingit, circa 1900. Photograph by Elbridge W. Merrill. (Courtesy of the Sheldon Jackson College Library, Sitka, Alaska.)

eyes of other members, and the aristocrats came to be considered in the manner of lineage and clan heads. As Kan notes (1985, 206), "They were expected to be generous, modest, dignified, honest, and careful, but eloquent, in their speech." Most important, the brotherhoods soon spread from Sitka to other major Tlingit communities. However, following the Russian Revolution in 1917, most Orthodox priests left Alaska, and as a result formal church services became rare. As an alternative, the Tlingit-led brotherhood meetings in villages came to focus the religious lives of Orthodox members. Through the 1950s local Indian leaders of the brotherhoods sustained their view of Orthodoxy with its particularly Tlingit aspects. A net result has been that the process of Americanization was thwarted and varied dimensions of Tlingit culture have thrived.

The Alaska Native Brotherhood (ANB) was founded in 1912 by established Presbyterian Indian leaders strongly committed to integration into the greater society. An important feature of the ANB, as presented by Philip Drucker (1958), was its regional focus. By the 1920s chapters (camps) were organized in most southeastern Alaskan Indian villages. The Alaska Native Sisterhood was founded by women in 1923 and initially comprised local church members. These organizations held a joint annual convention attended by three delegates from each local chapter, along with the officers and past presidents of the central organization.

The ANB official song was "Onward Christian Soldiers." Their primary goal was stated in the first article of the constitution: "The purpose of this organization shall be to assist and encourage the Native in his advancement from his native state to his place among the cultivated races of the world, to oppose, discourage, and overcome the narrow injustice of race prejudice, and to aid in the development of the Territory of Alaska, and in making it worthy of a place among the States of North America" (Drucker 1958, 165). The brotherhood advocated rapid Tlingit assimilation into Euro-American society. It strongly encouraged the use of English; in fact, eligibility for membership was restricted to English speakers, and the constitution was printed in English. The ANB also hoped to destroy the potlatch system.

The ANB concentrated on gaining rights for Indians equal to those of whites. The Russo–American treaty for the sale of Alaska stated that uncivilized tribes, including most Tlingit and other aboriginal Alaskans, were to be subject to such laws as the United States might pass. With the purchase, no attempt was made to negotiate treaties or to establish Indian reservations, and therefore the citizenship status of aboriginal Alaskans remained unclear. They were not "wards of the government" in the sense of reservation or treaty Indians. They came to consider themselves as citizens, but the whites in Alaska usually regarded them in the same light as Indians in the United States. Until they were declared citizens, the Tlingit could not file on mining claims, and this was a cause of resentment. Under the terms of the Dawes Act of 1887 or the Territorial Act of 1915, they could become citizens by demonstrating that they were following a "civilized" way of life, but few persons sought citizenship under these laws. The issue of citizenship was forced in 1922 by a Tlingit lawyer, William L. Paul, who was extremely active in brotherhood affairs. As a result of Paul's efforts, Alaskan Indians, in theory, had full voting rights before the federal government passed the Citizenship Act of 1924 granting full citizenship to all Indians who were not previously citizens. (In 1924 William Paul was the first Indian elected to the territorial legislature.)

By 1929 the ANB successfully challenged segregated white and Indian school systems, and in 1945 the territorial legislature passed an antidiscrimination law. The ANB began to recruit all native Alaskans beginning about 1962, but the Alaska Federation of Natives founded in 1966 became a more active cover organization working for Alaskan Aleut, Eskimo, and Indian causes.

The original brotherhood goal of doing away with aboriginal customs had been partially realized in the 1950s. The principal target, the potlatch, was regarded as heathen and was deplored; however, as Drucker pointed out, it was primarily a social, not a religious, ceremony. In reality some potlatch customs emerged within the structure of the ANB. These included addressing persons of the opposite moiety in a ceremonial fashion; fining individuals for infractions; and gift giving by the family of a deceased person for burial services provided by the opposite moiety through the brotherhood. In one sense the ANB served as a new institution through which moieties reciprocated. Furthermore, although the ideal of speaking English continued, the meetings of local chapters sometimes were conducted in Tlingit, especially

Figure 8-13 | The Sealaska Corporation office building in downtown Juneau was dedicated in 1976.

since the most active members normally were older and less likely to speak English with ease.

THE SETTLEMENT OF LAND CLAIMS   Because land and property rights were paramount in aboriginal Tlingit life, it is not surprising that the seizure of their lands by outsiders without compensation became a major issue. Originally, Euro-American settlement in southeastern Alaska was more widespread and intensive than elsewhere in the territory, and it seldom had clear legal justification. In 1935 the Tlingit and Haida in Alaska sued the federal government for land losses and sought a settlement of $80 million, but in 1968 the U.S. Court of Claims determined that they should be awarded only $7.5 million as compensation for the *sixteen million acres* of land involved.

The Alaska Native Claims Settlement Act (ANCSA) of 1971, described at the close of Chapter 4, included Tlingit claims not resolved by earlier court decisions. Under the terms of the act, the Tlingit and Alaskan Haida formed one of the original twelve regional corporations, the Sealaska Corporation (see Figure 8-13). As the largest of the regional corporations, Sealaska initially had about sixteen thousand stockholders, the vast majority of whom were Tlingit. Corporation assets were about $420 million in 1984, and revenues that year were $230 million. These statistics suggest that the shareholders were economically secure, if not wealthy; yet this was not the case. As far as a typical Tlingit was concerned, Sealaska failed them during the 1980s. Mismanagement to varying degrees by Tlingit and white employees caused substantial losses, which led to negative stockholder feelings. Not only were the well-paid managers a significant drain on corporation finances, but their life-styles alienated stockholders.

By the late 1990s, most Tlingit still were unhappy with Sealaska management. As one Tlingit said, "Sealaska has no soul or spirit." Timber sales brought in revenues of $23 million in 1996, the major source of income. However, some 8500 acres of timberland were clear-cut, even though the corporation position was that they practiced "careful management." It may take as long as two hundred years for the trees of a clear-cut area to become harvestable again. Even with the timber revenues, profits for shareholders remained modest—in 1996 they received $4.98 per share. It does appear, however, that current management is more competent than that of the comparatively recent past. Nevertheless, most Tlingit identify far more closely with their village corporation than they do with Sealaska.

| Current Developments and Issues

Culture may be broadly defined as the forms and norms of a people, including such aspects as their social and political life, religion, material culture, and language. In this book, the chapter-length discussions about particular tribes focus initially on their distinct cultures at the time of historic contact. For the Tlingit, as for many other tribes, the relative homogeneity of aboriginal culture had disappeared by the 1990s. According to one observer, Sergei Kan (1989b), three largely generational subgroups prevail: (1) elders with a traditional orientation; (2) progressive elders and middle-aged Tlingit speakers; and (3) middle-aged to young English speakers. These subgroups, although they are shifting, do not share a uniform sense of what it means to be Tlingit. It also appears that the capacity to speak Tlingit, and all that it implies, is a major divider. By the late 1990s the vast majority of fully fluent Tlingit speakers was over 65 years of age; they may have numbered 500 in a population total of about 15,000. Few individuals under 40 were fluent in their language. As Wallace M. Olson (1995, 71) noted, "there are many Tlingit who are more fluent in computer languages than they are in their traditional tongue." A logical conclusion is that as the number of older Tlingit speakers declines, many aspects of traditional Tlingit culture will become increasingly ephemeral.

Many contemporary problems engage Tlingit interests, some old and others new; some of these are examined in this section. In numerous contexts, what it means to be a Tlingit has been guided by the terms of the ANCSA and its amendments. Developments at the regional corporation, Sealaska, have been described, and it is also worthwhile to look at a village corporation that was created under the ANCSA. In addition, the most contentious issue uniting most Tlingit is their "subsistence rights" vis-à-vis the government, especially at the state level. These rights include "sovereignty" and such critical matters as day-to-day control over their landholdings, social programs, laws, and law enforcement. The chapter concludes with a brief historical overview of what it means to be a Tlingit.

A VILLAGE CORPORATION   No Tlingit village corporation is "typical," and Goldbelt Incorporated is less so than most others. It was created for the Auke kwaan ("tribe" in some contexts) in and around Juneau, the capital of Alaska and a major tourist stop. Goldbelt enterprises are increasingly tourist-oriented, but they do provide a good example of Tlingit adaptability to present-day realities.

The Auke kwaan had little direct local contact with the Russians who once occupied Alaska. When the United States purchased Alaska in 1867, the Auke may have numbered about 700. They were relatively isolated until 1880, when gold was discovered in the Juneau area. The sudden influx of miners, prospectors, and others led the U.S. Navy to establish a local presence to contain white lawlessness. The federal government previously had identified the area as "Indian country," meaning that trade and intercourse laws, including a prohibition on intoxicants, were in effect. Naval officers in charge recognized some aspects of Tlingit customary law and were impressed by its sophistication. However, before long the Tlingit were restricted to local areas; they were forced to settle at the margins of white-dominated Juneau.

With ever-expanding white control in southeastern Alaska during the early decades of the twentieth century, Tlingit rights became a pressing issue. The Auke were a principal participant in the lawsuit that eventually forced the federal government into a partial settlement of Tlingit land claims in 1959. With the ANCSA of 1971, as revised, a village corporation was permitted to claim 32,000 acres; but there was no block of land in the Juneau area for the Auke to claim. They became obligated to select acreage nearby. Initially they logged a great deal of timber from the area to pay stockholder dividends.

The assets of Goldbelt in 1996 were about $65 million, excluding the value of their landholdings. The board of directors included four women and four men, and the corporation and its subsidiaries employed about two hundred people. Alaska has become an increasingly favored destination for cruise ships in the summer months, and Juneau is a major stop; in 1997 about 500,000 people visited there. Understandably, Goldbelt management has invested heavily in tourist-related businesses. Their wholly owned subsidiaries included tour and travel operations, docking facilities, sales outlets for Tlingit crafts, and a boat for local sightseeing. In partnership with non-Goldbelt companies, it has developed a tramway to the top of a mountain in downtown Juneau and has formed a day-cruise company. Furthermore, plans include tour vessel trips to a reconstructed Tlingit village and the construction of a high-speed ferry system between Juneau and the ports of Haines and Skagway.

SUBSISTENCE ISSUES   Thomas F. Thornton (in press) justly maintains that "subsistence" has been the most contentious issue in Alaskan politics for over twenty years. Among Native Alaskans the word refers not only to the local harvest of wild food resources but to their right to determine harvest levels and to exercise general control over their landholdings. Thus subsistence and "sovereignty" are intimately associated. In essence, subsistence issues pit people in rural areas, Native and non-Native, against urban Alaskans. Alaska is home to nearly 600,000 people, about 80 percent of whom live in urban areas. Of the 20 percent who live in rural areas, about half are Native and half non-Native. Therefore, urban Alaskans, who are primarily Euro-Americans, have the greatest political power. Two additional sets of statistics further suggest the scope of the conflict. In rural areas during 1994, the average harvest of local edibles was about 375 pounds per person per year, while in urban areas it was 22 pounds. Equally significant, 4 percent of the fish and wildlife harvests throughout Alaska in 1990 was for subsistence use; 1 percent was taken by sportspersons; and 95 percent went to commercial interests, meaning primarily the fishing industry. Clearly, subsistence takes represented a small fraction of the total harvest.

The legal and political battles over subsistence usage among all interested parties are convoluted. A brief summary will suffice. The ANCSA and the Alaska National Interest Lands Conservation Act of 1980 indirectly and directly support Native preference in subsistence matters; about *60 percent* of Alaskan land is under federal control, a crucial statistic. The state of Alaska has argued that it has the right to manage all of its fish and wildlife resources. The federal government agreed to state management of subsistence on federal and state lands *if* they complied with federal laws. The state has not complied, and the federal government has assumed the responsibility for subsistence management on federal lands. The federal government also assumed control over subsistence fisheries management in late 1997. State officials are distressed over these developments, but resolution of the impasse remains elusive. The jury is out.

A related and even more far-reaching conflict between the state and Native Alaskans involves the definition of "Indian country" with respect to the Native community of Venetie (see also Chapter 4). The community attempted to tax a school-construction contractor, which led to a suit in the federal courts. In 1996 the Ninth U.S. Circuit Court of Appeals ruled that the villagers had the authority to levy taxes, regulate land use, and obtain policing authority on their lands. This ruling meant that the 226 federally recognized tribes (villages) would have the same status as Venetie. Officials of the State of Alaska were livid over this development and contributed $1 million in state funds to contest the decision. The reason is apparent: the state would lose control over most of Native Alaska. On the negative side for villagers, the state would probably stop contributing funds to most village projects. The powerful U.S. senator from Alaska, Ted Stevens, threatened to introduce legislation to nullify the ruling if the appeal by the state failed. However, early in 1998 the U.S. Supreme Court upheld the state's appeal and declined to recognize the status of Indian country in Alaska.

TLINGIT CONTINUITIES   The Westernization of the Tlingit has been somewhat eased by what might be called the "Tlingit factor." This factor comprises three sets of unique circumstances. First is the sophistication of aboriginal Tlingit culture. The second is the fact that they remained essentially free of effective Euro-American political control until the early 1900s. The third is the

Figure 8-14 | Tlingit art is especially apparent in Juneau, Alaska. The State Office Building includes the "Old Witch" totem pole made in the 1880s on Prince of Wales Island.

traditional Tlingit emphasis placed on trade for economic gain; this key value fit comfortably into the Euro-American concept of capitalism. As a result of these factors, the Tlingit could be reasonably discriminating in their acceptance of Western innovations, and they were adept at fitting new ideas into traditional patterns. As a result, selective sociocultural continuity becomes evident (see Figure 8-14).

As previously discussed, the Tlingit people made numerous early adjustments, such as replacing Chilkat robes with imported blankets and using silver dollars in potlatch exchanges to partially replace craft items. The Orthodox and Protestant brotherhoods provide examples of compromises that furthered Tlingit values. For many Tlingit, clan affiliations have lost their meaning, but identity with a moiety remains strong. Kan (1989b, 406) noted that modern potlatches retain many essential elements of the traditional versions. Old age and ritual expertise are now more important to hosting a potlatch than rank status, as in the past. Participation in potlatches, however, has declined. Memorial potlatches to release the spirits of the dead persist and often are ecumenical. Traditional Tlingit, Orthodox, Presbyterian, and Salvation Army participation may all occur in one ceremony, with little or no conflict.

The regional geographical clusters, or kwaans, have retained selective vitality, due in part to their incorporation into the structure of the ANCSA. Thus corporations such as Goldbelt remain a central factor in assuring Tlingit identity. Similarly, we find that traditional Tlingit artifacts are important identifiers for some clans and house groups. For example, the Eagle Nest House at Sitka has a comprehensive inventory of traditional ceremonial artifacts, while six other clans or house groups have similar holdings. In addition, many craftspersons make Tlingit artifacts for sale to tourists. Some twenty-five highly skilled craftsmen contract with individual buyers to produce artifacts, such as masks, helmets, and house post facings. The best artists may charge as much as $15,000 for a mask, and many have a backlog of orders of up to four years. In this general context, some Tlingit singers and dance groups, especially the Naa Ka Hidi Theater, are widely honored for their performance skills, and recognition of these groups continues to expand. Thus, Tlingit culture is far from moribund despite its losses.

| Additional Sources

The best brief overview of the Tlingit, past and present, is *The Tlingit: An introduction to their culture and history* (Juneau, 1995) by Wallace M. Olson. The best synopsis is by Frederica de Laguna in the *Northwest Coast* volume (7) of the *Handbook of North American Indians,* William C. Sturtevant, general editor (Washington, DC, 1990). *Cultures of the North Pacific Coast* (San Francisco, 1965) by Philip Drucker compares the cultures of the Indians in this region. An excellent Tlingit ethnography for the late 1880s is by Aurel Krause (1885), original in German, translated into English by Erna Gunther (1956). The only comprehensive ethnographic reconstruction of a kwaan was written about the Yakutat area by Frederica de Laguna (1972). Tlingit social life as it existed at Klukwan is brilliantly described in a book by Kalervo Oberg (1973). The best discussion of totem poles with reference to the Tlingit is by Edward Keithan (1963), and the best general work is the monograph titled *Totem Poles* by Marius Barbeau (National Museums of Canada, 1950; reprinted in 1964). *Northwest Coast Indian Art* (Seattle, 1965) by Bill Holm is the most insightful book-length discussion of the subject. Recent ethnohistorical studies by Sergei Kan are especially valuable for the Russian era and subsequent developments.

| Selected Bibliography

Bancroft, Hubert H. 1886. *History of Alaska, 1730–1885. The works of Hubert Howe Bancroft,* vol. 33. San Francisco.

Dauenhauer, Nora Marks, and Richard Dauenhauer. 1994. *Haa Kusteeyí, our culture: Tlingit life stories.* Seattle.

de Laguna, Frederica. 1960. *The story of a Tlingit community.* Bureau of American Ethnology Bulletin no. 172. Washington, DC.

————. 1972. *Under Mount Saint Elias*. Smithsonian Contributions to Anthropology, vol. 7. Washington, DC.

————. 1983. Aboriginal Tlingit sociopolitical organization. In *The development of political organization in native North America,* 1979 Proceedings of the American Ethnological Society, Elisabeth Tooker, ed., 71–85. Washington, DC.

Drucker, Philip. 1958. *The native brotherhoods*. Bureau of American Ethnology Bulletin no. 168. Washington, DC.

Emmons, George Thornton, with Frederica de Laguna and Jean Low. 1992. *The Tlingit Indians*. Seattle.

Jonaitis, Aldona. 1986. *Art of the Northern Tlingit*. Seattle.

Jones, Livingston F. 1914. *A study of the Thlingets of Alaska*. New York.

Kamenskii, Anatolii. 1985. *Tlingit Indians of Alaska*. Sergei Kan, trans. Fairbanks.

Kan, Sergei. 1983. Words that heal the soul. *Arctic Anthropology* 20(2):47–59.

————. 1985. Russian Orthodox brotherhoods among the Tlingit. *Ethnohistory* 32:196–222.

————. 1986. The 19th-century Tlingit potlatch. *American Ethnologist* 13:191–212.

————. 1989a. *Symbolic immortality: The Tlingit Potlatch of the nineteenth century.* Washington, DC.

————. 1989b. Cohorts, generations, and their culture: The Tlingit potlatch in the 1980s. *Anthropos* 84:405–22.

————. 1991. Shamanism and Christianity: Modern-day Tlingit elders look at the past. *Ethnohistory* 38:4:363–87.

————. 1996. Clan mothers and godmothers: Tlingit women and Russian Orthodox Christianity, 1840–1940. *Ethnohistory* 43:4:613–41.

Kashavaroff, Andrew P. 1927. How the white men came to Lituya and what happened to Yeahlth-kan who visited them. *Alaska Magazine* 1:151–53.

Keithan, Edward L. 1963. *Monuments in cedar* (rev. ed.). Seattle.

Krause, Aurel. 1885. *The Tlingit Indians*. 2 vols. Jena. Translated edition, Erna Gunther, trans., American Ethnological Society, 1956.

Lisianskii, Urey F. 1814. *A voyage round the world*. London.

McClellan, Catharine. 1954. The interrelations of social structure with northern Tlingit ceremonialism. *Southwestern Journal of Anthropology* 10:75–96.

Malaspina, D. Alejandro, and Don Jose de Bustamante y Guerra. 1885. *Political-scientific trip around the world* (translated title). Madrid.

Niblack, Albert P. 1890. The Coast Indians of southern Alaska and northern British Columbia. *Annual Report of the Smithsonian Institution,* 1887–88, 225–386. Washington, DC.

Oberg, Kalervo. 1973. *The social economy of the Tlingit Indians*. Seattle.

Olson, Wallace. 1995. *The Tlingit: An introduction to their culture and history*. Juneau, AK.

Porter, Robert P. 1893. *Report on population and resources of Alaska at the Eleventh Census: 1890*. Washington, DC.

Romanowsky, S., and E. Frankenhauser. 1849. Five years of medical observations in the colonies of the Russian-American Company. *Medical Newspaper of Russia* 6: 153–61. St. Petersburg. (Translated from German and reprinted in *Alaska Medicine* 4:33–37, 62–64, 1962.)

Swanton, John R. 1908. Social condition, beliefs, and linguistic relationship of the Tlingit Indians. *Bureau of American Ethnology, 26th Annual Report,* 391–512. Washington, DC.

Thornton, Thomas F. In press. Subsistence: The politics of maintaining a traditional way of life in a modern state. In *Public policy issues in Alaska: Background and perspectives,* Clive S. Thomas, ed. Fairbanks.

Veniaminov, Ivan. 1984. *Notes on the islands of the Unalaska district.* Lydia T. Black and R. H. Geoghegan, trans.; Richard A. Price, ed. Kingston, Ontario.

9 The Hopi: Farmers of the Desert

Your beautiful rays,
may they color our faces;
being dyed in them,
somewhere at an old age
we shall fall asleep old women.

Woman's prayer to the sun, for
a newborn girl. (H. R. Voth 1905, 53)

THE PUEBLO PEOPLES of the Southwest probably best typify Native American lifeways. Massive pueblos, painted pottery, colorful rituals, and kachina dolls characterize these people to most outsiders. Pueblo Indians, such as the Hopi of northeastern Arizona, continue to live in their desert setting, and most of them have clung tenaciously to their Indian identity. The survival of the Hopi as a people is remarkable in light of the forces that have been bent on their destruction over the centuries. As an example of the persistence of their culture, Christian missionaries began working among the Hopi in 1629, but by the 1950s fewer than 2 percent of the Hopi were practicing Christians.

There are additional reasons for devoting a chapter to the Hopi. Nowhere else are Indians so intimately associated with one locality. Nowhere else among Indians do the past and present blend into such a consistent whole. Furthermore, a wealth of information exists about the Hopi. They have long attracted the attention of ethnographers, resulting in excellent studies about their lifeways. The monograph titled *Old Oraibi* by Mischa Titiev (1944) is one of the best ethnographic studies of American Indians.

Pueblo peoples were distinguished from other Native Americans in the Southwest by their emphasis on maize cultivation, social and political complexity, and rich ceremonial life. Yet significant differences existed between the Eastern Pueblos, such as Isleta, Taos, and Zia, and the Western Pueblos that included Acoma, Hopi, and Zuni. Pueblo Indian linguistic diversity suggests that they had varied prehistoric backgrounds, and they differed by region in other ways. The Western Pueblo matrilineal emphasis contrasted with the patrilineal emphasis in some pueblos to the east. Western Pueblos were politically theocratic and less centralized than those to the east. Furthermore, kachinas (supernatural beings) were prominent in the west, whereas medicine societies tended to dominate in the east. Clearly it is incorrect to view Pueblo Indian cultures as uniform.

| People, Population, Language, and Habitat

Hopi, the word that these people apply to themselves, is often translated as "good" or "peaceful," but it more properly means "one who follows the right path," the ideal for all tribal members. The Hopi language is of the Aztec–Tanoan phylum and the Uto–Aztecan family. The aboriginal Hopi population numbered about twenty-eight hundred. After declining to some two thousand in 1907, it had reached about ten thousand by 1997. Their Arizona homeland is one of deserts and plateaus with sporadic and unpredictable rainfall (see Figure 9-1). Rainwater from the upland sandstone region seeps into a layer of shale and emerges at the ends of mesas as springs and moist areas. At higher elevations on the mesas, juniper and scattered pinyon grow. This flora is replaced by grassland nearer the valley floors, and in the lower areas desert vegetation, including saltbrush, greasewood, and sagebrush, dominates. In damp localities or along irregularly flowing streams, cottonwoods and willows grow.

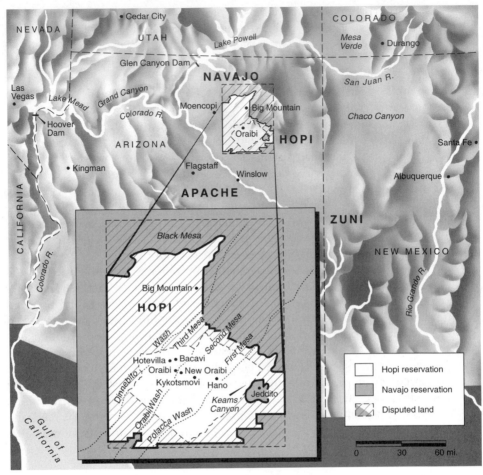

Figure 9-1 | Homeland of the Hopi Indians.

| Early Contact with the Spanish

In July of 1540 the Hopi saw the first Spanish. A small group under Pedro de Tovar arrived from the pueblo of Zuni, where Francisco Coronado, the expedition leader, rested. When de Tovar arrived at an eastern Hopi settlement, he encountered hostility and attacked the village, defeating the Indians. De Tovar then peacefully visited the six other Hopi communities, and later a party of the same expedition traveling to the Grand Canyon passed through Hopi country without meeting any resistance. The Spanish search for gold led Antonio de Espejo to enter the region in 1583, and he was welcomed by the people in the five villages. More lasting contact was made by Juan de Onate in 1598 when the Hopi grudgingly submitted to the authority of the Spanish king. The Spanish hoped to make these people Christians, but Franciscan missionaries did not settle among them until 1629. Churches were built at three settlements, and two more missionaries joined the first three. The Franciscans reported great progress, but the poisoning of one of the priests in 1633 suggests that not all Hopi were contented charges. Vigorous Franciscan efforts to destroy the old Hopi religion led to cruel punishments for backsliding Indians. In 1655 a missionary caught a Hopi performing an "act of idolatry." The man was beaten severely in public and again beaten inside the church; turpentine was applied to his body and ignited, and he died. The missionary was relieved of his post, but no punitive action was taken against him.

In 1650 the Hopi refused to join the other Pueblo peoples in a revolt against the Spanish, but they fully supported the Pueblo Revolt in 1680. Their major contribution was to kill the four missionaries stationed among them. The Hopi indirectly aided the insurrection by accepting refugees from the Rio Grande pueblos when the Spanish struck back. The Hopi feared Spanish reprisals, and three villages were relocated on mesa tops that could be better defended than could their valley bottom settings. The Spanish returned in 1692, and when the Indians willingly swore to support the Spanish king, peace was established. By 1699 the Spanish were in firm control of the Rio Grande pueblos, and this led a Hopi faction that favored Catholicism to request missionaries from the authorities at Santa Fe. A missionary visited, but after he left, the community was summarily destroyed by the anti-Catholic Hopi faction. The men who resisted were killed; their wives and children were scattered among the remaining settlements. The pagan Hopi under the leadership of a man from Oraibi went to Santa Fe and told the Spanish governor that the Hopi would make peace if they were permitted to continue their old religion. This, however, was unacceptable to the Spanish. In retaliation for the murder of Christian Hopi the Spanish in 1701 attempted to defeat the Hopi in battle, but the smallness of the Spanish force and the adequate defensive positions of the Hopi led the attackers to withdraw. The Hopi retained their freedom not so much by their military skill and determination as by the distance that separated them from Santa Fe and the difficulties the Spanish were having with other Indians. Throughout the 1740s and early 1750s the Hopi thwarted Spanish efforts to bring them under effective control.

Beginning in 1755 the course of Hopi history gravitated increasingly toward accepting the Spanish. When a sequence of dry years exhausted their reserve of food, they were faced with hunger. By 1779 many of them had abandoned their homeland and moved among the Zuni to survive. The next year most Hopi were so scattered that the local population was reduced to about eight hundred persons. In the midst of this struggle came the smallpox epidemic in 1781. In this same year, however, rain was plentiful, and the bountiful crops made it possible for the population to reconsolidate. Pressures by marauding Navajos forced the Hopi to request aid from the Spanish in 1818, but the Spanish, who were faced with their own survival problems, were unable to help. The most striking characteristic of Hopi historical contact with the Spanish was the ability of these Indians to withstand Spanish pressures toward acculturation, particularly in the religious sphere. Hopi resistance against the Spanish evidently was not unanimous, but the pro-Spanish faction seems to have been of minor importance.

| Aboriginal Life

Unlike the peoples discussed in earlier chapters, the Hopi were sedentary farmers whose lives centered in small, stable villages. They, possibly more than any other Pueblo people, display an appealing continuity with the past. Their ancestors settled in northern Arizona at least a thousand years ago, and the Hopi village of Oraibi is one of the oldest continuously occupied settlements north of Mexico.

ORIGIN MYTH Each Hopi clan had its own version of a creation story. In primeval times, according to a myth recorded at Oraibi, there was no light or living thing on earth, only a being called Maasaw (Death). Three caves beneath the earth's surface likewise were engulfed in darkness. In the lowest cave people existed in crowded and filthy conditions. Two brothers, The Two, lamented the plight of the people and pierced the cave roof; they grew one plant after another, trying to reach the second world. After a particular type of cane grew tall enough, the people and animals climbed it to the second cave world. This level finally was filled with people, and they ascended to the third cave. Here the brothers found fire, and the darkness was dispelled. Here the people built houses and ceremonial structures called kivas; but great turmoil developed when women began to neglect their duties as wives and mothers, preferring instead to dance in the kivas. Finally, the people, along with Coyote, Locust, Spider, Swallow, and Vulture, emerged at the fourth level, which was the earth. They wandered about with only torches to light their way. Together the people and the creatures with them attempted to create light. Spider spun a white cotton blanket that gave off some light. The people then processed a white deerskin and painted it turquoise. This skin was so bright that it lighted the entire world. The painted deerskin became the sun, and the blanket was the moon. Stars were released from a jar by Coyote.

Once the earth was lighted, the creatures realized that the land area was limited by surrounding water. The Vulture fanned the water with its wings, and as the waters flowed away, mountains appeared. The Two made channels for the waters through the mountains, and canyons and valleys were formed. The people saw the tracks of Maasaw and followed them to the east. They caught up with Maasaw, and a girl conspired with him to cause the death of a girl she envied. This was the first death among people, the conspirator was the first witch, and her descendants became the witches of the world. The dead girl was seen living in the cave world below the earth, which had become an idyllic place. The witch caused conflicts with people who had emerged on earth before the Hopi, particularly the Navajo and Mexicans. Another deity helped people by making their maize and other seeds ripen in a single day. Of the two brothers who led the people from the underworld, the younger brother was the ancestor of the Oraibi people. The older brother went east but promised to return when the Hopi needed him. After many generations and in accord with this promise the older brother's descendants, the Bahanas, were to return when the Hopi were poor and in need. The Bahanas would be rich and would bring food and clothing for the Hopi. The Hopi would reject them, but the Bahanas would treat them kindly.

APPEARANCE AND CLOTHING   A Hopi girl wore her hair long until she passed through a puberty ceremony; it then was put up in two disk-shaped bundles ("squash-blossom hairdo"), one over each ear. After she married, her hair was parted in the middle and worn long again. A woman's clothing consisted of a wraparound cotton blanket that passed under her left arm and was fastened together over the right shoulder. This garment extended a short distance below her knees, and she wore leggings as well as moccasins. Men wore headbands to control their hair, which might be relatively short or long and knotted behind the neck. Everyday male clothing included a breechclout of deerskin or cotton cloth and a cotton cloth kilt, belted at the waist. A man also might wear deerskin leggings and moccasins or sandals.

SETTLEMENTS AND MANUFACTURES   At the south end of Black Mesa are three tongues of land, and on the westernmost, called Third Mesa, the village of Oraibi is located (see Figure 9-2). This is the community where Mischa Titiev worked, and whenever possible the descriptions will focus there. The pueblo was laid out in a series of eight nearly parallel streets with scattered kivas and a plaza between two streets. In aboriginal times the square houses were made from stones dressed and set in place for the floor and walls by the men. The roof beams were placed on the uppermost course of stones, and the women for whom a house was being built prepared and applied a mud plaster to the inner walls. A woman and her friends completed the roof by adding brushwood, grass, and finally mud. Women owned the dwellings, and new ones were usually built next to the residence of a woman's mother or another close female relative. Houses were often windowless, and no doors opened on the street. They were often multistory, with access through an opening in the ceiling beneath which was placed a notched log ladder. Bin metates (milling stones) of different degrees of coarseness for grinding maize lined one side of a room (see Figure 9-3), and fireplaces completed the furnishings. Rooms without any outside opening were often used for storing food and material goods. A kiva was a rectangular subterranean room entered by descending a ladder from an opening in the roof. The section of the floor where observers sat was slightly raised, and the remaining portion included a fire pit and sipapu, a hole in the floor through which spirits were thought to enter.

Along most walls were stone compartments that held sacred objects. At Oraibi there were about fifteen kivas, each owned by a matriclan.

The most elaborate manufactures were textiles, usually woven by men. They carded and spun cotton into thread and then wove textiles on looms in their homes or in kivas. The fiber often was dyed black, green, orange, red, or yellow. On a vertical loom suspended between the ceiling and the floor they made square and rectangular cloth for blankets. Belts were made on a waist loom attached to a beam at one end and to the weaver's waist at the other, being held taut with his body. Women wove only rabbitskin blankets on vertical looms. The most important textiles woven by men for women were for wedding robes, belts, dresses, and shawls. For themselves, men wove kilts and sashes for ceremonies, and blankets, kilts, and shirts for daily use.

Pottery was made by women, both undecorated ware for cooking and storage and polished and decorated forms for other uses. They collected clay from nearby deposits, soaked it, and kneaded it into a paste, adding ground sandstone to the paste of utility wares. Long coils were added to a flat clay bottom, and each seam was pinched to join the preceding piece and then obliterated by hand-smoothing. The completed containers were dried, and undecorated utility ware was fired without further processing. If a pot was to be

Figure 9-2 | The village of Oraibi with melons and peaches drying on the roof in the foreground. (Courtesy of the Southwest Museum, Los Angeles, CA, neg. no. 24007.)

Figure 9-3 | A Hopi woman grinding grain in a bin metate. (Courtesy of the Southwest Museum, Los Angeles, CA, neg. no. LS. 6035-N42082.)

decorated, it was smoothed and thinned after drying with a piece of sandstone. Then it was moistened and polished with a stone in preparation for painting. Pottery was painted black, orange, red, white, and yellow, and the prevalent designs were quite similar to those used in early historic times, when old designs were revived after falling out of use. In 1895 an archaeologist excavated an abandoned Hopi pueblo. One of his Indian workmen was the husband of a woman who was widely recognized as one of the best Pueblo potters, Nampeyo. She found the beautifully executed, painted pottery unearthed at the site fascinating and studied the sherds to become familiar with the patterns. She developed a style based on these originals, and it became very popular.

SUBSISTENCE ACTIVITIES The Hopi farming year began near the end of February, when plots were cleared for planting. The time to sow was established by a Sun Watcher, who based his determination on the occurrence of the sunrise at a particular spot on the horizon. At the stipulated time, the men of a matriclan worked together as a unit from planting through the harvest. A married man planted the clan land allotted to his wife and her immediate family. Men owned the crops until the harvest was taken to a wife's house, upon which the harvested food became her property. Farmland at the foot of Black

Mesa was watered by ground seepage or from stream overflow (floodwater farming). A farmer prepared a plot by trampling the weeds or cutting them with a broad-bladed implement and breaking up the soil with a pointed stick. Maize, the most important crop by far, was planted in holes made with a digging stick. He dropped ten to twenty seeds into a single foot-deep hole; if a planting did not sprout in about ten days, he might reseed the plot. As plants grew, farmers weeded the plots and loosened the soil about the roots. Fields, which were about one acre in extent, were not rotated, nor was the maize hilled. They sometimes planted beans among the maize stalks but more often raised them in separate plots. Squash and cotton also appear to have been raised in separate acreage. During planting and harvesting, someone impersonating Maasaw, the God of Death, was usually present. Most other Hopi subsistence activities also were group endeavors, organized by individuals or societies to embrace some or all community members. One cooperative, communal task was to clear sand and debris from village springs that were owned by the Village Chief but used by everyone.

About forty plant species were cultivated in the 1930s. Of this number, five species were aboriginal (kidney and tepary beans, maize, cotton, and squash); four others may have existed prior to Spanish times but more likely were postcontact domestics (Aztec and lima beans, gourds, and sunflowers). Five species were introduced during the Spanish period (chili peppers, onions, peaches, watermelons, and wheat); all others were introduced by Mormon farmers or other Anglo-Americans. The Hopi cared for ten species of wild plants, but they apparently did not sow the seeds regularly. Seeds from two species of wild tobacco were sown when necessary to provide sufficient leaves for ceremonial uses. They used wild dock root for dye and sometimes planted the seeds. Fifty-four different wild plants were eaten, fifty were used to make or decorate artifacts, sixty-five were used medicinally, and forty had ceremonial or magical purposes. Although there is some overlap in these listings, the Hopi obviously used a wide variety of plant species. About two hundred wild flowering plants grew locally, of which half commonly were used.

The primary staple, maize, was the symbol of life to the Hopi, and they grew three varieties. In early historic times the flint variety was important since the hull of each grain was hard and not easily destroyed by weevils in storage. The flint variety was so difficult to grind, however, that it declined in importance. The most popular variety of maize in more recent times had been the flour type, which every farmer grew. They raised sweet corn of two named strains in small quantities.

They prepared maize for consumption in numerous ways. The harvested product was usually stored on the cob and shelled as needed. They made ground maize into gruel, dumplings, soups, and a breadlike product. Hominy was prepared by soaking shelled maize in a mixture of juniper wood ash and water, then boiling the grains and washing them to remove the hulls. Maize also was roasted on the ear, parched, or baked in pits. One important food made of maize, *piki,* was used as bread. They made it from a finely ground cornmeal mixed with water, using ashes as leavening, and cooked it on a special stone slab over a fire. The stone was heated and greased, and the bluish-gray liquid was poured onto it. After cooking, the piki was folded or rolled into "loaves" for later consumption. They often ate it by dipping one end into liquid food and biting off the moistened portion.

Compared with farming rituals, the ceremonial preparations for a hunt were elaborate. The most important species hunted were antelope, cottontails, and jackrabbits. They often hunted rabbits in the late summer, when crops did not require attention. A man organizing a hunt could be from any clan so long as he made prayer offerings to the God of the Hunt. A crier announced the details of the time for the hunt, and the next day the organizer performed further rituals. In the hunt, men formed a surround and moved in until they could kill the encircled animals with throwing sticks (boomerangs, rabbit-killing sticks) or with hurled clubs. The surround was formed repeatedly, and the game continued to be taken until the leader called an end to the hunt. When they returned to the village, each man gave his kill to his mother, sister, wife, or father's sister. The recipient made a ritual offering to the dead animal to restore the game to the God of the Hunt.

Before hunting antelope, deer, and mountain sheep, the organizer as well as all the others in the party made prayer offerings, and they practiced ritual smoking. The surround method was used to capture these animals in aboriginal times. The pattern seems to have been to run down and suffocate an antelope. A deer apparently was shot with arrows or clubbed to death but not stabbed. Once again, they made a ritual propitiation of the deceased animal. Coyote hunts were conducted by kiva members collectively, and as usual they employed the surround technique to catch and kill the animals. After a hunt they took each coyote to the kiva, gave it a lighted corn husk cigarette to placate the animal's spirit, and spoke to it as a child before the owner took the animal home.

DESCENT, KINSHIP, AND MARRIAGE   As already indicated, the Hopi traced descent through females (matrilineal), and grooms always joined the households of their brides (matrilocal). Matrilineages were very important in social terms, and matriclans were overwhelmingly important ceremonial units.

A male individual termed his mother the same as his mother's sister and did not distinguish between them in normal conversation. Father and father's brother were termed alike, but mother's brother was termed differently. The designations for females in the first ascending generation paralleled those for males, because father's sister was distinguished from mother and mother's sister (bifurcate merging terminology). This usage is reasonable since mother and mother's sister were of the same clan, and father was in the same clan as father's brother. In the cousin terminology, parallel cousins were termed as siblings, whereas mother's brother's children were termed as one's own children, and a father's sister's daughter was called the same as father's sister. Finally, a father's sister's son was termed father (Crow type cousins) (see Figure 9-4). The most distinguishing characteristic of the cousin term is the ignoring of certain generational distinctions. The kinship terminology provided the framework for

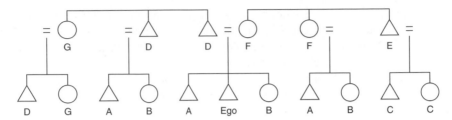

Figure 9-4 | The historic Hopi system of kinship terminology.

lifelong responsibilities, with particular forms of behavior expected in each set of relationships. One of the most bitter overt displays of anger against a relative was to renounce kinship ties.

SOCIAL DIMENSIONS   The Hopi knew of no term for household, yet this social unit dominated and guided the life of each individual. A child was born into this unit and retained a strong emotional identity with it throughout life. The household consisted of a core of women—grandmother, daughters, and daughters' daughters—plus unmarried sons and in-marrying husbands. All except the husbands belonged to the same matriclan; also members of the lineage were those males born into the unit but now married and living in the houses of their wives. When the members of a household outgrew its space, a room was added on to accommodate the newer members. This adjacent household retained its ties with the parent matrilineage, held farmland in common, and worshiped a common fetish (sacred bundle). The lineage fetish was in the custody of the oldest female lineage head, and the associated ceremonies were conducted largely by the old woman's brother or son. These ritual obligations were passed down the most direct maternal line. Common lineage problems were discussed at the original lineage residence, and it remained the heart of the matrilineage, sometimes after it was abandoned as a residence. From a leading matrilineage, with the greatest rights and duties, subordinate (daughter) lineages developed. As a daughter lineage grew, it might become socially removed from the original group and lose the underlying ties. The distant lineages would become separate clans if they created new bundles and acquired distinct names. Members of a named group who traced their ties through the same bundle formed a matriclan even though they could not trace connecting genealogical ties.

By 1906, about thirty named matriclans existed at Oraibi, a number that represented splits as well as the possible settlement there of new clans. The names, including Bear, Bow, Butterfly, and Lizard, were linked with happenings in mythological times or referred to clan ancestors. These ancestors were termed *wuya* and might or might not be tangibly represented by a clan bundle. A bundle sometimes included more than one wuya; this led to alternative names for the clan and probably represented the consolidation of two clans.

Clans formed nine larger groups (phratries) that were associated with the mythological past but not named; clans of the same phratry possibly stemmed ultimately from the same lineage base. Members of the same phratry shared common ceremonial and land-holding interests, and they could not marry within the group (phratry exogamy).

POLITICAL LIFE   Overall village control was in the hands of the Village Chief and the War Chief. The Village Chief was from the Bear clan, and a sacred stone in his possession verified his authority. The stone reportedly was brought from the underworld by the legendary village founder. The stone was engraved with motifs, including human figures, and their interpretation was the basis for a division of lands among the clans. The stone was inspected as a part of each Soyal Ceremony that the Village Chief headed. The Village Chief had not only the greatest sacred responsibilities at Oraibi but important secular duties as well. He settled land disputes, the most important differences between villagers. His sacred duties, in addition to those dealing with the Soyal Ceremony, included offering prayers for village welfare. It was the Village Chief who remained up late each night smoking and musing about pueblo conditions after most people had gone to sleep. For any critical community matter, his advice was sought, although he could not compel the actions of others. The office of the Village Chief was passed to a brother or to a sister's son after a long period of training. The Village Chief wore no badge of office, but he had a distinctive style of body painting for certain ceremonies and a sacred stick or cane of authority.

The only person at Oraibi with permanent power was the War Chief, who attained his position by being the most outstanding warrior. He had the right to inflict either verbal or physical punishment for nonconformity. On occasion, when parties of men were organized for a community project, men as kachinas assembled the workmen and directed their activities. (See the section "The Kachina Cult" later in this chapter.) A lazy man might be reprimanded or in extreme instances beaten by a kachina. The authority and power of the overt leaders never extended beyond the village. No means existed for uniting the Hopi as a tribe; in fact, the only time they clearly joined in a common cause was during the Pueblo Revolt of 1680.

The Hopi prided themselves on being a peaceful people who disliked shedding blood, and yet they were organized for armed conflict. They fought to defend their pueblo, and the role of a warrior was recognized as dangerous, important, and necessary. In primeval times, when the Hopi reportedly emerged from the underworld, the Kokop and Spider clans introduced a warrior society. Every man was a member, but not all were of the same rank. Members were divided into ordinary warriors and stick-swallowers. Boys were trained for warfare with a rigorous program of cold baths, races, archery practice, and early rising. The Warrior Society held a ceremony each fall, using the sacred equipment held by the Spider and Kokop clans. The two days of rituals involved making prayer objects, ritual smoking, offering prayers, and building altars. A war medicine was prepared and drunk, after which one branch of the membership gave exhibitions of stick-swallowing. For the real warriors, those who acknowledged killing and scalping an enemy, a special initiation that involved fasting and secret rituals took place.

Warfare was said always to have been defensive. Men went into battle clad in ordinary clothing but with the addition of caps made from mountain lion skin to which eagle feathers were attached. A warrior fought with a bow and arrows, stone club, spear, and throwing stick. Before a battle the men prayed to Maasaw and to long-dead warriors, and they sang songs to make themselves brave. Armed only with a stone club, the War Chief led them into conflict. A slain enemy was scalped to the accompaniment of a scalping song, and scalps were carried into the pueblo on poles. A Navajo scalp was considered worthless, but one from an Apache or Ute was valued. The permanent resting place for a scalp was in the home of its taker. A scalp was washed with yucca suds and intermittently "fed" by its owner.

RELIGIOUS SYSTEM   The Hopi religious system was precise, the ceremonial round was exacting, and the kachinas played a vital ceremonial role. To maintain the balance in nature and to sustain human relationship with the gods, each individual was obligated to contribute to the best of her or his ability. Through this effort an individual expressed a desire to be *hopi* or good, but being hopi involved more than goodness alone. A Hopi ideally was cooperative, self-effacing, and nonaggressive, and the particulars of such behavior were spelled out in detail. A Hopi had moral and physical strength and good health and accepted collective responsibilities while concentrating on good thoughts. Conversely, an evil or bad person was *kahopi,* with personality traits opposite those of the ideals.

Central Concepts   The basic tenet of the Hopi religion was the continuing relationship between the living and the dead, a duality expressed in many ways. A person not only had a physical body but also a "breath-body," spirit or soul. At death a soul journeyed to the underworld and continued to exist as it had on earth, with the exception that souls consumed only the essence of food. Preparations for the burial of the dead were similar to those for a newborn Hopi: a corpse was sprinkled with cornmeal, bathed, and received a new name. Because of their weightlessness, a soul could rise into the sky, where it would become a cloud to bring rain to the living. Thus, the God of Death, Maasaw, was in essence a god of fertility. The sun too was considered a god of fertility and was believed to have intimate association with the dead: it spent half of its time in the underworld with the dead and half of its time over the earth. Prayers and offerings to the sun and to the dead were thought to bring earthly blessings. Birth and death formed an endless cycle; in theory, death held no fears because it represented rebirth.

The sun's daily and yearly cycle in some ways mimicked the human life cycle. Each day on earth began as the sun left its eastern home in the morning and ended when it set in its western home; thus the sun gave light to both the earth and the underworld. A yearly cycle began with the summer solstice around mid-June. The summer solstice began the winter season because it was then that the days began to shorten. Summer, quite logically, began about mid-December, as the days grew longer. Earth and the underworld were thought to mirror each other: a summer solstice in one realm was a winter solstice in the other. Furthermore, when a major ceremony was held on earth, a minor one was being performed in the underworld, and vice versa.

Ceremonies The Hopi religious system required a series of annual and biannual ceremonies hosted by particular religious associations. Each important ceremony was controlled by a specific organization that was linked to a different matriclan. Each association was headed by a male elder of the leading lineage in the clan; this lineage also owned a bundle called the "mother" or "heart" of the clan, which consisted of an ear of maize, feathers, and coverings, as well as other sacred objects. Ceremonies were held in a kiva associated with the clan and at times established by phases of the moon, the location of the sun when it rose, or the number of days since a previous ritual had ended. The pattern for major ceremonies was similar. The rituals spanned nine days, during which kiva members were not permitted to eat fatty foods, meat, and salt. Sexual activities were restricted before as well as during these celebrations. The specifics of the ceremonies included the use of altars and associated wooden, stone, or clay tablets painted with motifs symbolic of animals, clouds, maize, and rain. Sand paintings and certain fluids with a water base likewise were important, and prayer offerings were left at the proper shrines (see Figures 9-5 and 9-6).

The performance of each major ceremony was the responsibility of a secret society, and it was essential for each Hopi to participate actively in the affairs of one or more of these societies. At about nine years of age, boys and girls were initiated into either the Kachina Society or the Powamu Society, the latter being more restricted in membership. Within the next few years, girls also joined one of several women's societies, and boys joined those for men. Occasionally, a woman joined a man's society and vice versa to fulfill a particular role, but by and large the ceremonial societies were divided along gender lines. The organization of women's societies was similar to that of men's: they were controlled by a lineage in a particular clan, possessed bundles, carried out secret rituals in a kiva, and performed certain ceremonies in public.

The ritual calendar may arbitrarily be considered to begin with the winter solstice or Soyal Ceremony. The Soyal was conceived around that mysterious moment each year when, in Hopi thinking, the sun rises at the same place for four days, and the days are shortest. The principal purpose of the Soyal Ceremony, which was conducted by those males who had completed the Tribal Initiation, was to induce the sun to begin the trip back to its summer home so that it would bring warmth enough for the crops to be planted. The ceremony had the complementary purposes of inducing fertility in both women and plants, and participation was villagewide. The typical smoking

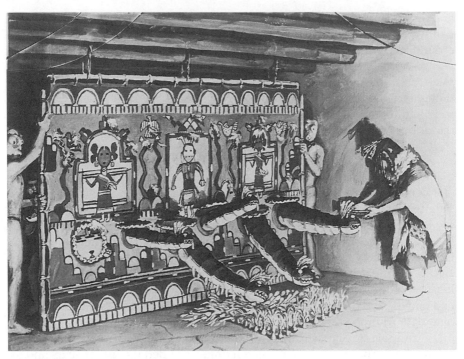

Figure 9-5 | A 1900 illustration of water serpents in a kiva being manipulated behind a screen in a symbolic harvest of small maize plants. (Courtesy of the Smithsonian Institution, National Anthropological Archives, neg. no. 1813-B.)

and prayers were accompanied by the manufacture of a large number of prayer offerings of corn husks, feathers, and prayer sticks. The kachinas performed, and select men and women danced.

The Powamu Ceremony began with the new moon of February and centered on the forced growth of beans in the kiva of the Powamu Society. After the beans sprouted, they were presented by kachinas to the grower's uninitiated offspring, his ceremonial children, and favored relatives. A child to be initiated into the Powamu Society saw some of the sacred rituals for the first time. This new knowledge was not to be revealed, under threat of punishment by men representing kachinas. Initiated children were permitted to impersonate kachinas, to participate in kachina rituals, and to become kachina fathers (ceremonial sponsors). Children who were not inducted into the Powamu Society became members of the Kachina Society.

Another high point in the ceremonial round came in August of every other year when the Antelope and Snake societies joined for a major ceremony. Together they manufactured prayer offerings, then went to their respective kivas to perform secret rituals. Snake Society members collected snakes to become a focal point of a dance. A Snake man held a snake's head

Figure 9-6 | Sand mosaic in the Antelope kiva. (Courtesy of the Field Museum, Chicago, neg. no. 480.)

with his lips or teeth as he danced around the plaza several times (see Figure 9-7). During the dance another man brushed the shoulders of the snake holder with a "snake whip," a short stick with eagle feathers attached. The man danced with each snake and then released it on the ground at the plaza. Afterward the snakes were gathered in a circle and sprinkled with cornmeal by women and girls of the Snake clan. Finally, younger men of the Snake Society picked up as many snakes as they could handle and took them to shrines in each of the four cardinal directions. The major goal of the ceremony was for the snakes to carry the message of the Hopi desire for rain to the underworld.

The public performances of Snake Society members have attracted more popular interest among Euro-Americans than any other American Indian ceremony. The reason is that the snake dancers carried prairie rattlers in their mouths as often as they did harmless species and did so with equal ease. Although prairie rattler bites could be fatal, illness or death from snakebite among the dancers was not reported. No evidence suggests that the handlers were immune to snake venom or that the snakes were charmed or drugged. Furthermore, laboratory tests showed that the Hopi did not have an effective antidote for venom. There appear to have been two reasons for Hopi success

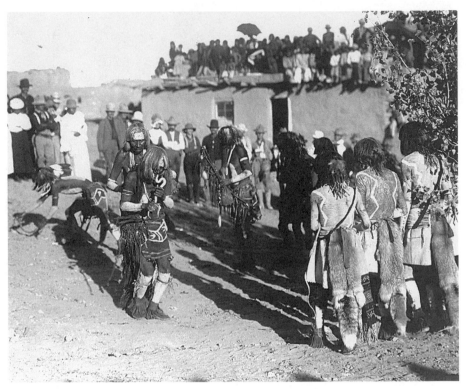

Figure 9-7 | A Snake Dance at Old Oraibi. (Courtesy of the Southwest Museum, Los Angeles, CA, neg. no. 20433.)

in handling rattlesnakes. In 1883 a herpetologist visited a kiva where rattlesnakes were being kept for a dance; he inspected the fangs of one rattler and found them intact. After the dance he sent two of the rattlesnakes that had been used to the U.S. National Museum, and the venom glands were found to contain poison. Thus, it would seem almost certain that the fangs were milked before the public ceremony. In 1932 and again in 1951, after a snake ceremony herpetologists recovered rattlesnakes that had had their fangs removed. These studies suggest that traditionally the Hopi had milked the poison from rattlesnake fangs but that between 1883 and 1932, they began to cut away the fangs. Presumably, as Anglo-American (English-speaking whites) knowledge about rattlesnakes became known to the Hopi, they cut out the fangs to eliminate the risk of poisoning from bites.

The final ceremony of major importance was the Tribal Initiation. Controlled by the Agaves Society, it was held only when this society had at least one candidate for initiation. During this ceremony, adolescent males were initiated into one of four secret societies: the Agaves, Horns, Singers, or Wuwuchim. It should be recalled that a male could not be a fully participating adult in Hopi society until he had passed through this initiation. The Tribal Initiation was the most complex of the ceremonies and a cornerstone of Hopi religion. It took place in November at a time established by the Sun Watcher. A new fire was made in the Agaves kiva by the kiva chief, and some embers were carried to the other participating kivas. A figure of Dawn Woman was brought from her shrine and exhibited on top of the kivas until the fifth day of the ceremony, when she was returned to her shrine after "delivering" her offspring. All candidates slept in their kivas. The dances performed on the third and fifth days were clearly associated with fertility; phallic symbols and simulated pregnancies were presented. These events, and many others, symbolized the ritual rebirth of male children into manhood and reaffirmed the integration between the living and the dead.

The Kachina Cult   Once long ago, according to Tawaqwaptiwa, a Village Chief of Oraibi, after the Hopi had departed from the uppermost level of the underworld, they wandered on earth with their gods, the kachinas. They were attacked by Mexicans, and all the gods were killed. The dead returned to the underworld, and the Hopi divided their ceremonial paraphernalia to impersonate them. From then on, impersonations of kachinas formed the core of Hopi rituals.

When a man wore the sacred apparel of a kachina, he became what he impersonated, and his basketry or leather mask (or "friend") was the most sacred item of his dress. As masks wore out, became soiled, or broke, they were replaced or repaired; however, this did not detract from their sacredness. The chief kachina masks were the only ones reportedly not replaced or duplicated. It was possible also to vary a new kachina mask from the original without impairing its supernatural associations.

Participation as a kachina was open to all village men under the general sanction of the Village Chief, and the activities of the kachinas were under the control of the Badger and Kachina clans. Kachinas were present at Oraibi from the winter solstice until the summer solstice, after which they were supposedly in the underworld except for Maasaw Kachina, representing the God of Death, who was about the earth all year long. While a Hopi adult did not believe that an impersonator was a god but rather a friend of the gods, small children were told that these were actual gods.

Kachina "dolls" have attracted widespread attention from whites and have been collected avidly for many years (see Figure 9-8). These carvings are stylized renditions of the disguises worn by the men who portrayed kachinas. They are small painted and adorned wooden images usually made by men prior to kachina performances. The figures were presented to children by kachinas and were considered by them as gifts from the gods. These kachina images were hung from the rafters of the homes to familiarize the children with the many different forms. Although kachina figures frequently are called dolls, this is a misnomer. They were not toys but served mainly to instruct uninitiated children about one aspect of the religious system. The Hopi made

Figure 9-8 | Model of the Prickly Pear Cactus Kachina. (© The Field Museum, Neg. A 95940.)

more than 240 different forms of kachina figures; they fit into six groups, including chief kachinas, clowns, and runners. A figure was carved from cottonwood tree roots, shaped, and then smoothed before appendages such as ears or horns were pegged in place. A thin layer of white clay was applied, and the clay was painted in vivid colors, the same ones used for the body paintings of real kachinas. Finally, feather adornments often were added to complete the figure.

Sorcery To the Hopi, community-wide prosperity indicated that each individual had contributed his or her utmost, and the ideals of the Hopi Way thus were achieved. But what about failures? Why was it that during some years rain did not fall, winds dried the ground and blew seeds away, and the streams did not flow with water? Obviously, it was essential to be able to explain why nature sometimes did not respond to the complex ceremonies. The burden of failure was said to rest largely with individuals, persons who were kahopi, thinking evil and doing evil; these persons were witches.

The origin of witchcraft was traced to Spider Woman, who caused the first human death. Hopi have reported that they believed a typical village included more witches than ordinary people. Witches might be male or female and from any clan; no one was considered to be incapable of witchcraft. A Village Chief or ceremonial leader might be suspect simply because he held an important office. Any self-assertive person was open to the accusation of being a witch because such behavior was not hopi. One could become a witch either by voluntarily practicing sorcery or by having been unknowingly inducted into a society of witches as a child. In the latter instance, existing witches reportedly carried off a related child while it slept and inducted it into a secret society that followed the pattern of other Hopi secret societies. The initiate was taught the witches' art of assuming the shape of an animal to pursue their nefarious craft by night. The power of a witch was derived from association with an animal familiar, such as a coyote, owl, wolf, or small black ant, from whom the greatest forces of evil emanated; quite logically, sorcerers supposedly possessed "two hearts," their own and that of their animal familiar. Sorcerers reportedly worked evil by sending pestilence to the fields, by causing land erosion, or by driving off rain clouds and replacing them with a conjured windstorm. A witch was not content with destroying crops but killed people as well. Murder probably was the most important activity of a sorcerer because it was believed that he or she extended his or her own life by killing one relative each year. In Hopi belief, a relative was killed or caused to be ill when a sorcerer shot stiff deer hairs, ants, a bit of bone, or some other object into his or her body without breaking the skin.

Ordinary people believed they could best protect themselves against a witch, who was most likely a near relative, by wearing stone arrow points regarded as the ends of lightning flashes associated with the clouds. The Hopi did not attempt to interfere with the activities of witches because they believed that they would die prematurely or encounter misfortune. A witch's spirit supposedly thirsted and hungered for the underworld and approached it by one step a year. The sanctions against a witch were not in this world but in the underworld; when his or her spirit arrived there, it was supposedly burned in an oven and became a beetle.

Shamans Some persons harmed and killed people by supernatural means, but others, shamans, cured people through their special abilities. A society of Hopi curers existed in early historic times, but it became extinct before being reported adequately. In any event there were curing specialists who relied on pharmacopoeia and massaging techniques. Some shamans were secular healers; they set broken bones and prepared herbs for patients. Their rather complex body of knowledge required specialized training, and a secular shaman was likely to pass his information on to a sister's son. In another category were the shamans who performed supernatural cures. These "two-hearted" individuals were supposed to employ their powers only for curing illness caused by witches. Obviously, such a person would be suspect in a sorcery case and considered a dangerous individual in any event. He would chew jimsonweed root or some other plant to induce a vision that aided in diagnosing the source of a malady.

LIFE CYCLE   As might be anticipated, the Hopi stress on fertility led to behavior considered conducive to pregnancy. A woman was supposed to pray to the sun at each dawn and was thought to be most likely to conceive if she had sexual intercourse while menstruating. Pregnancy was recognized by failure to menstruate, and if a woman suspected that she was carrying twins, she sought a shaman's aid to make the twins one. To bear twins was considered difficult, and it was thought that if both lived one parent would die. A pregnant woman prayed to the sun and sprinkled cornmeal while she prayed to ease the labor of childbirth. She was active during her pregnancy, and she as well as her husband observed diverse taboos.

A woman often gave birth in the same dwelling where she was born. She delivered in a squatting position over a layer of sand; the sand and afterbirth were covered with cornmeal and deposited in a special rock crevice. Following a birth the mother's mother cut the umbilical cord, and before long the father's closest female relative arrived to wash the head of the neonate. This woman was in charge until the naming ceremony twenty days later. Note that the relatives of both parents were involved with a newborn. The father was not present during the birth, and he usually lived in the kiva with which he was identified for forty days after an offspring was born.

An infant was nursed on demand and weaned after two to four years, sometimes longer. After a small child was able to walk, he or she was encouraged to urinate and defecate outside the home; if a child repeatedly defecated in a house, she or he might be scolded or slapped on the head. Since everyone slept in one small room, children soon learned about sex. Sexual activities, including masturbation by children, were accepted with casual regard. Small boys were taught jokes that we would consider obscene, and they told the jokes when performing as ceremonial clowns. Despite this casual attitude, young girls usually were shy, and a licentious person might be called "crazy."

Young children were taught that kachinas were gods, and in this role kachinas encouraged childhood conformity. Children were told that giants were coming to visit, and, if they had misbehaved, they were warned to prepare themselves. Girls were instructed to grind cornmeal and boys to trap small animals. A few days later, giant kachinas arrived at households wearing frightening masks and carrying weapons and baskets with which to carry off wayward children. The kachinas cited a child's specific transgressions— having been previously informed of them by parents—and threatened to seize particular children. Erring little girls offered the kachinas baked cornmeal; it was accepted, but the animals trapped by boys were rejected. Parents defended their children, and finally the kachinas left after receiving a gift of meat from the parents. Obviously the entire community was involved in childhood socialization. Children also had further contact with kachinas during formal ceremonies (see Figure 9-9).

There were no formal puberty ceremonies, but it was customary for boys in their early teens to begin sleeping in a kiva rather than at home. A girl was, however, expected to pass through a ceremony before she married. Each year

Figure 9-9 | Young children being introduced into the ceremonial round in a Flute Dance. (Courtesy of the Field Museum, Chicago, neg. no. 7020.)

girls between the ages of sixteen and twenty assembled at the house of a paternal aunt of one girl. The event usually was directed by a female who recently had passed through the rituals, and she was aided by two boys. For most of four days the girls ground maize in a darkened room; they observed food taboos and drank liquids only at midday. The boys organized a rabbit hunt on the third day, and the girls spent most of their time baking piki. Afterward, the girls appeared for the first time with new coiffures termed "butterfly wings" or "squash blossoms." A girl continued to wear her hair in this manner until she married. She was most likely to marry someone from within the community (village endogamy) soon after passing through this ceremony.

Premarital sexual relations between teenagers were expected and were formalized in the *dumaiya*. As a boy began sleeping in a kiva, he was free to roam the pueblo at night and did so wrapped in a blanket so that he could not be easily identified. As the members of his amourette's household slept, he crept in carefully to the side of the girl, who in a whisper asked who it was. The boy answered, "It is I," and from the sound of his voice, the girl identified her caller. If she were willing, which usually was the case since the boy went only where he thought he would be received, he passed the night with the girl, leaving just before daylight. A dumaiya supposedly was secret, but it could not remain so in a small community like Oraibi. The girl's parents did not interfere if they regarded the boy as an acceptable husband for their daughter. A girl was not likely to have only a single lover, and before long she might become pregnant. If this happened, the girl named the boy she liked best as the father, and the formalities of arranging a marriage were begun. It also was possible for a girl to propose directly to a boy during certain festive or ceremonial occasions. A couple did not court unless they stood in a proper social relationship with one another. A person could not marry another in the same clan or phratry and was not supposed to marry someone from his or her father's clan or phratry, but the latter rule was not observed with care.

After the relatives of a couple approved a match, the girl ground maize for three days at the groom's house to demonstrate her abilities as a homemaker. There was no comparable trial for the groom. While the girl was in the boy's home, his paternal aunts attacked the boy's mother and and her sisters with mud and water for permitting the girl to "steal" their "sweetheart." An atmosphere of jovial hostility surrounded the fight. On the fourth morning the couples' hair was washed in one container by their respective mothers and female relatives. A mingling of their hair symbolized the marital union. Once again the paternal aunts of the boy attempted halfheartedly to disrupt the ritual. After their hair had dried, the couple stood at the mesa edge to pray to the sun and later returned to the groom's home for a wedding breakfast. They were now man and wife, but they continued to live in the groom's house until the bride's wedding costume was completed by his male relatives and other men who offered to help. The men prepared the cotton and wove two sets of wedding garments, a small robe, and a white-fringed belt; in addition they prepared skins and sewed white moccasins and leggings. During the manufacture of these items the groom's family feasted the workers. After a month or more, the garments were completed; wearing one set and carrying the second in a reed container, the bride returned home. Her husband informally and unobtrusively took up residence in her household. The wedding garments were very important because they reportedly were required for entering the underworld after death.

All Hopi women appear to have married, but such was not the case for men. Indirect pressure was put on a girl by her brothers and her mother's brothers to bring another male into their economic unit. A boy's parents did not encourage him to marry because they then lost him as a productive family member. Any form of plural marriage was prohibited, but many unions were transient. It appears that over 35 percent of the people had from one to eight divorces. The most common grounds for divorce was adultery, followed by what we probably would call incompatibility. Divorce was a simple matter since it was only necessary for a man to rejoin his natal household or for a woman to order her husband from her household. The primary pressures against a divorce came from a girl's family, since they did not relish losing an economically productive male. The mother and her small children continued to reside in their old abode; an older offspring might join either parent.

The social core of a household consisted of a line of females. Within this setting the closest bonds were between a mother and her daughters. Daughters were destined to spend their lives in their mother's home or in an adjacent residence, and eventually they assumed their mother's role. From her mother a girl learned domestic skills and the norms of proper behavior. A mother guided the most important decisions in the ceremonial life of a girl and was likely to have a voice in the selection of her mate. As a girl's menarche arrived, she was instructed by her mother about caring for herself. The girl was not isolated at this time, nor at any other menstrual period; neither was she restricted from participating in ceremonies while menstruating. Were a mother to die, the mother's sister, who was called mother, replaced the biological mother in the girl's affection. Between a mother and her son the social bonds were not as close. A mother indulged an offspring of either sex, but a son in his early teens soon found his identity with a kiva group. A man's natal home remained the residence with which he felt most identified, however. He returned there if divorced and was a frequent caller in his mother's house. Like a girl, a man identified closely with his mother's sister, especially if the mother had died. A father was not overtly important in the upbringing of his children. He was, however, interested in having his daughter find a good husband, who by his farming activities could lighten the father's economic labors. A father took comparatively little active interest in a son until the latter's tribal initiation. Then the father selected the boy's ceremonial sponsor, which was an important decision. As a boy grew older, his father assumed a major role as his teacher. He imparted farming and ceremonial skills as well as advice about being hopi (see Figure 9-10).

The maternal uncle of a young boy was the only male of his parents' generation who was of the same lineage and clan as himself. If such an uncle were a ceremonial leader, a boy might follow him in office, which called for systematic training of the youth. A mother's brother was likely to be the most important figure of authority associated with the boy's home, and he did not hesitate to apply discipline. A mother's brother was not all sternness toward his sister's children, however. He often told them myths or tales about their clan and occasionally presented them with gifts. One very warm relationship was between a man's sister and his son. As a small child, a boy soon learned that he was always a welcome guest in this woman's home. Here he received favored foods and frequent demonstrations of love and affection. As he grew older, he took game to his paternal aunt and exhibited his warm feeling toward her. Sexual relations with this aunt and her daughters were possible, and Titiev suspects that in the recent past a youth may have been expected to marry a father's sister's daughter.

As death approached it was said that a person's body became swollen. Youths as well as most adults left the house because they feared being present

Figure 9-10 | An old man and a child. (Courtesy of the Southwest Museum, Los Angeles, CA.)

at the time of a death. The body and hair of a deceased person were washed, and then he or she was reclothed. After a man was wrapped in a deerskin or a woman in her wedding blankets, the corpse was flexed into a sitting position. Prayer offerings were fashioned by the father of the deceased or another male in his clan. A prayer feather was placed beneath each foot and in each hand, as well as over the navel, the supposed location of a person's spirit. The face was covered with cotton, symbolic of the time the dead become clouds, while food and water were placed with the body as sustenance on the journey to the underworld. The body was carried to the cemetery by men from the house of the deceased; here a hole had been dug just large enough to receive the bundled corpse, and soil was spread hastily on top. Men who attended the dead purified themselves afterward by washing in a boiled juniper preparation, and there was a ritual in the household of the deceased to protect members against spirits. The next day the man who had manufactured the prayer offerings took cornmeal and five prayer sticks to the grave. The prayer sticks were supposed to help the person on his or her travels to the land of the dead, and the food was to feed the spirit. A prayer was offered, and the spirit was told not to return for anyone else in the community. Later, household residents washed their hair and smoked themselves over hot coals on which pinyon gum had been placed. All possessions of the deceased were thrown away. A separate cemetery was provided for the stillborn, infants, and children. It was believed that the spirit of an infant did not travel to the underworld but lingered above the house, to be reborn again as a person of the opposite sex. The death of an adult was surrounded with misgivings and fear despite the fact that in Hopi belief most dead were to be reborn into a peaceful world that was an intimate part of the Hopi Way.

| More Recent Historic Changes

After early contacts and hostilities with the Spanish, the next serious problem faced by the Hopi was how to deal with another group of non-Indians who began to enter their country. Among the earliest Hopi and Anglo-American contacts was a conflict in 1834; white trappers raided Hopi gardens and killed about fifteen people. In 1850 the Hopi asked Anglo-American authorities in Santa Fe for help in controlling Navajo intrusions on their grazing lands, but the authorities took no action until later. Most Hopi took a cautious approach toward these whites. Everyone knew the origin myth in which an elder brother of the Hopi, a Bahana, departed and promised to return when the Hopi were in need. They reasoned that perhaps Anglo-Americans were the Bahanas, the prophesied whites; but no one knew for certain how to identify them. In the long run, contact with these whites did not aid the Hopi but set the stage for a serious rupture in Hopi society as well as conflicts over land.

ESTABLISHMENT OF THE RESERVATION   The Hopi were recognized by the federal government in 1870 when the Moqui Pueblo Agency was established, and a school supervised by missionaries was founded in 1874. The Moqui Pueblo Reservation (later changed to Hopi Indian Reservation) was created by an executive order in 1882, but the land set aside was for Indian, not exclusively Hopi, use. Passage of the Dawes Act in 1887 resulted in federal pressures on the Hopi to shift from family and community landholdings to individual allotments. Conflicts with the Navajo over grazing lands intensified, since there had been no boundary survey when the Hopi Reservation was established, and Navajo encroachment on Hopi lands continued. Through a series of executive orders the Navajo Reservation came to surround the Hopi, and about 1937 the BIA reduced the area officially designated as Hopi land to about one-fourth its original size, or one thousand square miles.

CHANGES IN THE SUBSISTENCE CYCLE By the early 1900s, the Hopi economy had undergone major changes. Their primary reliance on maize, beans, and squash continued, but new crops and animals became increasingly significant. The most important new animal was the sheep, and virtually every man had at least a small flock by 1900. Each animal was individually owned, but men herded cooperatively. Sheep were held as wealth and were butchered only for ceremonial occasions. Surplus meat was dried as jerky or dried, pounded, and mixed with fat as pemmican. Cattle were less popular because of their initial cost and because the pattern of allowing them to graze freely led to the destruction of crops. Although people owned horses, they were difficult to maintain. They had to be rounded up each day for pasturing, usually at considerable distance from the village. Like sheep and cattle, horses were individually owned, but men often tended them jointly.

THE RUPTURE AT ORAIBI Events between about 1870 and 1907 had a profound impact on Hopi life, especially at Oraibi. In the earliest contacts with Anglo-Americans it appears that the Oraibi chiefs were unfriendly, and in 1871 a government agent was well received everywhere except at Oraibi. For a number of years the interim chief had been a man serving only until one of his two eligible sons was old enough to assume the position. The younger son, Lololoma, became the Village Chief sometime prior to 1880. Initially, he continued his father's anti-white policies. He reversed his position following a trip to Washington, D.C., and became the leader of the progressive (friendly, pro-Anglo) faction. The conservative (hostile, anti-Anglo) faction was led by a man named Lomahongyoma but called Uncle Joe by Anglos. He was a leader in the Soyal Society, head of the Blue Flute kiva, and from the same phratry as Lololoma; this made his challenge to the latter's leadership legitimate. The progressives and conservatives had able leaders as the great drama at Oraibi began to unfold.

One of the critical issues was the precise identity of Anglo-Americans: were they the Bahanas who were to come to the aid of the Hopi? Each faction drew on sacred myths to validate its position. The hostile faction claimed that the real Bahanas would speak Hopi and could produce a stone matching the one held by the Village Chief at Oraibi. Obviously the Anglos were not Bahanas, and if the progressives accepted them, the anger of a supernatural would lead to a flood that would end the world. The progressives, on the other hand, traced Hopi difficulties to the underworld and witchcraft rather than to Anglo-Americans. An individual's choice of sides in this conflict was influenced by such factors as clan and phratry ties and kinship links to the leaders of the factions.

The conservatives categorically rejected Anglo-American ways. The year 1887 became crucial to the conflict when the Dawes Act was passed by Congress. As noted previously, this act was designed primarily to divide tribal lands into individual allotments. When soldiers arrived at Oraibi in 1891 to survey the village land in order to make allotments, the hostile faction disrupted their efforts. The soldiers then tried to unseat the leader, but they were surrounded. When the hostiles made a ceremonial declaration of war, the soldiers prudently withdrew. A larger U.S. military force sent to Oraibi shortly thereafter arrested both hostile and progressive leaders and imprisoned them temporarily at an army fort.

By 1891 the differences between the factions were beyond reconciliation. The hostiles were more numerous, and their leader Lomahongyoma declared himself the Village Chief. Neither side would cooperate with the other in holding the sacred ceremonies. In 1894 U.S. soldiers made another effort to survey Oraibi land. The hostiles resisted once again, and as a result their leader, Lomahongyoma, and others were imprisoned at Alcatraz; their confinement lasted from January 3 to August 7, 1895 (see Figure 9-11). The land was not allotted. By 1897 each faction held its own Soyal Ceremony without interference from the other.

What happened at Oraibi affected the entire tribe because the village housed twelve hundred of the twenty-two hundred Hopi listed in the census of 1890. Laura Thompson (1950) and John Loftin (1991) have pointed out that one factor behind the rupture at Oraibi was the problem of land. Loftin also emphasized that the two factions continued to disagree over how to interact with whites. There were other problems as well. The Hopi were embroiled in violent disputes with the Navajo over land boundaries. Oraibi soil was being eroded by an expanding arroyo that reduced the amount of farmland. Furthermore, a smallpox epidemic in 1897–98 killed many Hopi. Clan friction intensified, and a number of prophecies were advanced concerning problems among clans.

About 1901 there was a change in the leadership of the progressives. Lololoma died, and a younger sister's son replaced him. This young, aggressive man, Tawaqwaptiwa, was selected because of his forceful qualities. In September of 1906 open conflict developed. After some scuffling, the conservative leader, Lomahongyoma, by then back from Alcatraz, drew a line on the ground, and a push-of-war was launched. Before the pushing began it was decided that the losers would leave the pueblo. Lomahongyoma was the object to be pushed; people shoved him both from behind and in front. The conservatives lost, and that same evening about three hundred of them abandoned the settlement with their belongings. They founded the new village of Hotevilla, about seven miles to the north of Oraibi.

Figure 9-11 | The original caption on this picture reads: "Mosqui Indians Chief Lo-Ma-Hung-Yo-Ma, arrested at Oraibi, November 25th and 26th 1894, for seditious conduct and confined to Alcatraz Island, California, since January 3rd 1895." (Courtesy of the Southwest Museum, Los Angeles, CA, neg. no. 20086.)

BIA authorities arrived soon after the rupture. They sent the conservative leaders to jail and relieved Tawaqwaptiwa temporarily as chief. He was sent to the Indian school at Riverside, California, to learn to speak English and practice American ways. When he returned to Oraibi in 1910, he was extremely anti-American; Titiev (1944, 94) records accounts that describe him as "quarrelsome, stubborn, vindictive, and unusually licentious." Over the next twenty years, Tawaqwaptiwa managed to alienate most of the remaining residents of Oraibi; by 1933 only 109 Hopi remained there. Some had moved to New Oraibi, on the valley floor beneath Oraibi, and others had settled some forty miles to the northwest at Moencopi on the Navajo Reservation. As Thompson (1950) pointed out, the disintegration of Oraibi relieved the local pressures for land, but social cohesion did not develop in the offshoot communities. The most conservative community by the 1940s was Hotevilla. The people had had a nearly complete ceremonial cycle when they left Oraibi that September night in 1906. Through the years their resistance against whites became almost an end in itself, and for good reason: after the split, most of the Hotevilla men had been impounded by the federal government, and the women and children had found it difficult to survive until their return. Then, too, children had been forced by soldiers to attend school, and the people had been forcefully dunked in sheep-dip during a 1912 epidemic. These people scorned outside interference and wanted to be left alone.

After 1906 a complete ceremonial round could no longer be held at Oraibi because some clans were no longer represented, but Chief Tawaqwaptiwa faced the situation calmly as he aged. He maintained that the time would soon come when everyone would abandon him, and he alone would carry on the Soyal. Then there would be a great famine, and following it, all of the old ceremonies would be reinstituted at Oraibi. Again the village would thrive in all of its colorful glory. Tawaqwaptiwa waited and waited, and died still waiting.

| Emergence of the Modern Hopi

By the 1940s about four thousand Hopi lived in fourteen settlements, including Moencopi, on land set aside for them adjacent to the Little Colorado River. The critical problems facing the people were increasing land erosion and a population increase on a land base made smaller by Navajo encroachments. The erosion apparently resulted from a dry climatic phase and overgrazing by livestock. For many years the federal government had encouraged herding, and sheep had become essential in the Hopi economy. To remedy the erosion problem, federal efforts centered on a program of livestock reduction. The people of the Third Mesa area were required to reduce their holdings by nearly 45 percent, while reductions on the other two mesas were to be about 20 percent. This meant that residents of the Oraibi area were hardest hit by the program. They attempted to resist the reductions but were unsuccessful. Along with the reduction, the federal government introduced better stock management practices and organized cooperatives. Farming practices were not changed dramatically at this time; however, the plow was replacing the digging stick. As in the past, fields either were watered from stream flooding or were dry land plots. An effort made to irrigate farmland had limited success. Their essentially meatless diet consisted mainly of maize (see Figure 9-12), beans, potatoes, sugar, and coffee. The nutritive value of the diet was below the standard for children and barely sufficient for adults.

The most profound changes to affect the Hopi world during the emergence of the modern period occurred at Oraibi. Here all aspects of life underwent tremendous readjustments following the 1906 rupture. When the full ceremonial cycle no longer could be held, the kiva-centered life of males was altered, and the significance of the nuclear family increased proportionally. This lessened the position of men and strengthened that of women. The net result was the fostering of a previously unheard-of male individualism. Since the Oraibi land base was not adaptable to the accumulation of farmlands or to male control of such lands, ambitious men moved toward wage labor. Another avenue open to individual men was political leadership; however, personal achievement was still disapproved of among the Hopi.

Figure 9-12 | Hopi women cleaning corn. (Courtesy of the Field Museum, Chicago, neg. no. 368.)

One compelling reason why profound changes did not occur earlier and more rapidly among the Hopi was their remoteness from major Euro-American power centers. In sum, Hopi country was not readily accessible to outsiders for many years. Titiev (1972) proposed that abandonment of traditional Hopi life grew in intensity following the construction of paved highways linking Black Mesa with cities and towns in northern Arizona and New Mexico. No longer isolated physically, the Hopi turned outward toward the white world. Many people bought automobiles or trucks, ending travel by wagon or on the backs of burros and horses. Men began commuting daily to jobs in nearby towns or weekly to more distant cities, returning to the village on weekends. Some of these men continued to farm clan lands but only on the weekends. Surplus crops now could be transported over highways to be sold at distant markets, and in times of local food scarcity, a staple such as maize could be imported. Good roads also brought increasing numbers of tourists, especially during ceremonies such as the Snake-Antelope Dance.

In its physical aspects, Oraibi underwent less profound but equally far-reaching changes. The number of occupied houses was about the same as in the early 1930s, but larger houses were being built. Cinder block and cement were replacing local stone and adobe as building materials. As in the past, women performed lighter house-building tasks such as plastering. Outhouses became common, and most people owned store-bought furniture and appliances. The matrilocal marriage residence pattern and clan ownership of houses continued, but a woman no longer shared a household with her mother. When a woman married, she wanted an official American civil or religious ceremony to document the event, because experience had taught that documents were required in any legal dealings with whites. Each bride, even if she married elsewhere, still received traditional wedding garments from relatives.

The population of Oraibi was 112 in 1933 and had increased to about 130 in the mid-1960s. The emigration of young adults was more than counteracted by a decline in infant mortality attributable to Western medical practices. The young who remained at Oraibi became indifferent to the orthodoxy of the Hopi Way beyond participating in an occasional kachina dance. Gods of old had come to be displaced by technological forms; to obtain water had become a secular, not a sacred, process.

The consumption of alcohol traditionally was shunned by the Hopi. But some veterans returning from World War II were heavy drinkers, and intoxicants became increasingly popular, with accompanying drunkenness. Social life changed in yet another respect because numerous clans died out and some others were represented only by males. They, too, will become extinct unless outsiders who are members marry into Oraibi. Political life assumed an unprecedented turn when a woman became the Village Chief because the people could not agree on a male successor. Hopi religion has disintegrated, and the Soyal Ceremony is no longer performed. By 1955 at Oraibi the only remnant of this ceremonial event was that two men stayed up all night making prayer sticks for the sun.

| Contemporary Issues

The present-day Hopi face a number of issues that have deep and complex historical roots. In these issues, nothing less than Hopi lands and identity is at stake. Though they are presented separately, these issues are intricately interwoven.

HOPI FACTIONS   The Oraibi split in 1906 gave rise to the formation of five new villages on Third Mesa: Bacavi, Hotevilla, Kykotsmovi, and Lower and Upper Moencopi. In 1934 the Wheeler–Howard Act (the Indian Reorganization Act) was enacted by Congress to permit Native Americans to govern their own affairs within a structure proposed by the federal government. One of the first BIA programs encouraged each Indian tribe to form a tribal council to negotiate with the federal government in a way that the government could understand.

In 1936 the Commissioner of Indian Affairs, John Collier, persuaded the anthropologist Oliver LaFarge to try to convince the Hopi to form a tribal

Figure 9-13 | In the spring of 1994, Hopi Tribal Chair Ferrell Secakuku was inaugurated into office. (Courtesy of Gallup *Independent* newspaper.)

council. Initially only Christian Hopi and those employed by the BIA supported the plan. They prevailed in the election because many of those who were opposed to a tribal organization abstained from voting. The council is composed of elected officials from each village, with their number determined by a local census. Since the Hopi Tribal Council began in 1937, factions who favor the traditional clan-based Village Chiefs have objected to its existence. The idea of a tribal council was so controversial that at one point it was dissolved, only to be reorganized in 1951 (see Figure 9-13). Although the council has continued as the political forum for dealing with the federal government, it is criticized by various factions. Non-Hopi have labeled supporters of the tribal council as "progressives" and opponents as "traditionalists," but the Hopi do not make this distinction.

BLACK MESA COAL MINING   In 1969 the Hopi signed an agreement with the Peabody Coal Company to strip-mine coal on Black Mesa. Some traditionalists opposed the contract because it caused pollution of the earth. However, the Hopi had mined and burned coal as a fuel from the 1200s to the 1600s and may have been among the earliest coal miners in the world. Why they ceased is not really known. Under government pressure, most Hopi accepted the Peabody mine but were concerned about the air pollution from the generating plants. Equally or more critically, the Hopi were alarmed over the use of so much ground water to slurry coal from the mine to generating plants. A vexing problem was also that the federal government had forced them to accept royalties of mined coal that were well below market value. In 1982 the Hopi enacted a severance fee on coal mined from Black Mesa. The Assistant Secretary of the Interior for Indian Affairs vetoed the plan. By 1987, however, the tribal council negotiated a more favorable coal lease arrangement with energy companies that was far more environmentally responsible. Before long, coal royalty money provided more than 60 percent of tribal revenues.

THE HOPI-NAVAJO LAND DISPUTE (HOPI VIEW)   Another long-festering problem involves Hopi land rights and the Navajo. When the Hopi Reservation was created by executive order in 1882, the order did not specify that the land was for exclusive Hopi use. The Navajo who lived nearby grew rapidly in number and gradually came to occupy much of the land on the reservation that traditionally had belonged to the Hopi. In the 1930s about 1.8 million acres of Hopi land, from a total of 2.4 million acres, were made part of the Navajo Reservation. In 1962 the U.S. Supreme Court ruled that the land detached from the Hopi had in fact been set aside for both tribes; however, the Navajo continued their effective control. In 1974 the Navajo-Hopi Land Settlement Act was passed by Congress to separate the disputed lands, allotting one section for the exclusive use of each tribe. The act also created the Hopi Partitioned Lands to legalize the removal of 10,000 Navajo from Hopi land and the relocation of about 100 Hopi from Navajo land. The Hopi maintained that the Navajo Nation owed the Hopi tribe $23 million for use of land in the former joint-use area. In 1997 the Ninth U.S. Circuit Court entered a judgment against the Navajo. They are to pay the Hopi for Navajo livestock grazing and agricultural land use on lands that were occupied jointly between 1962 and 1979, plus interest, for a total of about $18 million. Furthermore, the Navajo are to pay the Hopi somewhat more than $3 million for damage to Hopi Partitioned Lands caused by overgrazing by Navajo livestock.

CONTINUITIES   Recent accounts by Richard O. Clemmer (1995) and John D. Loftin (1991) examine modern Hopi developments in detail and with sympathetic insight. They each emphasize the conflict between the attraction of traditional Hopi life and the realities of dealing with the federal government in particular and Euro-Americans in general. Loftin (1991, 84–6) views the Hopi situation as "compartmentalization," a temporary suspension of old values while partaking of Anglo culture, and adherence to traditional Hopi values in nontraditional ways. Clemmer (1995, 273) suggests that "segregative goals" characterize the Hopi as they try to maintain their unique identity while concurrently adapting Western institutions to their particular needs and desires. The approaches are complementary.

As the subsequent examples indicate, Hopi ambivalence toward Anglos is manifested in many ways. Fundamentally, the Hopi are opposed to tourists

Figure 9-14 | A Hopi from Second Mesa, Alphonso Numkena, makes and sells traditional-style gourd rattles. This 1998 photograph was taken at the Hopi Cultural Center.

visiting their villages, especially during religious ceremonies, and they are distressed when tourists attempt to take photographs. But the Hopi know that tourist dollars improve reservation economic conditions. Therefore, in 1971, they opened the Hopi Cultural Center, which has produced substantial profits for the tribe by selling craft items to tourists. Furthermore, arts and crafts businesses owned by individual Hopi have flourished from the tourist trade (see Figure 9-14). At the same time, because of pressure exerted by staunch traditionalists, villages and ceremonies periodically are closed to outsiders, only to be opened again by Hopi who seek compromise.

By 1986 about 80 percent of the Hopi lived on reservation land, and soon thereafter most homes had electricity from power lines. At Old Oraibi and Hotevilla, however, traditionalists resisted having power lines in their communities. One result was the installation of solar-powered electrical systems for some households. Whereas traditional houses were made from native sandstone and mortar, nontraditional building materials, especially cinder block, now predominate. Newer homes may look like the old type, but they are cheaper to build.

Religious ceremonies are now held largely on weekends because so many people hold down wage-earning jobs during the week. In a religious context, the money earned from jobs has been important because food sharing and gift giving are an integral part of ceremonial life. The greater amount of available cash seems to be responsible for an increase in the number of kachina dances performed. Thus adjustments and readjustments continue.

Are Anglos the Bahanas? The issue remains unresolved. Yet it is not clear whether prophecies, which are now prominent among the Hopi, were an integral part of their traditional culture or represent a comparatively recent development. Regardless, some Hopi, especially those on Third Mesa, contend that their actual white brother has not returned; Anglos are not Bahanas because they have not produced a stone to match the one at Old Oraibi. Hopi who subscribe to this position contend that the descendants of their *real* white brother have yet to appear.

| Additional Sources

Two publications in particular provide a good introduction to the Hopi. They are by Ernest and Pearl Beaglehole (1935) and Nancy Bonvillain (New York, 1994). The best works about a particular village are Mischa Titiev's studies made at Old Oraibi. Alexander M. Stephen's (1936) diary offers a wealth of information about most aspects of Hopi life, but it is difficult to use. The best biography of a Hopi man was edited by Leo Simmons (1942). *No Turning Back* (Albuquerque, 1964), the story of Polingaysi Qoyawayma (Elizabeth Q. White), as told to Vada F. Carlson, concerns a woman and her adjustments to the American and Hopi life-styles. The best ethnohistory is included in a book by Edward H. Spicer (1962), and Laura Thompson's (1950) work is a superior source of information about the emergence of the Hopi into modern times. One (9) of the two *Southwest* volumes of the *Handbook of North American Indians,* William C. Sturtevant, general editor (Washington, DC, 1979), includes a wealth of information about the Hopi and other Pueblo Indians in prehistoric, ethnographic, and historical contexts. John D. Loftin's *Religion and Hopi Life in the Twentieth Century* (Bloomington, IN, 1991) is a notable contemporary account of Hopi religion. Richard O. Clemmer's *Roads in the Sky* (Boulder, CO, 1995) is also an excellent source.

| Selected Bibliography

Beaglehole, Ernest, and Pearl Beaglehole. 1935. *Hopi of the Second Mesa*. American Anthropological Association Memoir no. 44.

Bonvillain, Nancy. 1994. *The Hopi*. New York.

Clemmer, Richard O. 1995. *Roads in the sky: Hopi culture and history in a century of change*. Boulder, CO.

Colton, Harold S. 1949. *Hopi kachina dolls*. Albuquerque.

Cushing, Frank H. 1923. Origin myth from Oraibi. *Journal of American Folklore* 36: 163–70.

Dozier, Edward P. 1970. *The Pueblo Indians of North America*. New York.

Eggan, Fred. 1950. *Social organization of the western Pueblos*. Chicago.

Forde, Cyril D. 1934. *Habitat, economy and society*. London.

Forrest, Earle R. 1961. *The Snake Dance of the Hopi Indians*. Los Angeles.

Geertz, Armin W. 1993. *The invention of prophecy: Continuity and meaning in Hopi Indian religion*. Berkeley, CA.

Jones, Volney H. 1950. The establishment of the Hopi Reservation, and some later developments concerning Hopi lands. *Plateau* 23:17–25.

Loftin, John D. 1991. *Religion and Hopi life in the twentieth century*. Bloomington, IN.

Lomatuway'ma, Michael, Lorena Lomatuway'ma, and Sidney Namingha, Jr., with Ekkehart Malotki. 1993. *Kiqotutuwutsi: Hopi ruin legends*. Lincoln, NE.

Oliver, James A. 1958. *Snakes in fact and fiction*. New York.

Ortiz, Alfonso, ed. 1979. *Handbook of North American Indians: Southwest*, Volume 9. William C. Sturtevant, gen. ed. Washington, DC.

Sekaquaptewa, Helen. 1969. *Me and mine: The life story of Helen Sekaquaptewa*. Tucson.

Simmons, Leo W., ed. 1942. *Sun Chief*. New Haven.

Spicer, Edward H. 1962. *Cycles of conquest*. Tucson.

Stephen, Alexander M. 1936. *Hopi journal*. Columbia University Contributions to Anthropology, vol. 23, 2 pts.

Thompson, Laura, and Alice Joseph. 1944. *The Hopi way*. Chicago.

Thompson, Laura. 1950. *Culture in crisis*. New York.

Titiev, Mischa. 1943. Notes on Hopi witchcraft. *Papers of the Michigan Academy of Science, Arts, and Letters* 28:549–57.

———. 1944. *Old Oraibi*. Papers of the Peabody Museum of American Archaeology and Ethnology, vol. 22, no. 1.

———. 1972. *The Hopi Indians of old Oraibi*. Ann Arbor.

Voth, H. R. 1905. Oraibi natal customs and ceremonies. *Field Columbian Museum, Anthropological Series*, vol. 6, no. 2.

Waters, Frank. 1963. *Book of the Hopi*. New York.

Whiting, Alfred F. 1950. *Ethnobotany of the Hopi*. Museum of Northern Arizona Bulletin no. 15.

Yava, Albert. 1992. *Big Falling Snow*. Albuquerque.

10 The Navajo: Transformations among a Desert People

Earth's feet become my feet, thereby I go through life.
Its legs become my legs, thereby I go through life. . . .
Long life happiness I am wherever I will go.
Before me it is blessed wherever I will go,
Behind me it is blessed wherever I will go,
It has become blessed again, it has become blessed again!

A part of the Blessingway chant, the purpose of which is to restore harmony and heal. (Wyman 1970, 224–25)

THE NAVAJO are by far the most populous tribe north of Mexico to maintain the essence of a traditional lifeway. There are about 250,000 Navajo, of whom some 150,000 speak Navajo; this is a good indicator of their cultural vitality. Equally significant, despite centuries of efforts by Christian missionaries, most Navajo still adhere to their own belief system.

The Navajo are possibly the tribe best known to non-Indians. Their blankets and silver jewelry have been appreciated and bought by generations of Anglo-Americans ("Anglo" refers to English-speaking whites). In recent years about one hundred films and videos have been released about the Navajo, far more than for any other tribe. They also have been studied by anthropologists more often than have any other Indians. Approximately 2600 authoritative articles, books, and monographs (book-length technical reports) had been published about them by 1987. A Navajo family has sometimes been defined as "a man, his wife, their children, and their anthropologist"!

An additional compelling reason to include a chapter about the Navajo is their remarkable cultural adaptability. For example, in the early 1860s the U.S. Army sought to subjugate and apparently to destroy them as a people. Soldiers herded most Navajo from their homeland to a distant fort, an infamous episode that the survivors termed the "Long Walk." During the course of their removal many people were purposely killed—including women in childbirth. When the surviving captives were released after five years, they had little more than hope and tenacity. Amazingly, despite continuing trauma, they not only persevered but began to thrive. One key aspect of Navajo history was their relative freedom from political control by Euro-Americans until the early 1900s. Another has been their capacity to adopt the ideas of other peoples and integrate them into their culture; at the same time, they themselves have been surprisingly uninventive. In sum, the modern Navajo possibly are the most remarkable example of cultural adaptation and readaptation among Indians north of Mexico.

Navajo country has both inviting physical beauty and stark cultural reality. Year-round splendor is visible in the colorful canyons and mesas, rock spires, broad valleys, and mountains. Nonetheless, living there requires constantly shifting adjustments. The low and erratic rainfall, sudden torrents from occasional storms, windstorms, the possibility of heavy snowfall, the high salt content of most soils, and expanses with little vegetation posed cultural challenges. In the Navajo portion of the Colorado Plateau, the landscape is high, ranging from about 3000 to 10,000 feet above sea level. At lesser elevations grama grass, a coarse western grass, prevails, but where there is water cottonwood and willows thrive. At higher elevations pine or pine and juniper dominate the mountainsides. A salient climatic feature is the low precipitation, sometimes as much as ten inches a year but more often considerably less. In the many small valleys, groundwater encourages the growth of tumbleweeds, which soon turn brown and blow away. This weed, a thistle, was accidentally introduced to the United States from Europe in 1873.

Fauna played an early and critical role in Navajo economic life. In addition to small game, such as cottontails and jackrabbits (actually hares), antelope and deer were important for food and hides. Bobcats, coyotes, black bears, and wolves were numbered among the predators. One touchstone of Navajo survival has been their capacity to exploit the resources in varied ecological zones.

This chapter is presented in a different format from the other chapters on particular tribes for a number of reasons. First, and most important, the Navajo did not appear as a clearly distinct tribe until around A.D. 1725, some 185 years after the Spanish first arrived in the Southwest. Hence, we cannot examine aboriginal Navajo life in depth. Second, in their historical emergence the Navajo absorbed so many Indians from other tribes that they justly have been identified as "biological and cultural hybrids" by Garrick Bailey and Roberta Glenn Bailey (1986, 15). Third, in the process of assimilating foreign elements, both Indian and European, the Navajo reworked them into a distinct configuration. Their culture cannot be understood without an appreciation of these factors. Therefore, the Navajo are introduced in an ethnohistorical account to emphasize their cultural "layering."

| The Background

The Navajo (Navaho) call themselves "Dine," meaning "the people." They identify northwestern New Mexico, their original home in the Southwest, as "Dinetah," or "land of the people." The word *Navaho* entered English from Spanish and is possibly derived from a Tewa Indian word that refers indirectly to cultivated fields. Despite a wealth of information about the Navajo, we know surprisingly little about their ancestors before they arrived in the Southwest. In linguistic terms, they belong to the Na-Dene phylum and the Athapaskan language family. Most Athapaskans lived and continue to live in a vast inland region of northwestern Canada (see also Chapter 3) and in interior Alaska. The close and early association between the Navajo and the Apache creates some confusion in following their movements, yet they both clearly came to the Southwest from the north.

FILTERING SOUTH   We justifiably think of human "migrations" as significant movements from one place to another. The migrants usually are numerous and their destination is known. In these terms, the Navajo and many other people did not migrate. Instead, small family groups or bands typically moved from one watershed to the next. They had no distant target destination in mind because they had no knowledge about far-off places. Why did they move? The reasons usually cited are food stress, overpopulation, disease, and internal or external conflicts. The northern ancestors of the Navajo may have responded to each of these conditions on their journey southward. They did *not* move south in search of a warmer land. They were as yet unaware that warmer land existed.

Neither the ancestral Navajo route to the Southwest nor the time of their arrival has been established with precision. When the precursors of the Navajo lived in the subarctic, they obviously adjusted to local conditions. Probable adaptations included a social life based on small family groups closely related by both blood and marriage. Hunting dominated their economy, while their material culture included tailor-made garments and cone-shaped dwellings. They may have begun to leave the far north around A.D. 1000 and may have descended along the eastern flank of the Rocky Mountains. Along the way, perhaps in the Plains, they learned about farming. Shortly before A.D. 1600 they appear to have arrived in Dinetah as a populous Athapaskan group but not as a distinct Navajo tribe (see Figure 10-1). A competing theory suggests that the Navajo presence in the Southwest goes back further. They may have entered the area and intermarried with the Anasazi (prehistoric Pueblo Indians) before A.D. 1100. If so, the blending of Athapaskan and Pueblo cultures into the historic Navajo may have taken place earlier than is generally believed.

THE SPANISH AND PUEBLO IMPACT   The Spanish era in the Southwest began with the Coronado Expedition of 1540 and ended in 1846 with the inception of the Anglo-American era. Reasonably clear evidence of direct Athapaskan–Spanish contact dates from 1582. Initially, relations were friendly, but soon conflict arose over the fate of captives held by the Indians. One of the markers of emerging Navajo culture became evident: they were aggressive and successful raiders for captives, edibles, and loot. Other early markers included trade with varied tribes and the cultivation of maize (corn) as an important food.

Spanish colonialism in New Mexico began in 1598, and Roman Catholic missions soon were established at pueblos; but missions to the Athapaskans failed. Athapaskans were soon raiding both Spanish and Pueblo communities for livestock, which they usually killed for food. In the Pueblo Revolt of 1680, the Spanish settlements were destroyed, some four hundred colonists were killed, and the survivors fled south. In 1692 the Spanish returned in force to reestablish themselves and seek revenge. The Spanish killed many Pueblo Indians and sold captives into slavery. At this juncture, thousands of Pueblo dwellers in New Mexico fled their homes, and most of them sought refuge in Dinetah. Athapaskan contact with these refugees was critical in the emergence of the Navajo. Pueblo refugees introduced weaving, possibly pottery, and a host of religious concepts, including ceremonial masks and sand paintings. Some modern Navajo clans originated at this time by assimilating particular Pueblo populations. From the Spanish they began to learn the complexities of herding goats, sheep, horses, and cattle. It also was from the Spanish that the proto-Navajo began to learn to process metal.

By 1696 the Spanish once again were entrenched in New Mexico, but Indians continued to raid their settlements. The Athapaskans in turn were

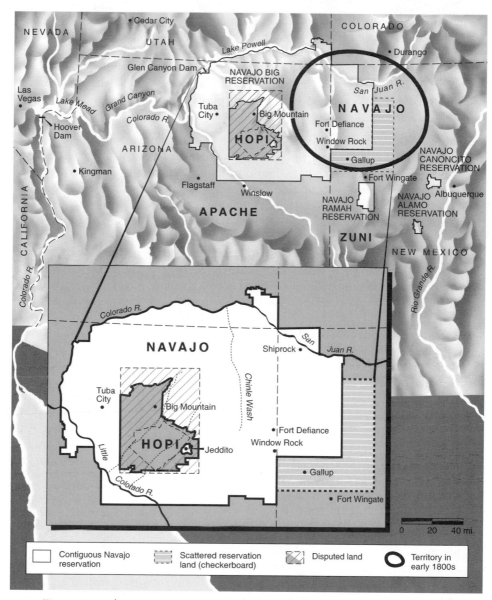

Figure 10-1 | Historic homeland of the Navajo Indians.

raided by the Ute Indians, who drove them south and west from Dinetah. During these years, around 1725, Navajo tribal identity was emerging. By the late 1700s they had increasingly turned from hunting and raising maize at home-steads to a more mobile life-style, with herding as a major economic focus. The mobility inherent in a herding economy, especially after horses were captured and raised in quantity for riding, enabled the Navajo to become even more formidable raiders. Peaceful negotiations with the Spanish seldom lasted for long, and the same was true after Mexico won independence in 1821. Because the Navajo had no overall political unity, some bands would make peace with the Spanish and Mexicans, whereas other bands continued to raid. The Navajo had become an independent people.

ANGLO-AMERICAN CONTROL In 1846 the United States seized New Mexico and inherited confrontations with Navajo raiders. In the early history of Navajo relations with Anglos, no date compares with August 31, 1849. An Indian agent, along with Colonel John Washington of the U.S. Army and his troops, met with a group of Navajo, including Narbona, a leader who sought peace with the Anglos. A disagreement arose when a Mexican man who was with the troops said he saw a horse that had been stolen from him. Washington demanded that the horse be returned to the Mexican. The Navajo refused and had begun to leave when the soldiers were ordered to fire on them. Seven Navajo were killed, including Narbona, who was shot in the back and scalped. No official action was taken against Washington, and Navajo mistrust of Anglos appears to have intensified. (See Figure 10-2 for a portrait of Narbona made on the day he was killed.)

In the first four years of Anglo-American control of New Mexico, an estimated 450,000 sheep were seized by the Navajo and Apache from Hispanic and Anglo settlements. Neither peace conferences nor military expeditions could stem the raids. The U.S. Army response was to build Fort Defiance deep within Navajo country in 1851. It was attacked unsuccessfully by the Navajo in 1860 and temporarily abandoned in 1861 at the beginning of the Civil War. Until the army returned there in 1863, the Navajo and other Indians, Anglos, and Hispanics fought for revenge, animals, slaves, and booty. By then the Navajo may have had 300,000 herd animals.

THE LONG WALK By the early 1860s the Navajo transformation from hunters and relatively sedentary farmers to mobile herders, raiders, and farmers was well developed. Most Navajo appear to have favored peace with the United States, but they were hostile to many other Indians in the region and to the Hispanics. Unfortunately, federal Indian policy was inconsistent and dominated locally by anti-Navajo military officers. One reason behind the periodic belligerence of the Navajo was that slave traders, including Hispanics, were seizing so many children. Brigadier General James H. Carleton, the commander of the U.S. Army troops, was determined to remove the Navajo from the 30,000 square miles they occupied and relocate them to Fort Sumner (Bosque Redondo) in New Mexico. The Long Walk of some 300 miles, beginning in 1863, was one of the most disreputable actions by the U.S. military against Indians. The army pursued a scorched-earth policy so that the Navajo had little food and few places where they could escape. They were herded to Fort Sum-

Figure 10-2 | A watercolor portrait of Narbona made from a sketch on the day he was killed. (Courtesy of the Library, the Academy of Natural Sciences of Philadelphia, Ms. Coll. 146, no. 44 Kern.)

ner. Those who could not keep up with the others were shot and killed, whether they were women giving birth, the ill, or individuals who paused to help another captive. About nine thousand Navajo were driven to Bosque Redondo. As many as two thousand Navajo may have avoided capture by the military, but some of them were found by slave traders and sold. At least another two thousand died during the Long Walk or at Bosque Redondo.

Fort Sumner was located in an area without adequate food or water and ill-adapted to farming, which was intended to help provision the prisoners. The army was poorly prepared to house and feed so many people in such a bleak setting. The prisoners were homesick; some became desperately ill, and some starved to death. They were raided by their enemies. Navajo boys reportedly went to where horses and mules were corralled, rooted around for undigested corn, and roasted it as food.

The army effort to transform captives into subsistence farmers failed. When they did plant crops, insects, disease, and drought led to repeated crop failures. As a result, the federal government spent more than $1 million a year to provision the captives, but the rations provided made many of them ill. Finally, the government decided to return the Navajo to their homeland because keeping them captive was a financial burden. A treaty was arranged with the

Figure 10-3 | Barboncito was the Navajo leader who was recognized by whites and who played an important part in the 1868 treaty negotiations. (Courtesy of the National Anthropological Archives, no. 55766.)

cooperation of a prominent leader, Barboncito (Figure 10-3); it was ratified by the U.S. Congress in 1868. The return trip of the Navajo was not without hardships. Children rode in wagons, some adults rode horses, and others walked.

This is an appropriate context in which to consider Navajo "warfare" in brief. What has been called warfare among them should more properly be termed *raiding;* conflicts typically involved a small number of warriors who approached an enemy covertly to seize livestock. True battles were rare. Men developed many skills to become successful raiders. They became adept at handling a bow, riding horses, tracking, controlling livestock, and performing the religious rituals associated with warfare. Men who aspired to be raid leaders underwent a prolonged apprenticeship under an older man who knew one or more highly complex war rituals. A leader organized a small group of family and friends to form a raiding party. As preparation, warriors often had a medicine man (a singer) perform an elaborate ceremony (a sing, or chant way) called the Enemy Way. More often, an Enemy Way was performed to purify returning warriors and to protect them from ghost sickness as a result of contact with the spirits of slain enemies. A large number of people from a warrior's clan would attend, requiring the warrior's family to slaughter many sheep as food. Outsiders referred to the Enemy Way as the "Squaw Dance" because in the social dancing that accompanied the ceremony, women chose dancing partners from among the men.

A small party of raiders set out on foot, hoping to return in a few days with at least as many horses as raiders and driving home a herd of sheep. They never wiped out an enemy's herd, however, so that it would eventually be replenished for future raids.

RESERVATION HISTORY TO WORLD WAR I   In their excellent study of the Navajo reservations up to 1975, Garrick Bailey and Roberta Glenn Bailey (1986) described the changes in insightful detail. The original reservation in northwestern New Mexico and northeastern Arizona, created by the treaty in 1868, included about 10 percent of what had been Navajo country before their confinement at Fort Sumner. Because the land base was so small, federal administrators permitted Navajo to live in adjacent areas. The resettlement program encouraged Navajo self-sufficiency because the government feared that they would revert to raiding. The government and Navajo alike dreaded the prospect of new hostilities, and both sought accommodations. To help them recover from their captivity, the people were provided with rations; they also received farming equipment and seeds, as well as substantial numbers of domestic animals, especially sheep. Federal support coupled with Navajo resilience led to unprecedented economic growth that peaked in the late 1880s.

This is not to say that few problems existed along the way. The scattered nature of the Navajo population, which was distributed over an area of about 25,000 square miles, created a lasting administrative problem. The two administrative centers, Fort Defiance and Fort Wingate, were understaffed, and the agents usually knew little about the Navajo. The federal employees, both civilian and military, could not possibly control the people under these circumstances. Their solution was to depend on Navajo leaders to act as a bridge to the general population. Because the Navajo had no tribal political organization, agents dealt with locally prominent men, charismatic leaders, whom the Anglos called "chiefs" but whom the Indians identified as "big men." The annuity compensation that was part of the resettlement terms, including such goods as coats, blankets, yard goods, tools, and farming equipment, was funneled through these men. Big men used the goods provided to further their power base. However, this treaty arrangement ended in 1879. When some Navajo resumed raiding, the government turned to the big men and hired tribal police to curb the raiders. Under some circumstances, big men accused raiders of being witches and killed them. The combination of big men and tribal police proved reasonably successful in curtailing raids.

After their resettlement, the people survived by hunting game, especially antelope, intensively and by collecting plant products. They seldom killed herd animals for meat. Before long, hunting and gathering depleted local food sources, and goats became the most important edible. Goats, who often bore two offspring at a time, were a good source of milk, cheese, and meat. Sheep began to multiply and eventually became the key herd animal, providing meat and wool that was woven into blankets and garments to wear or to trade. Horses, mules, and burros were ridden and provided a source of meat, but cattle were unimportant.

Trade with other Indians and Hispanics flourished and expanded as Navajo blankets became a major item for barter. Trading changed in character once Anglo traders on the reservation were licensed by the federal government in 1868. Initially, the people were poor; annuity payments did not begin to meet their needs. At the same time, local resources were overexploited. A case in point is the supply of skins used for moccasins. The people traditionally killed deer and used these skins to make moccasins, but hunting pressure soon depleted the deer population. Neither goat nor sheep skins were acceptable substitutes. At this time, however, Navajo sheep herds were increasing rather rapidly, and as a result they were able to exchange sheep wool, both with other Indians and at trading posts, for buckskins. Around this time, too, the Anglo-American demand for wool was increasing, and the railroad, which reached western New Mexico in 1881, provided an economical means to ship raw wool east to be processed. Before long the wool trade expanded dramatically, and trading posts both on and near the reservation became numerous and relatively stable enterprises.

By the early 1890s the Navajo owned an estimated 1,700,000 sheep and goats; they were also considered the best weavers in the region. Their blankets (Figure 10-4) had long been a premium craft item, but they also produced

Figure 10-4 | A Navajo "storm pattern" rug from the Tuba City, Arizona, area, circa 1920s. (Photo by Sharlotte Neely, 1994.)

a variety of other woven products, such as saddle blankets, sash belts, and women's dresses, both for their own use and for trading. They made use of changes in weaving materials and techniques introduced by Anglos, including commercial yarns and dyes and manufactured wool cards (to straighten tangled fibers and thus prepare the wool for spinning). These developments increased and modified the productivity of women, who were the weavers. A new market arose after a railroad was built through the southern sector of their country, thereby introducing tourists as customers for blankets and silverwork.

The Navajo learned the rudiments of silverwork from the Spanish, and the quality of Navajo jewelry grew in the 1870s as the inventory of production tools improved. In addition to and equally important as its appeal to the tourist trade, silver jewelry became a significant way for the Navajo to concentrate their wealth. In the 1880s they developed a pawn system with traders. Silverwork was pawned for goods in times of economic stress and was redeemed as individuals became more affluent.

The assimilation of the Navajo into the greater Anglo-American society became a long-range federal policy. Under the terms of the 1868 treaty, schools were to be provided for children, but the dispersed nature of the Navajo population and the limited federal resources allotted made this goal unrealistic. At that time Christian denominations were encouraged to open reservation schools. The Presbyterians founded a day school at Fort Defiance in 1869, but it was a failure, as was a local boarding school. Only a small number of children attended the Carlisle Indian School in Pennsylvania during the 1880s, in part because the people objected to sending their children so far away. By 1892 there were about 18,000 Navajo, but less than one hundred children attended school. Around this time only about fifty Navajo spoke English, and fewer still could read and write. Formal education obviously had failed to this point.

In the late nineteenth century a multitude of events over which the Navajo had no control impinged on their lives. The federal government granted land to railroads in a checkerboard pattern, along a right-of-way in the vicinity of Navajo lands. The eventual illegal exclusion of Navajo from public lands, the arrival of Anglo and Hispanic farmers and herders in their midst, and an expansion of the cattle industry by whites each had negative consequences. Furthermore, an increase in the Navajo population, expansion of their herds, and overgrazing by Navajo and non-Navajo stock created environmental problems.

The last decades of the nineteenth century proved a disaster. With the national economic Panic of 1893, livestock and wool prices fell precipitously. Repeated dry years and heavy snowfalls in Navajo country led to an alarming decline in goat and sheep herds; droughts resulted in crop failures. Many Navajo went hungry or starved despite considerable government aid. These hard times continued into the early 1900s. Overgrazing and competition with outsiders for land meant that most Navajo could no longer depend primarily on herds as their subsistence base. They developed alternative economic strate-gies. Gradually they improved the breeding stock of sheep, intensified farming activities, and turned increasingly to wage labor as an income supplement.

Federal control over reservation life became far more intense in the late 1800s. The General Allotment Act (Dawes Act) of 1887, as discussed in Chap-ter 2 and elsewhere, was a concerted federal effort to destroy the reserva-tion land base and assimilate Indians into the general population. The act had relatively little immediate impact on the Navajo, but federal domination in-creased as six regional administrative centers were created by 1909. Addition-ally, in the early 1900s the political appointees in charge of Indian reservations began to be replaced by career civil servants, who usually were more rigid in furthering federal policies. Federal agents sought to eliminate childhood mar-riages, plural marriages, and other "vices," but with poor results.

Navajo–Anglo conflicts varied from one sector of the reservation to an-other because of localized conditions. Throughout much of the reservation, Indians complained about their inability to graze stock on public lands and their restricted access to water. They were also concerned that the size of the reservation was inadequate for their needs, especially compared with the areas traditionally exploited. Reservation crowding became more acute as the population increased; by 1900 there were about 21,000 Navajo. The land problem was partially and temporarily alleviated by repeated expansion of the reservation. By the 1910s some Navajo claimed land allotments under the Dawes Act despite strong opposition from local whites, who anticipated that one day the reservation would be abandoned by the federal government and they would be able to homestead most of the land. When Arizona and New Mexico became states in 1912, Anglo political power vastly increased at the expense of Indians.

As mentioned previously, Navajo blankets had long been a major craft item both for personal use and to trade with other Indians. Blanket designs in-clude the Plain Stripe style based on Pueblo motifs, the "classic" Serape style of Spanish origin, and the Chief Pattern, which had numerous motif variations. The latter was possibly so named because they were traded to and worn by "chiefs" of other tribes; any Navajo might wear a Chief Pattern blanket. By the 1890s, with the encouragement of trading post owners, weavers began to pro-duce textiles for the Anglo market. Rug weaving soon had a major impact on reservation economic life following changes in weaving styles. An early "rug" measured about four by six feet, and many actually were blankets sold as rugs by traders. The Santa Fe Railroad and the Fred Harvey Company were instru-mental in fostering the Anglo passion for Navajo crafts. Navajo rugs and, to a lesser extent, silverwork designed for the Anglo market began to be sold in stores that featured Indian crafts. In 1903 the Navajo may have sold as many as 50,000 blankets and may have earned as much as $350,000 from their sale. The market continued to expand until around 1920, then declined during the Great Depression.

| Traditional Life

The preceding summary of Navajo ethnohistory up to the pre–World War I period points up a major problem when attempting to describe their "traditional life." Over more than two hundred years of Navajo tribal identity, the people changed repeatedly and dramatically. First they were hunters, farmers, and raiders who shifted to herding and then to herding supplemented by wage labor, which becomes increasingly prominent. In becoming "Navajo" they were profoundly influenced by the Spanish, Pueblo Indians, and Anglo-Americans, as previously emphasized. No comprehensive Navajo ethnography appeared until after they began to be dominated by the federal government. Hence, a "typical and traditional year" cannot be presented. Instead, the account in this chapter represents a mixture of customs both old and relatively new. The emphasis in this ethnographic reconstruction is on the decades surrounding the year 1900.

ORIGIN MYTH   Numerous varying Navajo accounts record their creation and emergence as a people. Narrators of and listeners to these tales accept the legends as legitimate, even with the textual differences. The myth recounted here represents a composite and differs significantly from some versions. Initially, we should note that the word used by the Navajo for themselves, Dine, literally means "Earth Surface People." They contrasted with the Holy People, who once lived beneath the present earth surface. Holy People are termed "Yei"; they exist at the zenith and nadir of the celestial sphere and at points of the compass. The Yei are associated with many things: features on the landscape, the weather, plant life, and some animals. The Yei are not gods in our sense because they may either help or hinder the people; to control them in rituals is a cornerstone of Navajo religion, crystallized in the Blessingway.

In a series of twelve stratified worlds beneath the earth lived the Holy People, but discord, usually resulting form witchcraft, forced them into one higher world after another. At one point men and women could not reconcile their differences and lived separately, but finally they learned to live together. In the last of the underworlds, a flood forced the Holy People to escape to the earth's surface. It was here that death originated.

The Yei created natural objects. They also originated the Earth Surface People, commonly referred to as "the ones with five fingers." The Earth Surface People were the ancestors of the Navajo and other peoples. The Holy People taught the Navajo how to live. The Holy People also were the parents of Changing Woman, the most prominent individual in Navajo mythology, who is identified with the earth itself. Changing Woman later conceived miraculously by the Sun and gave birth to two sons, the Twin Monster Slayers, who killed earthly monsters. The sites of these slayings are prominent features on the landscape. In this way the natural world was created.

APPEARANCE AND CLOTHING   Traditionally the hair of adults and children was brushed back, folded, and tied in place. Men followed a newer custom of keeping their hair in place with a rolled handkerchief in which they carried small items, such as tobacco and coins. Adults wore large silver earrings and locally made necklaces of silver or turquoise beads; alternatively, coral or shell beads might be obtained from a trader. Silver bracelets likewise were popular, as were belts made from heavy silver disks strung on leather straps.

Around 1900, new apparel styles were displacing older ones. However, low-cut moccasins with rawhide soles remained the universal footwear. White man's shoes were taboo; they could not even be touched. Similarly, some older people thought that garments manufactured by whites would produce illness if worn. This restriction began to disappear as factory-made yard goods, Pendleton blankets, and shawls became more readily available. Both sexes wore knit stockings. Navajo blankets were worn and also used as bedding, but their use declined as blankets became a popular tourist item.

Traditional woolen dresses were being displaced by homemade calico dresses or hand-sewn blouses and skirts. On special occasions a woman wore a heavy knee-length woolen tunic with border designs and knee-length leg wrappings of goat or buckskin. The tunic was held in place with a woven girdle. Apparently, velveteen blouses and satin skirts did not become popular until the 1920s. Men wore pants of wool or calico, calico shirts, and leggings of dyed deerskin held in place with garters of woven thread. On special occasions their leggings or pants were trimmed with buckskin fringes and silver buttons.

SETTLEMENTS AND MANUFACTURES   As the people became less mobile in the early 1900s, they created new dwelling types and modified old ones. The standard traditional winter house, or hogan, continued to dominate. It was cone-shaped and about fifteen feet in diameter. The frame consisted of three interlocking forked posts at the center that extended to the outer walls; a pair of additional posts and poles formed an entrance that always faced east. Pieces of wood and poles were placed against the frame, and the structure was covered with mud or earth. A shallow interior excavation became the floor, and a storage shelf extended around the inner walls. Smoke from a central fireplace escaped from a hole near the dwelling peak. Aboriginal American Indians did not make chimneys over fireplaces, but in some houses they installed a metal hood above the fireplace to draw smoke from the room. They also bought metal stoves from traders or fashioned homemade stoves from oil drums. A small number of houses included Anglo-style tables and chairs, but otherwise there were no furnishings. People worked and slept on sheepskins.

Another traditional hogan type had four interior posts to support crossbeams and a post and pole entryway. The frame was covered with small poles, bark, and finally packed earth. This flat-topped dwelling type was intimately associated with ceremonies. Hogans competed with new forms of housing that included log cabins, inspired by Anglos, and jacal dwellings of Hispanic origin; a small number of families occupied frame houses with either flat or gabled roofs.

Summer and temporary campsites consisted of improvised shelters. They included lean-tos, ramadas (open porchlike structures), and windbreaks, or tepee-style structures covered with canvas. Another prominent structure at a camp or winter settlement was a sweat house. This was a tepee-shaped structure with a pole frame covered with cedar bark and then with dirt. Rocks were heated in a nearby fire and transferred inside the structure for the bathers. A settlement also included wooden enclosures for securing livestock (see Figure 10-5). They also needed various items for the animals, such as saddles, quirts, lassos, and hobbles for horses and imported baby bottles of glass for feeding newborn lambs.

Imported artifacts were becoming increasingly popular. Iron axes had replaced those made from ground stone, and knife blades flaked from chert or chalcedony long ago had given way to imported metal knives. Near a homestead were looms on which women produced woven goods. Some people made and used clay cooking pots, but most containers were of metal and bought at trading posts. Locally made baskets and pottery were primarily produced for religious ceremonies, although some families continued to use relatively flat coiled baskets as food dishes.

Farming equipment of old, such as wooden digging sticks and wooden weed cutters, were being displaced by imported shovels and hoes. To harvest

Figure 10-5 | A Navajo camp as it appeared in 1944. (Photo by C. E. Purviance. Courtesy of the Museum of Northern Arizona.)

wild seeds a person might use a clublike wooden flail, and he or she could re-move kernels of corn from a cob by striking one ear against another. For grinding corn and other grains, they used a lava slab metate and round stone mano. These, however, were giving way to the hand gristmills that traders stocked. Roasting pits provided a traditional means for cooking meat, ears of corn, and ground cornmeal products.

Horses and burros had become beasts of burden, but some people con-tinued to use tumplines as an aid for carrying firewood, water containers, and other heavy loads. A tumpline was a strap made from buckskin or wool that could be slung over the forehead or across the chest of a male or female bearer to help support a burden. This form, however, appears to have been a relatively recent introduction. To carry water, they coiled sumac twig splints to form a somewhat globular basket that had loop handles near the top and that was covered with pitch. Goatskin water bags were a recent addition to their material inventory.

THE SUBSISTENCE ROUND   By the 1910s the economic round continued to depend most heavily on herd animals. Wealth, prestige, and security were linked primarily to the ability to meet the needs of livestock. The insightful discussion of Navajo stock by James F. Downs (1972) based on his fieldwork in the early 1960s is the primary source of information about herding in earlier decades.

One characteristic of Navajo pastoralism was their dispersion into small family groups at homesites. But as the population expanded, pressure on grazing land intensified. A key to their success was an ability to meet the par-ticular needs of cattle, goats, horses, and sheep in thoughtful combination. Efficient herding depended in part on having at least a few horses, and own-ing them increased one's social status. In practical terms, to keep at least one horse at a living site was highly desirable. A hobbled or tethered horse nearby provided immediate mobility for meeting various needs, especially for locating animals that had strayed. Yet keeping horses at hand meant that they must be fed and watered on a daily basis.

Sheep were most important as a food source, but they could also be converted into money, and they provided a major source of personal satisfac-tion. The care of sheep dictated the texture of Navajo life. Sheep required daily attention, but they also were the most domesticated and the least intelli-gent of the livestock raised. A herding instinct leads sheep to follow one an-other; a stray sheep is defenseless and will die of hunger, thirst, or predation, especially by coyotes. Sheep are nervous and react to the behavior of one an-other. To counteract this characteristic, a few goats usually were added to a herd because goats are more curious and self-reliant; they calmed and led the sheep. A small number, even hundreds, of sheep and goats could be managed by one person, adult or child, because after they were driven to grass the ani-mals could be ignored. In sum, sheep required a great deal of care but were readily controlled.

Yet sheep herding itself was demanding. Herders typically moved their flocks to high country in the summer and to lower land in the winter, a pattern termed transhumance. A heavy snowfall forced a family to dislodge the snow so that animals could graze, and cold winds made it difficult to find grass. Spring lambing required careful attention. Lambs were separated from a herd and tended at a homesite to increase the survival rate. Sheep were grazed on open range, penned each night, and taken out to feed shortly before dawn. This pattern may have originated in years past when other Indians raided Navajo herds. In addition, most Navajo feared the dark because of religious beliefs. Sheep were also penned during the heat of the day because in hot weather they would stop and refuse to eat or move despite vigorous efforts by a herder. The proximity to water was another crucial factor in the tending of sheep. Finally, if nearby land became overgrazed, a family was forced to move at least temporarily to more distant pasturage.

During World War I, the sizes of sheep and cattle herds increasingly responded to the market demands for lamb and beef. Cattle were raised to sell. Most families owned a few animals, but they were rarely slaughtered as food. Those families that placed at least some emphasis on cattle were constrained by a number of factors. Most important, a single cow required about four times as much rangeland as a sheep or goat. A few cows could be grazed together with sheep, but herds of cattle tended to stray widely. Considerable effort might be required to locate such animals and to drive them back again, especially if a man did not have a horse. Considering the importance of sheep as food, the fluctuations in cattle prices, and the far greater emotional identification with sheep, it becomes clear why cattle assumed secondary importance.

The only other important domestic animal was the dog. Often, each family member owned a dog and viewed it with considerable affection. One practical reason for owning a dog was to help herd sheep. Dogs usually aided a herder moving sheep in a particular direction, but they were not trained in the manner of Anglo sheep dogs. Perhaps the most important role of dogs was to keep coyotes away from sheep. They also served as scavengers around a homestead. Dogs were hungry most of the time and contributed to sanitation around a home by eating cow, horse, and human feces.

The arid nature of Navajo country meant that it was ill suited for intensive farming. At reasonably well-watered sites, family members, especially women, were largely responsible for raising maize and pumpkins as dietary supplements. Alternatively, a family might exchange sheep or sheep wool at a trading post or with the Hopi for maize, flour, and fruit. Planted fields were preferably near a homesite, but might be several miles away when the distant land was better suited. Despite the labor expended on clearing land, planting seeds, and controlling weeds, crops often failed for lack of moisture; or the seeds might wash away with heavy rains. After a few years the yield of a plot declined abruptly, and the process was repeated.

In another context, maize cultivation served a critical need unrelated to food. Corn pollen was considered an exceedingly sacred plant product, an idea borrowed from Pueblo Indians. Pollen was placed in small bags and used to bless individuals, animals, and hogans; it played a crucial role in all religious rituals.

SOCIAL STRUCTURE   Descent was traced through females and included about sixty named matrilineal descent groups (matriclans). These clans in turn were grouped into about fifteen unnamed phratries. A primary purpose of the clan and phratry was to regulate marriage. No one could marry into one's own clan, the clan of one's father, or a clan in the same phratry. Members of the same clan tended to be widely dispersed, and, possibly as one result, neither clan chiefs nor clan councils existed. A prominent man in a clan might influence the lives of nearby clan members and persons representing other clans in the vicinity; thus his authority was territorial and not based on clan affiliations per se. Furthermore, when a person traveled to another part of Navajo country, he or she could expect food, shelter, and other forms of aid from members of the same clan, irrespective of whether or not the persons had ever met previously.

Navajo kinship terminology not only is changing but also varies from one segment of the population to another. The version discussed is possibly the most widely prevailing system. A child was "born in" the mother's clan and regarded all the females of the mother's clan as "mothers." Whenever necessary for clarity of meaning, a person would identify a biological mother as his or her "real mother." A child likewise was "born for" the father's clan, and the males of this clan were "fathers." In addition, those *born for* a father's clan were siblings, whereas those *born in* a mother's clan were children. Mother and mother's sister were termed alike because they were women of the same clan. Similarly, father and father's brother were termed alike. Different terms existed for father's sister and mother's brother. The terms for the first ascending generation are bifurcate merging.

For siblings and mother's sister's children, distinctions were made by age and gender, and all were termed alike (e.g., an older sister and mother's sister's older daughter were both in a sense "older sisters"). Cross-cousins were termed alike with no gender distinction, and parallel patrilateral cousins were distinguished by gender. The terminology for cousins is basically Iroquois (see Figure 10-6).

The kinship terminology provided the framework for lifelong responsibilities, with particular forms of behavior expected in each set of relationships. Mother's brothers had important responsibilities toward their sisters' children, especially their sisters' sons, since many of the duties of raising children fell to the mother's brother. Adults who acted irresponsibly were said to bring shame on their families and, in fact, to act as if they had no families. Brother–sister relationships often overrode those of wife–husband in long-term importance.

Some relationships required polite, almost bashful, behavior, as was required of younger kin in dealings with older relatives. Women had high status

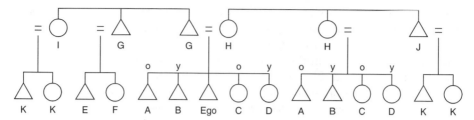

Figure 10-6 | The early historic Navajo system of kinship terminology.

and could address any man as "my son," while a man might address any woman by the more respectful term, "my mother." Daughters acted politely toward fathers. Intermediaries were often called upon to communicate with relatives who deserved extreme respect. When a brother married, his sisters might interact with him through their children or his wife. The social distance between a man and his mother-in-law was so great that a son-in-law was obliged to avoid her—he never spoke to her or remained in the same building or even in her vicinity. By contrast, relationships between a mother and her children were said to be "easy," warm, and affectionate. Sons enjoyed similar relations with their fathers. Some family ties were so familiar that joking was allowed, as between sisters and their unmarried brothers. In some relationships the joking could be of sexual content, as between cross-cousins or between a mother's brother and his sisters' sons.

A young couple was expected to live with the family of the wife's mother (ideally matrilocal residence). Despite this expectation, a newly married couple might live for a time with the husband's family unit (actually bilocal residence). Any number of factors determined the residence of a couple, such as whether a family could accommodate the newcomers or whether a family required the help of another male. For a couple to move back and forth before they settled down was not uncommon. As the population continued to grow, however, and the land base remained relatively stable, increasing numbers of couples lived apart from their parental families, especially when the husband had a wage-labor job.

Ideally, social and economic life centered around a "head mother," her stock, farmland, hogan, and the adjacent land that the family used. With her or close by lived her unmarried children, daughters and their husbands, and the children of these couples. Thus an ideal homestead consisted of matricentered hogans. The core residents were persons born into the matrilineage of the head mother. The stability of a homestead might be disrupted when the head mother died. In that case, her daughters might move away to found their own homesteads and in turn become head mothers. A less serious disruption occurred when an in-marrying husband was divorced by his wife or vice versa. In either case, the former husband left, usually to rejoin his mother's family at least temporarily; his children remained with their mother.

The nuclear family was the basic socioeconomic unit, and it was deeply enmeshed in kinship or marriage ties with other local families. A neighborhood ideally was dominated by extended family members of the core matrilineage. Additional matrilineage relatives probably lived at more distant localities. In combination, these matrigroups might form an "outfit." The term also has been applied to a more extensive territorial unit that did not have a strict basis in kinship; in this sense an outfit may be a comparatively recent development. In sum, social life focused on matricentered lineages.

POLITICAL LIFE   The Navajo did not emerge as a distinct tribal entity until about A.D. 1725. Furthermore, incipient political integration was initially thrust upon them following the treaty of 1868. It was then that the federal government appointed charismatic leaders, Navajo "big men," whom the administrators called "chiefs." This effort was largely unsuccessful. These points were made earlier, but they bear repeating to introduce more recent political developments.

In 1899 the federal government began to create regional administrative centers on the reservation, and soon thereafter career civil servants began to replace political appointees in Indian administration. These changes, as mentioned previously, meant that the United States was in a better position to assert greater political control over the people. As in the past, men who were appointed as "leaders" were those who did not actively oppose federal policies. There were thirty such appointees in 1900. In some sectors of the reservation, councils were organized that functioned on an intermittent or regular basis, but they were above all else the tools of Indian agents. Yet some agents opposed Navajo councils and sought instead to deal directly with individual Indians. These devices prevented the people from developing a unified political base. Even when an elected Navajo Tribal Council was launched in 1923, the purpose was to serve the interests of oil companies in lease negotiations. Broader Navajo interests were not considered.

RELIGION   The Navajo religion was based on the concept of *hozho,* which encompasses balance, beauty, goodness, happiness, harmony, and health. The purpose of ceremonies (chant ways), as well as the prayers and acts of individuals, was to maintain or restore hozho. By the early 1800s, their religion was a successful blend of curing practices associated with northern Athapaskan shamans and the Pueblo priest-based religion that focused on fertility.

A Navajo singer combined the traits of a shaman and priest. Singers, usually men, focused, like shamans, on curing the sick. In the manner of priests, however, singers spent many years as apprentices. By the early 1800s, there may have been as many as fifty basic ceremonies, each with numerous variations, requiring as many as nine days for a singer to perform.

Sand Paintings   Singers also learned how to make the accompanying sand paintings (dry paintings), of which there were more than 500 types, ranging in size from one foot in diameter to twenty feet across. The paintings encompassed a great deal of color and directional symbolism. Most sand paintings were made from pulverized black, blue, white, or yellow minerals. Many of the sand painting designs and behaviors during a sing relied on Pueblo fertility motifs of corn and rain. Among the most common symbols were Holy People, clouds, lightning, rainbows, and the four sacred plants—beans, corn, squash, and tobacco. A singer and assistants created sand paintings on buckskin or smooth, clean sand. Once completed, the singer instructed the patient to sit on the painting. Sand paintings were not permanent and typically were destroyed by sunset.

Navajo religion was mechanistic, in that complicated chant ways had to be performed flawlessly to attract the attention of Holy People and have the desired positive effect. A perfectly performed chant way coerced the supernatural to act in a specific way. The Holy People were seen as somewhat fickle and, like men, were portrayed in Navajo myth as alternately kind and cruel. Among the Holy People only Changing Woman was portrayed, like women in general, as consistently gratifying, nurturing, protective, and trustworthy. To perform a chant way correctly compelled the Holy People to be kind. To make a mistake in a chant or sand painting could create a dangerous situation. It was also important to make certain the correct ceremony was also chosen to be sung (Kluckhohn and Leighton 1946, 198).

To diagnose a problem and select the correct ceremony to restore hozho, the people consulted one of three types of shamanlike diviners: a hand-trembler, a listener, or a stargazer (crystal gazer). Each type had his or her unique way of analyzing a problem or illness to determine the correct ceremony. Hand-trembling was the most common method of divination. A hand-trembler would spread corn pollen along his or her hand and arm, say prayers and sing chants, and then enter a trancelike state as the hand began to tremble. Movements of the hand indicated which ceremony a patient required. Often a particular singer and a specific ceremony were recommended. The Enemy Way cured ghost sickness, for example, and the Life Way focused on bodily injuries.

To prepare for a chant way, the patient and all participants purified themselves by observing such procedures as consuming emetics and purgatives, ritual bathing in yucca suds, sexual abstinence, and sweat baths. All in attendance at a chant way thought only good thoughts. A ceremony properly prepared for and performed restored a patient, his or her family, and participants to hozho.

Ceremonies   All chant ways had elements in common. These included preceremony divination and purification, along with the use of bull-roarers, feather wands, herbal medicines, and incense. Medicine men, nightlong chants, prayers, rattles, and sand paintings were also customary. In addition, offerings were made of corn pollen, coral, shell, and semiprecious stones such as obsidian and turquoise. The shortest chant ways lasted one day and the longest nine (Frisbie and McAllester 1978).

One of the most impressive ceremonies was the five-day or nine-day Night Way. Included in it were masked dancers reminiscent of Hopi masked kachina dancers. A Night Way could be performed only after the first frost in late fall or early winter when there was no possibility of thunder or the presence of snakes.

Entrances to hogans always faced the rising sun, and events of daily life were surrounded by rituals. Mornings began with corn pollen offerings at dawn and prayers and songs from the Blessingway, the most widely performed of all chants. Throughout the day, people sang bits of chants as they herded sheep, worked at a loom, or performed other tasks. Additional songs from the Blessingway were sung at sunset (Wyman 1970).

The Navajo view of life was that the world could be dangerous. Illness and injury were thought to have a supernatural basis. Places struck by lightning were dangerous and avoided. Bears, coyotes, and snakes must never be killed. Ghosts were feared. Upon death, the evil part inside any person might linger among the living to disrupt hozho. Ghosts were thought to haunt death hogans and to wander at night and appear in the form of coyotes, dark objects, mice, owls, spots of fire, whirlwinds, or humans (Kluckhohn and Leighton 1946, 185). The names of the dead were never mentioned because to do so would call the ghost. Witches (skinwalkers) were living people who turned to evil, manipulating the supernatural to harm or kill the living. Sometimes witches were thought to roam at night disguised as bears, coyotes, crows, desert foxes, owls, or wolves (Kluckhohn 1944, 26). Persons asking questions about witches ran the risk of being accused of witchcraft. Only by depending on family ties and maintaining hozho could safety be achieved (Reichard 1950).

LIFE CYCLE   Ethnographic gems are unusual, and a flawless one is exceedingly rare. The autobiography of Left Handed, a Navajo male born in 1868, is a stellar example. Compiled by Walter Dyk and published as *Son of Old Man Hat* (New York 1938), the book recounts the life of Left Handed from his childhood until after he married, at about the age of twenty. The narrative style is compelling, as are the particulars. Although it is rash to depend on one man's view of growing up, a number of examples from his account ring true and provide details usually unrecorded or muted in a standard ethnography. In addition, at least some Navajo had the capacity to remember the precise wording of conversations for many years and thus provide another dimension of reality. Some events from Left Handed's childhood are described later in this section.

Children were valued by the Navajo, but no elaborate ceremonies accompanied birth. Corn pollen was sprinkled over a baby's head immediately after delivery. The baby then was bathed, wrapped in a blanket, and "shaped" by a midwife's kneading and molding. Within the first day of life, his or her ears were pierced. The afterbirth and everything stained with blood was buried, burned, or wrapped in a bundle and hidden in a tree to prevent a witch from using these items to harm the offspring. The umbilical cord was buried in the sheep corral or somewhere else near a family home so that the person's mind would be rooted to the family land. Although children were named, they were typically addressed by kin terms. Babies could be several months old before a name was chosen. They were indulged and kept in close physical contact with their mothers to nurse on demand. A baby's mother, as well as the other members of a household, were responsive to his or her needs and cries, and the baby was often held and cuddled.

A neonate spent most waking hours strapped with cotton cloths to a cradleboard, which could be carried easily. After a few months, he or she spent less and less time in the cradleboard and gradually learned to walk. A baby's first laugh led to gift giving and was a sign that his or her time in the cradleboard had ended. The person who first made a baby laugh was responsible for organizing a celebration.

Children could breast-feed until they were three or four years old or a sibling was born. Toilet training was not begun until a child could talk and typically was a slow and gentle process. Children decided what and how often to eat and when or where they would sleep. It was not unusual for a family to rearrange its plans to accommodate a child's wishes. Children seldom, if ever, were spanked or reprimanded; instead they were encouraged and taught with stories. They grew up feeling confident, loved, and valued and soon learned to respect those who were older. Small boys and girls helped with camp responsibilities by hauling water or firewood. Lambs were often given to children to raise. It was while herding that a child learned to value some measure of silence and solitude.

Left Handed was raised by his mother's sister and her husband, Old Man Hat. The family initially had few sheep and moved often from one semi-isolated hogan to another in search of pasture for the animals. Thus in his formative years Left Handed was primarily under the direct influence of his sociological parents above all others. They often provided formal guidance about growing up. Left Handed was told repeatedly to run each morning for good health and a long life. Old Man Hat said time and again that Left Handed should go to bed late at night and rise before the sun. By the time he was twelve he ran early in the morning, at midday, and in the evening. He put sand in his moccasins so his feet would toughen and he would be able to run in sand or snow.

Left Handed's life centered on herding sheep, and he was introduced to the task while quite young. He herded in the morning and evening near the family hogan. Because he was afraid, he stayed in the middle of the herd where he felt safe. Before long he learned to avoid soft ground in which the sheep might sink and not to allow the sheep to stray. By the time he was about eleven years old, he had a large sheep herd and many horses under his care.

As a child the daily cycle of the sun puzzled Left Handed. He did not ask about it but reasoned that the sun came up and went down in the same pattern each day. He thought that where the sun set, there must be many suns, or else they melted and disappeared. As he thought about the seasons, he wished for summer when it was cold and for cold when it was hot. He reasoned that when it was cold where they were living, they should return to the place they had been when it was warm. Similarly, when he was young he heard about the concept of a year, and it troubled him (e.g., one year as opposed to many years). He came to think that a year must have a body like an animal and he wanted to see it, but of course he never was able to see a year.

Sex puzzled Left Handed as a young child. He wondered, for example, why a girl had no penis. Did their parents cut them off? He asked his mother, who said that girls and boys were born as they are. When out herding, he met girls who also were tending sheep, but his mother told him to stay away from them. She said that girls and women had teeth in their sexual organs and could bite off his penis. He knew this was not so for sheep and reasoned that it possibly was true only for human females. It might be noted that the idea of a toothed vagina occurs in the mythology of many different people around the world.

Sometime between the ages of seven and thirteen, both boys and girls were initiated into Navajo ceremonial life during the next-to-last night of a Night Way. To prepare children for this event, their hair was washed with yucca suds. During the Night Way initiation, boys wore only breechclouts, while girls were fully clothed. The children were approached by two dancers, one in a black mask representing Maternal Grandfather of the Deities (Talking God) and the other in a white mask representing Female Divinity. Boys and girls first had their shoulders marked with cornmeal by Female Divinity. Then Talking God struck the boys on the shoulders with a bundle of reeds and handed the girls ears of corn wrapped in spruce twigs. Finally, the dancer representing Talking God placed the mask of Black God in turn over the face of each child, who then learned that the dancers were people impersonating deities. The children were instructed to keep the identity of the dancers a secret from the uninitiated.

At her first menstruation, a girl underwent the *Kinaalda* (girls' sing) ceremony that lasted four days during a Blessingway. The large number of kin that attended were housed and fed by a girl's family. During the Kinaalda a girl demonstrated her readiness for adulthood and willingness to accept hard times by observing many food and other restrictions. Each day a girl would rise early and at dawn run off to the east. She also would grind cornmeal, have her hair ceremonially washed, and be "shaped" by an older woman. Such molding was supposed to make a girl beautiful like the Navajo's favorite deity, Changing Woman (White Shell Woman).

After the Kinaalda, a girl was considered to be a woman and was ready for marriage a year or two later. At the social dances accompanying ceremonies such as the Enemy Way, a young woman had an opportunity to meet eligible young men. At these dances, "girl's choice" was the norm. Perhaps because women were seen as the appropriate ones to initiate interaction between the genders, rape was virtually unknown among the Navajo; women were treated with respect.

Although the young people involved had some say, it was older family members who arranged a first marriage. In the event of a divorce or death, an individual had far greater freedom in spouse selection. Marriage was the norm, and typically a man was somewhat older than his wife. The arrangements were initiated by a young man's father and maternal uncle, who approached a young woman's maternal uncle. If all parties agreed, the groom's family presented the bride's family with a gift of livestock (bride price). An unelaborate wedding ceremony was held at the bride's hogan, where the couple ate corn mush in a ritual context, an event followed by a feast for the families involved. A couple typically built their home near the bride's family (matrilocal residence). Marriage and raising children were the clearest indicators of adult status.

Domestic tasks such as child care, cooking, and sewing occupied the time of women, who also were responsible for weaving blankets and rugs for household use, trade, or sale. Women, men, or children might herd sheep, but men focused on herding. Men not only had responsibilities to their children, wife, and wife's family but also to their mother's and sisters' families in which the men had grown up. As members of their own clans, sisters' children received special attention from the men. Men helped arrange the marriages of their nieces and nephews and instructed them in clan responsibilities and religion. Men usually were the ones who dealt with outsiders for the family. Few responsibilities fell to the nuclear family alone; parents were responsible for clothing their children, and fathers worked to build up herds of livestock for their sons.

Occasionally a man had more than one wife at the same time (polygyny). If so the women, often sisters (sororal polygyny), were usually members of the same extended family. More rarely, a man might marry a woman and her niece or a woman and her daughter from a previous marriage. A widow was encouraged to marry her dead husband's brother (levirate), and a widower was encouraged to marry his dead wife's sister (sororate). In plural marriages each wife had her own hogan.

Divorce was easy and could be initiated by either gender. Putting a husband's saddle outside the hogan indicated that a wife had terminated a marriage, and the man returned to his mother's home. A woman retained all property and custody of the children, since they were members of her clan. A decision to divorce was not difficult for Navajo women, who depended on their extended families, rather than their husbands. A woman could also rely on her brothers and other relatives to help raise her children.

The Euro-American stereotype of American Indians is that they are stoic and devoid of humor, but nothing could be further from reality. In his study of Navajo humor, W. W. Hill (1943) found that it was rich and varied. A popular category of humor was based on accidental or ridiculous episodes. For example, a man might lie about his relationship with a woman, and she might accuse him of the lie in public. In another instance, a person caught stealing would have the stolen property in hand. Thus the offender appears ridiculous, and the episode might be told and retold to the enjoyment of the listeners. Practical jokes also were popular. For instance, when a horse race was scheduled for the following day, the horse that was a sure winner might be stolen the night before, ridden until it could hardly walk, and then returned to the corral of the owner. There also were what we might call "numbskull jokes." When a sheep was slaughtered, for instance, a man was told to obtain salt to process the meat; he might spend four days obtaining the salt.

Foreigners, especially Anglos, provided a basis for humor. When numerous Anglo tourists were watching a ceremony, a Navajo said he thought there must be many transvestites among whites since so many women wore trousers. Although the Navajo did not ideally approve of sadistic humor, it nonetheless existed, especially with reference to individual physical or behavioral characteristics. Nicknames such as Ugly Woman, Scum of Coyote Ear, and Hunchback are examples. Vulgar humor was also common, such as asking a man with a big belly how long it had been since he had seen his penis. Institutionalized humor, including "joking relationships," a form usually noted by ethnographers, was well developed among the Navajo.

Humor provides a fitting context in which to consider personality differences. The Navajo are well known for their individualism and flexibility; ideally, each person spoke for herself or himself. This behavioral variation extended to all aspects of their culture. One woman, for example, might consider a joke laughable, while another could regard the same joke as vulgar if not obscene. Or one man might take offense and become violently angry if a practical joke was played on him, while another would regard the joke as very funny. Admittedly, within any particular culture individual personality differences would be expected; the Navajo represent an extreme in their individual behavioral differences.

For men and women old age meant increasing respect and wisdom. A good life was one in which a married couple had raised responsible children, helped their families, acquired many sheep, and maintained hozho. If the elderly became infirm, they were well cared for, usually by a daughter, granddaughter, or niece.

The Navajo viewed death as frightful; the only exception to this fear was death in old age. If it were obvious someone was dying, the person was often taken from the hogan to a special shelter built for the dying. If someone died at home, a hole was made in the north side of the hogan for removal of the body. Subsequently the hogan was abandoned or burned. The body was pre-pared and disposed of at some distant spot as quickly as possible, usually by members of the deceased's clan. Personal possessions were left with the body. After the burial, mourners purified themselves by bathing and with incense.

The Navajo believed that at death whatever was praiseworthy about a person became an impersonal universal good; all that remained was an evil el-ement that could return as a ghost to harm the living. During the four-day mourning period the deceased's ghost was supposed to proceed to the after-world beneath the ground to the north, an unpleasant setting. Mourners avoided saying the name of the deceased because it might cause a ghost to linger around the living. An encounter with a ghost, which could happen only at night, required a sing to reestablish hozho.

| The Comparatively Recent Past

As historical changes are considered further, one variable in particular merits attention: the proximity of Navajo and Westerners to each other (see also Chapter 9). Navajo autonomy prevailed during the Spanish and Mexican eras because the people were so scattered and far from the administrative cen-ters. And so it was during the early Anglo era. Anglo expansion became more persistent as wagon trails were developed and as railroads penetrated the re-gion. Nonetheless, most of the reservation remained isolated. Much of the country was so rugged that most travel was on horseback. Remote sectors did not become accessible until adequate roads were built. In realistic terms, road construction began on a modest scale in the 1910s. As the network expanded, not only were Anglos able to reach distant places, but also local Navajo could travel afar with much greater ease. The popularity of wagons was followed by Navajo ownership of automobiles and trucks. Yet by the early 1930s many Navajo continued to depend on travel by horseback or horse and wagon.

Road access contributed to the construction of day schools in more iso-lated localities, and as the people came to realize that formal education for their children was desirable, school attendance was more regular. Proselytiz-ing by Christian missionaries became more widespread, though ineffective. At the same time wage-labor jobs expanded. With increasingly dependable roads, greater numbers of men either sought year-round jobs at distant towns or expanded their pattern of seasonal work on distant farms and ranches owned by whites. Roads and highways thus became enablers and facilitators. Yet it was not until after 1950 that more remote sectors became accessible by paved roads or highways.

NEW TRAUMA: LIVESTOCK REDUCTION A number of environmental concerns began to arise in the early 1900s. Both the Navajo population and their herds were perceived as increasing at a dramatic rate, even though herd numbers probably were relatively stable. But because the Navajo eventually were forced from nonreservation public lands that they traditionally had exploited, the impression was created that the number of livestock was increasing. From 1900 to 1934 the reservation land base was expanded several times in an attempt to keep pace with this presumed growth. In terms of actual use, however, the land base had declined. Nonetheless, livestock reduction became a major federal goal.

The Navajo justly viewed the stock reduction that began in the 1930s as comparable to the Long Walk of the 1860s. Yet the reasons for the federal government's desire to decrease livestock holdings were compelling. Flocks of sheep were increasing at an alarming rate given the quality of the semidesert grazing area. Land erosion from overgrazing had been evident for many years, and there were fears that soil runoff could clog Boulder (now Hoover) Dam. This also was a time of dramatic change conceived for the country by the federal government. The election of President Franklin D. Roosevelt in 1932 introduced the New Deal programs, including the Indian Reorganization Act (IRA), which was to serve as a cornerstone for changes among Indians. The BIA Commissioner, John Collier, felt strongly that traditional American Indian life must be preserved; but at the same time he advocated Navajo stock reduction. Federal representatives addressed the tribal council about the need for reduction. The Navajo were convinced, at least in part, that overgrazing was a temporary problem resulting from several years of drought. They felt that once the normal cycle of rains returned, the grasses would be replenished. Nevertheless, the federal government went ahead with its own plan. As a consequence, the Navajo rejected the Indian Reorganization Act.

Within a decade of the onset of livestock reduction, Clyde Kluckhohn and Dorothea Leighton (1946, 1974) chronicled its consequences. They suggest that the government failed to recognize the impact the program would have on the Navajo way of life. They also charged that it did not live up to the government's positive expectations and that it had in fact failed. From 1933 to 1937 livestock reduction was for the most part voluntary, and the tribal council urged everyone to reduce their herds by 10 percent; many of the sheep were sold to the government to feed hungry people elsewhere. The historian Peter Iverson (1990) noted that after 1937 the livestock reduction program became coercive and far-reaching. Commissioner Collier was convinced that the decrease was insufficient to offset the deterioration of the land base. Although committed to egalitarian values, Collier understood Navajo culture poorly. He was convinced that "wealthy" Navajo had too many sheep and that this situation was unfair to poorer families (see Figure 10-7).

It was true that in the late 1930s 10 percent of Navajo livestock owners possessed 40 percent of all livestock, but Collier failed to take into account the generosity of these so-called wealthy persons who shared their flocks with poorer families and provided large quantities of mutton for the participants at all-important ceremonies. The value placed on balance, cooperation, dependability, generosity, harmony, helpfulness, and productiveness assured the redistribution of sheep.

Figure 10-7 | For centuries Navajo life has focused on sheep. Here Margaret Grieve shears an animal. (Photo by Mark Middleton, 1980. Courtesy of the Museum of Northern Arizona.)

While poorer people continued to be harmed by livestock reduction, after 1937 it was the "wealthy" Navajo who became the main targets of government stock reduction programs. Their flocks were seized and reduced to the size of the herds owned by families of modest means. In many cases, animals were shot and left to rot. Ultimately, livestock permits were required that put a cap on the number of sheep (or their equivalent in grazing needs of goats, cattle, or horses) at 350 per camp. Since the ownership of some horses was essential, no family could obtain the maximum number of sheep. There were no longer herds large enough to redistribute sheep to the poor or to sponsor major ceremonies. Those who had owned large herds worked through the tribal council in an attempt to ameliorate some of the worst aspects of the policy. Among the poor, there often were violent confrontations when sheep were seized. Thousands of sheep were slaughtered, often with no compensation. The program continued until 1945 (Henderson 1989, 398–99).

Livestock reduction guaranteed that most herders could no longer subsist off the land. Social forms, such as the outfit (a group of cooperating extended families related through the same matrilineage and occupying neighboring territories), all but disappeared (Aberle 1981a, 2–6). As a result, some anthropologists studying the Navajo in the decades following livestock reduction debated whether outfits had ever existed.

Families turned to wage labor and later to welfare to supplement farming, herding, and crafts. During the Great Depression of the 1930s, however, jobs were scarce, and in the Southwest, Indians were discriminated against in hiring. Land-use patterns were changed, and the Navajo social system of old was destroyed. Many people went hungry. The status of women deteriorated as the economy shifted from the domestic scene to wage and welfare, in which women became largely dependent financially on their husbands and sons who had jobs off the reservation. Wage labor often was so far away that men could return home only on weekends. Thus, men had less influence in the day-to-day family life but greater financial importance.

Aberle noted that the negative psychological impact of livestock reduction was overwhelming. Feeling helpless, lost, unhappy, and out of hozho, many Navajo, especially those who formerly had the largest herds and who felt the greatest relative deprivation, turned to a religion new to them, the Native American Church. Criticized by white Americans and by some Navajo for its use of peyote as a sacrament, the Native American Church introduced a feeling of purpose in life and a remarkable serenity to people who had suffered greatly (Aberle 1966, 252–77, 315–33).

WORLD WAR II The Navajo considered World War I to be a white man's conflict and assumed a passive attitude; no more than perhaps a dozen individuals served in the military during the war. They could not be drafted because they did not become U.S. citizens until a congressional act was passed in 1924. Early in World War II, many Navajo did not register for the draft because they distrusted the federal government; some people thought that registration had a connection to stock reduction. After the Japanese attack on Pearl Harbor, however, their attitude changed, and most of them supported the war effort. By the end of the war about 3600 Navajo had served in the armed forces. About 15,000 others held war-related jobs locally and elsewhere. In 1945 the total Navajo population was about 59,000.

The most famous Navajo during World War II were the approximately four hundred "Code Talkers" in the U.S. Marine Corps. Searching for a code that the Japanese could not easily decipher, the military turned to Navajo servicemen. The code was used in Pacific-area campaigns largely to report the location of enemy artillery and to direct fire at it from marine positions. The code itself consisted of isolated Navajo words; the first letter of each word was translated into English to spell out the message in English. In the assault on Iwo Jima, over eight hundred transmissions were made without error. The Japanese were never able to break the code, and the success of the Iwo Jima campaign was attributed in large part to the Code Talkers.

World War II impinged on Navajo life in other ways as well. The federal government reduced its presence and influence on the reservation, and stock reduction programs were not enforced. More important, after the war, returning veterans and civilian war workers who held jobs off the reservation were far better able to cope with the white man on Navajo terms.

THE NAVAJO NATION EMERGES Stock reduction and World War II provided a partial background for a virtual cultural revolution beginning in the 1950s. It was then that reservation mineral resources—coal, gas, and oil—

began to be exploited intensively to supply power to the rapidly growing population centers in the west. By the 1960s the tribe was receiving an average of $14 million a year in bonuses, leases, and royalties from mineral resources, including uranium and vanadium (a mineral used in vanadium steel). The interest from tribal monies was more than $4 million in 1975.

The Navajo Tribal Council began to be controlled by the tribe rather than by the BIA in the 1950s, when it gained the right to allocate money earned from mineral resource development. The tribe likewise gained control over their police and the management of grazing land. Navajo court judges were elected rather than appointed by the BIA. Before long the council created its own infrastructure as a way to gain far greater authority over education, housing, and health services.

By the early 1970s fewer than half of the reservation families owned livestock, but the total number of animals steadily climbed, as a few stockmen owned large herds. Despite federal irrigation projects and other efforts, farming had little tribal importance by the 1970s. Craft income from the sale of rugs declined, although the prices were high. Fewer women were skilled weavers, and their hourly earnings were low. Silverwork sales to tourists, however, were relatively high, and a small number of silversmiths made a comfortable living. By the 1970s craft items accounted for about 6 percent of total individual income.

Wage labor, seasonal and year-round, on and off the reservation, became dominant in the 1950s. Nonetheless, for many Navajo work was hard to find, and welfare payments contributed somewhat less than did wage labor in the total economy. The availability of jobs in scattered locations, along with the mobility provided by roads and motor vehicles, led to a steady drop in the number of trading posts by 1970. Trading-post prosperity depended to a great extent on Navajo isolation and the trade in wool and craft items. As these declined in importance, many posts became local convenience stores.

Formal education developed so slowly that by 1945 the median attendance figure for adult schooling was about one year; understandably, most of these people did not have basic English skills. In the late 1940s a serious federal effort was launched to make schooling for children far more widely available. By the late 1970s reservation day schools, boarding schools, and public schools provided nearly all children with at least some formal education. Before 1950 few students had completed high school, but by the end of the 1960s the rate had improved, and higher education began to become available. The first Indian tribal college was launched by the Navajo themselves in 1968—the Navajo Community College (now the Dine College). Soon thereafter, universities in the region began offering programs to further Navajo higher education.

As is evident in this synopsis, Navajo culture became transformed in an erratic pattern. In the early 1900s direct control of the people and their lifeway diminished in fits and starts, depending on the degree of federal intrusion, national and regional economic conditions, and the accompanying Navajo responses. The extraction of reservation mineral resources beginning in the

1920s and the eventual control gained over much of Navajo life by the Navajo Nation president and the Navajo Nation Council heralded a new era that continues into the present.

| Present-Day Developments

Today the Navajo Reservation consists of approximately 32,000 square miles. The town of Window Rock, Arizona, is the capital of the Navajo Nation (see Figure 10-8). The "Big Reservation" is in Arizona, New Mexico, and Utah; the Ramah Reservation is near the Pueblo of Zuni in New Mexico; the Alamo (Puertocito) Reservation is eighty miles southwest of Albuquerque, New Mexico; the Canoncito Reservation is forty miles southwest of Albuquerque; and the "Checkerboard" consists of scattered tracks east and south of the Big Reservation. In addition, there are vast off-reservation areas to which the Navajo believe they hold the right for traditional use; their struggle to assert this right has met with mixed success. Many Navajo think that if they were allowed these lands, they would be better protected. In 1990 three branches of tribal government, executive, legislative, and judicial, were instituted; the office of tribal chair was replaced with the office of president. It has been estimated that the current reservation could support about 30,000 people living a 1920s-

Figure 10-8 | Today the Navajo Tribal Council meets in a large, modern building reminiscent of a hogan in Window Rock, Arizona. (Photo by Sharlotte Neely, 1994.)

Figure 10-9 | Regina Joe, a Navajo enrolled at the Crownpoint Agency, is typical in working off the reservation. After graduating from high school, she began work at the Gallup *Independent* newspaper. (Photo by Ted Rushton, 1995.)

style subsistence life. Today there are approximately 220,000 enrolled Navajo, most of whom live on or near the reservation (see Figure 10-9).

ENERGY RESOURCES   Although the fees from leases to energy producers have been a major addition to tribal coffers, the ultimate benefits to the tribe are somewhat questionable. Energy companies typically have not paid the Navajo as much as they would pay non-Indians. For religious reasons, traditionalists object to the land being spoiled in search of mineral wealth. Others on the tribal council wonder why, if most of the soft coal and uranium in the United States is on Indian reservations, the Navajo are not better off economically.

As tribal chairman, Peter MacDonald (1970–1982, 1986–1990) drew attention to the underpayment for reservation energy sources. A Christian convert, MacDonald became a Code Talker in World War II and later earned an engineering degree. In 1963 he returned to the reservation and soon became involved in tribal government. Despite his success in managing energy resources, MacDonald's tenure as chairman was blighted by corruption. He admitted receiving bribes and kickbacks and was convicted of conspiracy, extortion, fraud, and racketeering; subsequently, he was sent to prison.

Coal and uranium companies began operations on Navajo lands in the 1960s, but oil companies had preceded them by forty years. When the tribal council approved leases for strip mining coal, however, council members were unaware of the destruction involved. Once the coal was removed from a particular location, a vast, open pit remained. Subsequently the federal government required that the land be restored. The nearby coal-burning power plants produced an incredible amount of air pollution. Moreover, transporting the coal to the plants requires vast amounts of water, a scarce resource, and the water table is dropping at an alarming rate. Furthermore, a 1984 class-action suit over Navajo energy resource royalty management was finally resolved in 1995. The Navajo gained greater control over certain royalties, payments, and related matters.

In the 1970s, uranium production increased, and Navajo men worked in the mines. The companies, however, paid little attention to the safety of the miners. Many who were contaminated by high levels of radiation became sick or died. Improperly disposed-of uranium tailings also exposed children and other nonminers to radiation.

NAVAJO–HOPI LAND DISPUTE (NAVAJO VIEW)   The background to this conflict is provided in Chapter 9 in reference to the Hopi. The dispute crystallized in 1974 when Congress passed the Navajo–Hopi Land Settlement Act. The law ordered that a boundary be established to separate the respective use areas; this was accomplished in 1977. As a result, some 2000 families on the Hopi side of the line were to leave. By 1997 most families had complied with the "Accommodation Agreement," but ten families refused (see Figure 10-10). About half of the Navajo families moved to other parts of the already crowded reservation, creating a hardship for both the relocated people and their hosts. Most others were moved by a relocation commission to tract housing in cities such as Flagstaff. Unable to pay their property taxes, and sometimes tricked by unscrupulous real estate agents, many lost their homes. Those who did move had an exceedingly high rate of alcoholism, suicide, and unemployment, much higher than for the Navajo reservation as a whole. The Navajo made a serious tactical error in 1995 by withdrawing from discussions with the Hopi. As a result, they could not protect the interests of Navajo who refused to be relocated. For those people, life was hard; most of their livestock was seized and they were not allowed to repair their homes. That restriction, however, has since been eased.

THE CURRENT SCENE   One major issue facing the Navajo Nation is legal: the Navajo-Hopi land settlement. The Ninth U.S. Circuit Court returned a $21 million judgment in 1997 in favor of the Hopi for land overexploited by the Navajo. This decision is little short of catastrophic. Payment has not been made, and the interest due the Hopi is about $3000 a day. The Navajo also are

Figure 10-10 | Jenny Manybeads was among the many Navajo to be relocated as a result of the Navajo–Hopi land dispute. (Photo by Paul Natonobah, 1993. Courtesy of the Gallup *Independent* newspaper.)

distressed that those families who continue to live on Hopi land are under Hopi jurisdiction and that the Navajo Nation must pay for the services rendered. The Navajo seek to be the administrators of these people, but to date they have had no success.

Historically, the Navajo had been on friendly terms, both socially and economically, with the Hopi. One unfortunate result of the land dispute is that now there is a great deal of bitterness on both sides. The Navajo, however, do permit the Hopi to take eagles for ceremonial purposes from Navajo lands.

The 1998 Navajo tribal budget was nearly $88 million, most of which, nearly $68 million, was for the executive branch to provide social services. The tribe hoped to develop a new youth recreational center and nursing home facilities, but the amount of money available was less than it had been in recent years. The nation is also developing programs to attract greater numbers of tourists and to market only authentic Navajo arts and crafts (see Figure 10-11). Tourists are considered a largely untapped "gold mine." Some Navajo leaders feel that opening a casino on their land could provide a long-term solution to their economic problems. It was estimated that from $26 to $66 million each year could be obtained in revenue through gambling. Furthermore, a study suggested that some $35 million annually in goods and services could be realized by the private sector from gambling. However, in a 1997 ballot the Navajo people voted not to open a casino.

Figure 10-11 | David Tsinnie, in this 1998 photograph, is a Navajo artist living in the Coconino District of Arizona.

| Additional Sources

The best starting points for examining traditional culture are Ruth Underhill's *The Navajos* (Norman, OK, 1956) and James F. Downs's *The Navajo* (New York, 1972). Specialized key studies are *Navaho Religion* (New York, 1950) by Gladys A. Reichard and *Navaho Material Culture* by Clyde Kluckhohn, W. W. Hill, and Lucy Wales Kluckhohn (Cambridge, MA, 1971). Two remarkable Navajo life histories are *Son of Old Man Hat* by Walter Dyk (New York, 1938) and *Left Handed* by Walter Dyk and Ruth Dyk (New York, 1980). For a historical overview, the best starting place is *The Navajos* (New York, 1990) by Peter Iverson. The second *Southwest* volume (10) of the *Handbook of the North Americans Indians,* William C. Sturtevant, general editor (Washington, DC, 1983), also provides a fine overview of the Navajo in historical perspective. To examine the era of stock reduction, the reader should review *The Navaho* (Garden City, NY, 1946) by Clyde Kluckhohn and Dorothea Leighton and *The Peyote Religion Among the Navaho* (Chicago, 1966) by David F. Aberle. To understand the Navajo–Hopi land dispute, the reader should consider *The Wind Won't Know Me* by Emily Benedek (New York, 1992). To keep up with current affairs, a subscription to the weekly tribal newspaper, *The Navajo Times,* is recommended.

| Selected Bibliography

Aberle, David F. 1966. The *peyote religion among the Navaho.* Chicago.

———. 1981a. Navajo coresidential kin groups and lineages. *Journal of Anthropological Research* 37:1–7.

———. 1981b. A century of Navajo kinship change. *Canadian Journal of Anthropology* 2:21–36.

————. 1993. The Navajo-Hopi land dispute and Navajo relocation. In *Anthropological approaches to resettlement: Policy, practice, and theory,* 153–200. Boulder, CO.

Adair, John. 1944. *The Navajo and Pueblo silversmiths.* Norman, OK.

Bailey, Garrick Alan, and Roberta Glenn Bailey. 1986. *A history of the Navajos: The reservation years.* Santa Fe.

Benedek, Emily. 1992. *The wind won't know me: A history of the Navajo–Hopi land dispute.* New York.

Bingham, Sam, and Janet Bingham. 1984. *Between sacred mountains: Navajo stories and lessons from the land.* Tucson.

Brugge, David M. 1994. *The Navajo–Hopi land dispute.* Albuquerque.

Downs, James F. 1972. *The Navajo.* New York.

Dyk, Walter. 1938. *Son of Old Man Hat.* New York.

Dyk, Walter, and Ruth Dyk. 1980. *Left Handed: A Navajo autobiography.* New York.

Frisbie, Charlotte J., and David P. McAllester. 1978. *Navajo Blessingway singer: The autobiography of Frank Mitchell.* Tucson.

Henderson, Eric. 1989. Navajo livestock wealth and the effects of the stock reduction program of the 1930s. *Journal of Anthropological Research* 45:379–403.

Hill, W. W. 1943. Navaho humor. *General Series in Anthropology* No. 9.

Iverson, Peter. 1981. *The Navajo Nation.* Westport, CT.

————. 1990. *The Navajos.* New York.

Jett, Stephen C., and Virginia E. Spencer. 1981. *Navajo architecture: Forms, history, distributions.* Tucson.

Kelley, Klara B. 1993. A rebuttal to some negative stereotypes of Navajos and misconceptions about Navajo history and Navajo–Hopi relations. Typescript. Window Rock, AZ.

Kelly, Lawrence C. 1968. *The Navajo Indians and federal Indian policy: 1900–1935.* Tucson.

Kluckhohn, Clyde. 1944. *Navaho witchcraft.* Papers of the Peabody Museum of Archaeology and Ethnology. Volume 22. Cambridge, MA.

Kluckhohn, Clyde, and Dorothea Leighton. 1946 and 1974. *The Navaho.* Garden City, NY.

Kluckhohn, Clyde, W. W. Hill, and Lucy Wales Kluckhohn. 1971. *Navaho material culture.* Cambridge, MA.

Lamphere, Louise. 1977. *To run after them: Cultural and social bases of cooperation in a Navajo community.* Tucson.

Luckert, Karl. 1975. *The Navajo hunter tradition.* Tucson.

Lynch, Regina H., and the Rough Rock Demonstration School Navajo Curriculum Staff. 1993. *A history of Navajo clans.* Chinle, AZ.

McNitt, Frank. 1970. *Navajo wars.* Albuquerque.

McPherson, Robert S. 1994. From Dezba to "John": The changing role of Navajo women in southeastern Utah. *American Indian Culture and Research Journal* 18:3:187–210.

Parmon, Donald. 1976. *The Navajos and the New Deal*. New Haven, CT.

Reichard, Gladys A. 1928. *Social life of the Navajo Indians*. New York.

———. 1950. *Navaho religion: A study of symbolism*. New York.

Spicer, Edward H. 1962. *Cycles of conquest*. Tucson.

Sturtevant, William C., gen. ed. 1983. *Handbook of North American Indians: Southwest*. Volume 10. Washington, DC.

Tamir, Orit. 1991. Relocation of Navajo from Hopi partitioned land in Pinon. *Human Organization* 50:173–78.

Underhill, Ruth M. 1956. *The Navajos*. Norman, OK.

Walters, Frank. 1950. *Masked gods: Navaho and Pueblo ceremonialism*. Chicago.

Witherspoon, Gary. 1975. *Navajo kinship and marriage*. Chicago.

Wyman, Leland C. 1970. *Blessingway*. Tucson.

11 The Mesquakie: Warriors and Farmers of the Woodland Fringe

When I was perhaps seven years old I began to practice sewing for my dolls. But I sewed poorly. I used to cry because I did not know how to sew. Nor could I persuade my mother to [do it] when I said to her "Make it for me." "You will know how to sew later on; that is why I shall not make them for you. That is how one learns to sew, by practicing sewing for one's dolls." . . . And so I would always practice sewing for my dolls!

An anonymous Mesquakie woman describes her childhood. (Michelson 1925a, 295)

MOST INDIANS in the east central United States have disappeared, yet one small group, the Mesquakie (Fox), have survived as a tribe. In colonial times, the French attempted to exterminate the Mesquakie and nearly succeeded. Later some survivors fought tenaciously to defend their land against white settlement, and the turmoil climaxed in an Indian war. The survivors were displaced, and subsequently the Mesquakie were repeatedly forced to relocate, causing further privation and deaths. The Mesquakie were haughty, independent, and noble of purpose. Their actions in the 1850s provide a striking example of their resilience. After most Mesquakie had been forced to accept a reservation in Kansas, some of them began to return to Iowa, where a small number had remained. Here they *purchased* land from whites and attempted to resume an earlier lifeway. Although many of their traditions have changed over the years, the Mesquakie have retained their distinct identity and their Iowa lands to the present day. Their capacity to remain in the Midwest and to sustain an Indian heritage are compelling reasons to devote a chapter to them.

Two difficulties arise in preparing an account of past Mesquakie life. First, most pertinent information does not date from the period of early historic contact. Thus an aboriginal base line account, one describing them before their customs were altered by fur traders, cannot be presented. However, the Mesquakie are regarded as highly conservative, and except for many superficial changes, one may assume that reports about their relatively recent past are more representative of aboriginal patterns than would be the case for most American Indians. A second difficulty is their association with their allies, the Sauk (Sac). The Mesquakie were never integrated politically with the Sauk, although the U.S. government incorrectly perceived them as a single entity. As a partial result, it sometimes is difficult to separate the history of one tribe from another.

| Origin Myth, Population, and Language

The name Mesquakie, by which these Indians know themselves, translates as "Red-earth People" and is derived from the red earth in their origin myth. According to the myth, at a place that is not on earth and is so far away that no one is able to travel there, a place where it is always winter, lives Wisaka. In the remote past Wisaka had lived on earth with his younger brother. The *manitous* (supernatural forces) met in council and plotted to murder the brothers; they succeeded in killing Wisaka's younger brother. They tried to kill Wisaka first with fire and then with a flood, but Wisaka climbed a tall tree on a mountaintop. A canoe appeared at the top of the tree, and he paddled about on the water. A turtledove brought him twigs, and a muskrat brought mud from which he made a ball. He threw it into the water, and it grew into the earth as we know it. Wisaka created all the things on earth, including people. The Mesquakie, according to their traditions, have such great antiquity that they do not know when they first arrived on earth. They were the first people to dwell on the land made by Wisaka, and they lived by the sea. From the sea came a great fish with the head of a man. As this fish walked on the land, he became fully human, and he was followed by other fish who made the same transformation. These individuals established a community near the Mesquakie, and every aspect of Mesquakie life was copied by the fish-turned-to-men. These were the manitous of the world. When Wisaka formed the Mesquakie, they were red, the same color as blood. As time passed, people grew more distant from the manitous, and the world in which they lived changed. In recent times animals and birds have begun to disappear, and the manitous who control the universe are unhappy about this new state of affairs. Sometime in the future the manitous will destroy the earth, the Mesquakie will revert to their original red condition, and the world will begin again.

The Mesquakie appear to have received the name "Fox" when members of the Fox clan told a party of French that they were Fox. By the early 1730s, following the French campaign to destroy the Mesquakie, their core population may have consisted of 100 people. The population had reached 264 by 1867 and 403 by 1932. In 1970, about 500 lived in the vicinity of Tama, Iowa, and in 1997 the tribal roll included about 1250 persons.

The Mesquakie, Sauk, and Kickapoo were neighbors and spoke closely related languages in the Algonquian linguistic family, one of the nine families comprising the Macro-Algonquian phylum. Algonquian speakers occupied a vast sector of eastern Canada and a smaller area in the eastern United States. Remarkably, the other groups with whom they are affiliated linguistically include two small northern California tribes, the Yurok and Wiyot. Early historical records locate the Mesquakie along the Fox River of eastern Wisconsin (see Figure 11-1). The Mesquakie lived at a western margin of the Northeast culture area.

| Early Conflicts

Early historic Mesquakie contact with most other Indians and with non-Indians was characterized by unsettled and essentially hostile relations. Efforts by white settlers to drive the Mesquakie off their lands were repeated and bloody. The era of physical violence ended by the 1850s, when most Mesquakie settled in Iowa.

FRONTIER HOSTILITIES   The first direct contact between the Mesquakie and Europeans was in 1665 as the French entered the western Great Lakes region. In 1670 the famous Father Claude Jean Allouez founded a mission among them, but he could convert only the ill and dying. As the French pushed west, they armed the Ojibwa (Chippewa) and the Siouan-speaking enemies of the Mesquakie. This led to French and Mesquakie conflict, which tipped in favor of the French after they founded Detroit in 1699 and made peace with the powerful Iroquois a year later. Because the French continued to arm their enemies, the Mesquakie sought aid from the British and from

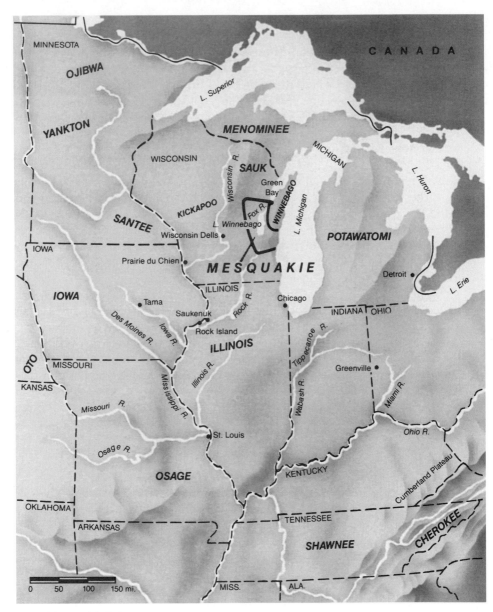

Figure 11-1 | Early historic range of the Mesquakie Indians.

friendly tribes. The Iroquois assured the Mesquakie of a home among them if they were defeated by the French.

Hostilities with the French began to peak in 1728 when nearly five hundred whites and twelve hundred allied Indians moved against the Mesquakie. The destruction of Mesquakie settlements was a severe blow, and by 1730 the

French and their Indian allies had killed nearly twelve hundred Mesquakie. The Mesquakie survived only because surrounding Indians released their Mesquakie prisoners and because the Sauk sheltered and protected them against the French; soon both the Mesquakie and Sauk were forced to flee south. Peace was made with the French in 1737. Subsequently the Mesquakie began returning to Wisconsin, but they did not feel secure until the British assumed control of the Great Lakes region and replaced the French at the Green Bay post in 1761. Before long the Ojibwa drove the Mesquakie from Wisconsin to Illinois, where they came into increasing conflict with white Americans around 1800. The influx of white settlers to the Northwest Territory increased pressure on the government to move all Indians from the Midwest. The position of the Mesquakie and Sauk was not favorable, since they had sided with the British during the American Revolution.

In 1804 a small party of Mesquakie and Sauk went to St. Louis, where the Sauk signed a treaty with the United States that relinquished their lands along the Mississippi River. The Mesquakie were bitter in the aftermath because *no* Mesquakie had signed the treaty. Furthermore, in this treaty the U.S. government "joined" the Mesquakie and the Sauk for administrative convenience even though they were separate tribes, each with its own council. Thus the Treaty of 1804 led the federal government to falsely view these two people as one. This treaty was the one document to which Euro-Americans referred constantly in asserting their claims to Mesquakie lands. The treaty was made, the damage done, but the bitterness in the minds of the Indians never died.

The most serious difficulty whites had in dealing with Indians stemmed from the conflicts between tribes. These not only disrupted trade but made white settlement of the country difficult. To end the fighting, in 1805 the government invited the major tribes in the upper Mississippi River drainage to a council held at St. Louis with Governor William Henry Harrison of the Northwest Territory. To impress the Indians with the power of the United States, select Indians were taken to visit Washington, D.C. About a third of the group were Mesquakie and Sauk. Even as some chiefs were in Washington, however, others were on the warpath against the Chickasaw and Osage. Thus this effort to bring a peaceful settlement of Indian differences failed. In 1805–6 Mesquakie and Sauk war parties roved along the Missouri River raiding Osage camps and killing whites. Settlers brought increased pressure on the government of the Northwest Territory to arrange a more effective settlement of Indian differences. To compound the governor's problems, additional settlers entered the Northwest Territory between 1806 and 1812. They were particularly active in clearing the land and establishing farms between the Ohio and the Mississippi rivers, precisely the region with the greatest Indian unrest.

RESISTANCE TO WHITES　By this time Indians in the Midwest were desperate, and they rallied around a Shawnee Indian leader best known as the Shawnee Prophet. He reportedly had died and been reborn; while dead he had visited the land of the spirits and been given a view of the future. This messiah saw contentment only for those who gave up white ways and re-turned to the old Indian way of life. With Greenville, Ohio, as the center of his activities, he received tribal representatives from the surrounding region. The movement coalesced into an effort to rid the country of the Long Knives, or white Americans. With the Treaty of 1804 as the rallying point for their griev-ances against white Americans, the Mesquakie and Sauk were ready and willing to follow this confederation organized by the Shawnee and actively fostered by the British. In the Battle of Tippecanoe Creek of 1811, the Shaw-nee Prophet's prestige was destroyed by Harrison's stand against the Indians. Although the battle was not decisive, it was unlikely that an Indian confedera-tion could emerge afterward. In early 1812 an Indian delegation that included Mesquakie and Sauk went to Washington, D.C., and this time they were well received because the War of 1812 had erupted into open conflict. The most white Americans could hope to do was to keep the Indians from joining in the conflict on the side of the British. To prevent Mesquakie and Sauk partici-pation, white Americans decided to move these Indians to Missouri, where they would be beyond effective contact with the British. They succeeded in moving approximately fifteen hundred members of the combined tribes to these new lands.

The fortunes of the Mesquakie and Sauk were soon guided by two Sauk leaders, the pro-British Black Hawk and Keokuk, who eventually became pro-American. Black Hawk (see Figure 11-2) had distinguished himself as a war-rior at the age of fifteen, and by nineteen he had led a party of two hundred warriors against an equal number of Osage. In this conflict nearly half the Osage had been killed; Black Hawk alone had killed six persons. By 1812 he had become the most respected leader of the combined tribes. Early in the War of 1812 he journeyed to Green Bay, Wisconsin, with two hundred war-riors, and was well received by the British. They convinced him that the first effort should be to secure the Great Lakes region.

While Black Hawk was away, American troops threatened to destroy the principal Sauk village of Saukenuk near the mouth of the Rock River in Illi-nois. The people had decided in council to flee, but an unimportant Sauk, Keo-kuk, asked to be heard. He was a fine orator and maintained that they should resist the white Americans. His persuasive speech convinced the people, and when the American force failed to arrive, Keokuk became a hero. By his abili-ties as an orator and his determined stand against the Americans he estab-lished himself as a rival to Black Hawk.

Black Hawk's effort to contain the Americans was moderately successful, but by the fall of 1814 the course of the War of 1812 had changed in the Northwest Territory. The Indian war was not well managed by the British, and the American forces were consolidating. The Treaty of Ghent brought an end to the conflict, but the Mesquakie and Sauk were deeply divided; those who had settled in Missouri had been largely neutral, whereas most of the others had fought the Americans. Despite the American victory, many Indians in the Northwest Territory still looked to the British for help in their struggle against

Figure 11-2 | Black Hawk, the Sauk warrior who allied himself with the British and led his people to resist white American control for twenty years. (After McKenney and Hall 1934.)

the Long Knives. Unsettled conditions among the Mesquakie and Sauk led to sporadic raids against frontier settlements and clashes with those Indians on whose lands they encroached. To end these killings, white Americans called a meeting in 1820 of Indians along the upper Mississippi. By now Keokuk had emerged as a powerful instrument of white appeasement in the central prairies. He was willing to abide by American decisions as long as they furthered his own interests, and the effective influence of Black Hawk had declined.

Finally, in 1825, the Treaty of Prairie du Chien was signed by the Mesquakie, Sauk, and Siouans. Boundaries were established, and Indians were to give up their ties with the British. Although the Mesquakie ceded lands that subsequently were occupied by whites, the Indians did not leave, causing further conflict. Five years and another treaty later found Black Hawk still determined to resist. Although many Mesquakie and Sauk were living in the vicinity of Dubuque, Iowa, Black Hawk and his "British Band" returned to Saukenuk in the spring of 1831 and maintained an uneasy peace with white settlers. Before long Black Hawk was forced to abandon Saukenuk and to accept Keokuk as the leader of the combined tribes. By then it seemed that resistance was no longer feasible, but Black Hawk's determination was renewed by a false report from one of his subordinates that other tribes and the British had promised support.

In the spring of 1832 the British Band, including five hundred warriors, crossed the Mississippi River and moved toward Rock Island. Turmoil broke out on the frontier. Militia and troops moved to prevent Black Hawk's band from reoccupying their traditional land. The American military effort to prevent the reoccupation was hopelessly confused. At the same time, Black Hawk remained unaware that he had been deceived by his lieutenant. As Black Hawk traveled up the Rock River, he finally learned that neither Indian nor British aid could be expected. Surrender was the only option. He sent a party of warriors carrying a flag of truce to the camp of the whites. The whites, who were not under any realistic military control, misunderstood the warriors' purpose and killed one of them. The survivors raced back to their encampment with the news. Thus Black Hawk was forced to fight. He rallied forty warriors who ambushed the approaching whites, causing them to flee in panic. After the skirmish, Black Hawk and his followers returned to the American camp, looting and mutilating the bodies of the slain whites. When a regular military contingent reached the battleground, they found that eleven individuals had been killed. As the Indians retreated, they massacred whites at a farm and sent scalping parties into the settlements along their path. The government responded with reinforcements. By the end of June, the U.S. military operation included about thirty-six hundred men, had cost about $300,000, and had failed to defeat the Indians.

Black Hawk made a desperate effort to survive. He reached the banks of the Wisconsin River before the Americans could attack; nevertheless, the whites were able to kill nearly seventy warriors. Despite earlier deaths from exposure and starvation, abandonment by their few allies, and casualties in battle, the British Band numbered 150 as it crossed the river bottom and reached the eastern bank of the Mississippi River. Before long, realizing that their situation was hopeless, 100 of them fled across the Mississippi. The remaining fifty, including Black Hawk himself, were captured near the Wisconsin Dells; thus the Black Hawk War ended.

The ensuing treaty required that the Mesquakie and Sauk forfeit about six million acres of land in Iowa; however, they were allowed to retain a small reservation. As immediate compensation for the ceded lands, they received the services of a blacksmith, a gunsmith shop, and an annual allotment of tobacco and salt. They also were given winter provisions and $40,000 for paying debts to traders. Over the next thirty years they were to receive further payment of $660,000 for the cession. The treaty stipulated that Black Hawk and other chiefs were to be taken to Fort Monroe on Chesapeake Bay as prisoners to prevent further violence along the frontier. Black Hawk arrived in Washington, D.C., in late April of 1832 but was a prisoner at Fort Monroe only briefly. He was released in the custody of Keokuk and was given a tour of the major cities in the eastern United States to impress him with American power. He was overwhelmed by the seventy-four-gun warship *Delaware,* amazed by the mobs of people that surrounded him, and awed by the arsenals that the Americans maintained. According to the historian William T. Hagan (1958), if Black Hawk had accompanied one of the earlier Indian parties to Washington, D.C., and had realized at that time the power of white Americans, the Black Hawk War probably would never have been fought.

| Early Historic Life

Information about the Mesquakie before 1730, when they lived in Wisconsin, is negligible, and much the same is true for the next hundred years. Thus, to reconstruct an aboriginal baseline ethnography for these people is impossible. This account is not as full as might be hoped because it is drawn from diverse sources, few of which considered the Mesquakie at length.

APPEARANCE AND CLOTHING   The appearance of Mesquakie men was striking, largely because of their roached hair style (as worn by Black Hawk; see Figure 11-2). A man shaved all the hair from his head except for a palm-sized tuft at the crown. Most of the tuft was about two inches long, but at the center grew a scalp lock that never was cut and usually was braided. From this braid hung an eagle quill, and along the middle of the tuft were attached lengths of deer hair that very frequently were painted red. The typical clothing of a male included a skin cape for cold weather, a buckskin breechclout, leggings, and high-topped moccasins. Women dressed their hair by parting it in the middle and drawing it to the back of the neck. Most probably, the women wore long buckskin dresses and short leather moccasins. Young children usually wore only a long, loose shirt, and older children followed adult clothing styles.

SETTLEMENTS   Summer villages were in lowlands along rivers and streams where the ground could be cleared and crops planted. The dwellings were oblong bark-covered structures with pole frames up to forty feet long and twenty feet wide. Along each interior sidewall was a raised bark- and skin-covered platform that served as seats and beds. In the open space at the center of the house were fires for cooking and heating. People occupied clusters of lodges from April through much of September, but in the winter small family groups dispersed to follow a wandering life. The winter dwellings were oval structures framed by placing the ends of poles in the ground, bending the poles, and tying them together at the top. Over the framework were placed reeds or mats, and at the doorway hung a bearskin.

SUBSISTENCE ACTIVITIES   The economic cycle around 1820, and most likely before, was divided into two phases. In the spring and summer the Mesquakie tilled lands adjacent to their lodges. Here the women planted and maintained the gardens while the men hunted. The principal hunting weapon was the bow and arrow; the bow was sinew-backed, and arrows were placed in a buckskin quiver. The most important game animal was deer, valued not only for its meat but for its skin and fat. They hunted birds and small game, as well as bear, which the Mesquakie considered a choice meat. The staples, however, were the maize, beans, and squash that the women cultivated and the wild plant foods that they collected. These foods were dried and stored in cache pits, in bark baskets, or in the rafters of a bark house. In mid-September when families left their summer settlement they took a small quantity of maize to a winter hunting area. The scattered families lived in dome-shaped structures until the number of game animal kills declined in late winter. They then assembled in large camps and were inactive until they began to trap beaver in the spring. Following the beaver-trapping season they traveled back to their villages, planning the trip so that they would arrive simultaneously. They did this to minimize the exposure of small groups to hostile peoples and to prevent anyone from taking provisions from another's cache.

By the time that reasonably complete records of food habits became available, we find that an iron kettle hung from a hook above the fire was the usual cooking utensil. The Mesquakies' primary staple was maize prepared in many ways. They boiled or processed it as hominy by leaching the shells with wood ash and washing away the lye. They parched it in a fire but most often ground it into meal and boiled it as gruel. They processed squash fruit for storage by cutting it into rings that were dried in the sun. Among the wild plants they collected were broad-leafed arrowhead corms, either gathered from the plant rootlets or robbed from muskrat caches. These "potatoes" were boiled, sliced, and strung on cords hung from the rafters of a bark house. The groundnut was a potatolike growth that grew along the plant roots and was as much as three inches in diameter; it was peeled, boiled, sliced, and dried to be cooked with meat in the winter. Additionally, the Mesquakie collected sugar-maple sap, which was an important seasoning in cooking, and used a few plants specifically for seasoning. They ate hickory nuts, butternuts, and walnuts, and consumed wild fruits either at the time of collection or after they had been dried.

DESCENT, KINSHIP, AND MARRIAGE   The most important Mesquakie kinship ties were traced through males (patrilineal descent); persons with a presumed but unknown common ancestor comprised a patriclan, the most important descent group. The members of any clan were obligated to seek spouses from another clan (clan exogamy). The leading clans were named Bear, Fox, Wolf, Thunder, Swan, Eagle, Sturgeon, and Bear Potato; the largest ones and possibly the oldest were the first four. The succession of paramount chiefs was from particular clans. The Fox, Thunder, and Bear clans contributed most chiefs, leaders of war parties, and council members; the other clans normally provided councilmen. The clans appear to have formed two groups (moieties) that rendered reciprocal services in ceremonial activities; the Bear and Wolf reciprocated with the Eagle, Fox, and Thunder clans. It must be added, however, that the exact nature of these mutual obligations is not known.

A second type of moiety division has been recorded. In this arrangement each person was assigned to one of two groups, the To'kana or Kicko, depending on birth order and the father's affiliation. A firstborn was usually assigned to the division to which his or her father did not belong, and the second to the group of his or her father's affiliation. The third belonged to the moiety of the first and so on. Assignment was irrespective of gender and did not influence marital arrangements. Between the members of the moieties, a friendly rivalry existed. They competed in games, and the division was important in certain festivities, hunting arrangements, and the assignment of camp police. As Charles Callender (1978, 640) noted, "This method of assigning membership had the great advantage of producing units that remained approximately equal under any circumstances and crosscut all other social groupings."

In the Mesquakie kinship terminology collected in the 1930s, we find that on a male individual's generational level specific terms existed for older brother and older sister, whereas younger brothers and sisters were grouped as younger siblings. These terms were extended to father's brother's children and to mother's sister's children. There were additionally distinct and separate terms for father's sister's son and daughter as well as for mother's brother's son and daughter. The terms for father's sister's son and daughter were the same as for sister's son and daughter (Omaha cousin terminology). On the generational level above the individual, we find that the word for father was extended to father's brother, but there was a different term for mother's brother, extended to all males in the direct line from mother's brother—for example, mother's brother's son, mother's brother's son's son. The terminology for males on the first ascending generation above the individual is bifurcate merging (see Figure 11-3). The most important observation to be made about the terminology is that there was the inclination to group individuals on both sides of one's family into a small number of categories and to ignore generations.

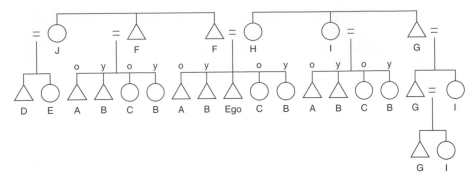

Figure 11-3 | The historic Mesquakie system of kinship terminology.

In kinship behavior, egalitarian relationships tended to exist between sets of individuals. For example, the behavior between a father and his son tended to be as between two brothers in the ideals of modern American society. Among the Mesquakie, the mother–son relationship was more like that between sister and brother. Again, between a father and his daughter, the brother-and-sister attitude prevailed, while the mother–daughter relationship paralleled that of a father and son.

SOCIAL OVERVIEW   According to the able analysis of early historic Mesquakie life by Natalie F. Joffe (1940), the most important social and economic unit was the small extended family. It might include about thirty individuals, since a man sometimes had two to five wives, and their children sometimes brought spouses into the household. In addition, there might be household members from other tribes who had been adopted or were considered captives. Female prisoners might marry Mesquakie men, and their offspring were regarded as Mesquakie. A family group also might include individuals adopted to take the place of deceased persons; these individuals did not take up residence in the household but were regarded as members of it.

POLITICAL LIFE   A dichotomy existed between the organizations devoted to peace and those in charge of warfare, although the membership of each group was much the same. Each had an overall chief, lesser chiefs, and a crier. A peace chief came from the Bear clan and was selected by the tribal council. The council made decisions about peace and war, but little is known about its composition or about most of its functions. The ideal was for the peace chief to be a placid consensus seeker who would guide the council in making ordinary decisions. The war chief typically seems to have been a member of the Fox clan with proven abilities as a leader in warfare. The war chief understandably had far more power than did the peace chief, although most often their actions were guided by tradition. As Walter B. Miler (1955) stressed, the Mesquakie were rugged individualists who knew what was expected of them, and in normal activities they strongly resented any attempt to direct their behavior. As the Jesuit missionary Father Allouez (Miller 1955, 286) wrote long ago, "These people are self-willed beyond anything that can be imagined!"

Conflict between clans appears to have been settled by respective clan members. For example, in one case a man killed his wife. She was, of course, a member of a different clan, and her male relatives summoned the murderer to appear at their main lodge. He did as he was directed and squatted on the floor while the men of the woman's clan seated themselves on the platforms. One man held an ax that would be used to smash the murderer's skull if he were to be executed. When the jury was assembled, a man at one end of the line silently nudged the person next to him; this was a vote to kill the murderer. This man nudged the one sitting on his far side and so on until one man failed to nudge his partner; this indicated that he did not approve of the death penalty. Because a unanimous verdict of guilt was required, the murderer was not doomed to die, and his relatives were permitted to offer gifts as compensation. This process demonstrates that murder was not judged on the tribal or village level but was considered an offense against the kin group of the deceased individual. The example also illustrates that alternatives of action—death or compensation—were possible.

WARFARE   One activity at which the Mesquakie excelled was physical combat with enemies, but this was war only in a loose sense of the word. Aggression against other Indians or against whites was organized by the tribe or by individual raiding parties. A national war such as those fought against the French, white Americans, or the Osage met with overall approval, but even these actions rarely involved large numbers of warriors and large-scale battles. Raids organized by individuals against a particular enemy to accomplish a specific purpose were most common. Warriors ventured forth to secure hunting areas against intrusion by others, to acquire new lands on which to hunt, to avenge the death of a Mesquakie, or to gain prestige and honor. A war leader was able to organize a raid if he had had prior success and possessed supernatural power. He supervised the strategy, but his authority was limited, since any warrior could return home at any time without a loss of honor. Even though a warrior might submit to the temporary control of a war leader and follow instructions, he was obliged to bend to the war chief's modicum of authority only during the period of the raid. The important point is that the Mesquakie war leader had more authority and power than any other individual at any other time, and yet his prerogatives were few indeed. As if to emphasize the temporary nature of his position, after returning from a raid he was not allowed to enter his settlement until he had been purified ceremonially.

Mesquakie society heaped a great deal of honor upon the successful warrior. To be a great warrior was a value instilled in boys from early childhood.

A male child was given portions of the eyebrow or heart of a brave but slain enemy so that he might eat them and acquire the qualities of the deceased. A boy attempted to join a war party as soon as possible so that he might boast of his exploits according to the custom for all warriors. Anyone could attempt to lead a war party; if he dreamed and his dreams were judged propitious by other warriors, they pledged themselves to join the raid. Before departure, the people sang war songs, and men abstained from the company of women. Although a woman might join her husband on a war party, she would not have sexual intercourse with him during the trip. A raiding party advanced slowly, hunting along the route and caching dried meat for the return trip. The party carried a sacred bundle (medicine bundle, sacred packet) for supernatural protection. Some men served as scouts, and one was designated as the cook. The raiders always planned an attack to surprise the enemy. If they were successful, the return was led by the man who made the first kill; in defeat, each warrior returned home as best he could. If the party took captives, they often killed the aged ones on the way home. A successful raid ended with a scalp dance and feasting at the village of the warriors. A woman could gain important status and rights among men if a male relative permitted her to club the head of an enemy he had killed. For a Mesquakie man to steal horses was considered honorable; however, horses were relatively unimportant, and such theft did not have the social value reported among most Plains Indians. A warrior could and usually did take new names repeatedly if he excelled in warfare. Warfare among the Mesquakie was not nearly as elaborate as among many Plains Indians, but it did manifest most of the important features found farther west.

RELIGION   The most distinctive characteristics of Mesquakie religious life were the importance of personal rapport with supernatural forces and the secondary role of group ceremonies. Supernatural matters centered in the concept of manitou, a fickle, mysterious, and pervasive quality in nature that persons communicated with for power. Manitou was approached with humility and apprehension, and it could impart to the seeker a sense of strength. The usual way to contact a manitou was by fasting for a prolonged period, but this force might be seen or heard at critical or even ordinary moments. It might manifest itself through a song, an object, or a ritual. The central religious concept of manitou was as an abstract, impersonal, and pervasive supernatural force. Yet it was received by an individual, and a personalized manitou was drawn into the experiences of an individual. The blessing and cooperation of a manitou had no built-in permanence. It could be lost at any time, and therefore an individual receiving such power always sought to reinforce it. The varieties of manitou were endless. The force could be animal, human, organic, inorganic, material, nonmaterial, natural, or supernatural.

To gain the cooperation of a manitou an adolescent boy darkened his face with ashes and fasted alone in the forest for four days and nights or perhaps longer. Near the end of his isolation he dreamed of a manitou or received a vision that included instructions. The receipt of power was contingent on following rules set down by the supernatural. These usually included the avoidance of menstruating women and a periodic offering of tobacco to the manitou. In addition, other instructions might be given, such as wearing a certain item of clothing, singing a particular song, or obtaining an object that would become the basis for a sacred bundle. The Mesquakie thought that if a boy behaved properly in his relationship with a manitou, the association was lasting, but if the boy failed in his duties, the manitou withdrew support. If this happened, a youth fasted and isolated himself again to obtain an affiliation with another manitou. A faithful manitou was believed to remain with a man not only during his life but also after death. Whether women had relationships with the manitou is not known.

The most important personification of a supernatural force was the *Gitche Manitou,* the Great Manitou. Another was the creator and culture hero Wisaka, addressed as "my nephew." Other creatures associated with mythology might be helpful; bears, deer, and snakes were thought to make one swift of foot. An individual's contact with these animals served as a basis for the emergence of a sacred bundle, the essence of Mesquakie ceremonialism. The founder learned essential rituals from a supernatural, and a cult developed around each bundle. Affiliation with a sacred bundle and its ceremonies was along a clan line, but an outsider could be incorporated into a group by learning the rituals and by being invited to participate.

The most important annual ceremonies were held by clans during the spring, summer, and winter. The spring and summer rituals were held in the bark house of a clan. Here singers and drummers consistently sat on the south side of the structure. Hoof or gourd rattles were used by certain clans, and rasps were used by others. Participants performed four dances and ate three times, with the main feast following the third dance. In all the ceremonies an emphasis was placed on dogs as special food, seating position according to moiety, and the sacrifice of tobacco. A ceremonial leader committed ritual speeches to memory and punctuated his delivery of them with accounts of other episodes. Such an individual followed established tradition in his performances, and his authority was limited to these specific times.

The most important supernaturals, apart from manitous, probably were witches envisaged as either human males or females. Witches reportedly were often from the Bear clan, and they learned their skills from other witches. The nearness of a witch at night was supposedly indicated by flashes of light or a hissing sound made as it passed. Witches' evil power took diverse forms: swelling of part of a person's body or death from no apparent cause was believed to be a witch's doing. If a person was bewitched, certain techniques could be used to turn the malevolent power back against the witch.

The Mesquakie considered most phenomena as supernatural. Thus, the sun was seen as a man, a manitou, and the grandfather of the Mesquakie; he was not always considerate of the people. The moon, as their grandmother, was thought to have a gentle quality and could be looked upon at any time.

The months were named and associated with the arrival of each new moon. The Milky Way was considered a river of stars, and other stars in the sky were thought to be either persons who had died and had gone to live in the sky, or else great manitous. The four stars forming the body of the Big Dipper were thought of as a bear, followed by three stars who were hunters. According to myth, they killed the bear in the fall, and its blood fell to earth, turning the leaves of some trees red and fading the color of others. Then the bear came back to life, and the hunters pursued it for another year. The color red symbolized the fall of the year; it also signified hostility and was used for decoration. Black was the color for winter, for fasting, and for mourning. Green was for spring and peace; it was the special color of the chief's clan. Yellow symbolized summer.

Curers among the Mesquakie used plant products and to a far lesser extent animal substances to heal patients. Whoever collected a plant had to follow certain rules. Songs were sung before removing roots, and an offering was placed in the ground where a root had been to appease Grandmother Earth, because plants were seen as the hairs on her head. The earth was considered the grandmother of Wisaka and the Mesquakie as well; her name was Mother-of-All-Things-Everywhere. Plants' conversation with one another supposedly was heard as the wind blowing through trees. The Mesquakie believed that plants could be happy or sad and that they mated in the spring and bore fruit in the fall. Wisaka was appeased so that plants would be potent cures. There were proper methods and a proper season for collecting medicinal plants, and only stipulated amounts were harvested.

LIFE CYCLE   The Mesquakie believed that a couple must have sexual intercourse repeatedly for a woman to conceive. During pregnancy, a woman observed many restrictions. For example, to ensure a normal birth, she abstained from eating nuts so that the embryo would not break through the membrane; she could not touch a corpse for fear her baby would die. A birth took place in a small nearby hut where a woman in labor knelt and leaned forward, supported by a rawhide strap. She did not cry out no matter how severe the pain. If a delivery was long and difficult, a shaman or woman sang around the outside of the hut but usually offered no other assistance. For ten days after a birth, the mother was cared for by an old woman, and for the next twenty days she slept in the main dwelling apart from the other occupants. A traditional personal name associated with the father's clan was chosen, but the name of a living person was never used.

A baby was carried on a cradleboard by its mother for nearly a year. As children matured, the parents might favor a boy who was becoming an outstanding hunter. Children were expected to be retiring and honest and not to visit other families often for fear that people would think they were always searching for something to eat. When a boy deviated from parental expectations, he was obligated to fast. This helped to prepare boys for fasting in later years, as fasting was considered a major gateway to manhood. Abstention from food was also emphasized for girls, especially as their menarche approached; the goal was for them to have a long and good life. These ideals constituted the normal expectations for children.

As mentioned earlier, the relationship between a father and his son was somewhat comparable to the behavior between brothers in our society. Hunting instruction began when a boy was about seven, and by the time he was twelve he had been given a gun and was expected to obtain small game. He was taught not only objective hunting skills but also associated magical practices. When a boy killed his first game, a feast was held in his honor, a widespread practice among North American Indians. A son who disobeyed was not punished physically but was instructed by his father to fast. To fast and seek solitude were not new to the child, but the requirement intensified as he grew. While the boy was young, he was expected to seek out a manitou. When he went alone into the forest on his quest, his parents mourned the loss of their son; after establishing this supernatural relationship, he would no longer be a child. Fasting and painting one's face with ashes made a young man able to approach a manitou and encouraged it to grant the young man success in the hunt and in war, and give him longevity as well.

A girl sought her vision at home and was taught domestic skills by her mother. She learned to sew, to cook, and to care for the garden. About the age of twelve, she began to acquire the more complex skills necessary for making moccasins and house mats. At her first menstruation she was isolated from the settlement in a small hut where she lived for ten days with a blanket over her head. Her companion during this isolation was an old woman who instructed the girl about adult behavior. At the end of this initial isolation the girl bathed in a stream, and her skin was pierced, especially about the back and sides, until she bled freely. The bloodletting was to ensure that the girl would not menstruate excessively. She then moved within sight of the settlement, living there for twenty days. After this time she took a second bath and finally returned to the family dwelling. During subsequent menstrual periods, a woman was isolated in a hut. She was believed to be potentially dangerous not only to herself but also to men and supernaturals. Supposedly, if she were to touch her hair, it might fall out; if she ate sweet or sour food, she might lose her teeth; and she could kill a tree with her touch or cause a crop to fail if she ran through a garden. Most important, manitous supposedly abhorred menstruating women, and men avoided such women so that they would not jeopardize their special powers.

A girl did not marry until she was skilled in making fine beadwork and ribbon applique. Her behavior was supervised carefully by her mother and her mother's brother. This man not only joked with her but made certain that she behaved properly since he would be shamed if she misbehaved. She was taught not to be promiscuous or to giggle, for giggly girls were open to sexual overtures. As a boy became a young man, he was expected to be respectful toward girls and to have sexual intercourse only with the girl he planned to marry. A young man sometimes courted a girl by playing a flute near her home, which was an attempt to lure the girl outside. The melody of the flute conveyed his desire, but for a girl to accept the lure invited seduction. The parents of a courting couple preferred to have the man visit their home openly to win their daughter in marriage.

The principal means for obtaining a wife was by bride service, but less commonly a couple might elope. A suitor usually established a friendship with the girl's brother and broached the subject to him. The girl of course was from a different clan than the man, and after the girl's family declared the match acceptable, they usually required the services of the groom until the first offspring was born. Alternatively, a man's family presented the girl's family with gifts in lieu of bride service by their son. This was attempted especially when the boy's parents did not want to lose him as a hunter. If gifts were accepted in place of bride service or when the service was completed, the couple was free to establish an independent household or to join either set of in-laws. An elopement occurred when a man persuaded a girl to join him on a summer hunt; on their return he presented the parents of the girl with gifts. Another less common arrangement was for a girl to be offered to a warrior by her father. This happened when a man had rendered extraordinary service to the family of the girl. For example, if a warrior prevented the scalping of a man's dead son, gave the son a warrior's interment, or rescued the son from an enemy, he might be offered the sister as a wife.

At least a few Mesquakie men remained unmarried and lived as transvestites. A dance held annually centered about and emphasized the position of such a person. The *berdache* ("man-woman") was surrounded in a dance by men who had had a sexual relationship with him (see Figure 11-4). A transvestite dressed like a woman, and because of his unusual role he was regarded as sacred.

The dissolution of a marriage usually resulted from sterility or from the inability of a couple to tolerate one another. Some personality characteristics such as extreme jealousy or ill temper led to divorce. When a marriage was dissolved, any presents that had been exchanged during the marital arrangements were returned, but each partner retained his or her personal property. Sometimes a husband left his wife after a few days of marriage; this was said to have occurred when the bride was not a maiden. In extreme cases of a wife's infidelity the offended husband might kill the couple; a milder alternative was for the husband to cut off his wife's ears or bite off her nose. A wife had no recourse in the case of a husband's infidelity.

A conspicuous characteristic of Mesquakie adult life was that it was dictated by tradition. Each individual knew what was expected of him or her and resented being directed by another person in any manner. He or she was responsible for all personal decisions and met institutional obligations without supervision. Communication with the supernaturals was by an individual, with no one standing between the person and the manitou. Because individualism was the norm, it is not surprising that the Mesquakie resented being told to do anything.

Figure 11-4 | Mesquakie and Sauk dance to the berdache, after an 1836 painting by Catlin. (From Donaldson 1886.)

When an adult died, three forms of interment were possible. The body might be placed on a scaffold or in a tree. An honorable interment for a warrior was to place him in a sitting position above the body of a slain enemy. Most common perhaps was to dig a shallow pit and arrange the body in a seated position with the head above the ground and covered with rocks or a small shed. Food and water were placed with the body, but weapons were not, since spirits might use them against the living. At the foot of a grave a stake was erected after the bark was peeled from it. Among the final acts were sprinkling tobacco on the body and killing a dog on the site of the burial. The dog's spirit supposedly protected and guided the dead to the next world. Just before the body of a warrior was abandoned, an old warrior recounted the number of persons the deceased had killed, which meant that their souls would serve as his slaves in the land of spirits. The ritual leader distributed the property of the deceased, along with items contributed by relatives of the dead person, to his helpers.

After disposing of the body, the clan to which the deceased belonged held a mourning ceremony. A second dog was killed and its hair singed by four firebrands taken from the hearth of the deceased. The dog was cooked, and the clan's mourning songs were sung until about midnight when the participants ate the dog. The principal mourners dressed in tattered clothing and blackened their faces. They remained in this state up to four years, which was the maximum time limit before an adoption ceremony and an end to mourning. The adoption ceremony was performed by the relatives of the deceased and served to release the soul of the dead permanently. According to Mesquakie belief, the soul had left the earth after four days but returned at intervals until the adoption rituals were completed. If this did not happen within four years, the soul became an owl. The adoption was of an unrelated friend of the deceased who was of the same sex and approximate age. This individual assumed the kinship position of the deceased but also retained her or his own prior kinship ties. If the deceased was a warrior killed by an enemy, the adopted warrior was obligated to kill an enemy in order to release the widow from mourning.

Each individual was believed to have two souls that served different purposes. A small soul came from a particular manitou and was equated with the individual's life; it left the body at the time of death and through subsequent adoption ceremonies was reborn three times. The larger soul, from Wisaka, had entered the neonate's body at birth and was never reborn. The world of spirits was believed to be divided into two sections: in one section lived persons who had been good on earth, and in the other, persons who were evil. Some of these concepts may have been inspired by Christian missionaries.

| From Iowa and Back

Following the end of the Black Hawk War in 1832, the Mesquakie had so little reservation land in Iowa that they could not possibly follow their traditional way of life for very long. They planted crops until the land was depleted, and, after exhausting local game sources, they turned west to hunt bison. This soon became an unprofitable subsistence base, and they began wintering among white settlers. Generally hostile whites, unscrupulous traders, and dishonest Indian agents compounded their difficulties, which also included diseases and the excessive consumption of alcoholic beverages. Furthermore, the Mesquakie were thrown into contact with their Siouan enemies, and the resulting raids led to an embittered attitude on both sides. To cap all of this, a local increase in the white population forced the Mesquakie to move again. In 1842 they were forced to relocate on nearly 400,000 acres at the headwaters of the Osage River in Kansas.

The Kansas reservation was prairie country to which their farming and hunting economy was ill adapted. They hunted bison and other game but depended largely on annuities from the government. Hunting on the prairies brought them into conflict with the Arapaho, Comanche, and Kiowa, who resented the intrusion. The Mesquakie were never reconciled to their land in Kansas; epidemics of cholera and smallpox no doubt contributed to their discontent.

In 1856 some of them returned to Iowa, where other Mesquakie had remained. They first bought and settled eighty acres of land in Tama County in 1857. Legal recognition of these Mesquakie was extended by the state government, and the land was held in trust by the governor. Soon others returned from Kansas. Amazing at it may seem, the Indians were welcomed by whites. Altruism was the motive of some, and interest in the annuity payments received by the Indians was the motive of others. When the Mesquakie in Kansas were forced by the federal government to give up their reservation and move to Oklahoma in 1869, still more returned to Iowa. By about 1870 some three hundred Mesquakie were in Iowa, and they began to settle down to a new way of life in the Tama area.

Figure 11-5 | Mesquakie men on horses with summer sun shade and reed-covered dwellings in the background, circa 1904, Tama, Iowa. (Courtesy of the State Historical Society of Iowa, Iowa City.)

By the 1860s the Iowa Mesquakie were miserably poor and sometimes reduced to begging. Their economy was based on hunting and trapping, gardening, and selling curios. Whenever they obtained surplus money, they purchased additional land. They remained extremely distrustful of whites. As late as the 1880s they still refused to send their children to school. They rejected modern farming practices, and Christian missionaries were largely ignored. In 1894, after the sale of land allotments that had been held for them in Oklahoma, they were able to expand their land holdings to twenty-eight hundred acres. Apparently at about this time they began to rent farmland to whites, and they used the rent money to pay taxes.

A visitor in 1897 and 1898 reported that at that time the population was about four hundred. The winter dwellings were oblong, pole-framed structures with mat coverings, just as in aboriginal times (see Figure 11-5). The ground inside a house was covered with old blankets, and a fire in a central fireplace provided warmth, light, and heat for cooking. The only items seen in one such dwelling were containers and food. The standard fare seems to have been flour, lard, and maize. The flour was fried in lard to make a bannock, which was eaten with dried sweet corn. Dogs remained an important source of meat for festive occasions. A few families, particularly those of younger men, lived in frame dwellings with adjacent outbuildings. In the summer the people lived along the bottomland near the Iowa River in dwellings covered with boards and bark topped with mats. Inside, a platform extended along the length of the room on both sides. An additional structure was a hut nearby for menstruating women.

By 1900 most Mesquakie had abandoned their old hair and clothing styles. Most men had long hair braided into a small pigtail from which silver ornaments and beadwork hung. A man's most important ornament was made from silver and protected his scalp lock. Men dressed in store-bought shirts and trousers except at home, where they wore a breechclout and blanket. Moccasins had changed from buckskin to cloth, and the skin cape was replaced by a blanket or shawl. The shirts and skirts of women were made from calico; women wore at least two shirts, which were loose at the waist and buttoned at the front. They wore two or more skirts, which hung loosely from the hips to just below the ankles for younger women and girls and just above the ankles for older women (see Figure 11-6). Women wore short woolen leg-

Figure 11-6 | A Mesquakie woman with her child, circa 1900. Although the dress is typical, the furniture is not, and thus the photo was probably taken in a photographer's studio. (Courtesy of the State Historical Society of Iowa, Iowa City.)

gings that reached their knees. They preferred beaded shawls, but those who could not afford shawls wore blankets. Men and women alike were partial to silver jewelry, which was considered "good medicine."

| Later Developments

Systematic studies by anthropologists were launched in 1932 and ended in 1959. The Fox Project, as it came to be called, was developed and guided by Sol Tax at the University of Chicago.

SETTLEMENT AND SUBSISTENCE   By 1937, Mesquakie lands near Tama, Iowa, consisted of a 3800-acre parcel where most people lived and another 520 acres that were leased to white farmers. The Mesquakie numbered 450 and supported themselves by farming or wage labor. The average family income from all sources in 1937 was about $500 per year. In the farming activities, women cultivated garden plots after the land had been prepared by men, and men raised the field crops, which were important sources of cash. If a family did not farm, its plot could be leased to another Mesquakie.

Families lived in frame houses with usually one or two rooms; adjacent outbuildings included a barn, corncrib, chicken coop, privy, and canvas menstrual hut. During their monthly periods or at childbirth, the women ate in the menstrual huts but slept in the houses. Another important structure had a rectangular pole frame covered with mats or canvas that resembled the old summer house. An accompanying arbor with a platform was often attached, and it was here that men sat and children played. Women typically cooked at a nearby outdoor fire.

They continued to maintain some traditional food habits. Dried and shelled maize was milled or made into hominy, and squash was sectioned, dried, grated, and stored for future use. The people still collected local plant products and took small game. New crops included oats, alfalfa, potatoes, beets, and onions. They obtained wheat flour and most meat and dairy products from a store, and their maize was ground at a commercial mill. They kept innumerable dogs, and young ones remained an important ceremonial food. About half of the families owned horses for hauling buggies and wagons or for plowing and riding, but it was primarily younger persons who rode horses. The material culture in the late 1930s seemed typical of rural Iowa. About half of the families owned automobiles, and families did most shopping in Tama, where the storekeepers made some effort to stock goods with an appeal to Indians, including shawls, silk neckerchiefs, and beads. Special items for use on festive or ceremonial occasions, such as seed beads, were purchased from mail-order houses; deerskins were obtained from other Indians.

By the mid-1950s about half of the men supported their families as skilled and unskilled laborers and artisans in communities surrounding the settlement. Most men commuted to work each day, but in some instances they returned to the settlement only on weekends. The Mesquakie had all the obligations of other United States citizens; they paid some forms of taxes and had the same rights to vote or to receive welfare if they were without economic means. At that time about eight families received aid from the state and federal governments. The Indians also received from the federal government some services not offered to non-Indians, such as health care.

SOCIAL DIMENSIONS   In the 1930s a typical residence unit included a husband and wife, their biological children, unmarried relatives, and perhaps children by a former marriage. These nuclear-core households were the economic and social units, although all residents might not contribute equally to the family's support and the near relatives of the couple were often transient. In general, a new household was established near the home of relatives and tended to be more closely linked to the wife's family than to the husband's. Yet relatives on both sides of the family (kindred) offered the typical individual a widespread network of kin, numbering between fifty and one hundred persons, distributed among about a dozen households. It is significant that although the Mesquakie were patrilineal, the important social ties in their daily lives were with both sides of the family. Family ties were expanded through adoption, which was of the same nature as in aboriginal times, a deceased relative being replaced by an adopted individual of approximately the same age and gender. Although adult life centered about the family, many forms of entertainment existed outside the family. Tama pool halls were frequented by men and boys; a men's baseball team and a girls' softball team were active; and during the winter gambling was an important form of diversion for men and women.

THE ANNUAL POW-WOW   One of the most pleasurable and lasting of all new Mesquakie institutions has been the Tama Pow-Wow held each August. From the time the Mesquakie returned to Iowa, whites probably had been invited to attend certain of the ceremonies. In later years nonreligious attractions were added, although the religious core of the celebration remained. In 1913, as a response to white enthusiasm, the Pow-Wow was organized formally as a four-day affair, primarily intended as entertainment for whites. The committee controlling the Pow-Wow was structured as a tribal council, with representatives selected from the fifteen major family lines. In 1922 the group was reformulated as a corporate body in a legal sense, with a constitution, officers, and committee members. By 1951 committee membership had been expanded, and even though the positions were elective, the idea of representation by major family groups was preserved. By the early 1950s the rather elaborate Pow-Wow arrangements were guided largely by the committee secretary, a person familiar with whites. Yet there was no real authority to guide the event; the participants followed traditionally established norms for the celebration, which resembled a county fair but had a strong Indian emphasis. By 1951 there were many family souvenir and food concessions and, most important, old dances and songs were performed (see Figure 11-7). In good weather it was not unusual for ten thousand people to attend the event, and most Indian families camped at the Pow-Wow (now spelled Pow Wow by the Mesquakie) grounds. All normal routine ceased as the time approached. This was the one time of the year that the people all worked together.

POLITICAL LIFE   Mesquakie political institutions understandably had changed a great deal by the 1930s. They were characterized by a factionalism that apparently originated in a controversy over recording individual names for a tribal roll in 1876. Members of the conservative faction refused to tell the Indian agent their names, but the progressives did so; this led to inequities in the annuity payments. In addition, a chief was appointed in 1881 who was not a member of the Bear clan. No issue was made of the fact at the time, but when the chief later led the progressives, the conservatives questioned his right to the leadership. This division continued to be important in the 1930s. Families, but not clans, tended to act as units in the factionalism, but these differences did not affect ceremonial activities in which clans were important. Marriages tended to be within a faction, but when they did cut across factional lines, it was most often the woman who joined the side of her husband.

In 1916 the last chief appointed a council that functioned until 1929, when it was replaced by an elected council. The elected members of the contending factions could not agree, however, and they never met. Although elections continued to be held, the council remained inactive owing to internal differences. Then in 1937 the tribe organized under the Indian Reorganization Act, and the seven elected council members began to work together. However, the details of council operations were not recorded. Mesquakie lands continued to be held in trust by the federal government but were subject to taxation, eminent domain, and other judicial procedures that applied to any individually owned land in the state. Personal differences usually were settled verbally, although women sometimes fought and one man might strike another on the head. The most common offenses prosecuted were drunkenness and differences over property rights. These legal actions often were brought by Indians, but they did not seek intervention from whites for problems such as theft.

The status of warrior revived once again during World War II. Nearly fifty Mesquakie served in the armed services, and about half of them became members of a local American Legion post. Initially, the Mesquakie veterans had joined the Tama post, but they resigned when they were refused intoxicants. The federal restriction against selling intoxicants to Indians was still in force, although it had been suspended when Indians were in the armed services. A Mesquakie post was founded in the hope that veterans would achieve greater recognition in white society. Although the Mesquakie community turned to members for leadership, it soon became evident that the veterans

Figure 11-7 | Young dancers at the Tama Pow-Wow, circa 1959. (Courtesy of Joan Liffring Zug.)

were no better able to cope with local problems than was any other segment of the community. The organization passed out of existence, partially because effective Indian leaders did not appear. Moreover, federal officials withdrew permission to use a government building for post meetings when they learned that the Indians were keeping beer in the building.

RELIGION   The concept of manitou has persisted, and formal religious activities have coalesced around the sacred bundles of the clans or voluntary religious associations. Christianity, the use of peyote, and the nonaboriginal Drum Society all offered limited opportunities for religious participation. The peyote cult, mentioned in Chapter 2, was small in 1937, although ceremonial use of the cactus had been known since around 1900. Peyote was valued mainly for its reportedly curative properties; a person who had tried other cures and then turned to peyote often continued to take it after he had recovered. The Drum Society was a religious group organized in 1932 and probably was derived from the Potawatomi. The members were from the progressive faction even though they believed the power of the ceremony to be derived from a manitou. The ritual involved the use of four drums, and the ceremonies were held four times a year. The drums were associated with particular leaders, each having specific functions.

Religion still focused on the sacred bundles, which were hereditary either in a patriclan line or across clan affiliations. Forty sacred bundle groups in eleven major categories existed, and within each category were major and minor bundle groups. Membership in a sacred bundle group could be acquired through an invitation, which most often was extended to an individual who was a good singer and knew the songs associated with the particular bundle group. Certain reciprocal functions linked the groups into various activities. The bundle affiliations did not regulate marriage, although this was apparently once an ideal. The ceremonies were held in summer longhouses and extended from morning until sunset of a single day. Food was prepared by the hosts, and the most important dish was stewed puppies that had been ceremonially killed with clubs. The stew was served by members of another sacred bundle group, and after the meal the bones were carefully collected and burned. The dances were in sets of four, and the sacred bundle was opened and various items used in the ceremony. Both men and women participated in the summer rituals, but only men were active in the winter festivities.

Witchcraft and sorcery were still very much a part of Mesquakie life in the 1930s. Malevolent power was obtained in a vision quest, and a sorcerer might take the form of a bear or snake. If a potential victim could shoot a gun at the spot where a witch was thought to be, the sorcerer supposedly would die within four days. One important use of sorcery was as love magic, and if properly employed, it was believed to lead to the irresistible attractiveness of the user. A nonresponding victim would be driven to insanity and eventual suicide. The ability to cure, which came from a vision, was limited to shamans, who employed a variety of techniques. A shaman visited the patient, and if he was compensated enough he accepted the case. The curing procedure entailed singing, administering herbs, and sucking out the disease. Because a bear or snake supposedly had given supernatural power to the medicine man, a claw or bone formed the core of his medicine bundle and might be used to suck out the substance causing the illness.

In the 1950s the traditional religion continued to be organized around the traditional ceremonials. Apart from the yearly Pow-Wow, clan-affiliated religious activities most often brought people together. The clan organization, which was weak and somewhat vaguely defined, served primarily as the structure around which the traditional religious ceremonies were organized. According to Charles Callender (1978), clans probably had served the same general function in the past. Community elders provided the greatest support for the old religious system, and some middle-aged persons followed their lead. Younger Mesquakie tended to be nonreligious, but some seemed ready to adopt Christianity if they were not restrained by elders. The forty Drum Society members still tended to be progressive. In the late 1940s about a dozen persons participated in the peyote rituals. About thirty Mesquakie were members of two Christian denominations, the United Presbyterian and Open Bible Gospel churches; both were maintained and encouraged by whites, although some meaningful Mesquakie leadership was beginning to emerge.

SETTLEMENT OF LAND CLAIMS   In 1969 the federal government partially rectified injustices of old. In that year the U.S. Indian Claims Commission awarded the Mesquakie and Sauk of Iowa nearly a million dollars for lands ceded in 1830 for which they had not received just compensation. Each adult received $500, with a like amount held in trust for each person under eighteen years of age. The Mesquakie Tribal Council held 60 percent of the settlement money for planning and development. Of the nearly 800 persons on the tribal roll, about 500 lived in or near their lands in Iowa at that time. With an inadequate land base, economic conditions had forced some persons to leave. A further settlement in 1976 ended a twenty-eight-year court battle over seventeen million acres of land taken by the federal government for which the Mesquakie had not been compensated. Of the $6.6 million payment, each adult received nearly $6000, and this amount was held in trust for each of the 329 minors to receive when they reached the age of eighteen. About $1.3 million was held in trust by the federal government for tribal projects. It does not appear that the cash received by the 573 adults will have any long-range impact on their lives (see Figure 11-8).

| The Recent Past

Before turning to the Mesquakie of the late 1990s, it is pertinent to cite select statistics from the comparatively recent past. In 1978 most families at the

Figure 11-8 | Adrian Pushetonequa, a Mesquakie artist, in 1972. (Courtesy of John M. Zielinski.)

settlement and nearby lived beneath the poverty level; in 1985 the vast majority of families received some form of welfare assistance. About a quarter of all their homes flooded in the spring, and about half of the houses did not have central heating or indoor plumbing or water. Finally, in 1986, when economic conditions were depressed in rural Iowa, the unemployment rate at the settlement was about 67 percent. These statistics are especially critical, as will soon become evident (see Figure 11-9).

After the Fox Project ended in 1959, the next systematic Mesquakie study was by Douglas E. Foley (1995), a white professional anthropologist raised in the Tama area during the 1950s. He knew local Indians through school contacts and was well aware of the varied opinions about them held by his family and peers. Thus Foley came from an unusual personal background when he visited the settlement repeatedly in the 1980s and early 1990s. By then Foley had become distrustful of the traditional "objective" and "scientific" approach to ethnography. Foley (1995, ix) wrote, "I make no claim that the tale I am about to spin is absolutely true. . . . I am characterizing people as I see them." His perspective was "postmodern," or perhaps more aptly, a return to the humanistic tradition of ethnographic reporting. In a robust combination of

Figure 11-9 | The Mesquakie had a new building as their tribal headquarters by 1981; it was managed by tribal members such as Don Wanatee.

historical reconstructions, vignettes, and interviews, Foley provided a vivid account of Mesquakie life.

RACISM   Some Fox Project investigators sought to expose and combat Indian and white racism at Tama. For Foley, racism was a focal concern. One example he cites goes back to the early 1940s. Beginning about that time and continuing for twenty-five years thereafter, the local newspaper repeatedly published stories about drunken Indians being killed by trains. A railroad from Tama runs through the Mesquakie settlement, where trains never stopped. Indians who had been drinking in Tama walked the tracks to their homes because the tracks provided a direct route. On cold nights the tracks were warm and less icy than the roads. The drunken Indian might be unable to make it back without resting on the tracks. The engineer aboard a speeding train could not see well in the dark, and therefore Indians were killed. The newspaper accounts detailed the mutilations ad nauseum. Foley (1995, 88) wrote, "For whites the train that passes through the settlement is an avenging angel. It brings death to those Mesquakis who disregard the power of white commerce, white technology, the white way of life. These stories always emphasize the link between alcohol and the mutilated body."

Indian versions of these stories contrasted with newspaper reports. In some cases, the Mesquakie said, a victim might be nearly blind, have poor hearing, or may have been suicidal. More often they thought that the victim had been placed on the tracks by whites. One version was that a Mesquakie was arrested for drunkenness in Tama, beaten in jail, and placed on the tracks as a means of destroying the body and concealing police brutality. In another variation, the members of a white gang beat up an Indian and placed him on the tracks to hide their crime.

Some whites, possibly many, in the 1950s and 1960s termed the Mesquakie "Squawkies" because they were always complaining. They were considered "welfare cheats," and stereotypes of this nature were not unknown even into the 1990s. A major white complaint was that Indians represented a financial burden on the school district budget because they did not pay local school taxes. Thus the Indians were freeloaders who depended on white benevolence. As Foley probed the tax situation, he found some whites who acknowledged that the school district received aid from Federal Impact funds for students from reservations (or military bases) to attend local schools. The school district also received state aid to compensate for taxes not paid by Indians. White administrators and school board members contended that these sources were *insufficient* to cover the cost of educating Indian students. Yet in 1990 each Indian was "worth" about $1200 *more than* the $3125 that the district spent each year per student. In addition, a school district received other state and federal funds for students from low-income families, whether white or Indian. These monies totaled in excess of $750,000 a year. Foley (1995, 57) observed, "In short, having Indian students has been a major financial plus for many years. Unfortunately, school leaders pandered to racist attitudes about the financial burden of having Mesquakie students" (see Figure 11-10).

SETTLEMENT POLITICS One critical question still predominates: Who is a real Mesquakie? Pure Mesquakie heritage was claimed by some families, but apparently every family had members who had married non-Mesquakie. Thus genetic heritage could not be an indisputable criteria. A legal definition was formulated in 1937, when the tribe organized under the IRA. The basic definition, in theory, excluded "outsiders," meaning primarily persons of mixed white or non-Mesquakie Indian ancestry, but in fact some such persons were tribal members. Being a tribal member was important, as was having tribal voting rights. An enrolled member could claim a homesite at the settlement and, with council approval, could obtain a house funded by the federal government. Enrolled members had free garbage pickup, free water and sewage hookups, free medical care, and other benefits denied non-tribal members.

From time to time, some "pure-bloods" had advocated ejecting persons who were clearly of mixed ancestry, or "blanket breeds," from the settlement; in fact, most of these people did not live in the settlement. Those who were residents were considered to be "guests," and they behaved accordingly. They avoided becoming involved in tribal politics, and only those among them who were most accepted participated in Mesquakie social and religious events.

Figure 11-10 | By 1981 the Headstart program at the Sac and Fox tribal complex near Tama was enjoying success.

The modern basis for at least some Mesquakie factionalism appears to date from 1895, when the chief was persuaded by an Indian agent to send young people to a boarding school. This decision by the progressives was deplored by traditionalists, and the chief's opponents claimed that he was not from the proper clan. By 1905 the Indian agent began appointing council members. Then in 1937 the Tama Mesquakie accepted a tribal government under the IRA. This decision placed political control in the hands of the Indians in a democratic election system that ignores the former rule by clan elders.

The successful effort to introduce casino gambling at the settlement in recent years conveys the push and pull of the traditional and progressive factions. Objections by traditionalists to commercialized gambling seem to have been relatively straightforward: it was not in keeping with their values. The progressives, by contrast, were attracted to the potential economic benefits. The conflict soon became convoluted; a brief synopsis is given here.

Beginning in the early 1980s, Ed Longknife (a pseudonym), an assertive Mesquakie with strong political opinions, had advocated tribal bingo. Yet it was the manager of a Winnebago bingo hall who brought the matter before the tribal council in 1983. He felt that he had made his case and would receive authorization to manage a new hall for the Mesquakie. However, Longknife supported a competing management contract and pressured the council to accept it. These developments were accompanied by accusations of mismanagement by the council in other matters, and a referendum on the bingo-management proposal failed. The debate went on for years, partially because some people objected to the percentage of profits sought by management companies. Finally, a development team was appointed by the council to examine the issues involved in a bingo operation. The team consisted of young college-educated Mesquakie who visited bingo halls of other tribes and worked hard at their mission. They recommended launching a small-scale hall that would be *managed by the tribe*. A referendum on the matter passed, and a bingo hall was opened in the tribal gymnasium. This enterprise provided a modest but acceptable economic return and led to the construction of a new $2.5 million, 35,000-square-foot bingo hall that opened in 1989 and was financed in part with bingo profits. The success of the young "progressive-traditionalists" was clear, and they were justifiably pleased with their success.

Longknife and his supporters, however, were dissatisfied with tribal bingo because they felt a great deal more money could be earned from casino gambling. Proponents and opponents jockeyed for advantage, each accusing the other, with some justification, of questionable manipulations. The conflict became acrimonious. Council meetings were often canceled because a quorum could not be obtained. Then in 1991 a council election produced enough pro-casino candidates to hold a referendum on the issue; the results decisively favored casino gambling. A gambling pact with the state was signed. The next question was whether the tribe or a management company would operate the casino. Longknife favored a management company, whereas the progressive-traditionalists favored the tribe. At this juncture, at least twelve management company representatives invaded the settlement to launch a fierce battle to win the contract. There were objections to each proposal. One plan seemed overly ambitious: it included a hotel and recreational-vehicle park and called for 40 percent of the profits from the casino to go to the management company. In the eyes of Foley (1995, 189), "All these casino management companies looked the same to me. They all needed tax-exempt Indian land to put up their neon money-making boxes."

Under questioning at a critical council meeting, the representative of the favored management company revealed that he would make $2 million if the contract was approved. Despite this admission—as gross as it was—some people continued to favor this company, while others were firmly opposed. The council vote was critical; the Mesquakie preferred to have unanimous council approval for key issues such as this one. Thus another impasse arose. The solution was to seek and sign a contract with a previously uninvolved management company. Ultimately, most of the bingo hall was converted into a casino. The management company provided executives, trained the Mesquakie in operations, and received a fee of 7 percent of the profits.

In 1992, "Las Vegas-style gambling" was launched at the 30,000-square-foot facility. By 1997, Meskwaki Bingo & Casino had more than 800 employees, about 200 of whom were Indian, primarily Meskwaki (another official spelling of Mesquakie). Some 40,000 gamblers visit the facility each week.

Figure 11-11 | In 1997 Meskwaki Bingo & Casino was expanding to include a larger gambling area and hotel.

An expansion of the bingo hall and casino to be completed in 1998 will provide additional floor area for gambling, as well as a 200-room hotel (see Figure 11-11). The positive impact of gambling on tribal life has been little short of astounding. The BIA no longer funds the tribe, nor are there any BIA representatives assigned to the settlement. Residents no longer need state welfare funds or federal money for housing. The percentages of tribal profits from gambling were allotted as follows: economic development, 25%; health care, 20%; education, housing, and tribal infrastructure, 15% each; and direct payments to enrolled members, 10%. In 1997 substantial monthly payments were made to the 1253 enrolled band members. Those living at the settlement did not pay federal or state taxes, but those living outside of its boundaries did.

Changes in the settlement land base suggest the scope of recent developments. The settlement land encompassed about 3800 acres in the early 1900s. By 1997 the Mesquakie had purchased about 3200 additional adjacent acres to incorporate into their holdings, a dramatic increase.

In the formal 1937 enrollment, 441 persons were considered "pure bloods"; they numbered 1132 in 1996. When one pure blood marries another, the children are Mesquakie. If a Mesquakie man marries a white woman, the children are Mesquakie. If these children in turn marry whites, their own children will not be considered Mesquakie. If a Mesquakie woman marries a white man, the children are not Mesquakie, as we would expect given their patrilineal system of inheritance. Because of the increasing tendency for Mesquakie men and women to marry whites or non-Mesquakie Indians, there are fewer children of pure Mesquakie heritage, a matter of great concern for the future. As a pure-blooded Mesquakie grandmother recently said, she loves all of her grandchildren, but she cherishes her Mesquakie grandchildren.

Looking to the future of the Mesquakie, it is notable that the resident population at the settlement has been relatively stable in recent years: it was 552 in 1986 and 527 in 1994. In the latter year, 369 additional enrolled members lived near the settlement, and the remaining 199 members resided in more distant communities. Thus the vast majority of the members continue to live on or near the settlement, a strong indicator of their ongoing Indian identity. The political factionalism that crystallized in the late 1800s continues as a "conservative" versus "progressive" dichotomy. It must be stressed that these factions continue to be largely political; they cross clan, religious, and socio-economic lines. Individuals may be fierce political adversaries but friends or congenial relatives in everyday life. This capacity to compartmentalize cultural differences is a clear and continuing source of Mesquakie strength.

The Mesquakie of old would not recognize their descendants in Iowa today, but at the same time these descendants are the only Indians in the general region who have survived as a distinct cultural entity. This is the view expressed by Johnathan L. Buffalo, the Mesquakie historian, in a 1997 conversation with Oswalt (see Figure 11-12). He emphasized that the progressives and conservatives alike seek tribal survival and that they have adapted far more to the white world than most outsiders realize. Yet the conservatives are changing only hesitantly—they are being dragged toward change. Buffalo pointed out that the most liberal (e.g., white-oriented) Mesquakie would be

Figure 11-12 | In 1997 Johnathan L. Buffalo was the historical preservation coordinator for the Meskwaki in Iowa.

labeled as "conservative" if they were members of most other tribes. He also feels that as long as individuals say, "I am a Mesquakie," there is hope for the future. Pure Mesquakie heritage is a critical factor: it is "as good as gold."

| Additional Sources

The best early account is by Thomas Forsyth (1912), who was the Indian agent for the Mesquakie and Sauk from 1812 to 1827. The best general book-length study is by William T. Hagan (1958). The best summary article is by Charles Callender (1978), titled "Fox," in the *Northeast* volume (15) of the *Handbook of North American Indians,* William C. Sturtevant, general editor. This volume also contains the best overview of other Indians in the region. For traditional aspects of Mesquakie life, the writings of William Jones (who was of Mesquakie and white ancestry) and Truman Michelson are superior. *The Fox Wars,* by R. David Edmunds and Joseph L. Peyser (1993), is the best source on the subject. Chapter-length studies by Natalie F. Joffee (1940) and Sol Tax (1937) provide a wealth of information about conditions in the 1930s. *The Face of the Fox,* by Frederick O. Gearing (1970), is the best account for the period from 1948 to 1959. The best recent publication is the book *The Heartland Chronicles* by Douglas E. Foley (1995).

| Selected Bibliography

Bicknell, A. D. 1901. The Tama County Indians. *Annals of Iowa* (3rd series) 4:196–208.

Callender, Charles C. 1978. Fox. In the *Handbook of North American Indians,* William C. Sturtevant, gen. ed., vol. 15, *Northeast,* 636–47. Washington, DC.

Catlin, George. 1844. *North American Indians,* vol. 2, 207–17. London.

Donaldson, Thomas. 1886. The George Catlin Indian Gallery in the U.S. National Museum. *Annual Report of the Board of Regents of the Smithsonian Institution, 1885,* pt. 2 appendix.

Edmunds, R. David, and Joseph L. Peyser. 1993. *The Fox wars: The Mesquakie challenge to New France.* Norman, OK.

Foley, Douglas E. 1995. *The Heartland Chronicles.* Philadelphia.

Forsyth, Thomas. 1912. An account of the manners and customs of the Sauk and Fox nations of Indian traditions. In *The Indian tribes of the upper Mississippi Valley region of the Great Lakes,* Emma H. Blair, ed., v. 2, 183–245. Cleveland.

Gearing, Frederick O. 1970. *The face of the Fox.* Chicago.

Gearing, Frederick O., Robert McC. Netting, and Lisa R. Peattie. 1960. *Documentary history of the Fox Project 1948–1959.* Chicago.

Green, Michael D. 1983. We dance in opposite directions. *Ethnohistory* 30:129–40.

Hagan, William T. 1958. *The Sac and Fox Indians.* Norman, OK.

Joffe, Natalie F. 1940. The Fox of Iowa. In *Acculturation in seven American Indian tribes,* Ralph Linton, ed., 259–331. New York.

Jones, William. 1905. The Algonkin manitou. *Journal of American Folk-Lore* 18:183–90.

———. 1911. Notes on the Fox Indians. *Journal of American Folk-Lore* 24:209–37.

———. 1939. *Ethnography of the Fox Indians.* Bureau of American Ethnology Bulletin no. 125, Margaret Welpley Fisher, ed.

McKenney, Thomas L., and James Hall. 1934. *The Indian tribes of North America,* vol. 2. Edinburgh.

Michelson, Truman. 1913. Review of *Folk-lore of the Musquakie Indians of North America* by Mary A. Owen. *Current Anthropological Literature* 2:233–37.

———. 1922. How Meskwakie children should be brought up. In *American Indian life,* Elsie C. Parsons, ed., 81–86. New York.

———. 1925a. The autobiography of a Fox Indian woman. *Bureau of American Ethnology, 40th Annual Report,* 291–349.

———. 1925b. Notes on Fox mortuary customs and beliefs. *Bureau of American Ethnology, 40th Annual Report,* 351–496.

Miller, Walter B. 1955. Two concepts of authority. *American Anthropologist* n.s. 57:271–89.

Polgar, Steven. 1960. Biculturation of Mesquakie teenage boys. *American Anthropologist* n.s. 62:217–35.

Rideout, Henry M. 1912. *William Jones.* New York.

Smith, Huron H. 1928. *Ethnobotany of the Meskwaki Indians.* Bulletin of the Public Museum of the City of Milwaukee, vol. 4, 175–326.

Stucki, Larry R. 1967. Anthropologists and Indians: A new look at the Fox Project. *Plains Anthropologist* 12(37):300–317.

Tax, Sol. 1937. The social organization of the Fox Indians. In *Social Anthropology of North American Tribes,* Fred Eggan, ed., 243–82. Chicago.

12 The Iroquois: Warriors and Farmers of the Eastern Woodlands

Great Spirit, who dwellest alone, listen now to the words of thy people here assembled. The smoke of our offering arises. Give kind attention to our words, as they arise to thee in the smoke. We think of thee for this return of the planting season. Give to us a good season, that our crops may be plentiful.

A portion of the Planting Ceremony speech of the Seneca that is typical of ceremonial prayers. (Morgan 1954, vol. 1, 188)

ANTHROPOLOGISTS HAVE LONG HAD a special fondness for the Iroquois, and not without good reason. They were the subject of the first essentially modern account of an aboriginal people, written by the Jesuit missionary Father Joseph F. Lafitau and published in 1724. However, because this work first appeared in French, it did not make an immediate impact on Americans. Then in 1851 Lewis Henry Morgan published a book about the Iroquois that became a model for ethnographic reports.

The Iroquois have also been of special interest because they played a decisive role in shaping the North American colonial empires of the British and French, and they continued to play an important role during the American Revolution. From colonial times to the present, distinguished members of Iroquois tribes have been known to the people of Canada and the United States. During the colonial period, Hendrick was an outstanding Mohawk military leader and warrior, Joseph Brant was a Mohawk warrior and politician, and Red Jacket, a Seneca, was a great orator. Kateri Tekakwitha, a Mohawk born about 1656, was canonized as a saint in the Roman Catholic church in 1980. General Ely S. Parker, a Seneca, served as secretary to General Ulysses S. Grant and drafted the terms of peace at Appomattox, Virginia, that ended the American Civil War. Jay Silverheels (Harold I. Smith), a Mohawk, was better known as Tonto of "Lone Ranger" fame, and the runner Tom Longboat was an Onondaga. The Iroquois, famous in war and politics and representative of the Northeast culture area, have retained their identity with a rare resilience, but now their battles are most often fought in courtrooms.

| People, Population, and Language

The Iroquois commonly are considered a tribe, but they are more properly termed a nation. The five original tribes were joined by a closely related one, the Tuscarora, in historic times, and unrelated tribes, such as the Delaware, were also absorbed through adoption. Individuals in such tribes were considered secondary members of the Iroquois community.

The Iroquois confederation known as the Five Nations or Iroquois League originally included the Cayuga, Mohawk, Oneida, Onondaga, and Seneca tribes. The word *Iroquois* is based on an Algonquian word, translated "real adder," with a French suffix. The aboriginal Iroquois lived from Lake Champlain and Lake George in the east to the Genesee River drainage and Lake Ontario in the west. The northern boundary was the St. Lawrence River, and the Iroquois domain extended south to the upper Susquehanna River (see Figure 12-1). Each group occupied an oblong strip of country, and it is estimated that collectively at the time of early historic contact they numbered ten thousand.

The Iroquois spoke languages of the Macro-Siouan phylum and the Iroquoian family. Each of the five original Iroquois League tribes had its own language. The Cherokee language, which is of the same family as the Iroquois

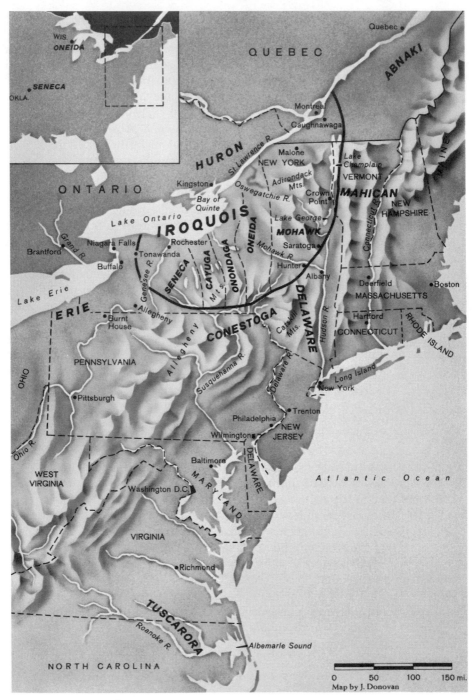

Figure 12-1 | Area of early historic Iroquois occupation.

languages, separated from Iroquois about 1500 B.C. The separation of languages within the Iroquois group took place after A.D. 700.

Around two thousand years ago, the Tuscarora split from what was later to become the League and settled along the Roanoke and nearby rivers in North Carolina and Virginia. Hostilities with white settlers erupted in the Tuscarora wars of 1711 and 1712–13. The second war ended with some Tuscarora moving north to join the League members. They were adopted formally by the Oneida in 1722 as members of the League, and the Iroquois then became the Six Nations. By 1904 the Six Nations numbered at least 16,000. In 1997 the total Iroquois population was possibly 80,000, most of whom lived in Canada. The largest concentration was at the Six Nations Reserve in Ontario with about 20,000 enrolled band members, of whom about 9500 lived on the reserve. In New York State there were nearly 19,000, and in Wisconsin the population was about 12,000.

Origin Myth

The Iroquois origin myth asserts that in the beginning there were six men who were carried about by the winds since there was no land. They learned of a woman in the heavens and decided that one of them should go there because they felt that they would perish without women. The man chosen was named Wolf, and he was carried high on the backs of birds to a tree near a spring where the woman went for water. When she appeared they talked, and Wolf gave her bear fat to eat. He soon seduced her, and the master of the heavens cast her out for this act. She fell onto the back of a turtle in a sea of water where otter and fish were digging clay from the bottom to form land. The land grew little by little to its present configuration. All people are descended from this woman, who gave rise to people identified with the wolf, turtle, and other species.

Early Involvements with Non-Indians

The French entered the St. Lawrence River system in 1534 with the explorations of Jacques Cartier, and they soon established contact with the Algonquian, Huron, and Montagnais Indians. By the time the imaginative and aggressive French explorer Samuel de Champlain turned his attention to the south, he had allied himself with the Algonquians against their enemies, the Iroquois League tribes. Little did Champlain realize what a powerful adversary he was to confront. As Francis Parkman (1901, 9) wrote, the League was "foremost in war, foremost in eloquence, [and] foremost in their savage arts of policy. . . ." In 1609 Champlain, with a group of Algonquians, canoed to the lake that bears his name and met a party of Iroquois. The Iroquois attacked with confidence, only to be defeated by the white men in strange garb who used exotic weapons (see Figure 12-2). Although they were initially defeated

Figure 12-2 | The defeat of the Iroquois by Samuel de Champlain and Algon-quians at Lake Champlain in 1609. (By permission of the Champlain Society.)

in battle, the Iroquois had political genius and a strategic location, so Europeans colonizing in the Northeast were obligated to work out agreements satisfactory to these Indians. The goals of member tribes sometimes differed from those of the League itself, and this required further European accommodations, especially in the seventeenth and eighteenth centuries.

THE FUR TRADE   Early Iroquois relations with the French, Dutch, and English focused primarily on the fur trade. These Indians were attracted to the fur trade because they sought European manufactures, especially the firearms that could advance their political interests. The Mohawk, as the easternmost Iroquois tribe, became middlemen in the fur trade; they obtained pelts from more remote Indians and exchanged them with Europeans for goods that they then traded to the other Indians for economic gain and political advantage. Thus the Mohawk increased their influence over other members of the League and over non-Iroquois. Yet the Mohawk were not powerful enough to conquer the other Iroquois, and they depended on them to obtain furs from more distant Indians. For example, the Seneca, the most numerous tribe of the League and the westernmost ɔne, partially controlled Mohawk access to furs. Among Europeans involved in fur trading, the French dominated to the north along the St. Lawrence River drainages; the Dutch, followed by the English, came to control the Hudson River sector and regions to the south. This distribution of European colonials forced the Iroquois to contend with the intense rivalry between the French and English.

QUEEN ANNE'S WAR AND KING GEORGE'S WAR As colonial Europeans began dealing with one League tribe after another, the tribes debated within the League about whom to choose as allies. These decisions usually led to raids and counterraids by both the Europeans and their Indian allies. During Queen Anne's War (the War of the Spanish Succession) between the English and French, beginning in 1702, the Iroquois as a whole remained neutral because their interests were divided. However, in 1704 those Mohawk who had been induced by French Jesuits to settle at St. Louis or Caughnawaga, near Montreal, accompanied a French-led party to Deerfield, Massachusetts, where about 110 English were taken prisoner and about 50 others were killed.

When Queen Anne's War ended in 1713, English control over much of eastern North America was consolidated, and members of the League were recognized as British subjects. For the Iroquois the most important implication was that the Mohawk valley was opened to white settlers. A Church of England missionary began working with the Indians but met with little success. One missionary complaint was the traffic in intoxicants from Dutch traders to the Indians. The Iroquois passion for alcohol is well documented, and the missionary unsuccessfully attempted to stem its flow. In 1719 he abandoned the mission. Incidentally, it was in 1712 that the Jesuit Father Lafitau arrived in New France and began his six-year stay at Caughnawaga, working among the Mohawk there.

In the 1710s, British traders expanded into Ohio under the protection of their Iroquois allies. These traders continued moving westward from 1740 to 1748 during King George's War (the War of the Austrian Succession) between the French and English. At that time the Iroquois attempted to remain neutral, although some Mohawk fought the French. When the war ended, an English missionary founded a mission among the Mohawk. The Indians were friendly and had retained at least some of what they had been taught by his predecessors. In fact, one Indian had taken it on himself to spend most of his time preaching and instructing others. The distressing aspects of the situation were that intoxicants had become popular among the Indians and that Roman Catholic priests at Fort Frontenac (Kingston, Ontario) had been successful in inducing more Mohawk to move to Canada.

THE FRENCH AND INDIAN WAR About 1750 the French sought to dominate the Lake Erie and Lake Ontario regions as well as to establish closer contacts with the Cayuga, Onondaga, and Seneca by building a mission at the junction of the Oswegatchie and St. Lawrence rivers. A major in the colonial militia, George Washington, unsuccessfully attempted to induce the French to abandon one post they had seized. He later fought the French to dislodge them from the upper Ohio River area but was defeated; this greatly strengthened the position of the French with local Indians. In 1756 a formal war, the French and Indian War (Seven Years' War), was declared between England and France. The English were defeated soundly until they took Fort Frontenac, which soon forced the French to withdraw from Fort Duquesne, later called Fort Pitt and then Pittsburgh. In 1759 the English began a two-pronged attack against the French that led to an end of French colonial power in Canada. At the famous battle for Quebec on the Plains of Abraham, the English line met the charging French and did not fire until the advancing army was thirty-five paces away. The French force nearly was destroyed, and a French effort to re-take Quebec ended in failure. In the spring of 1760 the English formulated a plan to take Montreal with converging armies. The plan succeeded, and by the end of the year the French had been forced to surrender their principal hold-ings in North America.

At the opening of the French and Indian War, the Iroquois sought neu-trality, but this proved impossible. It was in the best interest of some Mohawk to support the English, whereas the Seneca aided the French. With an English victory the political power of the Iroquois diminished because the English no longer needed them as a buffer against the French. As a result, English colo-nists now became able to settle Indian lands to the west without serious Iro-quois intervention.

The British government acted in 1763 to license traders to Indians and to prohibit the alienation of Indian lands except with the approval of the governor-in-council. These were two extremely important precedents in guid-ing Indian policies in Canada and the United States.

THE AMERICAN REVOLUTION AND JOSEPH BRANT The final political drama in which the Iroquois were to play a significant role in American his-tory began in 1775. In general, the Iroquois were loyal to the British, who sought their active support. The second Continental Congress created an In-dian Department, whose primary goal was to render Indians neutral. An Iro-quois leader loyal to the British, Joseph Brant, visited England in 1775. While there, he was made a captain in His Majesty's Army and pledged Iroquois aid to the British. On his return, Brant led a force of Mohawk against the Ameri-can rebels. With the Declaration of Independence in 1776, the political break with the British was complete, and war began. The League policy of unanim-ity broke down as a result of the conflict. The Mohawk and Onondaga were divided internally, some favoring each side; the Cayuga and Seneca supported the loyalists; the Oneida and Tuscarora in theory were neutral but aided the rebels.

After the successful attack by forces under Joseph Brant and Walter But-ler to the south of the Mohawk River, the Americans organized an army against these Iroquois. In 1779 the troops of General John Sullivan destroyed Iroquois communities, crops, and grain caches. Iroquois effectiveness was ended, and many fled to Canada, abandoning their traditional lands forever. In Canada the Mohawk settled temporarily near Montreal, where they were given lands. When the treaty of peace was signed in 1783, no mention was made of the In-dians and their future status. In recognition of Mohawk aid, the British granted these Indians land along the northern shore of Lake Ontario and along Grand

River, which flows into Lake Erie. About sixteen hundred Iroquois began moving to the Grand River drainage in 1784. A small portion of this area is the modern Six Nations Reserve. A separate treaty was made between the Six Nations and the United States, in which the Oneida and Tuscarora, who had remained relatively neutral in the conflict, were permitted to retain most of their land, but the other League nations, who had fought for the British, were forced to relinquish claim to most of their land.

THE WAR OF 1812 The last time the Six Nations asserted political power in an international dispute was in the War of 1812. The Americans were quick to assure the Six Nations members that invading forces would not disturb their interests, but the Iroquois were unimpressed. Yet they were unwilling to commit themselves wholeheartedly to the British cause for good historical reasons; an initial call to arms for the British brought forth fewer than fifty Iroquois. Later victories by the Canadians induced some five hundred Six Nations warriors to fight with distinction, but before the end of the war any effective Iroquois cooperation had ceased.

| Early Historic Life

One difficulty in assembling Iroquois sources is in separating information about the Iroquois in general from that pertaining to a single member tribe. The problem cannot be resolved successfully because we do not have parallel information for all the League tribes. The descriptions to follow represent a composite view stressing the Mohawk and Seneca. A second difficulty is in obtaining comprehensive accounts of early historic conditions; thus, this sketch represents a reconstruction of Iroquois life from diverse historic sources.

CLOTHING Iroquois garments were made principally from deerskins sewn with deer-bone awls and sinew threads. Women wore underskirts that hung from the waist to just above the ankles, with designs in porcupine quills along the lower border. Over this garment they wore long dresses with fringed sleeves and fringe along the bottom. From their knees to their moccasins they wore short leggings, and in cold weather they wore a skin cape about the shoulders. Men wore kilts that reached their knees, were belted at the waist, and were fringed at the bottom and decorated with dyed quills sewn on to form designs. Men also wore fringed shirts and long, fringed leggings; on their feet they wore quill-decorated moccasins.

SETTLEMENTS AND MANUFACTURES The Iroquois customarily built villages on hilltops and usually occupied a particular community for about ten years. After this period accessible farmland was relatively unproductive, firewood scarce, and dwellings decaying. About twelve Iroquois villages, each with three to six hundred residents, are reported before the turn of the eighteenth century. The Mohawk had three communities, and a series of major and minor trails connected these with the other settlements of the League. Villages were not dispersed widely but clustered along an east-west line. Specially trained runners could carry messages throughout the League in about three days.

A typical village was surrounded by a ditch and up to three rows of wooden palisades. Beyond the enclosure were many acres of cultivated fields. Dwellings, of the well-known longhouse type, were from 50 to 130 feet long and about 16 feet wide. A house was built of seasoned posts, poles, and bark. Bark was stripped from trees in sheets, and these were stacked to flatten as they dried. Four stout posts with forked tops, one at each corner, formed the outline of the structure. Smaller forked poles were spaced between the main posts, and in the crotches of the forks poles were strung; other poles were placed at right angles to form the rafters. The arched roof was made with bent poles, and an entire frame was covered with overlapping sections of bark lashed into place and held firm with retaining poles (see Figure 12-3).

A house interior was partitioned into two main sections, each about twelve feet long; between these main sections were compartments for storing

Figure 12-3 | Model of an Iroquois village with a longhouse under construction. (Courtesy of the Rochester Museum and Science Center, Rochester, NY.)

Figure 12-4 | Model of one portion of a Seneca longhouse. (Courtesy of the Rochester Museum and Science Center, Rochester, NY.)

maize and other provisions. Along the center of a longhouse were fireplaces, with each family occupying an apartment opposite a fire. Smoke from the fires drifted through an oblong roof opening that also admitted light. In windy or rainy weather bark slabs covered this opening. Each family had an apartment with two platforms, and there might be as many as twenty apartments in a house (see Figure 12-4). An upper platform, some five feet above the ground and six feet from front to back, was covered with bark, reed mats, and skins. The lower platform was of similar dimensions and was about two feet above the ground. On these platforms family members lounged or napped during the day and slept at night. At each end of a longhouse was a doorway leading into the storage rooms that opened to the outside. The outer doors were of bark and were hinged at the top. In the winter a skin covering was added to the door.

For a small family or as a temporary residence, a less permanent dwelling was built. It was triangular in outline, with poles at each corner converging at the top, and was covered with overlapping bark slabs. An opening in one side served as the doorway, and one at the top was for smoke from the interior fireplace.

Maize was stored in houses as well as in underground caches. Excavated pits were lined with bark, and the grain was placed inside. Bark slabs were added as waterproof roofing, and the cache was covered with soil. Similar underground caches were lined with deerskins to hold dry meat.

The semipermanent nature of settlements enabled the residents to accumulate considerable material property. Considering the adaptability of stone as a raw material, it might justifiably be assumed that when workable stone was available, it would be utilized extensively. Yet this was not the case among the Iroquois. Their most important use of stone was for arrow points and ax blades that they chipped (flaked) into shape; mortars and adz blades were produced by grinding and polishing stone. They preferred to work softer materials. For example, they made bark into storage containers, trays for mixing meal, deep trough-like vessels for maple sap, and ladles. Deep-bowled wooden ladles were used to eat soup or hominy. In addition grit-tempered pottery vessels were used for cooking and storage. Basketry was limited, but containers made from animal skins commonly were used to store household items. A skin bag that hung from the waist of a hunter or warrior contained most of the artifacts he required while traveling.

CONVEYANCES Summer travelers used overland trails, waterways, or a combination of the two. To carry a load, a tumpline was passed over the forehead and attached to a basket, cradleboard, or pack frame. A pack frame, made from sections of hickory, was fitted to the back and might be supported by a chest strap, a tumpline, or both. A canoe was covered with the bark of red elm or hickory since both trees were small in this area and the bark could be pried off in one piece. Canoes were from twelve to forty feet long and propelled with single-bladed paddles. The rounded ribs and the gunwales of a vessel were made from ash, and each end had a slight upturn. For winter travel, people wore relatively short and broad snowshoes made of hickory frames laced with babiche. Reportedly, a person could travel as many as fifty miles a day on snowshoes.

SUBSISTENCE ACTIVITIES Most food was cultivated, and the right to use a plot belonged to the persons who cleared and planted it. Farming was a primary activity of women, who appear to have cleared the land, sowed the seeds, cut the weeds, and harvested the crops. The most important plant raised was maize, at least fifteen varieties of which were identified. The women also planted varieties of beans and squash. In combination, the spirits of maize, beans, and squash were considered supernaturals, called the Three Sisters. The most important farming tools were the digging stick and a hoe made with a scapula blade. Tobacco was also raised for smoking in elbow pipes made from fired clay. Once planted, tobacco seeded itself and from year to year required only thinning. The leaves were picked in the fall after a frost and were dried before use. Tobacco was used only in pipes and often was kept in a weasel-skin pouch attached to a man's belt. Women collected wild plant foods, including over thirty different wild fruits and about fifty plant products ranging from roots to leaves. These were added to the maize-bean-squash diet and were important if crops failed.

Beyond the farmlands of a settlement were hunting, fishing, and collecting areas belonging to the community. From harvest time until midwinter, some people abandoned their villages and scattered to hunt; again in the early spring they left their villages to collect maple sap, fish, and hunt passenger pigeons. Deer were hunted communally by driving them between converging lines of brush with bowmen concealed at the end. The most effective means for taking a single deer was to set a spring-pole snare in the animal's trail. When the snare peg was tripped, the spring pole righted itself, and the deer was lifted into the air by its hind legs. Snares were set for bears on their trails, and as an animal became entangled, a heavy pole fell on its back to pin it down. Hunters might also chase bears for long distances until the animals tired and could be shot with arrows. When a large animal was killed in the winter near the home of a hunter, he brought it in on a toboggan improvised from bark. At other times the prey was butchered at the kill site; the meat was removed from the bones, dried before a fire, and placed in bark containers for transport.

In the late spring as women planted crops near the villages, men fished and harvested birds. A common fishing technique was to use cone-shaped traps about three feet long made from converging splints of black ash bound together with fiber cords. Such a trap was placed beneath the water facing a rapid or ripples, and the fisherman used a stick to guide fish downstream into it. Birds were snared with elm-bark nooses, and some species, especially quail and pigeons, were taken in nets made from shredded bark. After completing their spring subsistence activities, men spent most of the summer engaged in ceremonies, council meetings, and war.

The only scheduled meal was in the morning, and at this time men ate before the women and children. At other times people ate when they were hungry, but a woman always offered food to visitors and to her husband when he returned from working. Foods prepared from maize dominated, with hominy, cornmeal "bread," succotash, roasted corn, and boiled corn probably eaten most often. Of these the most important food was hominy gruel called *sagamite*, which is an Algonquian term. To prepare bread the kernels were taken from the ear, boiled in water with wood ashes to remove the hulls, ground in a tree-trunk mortar with a wooden pestle, passed through a sieve, and shaped into loaves that were boiled in water. For roasting, the ears were placed in a line next to a fire. After roasting, some ears were shelled and the grains further dried in the sun and stored. To store maize on the cob, they stripped back the husks and braided them into bundles of twenty ears each. To the maize diet, they might add meats and soups, as well as wild vegetable products.

DESCENT, KINSHIP, AND MARRIAGE   A longhouse was occupied by women of a matrilineage, their in-marrying husbands, and their children (matrilineal and matrilocal). The matrilineages were joined into fifteen named matriclans; among these were the Bear, Beaver, Deer, Hawk, Turtle, and Wolf clans. The clans of the Cayuga, Onondaga, Seneca, and Tuscarora were divided into moieties. The Mohawk and Oneida had only three matriclans. The

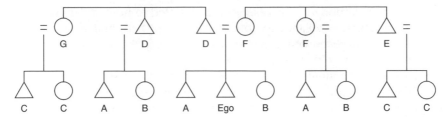

Figure 12-5 | The early historic Iroquois system of kinship terminology.

Turtle and Wolf clans formed one moiety, and the Bear the other. The matriclans cut across national lines so that members of the Wolf clan, for example, were found in each nation, in different villages within a nation, and in one or more households within a settlement. Where the moiety division existed, it once was said to have formed the exogamous unit; any combination of marriages between persons of opposite moieties was permitted. By Lewis Henry Morgan's time only clan exogamy and matrilineal descent prevailed. Inheritances were bequeathed by a man to his brothers, his sister's children, or some other person in his matriclan. The importance of the clan cannot be overestimated in Iroquois society; not only was it the property-holding unit, but it was empowered to invest, and renew if necessary, political leaders. Members cooperated in economic and political life and judged disputes with other clans. Furthermore, each clan had a common burial ground, held religious ceremonies, and could adopt outsiders.

In the kinship terminology, a person referred to her or his father and father's brother by the same word, and called the mother the same as mother's sister. There were separate and different words for father's sister and mother's brother (bifurcate merging terms). The words for parallel cousins (father's brother's or mother's sister's children) were the same as for biological brothers and sisters, but cross-cousins (father's sister's or mother's brother's children) were called cousins. This is a cousin terminology that has come to be known as the Iroquois type (see Figure 12-5). By extension, all individuals of one's matriclan, irrespective of their tribal affiliations, were drawn into the system as blood relatives. The basis of Iroquois political life was an extension of household and community kinship ties at the national and league levels.

SOCIAL DIMENSIONS   The Iroquois often have been characterized, especially in older writings, as one of the best examples of a matriarchy, but this is an unfortunate label. It does not appear that they were overtly controlled by women. Because the Iroquois were matrilineal and matrilocal and because women were a very powerful political force, it certainly is appropriate to label the Iroquois as a matricentered or matrifocal society. The position of Iroquois women in the early seventeenth century, and probably for many earlier years, was well summarized by Lafitau (1974, 69): "In them [women] resides all the real authority: the lands, fields and all their harvest belong to them; they are the soul of the councils, the arbiters of peace and war; they hold the taxes and the public treasure; it is to them that the slaves are entrusted; they arrange the marriages; the children are under their authority; and the order of succession is founded on their blood."

The Iroquois clearly distinguished between the activities of men and women, and no close bonds other than family ties joined members of the opposite sex. Men sought the company of men, and women preferred to associate with other women. The primary duties of women were to care for children; to plant, cultivate, and harvest crops; to collect wild food products; and to prepare meals. Men concentrated their energies on hunting, politics, and warfare. The behavioral ideals for each sex were set forth in their oral traditions, and children were taught these values by their parents. Each person was identified with the totemic group of his or her mother but also had a personal totem, or perhaps more aptly, a guardian spirit comparable to the Algonquian manitou. A guardian spirit, or *oki,* was acquired in a dream or vision; represented by an object in a personal medicine bundle, its purpose was to aid the possessor.

When a woman died, her farmland, along with her domestic property, usually was inherited by her children, although she might will them to other persons. A man's property normally was passed to his matrilineage, whose members disposed of his separate dwelling or apartment in a longhouse as well as his other material goods. The members might keep some items by which to remember the deceased. A man too could will his property to his wife or children if he made his desires known before a witness (see Figure 12-6).

An analysis of historical references to Tuscarora personality characteristics by Anthony F. C. Wallace (1958) provides what possibly are general traits of aboriginal Iroquois. Their "demandingness," which Wallace thought masked their extreme dependency, was best exhibited in their expectations of others; they never ceased, it seems, to expect goods and services. The same attitude was reflected in their use of intoxicants; their desire apparently knew no limits in early historic times. They blamed the difficulties resulting from intoxication on the white traders or on the rum itself but not on the person drinking it. Another striking characteristic of the Tuscarora and other Iroquois was the absence of fear of heights.

DREAMS Wallace (1958) studied early historic records about Iroquois dreams and found that the meanings they attached to dreams were in some respects similar to ideas developed by Sigmund Freud. The Iroquois in general believed that dreams expressed inner and symbolic unconscious desires, which if frustrated could cause psychosomatic illness. An individual could not always interpret his dreams properly, in which case he consulted a shaman versed in such matters. The dreamers most often mentioned in the literature

Figure 12-6 | A 1724 illustration of an Iroquois burial. (From Lafitau 1974.)

were adolescent boys who embarked on vision quests, warriors who feared torture, and the ill who feared death. The young boys had dreams of the visitation form, according to the twofold Iroquois dream classification of Wallace. In these, the supernatural communicated with the dreamer, bestowing power such as good fortune in hunting or war or some other inordinate ability. One of the most important powers given was a capacity to predict the future. Symptomatic dreams told one of the desires of his soul. Wallace (1958, 244) wrote that "the only way of forestalling realization of an evil-fated wish was to fulfill it symbolically. Others were curative of existing disorders, and prophylactic only in the sense of preventing ultimate death if the wish were too long frustrated. The acting out patterns can also be classified according to whether the action required is mundane or sacred and ceremonial." It was under the compulsion of fulfilling a symptomatic dream that men were tortured by their friends, sought some material object even if it meant great hardships, held traditional but special ceremonies, or introduced a new ritual.

In summary, Wallace's (1958, 247) concluding paragraph is best quoted.

The culture of dreams may be regarded as a useful escape-valve in Iroquois life. In their daily affairs, Iroquois men were brave, active, self-reliant, and autonomous; they cringed to no one and begged for nothing. But no man can balance forever on such a pinnacle of masculinity, where asking and being given are unknown. Iroquois men dreamt; and, without shame, they received the fruits of their dreams and their souls were satisfied.

ENTERTAINMENT Diversion in the form of games of chance and skill played an important part in Iroquois religious and social life. The contests were between individuals or teams organized within a community or beyond it, even including different tribes. The teams generally seem to have been divided along clan lines. These people were avid gamblers, and betting on the outcome of a game was intense: a man might gamble all of his property on the outcome of a game. The favorite game was lacrosse, played on a field about 450 yards long. Each of the six to eight players on a team carried a crook that had netting strung from the curved end to about halfway up the stick; the ball could be moved only with this racket. The object was to drive a deerskin ball from midfield through the opposing team's goal, which consisted of two poles near each other at one end of the field. The rules allowed a variation from five to seven in the number of goals necessary to win a game. Another game was to throw a javelin through a rolling hoop or to throw it farther than an opponent.

The snow snake game was played mainly by children. The snow snake was a thin, smoothed hickory shaft some six feet in length, with the forward end increased in diameter and slightly upturned. There were up to six players, with three to a side, and each hurled his snow snake across a snow surface. The game was scored according to the distance achieved until the specified number of points had been reached by one side. The snow boat game was based on the snow snake principle. A snow boat, constructed from a solid piece of beech wood, looked like a round-bottomed vessel with an upturned bow. The boat had small feathers at the top of the stern and an oblong central opening in which was placed an arched piece of wood hung with rattles. On a hillside each player trampled a runway in the snow, iced the depression, and propelled two or three boats down the chute and as far as possible across the snow below.

POLITICAL LIFE: THE LEAGUE OF THE IROQUOIS The League of Hodenosaunee or Iroquois was originated to bring peace among warring Iroquois tribes. The League was structured to handle civil affairs only; most military activities were pursued outside its framework. The date of the League's founding has long been disputed. Traditionally the date has been estimated as between A.D. 1400 and 1600. According to Barbara Mann and Jerry Fields (Johansen 1995), a much earlier date is more likely. Their primary supportive evidence is based on oral history and on the occurrence of an eclipse. Seneca oral history reports that the League was originated soon after a total eclipse of the sun. Mann and Field identify this eclipse as occurring on August 31, 1142.

The original League included fifty permanent offices that were filled with persons from each of the five member tribes. The Onondaga contributed fourteen; the Cayuga, ten; the Mohawk and Oneida, nine each; and the Seneca, eight. These representatives have been called sachems in the literature. This title is derived from a word used by diverse Algonquian language speakers in the eastern United States to refer to the holders of hereditary offices. Among the Iroquois a sachem was called Counselor of the People. Sachems were always men and were drawn from the matriclans of the tribes; for example, three Mohawk sachems were chosen from each of the three matriclans. The sachems collectively formed the Council of the League, which had legislative, executive, and judicial authority over the combined tribes. Historically, the first annual meetings were held at Onondaga to invest new sachems. In theory, and seemingly in fact, each member tribe had an equal voice. The unequal distribution of sachemships among the tribes was not a key to power because decisions made in the name of the League were by consensus. When the Tuscarora were adopted by the Oneida in 1722, they too became members of the League.

The stated purpose of the League was to avoid the kind of constant wars that had occurred before its foundation. League meetings were called to deal with internal and external affairs, to invest new sachems as well as mourn the ones replaced, or to carry out religious obligations. The influence of any particular sachem depended on his abilities as a speaker. Occasionally, conflict arose between different members of the same clan in different tribes. An individual's allegiance was strongest toward his own household, less important toward the clan in general, and least important beyond his tribe. Feuds sometimes erupted between clans of different tribes, but no doubt these quickly were brought before the League Council for settlement.

Sachems did not seek or gain distinction as individuals but acted collectively, and their achievements were reflected only in group judgments. At a League Council meeting, sachems could not decide an issue according to their personal feelings but were obligated to reflect their constituency. The frequency of interaction among member tribes and the close kinship bonds created a feeling of unity even when the organization was not in session. Member tribes frequently joined to hunt, fight, and participate in religious ceremonies. If a group of individuals, such as a band of warriors, chiefs, or women, thought a particular matter was important, they met to discuss the issue and appointed an orator to convey their views to a sachem. If the sachem considered the subject significant, he would introduce it at the next meeting. If an alien tribe desired to submit a question to the League, the foreign ambassador first went to the Seneca, who decided whether a question of foreign origin was important enough for a League meeting. If so, they sent runners to the Cayuga with a wampum belt into which had been "read" the time, place, and purpose of the meeting. Each member tribe in turn notified the one to the east. When the topic for consideration was of widespread interest, people came from all over the League territory. A meeting opened with prayers, and the matter at hand was put forth by the envoy, who then withdrew from the meeting. Discussions were held, and orators spoke about the issue. When the time to reach a decision arrived, groups of sachems debated among themselves until they agreed. The next step was for one from each group to act as a spokesman in consultations with other sachems who were similarly selected. Finally, the varying conclusions were offered. If consensus could not be reached, the matter was set aside. When a consensus decision was achieved, an orator summarized the proceedings and gave the decision to the envoy. Only once, it appears, was the principle of consensus set aside; this was when the Oneida sachems refused to agree with the others to side against the colonists during the American Revolution. The conclusion then was to permit each member tribe to determine its own position.

In the original League were the sachems Daganoweda and Hiawatha, the legendary founders of the League. Their offices were not filled on their deaths. Although in theory each sachem had the same power as any other, certain sachemships were more honored than others. The most notable example was the Onondaga sachem position titled Tododaho; this man had two other sachems as his assistants. The Seneca sachem Donehogaweh was the Keeper of the Door in the council house, and the Onondaga sachem Honowenato was the Keeper of the Wampum for the League. Certain obligations were attached permanently to a particular tribe of the League. The Onondaga, since they were centrally located in the League, were in charge of the council hearth and wampum. In ordinary session the Council of the League met each fall among the Onondaga. Special sessions, however, might be convened among any member tribe. The Seneca were the Keepers of the Door because they faced the hostile tribes to the west. The Mohawk, the easternmost Iroquois, were given the right to receive tribute, suggesting that the Indians to the east were subject peoples.

Any important decision was recorded through the medium of wampum. In treaties with whites as well as with other Indians, wampum belts were exchanged to bind the contract. The decision or agreement was "talked into" the beads, and the Keeper of the Wampum taught the texts to his successor. The wampum beads were spiral-shaped freshwater shells strung together or made into belts. The word *wampum* is derived from Algonquian and means "a string of white beads." In general, the Iroquois used white beads in a religious context and purple ones as a mnemonic device to recall the details of political decisions.

At the death, or removal from office, of a sachem, his successor was "raised up" at a council meeting. His former name, the one acquired as an infant, was dropped, and his new name designated the office he was to hold. The meeting was held at the council headquarters or capital of the tribe involved in the replacement, and the tribe of the sachem to be elevated served as hosts to the League. There were prayers, a mourning rite for the sachem to be replaced, recitations of ancient traditions by reading the wampums, and finally the investiture of the new sachem. The religious ceremonies were punctuated with feasting, games, and social dances that relieved the solemnity of the occasion. Sachemships were passed along matrilineal lines, with an office normally passing to a brother or to a sister's son. The abilities of logical successors were considered, and the person thought most fitted for the office was invested. If no such individual existed within a matrilineage, a rare occurrence, the selection was made from another closely related matrilineage. The most influential person in selecting a sachem was the oldest woman in the matrilineage through which the clan title passed. In the event that it was necessary to displace a sachem before his death, this action could be taken only by the clan council of the nation to which the sachem belonged.

Each nation handled its own domestic problems through its sachems. Thus, the nine Mohawk sachems were the final authorities on Mohawk internal affairs, and they functioned in the same manner as the League Council. Furthermore, if a sachem from one tribe visited another in the League, he was accorded the same status that he enjoyed at home.

After the League had been functioning for an unknown length of time, a nonhereditary office, that of chief, was created. Such a person was called Pine Tree Chief, An Elevated Name, or Brace in the Long House. Chiefs were elected by the clans of a nation for the lifetime of the individual. There was no set number of chiefs, and they were selected on the basis of such qualifications as oratorical skills or deeds in warfare. The chiefs first served as local leaders and as advisers to the sachems. Later they sat in the League Council and rivaled the sachems in authority; at this time they were invested by the sachems. According to tradition, the creation of the office of chief was the only innovation in League structure after it was founded. In general, the League was bound to follow as closely as possible the organization and purposes established at its founding.

WARFARE　It is fitting to examine some of the Iroquois's more vicious traits in warfare in order to place their practices in perspective. Methods of warfare among Europeans and Indians in eastern North America during the seventeenth and eighteenth centuries are briefly compared. The best study is by Thomas S. Alber (1992).

Scalping the dead, or in some cases the living, clearly was a custom of the pre-Columbian Indian. White explorers and colonists quickly learned to scalp their enemies. Although scalping was unknown in Europe, decapitating enemies and exhibiting their heads was reasonably common. For Indians, scalps had sacred associations, but this was not true of the European custom. Cannibalism among eastern Indians was not uncommon. Moreover, it also had sacred associations (e.g., to gain the supernatural power of a slain enemy). It was not practiced in Europe, nor did Europeans adopt the custom from Indians.

Torture in Europe was well known, not only to obtain confessions but also as a part of public executions to entertain English of French crowds. For example, in Paris in 1757 some prisoners to be hanged might first have their hands cut off or their tongues cut out. In this context, Iroquois torture techniques, soon to be described, may seem a little less barbaric.

Although not politically sanctioned in Europe, the rape of women was and remains a part of the European warfare complex. Indian warriors in eastern North America do *not* appear to have raped captive women. The evidence, slim as it may be, certainly suggests that the practice was unknown. One possible reason was that sex and warfare were incompatible ideas to warriors; they were considered to be separate domains. However, the rape of Indian women by whites occurred not infrequently.

It must finally be noted that on occasion the French in Canada during the latter seventeenth century tortured Iroquois prisoners as public spectacles.

The Iroquois League was structured to handle only civil affairs, and most military activity was pursued outside its framework. If a sachem planned to participate in warfare, he first was obligated to resign his office temporarily. When the League as a whole declared war against an enemy tribe, hostilities were coordinated by the sachem war chiefs, although these men did not necessarily play a part in the direct conflict.

The principal weapon used by the Iroquois was a wood stave or self bow with a slight outward curve at the ends; a bow was so rigid that it could be strung only with practice. The arrows were feather-vaned and tipped with antler or flint arrow points. About fifteen arrows were carried in a skin quiver that hung on a man's back. One club used in close combat was made from a two-foot length of ironwood with a large knot at the end. Another form of club had a slightly curved wooden handle, and set into the convex surface was a sharp, curved antler point. The famous tomahawk apparently was not an aboriginal Iroquois weapon, but it was known among the eastern Algonquians, from whom the word was derived. The blade was hafted in the manner of a modern hatchet. Tomahawks were soon manufactured from metal in Europe for the Indian trade, and they sometimes had pipe bowls at the heads (see Figure 12-7).

Near the center of each settlement was a war post, and a chief who sought to organize a fighting party whooped about the village, stuck a red tomahawk adorned with red feathers into the war post, and danced around it. Any man willing to join the party participated in the dance. After a band of warriors had been organized, women began preparing food for the venture. The standard fare was very dry, pulverized maize mixed with maple sugar and placed in a bearskin bag. A Pine Tree Chief customarily led a raiding party, and each was organized as a small contingent that might join one or more similar units. The units had no overall commander; each party leader was responsible for his group. Participants were free to act according to their personal feelings, and proper behavior could not be dictated. Before the

Figure 12-7 | An aquatint of an Iroquois warrior in 1787; note the war club, ax, and tomahawk. (Courtesy of the Library of Congress.)

warriors departed, at their camps, and on their return trip, they painted symbols on trees representing the number of raiders, the destination of the war party, and the outcome of the raid. When the combatants returned, the authority of the temporary leader ended. Since warfare focused the lives of men and brought them glory and prestige, the organizer of a war party could recruit a following easily. The Iroquois considered themselves at war with all Indians with whom they had no alliance; thus, there always were potential victims.

When a returning war party passed through a League village, its captives were forced to run the gauntlet naked, and according to Cadwallader Colden (1755, vol. 1, 9), "the Women are much more cruel than the Men." As the warriors approached their home village, they sounded a war whoop and danced as they led their captives. At the war post they were welcomed and praised by an elder. In reply, warriors narrated their exploits and performed the War Dance. Captives were repatriated only under extenuating circumstances. A man either was adopted into the tribe or was tortured to death. The one exception was to free an extremely brave enemy warrior. If the warriors had lost one of their number to an enemy, the Iroquois widow could adopt any male prisoner to take the place of her husband. First, however, he was obliged to run a gauntlet to his new home. The women and children lined up with whips, and the potential adoptee ran between the lines. If he stumbled and fell, he was considered an unworthy person and was killed; if he ran the lines successfully, he became a member of the tribe.

The fact that widows had first choice concerning the fate of captives has been cited as evidence that women were important in decision making. In addition, there are records of women inducing men to go on war parties or restraining them under certain circumstances. Evidence such as this has led to the generalization that Iroquois society was dominated by women. In a review of ethnohistorical writings about the status of Iroquois women, Cara B. Richards (1957) concluded that they gained dominance in relatively recent times. She notes that early reports state that the fate of captives was determined by the captor and the council. If a woman disagreed with their decision, she could not take effective counteraction until after the captor and council released the prisoner. Later in time the release of a prisoner by the council became an unimportant formality, indicating increased female authority. One factor leading to the expanding importance of women in decision making may have been the instability in village life after the introduction of firearms and the subsequent increase in mortality among warriors.

The general League pattern was to assimilate distantly related defeated tribes. Thus, after the Erie, Huron, and Neutral were conquered, they were brought into the League, but not with a voice equal to that of the original Five Nations.

The League tribes are famous not only for their complex political structure and its successful implementation, but for their treatment of prisoners. A summary of their methods prepared by Nathanial Knowles (1940, 188) gives a good idea of the variations. Among the techniques were: "applying brands, embers, and hot metal to various parts of body; putting hot sand and embers on scalped head; hanging hot hatchets about neck; tearing out hair and beard; firing cords bound around body; mutilating ears, nose, lips, eyes, tongue, and various parts of the body; searing mutilated parts of the body, biting or tearing out nails; twisting fingers off; driving skewers in finger stumps; pulling sinews out of arms; etc." Only the Onondaga tortured young and old, male and female; the other tribes reserved their tortures for men. The usual practice, except for a person slated for possible adoption, was to begin abusing a captive soon after he was taken, and to begin his systematic torture when he arrived in the settlement of the captor. The prisoner was forced to run around inside a longhouse as young men burned him, primarily on the legs, until he fainted. As he was slowly being tortured, he was expected to sing about his lack of fear. After a captive fainted, he was revived and the tortures repeated. Care was taken to see that he did not die from the tortures because he was to mount a platform at dawn. Here he was bound so that he could move about and was tortured more before the entire community. When the captive was very near the point of dying, he was stabbed to death or his head was smashed. Normally the body of a tortured person was cooked and eaten.

RELIGION   For the Iroquois, the world was occupied by a host of invisible spirits. The most powerful deity was the Great Spirit, who created people, other animals, plants, and forces for good in nature. The Great Spirit indirectly guided human affairs but could not be appealed to directly. He was capable of countering the Evil Spirit by applying his energies, and people passed through life between these competing fraternal deities. Among the lesser supernatural controlling forces for good was the Thunderer, who was capable of bringing rain or exacting vengeance, especially against witches. Associations of the Thunderer with productivity are reflected in prayers offered to him when crops were planted and thanks expressed after a harvest. The Spirit of the Winds commanded the winds and therefore could either help or harm people. The Three Sisters, the spirits of maize, beans, and squash, were conceived as lovely women and collectively called Our Life. Everything that aided people, including particular plants, fire, and water, had its spiritual associations. Some spirits assumed human form and were assigned specific obligations, and all bore the general name, the Invisible Aids. It was possible to communicate with the lesser spirits for good by burning tobacco, since it was thought that through this medium prayers and special needs could be made known to the gods. Gratitude was expressed in thanksgiving statements.

The Evil Spirit controlled a host of lesser spirit beings who brought pestilence to people and to crops, but few of these forces were systematized in the thinking of the Iroquois. One organized group of evil supernaturals was the False Faces, who were able to send death and destruction. They existed as contorted and evil-appearing faces and lived in out-of-the-way places; it was thought that anyone who chanced to see them would become paralyzed.

The most dreaded antisocial actions were believed to be performed by witches in league with the Evil Spirit. Anyone could conceivably assume the form of an animal, bird, or reptile in his or her desire to do evil. Witches were supposedly difficult to detect because they transformed themselves into inanimate objects at will. Witches were thought to have a society with regular initiations; to become a member an initiate supposedly had to kill his or her closest friend by supernatural means. Anyone who saw a witch practicing was free to kill him or her, and the normal punishment for unconfessed witches was death. It was possible to establish at a council meeting whether someone was a witch; if the accused confessed and promised to reform, he or she was freed.

Religious specialists, or Keepers of the Faith, were chosen by female and male elders of the matriclans and were expected to serve when requested. Both sexes were represented in nearly equal numbers, and all members held equal rank. Each was invested by being given a new name announced at the next general meeting of the nation. Their primary duty was to arrange and conduct the main religious ceremonies; sachems and chiefs were ex officio Keepers of the Faith. Among their other duties was the censuring of antisocial behavior; the strongest form of censure was to report serious transgressions to the tribal council. A person could choose to relinquish the obligations of Keeper of the Faith by assuming his or her old name.

Major Ceremonies The Iroquois held six major religious ceremonies; in sequence of occurrence they were the Maple, Planting, Strawberry, Green Maize, Harvest, and New Year's (Midwinter) ceremonies. The first five were similar in many respects, as in sharing the common feature of public confessions prior to group observances. During these confessions, confessors held a string of white wampum as a symbol of sincerity. The audience did not pass judgment on transgressions, but it was expected that future behavior would reflect renewed purpose and intent. On the day of any ceremony, sacred rituals were held in the morning. The religious aspects included speeches by the Keepers of the Faith about the precedent and purpose of the ceremony, offerings of burnt tobacco, prayers, and thanksgiving speeches. In the afternoon and evening, social festivities included dances and feasting. One of the most popular dances was the Feather Dance, which included not only a dance but accompanying songs of thanksgiving.

The seven-day New Year's Ceremony usually was held in early February. Before the rituals began, people who had dreamed went from house to house asking the residents to guess the nature of their dreams. When someone suggested a reasonable text and meaning for a dream, the dreamer ceased his or her quest for an interpretation. If the accepted text and its meaning included statements about the future behavior of the dreamer, she or he was obligated to behave as directed. Jesuit missionaries who witnessed the dream procedure in 1656 recorded it as a violent affair, with the dreamer threatening and actually destroying a great deal of household property until he or she was satisfied with an interpretation.

The formal New Year festivities, designed to drive away evil, were launched by two Keepers of the Faith disguised in skin robes and adorned with corn husks. On the first day, they visited each household on two separate occasions to announce the purpose of the ceremony and to sing a song of thanksgiving. The same day one or two white dogs, symbolizing purity, were sacrificed and hung from a pole. On the second day the Keepers of the Faith dressed as warriors and visited each household three different times to perform rituals that included prayer and song. The third and fourth days were devoted to dancing and visiting among the people. At this time, groups of boys, accompanied by an old woman carrying a basket, visited each house. The boys danced, and, if given presents, they all moved on. If no gifts were forthcoming, they stole whatever they could. If they were caught, they returned what they had taken. On the fifth day the sacrificed dog or dogs were placed in the council house and a speech was made about their dedication to the Great Spirit; later the dog or dogs were burned in a fire to carry a message of contrition to the Great Spirit. The Thanksgiving Dance was held on the sixth day, and gambling dominated the final day. Note that midway through and at the end of the ceremonies, time was set aside for entertainment, possibly as a relief from the intensity of the religious obligations.

False Face Society   The famous False Face Society was organized to counteract disease. A male became a participant by dreaming that he was a member and left the society by dreaming that he was no longer active. The only woman member was the Keeper of the False Faces, who not only kept the ceremonial paraphernalia but was supposed to be the only one who knew the identity of all the members. A False Face Society probably was represented in each village; its duties included curing illness and keeping evil spirits at bay. If someone was ill with a disease that was often treated by the society, and if he or she dreamed of false faces, it was a sign that the person could be cured by the False Face Society. The society was most noted for its ability to cure eye inflammations, nosebleeds, swellings, and toothaches. The Keeper of the False Faces was notified when someone hoped to be cured, and she assembled the members, each of whom covered himself with a face mask and blanket and carried a turtle-shell rattle. The members sprinkled the patient with hot ashes, performed a dance, and then withdrew. The main function of the False Face Society was to clear disease from a village at regular intervals.

The False Face Society masks were inspired by mythological beings and creatures seen during dreams. A mask was carved from a living basswood tree and portrayed one of about a dozen facial types. As the most distinguishing feature, some had crooked mouths, others a smile, some a protruding tongue, and so on (see Figure 12-8). They might be painted black, brown, red, or white. Another type of mask was made from braided and sewn corn husks.

Figure 12-8 | Two ceremonial items: a False Face mask and a cow horn rattle, shown by a dancer on his traveling rounds to private homes before a ceremony in the longhouse. (Photo by Annemarie Shimony, circa 1970.)

These represented important farming and hunting deities. Corn-husk masks also could be differentiated according to facial features.

| Later Historic Changes

The preceding chapters about specific peoples have each included sections about the life cycle, but comparable information for the Iroquois is not comprehensive for particular tribes and thus is difficult to assemble. Therefore, we now shift attention to historic changes in Iroquois life and especially to their innovative belief system, which is well documented.

THE NEW RELIGION   In the aftermath of the American Revolution, most Iroquois in New York State were forced to move because they generally had

supported the British cause. One Seneca leader, Cornplanter, and his followers eventually supported the Americans, apparently because they perceived
the Americans to be more powerful. During his official visits to Philadelphia to
seek support for the Seneca, Cornplanter became acquainted with the Quakers. In 1796 the Commonwealth of Pennsylvania granted Cornplanter a fee
patent title to three plots of land, each about one mile square, along the Allegheny River near the New York state line. Cornplanter and some four hundred followers settled at the plot called Burnt House, living in thirty dwellings.
Quaker missionaries went to Burnt House in 1798, and one of them, Henry
Simmons, stayed at the settlement. In a study of what happened at Burnt
House at this time, Merle H. Deardorff (1951) included information from Simmons's diary, an ethnographic gem, and other Quaker writings. We learn that
Simmons was asked by Cornplanter about his beliefs and that Simmons re-
sponded cautiously. As Deardorff (1951, 90) wrote:

> Questions about theology and morals had been referred to Simmons, and an-
> swered in the Quaker way: Look inside. You have a Light in there that will show
> you what is good and what is bad. When you know you have done wrong, repent
> and resolve to do better. Outward forms and books and guides are good; but they
> are made by men. The Great Spirit himself puts the Inner Light in every man. Look
> to it. Learn to read and write so that you may discover for yourself whether or not
> the white man's Book is true. Learn to distinguish good from evil so that you may
> avoid the pricks of conscience in this world and prosper; and that you may avoid
> punishment in the next.

The missionary, however, saw behavior by the Indians that was incompatible
with his beliefs. For example, Simmons objected when Iroquois trappers traded
furs for intoxicants that resulted in a community-wide binge of several weeks'
duration. Quaker reproval led the contrite Indians to appoint two chiefs to attempt to curb drinking.

At the home of Cornplanter, his half brother Handsome Lake (Ganio-
dayo) appeared to be near death in June 1799. Handsome Lake had a vision,
which Simmons detailed in his diary. Handsome Lake saw three men carrying
bushes with berries attached. The men had asked him to eat some of the
berries so that he could live to see berries ripen in the summer. They said that
the Great Spirit was unhappy about the drunkenness of the people, and if
Handsome Lake recovered, he was not to consume intoxicants. The man also
told him that he would be visited later by a fourth man.

After regaining consciousness, Handsome Lake asked Cornplanter to assemble the council, report the vision, and instruct each person to eat a dried
berry. These instructions were followed. Within a short time, Handsome Lake
had another vision in which the fourth man, presumably the Great Spirit,
pitied him and promised to end his suffering. When Handsome Lake awoke,
he sent for Cornplanter and after talking with him fell into a trance for seven
hours. Simmons (Deardorff 1951, 91) wrote, "His legs and arms were cold, his
body warm but breathless." Handsome Lake later revealed that he had been

led by a guide to meet his dead son and Cornplanter's recently deceased daughter. His son had revealed that he was sorry that he had not taken better care of his father. Cornplanter's daughter had told of her unhappiness because her father and brother argued. The guide had then said that sons should treat their fathers well and that Handsome Lake must give up intoxicants and all dances save the Green Corn Ceremony. Furthermore, Handsome Lake had been told that if the people agreed, it would be proper to accept whites as teachers. Finally, the guide had said that Handsome Lake was to return among the living and he would see no more of these things until he died; in death he would return to this setting if he behaved properly.

When Handsome Lake recovered, he began preaching his doctrine, which came to include the rejection of schools and a return to a subsistence-based economy. In 1802 his cause received American support when Handsome Lake went to Washington, D.C., with other Iroquois and President Thomas Jefferson condoned his teachings. Partly because of this official sanction, Handsome Lake became an acknowledged prophet. From the time of his recovery until his death, Handsome Lake visited Seneca communities to influence the behavior of others. By 1807 his fame as a prophet had spread widely among the Iroquois and to other eastern tribes. When the War of 1812 began, the Iroquois had learned their lesson, and most of them did not participate. Handsome Lake in particular preached neutrality because of his continuing close ties with the Quakers. In 1815 the prophet moved to Onondaga, and it was here that he died the same year.

As Deardorff has noted, the Handsome Lake revelations, or Gaiwiio (Good Message), came to be joined by a body of teachings that included biographical material, prophecy, law, parable, and anecdote. Believers called the entire system the New Religion. The Good Message was not the only basis for the New Religion; some of the more important changes proposed in the revelation had been initiated before Handsome Lake's trances. If the text of the revelations had been the only document to survive, Handsome Lake might have been assumed to be a great innovator; but from the diaries of the Quaker missionaries it is obvious that the revelations were in step with what were recognized and pressing problems at Burnt House. Although much of the Handsome Lake doctrine was influenced by Quaker and earlier Jesuit missionaries and although some aspects were novel, these teachings also had deep roots in Iroquois religious life of old. The emphasis on confession, the continuity in honoring traditional gods, and the prominence of the annual ceremonial round are examples. Furthermore, the Iroquois had long placed considerable emphasis on prophetic dreams, and this too was a critical element in the Handsome Lake revelations. Unlike many other Indian prophets, Handsome Lake was willing to adapt his basic ideas to accommodate Quaker beliefs and to accept certain material aspects of white culture, such as farming methods. This flexibility contributed to the stability of Iroquois life in his time and unquestionably aided the long-term survival of the Good Message. Soon after Handsome Lake's death, other Christian missionaries proselytized among the Seneca, and the Indians labored in council to establish a uniform approach to religion. The time-honored pattern of unanimity, however, could not be achieved, and by 1820 the New Religion had separated from other Iroquois religious systems.

The Good Message was not recorded systematically until 1845, and no single text became standard. By 1949 the New Religion was being taught in ten ceremonial structures, each termed a longhouse, on the meeting circuit of the Six Nations. Most of the preachers required four days to relate the Good Message. The Tonawanda Longhouse was called symbolically the Central Fire, and here were kept the most sacred strings of wampum that had belonged to Handsome Lake.

The New Religion includes the following tenets: the prohibition of intoxicants; obedience of children toward their parents and care of aged parents; faithfulness of married couples; reproval of gossiping or boasting; killing of witches; awareness of a hell for sinners and heaven for persons who have lived good lives or repented of having lived evil lives; and the acceptance of the ways of whites save for schools. As has been noted by Edmund Wilson (1960, 87), the New Religion "has a scope and a coherence which have made it endure as has the teaching of no other Indian prophet, and it is accepted at the present time by at least half the Iroquois world as a source of moral guidance and religious inspiration."

OTHER CHANGES The course toward modern Iroquois life was set in the early nineteenth century. Many of those Iroquois who sympathized with the British had moved to Canada, and the ones in the United States had settled on small reservations. Each of these two major groups had its own chiefs, councils, and wampum, and each became increasingly involved in reservation or reserve politics and relationships with the respective governments. In the early 1800s the Iroquois in both countries continued to hunt over broad areas that reached beyond their boundaries and to plant traditional crops in old ways. However, as increasing numbers of white settlers occupied nearby land, Iroquois life began to change in basic ways.

The ability of the Indians to hunt profitably declined as the supply of game diminished; furthermore, they no longer could move from one area to another as the productivity of their farmland declined. Consequently, they turned increasingly to plow agriculture, farming in the manner of whites. In New York State, the Iroquois depended heavily on annuities derived from the sale of land to obtain items of material culture such as blankets, guns, and farming equipment. Annuity payments unquestionably eased their transition to a more sedentary life-style. The greatest threat to their security was continued encroachment of whites on their lands; another concern was the conflict arising from the pull of traditional Iroquois culture and the attractions of white culture. This inevitably caused factions to develop on reservations and reserves that have continued into the present.

The Six Nations Reserve

One present-day Iroquois stronghold is in western Ontario, along the Grand River. As compensation for land lost in New York State following the American Revolution, the Mohawk war chief Joseph Brant received an original tract of 675,000 acres from the British. In 1784–85, about 1450 League members began to settle along Grand River; they were accompanied by nearly 400 persons from other tribes who had lived among the Iroquois before the American Revolution. Most migrants were Mohawk, but the other League tribes were also represented, exemplifying the ideal structure of the League.

Brant claimed that the land grant showed British recognition of Iroquois national sovereignty, and he felt free to do as he wished with the land. Soon he had sold about half of the acreage to whites. He felt that white farmers in their midst would encourage Indian men to farm. The Mohawk, Oneida, and Tuscarora lived largely along upper Grand River and became known as the Upper Tribes. Many had been Christianized before migrating to the reserve, and they were as a group reasonably responsive to becoming more like white Canadians. Down the river were the Lower Tribes, the Cayuga, Onondaga, and Seneca, who retained a far more traditional way of life and were receptive to the Good Message of Handsome Lake.

People in the Six Nations Reserve lived on scattered homesteads by the 1950s, and individual holdings were inherited by members. The stress placed by Canadians on paternal inheritance had confused the traditional matrilineal system. Inheritance rights, like individual rights to band membership, were calculated patrilineally according to the Canadian authorities but matrilineally by the Iroquois. Another difference was that Canadians considered the nuclear family an important social unit, and their emphasis on it robbed the clans of important functions. A newly married couple on reserve land now lived either with the husband's or wife's relatives only until they could establish an independent household (neolocal residence). The exogamous nature of the matriclans continued to be observed by some people, but others felt it was acceptable to marry anyone to whom close genealogical ties could not be established. The matrilineages remained important in selecting sachems and chiefs of the clan, but disputes arose over which were the leading lineages with the vested rights. Members of the leading lineages of a clan most often made an effort to retain their clan ties so that they would not lose their political and religious authority. A real difficulty, however, stemmed from the fact that even some conservative families could no longer trace their clan affiliations.

By 1956 the reserve population, most of whom were Mohawk and Cayuga, numbered about sixty-five hundred. Today the population exceeds twenty thousand. In the 1950s Annemarie A. Shimony first studied reserve Indians who had adopted some white ways but had categorically rejected assimilation into greater Canadian culture. No attempt is made here to summarize her wealth of information; instead, the focus is first on the New Religion and then on political developments since a critical year, 1924.

THE NEW RELIGION ON THE RESERVE   The New Religion had four local congregations, each symbolized by a type of fire and centered at a different longhouse. The Central Fire was the Tonawanda Longhouse in New York State. Here preachers on the longhouse circuit were invested, but the Central Fire had no jurisdiction over the Home Fires. The rituals of the four longhouses were essentially the same. Each longhouse had wampum to validate its legitimacy, and the particular one to which a person belonged was determined by matrilineage ties and by its proximity. Longhouses were the traditional rectangular wooden buildings, usually with doors and wood-burning stoves at each end and with benches along the walls.

Longhouse leaders were Keepers of the Faith or deacons, as they more commonly were called. Each longhouse had a leading male and female Keeper of the Faith, chosen on the basis of merit. They guided all longhouse functions. With a breakdown of the clan structure, Keepers of the Faith as a group had an increased voice in community affairs. A second longhouse functionary, the Keeper of the Fire, was the guardian of the longhouse wampum. His moiety and clan affinities were unimportant, but he had to be a staunch believer in the New Religion. The wampum was symbolic of the longhouse traditions, and the people believed that Canadian officials sought to destroy the wampum and thereby eliminate the longhouses. The final longhouse leader was the Speaker, who presented traditional and extemporaneous speeches to the congregation. Such persons did not hold a formal office, nor were they usually preachers on the longhouse circuit. A Speaker was required to have a talent for public speaking and knowledge of traditional speeches.

A longhouse served many functions in the members' efforts to resist becoming like other Canadians. The organization fulfilled social, medical, economic, and political needs. Social gatherings included softball or lacrosse games, raffles, and dances. Organized social activities sponsored outside the longhouse usually were closed to longhouse members by their own dogma. The longhouse ceremonial round was rich in detail; it was based on the Handsome Lake revelations, as well as the aboriginal planting and harvest ceremonies and the old and new means for curing. An important aspect of almost any longhouse function was the recitation of a formal address of thanks to the Great Spirit for the continued life of the persons attending and thanks to the participants for attending. In all longhouse activities the ritual and social language was Iroquois; speaking English was disapproved of in any context. To the members, participation in longhouse events gave real purpose to life and at the same time offered a systematic philosophy for living. People were encouraged to remember the teachings of Handsome Lake and to live good lives. At times the younger members were told not to imitate such fashion extremes of whites as high-heeled shoes and low-cut dresses for girls. Neither should one listen to the radio, watch television, or drink intoxicants, for such behavior was not in keeping with the New Religion. Behind it all was the real fear that the longhouse members would become carbon copies of their white

Canadian neighbors. The conflict of values seems often to have led to trauma at the time of death for those individuals who had at some time followed forbidden white ways.

For members of the New Religion and other Iroquois as well, there was a deeply rooted focus on death. Death supposedly could be caused by failure to accept a time-honored view about the spirit world, by showing a lack of respect for plants or animals, or by failing to hold rituals as directed. Furthermore, the dead had great power over the living, and to neglect them was an invitation to disease and death. In general, it was thought that souls resided in a pleasant upperworld or else suffered punishment. Souls bent on evil could assume animal forms, but ordinarily they were nonmaterial or a light vapor. All of this concern with death and the dead necessitated the proper performance of obligations to the dead. To avert death and illness for the community or the individual, the Ceremony for the Dead was held at least once and preferably twice each year.

The sachems, who were either Christians or members of the New Religion, represented traditional authority and formed the official political body of the Six Nations Reserve until 1924. The longhouse sachems considered that their Christian counterparts were not legitimate officeholders unless they had been invested at a longhouse ceremony, which was comparable to raising up a sachem in the old League. With respect to Canadian officials, the sachems were divided over whether or not they favored closer rapport. In 1924 some World War I veterans, especially those from the Upper Tribes, formed a group known as the Progressive Warriors and sought Canadian recognition of an elected council. During an ensuing investigation of Six Nations Reserve affairs, the sachems would not present their case to Canadian representatives; thus, the government heard from only the acculturated faction, which supported elected chiefs. The Canadians decided in favor of elected leaders, since they received little cooperation from the sachems, who represented the traditional confederacy council. An elected council was installed in 1924; the New Religion sachems were locked out of the council house, and Royal Canadian Mounted Police officers enforced the government's decision. The supporters of the confederacy were bitter against the Canadians as well as against their factional opposites, and the bitterness continues to the present. In an ethnohistorical account about the relatively recent past on the reserve, Sally M. Weaver (1972) has noted that the confederacy council refused to disband after the elected council was instituted and continued to hold regular meetings in the hope of being reinstated as the only legitimate authority.

POPULATION DISPERSAL AND DIVISIONS   Life became difficult on the Six Nations Reserve during the Great Depression (1929–39); some families left to find seasonal work, while others returned because on the reserve they could at least raise their own food. Again during World War II, the population dispersed, as many people left the reserve to find factory jobs or enlist in the services. Following this exodus came another change during the 1950s as increasing numbers of residents worked in nearby cities and the reserve itself became steadily more suburban.

Six Nations Reserve residents remain deeply divided, as some support a Christian life-style and others adhere to the longhouse traditions. The groups are socially distinct and antagonistic. Those faithful to the longhouse are proud of being Iroquois, adhere to the New Religion, and participate in the annual round of what have become traditional ceremonies. They follow the matrilineal descent system and support the confederacy, whose chiefs usually are longhouse members. Those residents who belong to the Christian group may identify themselves as Iroquois, yet their behaviors and beliefs appear to be much the same as those of white Canadians. Most residents, whether Christian or longhouse supporters, are preoccupied with local politics, and particular issues have varied combinations of supporters. Confederacy members in general resent the power of the band council, which began expanding its dominance in the 1960s. They likewise object to accepting social benefits, such as aid to the aged and to unmarried mothers, provided by the Canadian government, because to do so is to acknowledge federal control. However, they do accept this and other aid despite their philosophical objections.

| Recent Developments on the Reserve

In the bylaws of the Six Nations Reserve, the only legal residents are the approximately 20,000 band members, of whom about 9500 lived on the reserve in 1997. Thus, if a band (i.e., federally recognized) member marries a non-band member, the latter technically cannot reside on the reserve; however, the bylaw is not enforced on a consistent basis. This in turn has led to challenges in the Ontario court system based on racial rights in Canada. At issue is whether members of the reserve band can establish their own residence laws. It must be emphasized that they are legally defined as "allies" of the Crown, not subjects of the Crown, irrespective of Canadian law. The Six Nations own their land; it is not Crown land. To have their own residency laws on the reserve represents one effort to be more fully self-governing (see Figure 12-9).

In another context, the Canadian government has transferred the funding and partial control of some programs to the Six Nations band council. By 1994 the band had received nearly $21 million dollars from the federal government and nearly $8 million dollars from the provincial government. Most of this money supported the band council government, infrastructure, and social services. Thus, the Six Nations have gained and continue to gain greater local administrative power.

By the late 1990s, elected band council members were far less sympathetic to Canadian government policies than they had been in 1924. The traditional leaders as hereditary chiefs have maintained a "shadow government"

Figure 12-9 | Erik Bruce Isaacs, a Cayuga, won the "Typical Baby Indian" award at the Six Nations Fall Fair in 1983. (Courtesy of the *Brantford Expositor*.)

on the reserve up to the present. In some contexts, the traditional council leaders—with considerable authority but no formal power support the posi tions of the elected leaders in a more united effort to gain autonomy. One ongoing problem is that the federal, provincial, and local Canadian governments have refused to recognize the hereditary council. One instance in which the two councils are united is an effort to establish a traditional Iroquois justice system on the reserve despite Euro-Canadian opposition.

The potential of casino gambling sponsored by the Six Nations is currently a divisive political issue. The probable economic benefits appeal to some residents, whereas others object on moral or religious grounds. Supporters argue that the goal of self-government cannot be achieved without a sound economic base for the band and that gambling profits would be a relatively reliable source of revenue. The band intermittently operates relatively high-stakes bingo and is contemplating the construction of a permanent local bingo hall. Equally if not more appealing is an effort to launch a casino at Niagara Falls, Ontario. Niagara Falls already has a highly profitable casino operated by the province and a second provincial casino there is in the planning stage. It appears that the provincial government may have a difficult time blocking the construction of a Six Nations casino at Niagara Falls.

For most band members, a disturbing development emerged first in 1988 when a militant group, the Warrior Society, began patrolling the reserve as nonlegal police. The hereditary and elected chiefs alike denounced the Warriors, and the patrols soon ceased. By 1994 they had few members and sympathizers, perhaps a total of only forty individuals. One major problem, however, is that the Warriors, like the hereditary chiefs, seek far greater independence from Canadian government control. Both groups seek an Iroquois government. However, the Warriors have been known to engage in illegal activities such as smuggling alcoholic beverages, guns, tobacco, and drugs into Canada from Iroquois reservations in the United States. Traditional and elected band leaders alike fear that these Warrior activities will not only undermine the basis for band control on the reserve but may also provide the Canadian government with reasons for abrogating the rights of Six Nations Reserve members. Before the provincial government reduced the tax on tobacco products, smuggling them into Canada from the United States was a highly lucrative endeavor. Some smugglers on the reserve became multimillionaires. An example such as this one makes most reserve residents fear the corrupting influence of the Warriors on individuals and on the quality of reserve life.

In 1997 an estimated 9500 Iroquois lived on the reserve, and they have been increasingly concerned about the perpetuation of Iroquois culture. The Woodland Cultural Centre at Brantford includes a museum, archives, and numerous programs that stress traditional Indian life. One major fear is that their aboriginal languages will become extinct. In 1998 at the Six Nations Reserve no one spoke Seneca or Tuscarora, and the other Iroquoian languages combined were probably spoken by fewer than 350 persons altogether. Most important, longhouse ceremonial texts are traditionally delivered in an Iroquoian language, and about 50 percent of the reserve residents are members of a longhouse. Although a local radio station, CKRZ, includes Iroquoian-language texts and programs, these efforts do not appear to be very effective in language instruction.

In 1986 concerned parents launched a language program to teach Mohawk and Cayuga at a small number of reserve schools. Mohawk and Cayuga are taught in an immersion program. At one such school, more than half of the approximately three hundred students participate in dual-language instruction that begins in kindergarten. About fifteen students in eleventh grade who have been in the program since entering school are able to speak either Mohawk or Cayuga. When a white teacher refused to allow two students to speak Cayuga in her English class in 1996, parental protestors closed the school until the teacher was removed. Confrontations continue to be a powerful weapon on the reserve. The situation is currently at an impasse as the Six Nations strive to gain complete control over the educational system. They were scheduled to assume control in 1997, but action has been delayed by the federal authorities who fund the schools.

The Six Nations Reserve is among the strongest centers for the perpetuation of traditional Iroquois culture in Canada and the United States. Their sense of Indian identity, much greater than it was twenty years ago, continues to grow with each confrontation with Canadian authorities. The Six Nations willingly concede little to Euro-Canadians, not only because the reserve residents own the land they occupy but also because they continue to consider themselves "allies of the Crown," not its subjects. As the Mohawk linguist, longhouse member, and political activist Amos Keye says, "Lead, follow, or get out of the way!"

| Skywalkers

The word "skywalkers" refers to Indian ironworkers, especially Mohawk, who construct skyscrapers, bridges, and other high steel structures. Since the late 1940s ethnographic and popular accounts have praised their inordinate success in this dangerous occupation. The best overview of the skywalkers is by Richard Hill (1987), an ironworker.

Traditionally, as discussed earlier in this chapter, warfare was a primary focus among Iroquois men, but occurrences of war diminished rapidly following the War of 1812. Some of the men became canoemen (*voyageurs*) in the fur trade—a dangerous occupation, especially when in enemy country. This trade, however, began to decline about 1800. Adventurous men were next drawn to the timber industry; rafting logs through fast water and rapids was hazardous work. At about the same time, other men became farmers, and still others began to travel about New England selling Indian medicines.

Reports about the Mohawk dating from colonial times suggest that at least some men did not fear heights. They were observed crossing deep creeks by walking fearlessly on small poles and had been seen casually striding along the peaked ridge of a gabled house. Some outsiders have suggested that an absence of a fear of heights was inborn, but it seems more likely that the trait was learned. Irrespective of the basis for this propensity, it received a clear test in 1850 with the construction of a railway bridge near Montreal. The Victoria Bridge was to be buttressed on the Caughanawaga (Kahnawake) Reserve. In exchange for the building rights, the railway agreed to hire local Mohawk to quarry and haul stone to support the bridge. Before long the project construction engineer could not prevent Mohawk men from walking the iron support beams. The French construction workers were timid, and as a partial result, a Mohawk crew was hired. This appears to have been their introduction to ironwork (see Figure 12-10).

In realistic terms, however, the Mohawk did not begin to work iron systematically until 1886, when a cantilever bridge, known as the "black bridge," was built across the St. Lawrence River and buttressed on the Caughnawaga Reserve. The earlier experience on the Victoria Bridge was repeated. It appears that three crews were trained on the black bridge. In the construction of a bridge of this nature, precut and drilled beams and girders were hoisted in

Figure 12-10 | Iroquois ironworkers in 1983 at Niagara Falls, New York. (Courtesy of Richard W. Hill, Sr.)

place with a crane or derrick, temporarily bolted and plumbed, and then riveted. The Mohawk became members of riveting crews, both the most dangerous and the most lucrative work.

By 1907 there were over seventy skilled Mohawk ironworkers. Thirty-eight were working on the Quebec Bridge across the St. Lawrence River near Quebec City. On August 19, 1907, while still under construction, the bridge collapsed, killing ninety-six workers, thirty-three of whom were Mohawk. Bridge work then took on a new meaning; because it obviously was dangerous, it became an attractive type of employment to Mohawk men. Mohawk women, however, insisted that the gangs of ironworkers hire out on many different projects so that another disaster could not devastate so many families at the same time (see Figure 12-11).

Over the years, some Mohawk who attempted to become ironworkers failed because they feared heights or found the work unappealing. To others, however, it was exciting work, and the comparatively high wages were espe-

Figure 12-11 | Stan Hill, a Mohawk ironworker in 1973. (Courtesy of Richard W. Hill, Sr.)

cially attractive. In the early 1900s Mohawk and other Iroquois men began working on jobs in the United States and established skywalker colonies in such cities as Buffalo and Brooklyn in New York State. They were among the earliest modern urban Indian populations. Following World War II, Iroquois from each of the U.S. reservations and Canadian reserves had become skywalkers. By the late 1980s, about 7000 of an estimated 130,000 Indians from all tribes were ironworkers in the United States and Canada. Thus Indians, especially Mohawk, are the best known skywalkers, but they obviously represent a minority of the persons, including some women, who work in high steel. (The first steel-framed skyscraper dates from 1886.) Despite their smaller numbers, it appears that Indian skywalkers are maimed or killed in accidents at about the same rate as non-Indians.

In a search for the reasons behind Mohawk success as ironworkers, Morris Freilich (1958) learned that Mohawk men were not free from fear of heights but that they concealed their fear in order to behave as warriors and prove their courage. Also, work in high steel was highly compatible with many essential features of the old Mohawk way of life. The men left home to work for extended periods as they had left to hunt and fight in aboriginal times. There was danger and possible death in what they did, just as there had been of old.

When a man returned, he could boast of the tall buildings on which he had worked, just as he once had boasted of his skills in combat. The modern steelworker was subject to little authority, and if he was displeased he could quit his job, just as he formerly had been able to drop out of a war party. These and other parallels lent support to the traditional status of the male in a nontraditional setting. Yet when an ironworker retired, he was likely to return to a reservation or reserve. His adjustment to an uneventful and sedentary life was difficult. One response was to readopt Indian ways, to the point of refusing to speak English, and to become deeply involved in local social life and politics.

| Nationalism and Sovereignty

As the twentieth century progressed, the Iroquois increasingly asserted their nationalism. In World War I, the Iroquois in the United States, as a separate entity, declared war on Germany. In Canada, the people of the Six Nations Reserve had a forceful confrontation with the Royal Canadian Mounted Police in 1924 to assert their national sovereignty. In both countries, the Iroquois tend not to vote in non-Indian elections as a means of emphasizing their separate identity. In New York State, the Iroquois have forcefully resisted efforts by state officials to intervene in their affairs. Predictably, in the United States the Iroquois have avoided paying state and federal income taxes and fought varied efforts to use reservation lands for the St. Lawrence Seaway, the Power Authority of New York State, and the relocation of highways or the building of dams. These disputes have often been complicated by the fact that elected leaders cooperate with the whites, whereas hereditary leaders continue to support the Iroquois Confederacy (see Figure 12-12).

Yet times are changing! In 1976 the Seneca of the Allegheny Reservation signed an agreement with New York State *as equals.* This was the first time since the early 1800s that the state had recognized the sovereign or national status of the Seneca. To build a highway through the reservation, the state attempted to exercise its power of eminent domain, but the courts, including the U.S. Supreme Court, held that the state had no right to condemn reservation lands for the highway. As a result, the state negotiated with the Seneca and received an easement of, but not title to, 795 acres of land. In return the state agreed to pay $2 million, give the Indians *title* to 795 acres of land from the adjoining Allegheny State Park, and provide other benefits.

The Iroquois have long been adamant in asserting that the governments of Canada and the United States must acknowledge their distinct national identity and deal with them as a sovereign nation on the basis of negotiated treaties. In the recent past, the federal government of the United States had refused to entertain the concept of "nations within a nation," but as indicated in the previous paragraph, the federal courts began to be far more sympathetic to sovereignty cases in the mid-1970s (see also Chapter 2).

Among the Iroquois, other Indians, and Euro-Americans alike, Indian gambling has been and remains a divisive issue. Some Iroquois favor it, whereas others are clearly opposed. One early basis for Indian gambling was

Figure 12-12 | This statue of Joseph Brant was unveiled at Brantford, Ontario, in 1886. In a 1990 protest, the blindfold over Brant's eyes and the sign symbolized a major confrontation with the Canadian government. At the Oka Reserve, Quebec, the Mohawk contested the proposed construction of a golf course on an Iroquois burial ground. The conflict peaked in a standoff between the Iroquois and Canadian military forces. The golf course was not built. (Courtesy of the *Brantford Expositor.*)

on the Oneida Reservation in New York State, and the circumstances merit review. Public bingo was launched in 1975, but the prize money awarded was in greater amounts than the state permitted. The operation was soon closed by county authorities. However, this effort initiated gambling on reservations and led to many court cases before gambling was finally sanctioned by the federal government (see also Chapter 2). In 1993 the 1100 Oneida opened another gambling facility, the Turning Stone Casino. Soon after opening, the casino was employing about 1500 people and beginning to attract some 7000 visitors each day. Within a few years, gambling profits revolutionized the quality of reservation life. By 1996 some elderly people who had never dreamed of having adequate housing began to occupy up-to-date dwellings funded by gambling profits, as well as by Department of Housing and Urban Development funds. They built a new health care clinic, day care center, and recreational center for young people. Before the casino operation, only two Oneida had attended college; soon after, thirty-eight received scholarships. Furthermore, the Oneida have been buying available local farmland; as a result, the original 32-acre reservation now includes nearly 4000 acres. As the Oneida leader Ray Halbritter said (McAuliffe 1996, 8), "Our future depends on our ability to take care of ourselves, not on our ability to get anybody else to look out for us by either giving us money or having a law that protects you. We've really got to, number one, develop our own empowerment. Gaming gives us one step in that direction."

| Additional Sources

The book by Lewis Henry Morgan (New York, 1851; also 1901, 1904, and 1954 editions) remains the standard Iroquois source. The first systematic Iroquois study by Joseph François Lafitau, translated and edited by William N. Fenton and Elizabeth L. Moore (vol. 1, Toronto, 1974; vol. 2, Toronto, 1977), is an ethnographic classic. The most comprehensive recent study, concerning the Six Nations Reserve, is by Annemarie A. Shimony (Syracuse, 1961; revised, Syracuse, 1994). *The Mohawk* (New York, 1992) by Nancy Bonvillain and *The Iroquois* (New York, 1988) by Barbara Graymont provide overviews. A notable historical account is *The Ordeal of the Longhouse* (Chapel Hill, 1992) by Daniel K. Richter. Uneven presentations about the Iroquois tribes are included in the *Northeast* volume (15) of the *Handbook of North American Indians,* William C. Sturtevant, general editor (Washington, DC, 1978). A book of particular interest is *The Reservation* (Syracuse, 1978) by Ted C. Williams, an anthropologist and the son of a Tuscarora sachem; the text concerns life on the Tuscarora Reservation in the 1930s and 1940s. *The Death and Rebirth of the Seneca* (New York, 1970) by Anthony F. C. Wallace may be the finest ethnohistory by an Americanist. *The Iroquois Struggle for Survival* (Syracuse, 1986) and *The Iroquois and the New Deal* (Syracuse, 1981), both by Laurence M. Hauptman, examine aspects of relatively recent political life in perceptive detail. Furthermore, the writings by William N. Fenton about various aspects of Iroquois life are superior.

| Selected Bibliography

Alber, Thomas S. 1992. Scalping, torture, cannibalism and rape. *Anthropologica* 34: 3–20.

Beauchamp, William M. 1926. The principal founders of the Iroquois League and its probable date. *Proceedings of the New York State Historical Association* 24: 27–36.

Biggar, H. P., ed. 1925. *The Works of Samuel de Champlain,* vol. 2. Toronto.

Colden, Cadwallader. 1755. *The history of the Five Indian Nations of Canada.* 2 vols. London.

Deardorff, Merle H. 1951. *The religion of Handsome Lake: Its origin and development.* Bureau of American Ethnology Bulletin no. 149, 79–107. Washington, DC.

Fenton, William N. 1940. Problems arising from the historic northeastern position of the

Iroquois. *Essays in Historical Anthropology of North America*. Smithsonian Miscellaneous Collections, vol. 100, 159–251.

———. 1941. *Tonawanda longhouse ceremonies: Ninety years after Lewis Henry Morgan*. Bureau of American Ethnology Bulletin no. 128, 140–66.

———. 1951a. *Locality as a basic factor in the development of Iroquois social structure*. Bureau of American Ethnology Bulletin no. 149, 35–54.

———. 1951b. *The concept of locality and the program of Iroquois research*. Bureau of American Ethnology Bulletin no. 149, 1–12.

———. 1951c. Iroquois studies at the mid-century. *Proceedings of the American Philosophical Society* 95:296–310.

———. 1957. Long-term trends of change among the Iroquois. In *Cultural stability and cultural change,* 30–35. American Ethnological Society.

Freilich, Morris. 1958. Cultural persistence among the modern Iroquois. *Anthropos* 53:473–83.

Hewitt, John N. 1892. Legend of the founding of the Iroquois League. *American Anthropologist* 5:131–48.

Hill, Richard. 1987. *Skywalkers: A history of Indian ironworkers*. Brantford, Ontario.

Johansen, Bruce E. 1995. Dating the Iroquois Confederacy. *Akwesasne Notes,* new series, Vol. 1, nos. 3 and 4:62–63.

Knowles, Nathaniel. 1940. The torture of captives by the Indians of eastern North America. *Proceedings of the American Philosophical Society* 82:151–225.

Lafitau, Joseph François. 1974. *Customs of the American Indians compared with the customs of primitive times,* William N. Fenton and Elizabeth L. Moore, eds. and trans., vol. 1, Toronto, 1974; vol. 2, Toronto, 1977.

Lydekker, John W. 1938. *The faithful Mohawks*. Cambridge.

McAuliffe, Dennis, Jr. 1996. For many Indian tribes, the buffalo are back. *Washington Post National Weekly Edition*. Mar. 18–24, 8–9.

McKenney, Thomas L., and James Hall. 1933. *The Indian tribes of North America,* vol. 1. Edinburgh.

Mitchell, Joseph. (*See* Wilson, Edmund.)

Morgan, Lewis H. 1851. *League of the Ho-De-No-Sau-Nee or Iroquois*. 2 vols. New York. (Editions published in 1901 and 1904 were edited and footnoted by Herbert M. Lloyd and were reproduced in 1954 by the Human Relations Area Files.)

Parkman, Francis. 1892. *A half-century of conflict*. 2 vols. Boston.

———. 1901, 1902. *The conspiracy of Pontiac and the Indian war after the conquest of Canada*. 2 vols. Boston.

Richards, Cara B. 1957. Matriarchy or mistake: The role of Iroquois women through time. In *Cultural stability and cultural change,* 36–45. American Ethnological Society.

Richter, Daniel K. 1992. *The ordeal of the Longhouse: The peoples of the Iroquois League in the era of European colonization*. Chapel Hill, NC.

Shimony, Annemarie A. 1994. *Conservatism among the Iroquois at the Six Nations Reserve*. Syracuse, NY. (First published in 1961.)

Thwaites, Reuben G. 1898. *Travels and explorations of the Jesuit missionaries in New France,* vol. 13. Cleveland, OH.

Tooker, Elisabeth. 1978. Iroquois since 1820. In the *Handbook of North American Indians,* William C. Sturtevant, gen. ed., vol. 15, *Northeast,* 418–441, Washington, DC.

Voget, Fred. 1951. Acculturation at Caughnawaga: A note on the native-modified group. *American Anthropologist* n.s. 53:220–31.

Wallace, Anthony F. C. 1951. *Some psychological determinants of culture change in an Iroquoian community.* Bureau of American Ethnology Bulletin no. 149, 55–76.

———. 1958. Dreams and the wishes of the soul: A type of psychoanalytic theory among the seventeenth century Iroquois. *American Anthropologist* n.s. 60: 234–48.

———. 1970. *Death and rebirth of the Seneca.* New York.

Weaver, Sally M. 1972. *Medicine and politics among the Grand River Iroquois.* National Museum of Man Publications in Ethnology, no. 4.

———. 1978. Six Nations of the Grand River, Ontario. In *Handbook of North American Indians,* William C. Sturtevant, gen. ed., vol. 15, *Northeast,* 525–36. Washington, DC.

Wilson, Edmund. 1960. *Apologies to the Iroquois.* (Includes a reprinting of "The Mohawks in High Steel," by Joseph Mitchell.) New York.

13 The Eastern Cherokee: Farmers of the Southeast

*My companions, men of renown, in council, who
now sleep in the dust, spoke the same language [anti-
removal] and I now stand on the verge of the grave to
bear witness to their love of country. My sun of existence
is fast approaching to its setting and my aged bones will
soon be laid in the bosom of this earth we have received
from our fathers who had it from the Great Being above.
When I sleep in forgetfulness, I hope my bones will not
be deserted by you.*

Woman Killer, a man reportedly over eighty years of age in 1830,
argues against selling Cherokee land at the time of their pending
removal from North Carolina. (Strickland 1977, 379)

IN THE EARLY history of the Southeast, four tribes were larger and more influential than any others: the Cherokee, Chickasaw, Choctaw, and Creek. Along with the Seminole, who arose as a distinct entity in historic times, they have been called the Five Civilized Tribes. The largest aboriginal nation in the southeastern United States was the Cherokee; the one with the greatest political influence early in its history was the Creek. The Choctaw were soon divided internally, which dissipated their political effectiveness, while Chickasaw strength declined early in the historic period. Each nation owned land that white settlers coveted, and with the federal Removal Act of 1830 most of these Indians were moved west of the Mississippi River. They were often driven from their homes and their property was seized illegally; thousands died from the calculated cruelties and gross negligence of white oppressors. Some Cherokee who lived in the southern Appalachian Mountains refused to leave. They hid in the mountains, and when it was safe, they reestablished themselves in North Carolina, where they continue to live. This chapter primarily concerns these people because they successfully resisted removal and because they are the largest aboriginal tribe remaining in the Southeast culture area. Furthermore, they exhibit a vitality that is refreshing, and the numerous scholarly studies about them make it possible to plot the changes in their way of life with considerable precision.

| People, Population, and Language

Many theories, most of them fanciful, have been offered to account for the presence of the Cherokee in the Southeast. The archaeological record is sufficient for Joffre L. Coe (1961) to suggest that ancestors of the Cherokee occupied the southeastern area for thousands of years. At the time of historic contact their number was estimated at twenty-two thousand, but this may be an exaggerated figure. Cherokee is a corruption of Tsalagi, the Choctaw-French term for the Cherokee, which they adopted for themselves. Originally the Cherokee called themselves Ani-Yunwiya, "the principal people." Their language belongs to the Iroquoian family and to the Macro-Siouan phylum; thus their closest linguistic relatives are the Iroquois. When first encountered, the Cherokee were concentrated in western North Carolina (see Figure 13-1). They occupied the Great Smoky Mountains, and in part because of the rugged nature of the terrain, they lived in four regional groups that had a certain degree of mutual isolation reflected in dialectic differences. The ethnographic descriptions apply to all of the Cherokee before those now living in Oklahoma were relocated there following the Removal Act. The emphasis then shifts to those who stayed behind and are now known as the Eastern Cherokee. The Eastern Cherokee own about fifty-seven thousand acres in western North Carolina, and in 1997 they numbered nearly 12,000. (In Oklahoma, by contrast, the Cherokee population is almost 130,000.)

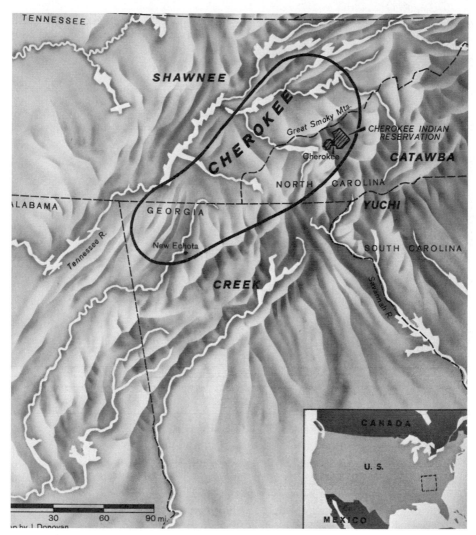

Figure 13-1 | Aboriginal range of the Eastern Cherokee Indians.

| Early Contact and Conflicts with Non-Indians

The expedition led by Hernando de Soto may have passed through a Cherokee community in 1540, but not until the late 1600s were white intrusions relatively common. Firearms and other trade goods became available about 1700, and shortly thereafter traders settled among them. It was not long before the Cherokee were embroiled in hostilities with white colonists from the eastern seaboard, and old rivalries with other Indians became intensified.

In a series of conflicts with English colonists in 1759–61, many settlements were destroyed, and the Cherokee were defeated. Soon thereafter intrusions by white settlers became increasingly common, and the Cherokee were forced to give up large sectors of land. In the American Revolution, they understandably fought on the side of the British because white settlers posed the greater threat. An alliance with the British, however, led to the repeated destruction of their settlements. Peace was made in 1794, and some Cherokee decided to settle west of the Mississippi River because they felt that whites would never be satisfied in their desire for more land. Most Cherokee remained, however, and became prosperous farmers, even organizing a government modeled after that of the United States. Yet pressures by whites for land never ceased, and by 1839 most Cherokee had been forced from their homes. About one thousand avoided removal, either by escaping into the mountains as fugitives or because they were protected as North Carolina citizens under an 1819 treaty. The descendants of these persons are the Eastern Cherokee, who now live in the North Carolina mountains.

| Early Historic Life

The Cherokee were not described in reasonable detail until the mid-1700s, and since their ties with traders and other whites were well established by then, an aboriginal base line ethnography was never assembled. The description that follows therefore focuses on their early historic life.

SETTLEMENTS AND MANUFACTURES   In reasonably early historic times, the Cherokee lived in scattered settlements because relatively level plots of ground suitable for cultivation were scarce. They built communities near streams and rivers to have access to fish and to game that was attracted to water and also for religious reasons. A large settlement might encompass 450 acres, but a typical community covered a much smaller area. A large village or a number of smaller ones formed a political aggregate, or band, of from 350 to 600 persons. As a group approached the larger number, the tendency was for a portion to separate and organize as a new unit. In the early 1700s some sixty settlements were represented by about thirty-five bands.

People lived in rectangular houses built by setting poles vertically, weaving twigs between them, and coating the walls inside and out with a mixture of moist clay and grass. These gable-roofed houses sometimes had two stories and often were divided into rooms. In one room was a fireplace, and above it a hole in the roof let the smoke out. The most prominent furnishings were raised beds made of poles with wooden crosspieces covered with mats and skins. A cone-shaped building, termed a hot house, appears to have been used as a bathhouse for purification or as sleeping quarters on cold nights. The most imposing structure was the council house used for religious, social, and political purposes; some of these buildings accommodated five hundred people. A council house was seven-sided, framed with logs, and had a roof supported by concentric circles of interior posts. The entire structure was covered with earth except for a narrow doorway and a smokehole at the center of the roof. Inside were benches and a central fireplace.

Among Cherokee domestic artifacts was a wide variety of well-made large and small baskets woven from split canes. These probably served as dishes, storage containers, carrying baskets, sifters, and winnowing trays. The Cherokee also made superior pottery containers for use in cooking food and for storage. Also outstanding were their pipes, made with long wooden stems and platform bowls of stone with sculpted figures of animals or persons.

CLOTHING AND APPEARANCE As was true for other Indians in the Southeast, the Cherokee made most clothing of deerskins sewn with sinew thread. A man's basic garment was a breechclout, and women wore knee-length skirts. Their moccasins were of deerskin, and they wore bison-skin robes during cold weather. They made summer capes of feathers attached to a fiber base. Buckskin shirts and cloth boots were added in early historic times. The most distinctive personal adornment was the ear decoration of males. A section of the outer border of each ear was cut free, stretched, and wound with wire to hold it in an expanded arc (see Figure 13-2). This aboriginal practice declined in popularity when silver jewelry became popular in the late 1700s. Wealthy persons wore collarlike bands of clamshell beads around their necks. Youthful warriors were tattooed by pricking the skin with a needle and rubbing bluish coloring in the openings. Designs of animals, flowers, and geometric forms were tattooed on the chest or muscular parts of the body. All the hair was plucked from a man's head except for a scalp lock at the back; it was decorated with beads or feathers. Women apparently drew their hair back into a very long bundle held with ribbons.

SUBSISTENCE ACTIVITIES AND CONVEYANCES The most important aboriginal crops probably were maize, beans, pumpkins, and tobacco. In early historic times the maize harvest was of critical importance, and if it failed people dispersed to hunt and collect plant products. Gardens were planted, tended, and harvested by women with the help of men. Wild plant products were also important in the diet, including berries, grapes, persimmons, plums, nuts, and roots.

The most important meat animals were bison, deer, and game birds, especially wild turkeys, killed with self bows. The reed arrows were tipped with points made from bone, fish scales, or metal. Hunters took small game with darts shot from blowguns; a nine-foot blowgun fashioned from a reed had an effective range of some sixty feet. The darts were not poisoned and so were not very effective. Blowgun use was widespread in the Southeast and probably was introduced either from Mexico or South America via the Antilles. They

The Three Cherokees, came over from the head of the River Savanna to London 1762.
Their Interpreter that was Poisoned

Figure 13-2 | Three Cherokee men during a visit to England in 1762. (By permission of the British Library.)

harvested fish with hooks, leisters, or traps, and any fish found in shallow water were driven into baskets. Dogs were the only aboriginal domestic animal, but in later times chickens, hogs, horses, and other species of European derivation were raised.

The only important conveyance was the dugout canoe. Made from a log up to forty feet long, the canoe was hollowed by burning one side and chipping out the charred wood. A vessel was about two feet wide, straight-sided, flat-bottomed, and capable of carrying twenty persons. Canoes made of wood frames covered with bark were known but were not important.

DESCENT, KINSHIP, AND MARRIAGE Descent was traced through females (matrilineal), and a person was prohibited from marrying a member of his or her own matriclan (clan exogamy) or father's clan. A man's preferred mate was from his father's father's or mother's father's clan. After a man married and moved to another settlement, he still was regarded as a member of the clan of his birth. The members of a localized clan segment made certain that a spouse was mourned properly and that men fulfilled familial obligations. Violations led to public whippings by the women of the clan involved. A widow was expected to marry her deceased husband's brother (levirate),

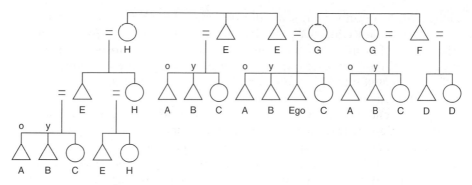

Figure 13-3 | The early historic Cherokee system of kinship terminology.

and a widower was supposed to take his deceased wife's sister as a spouse (sororate).

The aboriginal Cherokee kinship terminology reportedly was of the Crow system, meaning that the cousin terms were of the Crow type and descent was matrilineal. In this cousin terminology, a father's sister's daughter and mother's brother's daughter were termed differently from each other and from sisters or parallel cousins (mother's sister's and father's brother's daughters). However, a father's sister's daughter was classed with father's sister. The kinship terminology made it possible to distinguish precisely the four matrilineages that were most important to an individual: those of mother, father, mother's father, and father's father (see Figure 13-3).

SOCIAL DIMENSIONS Eighteenth-century Cherokee households usually consisted of a number of nuclear families related through females (matrilineal extended family). Ideally, the household included an elderly couple, their daughters, the daughters' husbands (matrilocal residence), unmarried males born into the household, and the daughters' daughters. The mutual obligations of household members and their relationship with the members of other such units were defined with precision. A father taught his son to hunt, but a mother's brother, who lived in another household, was a child's disciplinarian. An in-marrying male was respectful toward his in-laws but was expected to joke with his wife's brothers and brothers-in-law; through the jokes of others, one became aware of his erring ways. In-marrying males retained close ties with their natal households and the clans of their birth, yet a household's members formed the most closely cooperating economic unit in the society.

In social and political terms, matrilineages were less important than matriclans. Members of the same clan in a band acted collectively. Apparently seven named clans (Bird, Blue Paint, Deer, Red Paint, Twister-Long Hair, Wild Potato, and Wolf) were represented in each village, and members of a clan cooperated closely at the village level. The seven clans in a settlement allotted farmlands to member households and regulated marriage. Another important obligation of a clan was to settle disputes with the members of another clan. The most serious crime was murder. If someone killed a person in another clan, all local members of the murderer's clan were held responsible, and all males of the dead person's clan were obligated to seek revenge. Preferably the offender himself was killed in revenge, although one of his clan mates might be substituted.

Eighteenth-century Cherokee ideals about adult behavior emerge with clarity from an analysis of myths and ethnographic accounts. A good person interacted congenially with others to maintain harmonious interpersonal relations. As Fred Gearing (1962, 31) noted, a guiding principle behind behavior was embodied in the statement "thou shalt not create disharmony." In their ethos a person studiously avoided face-to-face conflict, he or she was cautious in dealings with others, and if overt conflict did arise she or he withdrew emotionally and physically if at all possible. Conflict was expressed at a distance through gossip and backbiting or more seriously in the use of magic to cast a spell over an adversary. An important means for eliminating personal animosities was a yearly ceremony to expose and purge ill feelings against other villagers.

The obligations of women tended to be much the same throughout the year. They cooked and prepared foods for storage, cared for children and the ill, and fashioned artifacts for domestic use. Farming activities introduced the greatest change from this routine. As Gearing has described the tempo of eighteenth-century Cherokee life, the routine of the males varied seasonally. In the summer after helping women plant the crops, young men played stickball, sometimes hunted, and constructed or repaired buildings. In the late summer they helped harvest the crops and then devoted three weeks to a series of ceremonies. In the fall and winter the young men hunted, fought, and held ceremonies.

Among the Cherokee and other Indians in the Southeast, stickball, the generic game from which lacrosse is derived, was a popular sport. Every player carried a stick that had a small loop and a pocket attached at the end. The object of the game was to carry a small ball across the goal of the opposite team. The ball could be carried in one hand, in the mouth, or in the mesh pocket of the stick. Any means, including the use of the stick, could be employed to obtain the ball; injuries, both purposeful and unintended, were difficult to prevent. They quite reasonably called the game "the little brother of war." Stickball games were social events but included many ceremonial aspects. For example, a man was not to have sexual intercourse with his wife for at least seven days before participating in a game, and if she was pregnant, he could not play. Several shamans were active for each side, and a rite was performed at running water. On the night before the game a dance was held, magic was invoked against opponents, and other rituals took place. During a game itself, each side tried to disable the best players on the other team.

POLITICAL LIFE Early in their history, the Cherokee political life was well-organized, although it was localized and did not unite the nation as a whole. This political organization changed as it was affected by both British influences and inclusion of warriors.

Early Organization   Each Cherokee village, with an average of about 325 residents, was politically autonomous. Control was in the hands of a council of elders, the heads of clans, and representatives of two organizations, called the Whites and Reds, that stood in opposition to one another. The Whites symbolized peace, and members were traditionally old, passive, and mild-mannered. White chiefs achieved their goals through diplomacy and reached decisions by consensus. The Reds, by contrast, symbolized war; members were expected to be young, active, and impetuous. Reds generally were young males who had married into a village and thus occupied a marginal position within the social system. As Reds aged, they became associated with the Whites and gradually found themselves integrated into community life.

Each fall, after the Harvest Ceremony and before rekindling a sacred fire, a white flag flew over the council house to indicate that the community was in control of the Whites. At an assembly, seating arrangements were by age, gender, and clan. Deliberations were guided by a general council composed of elderly men, called Beloved Men, and by priests. There was also an inner council of seven Beloved Men, one from each clan. Topics for discussion typically included relations with other Indians and non-Indians, matters of war and peace, and trade. With the priests as arbitrators, any question put before a council was stated and restated until a consensus was achieved. Apparently the members of each clan attempted to reach a unified position, but if it became clear that a clan could not support an emerging consensus, they withdrew to avoid open conflict.

A council served one large settlement or a cluster of smaller communities, but no larger political structure united the bands or the nation. Each village was an independent political entity that sought to live in harmonious relations with other such units. Gearing (1962, 83) has reasoned that prior to 1730 the Cherokee comprised a "jural community," meaning that they were united by cultural and social ties. The members of one village might cooperate with those in another, and they appear never to have fought each other, although they were often at war with adjacent tribes. Some villages were more important than others because of their strategic location, the learning of their priests, or the importance of a secular leader, but no village appears to have been dominant for very long. Conflict between Cherokee villages most likely developed if a man killed someone from another village. This was a matter to be resolved by the members of the clans involved, and since each clan was represented by fictive brothers in every other village, these ties, and the ideals of proper behavior in times of disputes, were enough to avert open conflict.

British Influences   In 1730 the village council functioned as it had in the past, but British colonial administrators began viewing the Cherokee as a single political unit rather than an aggregate of independent villages. Thus, when a raiding party attacked a white frontier settlement, all of the Cherokee were held responsible. To avoid reprisals, a tribal government began to form. The first person with political authority beyond the village level was Moytoy, an Overhill Cherokee, who presumably was a war chief. He was crowned "Emperor" of the Cherokee in 1730 by the British. The Overhill settlements had long been influential, and they became more important as the military effectiveness of the Chickasaw declined. This placed the Overhill communities on the French frontier and led to their strategic importance to the British and Cherokee alike. The influence of Moytoy was not acknowledged among all Cherokee, but his political office was widely recognized as legitimate. A smallpox epidemic in 1738–39 seems to have killed about half of the people, and as a result the curers, who probably were the war party doctors, lost their position of respect, so much so that they destroyed their ritual equipment. This resulted in even more power shifting to political leaders. With the death of Moytoy in 1741, his son Amouskositte became the leader. Presumably, it was he who threatened to destroy a Cherokee village and kill all the inhabitants if they did not kill a man who had murdered a trader. The pressure to take action against the murderer had come originally from the governor of South Carolina, who threatened to cut off trade to the Cherokee. Without arms and ammunition they would have been unable to defend themselves against the French and their Indian allies. Thus the actions of any one village began to be subordinated to *tribal* interests.

In this and other episodes, particular individuals emerged as spokesmen for the Cherokee, but only in dealing with alien powers. By 1753 a priest state was beginning to emerge, roughly paralleling the village-level organization. The capital settlement was the residence of the most notable leader and the chief priest. Other leaders from representative villages met there to deliberate. The major problem was how to prevent warriors from launching raids. The tribal council could punish raiders after the fact but had no institutionalized network to prevent raids. The inability of Amouskositte's successor to prevent raids against frontier settlements led to a war with the English that lasted from 1759 to 1761. The destruction of numerous villages forced the Cherokee to sue for peace. Raids continued to be a problem, however, and as white settlers boldly began farming Cherokee land, retaliatory raids increased.

Influence of Warriors By 1768 the Cherokee had decided to include outstanding warriors among the decision makers at the tribal council meetings. Heretofore warriors had played an integral part in council decisions only during preparations for conflict and when actually at war. Although the tribal council in theory remained opposed to reprisal raids, integrating the warriors into the tribal political organization meant that any activities they undertook would be legitimate. The American Revolution and the opening of Kentucky to white settlers split the Cherokee into two factions. Most young warriors sided with the British and were armed by them; the old men only sought peace. Decades of raids by warriors such as Dragging Canoe, leader of the Chickamaugas faction, led American military forces to destroy nearly all Cherokee settlements, but the people were not destroyed. When their villages were burned, they fled to the mountains, and after the conflict they returned to re-establish farming communities. Although they repeatedly were forced to give up land, in 1800 they still held title to about forty-three thousand square miles, about half of it in Tennessee and the remainder in adjacent sectors of Alabama, Georgia, and North Carolina.

WARFARE In the 1700s much of Cherokee energy was focused on raids and war as a direct and indirect result of white contact. When a council decided to make war, a red flag was raised over the council house, and the Reds began their preparations. Rituals by priests, fasting and dances by warriors, narrations of heroic deeds, and ritual bathing were all involved. An oration by the war speaker preceded the formal departure of a war party. When venturing forth, the warriors were elaborately painted red and black. The war club, with a projection at one end, was either hand-held or thrown. Warriors also used bows and arrows and spears when fighting. In early historic times, the metal tomahawk of European manufacture was popular, but these and earlier weapons were replaced by imported firearms and knives as they became available (see Figure 13-4).

Figure 13-4 | Pencil drawings of Cherokee men by George Catlin. (Courtesy of the New York Historical Society, New York City, neg. no. 33072.)

In enemy country, a war party erected a small post bearing carved symbols that indicated their past exploits; such a post appears to have been a declaration of war. If the raiders succeeded in an attack, they might carve symbols on a nearby tree to record their victory. Two categories of men, warriors and chiefs, probably fought, and some women were famous for their abilities in battle. A chief's advisors included at least one "War Woman," or "Beloved Woman," who helped make decisions about whether to go to war and to plot strategy. The most famous was Nanyehi (Nancy Ward, 1738–1822), whose valor in battle earned her the title while she was in her teens. The leader of a war party had only nominal control over his following, and apparently a warrior could leave at any time except during actual combat. A war party attacked stealthily, attempting to kill and scalp as many persons as they could before withdrawing with captives if at all possible. Before returning home, the raiders painted the scalps they had taken red and tied them to a pole that was carried ahead of the line of warriors as they entered their village. Captives might be adopted, but more often they were tortured to death slowly by males and females, young and old. Women whose relatives had been killed by members of the victim's tribe were the most persistent torturers.

RELIGION Many Cherokee activities in the 1700s were linked to a round of religious observances. In the fall, the first of three important ritual sets was the Harvest Ceremony. Held in late September after the maize crop had matured, this celebration included processions in which green boughs were carried and four days of dancing. Religious dances were held in the council house, along with social dances in which women participated. Soon after these festivities and when the moon was new, the council house became the center for ritual offerings to a sacred fire. Later a priest led the villagers to a river, where each person bathed seven times, and then they all feasted. About ten days after the completion of this ceremony, rituals were held to negate any ill feelings that a person might harbor against others. The purpose was for each individual to become ritually pure. Then the sacred fire in the council house was extinguished and rekindled. The members of each household lit new fires in their homes from embers of the new sacred fire. The people bathed in a river, permitted their old clothing to drift away, and put on new garments when they emerged. During the time between these ceremonies the most important political conferences of the year were held.

| Later Historic Changes

When George Washington initiated a policy of Indian assimilation in 1789, he expected the process to be completed within fifty years for all Indians east of the Mississippi River. Assimilation was to be achieved by teaching English to Indians, introducing the farming methods of whites, and imposing the concept of private land ownership. In 1794 the Cherokee signed a treaty of peace with white Americans. This was meant to end the bitter conflict that for twenty years had destroyed the aboriginal basis of Cherokee culture and had sapped the energies of the surviving Indians. Many of them concluded that the selective adoption of white ways was not only desirable but also essential for survival. However, the process of Indian assimilation was hampered by the anti-Indian attitude of many whites along the frontier.

Missionaries were to play a key role in Christianizing and "civilizing" the Cherokee. The first series of Protestant missionaries arrived among them in 1799. As the historian William G. McLoughlin (1984) noted in his seminal study of early missionary activities among the Cherokee, their resistance to becoming Christian was far greater than the missionaries had anticipated. Before long these Indians tried to revive their religion of old, but with little success. In the early 1800s the Cherokee were still attempting to adopt white ways on a selective basis and at their own pace, but the launching of the Jacksonian era in 1828 brought changes in federal policies toward Indians that doomed these efforts.

ADAPTATIONS   The Cherokee Nation founded in 1827 was modeled after the government of the United States, with executive, judicial, and legislative branches. A capital with buildings in the Euro-American architectural style was constructed at New Echota, Georgia, in 1825. Soon after the nation was founded, Sequoya (George Gist), who was of Cherokee and white ancestry, presented to the leaders a proposal for writing their language. In 1809 Sequoya had become impressed with the importance of writing, and he had originated a system whereby symbols represented syllables in the Cherokee language (see Figure 13-5). Within a few months after the syllabary was adopted in 1821, thousands of Cherokee had learned to read and write their

Figure 13-5 | Sequoya (circa 1760–1843) originated the Cherokee syllabary adopted by the Cherokee Nation in 1821. (From McKenney and Hall 1933.)

own language. The syllabary functioned to preserve traditions by allowing the Cherokees to transcribe the sacred formulas of priests and to write their own history. *The Chronicles of Wolfetown,* recorded between 1850 and 1862, are a good example of the archival data written in the Cherokee syllabary and later translated into English by Anna Gritts Kilpatrick and Jack F. Kilpatrick (1966). The syllabary also enabled the Cherokee to adapt to white ways. A print shop was established at New Echota, and the first issue of a bilingual newspaper, the *Cherokee Phoenix,* appeared in 1828. Missionaries translated the Bible and hymns into Cherokee, and by this time they were numbered among the Civilized Tribes. Their population was about 13,500 in addition to nearly 150 white men who had married Cherokee women and about 75 white women who had Cherokee husbands. At this time, too, they owned nearly 1300 black slaves, which indicates that some members of the nation were succeeding in the Southern economic system.

REMOVAL   Of all the Indian policies enacted by the United States, none was more heartless than "removal." In 1830 the U.S. Congress passed the Indian Removal Act, which provided for the relocation of all Indians in the southeastern states and the Ohio River drainage to Indian Territory west of the Mississippi River. The act was strongly supported by President Andrew Jackson, whose goal, at least in part, was to prevent the inevitable destruction of these Indians at the hands of whites. Cherokee resistance was strong but largely unsuccessful. They had adopted "civilized" ways, which was disconcerting to politicians in Georgia who yearned to bring their productive lands under state control. In 1829 the Georgia legislature passed a law making much of the Cherokee Nation land into state holdings. Under terms of the law, all previous federal legislation and regulations were to be null and void. In addition, Indians were prohibited from testifying in court cases involving whites, and prohibitions were established against interference with removal plans. About this time, gold was discovered on Cherokee holdings, and the governor declared that all gold-bearing lands belonged to the state. The actions of the Georgia legislature led to the famous *Worcester v. Georgia* case, which reached the Supreme Court in 1831. The court judgment, under Chief Justice John Marshall, was that the federal government, not the state of Georgia, was responsible for the Cherokee. Illegal seizures of land and other property by whites, conflicting policies of the Indian leaders, intrigue by unscrupulous whites and Indians, and harassment by state representatives finally led to the 1835 Treaty of New Echota and Cherokee removal.

Before the Cherokee treaty leading to their "legal" removal, gross injustices were perpetrated by citizens and representatives of the state of Georgia. Indians were forced from their lands at bayonet point, they were removed in chains without due legal process, they were sold intoxicants in violation of federal regulations, and their movable property was often stolen with impunity. A state law prohibiting a Cherokee from employing a white was used as a pretext for seizing plantations; these then were distributed to whites by lottery. The Cherokee were allowed by law to transfer land only to the state. When some families finally were forced to leave Georgia, much of the property they carried with them was seized and their money extorted. Food and shelter during the forced migration often were inadequate or nonexistent, and the weakened emigrants were struck by cholera, along with other diseases. Yet, by 1838 when all of these people were supposed to be gone, only two thousand had been deported; the other fifteen thousand still believed that somehow they would not be driven from their homeland. Such was not the case. About seven thousand soldiers under General Winfield Scott moved against the Cherokee, who had previously been disarmed. Scott ordered that within a month's time every Cherokee must be moving westward. Soldiers went from house to house, forcing people to leave at once. Often the Indians were not allowed to take anything with them, and they were impounded in stockades until they could be shipped west. Their journey to Oklahoma is known to the Cherokee as the Trail of Tears; about four thousand people died as a direct result of their forced removal. This episode in American Indian history is the saddest of the sad.

FORMATION OF THE EASTERN BAND OF CHEROKEE   About a thousand conservative Cherokee either escaped to the mountains or were granted sanctuary under an 1819 treaty. The state of North Carolina made no real attempt to remove the remaining Cherokee and in 1842 officially ceased any efforts to remove the Indians. As an indication of their traditional nature, it was recorded a few years later that only a few mixed-blooded and no full-blooded Indians spoke English. William H. Thomas, a white trader, attorney, and the adopted son of a chief, emerged as influential with this group. He spoke Cherokee, became the Indian agent, and eventually established the right of the Cherokee to remain in the locality. With the money paid to compensate for the illegal seizure of their property, Thomas and other sympathetic whites began buying parcels of land for the Indians, because Indians could not legally own land under the state constitution. The plots were held by Thomas in his name; when he became ill and in debt following the Civil War, his creditors claimed all this land. However, Congress sued the creditors to preserve the land for these Indians, and the matter was settled in favor of the Cherokee in 1874. To protect them in the future, the commissioner of Indian affairs was made their trustee, and a deed for their holdings was obtained in 1876. The Cherokee refugees who had reestablished themselves in North Carolina became relatively prosperous farmers. Yet they still spoke Cherokee, maintained their clan organization, and kept many traditions of old intact. During the Civil War those who fought did so for the Confederacy, although a few later joined the Union Army. Unfortunately, a returning Union soldier carried smallpox, and more than one hundred of the two thousand Indians died of the disease. By and large, the Cherokee lived throughout this period as self-sufficient farmers on scattered homesteads where they grew maize as their most important crop and raised livestock (see Figure 13-6).

Figure 13-6 | A North Carolina Cherokee home in 1888. (Courtesy of the Smithsonian Institution, National Anthropological Archives, neg. no. 1000-B.)

During the time that their right to the land was in question, the Cherokee drafted a constitution providing for a chief and two representatives for each of six settlements. In 1870 this body began to function as the Eastern Band of Cherokee, but it was not incorporated formally until 1889. The 1887 passage of the Dawes Act and separate efforts to allot Oklahoma Indian lands led to rumors that Eastern Cherokee land was to be allotted. A long-standing complaint, and one that would recur, was that some whites used devious means to become tribal members in the hope of obtaining land. Some whites reportedly became "five-dollar Indians" by paying this amount as a bribe to be entered on the roll. The enrollment of these whites, in addition to the children of white–Indian marriages, has, over the years, meant that there are a significant number of "white Indians."

SCHOOLS   Schools for Cherokee children were launched by missionaries in the early 1800s with modest success, but they were discontinued with Cherokee removal. In 1881 the Society of Friends opened a school on a contractual basis with the federal government, an arrangement that lasted until 1892. The Quakers succeeded in upsetting the pattern of Indian life, but not nearly as much as did their educational successors in the BIA. The pattern of formal education under the BIA was for a child to attend a day school through the fourth grade and then attend a local boarding school through the ninth grade; his or her education was completed at a distant boarding school such as the one for Indians in Carlisle, Pennsylvania. The goal of compulsory education was to destroy Indian life; children were punished for speaking Cherokee, chained to their beds if they repeatedly ran away, and forced to learn white ways.

POLITICAL, SOCIAL, AND ECONOMIC UNITS   When William H. Gilbert studied the Eastern Cherokee in 1932, the political units created after removal were continuing to function. The six townships had locally elected officers, and an elected band council regulated land usage. The state of North Carolina controlled taxation and law, and the federal government had jurisdiction over education and welfare. The townships not only were political units but also served important economic and social functions.

An organization called the free labor company or *gadugi* existed in most Eastern Cherokee communities. A typical gadugi had about a dozen members who annually elected officers, including one person who served as director. Although small, these companies were a source of pride among local residents, and they provided significant services to their membership. Participants contracted their labor as a unit and helped each other in farming and other activities; a number of women cooked for the workers. Members also could borrow money from the collective treasury. The gadugi was an important cooperative enterprise historically and apparently had an aboriginal base, but as it developed, the membership became limited to conservative Indians. As the free labor companies began hiring themselves out to whites with increasing frequency, around 1910, they were judged taxable by the state of North Carolina, which led to their decline.

The aboriginal Cherokee had performed a wide variety of dances, and by the early 1930s most of these were still remembered (see Figure 13-7). Of the large number still performed, one of the best known was the Booger Dance. The word *booger* had the same root as the English word *bogey* meaning goblin, but in its Cherokee context it closely approximated the idea of a ghost (see Figure 13-8). Masks worn during the dance were designed as caricatures of aliens. Originally the dance may have been performed to induce warriors to join war parties and to dilute the harmful effects of the spirits of foreigners. By the 1930s, however, the dance was almost free from religious associations. The masks at that time portrayed enemies: African-Americans; Chinese, who were identified with an old Cherokee myth; and whites. The dances were performed by a small number of men and sometimes by a few women, all of whom were disguised. The performers danced in a circle, frightened children, and joked with adults who stood in a proper joking relationship to them.

The gadugi, the dances, the importance of clans in regulating marriage, and much of the additional substance of traditional life were waning in importance by the late 1950s. Furthermore, as the Cherokee entered the modern era, earlier decisions about the qualifications of an Indian contributed to a reformation of what it meant to be an Eastern Cherokee.

Figure 13-7 | The Cherokee priest Swimmer (Ayunini) was the source of many dances, myths, and sacred formulas recorded in 1887. (Photo by James Mooney. Courtesy of the Museum of the Cherokee Indian.)

| Becoming Modern

As long as the Eastern Cherokee remained relatively isolated subsistence farmers, the federal government was only moderately interested in them, and they could, and did, maintain a traditionally oriented lifeway. However, as the network of roads expanded and as the people were drawn more firmly into the national economy, their capacity to resist external pressures declined. As a result, many Eastern Cherokee found their sense of being Indian increasingly challenged.

ECONOMIC BASE   The Eastern Cherokee lands consist of nearly fifty-seven thousand acres in western North Carolina adjacent to the Great Smoky Mountains National Park. Most of the reservation consists of mountain slopes with little rich bottomland. Until 1900 this land base was adequate for their subsistence-based farming. They also raised cattle and hogs, but stock-fencing laws and the chestnut blight, which depleted the prime source of food for hogs, ended these enterprises by the late 1920s. By then an increase in popu-

Figure 13-8 | Booger Dance mask. (Courtesy of Museum of the Cherokee Indian.)

lation resulted in economic hardship. At the same time, an expanding network of roads decreased their isolation. Wage labor opportunities increased, but there were few jobs. Thus the standard of living became further depressed. It was not until after World War II, when tourists began to visit the area in great numbers, that the local economy expanded significantly. By the late 1950s, over two million automobiles were passing through the town of Cherokee, North Carolina, each summer.

The landholdings of the Eastern Band of Cherokee were *owned* by these Indians collectively, not by the federal government. Some family lines had occupied the same acreage for generations, but it was the tribal council that dealt with land allotments and reallotments as well as land leases to non-Indians. Leases to business establishments provided about 80 percent of the money received by the council. One function of the council was to settle disputes over land; these were made more difficult by the fact that some boundaries were ill-defined.

During the late 1950s a majority of the approximately seven hundred households depended on subsistence farming for most of their food, and intermittent wage labor in the summer was the major source of cash. Some families relied on welfare payments during at least part of the winter; this also was charactcristic of non-Indian farmers in the region. Very few individuals had full-time jobs that provided their sole income, and conservative families had the most difficulty in making the transition from subsistence farming to a cash economy. Despite the depressed standard of living for most persons, very few Eastern Cherokee were willing to move away permanently. Most of those who left temporarily did so after World War II, for reasons including residence at boarding schools, time spent in the armed service, or temporary jobs elsewhere.

In 1972 the Eastern Cherokee met in a general council for the first time since 1838. They gathered to decide whether they should accept nearly $2 million from the federal government for twenty-five million acres of land lost to whites. They agreed to receive the settlement and divide the money; each person received less than $300. This finally resolved an old grievance, and other factors were beginning to favor them as well. The tourist industry continued to expand broadly, and two-thirds of the nearly 175 enterprises, although not the most lucrative, were Cherokee-owned. Light industries were being introduced, there was a surge in construction jobs, and tribal assets had increased significantly. However, as a group their average income was still only 60 percent of the national average.

EDUCATION   The New Deal for Indians that began in 1934 was a concerted effort to accept the diversity in cultural and historical background of the different tribes under federal control. It was a humanistic endeavor to respect the integrity of Indian cultural traditions and to encourage their ongoing vitality. An effort was made to teach the Cherokee syllabary in federal schools, but the program was abandoned because of a lack of local interest. Some local programs did succeed, however. Attempts to do away with boarding schools were not successful until 1954 because of the distance separating some homes and school facilities. A study by Sharlotte Neely of Eastern Cherokee education indicates that in 1954 some high school students began attending county schools. With reference to the previous pattern, Neely (1971, 44) wrote, "The students were boarded at schools so that their association with Anglo-American cultural phenomena would outweigh their exposure to Cherokee culture in their homes." Further changes included the consolidation of four grade schools into the Cherokee Elementary School in 1962 and the end of the last Indian day school in 1965.

In the 1950s the educational stress continued to be on vocational training with an emphasis on farming skills; academic courses were similar to those in other sectors of rural North Carolina. Because wage labor employment was difficult to obtain and the farms were declining in value, it was hard for high school students trained in this way to succeed locally. As the tourist business increased and some industries began to move into the area, employment opportunities expanded, but because the Indians tended to be noncompetitive in terms of white values, they were at a distinct disadvantage in the job market.

In the early 1970s a new direction for Eastern Cherokee education emerged through the Headstart and Follow Through programs. The small classes, well-trained teachers, predominantly Cherokee teacher aids, and community-wide interest suggested an intensity of concern over education that was far greater than in the recent past. Over 90 percent of the children spoke English at home, and thus they did not have to learn a "school" language. Furthermore, there were physical reminders of their Cherokee heritage, such as paintings of Indians along the halls and Indian as well as white dolls with which to play. Classroom instruction included Cherokee culture when appropriate, and instruction in the aboriginal language was initiated in the Follow Through program. In the fall of 1990 the Eastern Band of Cherokee Indians assumed direct control from the BIA of their school system on the main reservation, and shortly thereafter they incorporated a computer-assisted Cherokee-language program in the schools. In the remote reservation community of Snowbird, Cherokee children attended integrated Graham County public schools. If financial resources become available, Cherokee-language instruction may be incorporated into the county school curriculum. Cherokee-language computer software is already available in the schools.

VOLUNTARY ASSOCIATIONS   The game of stickball remained a popular sport, and each township fielded a stickball team until they were done away with in the 1930s at the insistence of the BIA. Two reasons appear to have accounted for the repression. One was that the games were played as battles, which resulted in many injuries, and the other was that spectators were so unruly that serious disturbances sometimes resulted. Softball games replaced the stickball contests but did not serve as a direct substitute. The teams were organized by township, and attendance was good, but the rivalry and spectator participation were subdued. In 1959 the Chamber of Commerce began sponsoring weekly stickball games played by teams representing all the townships. The frequency of the encounters led to increased competitiveness, which resulted in some serious injuries to players, and spectator involvement recalled the problems of the 1930s.

In 1914 the Cherokee Indian Fair began to be held on an annual basis in the fall and was attended by all Cherokee. Later, rides and games of chance were provided by a traveling carnival company. The most important dimension of the fair, however, was that fostered by the Fair Association, whose president was the tribal chief. The association's goal was to show progress in farming and business enterprises, and diverse exhibits for which there were competitive prizes became important. The fair also featured a stickball game with twelve players, apparently drawn from the conservative population, on a team. Some teams still observed rituals before a game, as in aboriginal times. Later the fair's name was changed to the Fall Festival, and in the 1970s performances of traditional dances were added.

LANGUAGE   Almost all Cherokee spoke English in the late 1950s, but some older persons rarely conversed in it, and although their aboriginal culture had long since disappeared, a large percentage of the population, especially those identified as conservative, spoke Cherokee as well. In one sector, about 40 percent of the households spoke Cherokee by preference. Households in which the aboriginal language was used most often were composed of full-blooded Indians or those who were of only one quarter non-Indian heritage. John Gulick (1960) reasoned that the prevalence of spoken Cherokee was, and will continue to be, sustained as long as such persons marry one another. The persons who had retained their language of old appeared to have done so because it symbolized their Indian identity. The syllabary developed by Sequoya was still in use, and the Bible printed in it continued to be available; the minutes of the Tribal Council were recorded both in Cherokee and in English. Some of the free labor companies recorded their minutes in the syllabary, but its most important use appears to have been to record the formulas of priests (see Figure 13-9). Today the Cherokee language is taught in the schools with the help of traditional speakers and computer programs. As intermarriage with nonspeakers continues, the number of households who use Cherokee as their primary language declines, even in the traditional Snowbird community where most people still speak the language (Neely 1991).

KINSHIP AND FAMILIES   The old kinship terminology was known only to some of the most elderly Eastern Cherokee in the late 1950s. The majority of persons familiar with the Cherokee terms used them in a way comparable to English usage. In other words, the terminology that had made it possible to distinguish relatives according to lineage and clan lines had been modified for bilateral usage.

It appears that these people preferred nuclear family household units, and most houses were so occupied. A significant number of households contained a number of related nuclear families—that is, small extended families. These extended families often included the nuclear families of siblings or a nuclear family plus grandchildren. The larger living units tended to occur more often among conservative families, and one reason might have been because they placed a high value on hospitality. These people also tended to be poor and lived together out of necessity. Then, too, daughters with illegitimate children often lived in their parents' households. Yet no clear evidence suggests that large households represented continuity with former residence patterns.

The matriclans that had regulated marriage in aboriginal and early historic times had declined. In the early 1950s older people were still familiar with the clan system, and about 80 percent of the marriages were in accord with it. By the mid-1950s the percentage had dropped to 20, and it was not certain that all of these marriages had in fact taken clan regulations into conscious consideration. Common-law marriages seemingly were typical, and illegitimate offspring were not stigmatized. Notably, those young adults with a minimum percentage of Indian genetic heritage tended to marry persons

Figure 13-9 | A bilingual cross at the Little Snowbird Baptist Church includes the Cherokee syllabary. (Photo by Thomas C. Donnelly, 1990.)

with a greater proportion in order to ensure Eastern Cherokee rights for their children.

DIVERGING VALUE SYSTEMS   In the 1950s, when persons identified as Eastern Cherokee considered their Indianness in abstract terms, they expressed a clear dichotomy between "full-bloods" and "white Indians." A full-blood was genetically Indian or nearly so, spoke Cherokee, belonged to a free labor company, and subscribed to the traditional Cherokee value system. White Indians had the attitudes and values of whites, spoke English, and had comparatively little Indian genetic heritage. This dichotomy was neat, but it did not always appear valid even to the Cherokee themselves. A person might be judged an Indian in one context and white in another; clearly, there were gradations of Indianness, and context was an important consideration.

This led Robert K. Thomas to define four value systems among these people (cited in Gulick 1960). The conservatives, who possibly numbered about one-fourth of the population, were "true Indians" in heritage, language, and behavior. "Generalized Indians" thought of themselves as Indian but, unlike conservatives, attempted to accommodate the white world. They accepted important values of conservatives and whites alike. "Rural-white Indians" did not look like Indians, had a minimal amount of Indian genetic inheritance, and patterned their general attitudes after those of whites in the rural South. Such persons were seldom active in purely Cherokee institutions but were likely to be members of such white organizations as the 4-H Club. These individuals might interact with "generalized Indians" but did not usually function well with conservatives. Finally, the "middle-class Indians," the smallest group in numerical terms, were involved in nonfarming businesses or were office workers. They tended to socialize with non-Indians holding similar jobs.

The behavioral system of the conservative segment was analyzed by John Gulick and his associates (1960) and found to be *not* an odd assortment of "survivals," but an integrated configuration, which Gulick termed the Harmony Ethic. A critical component was the minimization of overt and direct aggression in face-to-face situations; the aggression that did occur was expressed indirectly as gossip and sorcery. A high positive value was placed on being generous with other people in terms of rendering personal services and providing food. Conservatives did not assert themselves; they withdrew in the face of potential conflict and made a point of minding their own business. Given these attitudes, no well-defined leaders held sway even in situations where they might be expected to. For example, the officers in a free labor company worked together as a group rather than in a hierarchical decision-making structure, and tended to render decisions that reflected common consent. Because the concept of disagreement ran contrary to this value system, conservatives tended to cast an affirmative vote or not to vote at all.

| The Contemporary Scene

Unquestionably, the factor having the greatest impact on contemporary Eastern Cherokee life is tourism. In July 1997 alone, 1.7 million people visited Great Smoky Mountains National Park, which borders on Cherokee landholdings. One reason for the popularity of the Smoky Mountains park is that the area is within a two-day drive for two-thirds of the people in the United States.

While at the park, many tourists visit the town of Cherokee. Major attractions include the Museum of the Cherokee Indian, the Qualla Arts and Crafts Center, and the Oconaluftee Indian Village, as well as Indian gambling operations. In and near Cherokee are many motels, campgrounds, and souvenir stores. Many tourist-oriented shops have an official greeter dressed in

Figure 13-10 | Millions of families visit Cherokee, North Carolina, each year, and many enjoy taking a picture of their children with an Indian. This photograph was taken in 1984.

traditional Indian attire, who for a fee can be photographed next to a totem pole, a tepee, or a tourist (see Figure 13-10).

The Cherokee Historical Association has been largely responsible for major tourist promotions in the town of Cherokee, including the presentation of a play, *Unto These Hills*. Contrary to what might be expected, the association is not owned and operated by the Cherokee Indians but by white businesspersons. The Eastern Cherokee accuse the Cherokee Historical Association of unjustly implying that its enterprises are owned by the Indians. Some Indians also are distressed by the manner in which Cherokee history is presented in *Unto These Hills*. The play presents them as simple savages until their Great White Father, William H. Thomas, and white missionaries save them and their land at the time their removal is threatened. The drama suggests that the current status of the Cherokee is dependent on whites, a concept not considered accurate by many living Cherokee.

One long-standing objection of the Cherokee to the tourist-oriented businesses owned by whites has been that they hired Indians for primarily low-paying service jobs. One result was that when the Indians launched a tribal enterprise, Cherokee Bingo, in 1982, they were determined to control the operation. Over the years, the bingo business expanded so that ultimately jackpots of $50 thousand and $1 million were offered. Thousands of bingo players from cities in the eastern United States and Canada traveled to Cherokee by chartered buses. The bingo hall has been expanded to hold over one thousand people, and it employs about two hundred persons. The profits in 1986 were about $400 thousand.

Although bingo was the first tribal venture into gambling, it pales compared with a recent undertaking. In 1997 the $82 million Harrah's Cherokee Casino opened as an entertainment complex that includes gambling areas, restaurants, and a child care facility. The complex has about 1100 employees, and Indians are given preference for jobs. Early projections suggest that the casino will attract about 3.4 million customers each year.

Of some economic concern to the tribe, however, are efforts currently being made by the state-recognized Georgia Cherokee to create a business partnership with the federally recognized Ketoowah Band of Cherokees from Oklahoma. The Ketoowah Band hopes to convince the Georgia legislature to recommend that a small plot of land north of Atlanta be given federal reservation status. The plan is to build a casino that would be run by the Georgia Cherokee. Located on Route I-75 so close to Atlanta, such a casino would draw crowds that might otherwise visit the casino in Cherokee, North Carolina.

The profits from gambling are increasingly critical in tribal operations; in 1997 they amounted to millions of dollars. The same year a portion, presumably 50 percent, of the profits was distributed to tribal members on a per capita basis, as required by the tribal council. The bludgeoning impact of gambling shows no sign of relenting; quite the contrary. Once the Harrah casino is fully operational, far greater profits are anticipated.

Gambling appears to be changing the foundation of tribal politics. For many years, political issues had focused to a great extent on local problems confronting small communities as voting units. The Harmony Ethic of old is increasingly under pressure from new realities in tribal politics. Cooperation, consensus seeking, persuasion and compromise, fair treatment, and working together are words and phrases still used by tribal politicians. At the same time, these politicians openly, and sometimes forcibly, accuse one another of fraud, of using political office for personal gain, of political favoritism, and of similar infractions. For example, in 1997 the board appointed by the principal chief to exercise control over gambling resigned en masse to protest a tribal council decision. The council chose to reinstate the daughter of a council member who had been fired from her job at Tribal Bingo. The board members acted in terms of the Harmony Ethic—they withdrew when they could not support the council decision. The principal chief refused their resignations while at the same time unsuccessfully seeking replacements for them. Thus the give and take, compromise and openness, of this and many other decisions in the Cherokee political process reflects a vigorous vitality (see Figures 13-11 and 13-12).

Figure 13-11 | Cherokee lands today are overcrowded. One of the advantages to living on the reservation is access to modern housing. The Cherokee Tribal Council's house building program has significantly upgraded housing over the last thirty years. In the Snowbird community the house on the left replaced the one on the right. (Photo by Sharlotte Neely, 1974. Courtesy of University of Alabama Press.)

Figure 13-12 | Cherokee Lou Ellen Jackson inside her newer home in Snowbird. (Photo by Kenneth Murray, 1991.)

The most important political issue facing the Eastern Cherokee today is the development of a new constitution at the urging of the federal government. By 1997 a draft had been developed that challenged old ideas about Cherokee identity. The new constitution, if approved, would make a distinction between Eastern Cherokee members and citizens. Everyone currently enrolled and their descendants who have one-sixteenth or more Cherokee genetic heritage would continue to be members of the tribe. Citizens are defined as members who also live on Cherokee reservation land. Only citizens would have full voting rights. As more traditional Cherokee are forced to move off the reservation for jobs, the concern is that the percentage of voters who are traditionalists will decline.

| Additional Sources

The best starting place is *The Cherokee* (New York, 1989) by Theda Perdue. The best comparative study about the Cherokee and other Indians in the Southeast is by John R. Swanton (Washington, DC, 1946). The *Southeast* volume (14) of the *Handbook of North American Indians,* William C. Sturtevant, general editor (Washington, DC, forthcoming), also provides an overview of these people. Historical information about the Cherokee published first in 1900 by James Mooney has been republished as *Historical Sketch of the Cherokee* (Chicago, 1975). Another reprint is of the 1887 publication, *The Cherokee Nation of Indians,* by Charles C. Royce (Chicago, 1975). A more recent study is by John R. Finger, *The Eastern Band of Cherokee, 1819–1900* (Knoxville, TN, 1984) and *Cherokee Americans* (Lincoln, NE, 1991a). William O. Steele, in *The Cherokee Crown of Tanaassy* (Winston-Salem, NC, 1977), examines the exploits of Alexander Cuming in early English–Cherokee relations. Fred Gearing's (1962) analysis of historic Cherokee political developments is worthy of careful study.

William G. McLoughlin describes early acculturation by missionaries in *Cherokees and Missionaries 1789–1839* (New Haven, CT, 1984). The most insightful studies of more recent culture change are by John Gulick (1960), Harriet J. Kupferer (1966), and Sharlotte Neely (1991). Theda Perdue's *The Cherokee* (New York, 1989) and Neely's *Snowbird Cherokees* (Athens, GA, 1991) provide an overview of Cherokee history and contemporary life. *The Journal of Cherokee Studies,* which began publication in 1976, is a valuable source for varied articles about the Cherokee.

| Selected Bibliography

Anderson, William L., ed. 1991. *Cherokee removal: Before and after.* Athens, GA.

Coe, Joffre L. 1961. *Cherokee archaeology.* Bureau of American Ethnology Bulletin, vol. 180, no. 7. Washington, DC.

DePratter, Chester B. 1991. *Late prehistoric and early historic chiefdoms in the southeastern United States.* New York.

Ehle, John. 1988. *Trail of Tears: The rise and fall of the Cherokee Nation.* New York.

Finger, John R. 1984. *The Eastern Band of Cherokees: 1819–1900.* Knoxville, TN.

———. 1991a. *Cherokee Americans: The Eastern Band of Cherokees in the twentieth century.* Lincoln, NE.

———. 1991b. Termination and the Eastern Band of Cherokees. *American Indian Quarterly* 15:2:153–70.

Fogelson, Raymond D., and Paul Kutsche. 1961. *Cherokee economic cooperatives: The gadugi.* Bureau of American Ethnology Bulletin, vol. 180, no. 11. Washington, DC.

French, Laurence, and Jim Hornbuckle, eds. 1981. *The Cherokee perspective.* Boone, NC.

Gearing, Fred. 1962. *Priests and warriors.* American Anthropological Association Memoir no. 93.

Gilbert, William H. 1943. *The Eastern Cherokee.* Bureau of American Ethnology Bulletin no. 133, 169–413. Washington, DC.

———. 1965. Eastern Cherokee social organization. In *Social anthropology of North American tribes,* Fred Eggan, ed., 283–338. Chicago.

Gulick, John. 1960. *Cherokees at the crossroads.* Chapel Hill, NC.

Hudson, Charles. 1976. *The Southeastern Indians.* Knoxville, TN.

Kilpatrick, Anna Gritts, and Jack F. Kilpatrick, eds. 1966. *Chronicles of Wolfetown: Social documents of the North Carolina Cherokees, 1850–1862.* Bureau of American Ethnology Bulletin 196, No. 80. Washington, DC.

King, Duane H., ed. 1979. *The Cherokee Indian nation: A troubled history.* Knoxville, TN.

Kupferer, Harriet J. 1966. *The "Principal People," 1960.* Bureau of American Ethnology Bulletin, vol. 196, no. 78. Washington, DC.

Leftwich, Rodney L. 1970. *Arts and crafts of the Cherokee.* Cullowhee, NC.

Malone, Henry Thompson. 1956. *Cherokees of the old south: A people in transition.* Athens, GA.

McKenney, Thomas L., and James Hall. 1933. *The Indian tribes of North America,* vol. 1. Edinburgh.

McLoughlin, William G. 1984. *Cherokees and missionaries, 1789–1839.* New Haven, CT.

Mooney, James. 1900. Myths of the Cherokee. *Bureau of American Ethnology, 19th Annual Report,* pt. 1. Washington, DC.

Neely, Sharlotte. 1971. *The role of formal education among the Eastern Cherokee Indians, 1880–1971.* M.A. thesis, University of North Carolina at Chapel Hill.

———. 1978. Acculturation and persistence among North Carolina's Eastern Band of Cherokee Indians. In *Southeastern Indians since the removal era,* Walter L. Williams, ed., 154–73. Athens, GA.

———. 1991. *Snowbird Cherokees: People of persistence.* Athens, GA.

———. 1992. Adaptation and the contemporary North Carolina Cherokee Indians. In *Indians of the Southeastern United States in the late twentieth century,* J. Anthony Paredes, ed., 29–43. Tuscaloosa, AL.

———. 1995. The Role of Christianity in the Snowbird Cherokee community. In *Religion and the contemporary south,* Southern Anthropological Society Publication No. 28, O. Kendall White, Jr., and Daryl White, eds., 46–55. Athens, GA.

Reid, John Phillip. 1970. *A law of blood: The primitive law of the Cherokee nation*. New York.

Speck, Frank G., and Leonard Broom. 1951. *Cherokee dance and drama*. Berkeley and Los Angeles.

Steele, William O. 1977. *The Cherokee crown of Tanaassy*. Winston-Salem, NC.

Strickland, Rennard. 1982. *Fire and the spirits: Cherokee law from clan to court*. Norman, OK.

Strickland, William. 1977. Cherokee rhetoric. *Journal of Cherokee Studies* 2:375–83.

Swanton, John R. 1946. *The Indians of the southeastern United States*. Bureau of American Ethnology Bulletin no. 137. Washington, DC.

14 The Natchez: Sophisticated Farmers of the Deep South

Dance générale.

A great number of years ago there appeared among us a man and his wife, who came down from the sun. Not that we believe that the sun had a wife who bore him children, or that these were the descendants of the sun; but when they first appeared among us they were so bright and luminous that we had no difficulty to believe that they came down from the sun.

A priest described the origin of the Great Sun and his lineage. (Le Page du Pratz 1947, 312)

ALONG THE EASTERN bank of the lower Mississippi River developed the most elaborate Indian cultures reported to the north of Mexico. Nowhere else were similar heights of cultural complexity reported. In essence, the Natchez had achieved a chiefdom level of sociopolitical development. Fortunately, their culture was recorded in considerable detail, unlike those of other Indians in the area who probably exhibited comparable complexity. Natchez political life was dominated by a royal family, and the people had inordinately complex religious and social conventions. In addition, their relations with the French passed through well-defined stages that were often similar to European–Indian historical contacts elsewhere.

People, Language, and Population

The word *Natchez* is apparently derived from a French interpretation of the name of their settlement called Naches, but these people called themselves the Theloel. The language of the Natchez is classed in the Macro-Algonquian phylum and the Algonquian family, but it is distinct and has no close ties to any other. It is interesting to note that while the women spoke the same language as the men, women were said to "soften and smooth their words, whereas the speech of the men is more grave and serious" (Le Page du Pratz 1758, 312). Because the French learned the language from women, their pronunciation was feminine and was ridiculed by both Natchez men and women. At the end of the seventeenth century, the Natchez numbered about thirty-five hundred, and in 1720 they could assemble twelve hundred warriors, including refugees they had absorbed and the Tiou, who were a dependent people. By 1731 only three hundred warriors could be mustered, and by a few years later they had become a remnant people, although a few survived into the 1900s (see Figure 14-1).

History of Natchez–French Relations

The Natchez attacked the Spanish expedition under the original command of Hernando de Soto as it descended the Mississippi River in 1542. The next known contact was with the French explorer Sieur de La Salle in 1682. In an important study of the course of French–Natchez relations, Andrew C. Albrecht (1946) labeled this as a first phase, one of visiting explorers. The Natchez were gracious hosts to the La Salle party. They provided the French with food and smoked the peace calumet with them, but these Indians were not overawed by the Europeans. La Salle was respectful toward them since he was well aware that they were the most powerful tribe in the region. Friendly relations were disrupted temporarily when two Frenchmen were killed in 1690, but in 1698 four missionaries sent from French Canada to the lower Mississippi remained briefly among the Natchez. In 1700 one baptized 185 children. In the same year Pierre de Iberville established friendly relations between the

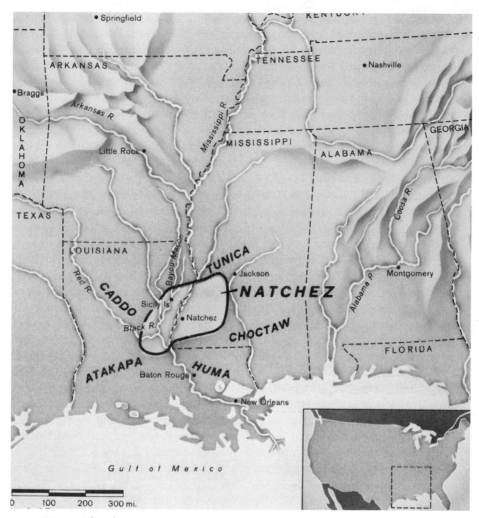

Figure 14-1 | Aboriginal range of the Natchez Indians.

Natchez and the French who were penetrating from the lower Mississippi River. De Iberville attempted to wrest political control from the French in Canada to establish an independent colony.

With the arrival of missionaries and fur traders from Canada, a second phase of contact began, but neither the traders nor the Roman Catholic missionaries were very successful. As will be understood later, the religious system of the Natchez was so highly integrated with social and political life that the task of making Christians of these people was nearly impossible. In addition, the great distance between the lower Mississippi River and eastern Canada made these trading and mission ties tenuous. The French administration that was established by de Iberville independent of Canada became the most influential force in the lives of the Natchez. During the early 1700s English traders operating from the Carolinas were successful in winning the support of a leading Natchez called Bearded Chief, who apparently dominated the communities of White Apple, Hickory, and Grigras. The settlements of Grand Village, the home of the Great Sun who was the reigning ruler, and Flour were loyal to the French.

The third phase of Natchez–French relations began in 1713 with the establishment of a French trading post in the midst of the Natchez. Antoine Crozat was granted a monopoly on all the trade in Louisiana, with the stipulation that he was to bring slaves from Africa and settlers from France. The post built by Crozat may have been at Grand Village, but it did not succeed. Intrigue by English traders and Bearded Chief apparently led to its being plundered in 1715. The French now found themselves in a tenuous position; the obvious solution was to subjugate the Natchez and establish military control over the area.

The fourth phase, military control, began in 1716 when Jean de Bienville, with a force of no more than fifty men, tricked the Indians so that he was able to seize and kill those who had plundered the trading post and had killed some Frenchmen. The Natchez agreed to peace with the French and aided in the construction of the stockaded Fort Rosalie, which was built to the west of their villages and overlooked the Mississippi River. For the moment, relations temporarily became stabilized, with the Natchez controlling their settlements and the small French garrison representing the outpost of an empire. In 1717 Crozat terminated his monopoly, and soon afterward the Western Company of John Law assumed the responsibility for trading and colonizing. It obtained the right to grant lands to private individuals and proceeded to do so. The company attempted to settle the country with a French landed nobility who would bring with them tenants, skilled craftsmen, and slaves.

In 1718 the fifth phase began when concession holders began arriving, and two years later French immigrants were well established. The French farmers prepared the land for raising tobacco, and Indian–French relationships were quite congenial. In 1718 the colonist to whom we are most indebted for our knowledge of the Natchez settled in the area. He was Antoine S. Le Page du Pratz, a Dutchman by birth, who remained in Louisiana until 1734. The French were provided land and food by the Indians, who in turn were offered guns, powder, lead, intoxicants, and cloth; this was highly satisfactory to both parties. Then in 1723 at Fort Rosalie an old Natchez warrior was killed needlessly by a soldier, and his murderer went unpunished by the French commander of the fort. In retaliation the Natchez killed some French settlers. Peace was reestablished within a few days, but a course toward further hostilities had been set. After the peace the French attacked White Apple, demanding and receiving the head of a leader who had been hostile to them. The Natchez could not understand this deception by the French and subsequently avoided contact with them.

At this crucial point in Natchez–French relations two deaths occurred among the Natchez that quite possibly led to temporary Indian disorganization. In 1725 the younger brother of the Great Sun, Tattooed Serpent, died, and three years later the Great Sun himself died. Thus, in 1728 a young and inexperienced Great Sun was in power. In the next year, 1729, a new commander of the Fort Rosalie garrison decided quite arbitrarily that he required the land of White Apple for settlement. When he told the Natchez leader of the community to forfeit the village, the noble refused, and the commander became furious. The Natchez parleyed to decide what course of action should be taken. They decided that because the French were becoming more numerous, were corrupting the Natchez youth, and were breaking their promises, the French should be destroyed. Thus began the sixth and final phase, the Natchez revolt. The Great Sun agreed, and the Natchez sought the aid of neighboring tribes. In spite of an attempt by the leaders to keep their decision from the women, one noblewoman, Tattooed Arm, the mother of the Great Sun, prodded her son into revealing the general plan. She warned the French, but the commander would not take this and other warnings seriously. Finally the Natchez fell upon the French and killed more than two hundred persons who were at or near the fort. As an aside, it is perhaps noteworthy that the Natchez warriors had such great contempt for the French commander that he was not killed until late in the massacre and then was beaten to death by a commoner with a wooden war club.

The Yazoos, allies and neighbors of the Natchez to the north, killed the small number of French among them but not until after the massacre by the Natchez. Apparently Tattooed Arm, the woman who had warned the French, altered the time of the attack and made the Natchez uprising premature, which angered their allies. The Choctaw were to have aided the Natchez but could not do so because of the time change. They were angry, too, because the Natchez did not share the spoils with them, and so the Choctaw subsequently aided the French against the Natchez. In late January 1730 a French and Choctaw force, estimated at between seven hundred and sixteen hundred, attacked the Natchez at two forts they had constructed. A larger French force arrived in mid-February and bombarded the Natchez with cannon fire. Before long, however, the French began to run low on ammunition, and their Choctaw allies talked of withdrawing. By mutual agreement the Natchez released the captives they still held, and the French withdrew to the Mississippi River. Then the Natchez with their loot slipped across the Mississippi River and escaped. They ascended the Red River to the Black River and built a fort at Sicily Island. In 1731 another French and Indian force was sent against the Natchez, and about four hundred, including the Great Sun, were forced to surrender. Some of these Natchez were sold into slavery in the West Indies, and what happened to most others is not known.

| Aboriginal Life

The Natchez clearly stand apart from all the Indians reported on in earlier chapters. Natchez social conventions, political organization, and religious institutions survived into historic times, whereas other mound-building

Indians in the Southeast with similar cultures soon disappeared. It is assumed, and with good reason, that the Natchez had deep prehistoric roots in the Southeast. Fortunately, one careful observer, Le Page du Pratz, lived among the Natchez at the time their culture was flowering, and his writings from the early 1700s are the material on which the following account is based.

ORIGIN MYTH   The mythological beginnings of the Natchez offer special insight into the form of sociopolitical structure that they developed. According to tradition, a man and his wife entered an already established community to the southwest of historic Natchez country. The newcomers were so bright in appearance that they seemed to have come from the sun. The man said he had noted that the people did not have effective means for governing themselves and that he had come from the sky to instruct them. He told the people about the Great Spirit and what they must do to please him. Among the rules of behavior were a series of prohibitions: do not kill except in self-defense; do not have sexual intercourse with a woman not one's wife; do not steal, or lie, or become intoxicated. Finally, he said that the people should give freely of what they had to those in need. After hearing these rules of conduct, the people agreed to their wisdom and asked the man to be their leader. He said he would do so only under certain conditions. Among these were that the people must obey him but no other and they must move to another country, to which he would lead them; finally, he set forth the rules for selecting his successor. He said too that they should build a temple in which the leaders could communicate with the Great Spirit. In the temple would be an eternal fire that he would bring from the sun. The people agreed to these and other conditions, and the sacred fire was brought from the sun. This man then became the first Great Sun.

SETTLEMENTS AND MANUFACTURES   The main area of Natchez settlement was along the eastern bank of the Mississippi River near the present city of Natchez, but the Natchez also seem to have controlled adjacent land on the western bank of the river. During the French period, the main settlement area was a rolling plain of black soil covered with grasses, hickory forests, cane thickets in the draws, and adjacent pine or hardwood forests. Nine communities may have existed in the early historic period, but five usually are mentioned by later sources. Grand Village, the principal settlement and the one that may have been termed Naches, was the residence of the Great Sun. The other villages were nearby. These included Grigras, a community of refugees among the Natchez; Hickory, sometimes termed Walnut; Flour; and White Apple, which has also apparently been called White Earth. That there were five distinct villages is by no means certain; the designations simply may have been references to neighborhoods around Grand Village. The only site identified with reasonable certainty is Grand Village, which has been partially excavated. It is difficult to reconstruct the configuration of a typical settlement, and the following account is a composite of reported characteristics.

Figure 14-2 | Diorama view toward the east of Grand Village. The Great Sun's mound is in the lower left foreground; the Temple Mound is in the lower right. St. Catherine Creek flows from left to right, with the Sandy Branch coming in from the center. Other Natchez settlements are shown in the distance. (Courtesy Grand Village of the Natchez Indians, Mississippi Department of Archives and History.)

In the center of Grand Village was an open plaza measuring 250 by 300 paces with a flat-topped mound at each end. On top of one mound was a temple, and on the other was the home of the Great Sun. The temple mound was about eight feet high, relatively steep on three sides, and sloped gently to form a ramp on the side toward the open plaza. The temple on top probably was about thirty feet long and somewhat narrower (see Figure 14-2). This structure was built of thick logs ten feet in height and plastered on the outside with mud. The roof was ridged, and three large wooden figures of birds adorned the peak. Entered through a rectangular doorway, the temple was divided into two rooms. A perpetual fire burned in the larger outer room, and on a nearby platform was a cane coffin containing the bones of the most recently deceased Great Sun. In the inner room were two special boards with unidentified items attached. The wooden box that contained the stone statue of the first Great Sun probably was kept here. Reportedly, he turned himself into stone because he feared that his remains would be tainted if placed in the ground. The bones of other persons probably were stored in this room.

The home of the Great Sun was on an earthen mound some eight feet high, and the house itself was twenty-five feet wide and forty-five feet long.

All other houses were at ground level, but the eight homes nearby were larger than the other houses. At the death of a Great Sun his house was burned, and the same mound probably was increased in size and used as a foundation for the home of his successor. The houses in general appear to have been square, rectangular, or, less often, round. Their straight walls were not less than fifteen feet high, and they had rectangular doorways but no windows. Hickory timbers were embedded in the ground at the four corners; they were bent over at the tops and tied to form a dome. Along the sidewalls similar poles were embedded in the earth, bent, and tied to the primary dome branches. Poles forming the inner walls were tied in place, and the inner as well as outer walls were spread with a clay and moss plaster and covered with split cane mats. The roof was covered with a mixture of sod and grass and topped with cane mats. In the winter the inhabitants built a fire for warmth. Recent experiments in a reconstructed Natchez dwelling suggest that the fire drew air *into* the building, and the smoke filtered out through the roof. It appears that the houses may have been scattered widely. Somewhere near a village were raised platforms on which the bodies of deceased persons were placed. A woven mat smeared with mud covered the body; the head of the individual was left uncovered so that food offerings might be placed beside it. After the flesh had decayed, the bones were moved to the temple.

A number of household artifacts were reported among the Natchez, and others were excavated from a historic site. Within the cane-walled dwellings were household goods not usually reported north of Mexico. The most prominent furnishings were beds made from poles and cane with bearskins over the frame, a bison skin cover, and log pillow. When relaxing during the day, the people sat either on the beds or on short-legged wooden stools. Pottery vessels were commonly used, including some with shallow bowls decorated with incised scrolls or meanders. Some large pots held up to forty pints of bear oil. A wide variety of cane basketry included sieves of various grades for sifting maize, containers for small items of adornment, and hampers for maize. Knives were made from split sections of hard cane, and stone-bladed axes served for heavy woodworking.

APPEARANCE AND CLOTHING   The Natchez were striking in appearance, according to the French. Their proud air and noble bearing became the American Indian stereotype among Europeans. Le Page du Pratz (1947) described them as 5½ feet or more in height, lean, sinewy, with rectangular features, coarse black hair, and black eyes. To him they were "naturals," but to other French observers they were "savages." As infants their foreheads were flattened by the straps that held them in cradleboards. A woman wore short bangs in front and bound her long hair in a mulberry thread net with tassels at the ends. Her ears were pierced, and from each large hole hung an elongated shell ornament. Around her neck she might wear strings of small stones or perforated shell disks. Around a man's head was a band of short hair. A few hairs were allowed to grow long at the crown, and white feathers were worn in these scalp locks. Often the young Natchez dandies painted themselves red and wore bracelets made of steamed deer ribs bent in circles and then polished to a high luster. They might carry fans of turkey tail feathers, and they wore necklaces of stone beads like those of the women. The people plucked their axillary hair, and the men plucked their whiskers.

The tattoos of these people were impressive in their diversity and complexity. Youthful males and females were tattooed with lines on the face. Persons of the nobility and warriors were elaborately tattooed on the body, head, and limbs. The patterns were of serpents, suns, and other undescribed forms. Warriors who had slain an enemy were permitted to tattoo themselves as evidence of their kills, and for a brave deed a man had the right to tattoo a war club on his shoulder with a sign beneath symbolizing the people involved in his conquest. The tattooing method was to prick the skin until blood flowed freely and then rub charcoal, red pigment, or blue pigment into the openings. Warriors pierced their earlobes and expanded the holes until they would hold decorative plugs about an inch in diameter.

Males younger than twelve years and girls younger than nine went without clothing. An older girl's primary garment consisted of a short fringed skirt made from the threads of mulberry inner bark. An adult woman wore a deerskin that was fitted about the waist and reached the knees. Some high-status women wore cloaks of netting made on a loom from mulberry inner bark. The netting was covered with overlapping rows of bird feathers. In cold weather a woman wore a cape, probably of skins, that passed under her right armpit and fastened over the left shoulder. Ordinary men wore skin breechclouts that were belted and colored white; breechclouts of nobles were black. The leggings of men reached from their thighs to their ankles, but they wore skin moccasins only when traveling. In cold weather a man wore a poncholike shirt of deerskin that was sleeved and reached below the knees. In severe weather a bisonskin robe with the hair intact and facing inward was worn. Deerskin garments were sewn with sinew after an awl was used to pierce the skins. Class distinctions in dress and adornment included elaborate tattoos for the nobility, feather-covered mantles for noblewomen, and black breechclouts for the chiefs or nobles. Infants of the nobility wore two or three pearls about their necks. These ornaments were taken from the temple and were returned when a child was about ten years old.

SUBSISTENCE ACTIVITIES AND CONVEYANCES   Cultivated crops were the most important source of food; hunting and fishing clearly were secondary. A farm plot was cleared of cane, which was dried and burned, and the ground was broken up with an L-shaped mattock of hickory. Maize was planted by making holes in the ground with a digging stick and dropping a few grains of corn into each hole. The Natchez probably cultivated their crops with a hoe made by hafting a bison scapula blade at right angles to a wooden handle.

The principal cultigen was maize, and from two varieties some forty named dishes were prepared in the Natchez area. Maize was mixed with beans, smoke-dried, ground into meal, prepared as hominy, or parched. Ground meal was made into cakes that were roasted in ashes, baked, or boiled in water. Additional crops included pumpkins and beans, while two species of wild grass were cultivated along riverbanks. The Natchez consumed walnuts, chestnuts, and acorns, but these were not important dietary items. There were no set mealtimes except for feasts. When an ordinary meal was served, the males, including those who were very young, ate before the females.

One of the primary reasons the French established plantations in the Natchez region was for the cultivation of tobacco. The Indians had raised to-bacco in aboriginal times, and the people were described as avid smokers. They smoked pipes of unknown form and inhaled the smoke. Smoking was not merely a pleasant activity; pipes and smoking played an important part in events surrounding war and peace.

Hunting was most important in the fall, and deer sometimes were pursued by about a hundred men at a time as a sport. Once they had located and surrounded a deer, men forced the animal to run back and forth until it was exhausted. It was taken alive to the Great Sun or his representative, who killed it and divided the meat among the leaders of the hunt. In ordinary hunting a man wore a deer disguise when animals were cautious, and imitated the deer's call to attract an animal closer. Hunters used self bows of locust wood strung with plant fiber or twisted sinew. Arrows of cane or wood had feather vanes and heads made from splinters of bone, garfish scales, stone, or a fire-hardened shaft tip. Cane-shafted spears were tipped with flint points and used when hunting large game such as bear, bison, and deer. When a kill was made near a settlement, the hunter returned with the choice parts and sent his wife to retrieve the remainder of the animal. Meat was either cooked or smoke-dried for future use. They ate bear meat only if it was lean, but bears were killed when they were fat to obtain the oil. These animals were smoked out of their holes in trees, and if a cub was found, it was sometimes taken alive to the village and tamed. The only domestic animal of the Natchez was the dog. It was used to tree turkeys so that they could be killed with arrows. Fishing was a less important means of obtaining food than either farming or hunting. Among the fishing devices were gill nets made from organic fibers and fish arrows that had pointed bone tips and wooden floats attached by a cord to the shaft. They also used hooks, and the species they took most often were suckers and catfish.

For water transportation, they used both rafts and canoes. Rafts were used to carry relatively light loads and were made from bundles of cane lashed together. For transporting heavy loads, large canoes were made from hollowed-out cypress or poplar logs. The interior of the log was removed by controlled burning, after which the charred wood was chipped away. These dugout canoes were some forty feet long, had three-foot beams, and could carry up to twelve tons.

SOCIOPOLITICAL DIMENSIONS   For years the accounts of Natchez sociopolitical life had been confused and contradictory. Thanks to Douglas R.
White, George P. Murdock, and Richard Scaglion (1971), particulars about
their descent and ranking system have been clarified. The Great Sun ruled as
a divine king and administered Grand Village. He appointed administrative
officers, including the Great War Chief, a supervisor of public works, the
leader of temple ceremonies, and others. The Great Sun also appointed the
War Chief in each of the other major villages.

The Suns constituted a royal family, and in 1700 they numbered seventeen individuals. Inheritance was through the matrilineal line for the royal
family; it was extended to only three collateral generations. The fourth generation of collaterals became Nobles, and three generations after that they became Stinkards (commoners). Furthermore, the male children of Noble men
became Honored men; women could only achieve Honored status as the
wives of Honored men. The Honored title could not be passed on to either
male or female children; thus, there were no Honored women by birth. The
summary of descent and rank provided by White, Murdock, and Scaglion
(1971, 373) follows:

Parent(s)	Offspring
Sun mother	Sun rank, Noble class
Sun father	Noble class
Noble mother	Noble class
Noble father	sons: Honored rank, commoner class
	daughters: Stinkard (commoner) class
Honored father	Stinkard (commoner) class
Stinkard parents	Stinkard (commoner) class

The sons of highest rank, from oldest to youngest, held the key political
offices. Noble men in turn filled lesser offices, and Honored men also appear
to have served in lesser offices. As will later become apparent, under special
conditions, a male commoner could be elevated to the rank of an Honored
person.

WARFARE   Judging by the respect the French gave the Natchez, it is apparent that their military power was considerable. A Great War Chief, appointed by the Great Sun, was in charge of warfare. Ideally, it appears, warfare
was controlled at the tribal level. The rationale for aggression might be real—
for instance, another tribe may have been hunting on Natchez land—or an offense might be fabricated. Subordinate to the Great War Chief were three
grades of combatants: apprentices, warriors, and old warriors. Old warriors
played a critical role in military matters, and one of these men led a delegation
to confront a potential enemy. They carried a peace calumet but offered no
gifts so that they would not be thought of as appeasers. A delegation of this

nature was usually well received, gifts were presented to them, and the matter was closed. If this effort failed, the Natchez prepared for offensive combat.

To prepare for combat, the military hierarchy performed numerous formal rites and ceremonies that lasted for three days. A pole with a war calumet attached, representing the enemy, was raised near the house where the plans were being formulated. The Great Sun, lesser war chiefs, warriors, and old warriors met, and the Great War Chief described the grounds for launching an attack. The opinions of the old warriors were decisive. If the presentation was accepted as valid, they proceeded with preparations for combat. Each warrior painted his body in different colors and carried a bisonskin shield and war club into combat. A meal was prepared of coarse food to remind warriors that they did not require dainty edibles, and later a dog was roasted for ceremonial consumption. Subsequently, as an act of purification, a war drink that was a powerful emetic was drunk by each man, who then vomited violently. The three-day ceremony also included dances, recitations of personal achievements in warfare, and the singing of death songs.

A war party could include as many as three hundred warriors, who traveled only by night. If they interpreted any sign as an ill omen for an attack, the men returned to their villages, despite all of the preparations. Similarly, if they met an unanticipated enemy party, they withdrew. Attacks were launched at daybreak. The intent was to kill and scalp as many men as possible and to take one male captive, along with all of the women and children. If an enemy had been forewarned and had prepared a defensive position, the Natchez searched for hunting parties to attack. Whenever possible, a Natchez killed in combat was scalped by his comrades to prevent an enemy from obtaining a Natchez scalp. The raiders returned home in honor if they had taken a living enemy man as a captive. On their return, the Great War Chief would compensate the families of any warriors lost in battle.

Back in their own village, the warriors planted two poles in the ground if a male captive had been taken; on them a crosspiece was lashed near the ground and another somewhat higher than a man's head. The captive was stunned with a blow at the base of the skull and was scalped by his captor. The victim's naked body was tied in spread-eagle fashion on the pole frame (see Figure 14-3). The young persons in the assembled throng gathered canes and lighted them; the first flaming cane was applied to the captive by his captor. The torturer was free to apply the cane anywhere he chose, and it was most likely to be on the arm with which the victim had best defended himself. The victim was then burned by the others as he sang his song of death. Some sacrificial victims were reported to have sung for seventy-two hours without pause before dying. However, not all captive males were dealt with in this manner; if a young woman whose husband had been killed claimed the captive, he was given to her as a husband. Captive women and children had their hair cut short and became the servants of their captors.

When an attack was anticipated, the Natchez usually decided in council to defend themselves rather than appease the aggressors. They warned out-

Figure 14-3 | The plan of a fort and illustration of methods of torture. (From Le Page du Pratz 1947, vol. 2.)

lying families to join the main group and posted guards at the approaches to their settlements. Another defensive move was to build palisaded fortifications. Forts were rather complex structures built around a tall tree that served as a watchtower. The trunks of trees were stripped of branches and were set in the ground to reach a height of about ten feet. The palisades were arranged in a roughly circular form with an overlap at the ends. Inside were structures to protect the women and children from arrows. The entrance was protected by towers, and in the passage to the outside were placed brambles and thorns. When an attack was imminent, emissaries carrying a peace calumet were sent to enlist the aid of friendly peoples. In the meantime the Great War Chief cited in council the reasons for defending themselves. He sought the support of warriors by reminding the older ones of their honor and pointing out the vengeance they could obtain, and holding out for youths the hope of glory.

Warriors who had distinguished themselves were given new names by the Great War Chief. These denoted particular levels of achievement in warfare. For example, the name Great Man Slayer could be claimed by a warrior after he had taken twenty scalps or ten prisoners. A warrior also might tattoo his body to commemorate an achievement and might be elevated to Honored status.

RELIGIOUS SYSTEM The Natchez religious system was a formalized network of beliefs, ceremonies, and dogma maintained by specialists who devoted all their time to supernatural matters. These persons, who were priests in a generic sense, served as guardians of the major temple. One of these men explained Natchez religion to Le Page du Pratz. The latter recorded that they

Figure 14-4 | The Great Sun being carried on a litter. (From Le Page du Pratz 1947, vol. 2.)

believed in an all-powerful Great Spirit who created all things good and was surrounded by lesser spirits that did his bidding. A particularly malignant spirit led the spirits of evil, but because it was tied up forever by the Great Spirit, it could do no great harm. The Great Spirit reportedly molded the first man from clay, and the figure grew to the proportions of a normal man. It was believed that woman probably was created in the same manner, but since man was created first, he was stronger and more courageous.

The reigning Great Sun, the highest authority on earth, combined the qualities of a god and a king. His power and authority over things religious were paramount, and his decisions were very important in secular matters. In this theocratic state, all religious, social, and political control was, in theory, in the hands of this individual. The Great Sun was surrounded by warriors and retainers wherever he went. When he traveled about, he was carried on a litter by eight warriors (see Figure 14-4); in his dwelling he sat on a small wooden throne. The Great Sun was distinguished in his dress from others; for example, his normal headdress was a net covered with black feathers and bordered in red decorated with white seeds; hanging from the top of the headdress were long white feathers in front and shorter ones behind. Lesser Suns appear to have worn similar headpieces.

The core of religious life was a sacred temple fire tended by eight elders; two of them cared for the fire continually, and they were killed if they permitted the fire to go out. When ordinary persons walked in front of a temple, they put down any load that they might be carrying and extended their arms toward the temple as they wailed loudly. The same type of behavior was followed when they passed before the Great Sun. The Great Sun visited the temple daily to make certain that the fire still burned, and each morning at sunrise he faced the east, bowed to the ground, and wailed three times. With a special calumet he blew smoke first toward the rising sun and then in each of the other cardinal directions. Thus, the Great Sun venerated the sun and was in turn venerated by all other persons in the tribe. What we see is a direct line of continuity from the past functionally linked to the Great Spirit, the Great Suns, and an eternal fire.

Ceremonies   The heads of families took their first harvest of any food to the temple; the guardians received it and conveyed it to the Great Sun, who could distribute it as he chose. Seeds to be sown were blessed at the temple before they were planted. The thirteen months of the calendar were named for the most important food of the prior month, and the beginning of each month was celebrated by a feast where either the Great Sun or a lesser Sun presided. The feast of the first month, corresponding roughly to March, was called Deer, and marked the beginning of a new year. Each year during the month of Deer a celebration was held to commemorate the liberation of a former Great Sun who had been captured by enemies. After ceremonies and ritual acts, gifts were presented to the Great Sun as he sat on his throne.

The seventh or Great Corn month was ushered in by the most important yearly ceremony, the one that celebrated the first harvest of maize. The corn used in the ceremony was from virgin ground and had been sown and tended by warriors. When the crop was harvested and stored in a granary of cane, the Great Sun was notified. All the villagers assembled at the cache to receive the Great Sun, who arrived on his litter with a canopy of flowers. After a fire was kindled by rubbing sticks together, maize was presented to the female Suns and then to all other women. The maize was cooked and eaten during a feast that was followed by speeches and dancing throughout the night to the accompaniment of a drum and gourd rattles. When dancing, the women moved in one direction and the men in the opposite direction (see Figure 14-5), and as a person tired he or she was replaced by someone from the audience. The next day a ball game was held. The warriors were divided into two teams, one led by the Great Sun and the other by the Great War Chief. In the hair of the Great Sun's men were white feathers, and the other team wore red feathers. The object of the game was to force a ball to one end of the plaza. The winning team was presented with gifts by the captain of the losing team, and the winners were permitted to wear their feather headdresses until the game was played again. After the ball game, a war dance was performed by the warriors. The festivities were not over until all of the harvested maize had been consumed. The celebrations just described were at the capital settlement, but similar festivities were led by local Suns at other settlements.

Religion embraced more than the temple cult, for there were thought to

Figure 14-5 | A dance scene. (From Le Page du Pratz 1947.)

be a host of spirits that probably were lesser agents of the Great Spirit. Power existed in the honey locust tree, and under one such tree near the temple the wood was kept for the sacred fire. Any tree struck by lightning was burned completely by the Indians, and snakes were regarded with terror. The Great Sun and people of all classes fasted to bring rain. When commoners fasted on certain days, they smeared black paint on their faces and did not eat until the sun had set.

Shamans The position of Natchez shamans is obscure, but they appear to have functioned outside the Sun-centered theocracy. An individual aspiring to become a shaman went into isolation for nine days and consumed nothing but water until a spirit appeared. During this time he or she reportedly learned certain skills, such as how to change the weather or cure illness. Spirit aids were kept in a small basket and included such tangible objects as owl heads, animal teeth, small stones, and hair from a deer. Shamans had very real obligations to those they served. Were a patient to die, the shaman might be killed, but success brought material gain. Among the techniques for curing and for changing weather were fasting, smoking, singing, and dancing. One cure included making an incision at the locus of an illness and sucking blood from the wound. When the shaman spit the blood into a container, not only blood was seen but also a foreign object such as a piece of wood, straw, or leather; the illness was attributed to this item.

LIFE CYCLE   Soon after babies were born, they were tied to a cradleboard, and strips of deerskin were bound over their foreheads to flatten them. The cradleboard was placed in a bed beside the baby's mother. Infants were smeared with bear oil to keep flies off and to make them supple. When nearly a year old, infants were encouraged to walk; they were nursed until they weaned themselves or until the mother again became pregnant. As children grew they came under the influence of an elder male in their extended family; this man counseled all the nuclear families within his group. A child termed this man father, but he might be a great-grandfather or even a great-great-grandfather. Children were discouraged from fighting with the threat that they would be sent away from the Natchez. Boys were encouraged to exercise and gradually acquire adult skills from about the age of twelve, and the gender division of labor was instilled at this time. Hunting, fishing, fighting, some farming, and the manufacturing of most artifacts were male activities. Carrying home game or fish, most of the farming, preparing food, and manufacturing clothing, baskets, or pottery were female responsibilities, along with raising children.

Following puberty, youths were free to have sexual intercourse, and girls apparently did not bestow sexual favors without material gain. A potential husband was proud of the amount of property his bride-to-be might accumulate in this manner. Males did not marry until they were about twenty-five, but females appear to have been somewhat younger. Once the couple decided to marry, the man went before the heads of their respective families to be questioned. If no close blood ties existed and if the pair loved each other, the elders sanctioned the marriage. On the wedding day the woman was led by the elder of her family, and followed by the remainder of her family, to the home of the man. Here they were greeted and invited into the house, where, after a pause, the elders of both families asked the couple whether they loved each other and were willing to be husband and wife. The ideals of domestic harmony were set forth, the couple exchanged vows, and a gift was made to the bride's father. The bride's mother handed her a laurel branch to hold in one hand and an ear of corn to hold in the other hand. She gave the corn to her husband, and he said, "I am your husband," to which she answered, "I am your wife." Finally the husband told his wife, "There is our bed, keep it tight," which was an injunction against committing adultery. After a special meal the couple and their guests danced from early evening through the night. This description of a marriage by Le Page du Pratz does not specify whether or not these customs were observed by everyone. The need for such clarification is evident, since other descriptions of Natchez marriages differ from this form.

Plural marriages were known, with sororal polygyny being the most common form, although nonsororal polygyny was also practiced. Plural marriages were more common among the nobility than among commoners. A noble with many wives retained only one or two in his house; the others lived at their natal homes where they were visited by him. In polygynous households, the wife who bore the first offspring supervised the other wives. Divorce was extremely rare for most persons, but an upper-class woman married to a common man was free to take other husbands. Furthermore, such a woman could have her husband put to death if he committed adultery. This is an unusual form of the double standard of morality. Berdaches (transvestites) were reported, but their position in the society is not clear.

The writings of Le Page du Pratz and a few others convey the essence of the ideals that guided adult life. Tribal unity did not prevail during the brief historical era, and there is good evidence of a power struggle among leading upper-class persons that influenced intervillage affairs. Some communities were friendly to the French while others were hostile, suggesting that the Great Sun could not, or did not, effectively control all the members of his lineage. Yet it appears that villagewide harmony existed and that the upper class did not abuse its power. The people in general were honorable in their dealings with each other and with the French. Recall that in the myth about the acceptance of the first Great Sun, certain specific rules of behavior were stated; they were maintained insofar as possible by the priests and the upper class in general.

One of the most vivid descriptions by Le Page du Pratz was of the funeral for the Great War Chief, Tattooed Serpent, who was the brother of the Great Sun and nearly as powerful. When he died everyone was greatly distressed because each brother had vowed to kill himself at the death of the other. The temple guardians urged Le Page du Pratz, who was influential among the Natchez and a friend of the Great Sun, to avert the leader's potential suicide. Le Page du Pratz and other whites went to the home of the Great Sun and talked with him. The Great Sun was deeply grieved over the death of his brother but was successfully restrained from committing suicide.

At the house of Tattooed Serpent, his corpse lay on the bed he had occupied while alive. His face was painted red, and he was clothed in his finest garments, including a feather headdress. Beside the bed were his weapons and the peace calumets he had received during his life. From a pole stuck into the ground hung forty-six linked sections of red-painted cane representing the number of enemies he had killed. Gathered around the body were his "chancellor," physician, chief domestic, pipe bearer, two of his wives, some old women, and a volunteer from among the noblewomen, all of whom were to be killed as a part of the funeral ceremony. The next day included a Dance of Death and two rehearsals for the deaths of persons to be killed. At about this time, two commoner parents strangled one of their offspring out of respect for Tattooed Serpent; by doing so they were raised to noble standing and would not be killed when the Great Sun died. Some warriors also had apprehended a common man who had been married to a Sun woman but had fled at her death to avoid being killed. His capture once again slated him for death, but three old women related to him offered themselves to be killed in his place. The man in turn was elevated to the upper class by the women's sacrifice.

On the day of the funeral, the "master of ceremonies" was painted red above the waist and wore a garment about his waist with a red and white feather fringe. On his head was a crown of red feathers, and he carried a red staff with black feathers hanging from the upper part and a crosspiece near the top. When this impressively arrayed individual approached the house of the deceased, he was greeted with "hoo" and by wailing indicating death. A procession formed behind the master of ceremonies; he was followed by the oldest warrior carrying the staff from which hung the red cane rings and a war pipe that reflected the honor of the dead man. These men were in turn followed by six temple guardians who carried the body on a litter (see Figure 14-6); then came those who were to be killed, each accompanied by eight relatives who served as executioners. Each of these relatives was subsequently freed from the probability of being killed at the death of the Great Sun and seemingly was raised to Honored status. The procession circled the house of the deceased three times, and then the litter bearers walked in intersecting circles to the temple. The dead child was thrown repeatedly in the path of the bearers and retrieved by its parents. After the body of Tattooed Serpent was placed in the temple, the sacrificial victims, their hair covered with red paint, were drugged with tobacco and strangled. Within the temple the two wives of Tattooed Serpent and two men were buried in the grave with him. The other victims were buried elsewhere, and the funeral ended by burning the home of Tattooed Serpent.

With a great man's death, pomp, pageantry, and human sacrifice unrolled; the death of a Sun was a tragic highlight to life. The number of persons killed at the funeral of Tattooed Serpent unquestionably was fewer than would have been considered fitting before the French arrived. For other people to die was of lesser moment, and yet any death was surrounded with further deaths. When an outstanding female Sun died, her husband, a commoner, was strangled by their eldest son. Then the eldest surviving daughter ordered twelve small children killed and placed around the bodies of the deceased couple. In the plaza fourteen platforms were erected, and on each was a man who was to die during the funeral. These men danced before the house of the deceased every fifteen minutes and then returned to their platforms. It was said that after four days the March of the Bodies ritual took place. The dead children previously had been placed outside the dead woman's home, and with them were the live victims. The woman was carried out on a litter, and the small bodies were dropped repeatedly before the procession so that by the time the litter reached the temple the corpses of the children were in pieces. After the woman's body was inside the temple, the fourteen victims were strangled, but not before they had received water and wads of tobacco

Mort. et Convoi du Serpent piqué

Temple .

Figure 14-6 | The burial of Tattooed Serpent, brother of the Great Sun. (From Le Page du Pratz 1947.)

that drugged them into unconsciousness. The living mourned for an important deceased person by weeping for four days. In general, mourners cut their hair but did not paint their faces, and they avoided public gatherings. The temporary grave was on a raised platform. A shelter of branches formed a vault over the body, and there was an opening at the end near the head where food was placed. The mourners grieved at the grave each day at dawn and at sunset for a month. After the flesh had decayed, the bones were placed in a basket in a temple.

The custom of executing persons at the death of the Suns and other upper-class individuals may seem barbaric and senseless, but they believed that it had very real advantages to the individuals involved. In their belief system, one's spirit under such circumstances would accompany the deceased upper-class person to the world of the dead and serve him or her there in perennial happiness. The same future awaited all others who observed the rules of the society during their lifetimes. It was thought that a person who had broken the rules of the people would go to a place covered with water; naked, she or he would be bitten by mosquitoes and have only undesirable foods to eat.

| Tattooed Serpent's Oration

Only a few short years following the dramatic burial ceremonies for Tattooed Serpent, the Natchez were nearly extinct. It seems fitting to record a speech that Tattooed Serpent made to Le Page du Pratz (1947, 40–41) after a war with the French and shortly before the Natchez were destroyed.

> I did not approve, as you know, the war our people made upon the French to avenge the death of their relation, seeing I made them carry the *pipe of peace* to the French. This you well know, as you first smoked in the pipe yourself. Have the French two hearts, a good one to-day, and to-morrow a bad one? As for my brother and me, we have but one heart and one word. Tell me then, if thou art, as thou sayest, my true friend, what thou thinkest of all this, and shut thy mouth to everything else. We know not what to think of the French, who, after having begun the war, granted a peace, and offered it of themselves; and then at the time we were quiet, believing ourselves to be at peace, people come to kill us, without saying a word.
>
> Why . . . did the French come into our country? We did not go to seek them: they asked for land of us, because their country was too little for all the men that were in it. We told them they might take land where they pleased, there was enough for them and for us; that it was good the same sun should enlighten us both, and that we would walk as friends in the same path; and that we would give them of our provisions, assist them to build, and to labour in their fields. We have done so; is not this true? What occasion then had we for Frenchmen? Before they came, did we not live better than we do, seeing we deprive ourselves of a part of our corn, our game, and fish, to give a part to them? In what respect, then, had we occasion for them? Was it for their guns? The bows and arrows which we used, were sufficient to make us live well. Was it for their white, blue, and red blankets? We can do well enough with buffalo skins which are warmer; our women wrought feather-blankets for the winter, and mulberry-mantles for the summer; which indeed were not so beautiful; but our women were more laborious and less vain than they are now. In fine, before the arrival of the French, we lived like men who can be satisfied with what they have; whereas at this day we are like slaves, who are not suffered to do as they please.

| The Demise of the Natchez

John R. Swanton (1946), in his study of Natchez sources, stressed that these people were not destroyed by the two French campaigns against them; in fact, the French efforts were quite clumsy. What did destroy the Natchez were frequent skirmishing with other Indians and the illness and death caused

Figure 14-7 | Nancy Taylor, one of the last Natchez speakers, in 1908. (Courtesy of Smithsonian Institution, National Anthropological Archives, neg. no. SWANTON BOOK IV 180-A.)

by physical exposure in the swamps where they took refuge. Those who escaped or were not at the fort at Sicily Island when the French made their 1731 attack, some 180 warriors, eventually joined the Chickasaw, against whom the French turned for having received these refugees. Some of the Natchez did not remain with or join the Chickasaw after their defeat, but lived with the Creek. This group probably included the largest number of survivors. They came to occupy a town near the Coosa River in Alabama, and in 1764 they had about 150 warriors. In 1832 the Natchez and the Creek were displaced to Indian Territory as a result of the federal removal policy. To complicate the matter further, some of the Natchez who joined the Catawba after their wars with the French later left them and lived with the Cherokee. In 1907 Swanton located some Natchez near Braggs, Oklahoma, in the southwestern part of the Cherokee nation; five of the individuals he found still knew some of the language (see Figure 14-7). In 1934, when Mary R. Haas worked among the Natchez living near Braggs, she found that only two Natchez speakers had survived among the postremoval Oklahoma Cherokee. Today a few rituals are pre-

Figure 14-8 | Matthew Creel and Andy Spell, Edisto-Natchez-Kusso Indians, at their festival. (Photo by Gene Joseph Crediford, 1992.)

served in Cherokee and Creek communities into which Natchez survivors intermarried. The descendants of these Natchez identify themselves as Cherokee or Creek and no longer perform these rituals in the Natchez language (Moore 1994, 371). Today in Natchez, Mississippi, the Grand Village of the Natchez has been reconstructed as a state park.

In 1747 Natchez survivors living among the preremoval Cherokee petitioned the colonial government in Charleston, South Carolina, to become "settlement Indians." They were given land near Charleston along the Edisto River. Today in South Carolina the 450 people in the communities of Four Holes and Creeltown are petitioning for federal acknowledgment as the Edisto-Natchez-Kusso Indians (Taukchiray and Kasakoff 1992, 95; Blumer 1994, 182) (see Figure 14-8). As an independent tribe, however, the Natchez are extinct, like so many Native American tribes.

| Additional Sources

The most worthwhile source is by Le Page du Pratz (1947); this was the primary source consulted for this chapter. For additional details and a comparative view of the Natchez and other Indians in the Southeast, the best source is the 1946 publication by John R. Swanton. The *Southeast* volume (14) of the *Handbook of North American Indi-*

ans, William C. Sturtevant, general editor (Washington, DC, forthcoming), also provides an overview of these people.

| Selected Bibliography

Albrecht, Andrew C. 1946. Indian–French relations at Natchez. *American Anthropologist* n.s. 48:321–54.

Blumer, Thomas J. 1994. Edisto. In *Native America in the twentieth century: An encyclopedia,* Mary B. Davis, ed., 181–82. New York.

Crediford, Gene Joseph. 1993. *Those who remain: Native Americans in South Carolina 500 years after Columbus.* Columbia, SC.

Fogelson, Raymond D. (forthcoming). *Handbook of North American Indians: Southeast.* Volume 14. Washington, DC.

Ford, James A., and Clarence H. Webb. 1956. *Poverty Point, a Late Archaic site in Louisiana.* Anthropological Papers of the American Museum of Natural History, vol. 46, pt. 1. New York.

Haas, Mary R. 1939. Natchez and Chitimacha clans and kinship terminology. *American Anthropologist* n.s. 41:597–610.

Le Page du Pratz, Antoine S. 1947. *The history of Louisiana.* Paris. (Published in London, 1758; reprinted at New Orleans, 1947.)

Moore, John H. 1994. Natchez. In *Native America in the twentieth century: An encyclopedia,* Mary B. Davis, ed., 370–71. New York.

Neitzel, Robert S. 1965. *Archaeology of the Fatherland site.* Anthropological Papers of the American Museum of Natural History, vol. 51, pt. 2. New York.

Swanton, John R. 1946. *The Indians of the southeastern United States.* Bureau of American Ethnology Bulletin no. 137. Washington, DC.

Taukchiray, Wesley DuRant, and Alice Bee Kasakoff. 1992. Contemporary Indians of South Carolina. In *Indians of the Southeastern United States in the late twentieth century,* J. Anthony Paredes, ed., 72–101. Tuscaloosa, AL.

White, Douglas R., George P. Murdock, and Richard Scaglion. 1971. Natchez class and rank reconsidered. *Ethnology* 10:369–88.

15 Current Realities, Fears, and Hopes

This sign, photographed in 1997, is at the entrance to the Pass Cahuilla Reservation in California.

Survival = Anger × Imagination.
Imagination is the only weapon on
the reservation.

The Lone Ranger and Tonto Fist Fight in
Heaven, Sherman Alexie, 1994, 150.
(Courtesy of The Atlantic Monthly Press.)

THE TWO INTRODUCTORY CHAPTERS of this book primarily summarize the cultural diversity among Native Americans living north of Mexico and report major ethnohistorical developments. The twelve chapters about specific tribes describe major variations in Indian lifeways, past and present. To achieve these goals, we have presented many dates, treaties, and other particulars because Indian life and history are complex subjects. No apology is offered for this detailed approach; it is but one of numerous ways in which to present ethnographic data. The accounts of specific tribes have one clear limitation: generalizations are usually restricted in scope. Thus the previous chapters about tribes beg for an overview that focuses not so much on the past as on the present and the future.

To generalize about contemporary Native Americans is a precarious endeavor because there is such wide variation in what it means to be an "Indian." For instance, the life-style contrast is great between a Chipewyan couple living in a relatively remote sector of northern Canada and an Oklahoma Cherokee man married to a white woman and living in an upper-class suburb of Tulsa. Regardless of how significant such differences may be, it is desirable to characterize Indian identity in a broad context. The observations in this chapter combine facts with impressions; the latter are partially based on Oswalt's contacts with Indians who represent the tribes described in detail in this book.

| Current Realities

Aboriginal Indian life has disappeared. Perhaps this is obvious, perhaps not. Europeans and other outsiders have been responsible. Today's Indians are from about eight to twenty-five generations removed from their early historic contacts with Westerners. When mortality rates from epidemics of exotic diseases, the cultural trauma represented by multiple epidemics, and the impact of Western cultural imperialism are factored in, the disruption of traditional Indian life has ranged from great to tribal extinction. Understandably, the amount of cultural knowledge about Indians across the generations has diminished, has been altered in content, or has disappeared. The "old ways," meaning configurations of aboriginal traits, have by and large vanished. A contemporary Indian elder might say, "My grandmother told me. . . ." Yet this does not assure a listener that the grandmother's statement represented an "old" Indian custom.

"Remembered culture" is just that; it is often difficult to demonstrate that a particular trait is old. For ethnographers to distinguish the old from the new is nonetheless essential to obtaining a historical perspective. This is not to deny that folktales, myths, and aspects of religious or social life, for example, may have been unchanging for generations. Long-term continuity and stability of cultural knowledge is usually difficult to validate in nonliterate societies.

To distinguish between old and new traits is clearly essential to providing an ethnographic time line for changes. But what does this mean for most Native Americans today? Probably nothing at all, or at least not very much.

This is fully understandable. If a modern Crow regards a specific convention as Crow, does it really matter to her or to him whether the trait is ancient, has been borrowed from other Indians, or has been reintroduced by individuals who read ethnographic reports about the Crow? For them it is only of consequence that a particular trait is a part of their culture. This perspective merits respect from outsiders, especially anthropologists and historians, even though it is not typical of the Crow's perspective.

Are Indian reservations and reserves really necessary? The most fervent critics of setting land aside for Native Americans call reservations and reserves "human zoos," a cruel word combination, and one that represents a flawed perception. Indians are free to leave their reservations or reserves, and they may place local restrictions on the activities of outsiders, tourists, anthropologists, and others. Historically, it is informative to know that there once existed what were essentially zoos for Native Americans, such as the one built at Bordeaux, France, in 1565. Here a Brazilian Indian village was recreated, and several hundred Indians were placed on exhibit. (See Margaret T. Hodgen, *Early anthropology in the sixteenth and seventeenth centuries,* 1964, Philadelphia.)

What is especially striking about Native American reservations in the United States but not most of those in Canada is their locations. At the time when most reservations were created, the land set aside for Indians was less desirable than was the nearby countryside. Reservations were typically created from land that had fewer resources than the aboriginal holdings of the Indians had. This has been an exceedingly critical factor. Indians have often had, and still have, a difficult time living on their assignments. The depressed standard of living on a typical reservation is often inherent in its location. One partial result is that most Indians enrolled on reservations do not live there, as is evident in the previous chapters.

As small and inadequate as most reservations may be, if they did not exist, a far greater number of Native American tribes in the United States probably would have disappeared long ago. Thus it hardly seems proper for Euro-Americans to begrudge Indians the comparatively small parcels that they now occupy.

It is notable that some tribes, such as the Yurok of California, are systematically documenting traditional place-names on the landscape of areas of aboriginal occupancy and use. This could become a step toward reclaiming this land, especially when the legal basis for its original loss is questionable.

Pan-Indianism is increasingly dominant. As described in Chapter 2, Pan-Indianism (or pantribalism) draws features from many tribes. Common characteristics include Plains Indian headdresses and apparel, particular styles of music and dance, foods, and social identity. Tribal members who seek a broad sense of being Indian find Pan-Indian identification personally satisfying. The most visible and widespread manifestation is the Indian powwows that have vastly increased in number over the past twenty years. Each year at least two thousand powwows are held in the United States and Canada combined. Pantribalism represents a present-day Indian melting pot.

Another salient aspect of pantribalism is the acceptance by federally recognized Indians (considered the only "real" Indians by some tribal members) of persons who are part-Indian and "wannabe" Indians. "Real" Indians typically have a sympathetic understanding of such persons and accept them in varied contexts. The powwow is an example.

Political factionalism is pervasive on reserves and reservations. As Westerners increasingly came to dominate Indian tribes, some tribal members staunchly supported their traditional lifeway, whereas others were willing to accommodate at least some of the goals of colonial intruders. This sooner or later produced factionalism within a tribe. One group came to be labeled "conservative" (traditional, hostile), while the opposition was called "progressive" (friendly, acculturated), irrespective of the gradations between these extremes. The dichotomy is often divisive as one faction competes with the other for recognition and power. The frequent result, however, is compromise. In some contexts, the dichotomy reminds one of the differences between the Democratic and Republican parties in the United States. Just as with these political parties, one Indian faction often, justly or unjustly, accuses the other of nepotism, favoritism toward allies, corruption, and fraud.

An involuntary sodality exists between Indians and curators. The U.S. Congress enacted the Native American Graves Protection and Repatriation Act in 1990. The act established a process for both public and private museums, colleges, and universities that receive federal funds to repatriate Indian skeletal remains and artifacts. The attitudes of collection curators ranged from sympathetic and cooperative to hostile and obstructionist. At the same time, museum curators often faced the daunting task of not only compiling appropriate inventories but also, and equally as important, identifying the legitimate owners.

For some tribes, the return of tribal member skeletal material for appropriate burial has been a major concern. Museums have been reasonably or very cooperative in meeting this condition of the act. Yet skeletal material that is thousands of years old may be difficult or impossible to identify with a particular tribe. This can lead to conflict between Indians, archaeologists, and other interested parties.

As far as the return of artifacts is concerned, Indians have been far less successful in their repatriation than in that of skeletal remains, no matter how sacred a particular artifact may be to a specific tribe.

What does all of this mean in terms of present-day realities? Foremost it means that in yet another context the federal government formally recognizes tribes as distinct legal entities. The act fosters tribalism in a highly ethical sense. Second, it means that museums and tribes must cooperate. This is important because of the institutional, curatorial, and personal responsibilities of both sides. In sum, human bones and artifacts represent invaluable assets for Native Americans as well as for museum curators, archaeologists, anthropologists, and the general public. Hopefully, the greater the dialogue, the greater the mutual understanding.

Indian political muscle is expanding. For many years in the United States, Indians were relatively passive recipients of federal treaties, rules, and regulations. In crisis situations, tribal members would travel to Washington, D.C., to voice their concerns. For the President of the United States to meet with Indian delegates is an old tradition.

In recent years, however, some Indians have become far more systematic in their lobbying efforts, especially with the expanding scope of, and profits from, Indian casinos. This trend led to the creation of the National Indian Gaming Association, based in Washington, D.C. Their charge is to protect the ongoing interests of Indian gambling operations. Thus they represent a lobby comparable to those of other businesses and political action groups centered at the capital.

Indian gambling has also led to Indian-versus-Indian lobbying battles. It is becoming increasingly common for a tribe with a casino to fight the establishment of a casino by another nearby tribe. Significant sums of money are donated to both the Democratic and Republican parties in an attempt to influence the decision at the federal level. In the same general context, efforts are being mounted to influence political decisions on casinos at the state level. For instance, in 1996 a Michigan tribe spent $3.5 million dollars to encourage state legislators to expand gambling in the Detroit area. In sum, Indians are rapidly becoming players in the U.S. political process with a weapon new to them—money.

Most Indians do not speak their tribal language. At the time of historic contact with Europeans, there were fifty-eight Indian-language families that were represented by one or more languages. At present, few of these language families can boast very many speakers, young or old, who learn a tribal language at home as their first language. Some of those who do are speakers of Cherokee, Chippewa, Cree, Inuit, Navajo, and Yupik, with varying degrees of vitality. Efforts to reintroduce tribal languages range from those that are modest and cursory to a few programs that are intense and systematic.

Is speaking a tribal language essential for Indian identity? Systematic studies of the question have apparently not been made, a situation that encourages speculations of uncertain merit. It would appear that the members of at least some tribes have retained a strong sense of Native American identity without speaking their aboriginal language. The following conditions are important variables in determining whether tribal identity can be maintained: living on traditional lands, especially when land is held collectively; being relatively isolated from strong Western influences; having a reasonably viable economy; possessing at least a certain degree of religious and social separateness; and perpetuating public displays, such as songs, dances, and other rituals. It must also be remembered that it is difficult for the members of "a nation within a nation" to retain their language, if only because English speakers are overwhelmingly dominant economically and politically.

The Indian population is youthful and is growing rapidly, becoming increasingly urban and less Indian racially. In the 1960 U.S. census, about

524,000 persons were identified as Indian. In the 1990 census, the number was nearly two million. In this context, Euro-American racial prejudice requires brief elaboration. As has been discussed earlier (Chapter 2), the black civil rights movement of the 1960s had a positive impact on Indians as well. Many Native Americans who had been "ashamed" to admit their heritage "came out of the closet." By 1990, an unknown number had become proud of their racial background. This factor alone no doubt led to some of the increase in the recorded Indian population in the 1990 census.

In 1990 less than a fourth of the U.S. Indian population was living on lands held in trust for them by the federal government, and more were living in urban environments. It also appears that the Indian population is young: according to census data, the average age of the Indian population is between twenty and thirty years, whereas that of the non-Indian population is between thirty and forty years.

Conversations with Indians representing varied tribes suggest that there is an expanding tendency to marry outside of one's own tribe. Marriages between Indians from different tribes or between Indians and whites or blacks are apparently more common than they were in the comparatively recent past.

In combination, these developments do not necessarily weaken the sense of what it means to be an Indian, but they do suggest that that sense may no longer be as strong as it once was.

Hostility against Indians prevails at the state, provincial, and local levels. These governmental units deeply resent federal protection of Native American rights. These rights include the ability to tax, the partial control of subsistence resources, and the maintenance of casino gambling; the latter is an issue of growing importance in Canada. State, provincial, and local governments support anti-Indian legislation. Alternatively, they often obstruct federal legislation favorable to Indians. In sum, as a minority, Indians invoke little sympathy or positive support at the nonfederal level. In the short term, it is doubtful that this condition will become favorable for Indians.

| Fears and Hopes

Tribes are deeply concerned about unilateral federal legislation to diminish Indian rights and sovereignty. An excellent example of one such assault occurred in the United States in 1997.

Senator Slade Gorton (R-Wash.), chair of the Senate Interior Appropriations Subcommittee, made two proposals in the 1998 Senate Interior Appropriations Bill. One was to allocate federal funds to Indians according to the wealth of a tribe. This proposal would punish tribes for economic development and represents a not-so-subtle effort to "tax" tribes with successful gambling operations. The proposal ignores the distressing economic conditions that have existed for so long on most reservations.

The second proposal put forth by Gorton would require a tribe to waive its sovereign immunity as a condition of BIA funding. This proposal strikes at the heart and soul of Indian law. Before Western intervention, virtually all tribes were independent and self-governing (i.e., sovereign) with respect to the conduct of their members. Currently, tribal governments have the independent power to control themselves except for certain restrictions under federal law. Federal restrictions have limited the sovereign powers of tribes in the United States in particular situations. For example, tribes are prohibited from making treaties with foreign nations and from allowing private parties to gain jurisdiction over Indian land without federal approval. Federal criminal law also extends to reservations. The Gorton proposals would go far beyond reasonable restrictions such as these.

The Gorton proposals were finally rejected by the Senate, but Senator Gorton has vowed to support the proposals in future legislative sessions.

In Canada, a current dispute addresses two critical issues in combination: sovereignty and sexual discrimination. Bill C-31, passed in 1985, was a far-reaching reassessment of the rights of First Nations members. One of its provisions gave Indian women who had been denied aboriginal status (e.g., after marrying a white) the ability to regain their Indian status. However, bands (i.e., enrolled members of reserves) had the power to accept or reject applications for Indian status. Band chiefs and councils sometimes rejected the applications of women whom the federal government had declared eligible for band membership. As a result, Bill C-31 was modified to permit federal authorities to decide who could become a band member. The conflict resulted in a legal battle launched in 1993. At present, the case is before the Supreme Court in Canada, and its decision is eagerly awaited. If the court decides to allow bands to select their own members, the bands "win" a major sovereignty dispute; if not, federal government control over bands will expand further, but discrimination against women will be diminished.

The impact of casino gambling has been wondrous in many respects, but not in others. Vastly improved housing, programs for youth, facilities for the aged, and dramatically reduced unemployment rates are among the beneficial by-products of Indian casinos. In addition, direct payments to tribal members based on gambling profits have been a godsend to many desperately poor Indians. Nonetheless, as mentioned elsewhere, eight casinos account for about 40 percent of the gambling income for tribes. Thus the benefits are not widely shared by reservation members across the country.

Conversely, the problems that accompany gambling can be frightening. Compulsive gambling among Indians have in some instances devastated their lives and the well-being of those close to them. Child and spouse abuse have increased dramatically on some reservations with casinos, as has violent crime. Alcoholism and the use of illegal drugs have expanded, as some young people and adults have far more money than ever before. Solutions to concerns such as these will not come easily.

All in all, Indians today might well plead *"Help us, white people, with unabridged ethical support, but otherwise LEAVE US ALONE!"* These are not contradictory ideas.

Indians are the longest oppressed minority in North America and the only persons with a fundamental right to own and control this country. In ethical terms, the uncontested poverty and poor health conditions for persons on many reservations merit a strong and positive commitment. Lest we forget, treaties, laws, agreements, and regulations underpin the merit of their cause.

Why should Indians not have far greater sovereignty in managing their internal affairs? What is fundamentally wrong with outsiders being subject to Native American laws when they are on reservation land? Why cannot Indians have more expansive control over reservation resources? Would such concessions really be unfair to non-Indians? Would fostering Indian cultures really hurt outsiders?

Native Americans are not cultural imperialists; they do not seek to make outsiders into Indians. Contrariwise, most Euro-Americans, racial prejudice aside, strive to re-form Indians in a white image. There is no compelling moral reason why we should not help Indians in a manner that they desire. Above all else, we all should strive to do Native Americans no greater harm.

Glossary

acculturation changes in the culture of Native Americans and other indigenous peoples in response to the presence of colonialists such as Euro-Americans

Anglo or Anglo-American English-speaking whites or Euro-Americans; the term is used most commonly in the Southwest

ashammaleaxia a Crow Indian word meaning "as driftwood lodges"; used to refer to solidarity among clan members

atl a word meaning "water" among Indians in one sector of Mexico

babiche thin, dehaired strips of caribou skin or the skin of other animals; used primarily as a binder

Bahana the Hopi word for the mythological older brother of the Hopi, whose descendants would someday return when the Hopi were in desperate need

band a small, family-oriented group of foragers; the word also is used in Canada and the United States to refer to a federally recognized group of Native Americans, for example, the Six Nations Band

baseline ethnography the description of a tribe before the members had significant contact with representatives of a literate society; thus the time frame varies widely depending on the geographical area

berdache a male transvestite who often assumed the clothing, mannerisms, and status of a woman; a "man-woman"

biculturation participation by a person in different cultures simultaneously; for example, a Crow Indian shares in both Crow and Euro-American cultures at the same time

bifurcate collateral kinship terms (for parents and their siblings) an uncle, aunt, mother, and father are each given separate terms

bifurcate merging kinship terms (for parents and their siblings) father and father's brother are called by one term, mother and mother's sister by another term, but mother's brother and father's sister terms are distinct

bilateral descent relatives are traced through both the male and female lines; the descent system used in the United States today

bilocal residence the establishment of residence by a married couple with or near either the husband's or the wife's parents

booger mask a Cherokee term, with the same root as the English word "bogey"; used to refer to enemies depicted on dance masks

bow, composite *See* composite bow

bow, self *See* self bow

bow, sinew-backed *See* sinew-backed bow

bride price an alternative term for bridewealth

bridewealth material property presented by a man or a man and his kin group to validate a marriage and thus reward a woman's family for the loss to her natal group

bull-roarer usually a piece of wood tied to the end of a cord that is twirled around to make a roaring sound; the sound produced may have supernatural associations

cariole a French word to refer to a toboggan with side panels and stanchions at the back; the cariole is a French innovation. *See also* toboggan

charismatic person an individual with an inordinate personal capacity for leadership

Chilcat robe a woven woolen dance robe made by Chilkat (Tlingit) women

clan a unilineal descent group in which relatives are traced primarily along the male or female line to a presumed common ancestor. *See also* the note at the end of Chapter 5

Code Talkers Navajo in the U.S. Marine Corps during World War II who used Navajo words as a code in frontline radio transmissions in the Pacific campaign

composite bow sections of antler or horn glued together to form a bow; it may be backed with strands of sinew

count coup a means of exhibiting bravery in warfare by striking or touching a live enemy; associated primarily with Plains Indians

cousin terms *Crow type:* father's sister's daughter and mother's brother's daughter are termed differently from sisters and parallel cousins, but father's sister's daughter is termed the same as father's sister and/or mother's brother's daughter is termed the same as brother's daughter

Eskimo type: parallel and cross-cousins are termed the same but with a separate term from those used for siblings; this is the cousin terminology used in the United States

Hawaiian type: parallel and cross-cousins are termed the same as siblings; thus "uncles" and "aunts" are termed the same as "mother" and "father"

Iroquois type: father's sister's daughter and mother's brother's daughter are called by the same terms, but different terms are used for parallel cousins and for sisters

Omaha type: father's sister's daughter and mother's brother's daughter are called by terms different from each other and different from those used for parallel cousins and sisters; however, father's sister's daughter is termed the same as sister's daughter and/or mother's brother's daughter the same as mother's sister

cross-cousins the children of siblings of the opposite sex; father's sister's children and mother's brother's children

Crow-type cousin terms *See* cousin terms, Crow type

cultural blindness a trait that appears to be illogical in its cultural context; for example, the long, slim olive jars in the United States today that make it difficult to remove the olives

cultural relativism the view that any human behavior occurs in the context of a particular culture and should be considered within that framework

culture area a geographical sector of the world whose occupants exhibit more cultural similarities with each other than with the peoples in other culture areas

deadfall a trap with a baited and triggered entry and a weight above that falls on an animal when it attempts to take the bait

descent, bilateral *See* bilateral descent

descent, unilineal *See* unilineal descent

Dinetah the Navajo word for their traditional homeland in the Southwest

dip net a bag-shaped net with rigid support around the mouth and a long handle used to scoop fish or other aquatic species from the water; broadly similar to a butterfly net used in the United States

dumaiya the Hopi word applied to a young man who secretly visits a young woman in her home at night to have sexual intercourse

encomienda a land grant in the Southwest given to Spanish colonists as a reward for services rendered

endogamy marriage to someone within a defined group, for example, band or village

Eskimo-type cousin terms *See* cousin terms, Eskimo type

ethnoarchaeology the use of archaeological techniques to acquire ethnographic data about a particular population; the term also refers to experiments in making replicas of prehistoric artifacts that are similar to those reported in ethnographic context

ethnocentrism the attitude that one's own culture is superior to all others

ethnographic present the use of the present tense when describing past forms of behavior; a literary device to convey the vitality of an ethnographic account

ethnography a descriptive framework for behavioral information about a population at a particular point in time, usually a year

ethnography, baseline *See* baseline ethnography

ethnohistory the presentation and interpretation of ethnographic information in historical context

ethnology the systematic comparison of cultures to establish how and why they are similar or dissimilar

False Face Society an Iroquois sodality whose members were primarily curers

family, nuclear *See* nuclear family

first fruit   the ceremonial distribution of the initial harvest for a plant product or animal species

First Nations   the designation for the Eskimo (Inuit) and Indian populations
of Canada

fish trap   an arrangement usually of stones or wooden splints, often funnel-
shaped, set in conjunction with a weir to capture and hold, but not
kill, fish

Five Civilized Tribes   the Cherokee, Chickasaw, Choctaw, Creek, and Seminole

foragers   people who depend on wild species for food; they hunt, fish, and
collect for a living

gadugi   the Cherokee term for a free labor company, a sodality

Gaiwiio   an Iroquois word for the Good Message, the teachings of Handsome Lake and subsequent texts added to his teachings

generational kinship terms (for parents and their siblings)   the father term
is extended to uncles and the mother term is extended to aunts

gill net   a fishing device that looks somewhat like a tennis net with floats attached at the top and weights at the bottom; as a fish of appropriate size
attempts to swim through the mesh, it is caught by its gills; may be used
to entangle other species, such as beaver

Harmony Ethic   the Cherokee ideal for people to be nonaggressive and
generous with one another

harpoon, toggle-headed   *See* toggle-headed harpoon

Hawaiian-type cousin terms   *See* cousin terms, Hawaiian type

hogan   the Navajo word for their pole-framed and earth-covered types of
dwellings

hominy   from an Algonquian word that now refers to a food prepared from
kernels of corn whose shells have been removed

hooch   a distilled alcoholic beverage originally made by Indians

hopi   a Hopi term for a person who is good, honorable, and nonaggressive

hozho   the Navajo word that means balance, beauty, goodness, happiness,
harmony, and health

Indian   an aboriginal or indigenous (as opposed to an immigrant) inhabitant
of the Americas; an American Indian or Native American

infanticide   the killing of a newborn offspring, or sometimes a young child

Iroquois-type cousin terms   *See* cousin terms, Iroquois type

kachina doll   the small-scale representation of mythological, ancestral, or
historical figures; the figures are not "dolls" as toys but are designed to
teach children the differences among the many types of kachinas

kahopi   a Hopi word for a person who is dishonorable and aggressive

kashgee   or kashim; a men's house among Western Eskimos where most
men and older boys live; it is also a workshop and ceremonial chamber

kayak   a small wood-framed and skin-covered Eskimo vessel with a covered
deck, designed for one person

kinaalda   the Navajo word for the ceremony that a girl underwent at her menarche

kindred   close bilateral relatives along the male and female lines; a kindred is ego-centered, meaning that a particular kindred is shared only by siblings; the kindred is an important kin group in the United States today

kiva   a Pueblo Indian ceremonial structure that is often beneath the ground

kueex   the Tlingit term for a potlatch

kwaan   a major geographical area identified by the Tlingit; comparable in many ways to a "tribe"

labret   or lip plug; an artifact, often made from wood, worn in a perforation above, below, or at the sides of the lips; multiple labrets may be worn

leister   a fish spear, often with multiple barbed heads

levirate   the marriage of a woman to her deceased husband's brother

lineage   a consanguineal kin group with descent traced along either the female or male line from a known common ancestor

lineal kinship terms (for parents and their siblings)   father's brother and mother's brother are given one term, father's sister and mother's sister are given a different term; both terms are different from those for parents; this is the "uncle" and "aunt" classification used in the United States today

lip plug   *See* labret

Long Walk   the forced removal beginning in 1863 of Navajo to Fort Sumner (Bosque Redondo) by the U.S. military; the captives remained there under military control until 1868

manitou   an Algonquian word for a supernatural force

mano   *See* milling stones

matriclan   relatives traced through the female line to a presumed common ancestor

matrilineal descent   relatives traced through the female line

matrilocal residence   the establishment of residence by a married couple within or near the wife's mother's household

medicine bundle   or sacred bundle; a packet of sacred objects for an individual or for a group such as a clan

menarche   the initial menstruation of a female

metate   *See* milling stones

metis   the term widely used in Canada to refer to a person of mixed Indian and non-Indian ancestry

milling stones   used to pulverize seeds or animal materials in the preparation of edibles; the base stone may be termed a milling stone, metate, or quern; the hand-held stone may be termed a hand stone, mano, or rubbing stone

moiety   a social group that is one of two larger groups; for example, one moiety within a tribe is comprised of clans A, B, and C, and the second moiety is represented by clans D, E, and F

moiety exogamy   the convention that an individual must marry someone from the opposite moiety

neolocal residence   the establishment of a separate residence by a married couple apart from the husband's or wife's parents

neonate   a newborn human offspring less than twenty-eight days of age

net   the male leader of a Cahuilla clan

nuclear family   same as the basic or elementary family; a person, the person's spouse, and their offspring

oki   an Iroquois term for a personal guardian spirit

Omaha-type cousin terms   *See* cousin terms, Omaha type

paha   a male ceremonial leader among some groups of Cahuilla

Pan-Indianism   or pantribalism; a sharing of traits among the members of different tribes, for example, apparel, dances, foods, and ceremonies

parallel cousins   the children of siblings of the same sex; father's brothers' children and mother's sisters' children

patriclan   a group of families related through males to a presumed common ancestor

patrilineage   a family line that is traced through males to a known common ancestor

patrilineal descent   relatives traced through the male line

patrilocal residence   the establishment of residence by a married couple within or near the husband's family's household

pemmican   a Cree word that refers to dried, pulverized meat and fat used mainly as food for travelers

peon   a guessing game played by the Cahuilla

phratry   an exogamous group of clans

piki   a Hopi word for finely ground cornmeal mixed with water and ashes and cooked on a heated stone slab

polyandry   a form of marriage in which a woman has two or more spouses at the same time

polygyny   a form of marriage in which a man has two or more spouses at the same time

potlatch   from the Nootka word "gift"; a ceremonial occasion in which wealth is displayed and gifts presented to honor a person and validate the claim to a title

powwow   a Narraganset word originally referring to the activities of shamans; presently used to refer to a public Indian gathering that focuses on feasting, dancing, other performances, and the sale of Indian craft items

primogeniture   inheritance by the firstborn male or, less often, by the firstborn female

sachem   based on an Algonquian word and used widely to refer to a hereditary male leader; a matriclan leader among the Iroquois

sacred bundle   or medicine bundle; a packet of sacred objects for an individual or group such as a clan

sagamite   an Algonquian word applied to corn porridge; a hominy gruel

self bow   a bow made from a wooden shaft

shaman a word from the Tungus in Russia; a part-time specialist in the supernatural; "shaman" does not mean sha*man,* a shaman may be male or female; the plural is shamans

sinew-backed bow a wooden bow shaft or composite bow strengthened with strips of sinew along the back

skywalker a term used to refer to Indians, especially Mohawk, who work in high steel

slave the subordinate status of a person that is passed on to his or her descendants; a captive in warfare, an individual purchased, or the child of an indebted person often were slaves

sliding historical baseline the beginning of history on a regional basis; for example, in area A historic contact with Euro-Americans may have taken place in A.D. 1600, whereas in area B it came in A.D. 1800; the time difference is ignored when establishing the beginnings of written history in the respective areas

snare a running noose of babiche or other strong material, firmly anchored (e.g., to a bush or tree) to hold a bird or other creature that is caught in the noose

sodality a secondary, special-purpose association with either voluntary or involuntary membership

sorcery the use of power gained with the assistance or the control of evil spirits; witchcraft is the use of sorcery

sororal polygyny a form of marriage in which a man marries two or more women who are sisters

sororate the marriage of a man to the sister of his wife, either while he is married to or after the death of his first wife

storyknife a knife-like artifact used by Western Eskimo girls in some areas to illustrate stories in mud, sand, or snow

surround a structure often made from stone or poles and brush into which big game was driven to become impounded and killed by other means

sweat bath bathing in the heat produced by coals from a fire or fire-heated stones, either for pleasure or for a supernatural purpose; often a small structure; water may be placed on stones to produce a steam bath

taboo a Polynesian word meaning "sacred"; it commonly refers to something that is both sacred and forbidden

teknonymy naming a parent after a child, often the firstborn; for instance, if the child's name is Alfred, his mother is called "Alfred's mother"

throwing stick also boomerang or rabbit-killing stick; used to hurl at birds or small game to stun or kill; the self-returning boomerang did not exist in North America

toboggan an Algonquian word; a flat-bottomed sled usually made from thin strips of wood bound together and bent upward at the front; *see also* cariole

toggle-headed harpoon a weapon, typically associated with Eskimos, designed to pierce the skin of an aquatic species and then to toggle (somewhat in the manner of a button passing through a buttonhole); a harpoon usually holds but does not kill prey

tolache   from a Nahuatl word adopted by the Spanish; among the Cahuilla it refers to a narcotic, jimsonweed, used by some Cahuilla in a male initiation ceremony

tomahawk   an Algonquian word for a light stone ax used as a weapon; following European contact a tomahawk head was manufactured from metal as a trade item and could include a pipe bowl at the head

totem pole   a pillar facing or pole with carved and painted symbols representing a clan and based on mythological or historical events

Trail of Tears   the Cherokee designation for the removal of most Indians from the Southeast to Indian Territory in the 1830s

trait   an act, object, or thought identified with a specific culture

transhumance   the movement of livestock by herders from one area to another at different seasons

travois   a French Canadian word for a vehicle consisting of two trailing poles with a platform for a load; a travois was initially pulled by a dog, and later by a horse

tribe   in general, a small-scale society with a name, dialect, and a territory

ulu   an Eskimo word for a knife with a semilunar blade; usually associated with women

umiak   a large open wood-framed and skin-covered Eskimo boat

unilineal descent   relatives are traced through the female line (matrilineal) or the male line (patrilineal)

universalism   the approach to human behavior based on the acceptance of value categories applicable to all cultures

value   a shared concept of what is desirable or undesirable

village endogamy   marriage to someone within one's own community

wampum   based on an Algonquian word for a string of white beads; the bead patterns of a wampum belt were "talked into" as a means of keeping records; for example, a particular bead pattern might refer to a tribe, whereas a second bead pattern might refer to the place of a treaty arrangement

weir   an obstruction of stone, brush, or other material across a stream or river to block the progress of fish; it may form a dam and be used with fish spears or have openings for fish traps

Wisaka   a Mesquakie creator and culture hero

witchcraft   employing sorcery; sorcery is the use of power gained with the assistance or control of evil spirits

Yei   the Navajo word for their mythological Holy People

| Pronunciation Guide*

Akiachuk (Kuskowagamiut village)   AH-kee-ah-chuk

Akiak (Kuskowagamiut village)   AH-kee-ak

Amouskositte (early Cherokee tribal leader)   ah-mos-ko-SIT-tee

Anasazi (archaeological tradition in the Southwest)   ah-nuh-SAH-zee

Apsaalooke (Crow name for themselves)   ap-SOO-laa-ka

Arapooish (Crow leader)   AARLA-push

ashammaleaxia ("as driftwood lodges," Crow term for clan solidarity)   aash-AMMA-lee-a-haheea

Auke (Tlingit geographical unit)   AA-kay

babiche (strip of skin used as a binder)   bah-BEESH

berdache (transvestite, "man-woman")   BEHR-dash

Cahuilla   kah-WEE-yuh

calumet (ceremonial pipe)   KAL-u-meht

cariole (type of toboggan)   KAHR-ee-ool

Caughnawaga (Iroquois reserve near Montreal)   gon-na-WAH-ga

Cherokee   CHER-ah-kee

Chilkat (Tlingit subgroup)   CHIL-cat

Chipewyan   chip-eh-WAH-yan

coup (touching an enemy in warfare)   koo

coureurs des bois (French or French and Indian hunter and trapper, especially in Canada)   koor-yuhr-duh-BWAH

Daganoweda (cofounder of the League of the Iroquois)   da-gon-na-WEE-dah

Dine (the Navajo's name for themselves)   di-NAY

Dinetah (Navajo homeland)   di-NAY-tah

dumaiya (Hopi courting practice)   doo-MIY-yuh

gadugi (Cherokee free-labor company)   gah-DOO-gee

Hiawatha (cofounder of the League of the Iroquois)   hi-uh-WAW-ta

Hodenosaunee (Iroquois term for the League of the Iroquois)   ho-dee-noh-SO-nee

hogan (Navajo dwelling)   HO-hwahn in Navajo; HO-gon in English

Honowento (Onondaga sachem)   ho-no-we-RAY-tow

hooch (distilled alcoholic beverage)   hootch

---

*AUTHOR'S NOTE: Some Aboriginal languages have sounds that are quite different from those of American English.

Hopi   ho-PEE in their language; HO-pee in English
Hupa (tribe in northwestern California)   HOO-pah
Inupik (Eskimo language group)   IN-yoo-pik
Iroquois   IR-uh-kwoi in English
kachina (Hopi mythological, ancestral, or historical supernatural)   kaht-SEE-nuh in Hopi; ka-CHE-na in English
kahopi (Hopi word for a dishonorable person)   kah-HOH-pee
kashgee (Western Eskimo men's house, alternative word for kashim)   KASH-gee
kashim (Western Eskimo men's house, alternative word for kashgee)   kah-SHIM
Kepel (former Yurok village)   kep-EL
Ketoowah (band of Oklahoma Cherokee)   kah-TOO-wah
kinaalda (Navajo term for a girl's puberty ceremony)   ki-nahl-DAH
Klukwan (Tlingit village)   KLUCK-ahn
Kolosches (Russian word for the Tlingit)   KO-losh
kueex (Tlingit word for potlatch)   qu-EEX
Kuskokwim (Alaskan river)   KUH-skoh-kwim
Kuskowagamiut   kuhs-ko-WAH-guh-myoot
kwaan (major Tlingit geographical unit)   QU-aan
Kwethluk (Kuskowagamiut village)   KWEETH-luhk
Lolooma (Hopi leader)   loh-LOO-oo-mah
Lomahongyoma (Hopi leader)   loh-mah-hohn-GYOH-mah
Maasaw (Hopi god of death)   maah-SAHW
Manitou (a supernatural force)   MAN-i-too
Mesquakie   mehs-QUAH-kee
Moytoy (early Cherokee leader)   MOY-TOY
Mukat (one of the twin Cahuilla creators)   MU-kat
Naa Ka Hidi Theater (Tlingit performance group)   naa-kah-HIDI
Nampeyo (Hopi woman)   naum-PEH-yoh
Nanyehi (Cherokee name for Nancy Ward)   nan-YEE-hee
Napaskiak (Kuskowagamiut village)   nuh-PAH-skee-ahk
Natchez   NACH-iz
Navajo   NAV-eh-hoh
net (a Cahuilla clan leader)   net
Oconaluftee (reconstructed Cherokee village)   oh-KOE-nah-LUF-tee
Oraibi (Hopi village)   oh-zhiy-VHEE in Hopi; oh-rye-be in English
pah (a Cahuilla leader)   PA-ha
parfleche (container made of folded skin)   PAHR-flehsh in English
pemmican (dried meat as food for travelers)   PEHM-i-kehn in English
peon (Cahuilla guessing game)   pe-ON in Cahuilla
piki (a Hopi ground cornmeal "bread")   PEE-kee
poncho (garment)   PAHN-choh
potlatch (ceremonial wealth display and gift giving)   POT-lach

Powamu (Hopi ceremony)   poh-WAH-moo

Requa (Yurok village)   req-WAH

Saa or **Sa'a** (Yurok place-name)   SAAH

Soyal (Hopi ceremony)   soh-YAHL

Tamaiot (one of the twin Cahuilla creators)   tim-a-YO-hwit

Tawaqwaptiwa (Hopi leader)   tah-wha-GWAHP-tee-wah

Tekakwitha, Kateri (Mohawk, became a Roman Catholic saint)   de-ga-
   GWEE-ta, ga-de-LEE

Tlingit   CLING-kit

Tododaho (Onondaga sachem)   ta-do-DAH-hoe

Tuluksak (Kuskowagamiut village)   TOO-luhk-sak

Venetie (Alaskan Indian village)   VEE-na-tiy

Weitspus (Yurok village)   WEET-puss

Wuwuchim (Hopi secret society)   woo-WOO-tsim

Wuya (Hopi clan ancestors)   WOO-yuh

Yei (Navajo mythological Holy People)   yay

Yupik (Eskimo linguistic group)   YOO-pik

Yurok   your-ROCK

| Name Index

Subject Index

Location of North American Indian Groups

SIBERIAN ESKIMO

BERING SEA ESKIMO

KUSKOWAGAMUIT

ALEUT

PACIFIC ESKIMO

KOYUKON

INGALIK

TANANA

TANAINA

EYAK

AHTENA

NABESNA

NORTH ALASKAN ESKIMO

KUTCHIN

MACKENZIE ESKIMO

HAN

TUTCHONE

MOUNTAIN

HARE

SATUDENE

COPPER ESKIMO

YELLOWKNIFE

DOGRIB

TILINGIT

KASKA

SLAVEY

TAHLTAN

TSETSAUT

HAIDA

TSIMSHIAN

SEKANI

BEAVER

C

CARRIER

SARSI

BELLABELLA
BELLACOOLA

KWAKIUTL

1

SHUSWAP

NOOTKA

2

3

6   4

5   7

8

LAKE

KUTENAI

BLACKFOOT

GROS
VENTRE
AS

9

10

11

12

13   14

17

18

FLATHEAD

15 16

20 21 22

19

23   NEZ
PERCE

1	CHILCOTIN
2	COMOX
3	LILLOOET
4	NICOLA
5	COWICHAN
6	THOMPSON
7	OKANAGON
8	KLALLAM
9	QUILEUTE
10	QUINAULT
11	TWANA
12	COLUMBIA
13	SANPOIL
14	KALISPEL
15	KLIKITAT
16	YAKIMA
17	SPOKAN
18	COEUR D'ALENE
19	WALLAWALLA
20	WISHRAM
21	TENINO
22	UMATILLA
23	CAYUSE

Map by J. Donovan